The Political Economy of World Energy

The Political Economy of World Energy

A Twentieth-Century Perspective

by
John G. Clark

The University of North Carolina Press
Chapel Hill and London

First published in the United States 1991
by The University of North Carolina Press

95 94 93 92 91   5 4 3 2 1

Library of Congress Cataloging-in-Publication Data

Clark, John Garretson, 1932–
    The political economy of world energy: a twentieth-century
perspective/John G. Clark.
       p.   cm.
    Includes bibliographical references and index.
    ISBN 0-8078-1944-1. — ISBN 0-8078-4306-7 (pbk.)
    1. Energy policy — History — 20th century.   2. Energy industries —
Political aspects — History — 20th century.   I. Title.
    HD9502   A2C53   1991
    333.79′09′04 — dc20   90-37657
                                                                                              CIP

First published in Great Britain 1990
by Harvester Wheatsheaf
Simon & Schuster International Group
Wolsey House, Wolsey Road
Hemel Hempstead
Hertfordshire HP2 4SS

Typeset by Excel Typesetters Co., Hong Kong
Printed and bound in Great Britain

Dedicated to the memories of my mother and father and to the memory of Robert Oppenheimer, and to past and present influences on my life:

Frank, Roland, and Don and the other boys of Park Terrace
The bons vivants of Nickel Hall, Park College, Missouri
"B" Company, 501st CommRecon Bn, I Corps, Korea
Members of the Hatchet Club, Department of History,
    University of Kansas
Teammates on Clio's Pups, fast-pitch champions
My tennis chums
My granddaughter, Emily Layton Nightingale
Lois, the kids, and the other grandchildren

Contents

Tables

xii *Tables*

Maps

Abbreviations

AEG	Allgemeine Electrizitäts Gesellschaft
AIOC	Anglo–Iranian Oil Company
BNOC	British National Oil Company
BP	British Petroleum
CIA	Central Intelligence Agency
CFP	Compagnie Française de Pétrole
CGEC	Commissariat Général aux Essences et Combustibles
CMEA	Council for Mutual Economic Assistance
CVP	Corporación Venezolana del Petroleo
DOE	Department of Energy
EC	European Community
ECA	Economic Cooperation Administration
ECO	European Coal Organization
ECSC	European Coal and Steel Community
EEC	European Economic Community
EIA	Energy Information Administration
ENI	Ente Nazionale Irdocarburi
ERAP	Entreprise des Recherches et d'Activités Pétrolières
GDP	gross domestic product
GE	General Electric
GNP	gross national product
IADB	Inter-American Development Bank
IAEA	International Atomic Energy Agency
IEA	International Energy Agency
IMF	International Monetary Fund
IMR	infant mortality rate
IOC	Interstate Oil Compact
IPC	Iraq Petroleum Company

JPDC	Japanese Petroleum Development Corporation
LDC	lesser developed country
LNG	liquefied natural gas
MITI	Ministry of International Trade and Industry
MNOC	multinational oil company
NATO	North Atlantic Treaty Organization
NEI	Netherlands East Indies
NIOC	National Iranian Oil Company
NPT	Non-Proliferation of Nuclear Weapons
OAPEC	Organization of Arab Petroleum Exporting Countries
OECD	Organization for Economic Cooperation and Development
OEEC	Organization for European Economic Cooperation
OPEC	Organization of Petroleum Exporting Countries
PEMEX	Pétroleous Mexicana
PEP	Political and Economic Planning
PRC	Petroleum Reserves Corporation
R & D	research and development
RDS	Royal Dutch–Shell
RWCS	Rhenish–Westphalian Coal Syndicate
SOCAL	Standard Oil of California
SOEC	Statistical Office of the European Communities
SOIND	Standard Oil of Indiana
SONJ	Standard Oil (New Jersey)
SONY	Standard Oil of New York
TELC	Tokyo Electric Light Company
TPC	Turkish Petroleum Company
TPER	total primary energy requirements
UAE	United Arab Emirates
UN	United Nations
USDOE	US Department of Energy
USFA	US Fuel Administration

Preface

Someone in the United Kingdom suggested to Harvester Wheatsheaf that I might be able to write a history of energy in the international economy during the twentieth century. The project seemed fascinating. It proved to be a significant learning experience. Still, I am just as happy to remain ignorant of my sponsor's identity.

At the time that I agreed to do this, there existed no similar history. While this is not necessarily an argument supporting the writing of one, I believed that in this case, it might be a useful venture. There were dozens, scores of estimable books on aspects of the energy scene during the twentieth century and their number increased geometrically after 1973. Some covered relatively short chronological periods. Others spanned significant time periods but focused on a particular country, a company, a fuel or energy source or process, or a crisis. Historians are supposed to place time frames and their events in context so their readers can better understand them. I thought this would be possible for energy as it moved across state borders and worked its influences around the globe. In any event, I have tried to explain some of the ramifications for the present of the often critical events of the past.

Many people helped me in my task. Some even wished I were working on something that I was more suited to, at least that is the way I interpreted criticisms of first drafts. Those who agreed to read portions of this study are not at all to be blamed because I perservered.

Among the folk providing indispensable support were the staffs of the libraries at Leicester University, Leicester, UK, London University, and the University of Kansas, Lawrence, USA. An opportunity to review sources that would not have been available to me was offered by the Economic and Social History Department at Leicester University.

They agreed to have me as a visitor while one of their own taught at the University of Kansas. Richard and Susan Roger, of Leicester, lived in my house. My wife, Lois, lived in Ann Schofield's house, in Lawrence. I lived in the Rogers' house. Ted and Judy Wilson joined me there in December. We all had a wonderful time.

Derek Aldcroft, Head of the Department at Leicester, his colleagues, and the staff all helped make my stay enjoyable. In particular, I would like to thank Peter Fearon of Leicester for reading drafts of the early chapters and, along with Tricia Fearon, for easing my way and feeding me frequently. A sabbatical from the University of Kansas allowed me to remain in England to complete much of the research after my teaching assignment was over.

Tom Weiss, Department of Economics, and Theodore Wilson, Department of History at the University of Kansas, both read the entire manuscript and offered essential criticisms and suggestions. Others who helped with portions of the study include the Economic and Social History Seminar at the University of Kansas, especially Deborah Gerner of the Department of Political Science.

There is no final bibliography. Full bibliographic details are provided at the first citation of each title in each chapter.

J.G.C.
1990

1
A prospectus

To fashion a study of energy in the international economy during the twentieth century requires consideration of myriad complex events and developments from every corner of the globe. During this century, people around the world, but first and most intensively in the industrial nations along the Atlantic's rim, experienced an ever widening choice of uses for energy derived from extended and improved access to inorganic sources. It is no coincidence that several nations reached industrial maturity at the close of the nineteenth century simultaneously with the emergence of increasingly sophisticated energy systems of broad application and but partially recognized potential. Alastair Buchan writes that "developments in the use of energy...have shaped the course of modern history more than other forms of technological change...."[1]

As a physicist knows, energy is ubiquitous. The universe is awash with pure and untapped energy. But the energy that I am interested in lights my study and is as intrinsic to each second of my life as air and water and various emotional states. Energy works for humanity but it must also be worked for. It is mined, processed, turned into innumerable useful products, bought and sold, all in extremely large quantities. In these processes and in the final use, the end use, of energy, specific energy forms — wood and other biomass, coal, oil, natural gas, electricity from thermal fuels or nuclear fission — enter societies and cultures and shape them. In places in Africa, once lush ground cover has been stripped so bare that people must walk for hours to find a day's supply of firewood. The lives of these people have been radically altered as they adapt to such scarcity.

Historically, it is important to know the volume and value of energy producing materials that pass from party to party and across national

1

borders. But that is hardly the entire story. This study provides an overview, covering roughly a century, of the energy industry systems of key producing nations as well as of the efforts of non-energy producing nations to become producers or otherwise to share in the profits and/or control the processing of raw fuels. In the twentieth century, societies learned that modernization — urbanization, industrialization, and attendant socio-political change — did not come automatically but had to be planned and worked for. Efficient energy systems were fundamental to the process, indeed, modernization could not occur without them. Societies also learned that the control of energy systems opened Pandora's box. Societies had to learn, and did so only imperfectly, to master these newly applied and powerful technologies. Even the most modern societies, the USA, Japan, and western Europe, must receive low marks for energy management. To compound their failures, they actively hawked their imperfect energy systems among the lower income and less technologically sophisticated nations.

At appropriate points, and among many other details and considerations, this study deals with: domestic, national, regional, and global energy demand and supply; the relations between nations that are linked by energy as well as other interests; movement across borders of capital and its products, technology and managerial expertise and pollution; questions of power, of who controlled the international movement of energy and capital; the specific companies, particularly the multinational oil companies (MNOCs) that were the epitome of power until the 1970s.

Thomas Hughes presents electric power systems as the embodiment of the physical, intellectual, and symbolic resources of the society that constructs them. Just as economic and social arrangements differ among societies, so, too, Hughes suggests, do technical components.[2] Does Professor Hughes claim too much? Perhaps, the devices of technical wizardry are merely the baubles and bangles of society, specious things, worn lightly, imperfectly reflecting the culture within. People *do* adopt technologies while preserving their own rhythms. On the other hand, things do ride mankind. Individuals and societies become captive to the very systems initially harnessed for their benefit. We constantly employ items that in the using are harming us.

Nonetheless, Hughes' imaginative and provocative study has required that I explore production and delivery systems as well as end uses since both might reveal something about prevailing economic and social systems, their resistance or adaptability to change, and the relative social losses or gains accompanying various energy uses. Measurement becomes a problem. Company economists are happy to note less energy use per unit of output. Society also gains because less energy use means less pollution. These relationships can be quantified and compared with less progressive situations. But how do we measure the cost of a dead otter or sea bird, the victims of an oil spill? Industrial society tends to measure only goods that are produced. While methods exist to translate into dollars the destruction of forests by acid rain or of sea creatures by an oil spill, few governments acknowledge such losses in their accounting. We must be constantly reminded of the possible consequences when a species or even an entire ecology disappears because of human action.

End uses of energy in a society are not impervious to change. They only seem to be intrinsic to its culture. But reduced costs and assured supply of a superior energy technology results in the rapid displacement of the traditional technology. In the USA, individual homeowners and businessmen switched as rapidly as they could from coal to less dirty oil and clean natural gas. Who, after all, wanted tons of black dirt poured into their basements each quarter? Natural gas became particularly desirable as states and the federal government maintained gas prices, and electric prices, too, at artificially low levels. Far from the USA, a Kikuyu chief, Kabongo, in the 1920s, questioned the value of the new ways adopted by his young men. They forget their own ways, he lamented. "They ride in fast motor-cars, they work with fire-sticks that kill, they make music from a box. But they have no land and no food and they have lost laughter."[3] Americans made choices and the Kikuyu did as well, but the options opened to Americans were infinitely greater than those the Africans enjoyed. Chief Kabongo and his people, ruled by British masters, recognized that the colonial system as a whole, not gadgetry, perverted and overturned traditional ways. But the yearning for the gimcracks of the modern world penetrated Kikuyu country as well as New York, Berlin, and Tokyo. Fulfillment came less swiftly to the Kikuyu than to the West.

Energy technologies symbolize modern times and come in various sizes—gigantic, as in an electric grid, or small, like a gasoline-powered vehicle. These technologies came on like an avalanche during the last years of the nineteenth century. Culture proved an imperfect defense against such threats to traditional ways of living. Cost and availability determined the degree to which a technology penetrated a society. Rural people in India do not prefer *uplie* (dried cow dung) as a cooking fuel to coal or wood; uplie is all they can afford.

Scrutiny of the end uses of energy, then, offers a view of the inner structure of societies. Those structures, after 1900, determined how much of which form of energy, of energy-targeted capital, of energy technology, and of energy expertise traversed national borders.

This study is a work of history by a historian. It adopts the form of political economy because the history of international energy can only be understood if political, institutional, social, and economic factors, all inextricably linked, are attended to. The organization of the book reflects my opinion that a credible explanation of energy affairs requires a focus on nation-states, and such domestic units as public and private energy companies, and regional groups of nations. During the course of my research, I learned that political explanations are more useful than economic in understanding energy transactions. Prices of energy are constantly manipulated by companies and/or governments to achieve institutional goals that have little to do with the actual cost of anything. Immediately after the *Exxon Valdez* oil spill in April 1989, wholesale prices of gasoline rose, not only at Exxon pumps but all over the USA. Yet only Exxon's supply had been marginally affected by the oil loss. Gasoline price manipulation like this has been recorded for decades in American markets, at least often enough to call into question the explanations of market competition that the oil companies offer for this or that price. In April, Exxon blamed American motorists and the Organization of Petroleum Exporting Countries (OPEC) for the sudden rise in price.

The approach here, then, is primarily institutional and political, and then economic. Of course, economics is essential. Energy purchasers, when they can, use costs as one reason for preferring this fuel over that. In local markets, real competition does occur. But at the global level, too many instances of cooperation between oil companies in pricing are recorded to permit much market competition. Before World War II, the giant MNOCs frequently made contractual arrangements to share and divide markets so as to forestall competition. The powerful German coal cartels acted similarly. Of course, after 1973 the pricing of oil by OPEC was disassociated from such theoretical considerations as the cost of production. Generally, then, the market forces encountered during the course of my research seemed more functional in a local than in a global context.

Readers should find the going rather easy. I adopt conventional chronological periods, punctuated by wars, depressions, and sundry crises. Conventional divisions work. The technological world after World War I — synthetics, radio, hybrid corn, the auto explosion, and other wonders — seemed far in advance of prewar technologies. After the war, the gold standard succumbed to depression. Nations became, or tried to become, more autarchic, with consequences for international energy traffic and internal energy mixes.

Chapters 2 and 3 carry the story from the advent of modern energy systems, characterized most notably by the transition from coal to oil and the dominance of the latter and its purveyors. World political and economic polarization provides the context, in Chapter 4, for an exploration of the consolidation of power by the great oil companies ensconced in various underdeveloped areas of the world and explains the emerging energy regimes of developed and developing nations. Chapters 5 and 6 deal with the linkage between western dominance in international energy, the increasingly embittered relationship between the producing states and the MNOCs and their home countries, and the energy transitions in the West that led directly to acute oil-import dependence upon the Middle East. Supply and price crises, first in 1973 with the embargo imposed by the Organization of Arab Petroleum Exporting Countries (OAPEC) and the price hike engineered by OPEC and, secondly, the more severe price rise occasioned by the Iranian Revolution of 1978, form the substance of Chapters 7 and 8. The first energy crisis terminated western hegemony in energy and hurried the eclipse of the United States as the undisputed world economic leader. These chapters contain discussions of the responses of developed and lesser developed states to inflationary pressures exacerbated by oil price escalation. (The price of a barrel of oil moved from less than $3 in 1972 to above $40 in 1979.) Chapter 9 deals with the same group of states during the 1980s, when energy prices peaked and then fell precipitously. Several themes, which had been introduced earlier, run through this chapter, including the fall and rise of OPEC, the plodding and fatally marred efforts of the western nations to achieve energy supply security, the neglect of energy conservation, and the accumulating evidence linking fossil fuel consumption with dangerous environmental pollution.

I have written a narrative history. I did not divide the several chapters into narrative and analytic sections, but chose to discuss issues as I went along. The study is not tied to any particular theory, although several theories are studied at appropriate points. Theories offered to explain large or small trends all failed the supreme test: they did not account for what happened. In discussing the several models purporting to explain energy changes and even to predict the future, I hope that the benefits of broad historical analysis are demonstrated. I would have been delighted to hang everything on a theory or two, but I was unable to create anything superior to those encountered. However, the facts are not simply laid out, one after another, like bathroom tiles, and left to their own devices. I package them and speak from them and for them. This book is not altogether "objective."

Within the several chapters, analyses of energy sectors are offered for four broad groups of states: the West (roughly the states belonging to the Organization for Economic Cooperation and Development (OECD)); the USSR and Soviet bloc, treated occasionally as lesser developed countries (LDCs); the producing states, largely LDCs but including the USA, the USSR, and, by the 1970s, the North Sea states; and the energy importing LDCs. From time to time, these groups are reconstituted into energy importing and exporting nations. Joined to these states are the energy industries, particularly the multinational oil companies (MNOCs) and such large units as electric utilities and electrical equipment manufacturers.

An investigation of the oil industry suggests that political–institutional arrangements — power — more satisfactorily explain the structure and function of international energy transactions than so-called free market pricing. The relationship between competitive markets and political solutions and the impact on both of events and the consequent impact of all on price receives constant attention. In the north German coal market before World War I, the Rhenish–Westphalian Coal Syndicate waged war with British coal imports. The coal cartel raised and lowered prices as necessary to undersell the British. Losses were made up by charging higher prices in non-competitive markets. Cartel power manipulated price, frequently charging less than the cost of production. Between the two world wars, most advanced nations adopted prohibitively high tariffs to protect domestic economic sectors. Coal and oil trades were affected by those policies.

Other centers of power in the energy industries are described and their checquered fortunes explained. An oligopoly of MNOCs, backed by western might, especially American and British, ruled the oil industry by World War I and continued to do so for the next five decades. But then, an oligopoly of producing states replaced the great companies. This study explains this apparently sudden change in energy centers of power and the consequences for production, pricing, national security, and so on.

Assiduous attention is devoted to the transformation of domestic energy mixes and to energy policy formation. Energy resource endowments of particular nations at different stages of economic development are scrutinized, normally from a comparative context. Shifts from fuel to fuel, including nuclear power, are chronicled and explained. From this investigation, a theme of sorts emerges: nations have, by and large, acted inefficiently and myopically in managing their energy resources and energy requirements.

In an earlier study, I concluded that US energy policy could be characterized as minimalist, uncoordinated, and based on the erroneous principle that correct policy guaranteed the lowest possible price.[4] In this the USA was not alone. Other industrialized states invariably chose cheapness over energy efficiency. Until 1973, this critical choice rested upon the superior power that the West brought to bear upon the LDC producing states. Oil's cheapness also affected coal, natural gas, and electric industries. Each chapter contains vital elements of this story.

Implicit within the above, yet separate thematically, is the conscious search, especially in the West, for energy supply security. The embargo of 1973 intensified this quest. Chapter 4 and subsequent chapters attempt an assessment of the results of this mission. Among the considerations necessary to conduct such an evaluation are the consequences of seeking oil supply security by developing such fields as Alaska's North Slope, the North Sea, and, perhaps, Antarctica and other equally fragile environments. The *Exxon Valdez* spill, the spill in Antarctic waters and the not infrequent disasters on North Sea rigs may be part of the price paid for seeking security only through increased production.

A theme, largely developed in the last half of the study and flowing directly from the above, suggests that the real energy crisis is one of overconsumption of fossil fuels and inexcusable neglect of renewable energy and conservation. The profligate and careless use of fossil fuels, fostered by cheapness, threatens the global environment. For a century or more, billions upon billions of tons of pollutants have been released into the atmosphere, dumped into the sea and buried in the earth. The diverse sources and causes of this assault are explored in subsequent pages as are the choices that must be made by both developed and developing states if the pace of environmental degradation is to be slowed.

Global energy transactions have, in this century, composed a significant aspect of geopolitical and routine diplomatic maneuvering. A consistent trend, since the early years of this century, has been the increased participation of governments in the energy business. What were once transactions between oil producing companies, which may also have refined and distributed petroleum, and other private parties, have largely become state to state transfers. Aramco, once ruler of the roost in Saudi Arabia, is now, in effect, a subsidiary of the Saudi national oil company. The preconditions for this and similar extreme swings in power had been building since before World War II. Why was the West unprepared for the supply and price crunch of 1973? Why did the Iranian Revolution create such economic havoc in the West, already once burned?

Individual states and shifting coalitions of states seek comparative advantage over states and competing blocs. Given the record, leaving global energy-resource development up to private companies or to individual nations or blocs seems unwise. National or bloc policies, as demonstrated in later pages, pay little attention to equity considerations in the international distribution of non-renewable energy and other resources or to ecological imperatives.

In energy and mineral production, rights are frequently pitted against rights. What rights do those nations with powerful technologies have to the resources of Antarctica *vis-à-vis* those nations with no technologies? Does Brazil possess the uninhibited right to cut down every tree in its Amazonian rain forests? How will such issues be resolved? Will western nations show restraint in criticizing the development policies of the lesser developed nations? How much leverage does the United States or the United Kingdom, among the leading polluters in the world, enjoy in admonishing Brazil or Nigeria to lavish greater care upon their environments? Among the highly developed economies, one searches in vain for signs of a dynamic and imaginative campaign to confront these issues.

There is no end to the energy problem. The only reasonable basis for predicting the future course of energy developments and the repercussions of such development is the historical record. But this record speaks with a forked tongue. Like the Bible there is something in it for everyone. Some look at the modern history of energy and are hopeful about the future. Others are less sanguine. Still others are downright pessimistic. One can only hope that a better understanding of energy history will promote a more rational approach to the future. Historians like to suggest this in order to lay claim to some relevance. I would not hazard a large bet on it, though.

Notes

1. A. Buchan, "Technology and World Politics," in B. Porter, ed., *The Aberystwyth Papers. International Politics, 1919–1969*, London: Oxford University Press for the University College of Wales (1972), p. 163.
2. T.P. Hughes, *Networks of Power: Electrification in Western Society, 1880–1930*, Baltimore: Johns Hopkins University Press (1983), p. 2.
3. From "The Coming of the Pink Cheeks. Part II," in L.E. Clarke, ed., *Through African Eyes: Cultures in Change. Unit IV. The Colonial Experience: An Inside View*, New York: Praeger (1970), p. 38.
4. J.G. Clark, *Energy and the Federal Government: Fossil Fuel Policies, 1900–1946*, Urbana: University of Illinois Press (1987), i.

2

Energy and the maturation of industrial economies in the West, 1900-18

Day and night, coal-laden trains rumbled over the tracks connecting the deep and rich mines of Wales and northeastern England with coastal ports. At the docks men and steam-driven equipment poured coal into the holds and engine rooms of waiting colliers. From Newcastle-upon-Tyne, many colliers nosed eastward toward North Sea or Baltic Sea destinations. At Hamburg, the leading German coal port, importers distributed the coal to buyers in Berlin and other interior cities where British coal was cheaper than coal from Germany's Ruhr fields during the years prior to World War I.

During those years, European-bound vessels from Philadelphia and New York included in their cargoes rising volumes of crude oil and petroleum products. Cans and barrels of kerosene, lubricants, and paraffin wax were off-loaded at London, Le Havre, Rotterdam, and Hamburg. Wholesalers and retailers, some owned by the shippers, then distributed these products to countless consumers who also availed themselves of competitive goods shipped in from Russia, Galicia, and Romania.

In 1907, the value of the UK's coal trade surpassed £52 million while the total value of all petroleum exports from the USA amounted to some £19 million. The UK alone accounted for some sixty percent of the world coal trade so in all likelihood the value of that trade surpassed £100 million. Oil companies in the USA supplied an estimated twenty-five percent of a global traffic in oil valued at £70 million.[1]

The monetary value of the world coal trade continued to exceed that of the oil trade through World War I. Coal remained the premier industrial fuel into the 1950s and the primary fuel for motive power at least into the 1930s. The application of the coal-burning steam engine to

9

both motive and stationary work tasks fueled the creation of a vast industrial complex, first in the UK, then in western Europe and the USA, and finally, in the early twentieth century, in Japan. Industrialization elsewhere proceeded more slowly, in part because of the comparative economic advantages and political power of the initial entrants. Coal-burning locomotives and vessels vastly increased the tonnage that could be hauled economically over long distances, thus reducing freight rates. Stationary engines made possible the deep mining of coal, accelerating coal production to levels sufficient for the development of a giant iron and steel industry in the West during the latter years of the nineteenth century.[2]

Among the industrial nations of the West, perhaps only the USA before World War I approached self-sufficiency in fuels, iron ore, and other critical industrial minerals. The leading European coal producers imported vast amounts of other raw materials. Germany, the world's third largest coal producer and second-ranked coal exporter, imported significant quantities of coal. Western Europe contained little oil and, by 1900, depended upon imports from eastern Europe and the USA.

The following section will discuss some of the changes wrought by the application of increasing quantities of non-renewable energy in several urban centers around the world. Attention will then shift to coal and oil. In both cases, the discussion is directed toward production, industrial organization, distribution, and marketing. While coal was more significant in foreign exchange, the oil industry developed greater complexity, tending toward vertically integrated organizations, the most important of which operated transnationally. Toward the end of the chapter, the international migration of the electric generating and equipment industry will serve as an example of an industry that smoothly orchestrated cross-boundary transfers of capital and technology. Consideration of the immediate effects of World War I on energy industries in several nations serves as a conclusion to Chapter 2.

Energy transitions

The West enjoyed access to the fossil fuels necessary to supplement domestic production. Exports of goods and services paid for the energy imports. An expanding population, increasingly urban, demanded greater quantities and varieties of goods and services, a demand met swiftly by the creation of such new and high energy consuming industries as electricity, synthetics and petrochemicals, and, emerging even before World War I, the automotive industry. Demand in these leading industrial sectors combined with the enhanced use of fossil fuels in households and transportation between 1883 and 1913 spurred the tripling of world coal production and the rise by ten times of crude oil production (Tables 2.2 and 2.7; see pages 16 and 30).

Abundant and relatively cheap energy stimulated the evolution of high energy-use societies in the USA, western Europe, and a few other areas before World War I. A dynamic and unceasing energy transition swept across the West, variously affecting other peoples of the world. International sales of fuels and international transfers of energy capital, technologies, and personnel comprised the key energy related goods and services moving across borders.

Vast differences distinguished the energy options available in Berlin, London, and American cities from those accessible to the residents of Cairo or São Paulo. Even sharper distinctions separated urban from rural people. Many rural folk lived beyond the reach of modern energy systems, and in the non industrial regions remained so even late in the twentieth century. In the cities of the West everything was available: coal or kerosene or wood for household heating and cooking, manufactured gas for street and commercial lighting, and, spreading rapidly, electricity for all lighting and for transportation. Coal, oil, and electricity (and natural gas in a few states of the USA), powered enormous industrial complexes.

In prewar Cairo and São Paulo, representative of colonial and/or pre-industrial cities, the skeleton of a modern energy system emerged during the late nineteenth century. Both centers experienced substantial population growth with São Paulo transformed from a town of 23,000 in 1872 to a major city of 580,000 by 1921 and Cairo, long the central place of Egypt, growing from 320,000 in 1897 to 791,000 in 1917. In both cities, local and national governments, foreign capital, and the rich, foreign and native, acted as agents of modernization.

Shortly after Cairo and Alexandria were connected by rail in 1865, the Egyptian government contracted with Lebon & Co., a French firm, to furnish manufactured gas to both cities. At the end of the century, Lebon received a franchise to provide electric service in both places and Port Said. While foreign capitalists founded some forty steam powered factories in Egypt between 1884 and 1918, only a handful were located in Cairo which remained an administrative and commercial center. British occupation of Egypt in 1882 unleashed a hectic era of modernization in Cairo, resulting in the creation of two distinct communities by 1900. One, a modern European-styled city, enjoyed gas and electric lighting, new sewer and drainage systems, a waterworks using coal and oil in the pumping stations, and an excellent electric tramway service. By 1914, 58 kilometers of track and wires crisscrossed the city. The tramways permitted the development of peripheral residential districts for the middle and upper classes, including the elegant and fully serviced suburb of Heliopolis.

The old medieval city remained as it had been except for the tramways. Few of the thousands of small stores, inns, workshops, or warehouses located in the old quarter were hooked into the electric, gas, sewer, or water systems. Mass transit and the advent of new industries such as power printing, mechanical weaving, and the railways and utilities probably improved employment opportunities for some. But the round of life for most Carenes, so far as can be discerned, remained basically unchanged. Residents drew water from neighborhood wells, cooked in charcoal burning mud ovens or braziers, and disposed of their wastes as best they could.

Much the same pattern described São Paulo which, unlike Cairo, experienced some industrialization before 1914. The great expansion of the coffee industry triggered São Paulo's rise to industrial pre-eminence in Brazil. The mechanization of newly constructed factories created new jobs, attracted rural migrants, stimulated the modernization of Santos, São Paulo's port, and encouraged the construction of urban services. Electric power companies and tramways, coal and oil firms, most financed and owned by foreign interests, appeared in the city before the Great War. As in Cairo, new middle or upper class suburbs arose, all tied to the various utilities while working class districts, unless near a tramway, remained essentially unimproved. Workers lived in small houses, a family to a room, without indoor plumbing. Wages were low, rents high, and light bulbs rare. As in other parts of the world, including the West, industrialization brought marginal economic or amenity benefits to Paulista workers.[3]

Among non-western nations, the drive to modernize proceeded most swiftly in Japan. By World War I, its level of economic development more closely resembled western than non-western models. Urban growth rates in Tokyo, Osaka, Yokohama, and Kobe replicated those in western cities. Tokyo's population reached 1.3 million in 1897, twice that of 1870 while half as many lived in Osaka. Industrialization in Japan, stimulated by victorious wars against China and Russia, rested upon domestic coal and oil production, the efficient application of such older technologies as the steam engine, blast furnace, and railroads, and upon the rapid adoption of newer chemical and electrical processes. New energy systems encouraged the mechanization of industry and mining and the construction of a comprehensive urban and interurban transportation network. While Japan imported most of the heavy machinery and equipment, Japanese technicians proved skillful in replicating and improving upon the new techniques. By 1918, 15,700 of 23,000 factories were mechanized, using equipment bought from such firms as Allis-

Chalmers Mfg. Co. and Otis Elevator Co., compared with 3,700 of 8,200 factories in 1904.

Industrialization affected Osaka, Kobe, and smaller cities more acutely than Tokyo. But the capital introduced the new energy systems more rapidly than elsewhere. The Tokyo Gas Company (1885) diffused its service throughout the city, lighting 1.5 million lamps in 1915 and supplying one million heating installations, mostly small domestic gas heaters. Electric service, available in Tokyo in 1888, proved too expensive for householders compared with either gas or kerosene until the development of hydroelectric power after 1907. Then, electricity penetrated every nook and cranny of Tokyo. By 1918, virtually every home in Japan contained at least one light bulb and countless factories and shops used electric motors. The electric railway service spread quickly, doubling the number of passengers carried between 1908 and 1917. Exploiting the rapid transit system, merchants in downtown Tokyo transformed the Ginza, a nondescript road, into the most exciting shopping street in the Orient.[4] Tokyo's residents became habitual tramway riders at about the same time as urbanites in Berlin, London, and many American cities.

Relative to the USA, Germany, France, and Britain, Japan may appear as a late starter in economic development and to have successfully exploited the advantages of that position. In an Asian context, however, Japan appeared as an early initiator of modernization and rapidly widened the economic gap between itself and other Asia-Pacific nations, the largest of which were colonies of or otherwise dependent upon the West.

As early as the mid-nineteenth century, the use of manufactured gas spread throughout the larger cities of Europe and America. In London, many city streets, theaters, restaurants, and middle class homes were brightly lit by gas. The prepayment meter, introduced in the 1890s, encouraged gas use in London's low income homes. The very efficient town gas system of England may have created a disincentive for electrification. By World War I, Berlin and the larger American cities were more thoroughly electrified than London. There, a decentralized system of dozens of small firms experienced difficulty in selling electricity to businesses and industries reluctant to shift to the new technology. London's electric companies carried a much smaller power load than Berlin's or Chicago's. Indeed, six large consumers in Chicago purchased one-third as much electricity as was sold in all of London in 1911 while the New York metropolitan region generated more electricity than all of the UK.[5]

In prewar London, Berlin, New York, Cairo, São Paulo, and Tokyo, suburban and industrial growth owed much to new energy techniques.

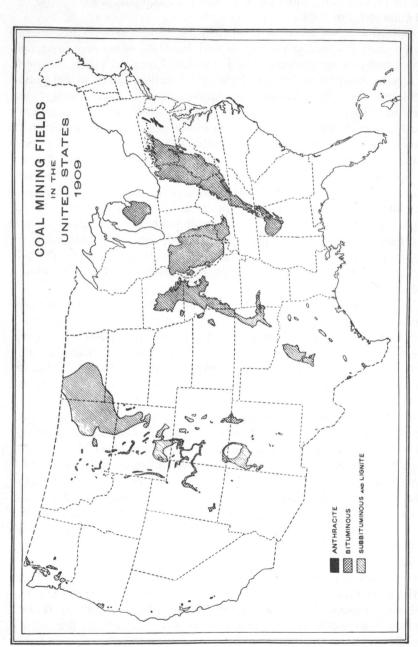

Map 2.1   Coal mining fields in the United States, 1909–19. (*Source:* US Bureau of the Census. *Statistical Atlas of the United States*, Washington, D.C.: GPO (1942), Plate no. 452.)

But in those cities and elsewhere, many people remained outside or only partially absorbed by the new technological society. In Egypt, 90 percent of the population were in no position to further the energy revolution. In Tokyo, 47 percent of the households were without public water. Low income families in the United States lived in squalid conditions. In smaller places such as Springfield, Illinois or Topeka, Kansas living conditions replicated those in major cities. Less than one-half of Topeka's households received city water in 1914, 75 percent of the homes used outdoor privies with drinking wells nearby, and 64 percent of the wells were polluted. As late as 1920, a survey of Springfield revealed that more than one-half of all families lived in very small houses without electricity, gas, or city water. The promise of an improved quality of life implicit in electric, gas, and other technologies materialized with painful slowness, even in the West where mass rural electrification awaited the post World War II years.[6]

The world coal industry

The maturing industrial centers in the West, the rapidly developing industry of Japan, and the youthful industries of such places as São Paulo all ran on coal. By 1900, coal fueled stationary and motive steam engines with a capacity of 66 million horsepower, compared with 1.6 million horsepower in 1840. The correspondence between rising iron and steel production and the output of coal, an essential chemical input as well as a fuel, was striking. Coal production in the USA grew by 411 percent between 1886 and 1913 (Table 2.2; see page 16) while pig iron output expanded by 421 percent; in Germany, this relationship stood at 283 percent and 533 percent, respectively.[7] Notwithstanding the intense competition of hydroelectric power, petroleum, and gas, coal remained the world's pre-eminent fuel until the mid-twentieth century (Table 2.1).

China's estimated 23 percent of world coal reserves[8] were of small consequence to the international coal trade compared with the 5 percent buried in Germany or the 17 percent in Europe. World production and consumption of coal was highly concentrated in a handful of states, those very states undergoing the most intense industrialization and urbanization. Total world coal production* rose by 90 percent between 1886 and 1900 and by another 75 percent by 1913 (Table 2.2). World

---

* Unless otherwise noted all types of coal — anthracite (hard), bituminous (stone), and lignites (soft) — are included, and all coal and oil tons are metric.

Table 2.1   World and USA primary energy use by fuel, 1900–35 (percent)

	World coal	USA coal	World oil	USA oil	World natural gas	USA natural gas	World wood	USA wood	World hydro-power
1900		0.70		0.04		0.02		0.23	
1913	0.74		0.04		0.01		0.18		0.02
1915		0.75		0.08		0.04		0.09	
1925	0.68	0.65	0.11	0.19	0.02	0.07	0.14	0.07	0.04
1929	0.66		0.13		0.03		0.12		0.05
1930		0.59		0.22		0.09		0.06	
1935	0.60	0.52	0.16	0.27	0.04	0.10	0.13	0.06	0.07

Sources: International Labour Office, *The World Coal-Mining Industry*. Studies and Reports. Series B. No. 31, Geneva: ILO (1938), pp. 496–7; S.H. Schurr *et al.*, *Energy and the American Economy, 1850–1975, an economic study of its history and prospects*, Baltimore: Johns Hopkins University Press for Resources for the Future (1960), pp. 496–8.

Table 2.2   Production of coal in world and in selected nations, 1886–1938 (million metric tons)

	World	USA	UK	Germany	Europe[c]	Japan	Russia
1886	403	101	157	73	294	na	
1900	767	245	230	153	na	10	
1907	1098	436	268	205	609	15	
1913	1341	517	292	277	684	21	30
1920	1348	595	231	252	na	29	8
1921	1160	459	163[b]	265[a]	na	26	9
1922	1237	433[b]	252	267	na	28	9
1923	1361	597	276	181	572	29	14
1924	1359	519	243	243	652	30	16
1925	1372	531	221	272	645	31	26
1926	1365	596	126[b]	293	628	32	32
1927	1470	542	280	304	853	33	
1928	1440	522	219	339	821	34	
1929	1559	552	239	350	873	34	48
1933	1174	348	191	246	622	33	90
1937	1582	451	224	368	716	45	151
1938	1504	358	210	380	720	49	160

[a] Treaty of Versailles boundaries
[b] Strike
[c] Not including Russia or Austria-Hungary

Sources: League of Nations, Economic and Financial Section, International Economic Conference, Geneva, May 1927, *Memorandum on Coal, Vol. 1*, Geneva: League of Nations (1927), pp. 43–52, 65; ILO, *World Coal-Mining* (1938), pp. 54, 76; E.B. Schumpeter, ed., *The Industrialization of Japan and Manchukuo, 1930–1940: Population, Raw Materials, and Industry*, New York: Macmillan (1940), p. 266; S. Takahashi, *Japan and World Resources*, Tokyo: Kenkyusha Press (1937), pp. 27; S. Uyehara, *The Industry and Trade of Japan*, London: P.S. King & Son (1926), p. 194; US Bureau of the Census, *Historical Statistics of the United States, Colonial Times to 1970, Part 1* (1975), pp. 589, 592; J. Darmstadter *et al.*, *Energy in the World Economy: A Statistical Review of Trends in Output, Trade, and Consumption Since 1925*, Baltimore: The Johns Hopkins University Press for Resources for the Future (1971), pp. 185–223.

coal production reached 1.3 billion metric tons in 1913 of which the USA produced 39 percent and Europe 51 percent. The respective contributions of the UK and Germany stood at 22 percent and 21 percent. Japan, India, China, and Australia supplied another 4 percent. Three nations, the USA, the UK, and Germany accounted for 82 percent of the world's coal output in 1913. Sixteen years later the USA and Europe still produced 90 percent of world coal.[9]

While coal strengthened its primacy as an industrial and household fuel in the West during the prewar years, its relative position deteriorated after the war (Table 2.1). For now, coal's years of supremacy will be investigated, beginning with a review of national coal industries and consumption patterns and then tracing the flow of coal in international trade.

Coal and national economies

In 1907, sixteen countries mined one million or more metric tons of coal valued at about £418 million, or 45 percent of the value of the world's output of minerals. Coal varied in quality and therefore value from mine to mine in the same producing districts. In America, householders prized Pennsylvania anthracite as a cleaner burning fuel than bituminous. The Ruhr fields of Germany produced ideal coking coal for blast furnace use, equivalent in quality to that produced in America's Pittsburgh district. Coal quality influenced the organization of national coal industries as did historical business precedents and preferences, the location of mines relative to markets, technological advances, and government policies.

Coal industry organization in the UK and the USA (except for anthracite) was quite similar while in Germany the coal industry evolved along different lines. In America, the anthracite industry must be distinguished from bituminous. The anthracite fields were located in a narrow belt in northern Pennsylvania, centering around Scranton and Wilkes-Barre. While anthracite production advanced from 52 million metric tons in 1900 to 83 million in 1913, its share of total coal production declined from 21 percent to 17 percent. Compared with bituminous, a small number of firms controlled the hard coal industry. In 1916, the largest thirteen companies — eleven owned by railroads — produced 79 percent of total production. The mines of the Reading Railroad, part of the J.P. Morgan system, yielded 20 percent of the anthracite. Political controversy swirled around these captive mines but, in the end, consumer abandonment of anthracite as a household fuel terminated the issue.[10]

Map 2.2   Coal mining fields in Europe. (*Source:* R.C. Smart, *The Economics of the Coal Industry*, London: P.S. King and Son (1930), facing p. 156.)

In contrast with anthracite, production of bituminous in the USA and the UK was diffused among thousands of firms. In America, 5,887 mines operated in 1911, two-thirds of which produced under 100,000 metric tons annually and cumulatively contributed about 10 percent of total output. In the UK, 1,500 firms operated 3,198 collieries. The coal industry in both the nations was intensely competitive. The many small firms lagged behind the larger in the introduction of coal-cutting machines, mechanical conveyors, sorting or sizing equipment, and automated tipples. Unable to increase production through mechanization, smaller firms often resorted to wage shaving tactics to remain competitive. Volatile labor-management relations characterized the coal industries of the USA and Britain.

American and British mine owners sold directly to such major consumers as railroads, utilities, and heavy industry and to wholesalers who disposed of the coal at home and abroad. Individual mine owners, unable or unwilling to cooperate, suffered from sudden fluctuations in demand. Demand instability, particularly from the large consumers affected by swings in the economy, combined with a relatively inelastic supply to heighten the vulnerability of the coal industry. For the most part though, an expansive economy prevailed before World War I and the coal industry appeared sound.[11]

Beginning in the mid-1870s as a response to depression and price deflation, the German coal industry consolidated into large producing companies, especially in the dominant Ruhr district where a buoyant iron and steel industry began to integrate at the same time. Halting and ineffective efforts to reduce production and stabilize prices during the 1870s and 1880s bore fruit in 1893 with the organization of the Rhenish–Westphalian Coal Syndicate (RWCS). Members agreed to deliver their entire production at a fixed price to RWCS which marketed the coal.

The refusal of the integrated iron and steel industry to join the cartel and the purchase of Ruhr mines by the Prussian government weakened RWCS which controlled some 85 percent of Ruhr production through 1903. In that year, the reorganization of RWCS brought the steel industry into the syndicate so that RWCS controlled above 90 percent of Ruhr production by 1914. RWCS also created a network of wholesale companies, three of which concentrated on foreign markets. Coal price stabilization after 1903, the failure of foreign coal to expand its share of German markets, and German coal exports which rose by 143 percent from 1905 to 1913 attested to the success of RWCS. Lesser coal cartels and cartelization in other industries permanently embedded cartels in the German economy.[12]

French and Belgian coal operators organized cartel-like organizations as well, but in both cases import dependency precluded effective price

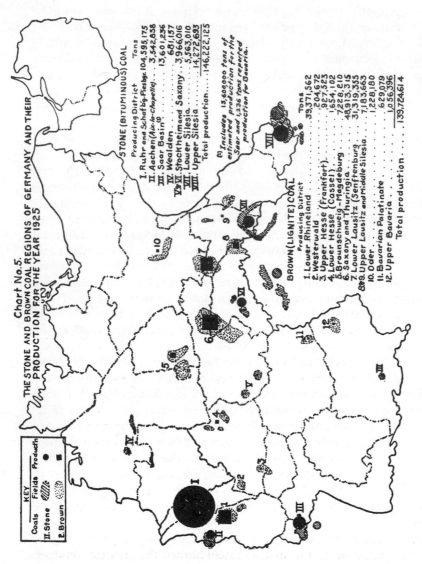

Map 2.3 The stone and brown coal regions of Germany and their production for 1925. (*Source:* A. Stockder, *Regulating an Industry: The Rhenish–Westphalian Coal Syndicate, 1893–1929*, New York: Columbia University Press (1932), p. 59. Reprinted with permission.)

Table 2.3 *Per capita* consumption of coal, 1901 and 1913 (metric tons)

	1900	1913
World	0.47	0.70
UK	4.00	4.20
France	1.20	1.60
Belgium	3.00	3.50
Holland	1.20	1.40
Germany	2.70	2.80
Russia	0.20	0.30
Italy	0.20	0.30
USA	4.40	5.10
India	na	0.05
China	na	0.03
Argentina	na	0.50
Brazil	na	0.10
Chile	na	0.80

Sources: As for Tables 2.1 and 2.2.

or production control. In Japan, however, a net coal exporter until 1923, horizontally and vertically integrated firms dominated by a kinship group (*zaibatsu*) moved forcefully into iron and steel, ship building, and coal and oil. By 1916, two powerful zaibatsu, Mitsubishi and Mitsui, owners of ten of the twenty-six principal Japanese coal companies (producing 87 percent of coal output), raised 26 percent of Japanese coal. The decentralized coal industries of the USA and the UK were somewhat anomalous by World War I, but so were their decentralized governments.[13]

National energy consumption by fuel or category of user is impossible to calculate for the prewar years. However, the per capita consumption of coal in several nations (Table 2.3), probably accounting for 80 percent of total energy use in the West and in Japan, reflects the great spread between the most highly industrialized nations and the others. Differences between Belgium and France and Holland mirror the more intense urban-industrial society fashioned by the Belgians. Only fragmentary evidence, usually non-comparable, is available to measure coal use in the West. Global and comparable data identifying categories of coal consumers are even more scanty. Table 2.4 reflects the data available.[14]

Without exception, industry consumed the largest proportion of coal; within the industrial sector, iron and steel burned the greatest tonnage. Such process heat industries as copper, lead and zinc, clay products, cement, glass, and chemicals, together, probably consumed as much coal as transportation and residential–commercial, except in the USA. There, the railroads, with 327,000 miles of track in 1914, burned

Table 2.4 Internal coal consumption of selected nations, by users, 1909–29 (percent)

	Industry	Transportation	Residential and commercial	Manufactured gas and electricity	Coal, coke and by-products
1909					
Rhenish–Westphalian Coal Syndicate	58[a]	15	15	5	7
France	49	16	19	8[b]	8
1913					
France	50	17	18	7[b]	8
United Kingdom	47	8	21	12	10
Japan	33	44[d]	na	na	na
1915					
United States[c]	34	30	17	na	16[a]
1921					
Japan	48	36[f]	na	na	na
1923					
France	16[g]	17	na	na	na
United States[ci]	50	25	na	8[h]	16
1925					
United States[ci]	52	25	na	8[h]	15
United Kingdom[j]	34	6	18	11	7
1926					
Italy	43	36	7	14	na
1929					
United States[c]	28	25	23	8[h]	17

[a] 70 percent metallurgical
[b] All gas
[c] Percent of coal available for internal consumption
[d] 75 percent marine use
[e] 88 percent coke and by-products
[f] 67 percent marine use
[g] Metallurgical only
[h] All electricity
[i] Bituminous only
[j] Exports accounted for remaining 24 percent

Sources: A. Stockder, *German Trade Associations*: *The Coal Kartels*, New York: Henry Holt (1924), pp. 16–17; S. Uyehara, *The Industry and Trade of Japan*, London: P.S. King & Son (1926), pp. 198–9; League of Nations, Economic and Financial Section, *International Economic Conference, Geneva, May 1927, Memorandum on Coal*, 2 vols., Geneva: League of Nations (1927). p. 48; R.C. Smart, *The Economics of the Coal Industry*, London: P.S. King & Son (1930), pp. 84–5; John G. Clark, *Energy and the Federal Government: Fossil Fuel Policies, 1900–1948*, Urbana; The University of Illinois Press (1986), Table 3; US Bureau of the Census, *Historical Statistics of the United States, Colonial Times to 1970, Bicentennial Edition, Part 1*, Washington, DC: GPO (1975). p. 591; S.H. Schurr and B.C. Netschert *et al.*, *Energy in the American Economy, 1850–1975, an economic study of its history and prospects*, Baltimore: The Johns Hopkins Press for Resources for the Future (1960). p. 82.

enormous quantities of coal. Domestic demand in the USA also exceeded a comparable demand elsewhere because incomes were higher and more single- and multi-family dwellings adopted central heating systems. Specialized demand for certain types of coal unavailable domestically were filled by imports. American anthracite supplied residential–commercial demand in Canada. Germany exported its superior coke and imported Austrian lignite, the principal coal used in German households. Great Britain, with its imperial and worldwide commercial network, shipped coal to Europe, Africa, South America, and Asia for industrial, railroad, and utility use.

Coal in international trade

Global coal production tripled between 1886 and 1913 (Table 2.2), principally responding to Western demands (Table 2.4). In the West, American and British coal mines filled all domestic needs and provided a significant surplus for export. For the five years, 1909–13, the average annual tonnage of coal exported amounted to 184 million, or 15 percent of all coal produced. Britain contributed 49 percent of exports and the USA and Germany, 12 percent each. Belgium and the Netherlands, Austria–Hungary, Czechoslovakia, Japan, and Australia accounted for an additional 18 percent. Britain's coal exports earned about £51 million in 1913, about 11 percent of all earnings from domestic exports. Coal exports contributed about 6 percent of the value of all German exports (from which the cost of coal imports must be deducted). American coal and coke exports, largely to Canada, were valued at about £15 million. Thus, the stake of the UK in the foreign coal trade far surpassed that of any other country.[15]

In 1913, Europe produced 63 percent of the global supply of coal (Table 2.5). One-third of the coal moved in foreign trade. The European market alone absorbed 115 million metric tons of the 131 million metric tons exported by European producers. France, Germany, Belgium, and Holland, the most highly industrialized states, received 52 percent of intra-European shipments. One other sizable coal market existed in Canada which imported 16 million metric tons in 1913, 99 percent from the USA. In effect, western Europe comprised the world coal market.

While all the nations in Table 2.5 produced coal, only one, the UK, enjoyed total self-sufficiency in coal. Of the major producers that imported and exported, only Germany was a net exporter. France, Austria–Hungary, and Russia produced relatively large tonnages of coal but were net importers (Table 2.5). The requirements of specific industrial consumers for coals of prescribed qualities, coke or coking coal for

Table 2.5   The western European coal market, 1913 (million metric tons)

	Production	Imports	Exports
UK	287	0	75
Germany	277	18	35
France	45	25	2
Belgium	23	10	7
Holland	2	8	0
Spain	4	3	0
Czechoslovakia	37	8	4
Austria–Hungary	54	15	8
Russia	36	8	0
Total above	765		
Sweden	<1	5	0
Norway	<1	2	0
Denmark	<1	4	0
Italy	<1	11	0
Portugal	<1	1	0
Switzerland	<1	3	0
Total above		115	131

Sources: B.R. Mitchell, ed., *European Historical Statistics*, second revised edition, London: Macmillan (1981), pp. 383–5, 430–2.

example, necessitated the exchange as did the location of European coal fields relative to markets. The vagaries of international boundaries shaped the pattern of coal exchange among nations and, as borders shifted, compelled the redefinition of trade relationships.

A feature distinguishing the coal from the oil trade was its predominantly national ownership. Britons, Germans, Belgians, and French owned their domestic mines and the wholesale and retail outlets. Although the large wholesale companies of the RWCS established branches in Utrecht, Holland and Antwerp, Belgium, RWCS encountered stiff competition from Belgian and Dutch wholesalers and eschewed entry into the retail market.[16] Commonly, imported coal passed into local hands at the receiving port or railhead. In oil, integrated multinational firms quickly blanketed the globe with subsidiary marketing units.

Linked to this feature of national ownership was the insignificant international movement of coal investment capital. British investors did not hold stock in western European coal companies. European capital did develop the Donets coal basin of western Russia. Donets coal, consumed internally, reduced somewhat the Russian market for imported coal. In China, too, a few rich coal fields attracted British, German, and Japanese capital but, like Russia, China was a peripheral area.[17] The movement of capital, partly in the form of new equipment and technical and managerial expertise was very small compared with the foreign money poured into the Baku, Romanian, or Mexican oil fields.

Britain's coal trade

Britain sold 61 percent of its coal exports to European purchasers. Each major European customer obtained a large proportion of its imported coal from the UK (Table 2.6). Britain's comparative advantages included: high quality coals suitable for coking and steam raising; easily mined seams and labor productivity superior to that of France or central Germany; lower mine-head prices than competitors; mines located near ports with easy and cheap access to Europe and South America; ownership of 40 percent of world shipping tonnage in 1914; declining ocean freight rates and the availability of coal as an out-bound cargo; a worldwide commercial and investment network; and an accelerating demand for coal.[18]

British coal dominated those European markets supplied through Atlantic, North Sea, Baltic Sea, and Mediterranean ports. Germany mounted effective competition in those parts of northeastern Europe easily and cheaply reached by Ruhr coal, notably France and the Low Countries (Table 2.5). In France, the mines of the Nord and Pas-de-Calais filled 65 percent of domestic demand in 1913, leaving a shortfall of 23 million metric tons (Table 2.6). The Ruhr mines provided eastern France with 4 million metric tons of coke and briquettes and another 5

Table 2.6   World markets for British coal, 1909–13

	1909	1910	1911	1912	1913
British exports	78	77	80	83	93
(million metric tons)					
% to France	13	12	12	12	14
% of above imports	54	—	—	—	60
% to Germany	12	11	11	10	9
% of above imports	44	—	—	—	46
% to Italy	11	11	11	11	10
% of above imports	95	—	—	—	90
% to Sweden and Denmark	8	8	8	8	8
% of above imports	96	—	—	—	95
% to Belgium and Holland	5	4	4	5	4
% of above imports	31	—	—	—	20
% to Russia	4	5	5	5	6
% of above imports	40	—	—	—	72
% to all other Europe	10	—	—	—	10
% of above imports	na	na	na	na	61
% to South America	7	7	8	8	7
% of above imports	na	na	na	na	85
% to Africa	6	—	—	—	7
% of above imports	na	na	na	na	na
% for bunkers	24	—	—	—	22
% to all other markets	<1	—	—	—	<2

Sources: League of Nations, *Memorandum on Coal*, I, pp. 53, 56–7, 67; Smart, *Economics of Coal*, p. 177; Jones, *Coal Industry*, p. 55; Jackson, *Price of Coal*, p. 178.

million metric tons of stone coal. Britain supplied the remaining 14 million metric tons through such ports as Le Havre, Rochefort, Bordeaux, and Bayonne. The Ruhr coal syndicate reigned supreme in Low Country coal markets, although the excellent coking coal of Belgium's Liege fields competed favorably with Ruhr coal in northern France and Holland.[19] The RWCS and other Ruhr companies competed weakly with British coal in eastern Germany.

From Hamburg east to the Baltic port of St. Petersburg, Britain's coal merchants ruled. Scandinavia, with a tiny coal production, depended almost entirely on British coal. Russia's Donets field lay too far south to supply the hinterlands of the Baltic ports. A complicated coal trade evolved in the eastern half of Germany, the destination of the bulk of the 18 million metric tons imported by Germany in 1913.

Demand between Hamburg (receiving one-half of British coal imports) and Hanover and Berlin was met by British coal, German brown coal from fields adjacent to Leipzig, and some Czechoslovakian brown coal. British stone coal, preferred for steam raising purposes, was competitive with brown coal for household purposes in areas as far south as Berlin. Berlin burned about 3.5 million metric tons annually before World War I. By then, British coal had captured 28 percent of the market. To the south of Berlin, brown coal from southern Germany, Czechoslovakia, and Austria met the larger part of demand. Austria, in return, received over 90 percent of its stone coal requirements from Germany.[20]

Italy's inferior natural resource endowment and its easy access to water assured the UK of a large coal market, averaging about 10 million metric tons annually for the years, 1903–13, or 90 percent of total Italian coal imports. Spanish ports unloaded an additional 2.5 million metric tons annually during the last peacetime years. Together Spain and Italy purchased 14 percent of Britain's coal exports.[21]

Imports by coal-poor South American nations, beyond the reach of more expensive US coal, accounted for about 8 percent of Britain's coal exports. American coal, cheaper at the mine-head than British, lost its price advantage on the long rail haul between mine and port. Welsh coal cost less delivered in Buenos Aires than American coal. With an enormous and growing domestic market, the American soft coal industry ignored development of the fairly small Latin American coal market. Argentina, totally dependent upon imports for fuel, received 98 percent of its coal from the UK with whom it had intimate banking and credit ties. British ownership of Latin American railroads, utilities, mines, and other industries generated a large part of the demand for coal, railroad equipment, and other goods. In return, Britain received grain, meat, coffee, tin, rubber, and copper.[22]

Britain marketed coal in Asia but the potential was limited by distance, a marginal demand, and competition from South Africa, Australia, and Japan. Those three competitors produced a surplus of close to 5 million metric tons in 1913. The Japanese surplus plus Chinese production supplied major Chinese ports, including Hong Kong. British coal met Australian coal in Singapore while South Africa and Australia shipped coal to India's coastal cities. This coal trade was far more important to the modernizing countries than to the UK. Japan's coal production in 1913 was valued at 70 million yen ($35 million), or one-half of the value of all mineral products. Domestic coal fueled a rapidly developing industrial sector centered on iron and steel. Japanese coal exports helped pay the bill for imported iron ore.[23]

By far the largest share of Britain's coal export earnings derived from the European trade, including most of the 21 million metric tons of bunker coal that powered merchant vessels. Earnings from coal exports helped the UK to feed itself and obtain from overseas other necessary natural resources. Imports of raw materials were substantial, amounting to about one-third of the value of all imports during the prewar years.

Some argue that Britain's large overseas investments reflected the failure of British capital to exploit internal opportunities. But Britain's economic performance between 1900 and 1913, others insist, cannot be described in wholly negative terms. Britain's share of world trade stabilized at 16 percent. From 1900 to 1913, exports of coal and iron and steel each rose in value by 92 percent. Exports of manufactured metal goods doubled in value while the increment for textile and clothing exports was 80 percent. The UK, however, suffered the penalty of being the founder. Germany's iron and steel production, equal to Britain's in 1900, far exceeded Britain's by 1913. The UK's share of world iron and steel exports diminished. Germany and the USA pulled abreast or surpassed Britain in several industries, denoting the strength of newcomers but not necessarily the inherent weakness of the first-comer. On the eve of the twentieth century, such older British industries as shipbuilding and steel were retooling while capital flowed into such newer industries as automotives and petroleum engineering.[24]

Clouds on coal's horizon

The industrial and transportation base of the early twentieth century rested on coal. But alternative fuels and energy sources challenged coal's supremacy even before World War I. In the USA, oil, natural gas, and electricity performed work tasks as efficiently as coal, prompting many industries to experiment with those fuels. The application of diesel motors to railroad and marine transportation proceeded rapidly. Fuel substitution on a mass scale only awaited increases in fuel oil production. Electricity could be generated efficiently by water, oil, and natural gas. Improved boilers burned less coal per kilowatt or British thermal unit (Btu) produced.

Prior to the advent of fuel oil as a competitor, coal faced only the marginal competition of wood, a more expensive and less efficient fuel and, in the larger cities, manufactured gas, also more expensive. Supply and conditions in local markets determined coal prices. The highly competitive bituminous industries in America and Britain, consisting of thousands of mines, fought to protect market shares.

Britain's mine owners contended with intensified government involvement, particularly during the years, 1910–13, when miners became increasingly militant. Government legislation in the areas of wages, mine safety, and working hours contributed to a decline in coal miner productivity which, in Europe, improved the competitive position of Ruhr coal. Mine owners in America, unable to stabilize markets through association, engaged in cutthroat competition and wage slashing. The American strikes of 1897 and 1902 reduced supply and propelled prices upward, as did the strike of 1912 in Britain. Normally, however, coal prices before World War I responded to intra-industry competition and market wide economic conditions.

The appearance of large volumes of fuel oil in traditional coal markets, apparent in the USA even before the war, transformed the competitive position of coal. Fuel oil was cheaper to produce, transport, refine, store, and handle than coal. Moreover, it produced more energy and less dirt per comparable unit burned. But coal production continued to grow because oil was a relatively new product to which people were unaccustomed, because not enough fuel oil was produced to meet industrial demand, and because of steel's coke requirements and the electric utilities' preference for coal.

During the late nineteenth century, the oil industry focused upon the production of kerosene and lubricants. Seizing upon the appearance of the internal combustion engine and the automobile, the industry revolutionized its array of products. As gasoline production soared, so too did its residue, fuel oil, which the oil industry aggressively marketed. Western coal industries, decentralized, unintegrated, and technologically regressive compared with oil, responded weakly to the competition from substitutes. Consumers turned away from coal when they could. While strength and a relatively uninhibited foreign trade in coal characterized the industry before the war, commentators labeled most postwar national coal industries as ill and in decline.

The world petroleum industry

Western European and American capital and management exercised dominion over all phases of the petroleum industry. Western Europe contained little oil. Even though the USA led the world in production from 1902 until the 1970s, a large proportion of oil derived from fields located in colonial territories and undeveloped or lesser developed nations. The inability of those societies to finance the exploration, recovery, refining, and distribution of their oil resulted in an influx of foreign capital controlled by a few foreign multinational oil companies (MNOCs). This imbalance of power set the stage for rivalry and enmity between nations seeking crude oil supplies, between the producing nations (except the USA) and the MNOCs over concessionary terms and ownership, and between the MNOCs for oil fields and markets

Centers of production

In 1900, world oil production centered in the Appalachian and Lima-Indiana fields of the USA, producing 40 percent of world oil, and the Baku fields of Transcaucasian Russia, producing 55 percent of world supply. By 1909, the center of American production had shifted to the great Mid-Continent fields of Kansas and Oklahoma and to California, together accounting for 58 percent of American production and 37 percent of world output. The world share of the USA reached 61 percent. Production in Russia declined to 22 percent of world production. Oil fields in the Netherlands East Indies (NEI), Mexico, Romania, and Burma produced commercial quantities by 1909. In 1913, those fields supplied 15 percent of the world's oil. Russia's share had further declined to 16 percent. The prolific Mid-Continent and California fields yielded 49 percent of the world's oil while the USA produced 64 percent.[25] World oil production is summarized in Table 2.7.

Sterile aggregate production figures hardly evoke the speculative risk, difficulty, hardship, and danger inseparable from oil exploration and recovery. While the geologists, engineers, and drilling crews employed the newest knowledge, techniques, and equipment, the alchemy of exploration consisted of good measures of luck, guesswork, and probability. Even in the easily traversed USA, one of every four or five holes drilled between 1900 and 1919 turned out to be dry while depletion caused the abandonment of thousands of wells each year. In the USA, wildcatters (small outfits of limited capital) rather than the large companies pioneered the drilling of new holes. Exploration and recovery in the deserts of the Middle East or the tropical forests of

Table 2.7   Crude production in selected countries, 1900–39* (thousand metric tons)

	World total	USA	Russia	Romania	Mexico	Persia	Venezuela	Colombia	Iraq	Bahrain
1901	20 018	9 314	11 432	*						
1902	22 475	11 915	10 811							
1903	24 404	13 485	10 146							
1904	26 158	15 716	10 542							
1905	29 255	18 083	7 377							
1906	28 871	16 979	7 906							
1907	35 430	22 295	8 302	1 090						
1908	38 294	23 963	8 347	1 108						
1909	40 095	24 587	8 855	1 252						
1910	43 995	28 128	9 441	1 305						
1911	46 223	29 590	8 884	1 491	1 685					
1912	47 308	29 924	9 130	1 742	2 223					
1913	51 724	33 348	8 434	1 819	3 449					
1914	54 704	35 673	8 996	1 722	3 521					
1915	57 991	37 732	9 201	1 615	4 418					
1916	61 404	40 371	8 834	1 201	5 442					
1917	67 502	45 009	8 466	499	7 422					
1918	67 586	47 776	3 647	1 172	8 568	1 157				
1919	74 614	50 787	4 262	888	11 688	1 361				
1920	92 468	59 454	3 413	998	21 083	1 641				
1921	102 819	63 380	3 889	1 123	25 959	2 238				
1922	115 288	74 836	4 792	1 321	24 467	2 986				
1923	136 340	98 310	5 256	1 458	20 079	3 386				
1924	136 151	95 831	6 099	1 794	18 749	4 345	1 214			
1925	143 481	102 516	7 052	2 235	15 505	4 703	2 643			
1926	147 225	103 473	8 657	3 129	12 137	4 811	4 954			
1927	169 474	120 957	10 397	3 539	8 607	5 327	8 474	2 015		
1928	177 822	121 003	11 466	4 131	6 732	5 834	14 194	2 671		
1929	199 445	135 211	13 509	4 666	5 998	5 657	18 453	2 723		
1930	189 267	120 538	17 095	5 587	5 306	6 151	18 345	2 731		
1931	184 232	114 239	22 225	6 594	4 435	5 956	15 653	2 448		
1932	176 796	105 390	21 073	7 223	4 403	6 640	15 643	2 203		
1933	192 286	120 754	20 996	7 202	4 533	7 252	15 696	1 621		
1934	202 971	121 075	23 623	8 325	5 089	7 713	18 147	2 312	1 025	
1935	220 599	132 879	24 657	8 174	5 365	7 637	19 767	2 346	3 654	
1936	238 872	146 624	25 255	8 487	5 470	8 362	20 639	2 500	4 054	
1937	271 897	170 554	26 242	6 993	6 254	10 373	24 830	2 746	4 244	1 034
1938	265 072	161 914	27 836	6 464	5 134	10 449	25 089	2 887	4 352	1 106
1939	278 154	168 661	29 448	6 086	5 719	10 420	27 529	3 180	4 105	1 011

* Empty spaces denote less than 1 million metric tons

Sources: Ferrier, *History of BP*, pp. 638–9, for 1901–32; *Twentieth Century Petroleum Statistics, 1974*, Dallas, Texas: De Golyer and MacNaughton (1974), pp. 4–10, for 1932–39.

Venezuela required substantial injections of development capital which only the large companies could marshal. Often years passed—or even decades—between the first drilling and commercial flow. Concessions granted in northern Iraq in 1903 produced commercial quantities of oil only in the mid-1920s.

Domestic politics and international rivalries inhibited the exploration and development of promising fields and determined winners and losers in the search for oil. One tragic consequence of the revolution in Russia in 1905 was the slaughter of Armenians in the Transcaucasus, accompanied by the destruction of two-thirds of the wells in the Baku field. Russian production plummeted, falling by over 3 million metric tons from 1904 to 1905, and had not fully recovered when world war and another more violent revolution swept the old regime into the void. The Russian bear and the British lion growled at one another over spheres of interest in Persia. All Europe lusted for and encouraged the demise of the Ottoman Empire. The smell of oil as well as larger national or imperial interests shaped the actions of contending parties. Oil exploration awaited the settlement of complex territorial issues. Americans protested their exclusion from oil fields in Sumatra and Burma by the colonial masters while scheming to achieve hegemony in Mexico and South America. Decisions to explore, to drill, to produce depended as much upon political as economic calculations.[26]

Oil and national economics

The world did not run on oil before World War I. In 1913, oil provided under 5 percent of world energy supply while coal contributed 74 percent (Table 2.1). Illumination and lubrication were the key uses of oil. While the demand for lubricants increased during the next decades, the days of kerosene or illuminating oil as the primary oil product were numbered. Electric and gas lighting reduced the use of kerosene in the larger markets of Europe and the USA. Simultaneously, the advent of the automobile, even before the war, resulted in the rapid increase of gasoline (naphtha) and fuel oil production.

In 1900, kerosene production in the USA accounted for 62 percent of refinery output, compared with 29 percent for gasoline and fuel oil. By 1914, the respective proportions were 25 percent and 67 percent. Fuel oil use rose swiftly as navies and merchant marines converted from coal to oil and as railroads adopted the diesel engine. Industries and electric utilities in the USA gradually discovered the cost and convenience advantages of fuel oil. Some portion of rising fuel oil consumption resulted in the direct substitution of oil for coal.

The auto demanded enormous quantities of gasoline. Inventive minds responded with new refining techniques, notably thermal cracking which greatly improved the refinery yield of gasoline and light fuels from each barrel of crude. Unlike the coal industry, oil firms invested significant capital in research and development, seeking new processes with which to manufacture new products. The improved heating capabilities and comparative cleanliness of oil burning furnaces for home, shop, and factory further reduced coal use.[27]

Like a good lubricant, petroleum penetrated deeply into the moving parts of national economies. Consciousness of rising oil use and its implications awakened gradually between the 1870s and World War I. Leo argues that governments generally treated oil as just another commodity until World War I. The wartime experience transformed oil into a strategic resource and governments thereafter directed much attention toward obtaining a secure supply.[28]

Before World War I, producing and non-producing states recognized oil as a prerequisite for national security and/or as a powerful contributor to the national welfare. In each nation, ideas about security and welfare inevitably confronted the reality of a domestic industry dominated by a small number of large firms and as international trade controlled by a few multinationals. Brief examples from the USA, Romania, and Great Britain elucidate the linkage between oil and attitudes toward security and welfare. The USA was a developed country with its own oil, Romania a slowly developing producing nation with oil markets throughout Europe, and the UK a developed nation without domestic oil resources.

In the USA, the Standard Oil Company, a colossus, won dominance by the 1880s in the transportation, refining, and marketing of oil both at home and abroad. The nation's proven and probable reserves seemed sufficient for all time. The domestic market consumed ever increasing proportions of total output, 59 percent in 1899 and 75 percent in 1914. The phenomenal growth of consumption ultimately compelled Standard and its few competitors to seek foreign sources of production to serve foreign markets, but this was of little moment to most Americans. The sheer size of Standard and its power over price, demonstrated by the success of its Draconic wars against domestic competition, aroused intense hostility in several states and within the federal government. In 1911, the US Supreme Court, invoking the Sherman Anti-Trust Act (1890), ordered the dissolution of Standard. Only in the USA were the giant domestic firms attacked because of their size and power. Elsewhere, when large firms suffered political assault they were invariably foreign, and mostly American. Public notions of national welfare in the USA required that Standard be dissolved into smaller units, presumably assuring a competitive marketplace. National security objectives played no part in this campaign.[29]

Foreign capital developed the Romanian oil industry. In 1914, three firms, Steaua Romana (owned by the Deutsche Bank), Romano Americana (a Standard Oil subsidiary), and Astra Romana (a Royal Dutch–Shell subsidiary) produced 71 percent of total output, owned the largest refineries, and monopolized both internal and export markets. The Deutsche Bank and other German oil groups underwrote oil development in Romania as a means of lessening German dependence upon Standard. Royal Dutch–Shell (RDS) entered Romania in 1907 in order to compete with Standard in European markets. By 1914, RDS was the largest producer in Romania. The Romanian state, urged on by indigenous oil interests and widespread nationalistic sentiments, challenged foreign domination through laws that assigned a greater share of the domestic market to home owned refiners and that regulated the exploitation of state oil lands. In debates over these measures, Standard Oil played the role of *bête noire*, even though RDS was the largest producer and Germany the primary source of development capital. Agitation for a national oil industry emerged as a central issue in Romanian politics after World War I.

Argentina created a national oil company in 1907. The Mexican Constitution of 1917 endowed the government with expropriatory authority. As in Romania, these nations identified Standard Oil as a national enemy. Each nation considered independence from Standard as a security–welfare imperative. Each reacted adversely to the expatriation of oil industry income. They demanded a larger and more direct flow of oil income into the national economy, believing that the nation should be the prime beneficiary of its oil wealth.[30]

The firmest bonding of oil policy with national security occurred in Great Britain, a nation with no domestic oil fields and imperial and global trade commitments. Numerous authors have discussed the involvement of the British government in the scramble for oil concessions in Mesopotamia and Persia, the support granted to the British Burmah Oil Company and the latter's participation in the formation of the Anglo-Persian Oil Company (APOC) in 1909, and the purchase by the British government in 1913 of controlling interest in APOC. Naval demands for a secure fuel oil supply, APOC's inability to finance expansion, and an alleged scheme by RDS to purchase APOC precipitated the government's direct involvement. Thereafter, the British government was suspected of influencing, if not directing, the exploratory activities of all British owned oil companies, including RDS.

Britain imported its oil from Mexico, the USA, Romania, and Russia. Marketers competed without hindrance in the UK, with RDS and Standard capturing the lion's share of the market. Britain's refining industry was weak. An open market served the national interest. The purchase of APOC protected national security by assuring that the firm would not fall into foreign hands. These policies, tempered by the war, bore fruit during the interwar years.[31]

Governments reacted to the enhanced importance of petroleum by appealing to notions of security and welfare, mixed liberally, especially in lesser developed producing states, with politically compelling nationalism. Argentina, Romania, and Mexico acted with more foresight than Russia which imposed tax and freight burdens on domestic oil that obstructed domestic sales. The major non-producing states did not hamper and frequently encouraged the formation of firms that sought oil concessions in foreign lands and, if an imperial power such as the UK or Holland, discouraged foreign exploration in their territory. France, an exception, neither staked out oil properties abroad nor nurtured a domestic refining industry. Indeed, French tariff policies virtually destroyed domestic refining before World War I.[32] Most non-producing countries—Japan (with increasingly inadequate domestic oil) and Germany—recognized the need to protect or at least not inhibit the growth of domestic refining. For the most part, crude oil and refined products moved about the world in response to demand. A handful of fully integrated MNOCs directed this flow. Governments in producing and non-producing states took notice of the power of the MNOCs, but as of 1914 had not formulated consistent or comprehensive policies toward them.

Oil in international trade

Western Europe and the USA housed the most powerful oil companies. Standard Oil enjoyed world market supremacy by 1890. Thereafter, vigorous competitors challenged Standard in markets outside America. By the late 1890s, the Royal Dutch Company (Royal Dutch–Shell in 1907), incorporated in 1890, was firmly entrenched throughout Asia and harbored ambitions to produce and market globally. The Société de Frères Nobel (1874), the Société Commerciale et Industrielle Caspienne et de la Mer Noire (1886), a Rothschild company, and a few large firms organized by German, British, and Dutch investors controlled the Russian oil industry by 1900. In 1913, three large firms, one an amalgam of British and Russian companies, RDS, now the owner of the Rothschild properties, and the Nobels produced 60 percent of Russian output and accounted for 75 percent of internal sales.[33]

Mergers and new organizations added to the roster of MNOCs

between 1900 and 1914. The Deutsche Bank controlled producing and refining companies in Russia, Romania, and Galicia, a marketing network in Germany and the Low Countries, and oil concessions in Mesopotamia. Anglo-German competition for oil (and other) concessions in Turkey led in 1912 to the formation of the Turkish Petroleum Company (TPC), a partnership consisting of the Deutsche Bank, RDS, and the National Bank of Turkey, owned by British capitalists. One year later, APOC merged with TPC, thereby vesting stock control overwhelmingly in the UK and stimulating further accusations of British oil imperialism.[34]

The Deutsche Bank, sensitive to Standard's market power in Germany and western Europe, orchestrated in 1906 an amalgamation of oil interests, including those of the Nobels and Rothschilds, into the European Petroleum Union (EPU), a pooling arrangement. EPU contested with Standard in kerosene and gasoline markets, but was ultimately compelled to purchase Standard products to meet European demand.[35]

A key merger in 1909 joined the Burmah Oil Company with the primary concessionaire in Persia to form the APOC. In the US, Sun Oil Company, the Texas Company, Pure Oil, and, after the dissolution of Standard Oil in 1911, such former Standard affiliates as Standard Oil (New Jersey) (SONJ) and Standard Oil of New York entered world markets. Without doubt the most momentous event in the oil world involved the merger in 1907 of the Shell Transport and Trading Company and the Royal Dutch Company to form RDS.[36]

Oil industry organization and competition

The strength of Shell Transport consisted of its tanker fleet and its storage facilities in Asia. Royal Dutch, the largest Sumatran producer, marketed throughout the Far East but possessed few tankers and inadequate storage. Both had survived the takeover efforts and price cutting tactics of Standard. Both were ambitious to enter the European market, but recognized that such a venture would require substantial capital investment in producing fields close to those markets. With problems and plans in common and with complementary organizational strengths, Shell and Royal Dutch discussions in 1900–2 produced a joint marketing agreement. In 1907, the two firms fused into RDS.[37]

The structure of RDS typified the fully integrated MNOC. RDS served as the holding company — and soon as the financier — of a large number of subordinate units. Three management subsidiaries received specialized responsibilities. The Batavian Oil Company owned and managed all producing lands and refineries. The Anglo-Saxon Petroleum

Company controlled the tankers and distribution while Asiatic Petroleum Company was the marketer. Each managed the various companies that engaged in those operations. Astra Romana in Romania and all producing companies in the NEI fell under the aegis of Batavian. Jersey Standard was similarly structured. SONJ, a holding company, owned the stocks and bonds of subsidiaries and other securities. Beneath SONJ, a regiment of subsidiaries performed the functional tasks.

In the UK, RDS marketed through its subsidiary, the British Petroleum Company, while SONJ operated through the Anglo-American Oil Company. In Germany, SONJ's subsidiary, the German American Petroleum Company, competed with the EPU pool, other Deutsche Bank companies, and subsidiaries of Asiatic. SONJ's subsidiaries purchased refined products from affiliates in the USA, only a fraction of supply coming from Romania. Of the foreign subsidiaries of SONJ, Imperial Oil of Canada, the West India Oil Refining Company (Havana), and Romano Americana operated large refineries. RDS also lacked refineries in its key European markets, preferring, as did SONJ, to locate refineries close to producing fields. Both firms, then, depended heavily upon efficient transportation from field to refinery to marketing units and, finally, to consumers. Even before 1900, Standard innovated in marketing by introducing credit sales and by delivering kerosene and fuel oil to customers. In China, Standard sold kerosene lamps at below cost, and even gave them away, in a campaign to expand lamp oil use. RDS and SONJ battled furiously for the Chinese and Japanese markets. As of 1913, RDS possessed the greatest advantage, producing fields in Sumatra.

Before the dissolution of Standard, the Rockefeller giant engaged in selective price cutting tactics, both at home and abroad, to eliminate competition. Predatory pricing in competitive markets in the USA combined with the ability of Standard to extract favorable railroad freight rates to give Standard the advantage throughout America. Abroad, however, and particularly in Europe, RDS, the Nobel interests, and other foreign conglomerates strenuously resisted Standard's relentless price cutting. By the time of Standard's dissolution, the products of Standard, RDS, or APOC were similar in quality and no one MNOC enjoyed a marked advantage in the efficiency of production, refining, transportation, or distribution. Essentially, the MNOCs accommodated one another in Europe and in America, where Standard's children and a few other firms dominated markets. Because of the large number of independent (non-MNOC) producers, refiners, and marketers in America, the market there remained more competitive than in Europe or elsewhere. Independents sought to maintain product prices below those of the larger firms. During the 1920s and after, such localized competition featured the "branded" products of the major firms and the "non-branded" products of the independents. In Europe, non-price competition characterized the contest for markets between the few large firms supplying crude and petroleum products.

Motor gasoline (petrol) met no competition; petroleum lubricants confronted no substitutes. Of the key petroleum products, only kerosene and fuel oil faced competition from manufactured gas, wood products, and coal. Kerosene ultimately lost out in the developed West to centrally distributed gas and electricity. Fuel oil battled coal for industrial and residential customers into the mid-twentieth century. In America and Europe, coal gradually lost out, except in electric generation and steel, not because of basic cost but because of efficiency and convenience. But prior to World War I, fuel oil marketers were only devising the strategies that would damage the coal industry after 1920.

Sales in Europe before the war accounted for one-half of Standard's total net earnings from marketing. In competing for European customers, SONJ's advantages consisted of customer recognition of quality brand name products and finely tuned distributing and marketing subsidiaries. But the dissolution decree of 1911 had stripped SONJ of its producing properties. As a consequence, SONJ purchased 87 percent of its crude from former domestic affiliates. Those firms would soon integrate forward into refining and marketing. In response, Standard integrated backwards to production, seeking oil fields around the world. A similar compulsion motivated RDS which raised the competitive stakes by acquiring producing properties and opening sales operations in the USA prior to the war. RDS also purchased a successful producing company in Mexico just before the outbreak of the Mexican Revolution. Already engaged in head-to-head competition in Europe and Asia, SONJ and RDS met, after World War I, as virile suitors for oil concessions throughout the Middle East and South America.[38]

Overall, the organizational structure of the western oil industry varied little among the larger firms. In America, however, small and unintegrated firms proliferated in production, refining, and marketing. Favored by anti-trust laws and the oil producing states, this layer of so-called independents (some of which grew to large size) provided a measure of competition and a distinct political challenge to the giant firms which the European MNOCs did not face. In other ways, the competitive climate varied from one national market to another. Neither Britain, Germany, nor the USA dissuaded foreign involvement in the oil industry. In Russia, ill-devised tax policies on Baku oil permitted Standard to capture markets via St. Petersburg. French tariff policies during the late nineteenth century protected domestic refiners by reducing the import of refined products. However, the French government reversed this policy in 1903 by reducing the duties on refined products. The refiners — known as the Cartel de Dix — abandoned their plants and seized control of marketing. Standard served as the primary supplier.

The inadequacy of Japanese domestic production presaged oil import dependency. But integrated Japanese-owned companies emerged, utilizing domestic production to compete with the subsidiaries of SONJ and RDS. By 1912, four sizable Japanese firms shared 50 percent of the domestic market while the two foreign firms controlled the other 50 percent. Only in the 1930s, when Japan sallied forth to win empire in the Far East, did the government discriminate against the foreign firms.[39]

As in the foreign coal trade, oil moved with relative freedom to wherever demand existed. Non-producing countries might encumber crude or refined products with tariffs but this did not obstruct the international flow of oil. Among the lesser developed producing countries, however, political signals flashed warnings of hostility toward foreign control of oil resources. The Peruvian government in 1914 levied taxes on a subsidiary of SONJ that the latter labeled as confiscatory. During the Mexican Revolution (1910–17), RDS and SONJ funded opposing revolutionary leaders. Oil company intervention, bitterness toward the Mexican policies of the USA, deep resentment over the favorable terms awarded foreign concessionaires, and demands that Mexico share liberally in the proceeds of its oil wealth shaped the writing of the Mexican Constitution of 1917. It asserted inalienable state ownership of all subsurface minerals and declared that foreigners could own property only if they submitted to Mexican law and abjured appeals to their national governments. The revolutionary turmoil, however, had no apparent effect upon Mexican oil production which increased five-fold between 1911 and 1918 (Table 2.7).[40]

Neither producing nor non-producing nations formulated clearly defined objectives about petroleum, other mineral resources, or the MNOCs. The resistance encountered by the transnational firms hardly deflected them from their chosen course. Mexico articulated the strongest expression of national interest, but implementation proved difficult. World War I altered the situation in oil as in coal. The power and reach of the MNOCs expanded exponentially, triggering unfriendly responses in many nations and proto-nations. More so than in the prewar years, governments justified their actions by appealing to security and welfare imperatives.

The transnational electric industry

Tokyo Electric Light Company (TELC) constructed in 1888 a modern central generating station equipped by the Edison Electric Company

(General Electric (GE) in 1892). TELC and GE negotiated a patent sharing and licensing agreement, permitting the former to open several large factories producing light bulbs and other electrical equipment. GE agreed not to export those goods to Japan while TELC confined its exports to China and Manchuria. By 1909, TELC had relinquished controlling financial interest to GE in return for investment capital, technological assistance, and new patent rights. Japanese managers, however, continued to establish policy and guide an ambitious expansion program.

A similar pattern prevailed in arrangements between Japanese firms and other western European and American electric companies. Westinghouse Electric & Manufacturing Company, GE's chief American rival, concluded a patent sharing agreement with Mitsubishi Electric Engine Company, a component of Mitsubishi zaibatsu. By the 1920s, GE, Westinghouse, and Siemens of Germany held majority interests in several Japanese electrical equipment and generating companies but did not dictate policy. Japan succeeded in domesticating these industries even while absorbing foreign capital and technology.[41]

The new technology of electricity stimulated major innovations in transportation and industrial techniques, created an entirely new domestic and international capital investment market, and sparked subtle but penetrating changes in urban life styles and urban forms. In Germany, electric output soared from one billion kwh (a gigawatt) in 1900 to almost nine gigawatts in 1914 while output in the UK jumped fifteenfold. In Japan, the capacity of hydroelectric and thermal power plants reached 876,000 kw in 1917, an increase of 7.5 times since 1907.[42] By 1913, the value of manufactured electrical products probably approached £150 million of which Germany accounted for 35 percent, the USA, 30 percent, and the UK, 16 percent. Germany exported a substantially larger proportion of its electrical goods than either the USA or the UK. As in petroleum and coal, the enormous domestic market in the USA consumed by far the greater part of the electrical goods produced. European nations were the leading importers, purchasing 55 percent of the value of electical goods entering the foreign trade.[43]

Western European and American firms, notably the "big four" — GE, Westinghouse, Siemens, and the Allgemeine Electrizitats-Gesellschaft (AEG or the German General Electric Company) — achieved an even greater dominance in the electric industry than did the MNOCs in oil. GE led the field in Japan, Siemens in much of Latin America, and both competed with Westinghouse and smaller British, Dutch, Belgian, Swiss, and Austrian firms in the UK and continental Europe. Patent sharing and licensing agreements required a lessor to use the lessee's equipment. The big four also invested directly in generating stations in order to develop markets for their equipment. Before World War I, the big four had established manufacturing plants in the UK, France, Italy, Austria, and Russia.[44]

The transnational electric holding companies sought opportunities to construct generating plants throughout the world and, of course, vigorously merchandized their generators, batteries, and bulbs. Their virtual monopoly of state-of-the-art technology and their financial strength allowed them to determine the pace, scale, and direction of electric development. British engineers and managers introduced electricity in Lagos, Nigeria in 1902, erecting a central generating station adjacent to the port's coal bunkers. In the three years, 1911–13, Britain's possessions received an annual average of 47 percent of British electrical machinery exports.[45]

European and American firms pioneered in the electrification of Latin America. Britain and Germany shared the market in Argentina while Germany supplied 75 percent of Chile's electrical goods imports. American firms entrenched themselves firmly in the Mexican and Brazilian power and electric railroad industries. Canadian financiers, importing equipment from several American manufacturers, organized the first power and light companies in Mexico City and São Paulo. German and Swedish firms, drawing on Deutsche Bank and Rothschild capital, participated in the installation of hydroelectric facilities in the São Paulo region. Gradually, the investment companies sold out to subsidiaries of the large electric manufacturers. By the early 1920s, the Electric Bond and Share Company, GE's utility holding company, owned and operated central stations throughout the USA and the world.[46]

Although British capital and electrical goods firms successfully pursued economic opportunities in Latin America and the colonies, the leading German and American firms carved out a large market share in the UK. Annual imports of electrical goods into the UK between 1908 and 1913 averaged about 61 percent of average annual exports of electrical goods. Foreign suppliers, Byatt estimates, furnished the equipment for 66 percent of Britain's installed generating capacity. Byatt attributes Britain's import vulnerability to the policy of free trade. Other factors also intervened. The relatively small scale of industry — three-fifths of London's factories employed fewer than twenty-five people — discouraged electrification since gas provided light. Some 40 percent of London's factories were at least partially electrified by World War I. But uncertainty as to the ability of small generating companies to supply sufficient electricity discouraged many firms from substituting electric for steam driven power. Many attributed the relatively slow adoption of electricity to the control over electric supply exercised by numerous local authorities. In short, slow electrification in Britain may be attributed to a general commitment to a steam–gas energy system and a reluctance to invest the capital necessary to switch to electricity. No doubt the town gas system was efficient. However, in 1913, less than one-half of the UK's industrial establishments were electrified, compared with 70 to 80 percent in Germany and the USA.[47]

Technological and organizational superiority assured the supremacy of the "big four" into the 1930s. Nations such as Mexico, Brazil, and Argentina, lacking indigenous technologies, technical personnel, and capital, only gradually replaced foreigners with local managers. These and other lesser developed countries, moreover, remained for many years potential rather than actual markets for the mass selling of household appliances. Japan, however, dispatched increasing numbers of young men to American universities and companies for a technical–scientific education and job experience. Japanese zaibatsu negotiated favorable patent and licensing contracts with the electric and petroleum firms, but retained managerial control. World War I shortages prompted Japanese manufacturers to reproduce scarce western equipment. By the 1920s, Japanese utilities and electric goods manufacturers were supplying a widening share of domestic demand and finding new outlets in Asia.[48] A deep sense of national unity, a stable central government, the high value assigned to education and science, a dynamic economy, and other qualities lacking or stultified in many nations protected Japan against foreign control of strategic industries.

Governments, World War I, and energy

World War I disrupted normal channels of trade for four years, compelling states to exploit national resources or do without. Among the Allied powers, the UK and France drew heavily from the American cornucopia. But even bountiful America could not maintain a stream of supplies to favored European nations sufficient to sustain consumption near prewar levels. Gigantic armies chewed up supplies and one another at a horrible rate. Fuel supply became a paramount concern to both warring and neutral nations.

In Argentina, wood use rose and energy prices escalated while coal imports of 4 million metric tons in 1913 fell to 707,000 metric tons in 1917 and oil imports tumbled. Fuel shortages broke Argentina's development momentum. The Argentine state oil industry failed to progress during the war, starved as it was of funds by the government. The military and some politicians viewed the wartime energy emergency as a direct threat to national security. They actively promoted intensified utilization of state oil fields. But, the end of the war and the availability of Mexican oil dissipated any feeling of urgency.

Japan, a minor belligerent experiencing a diminution of normal industrial imports, expanded in such key sectors as shipbuilding, steel, and oil refining. But domestic coal mines and oil fields yielded reduced proportions of demand. Japan, too, investigated strategies to strengthen the national resource base. The Japanese solution would differ radically from Argentina's.[49]

Coal and oil figured prominently in the logistics of the war and in its settlement. Most military planners envisioned a short war of a year or less. As a result none of the major belligerents—the UK, France, Russia, and Germany—stockpiled fuels or other essential primary products. Prior to the war, the British navy and other fleets switched rapidly from coal to oil burning marine engines. Tanks, airplanes, and lorries, all part of mobile armies, required gasoline and lubricants. Critical industries such as steel consumed coal and lubricants. As the war dragged on, diminishing fuel supplies threatened the productive capacity of Europe's fully mobilized societies.

Inconclusive findings characterize discussions of the significance of fuels to the mapping out of wartime objectives. During the interwar years, numerous analysts linked grand strategy to the quest for oil. They emphasized Germany's drive into Romania in 1916, the British invasion of Mesopotamia, and German–Turkish and British efforts to occupy the Baku oil fields or at least deny them to the Bolsheviks. But these were mere sideshows in a struggle won or lost on the western front. Germany invaded Romania only when Romania, at Britain's insistence, entered the war on the Allied side. The UK invaded Mesopotamia to deny it to Turkey, to extend her hegemony in the Middle East, to protect both India and the facilities of the APOC, as well as to assure access to the oil potential of northern Iraq.

The wartime experience did precipitate, as Heyman writes, "a real oil frenzy...which greatly influenced international relations after the...war."[50] However, this differs from the assertion that fuel supply considerations determined grand strategy. Beyond doubt, nations, particularly the victorious Allies, recognized the essentiality of fuels to national security. The Versailles settlement reflected this awareness. But the "oil frenzy" also mirrored pessimistic estimates of US oil reserves, the sudden removal of Russian crude from world markets, the unproven magnitude of Iraq's fields, and the correct assumption of oil companies that demand would soar with the coming of peace. These factors motivated the active exploration initiated by RDS, SONJ, and other MNOCs in Latin America and the USA.[51]

Dangerously depleted fuel stocks compelled the governments of the UK, France, Germany, and the USA (a belligerent in 1917) to intervene directly in their coal and oil industries. Each government established special agencies to increase production, assure the highest priority to the military and essential industries, check severe price inflation, and equitably distribute remaining supplies to civilians. All moved cautiously and only in 1918 were the systems fully developed. In the UK, as Kirby observes regarding coal, wartime exigencies, including a five-day strike by 200,000 miners in 1915 strengthened the case of those pressing for permanent and expanded government involvement. Nationalization of the coal industry took its place on the agenda.[52]

Oil companies in the USA provided over 90 percent of the oil reaching France and Britain during the war. An inter-allied petroleum council arranged transport and the fair distribution of the enormous quantities shipped to the UK, France, and Italy. Allied armies on the western front consumed an estimated 700,000 metric tons annually while the British navy burned over 2 million metric tons annually (40 percent of total imports). Military demand in the UK was double normal annual prewar consumption. Both the UK and France established agencies to control imports, ration civilian use, and regulate prices. In France, the Commissariat Général aux Essences et Combustibles (CGEC), with full power to move oil within France, broke up the inefficient Cartel de Dix. Although terminated in 1921, CGEC fought Jersey Standard and provided an immediate precedent for the evolution of the state dominated oil industry that functions in 1990. In Britain, the Petrol Control Committee drafted long-term policy proposals to protect imperial oil fields against foreign control and to obtain control of foreign oil fields. These discussions defined the parameters of British oil policies after the war.[53]

The USA, UK, France, and Germany suffered coal shortages caused by abnormal demand, overburdened transportation, the conscription of miners, labor management disputes, and, in France, by the cessation of imports from Germany and German destruction of mines that produced 50 percent of French coal. By 1917 and 1918, these governments had assumed almost total control of their coal industries. In America, the US Fuel Administration (USFA) set mine-mouth prices, established consumption priorities, reorganized the transportation system, limited wholesale and retail price margins, and promoted conservation.[54] Germany, blockaded by Allied fleets, and Britain imposed even more rigorous controls.

Germany, in 1915, compelled each coal and coke producer to join a coal syndicate, the better to regulate production and distribution. By 1917, these cartels, including RWCS, functioned under the control of the War Office. Government intervention in coal was all-encompassing by 1917. In March 1917, Britain assumed control of the output and distribution of all mines, regulated prices, licensed exports, and, in part, determined colliery profits. Britain carefully limited exports to neutral countries, a necessary tactic but one which damaged the postwar British coal trade. Despite these measures, severe coal shortages plagued the warring nations in 1918. As the war ended, American officials were preparing to ration coal. In Germany, nationalization of the industry was seriously considered and the British were investigating schemes to force the amalgamation of collieries.

With the Armistice, the USA quickly abandoned its fuel control regulations. In Britain and Germany, government controls persisted, gaining an acceptance in the UK that led to nationalization after World War II. The German coal industry, unaffected by an unimplemented nationalization act passed by the Socialists in 1919, retained its cartel structure until the next war. The French government, too, adopted interventionist policies in both the oil and coal industries. Of the major powers, only the USA sought to return to prewar arrangements.[55]

The war convinced many governments that national energy needs demanded legislative regulation and administrative oversight. This was especially apparent in the coal industry during the interwar years. Wartime coal demand precipitated an expansion of productive capacity far beyond peacetime demand. Britain's stringent wartime export controls forced traditional customers to look elsewhere for coal; many of those customers were permanently lost. To shore up domestic coal industries, many governments actively promoted foreign sales. They met attenuated demand and one another. Britain suffered most severely from this competition.

While the coal industry in several nations seemed stricken by an incurable malaise during the interwar years, the oil industry struggled to meet demand. Because they were winners, the UK and the USA, through their MNOCs, brought new fields under their hegemony and solidified their position in all old fields except Baku. The war hardly affected developmental trends in the US oil industry. The government's influence over domestic supply and demand was almost imperceivable. The governments of nations without domestic oil took steps to assure supply. In the lesser developed producing countries, host government demands for more equitable sharing of the wealth clashed with oil company insistence on the sanctity of contract. A rising nationalism, whether born of the war or not, fortified the weaker powers in challenging the claims of the MNOCs and their home governments.

Notes

1. A.D. Webb, *The New Dictionary of Statistics...*, London: George Routledge and Sons (1911), p. 90; US Bureau of the Census, *Historical Statistics*

of the United States, Colonial Times to 1970, Bicentennial Edition, Part 1, Washington, DC: GPO (1975), p. 898; H.F. Williamson *et al.*, *The American Petroleum Industry: Volume II, The Age of Energy, 1899–1959*, Evanston, Ill.: Northwestern University Press (1963), pp. 245–7.

2. Representative of those noting the linkages between the industrial revolution and access to cheap energy are: P. Deane, *The First Industrial Revolution*, Cambridge: Cambridge University Press (1979); D. Landes, *The Unbound Prometheus: Technological Change and Development in Western Europe from 1750 to the Present*, Cambridge: Cambridge University Press (1972); E.A. Wrigley, "Supply of Raw Materials in the Industrial Revolution," in R.M. Hartwell, ed., *The Causes of the Industrial Revolution in England*, London: Methuen (1967), pp. 97–120. The "West" includes the USA, the UK, and western Europe, including Germany and Italy but not Spain and Portugal.

3. For the above four paragraphs: for Cairo see J.L. Abu-Lughod, *Cairo: 1001 Years of the City Victorious*, Princeton: Princeton University Press (1971), pp. 94–117, 128–39, 174, 186–9; K.M. Barbour, *The Growth, Location, and Structure of Industry in Egypt*, New York: Praeger (1972), pp. 28, 49, 55–60; A.E. Crouchley, *The Investment of Foreign Capital in Egyptian Companies and Public Debt*, Cairo: Government Press (1936, reprinted by Arno Press, 1977), pp. 35–42, 73, 96, 114–19. For São Paulo see W. Dean, *The Industrialization of São Paulo, 1880–1945*, Austin: University of Texas Press for the Institute of Latin American Studies (1969), pp. 4–13, 38, 83, 91, 132–5, 152; P. Monbeig, *La Croissance de la Ville de São Paulo*, Grenoble: Institut et Revue de Géographie Alpine (1953), pp. 52–6, 62–6.

4. For Japan and Tokyo, see H. Uchida, "Western Big Business and the Adoption of New Technology in Japan: The Electrical Equipment and Chemical Industries, 1890–1920," in A. Okochi and H. Uchida, eds, *Development and Diffusion of Technology. Electrical and Chemical Industries. Proceedings of the Fuji Conference*, Tokyo: University of Tokyo Press (1979), pp. 145–8; Y. Takenob, ed., *The Japan Year Book...1920–21*, Tokyo: The Japan Year Book Office (1921), pp. 367, 612–13; T. Yazaki, *Social Change and the City in Japan from the Earliest Times through the Industrial Revolution*, translated by D.L. Swain, San Francisco: Japan Publications (1968), pp. 306–15, 355–6, 376–81, 443–6.

5. For the Western cities, see I.C.R. Byatt, *The British Electrical Industry, 1875–1914. The economic return to a new technology*, Oxford: Clarendon Press (1979), pp. 4, 211; *The Electrician* (London), 72 (5 December 1917), p. 354; T.P. Hughes, *Networks of Power: Electrification and Western Society, 1880–1930*, Baltimore: Johns Hopkins University Press (1983), pp. 227–31; T.I. Williams, *A History of the British Gas Industry*, Oxford: Oxford University Press (1981), pp. 31–5, 56–64.

6. Pierre Arminjon, *La Situation Economique et Financière de L'Egypte*, Paris: Librairie Générale de Droit & de Jurisprudence (1911), p. 150; Takenob, *Japan Year Book, 1920–21*, pp. 33, 337; T.J. Jones, *The Sociology of a New York City Block (Columbia University Studies in History, Economics and Public Law, XXI, No. 2)*, New York: Columbia University Press (1904), pp. 259–390; Shelby M. Harrison, *Social Conditions in an American City. A Summary of the Findings of the Springfield Survey*, New York: Russell Sage Foundation (1920) and *The Topeka*

Improvement Survey, Topeka, Kansas: Topeka Improvement Survey Committee (1914).

7. Landes, *Unbound Prometheus*, pp. 220–1; League of Nations, Economic and Financial Section, *International Economic Conference, Geneva, May 1927, Memorandum on Coal, Vol. II*, Geneva: League of Nations (1927), pp. 6–7.

8. F.R.E. Mauldon, *The Economics of Australian Coal*, Melbourne: Melbourne University Press (1929), p. 11. In 1977, coal experts guessed that China contained 1.4 trillion tons of coal, 7 percent of which was currently recoverable.

9. Webb, *Dictionary of Statistics*, p. 398; N.J.G. Pounds and W.N. Parker, *Coal and Steel in Western Europe: The Influence of Resources and Techniques on Production*, Bloomington, Ind.: Indiana University Press (1957), pp. 282–6.

10. *Historical Statistics, Part I*, pp. 589, 592; US Bureau of the Census, *Fourteenth Census of the United States, 1920, Vol. 11, Mines and Quarries, 1919*, Washington, DC: GPO (1922), p. 267; J.G. Clark, *Energy and the Federal Government: Fossil Fuel Policies, 1900–46*, Urbana: University of Illinois Press (1986), Chapter 1.

11. *ibid.*, Chapter 1; for the UK coal industry, see N.K. Buxton, *The Economic Development of the British Coal Industry from Industrial Revolution to the Present Day*, London: Batsford Academic (1978); M.P. Jackson, *The Price of Coal*, London: Croom Helm (1974); J.H. Jones *et al.*, *The Coal Mining Industry: An International Study in Planning*, London: Sir Isaac Pitman & Sons (1939); I. Lubin and H. Everett, *The British Coal Dilemma*, New York: Macmillan (1929).

12. American antitrust laws, British hostility toward consolidation, and the strong entrepreneurial habits of American and British mine owners obstructed any form of coal industry cooperation throughout the 1920s.

13. For the above three paragraphs, see League of Nations, *Memorandum on Coal*, I, p. 49–52; A.H. Stockder, *German Trade Associations: The Coal Kartels*, New York: Henry Holt (1924) and *Regulating an Industry: The Rhenish–Westphalian Coal Syndicate, 1893–1929*, New York: Columbia University Press (1932); Pounds, *Coal and Steel*, pp. 321–4; Takenob, *Japan Year Book, 1920–1*, pp. 559–66.

14. The sources defined twelve categories of coal consumers. The data for France distinguished between "metallurgical industries" and all other industries. US data did not. When the US figures included all coal, a residential/commercial category appears; when only bituminous distribution is traced, as in 1923 and 1925 (Table 2.4), the residential/commercial category is missing. Table 2.4 may be most useful as an example of data inadequacy and non-comparability.

15. International Labour Office, *The World Coal-Mining Industry. Studies and Reports*, Series B, No. 31, Geneva: ILO (1938), p. 116; League of Nations, *Memorandum on Coal*, I, pp. 25–7, II, pp. 8–9; W.W. Rostow, *The World Economy: History & Prospect*, Austin: University of Texas Press (1978), p. 382; *Historical Statistics, Part II*, p. 898.

16. Stockder, *RWCS*, p. 86; Pounds, *Coal and Steel*, pp. 322–4.

17. R. Billiard, *La Belgique industrielle et commerciale de demain*, Paris: Berger-Levrault (1915), p. 137; A.E. Probst, "Electrification and the Reconstruction of the Fuel Supply of the U.S.S.R.," in USSR, Committee

for International Scientific and Technical Conferences, *Electric Power Development in the U.S.S.R.*, translated by L.E. Mins, Moscow: Irna Publishing Society (1936), pp. 147–9; E.C. Carlson, *The Kaiping Mines (1877–1912)*, Cambridge: Chinese Economic and Political Studies, Harvard University (1957), pp. 47–53; K. Wang, *Controlling Factors in the Future Development of the Chinese Coal Industry*, New York: King's Crew Press (1947), pp. 23–4.

18. Buxton, *British Coal Industry*, pp. 94–7; J.P. Dickie, *The Coal-Problem, A Survey, 1910–1936*, London: Methuen (1936), pp. 178–80; Lubin, *British Coal Dilemma*, p. 24; A.J. Sargent, *Coal in the International Trade*, London: P.S. King & Son (1922), pp. 29–30.
19. League of Nations, *Memorandum on Coal*, I, p. 55, II, pp. 38–41; Sargent, *Coal in International Trade*, pp. 22–5; Buxton, *British Coal Industry*, p. 93; US Bureau of Foreign Commerce, *Foreign Markets for American Coal, Vol. 21-Part I*, US House of Representatives, 56th Cong., 1st Sess., Doc. 741, Washington, DC: GPO (1900), pp. 39 76, 136–42.
20. Sargent, *Coal in International Trade*, p. 26; BFC, *Foreign Markets for American Coal*, pp. 159–63; Stöckder, *German Coal Kartels*, pp. 29 32 and *RWCS*, pp. 67–73; League of Nations, Memorandum on Coal, I, p. 54.
21. *Ibid.*, pp. 58–63.
22. C.E. Solberg, *Oil and Nationalism in Argentina: A History*, Stanford: Stanford University Press (1979), pp. 5–7; BFC, *Markets for American Coal*, pp. 259–67; D.C.M. Platt, *Latin America and British Trade, 1806–1914*, London: Adam & Charles Black (1972), pp. 246–51, 266–8, 278–9, *passim*.
23. S. Uyehara, *The Industry and Trade of Japan*, London: P.S. King & Son (1926), pp. 189–97; League of Nations, *Memorandum on Coal*, I, pp. 43, 53, 72; Mitsubishi Economic Research Bureau, *Japanese Trade and Industry Present and Future*, London: Macmillan (1936), p. 196; Webb, *Dictionary of Statistics*, pp. 87–8.
24. For the above two paragraphs: for an outline of the contentious debate over Britain's economic performance, see D.N. McCloskey, *Enterprise and Trade in Victorian Britain*, London: Allen & Unwin (1981), pp. 94–131; Rostow, *World Economy*, p. 72; Webb, *Dictionary of Statistics*, p. 99; J. Foreman-Peck, *A History of the World Economy: International Economic Relations since 1850*, pp. 95–6; B.R. Mitchell, ed., *European Historical Statistics*, 2nd revised edition, London: Macmillan (1981); R.N. Adams, *Paradoxical Harvest: Energy and Explanation in British History*, Cambridge: Cambridge University Press (1982), p. 42–3.
25. Williamson, *Age of Energy*, pp. 16–7; R.W. Ferrier, *The History of the British Petroleum Company: Vol. I, The Developing Years, 1901–1932*, Cambridge: Cambridge University Press (1982), pp. 638–9; P. Apostol and A. Michelson, *La Lutte pour Le Pétrole et La Russie*, Paris: Payot (1922), pp. 104, 118–9.
26. For the above two paragraphs: Williamson, *Age of Energy*, p. 43 and Ferrier, *History of BP*, pp. 18–67. For a lively account of exploration in Venezuela, see R. Arnold *et al.*, *The First Big Oil Hunt: Venezuela— 1911–1916*, New York: Vantage Press (1960). J.D. Henry, *Baku: An Eventful History*, London: A. Constable (1905).
27. For the above two paragraphs: Williamson, *Age of Energy*, pp. 111,

136–62; S. Schurr and B. Netschert *et al.*, *Energy in the American Economy, 1850–1975, an economic study of its history and prospects*, Baltimore: Johns Hopkins Press for Resources for the Future (1960), pp. 106, 499; F.C. Gerretson, *History of the Royal Dutch*, Leiden: E.J. Brill (1958), III, p. 267, for estimates of the European gasoline market in 1908.

28. P.M. Leo, *The Emergence of Strategic Resources in World Politics: A Study of Petroleum and the International System, 1859–1928*, Ann Arbor, Mich.: University Microfilms (1978), pp. 2.11, 139–43, 150–2.

29. For sympathetic accounts of Standard, see R.W. and M.E. Hidy, *History of Standard Oil Company (New Jersey): Pioneering in Big Business, 1882–1911*, New York: Harper & Brothers (1955), pp. 676–98; G.S. Gibb and E.H. Knowlton, *History of Standard Oil Company (New Jersey): The Resurgent Years, 1911–1937*, New York: Harper & Brothers (1956), pp. 6–10; G.T. White, *Formative Years in the Far West: A History of Standard Oil Company of California and Predecessors Through 1919*, New York: Appleton-Century-Crofts (1962), pp. 363–85. For contemporary criticism of Standard see, H.D. Lloyd, *Wealth Against Commonwealth*, New York: Harper & Row (1894) and I. Tarbell, *The History of Standard Oil*, New York: Macmillan (1905). For an overview see, R. Sobel, *The Age of the Giant Corporation: A Microeconomic History of American Business, 1914–1970*, Westport, Conn.: Greenwood (1972).

30. For the above two paragraphs: M. Pearton, *Oil and the Romanian State*, Oxford: Clarendon Press (1971), pp. 18–33, 111–29; Hidy, *Standard Oil, 1882–1911*, pp. 515–8; A. Mohr, *The Oil War*, New York: Harcourt, Brace (1926), pp. 77–9; Solberg, *Oil in Argentina*, pp. 10–21; A.J. Bermúdez, *The Mexican National Petroleum Industry: A Case Study in Nationalization*, Stanford: Institute of Hispanic American and Luso-Brazilian Studies (1963); E. Chester, *United States Oil Policy and Diplomacy: A Twentieth Century Overview*, Westport, Conn.: Greenwood Press (1983), pp. 109–14; L. Meyer, *Mexico and the United States in the Oil Controversy, 1917–42*, translated by M. Vasconcellos, Austin: University of Texas Press (1972).

31. E.H. Davenport and S.R. Cooke, *The Oil Trusts and Anglo-American Relations*, New York: Macmillan (1924), pp. 3–23; Leo, *Petroleum and the International System*, pp. 184–8; Ferrier, *History of BP*, pp. 102–13, 158–99; Hidy, *Standard Oil, 1882–1911*, pp. 497–503; Mohr, *Oil War*, pp. 110–25.

32. For bitter denunciations of French policies, see R. André, *L'Industrie et le Commerce du Pétrole en France*, Paris: Librairie Nouvelle de Droit et de Jurisprudence (1910) and F. Delaisi, *Oil, Its Influence on Politics*, translated by C.L. Leese, London: The Labour Publishing Co. (1922).

33. The Rothschilds sold out to Shell Transport and Trading Company in 1902 and Shell and Royal Dutch merged in 1907. See Apostol, *Le Pétrole et La Russie*, pp. 151–4, 165–72.

34. Mohr, *Oil War*, pp. 80–93; Leo Muffelmann, "Le monopole d'état en matière de pétrole en Allemagne," *Revue économique international*, II (Avril 1914), pp. 7–33; Davenport, *Oil Trusts*, pp. 26–7; P. Sluglett, *Britain in Iraq, 1914–1932*, London: Ithaca Press (1976), p. 133.

35. P. de la Tramerye, *The World Struggle for Oil*, London: Allen & Unwin, 3rd edn (1923), p. 78; Gerretson, *Royal Dutch*, II, pp. 91–107; R.W. Tolf,

The Russian Rockefellers: The Saga of the Nobel Family and the Russian Oil Industry, Stanford: Hoover Institution Press (1976), pp. 183–6.

36. Ferrier, *History of BP*, pp. 69–88, 94–6; A.W. Giebelhaus, *Business and Government in the Oil Industry: A Case Study of Sun Oil, 1876–1945*, Greenwood, Conn.: JAI Press (1980), p. 49.

37. Gerretson, *Royal Dutch*, II, describes this in awesome detail. For a more digestible account, see K. Beaton, *Enterprise in Oil: A History of Shell in the United States*, New York: Appleton-Century-Crofts (1957), pp. 30–53.

38. For the above five paragraphs: Gerretson, *Royal Dutch*, III, pp. 190–6, 201–6, facing p. 228; Hidy, *Standard Oil, 1882–1911*, pp. 220–2, 324–5, 524–8, 573–9; Gibb, *Standard Oil, 1911–1927*, pp. 46–8, 75, 181–2; Beaton, *Shell in the US*, pp. 60–70; *World Petroleum Directory, 1937*, New York: R. Palmer (1937), p. 583; Williamson, *Age of Energy*, pp. 235–40.

39. For the above three paragraphs: Anglo-American Petroleum Products, Ltd, *Mexican Fuel Oil*, New York: np (1914), pp. 13–15; Hidy, Standard *Oil, 1882–1911*, p. 328; Ferrier, *History of BP*, p. 683; André, *Pétrole en France*, pp. 100–8, 114–30; Delaisi, *Oil*, pp. 47–53; Uyehara, *Industry and Trade of Japan*, pp. 203–5, 210.

40. A.J. Pinelo, *The Multinational Corporation as a Force in Latin American Politics: A Case Study of the International Oil Company in Peru*, New York: Praeger (1973), pp. 12–14; Leo, *Petroleum and the International System*, pp. 188–92; Bermúdez, *Mexican Petroleum Nationalization*, pp. 5–8; Meyer, *Oil Controversy*, pp. 42–53.

41. For Japanese developments: K. Imazu, "Modern Technology and Japanese Electrical Engineers," in Okochi and Uchida, eds, *Diffusion of Technology*, pp. 135–7; Uchida, "Adoption of New Technology in Japan," in *ibid.*, pp. 148–51, 161–6; J. Hirschmeier and T. Yui, *The Development of Japanese Business, 1600–1980*, London: Allen & Unwin (2nd edn, 1981), pp. 232–4; M. Wilkins, *The Maturing of Multinational Enterprise: American Business Abroad from 1914 to 1970*, Cambridge: Harvard University Press (1974), pp. 28–9; E.B. Schumpeter, ed., *The Industrialization of Japan and Manchukuo, 1930–1940: Population, Raw Materials, and Industry*, New York: Macmillan (1940), pp. 544–8; Uyehara, *Industry and Trade of Japan*, pp. 203–5.

42. Hydroelectric facilities in Japan provided one-third of the electricity in 1907 and almost 60 percent in 1917. Norway, Italy, and Brazil also harnessed their excellent water power resources before and after World War I.

43. Mitchell, ed., *European Historical Statistics*, pp. 500–1; Takenob, *Japan Year Book, 1920–1*, p. 613; *Historical Statistics, Part 2*, pp. 700–1; Landes, *Unbound Prometheus*, p. 290; League of Nations, Economic and Financial Section, International Economic Conference, Geneva, May 1927, *Electrical Industry*, Geneva: League of Nations (1927), pp. 21–6.

44. *Ibid.*, pp. 68–70. For the initial transfer of Edison Electric Company technology overseas and the subsequent disassociation of the German firms from the Edison organization see, Hughes, *Networks of Power*, pp. 47, 54–66. For Siemens, see S. von Weber, "The Rise and Development of Electrical Engineering and Industry in Germany in the Nineteenth Century," in Okochi and Uchida, eds, *Diffusion of Technology*, pp. 23–44.

45. N.S. Miller, *Lagos Steam Tramway, 1902–1933*, Lagos: Lagos Develop-

ment Board (1934); Byatt, *British Electrical Industry*, pp. 168–9.

46. Platt, *Latin America and British Trade*, pp. 242–3; Wilkins, *Multinational Enterprise*, p. 16; Solberg, *Oil in Argentina*, pp. 2–5; Monbeig, *São Paulo*, pp. 50–1; C. Armstrong and M.V. Nelles, "A Curious Capital Flow: Canadian Investment in Mexico, 1902–1910," *Business History Review*, 58 (Summer 1984), pp. 178–203; Dean, *São Paulo, 1880–1945*, pp. 21, 55–7.

47. Byatt, *British Electrical Industry*, pp. 4, 66–72, 138–43, 168–9, 209–10; Hughes, *Networks of Power*, pp. 229–31.

48. Uchida, "Adoption of New Technology in Japan," pp. 152–66; Imazu, "Japanese Electrical Engineering," pp. 138.

49. Solberg, *Oil in Argentina*, pp. vii–viii, 22–8, 37–49; Uyehara, *Industry and Trade of Japan*, pp. 54–5, 183–8, 210.

50. L. Heyman, *The New Aspect of the Oil Problem*, London: Petroleum Times (1933), p. 18. For representative interwar commentaries, see Delaisi, *Oil*; de la Tramerye, *Struggle for Oil*; L. Fischer, *Oil Imperialism: The International Struggle for Petroleum*, New York: International Publishers (1926); Mohr, *Oil War*. Leo, *Petroleum and the International System*, pp. 226–33, offers a balanced assessment of the search for oil.

51. W. Stivers, *Supremacy and Oil: Iraq, Turkey, and the Anglo-American World Order, 1918–1930*, Ithaca, N.Y.: Cornell University Press (1982), p. 105, emphasizes the stategic importance of Iraq to the defense of Persia and India. Sluglett, *Britain in Iraq*, pp. 3–6, 104, attributes British interest in Iraq as much to its oil potential as to its strategic position. Descriptions of wartime exploration are found in Beaton, *Shell in the US*, pp. 77–112, 166–70; Gibb, *Standard Oil, 1911–1927*, pp. 98–105; Wilkins, *Multinational Enterprise*, pp. 13–16, 27.

52. M.W. Kirby, *The British Coalmining Industry, 1870–1946. A Political and Economic History*, Hamden, Conn.: Archon Books (1977), p. 24–7.

53. Mohr, *Oil War*, pp. 141–2, 151; J. Rondot, *La Compagnie Francaise des Pétroles du franc-or au pétrole franc*, Paris: Plon (1962), pp. 33–5; de la Tramerye, *Struggle for Oil*, pp. 159–61; Leo, *Petroleum and the International System*, pp. 233–6; Ferrier, *History of BP*, pp. 243–52, 681.

54. The USFA exercised a similar authority over oil, with an important exception. The USFA lacked a legislative mandate to fix crude oil prices.

55. For the above two paragraphs: S. Osborne, *The Saar Question: A Disease Spot in Europe*, London: Allen & Unwin (1923), p. 46; Clark, *Energy and the Federal Government*, Chapters 3–4; Stockder, *German Coal Kartels*, pp. 170–92; Lubin, *British Coal Dilemma*, pp. 33–5; Buxton, *British Coal Industry*, pp. 159–68; Kirby, *British Coalmining*, pp. 24–35.

3

The search for energy during the interwar years

Economic and political crises buffeted many nations during the interwar years, deflating ambitions and ultimately persuading a few of the expedience of war and conquest. The economies of the powerful nations of the West proved fragile to an extreme. The former Allies each endured postwar depressions, recovered gradually but enjoyed only an abbreviated period of moderate prosperity between 1924 and 1929. This prosperity, built on foundations of sand, collapsed in 1929, plunging tens of millions around the world into the abyss of depression and shattering their hopes for a more secure life. The industrialized West tumbled further than the underdeveloped nations, but for the latter, in Latin America for instance, essential development projects were necessarily postponed.

The impermanent prosperity of the 1920s failed to bring equal benefits to all. The consequences of the war, compounded by the Versailles settlement, mired Germany in an inflationary cycle only broken by the depression. The Soviet Union, shattered by wartime losses, battled against indigenous counterrevolutionaries and a motley coalition of the former Allies to secure the revolution and then strove, in virtual isolation, to rebuild and modernize. A revolutionary regime in China proved incapable of uniting the nation or defending its sovereignty. The Middle East fell almost completely under the sway of western Europe, notably the UK, while sub-Saharan Africa languished under repressive colonial regimes. In Latin America, splendid potential was negated more often than not by political instability, the rise of tyranny, a parasitical upper class, the urgent need for western development

51

capital, and dependence upon export earnings from a single crop or mineral.

In the dominant West, depression subsided with painful slowness. Unfortunately, recovery was precipitated more by the military threat posed by Germany, Italy, and Japan than by the anti-depression policies of governments. As the depression eased in 1939, the terrors of still another war engulfed large parts of the world.

During the unstable interwar years, the USA and western Europe became increasingly energy intensive societies. The energy transitions of the prewar years progressed rapidly during the 1920s, slowed perceptibly during the worst of the depression, and accelerated once again just prior to the outbreak of World War II. The leading industrial sectors of the interwar years were basically new industries. Automotives and such collateral industries as rubber and glass, petrochemicals, particularly gasoline, and electrical generation and electrical equipment, all energy intensive, were highly interdependent. Automotives created the gasoline and rubber tire industries while petrochemicals and the new metals industries quickly applied electricity to the manufacturing process.

Chronic debility characterized the coal industries of the leading producing nations. Competition from more efficient fuels and more efficient coal burning systems eroded demand for coal. Fuel substitution and intense competition for overseas markets ravaged the hitherto dynamic foreign coal trade of Britain. During the interwar years, petroleum replaced coal as the primary energy product traded internationally.

A booming oil industry exploited expanding consumer demand for motor fuel — a ravenous demand in the USA — and heating oils. Flush fields in the USA, Venezuela, and Iraq and the ever larger refineries of the major oil companies poured forth enormous volumes of petroleum. The governments of lesser developed producing states, embittered by their inability to turn their resource wealth to national advantage, viewed with enmity the power of the multinational oil companies. Unparalleled oil industry growth coupled with mounting producing-state hostility toward MNOCs roiled the waters of international oil politics. The depression further exacerbated these relationships with regard to oil while coal producing states hastened to enact measures protective of domestic markets and stimulative of exports. Heightened consciousness of the essentiality of natural resources to national security and welfare fostered intense resource-based nationalism. During the 1930s, Germany, Italy, and Japan accused the USA, UK, and others of conspiring to deny them a fair share of natural resources. This argument became a core element of the rationale for German and Japanese expansion.

General trends in energy use

Aggressive marketers of petroleum, electricity, and natural gas captured ever-larger shares of coal's traditional markets. In America, New England coal retailers fought back, developing sales campaigns emphasizing published reports of diminishing oil reserves. "It is our firm belief," the New Englanders intoned, "that oil as a house heating fuel will not be permanent. . . Anthracite is really the only Fool Proof Fuel For The Home."[1] The New Englanders were wrong. Coal as an input to total energy use in the USA plunged from 74 percent in 1925 to 54 percent in 1938. This dramatic reduction, unequaled in other countries, contributed strongly to the aggregate drop in coal's share of world energy consumption shown in Table 3.1.

In Britain and Germany, Europe's leading coal producers, coal remained the key domestic and industrial fuel (Tables 2.2 and 3.1). *Per capita* coal use fell only marginally in the UK and Germany and even rose in France and Belgium. *Per capita* coal consumption in Japan also rose even as the proportion of coal use to total energy use diminished by some ten percentage points. Elsewhere in the world, coal use tumbled most sharply in Latin America. The pattern is clear: those nations — the USA, Venezuela, Colombia — richly endowed with oil fields shifted quickly to oil. Nations without domestic oil supplies but with surplus coal — Germany and Britain — continued to rely on coal. Coal importing nations such as France and Japan, both ambitious to match the industrial growth rates of Britain and Germany, imported a rising tonnage of coal while oil imports rose even more sharply.[2]

The consumption of energy produced from fossil fuels and electricity remained highly concentrated in a handful of western nations and Japan. The USA consumed 48 percent of world energy in 1925. Britain and Germany used another 23 percent, and France, Japan, Canada, and the USSR consumed 10 percent. Seven nations, then, accounted for 81 percent of global commercial energy consumption. By 1938, those countries still used 80 percent of world energy, although the relative rank had shifted substantially. As Table 3.1 indicates, the USA retained its position as the leading consumer, but the depression had occasioned an absolute diminution of energy use. Germany surpassed the UK; the USSR, consuming only 14 percent as much energy as the UK in 1925, used 90 percent as much in 1938, or more than two times as much energy as France or Japan.

Per capita consumption of energy, expressed in metric tons of coal equivalent, reveals the enormous differences in energy use between the industrialized countries and lesser developed societies (Tables 3.1 and 3.2). Within such non-industrialized states as Egypt and Brazil, *per*

Table 3.1 Consumption and imports of energy for the world and for selected countries,* 1925, 1929, 1938

		Total energy consumed (000)*	Total energy imports (000)*	% coal use to total energy use	% coal imports to total energy use	% oil imports to total energy use
World	1925	1 484 533	199 633	0.83	0.09	0.04
	1929	1 755 981	277 671	0.79	0.10	0.06
	1938	1 790 056	282 142	0.72	0.07	0.09
USA	1925	717 714	18 526	0.74	<0.01	0.02
	1929	819 935	24 941	0.68	<0.01	0.03
	1938	669 439	12 847	0.54	<0.01	0.02
UK	1925	182 279	9 128	0.96	<0.01	0.05
	1929	189 993	11 954	0.95	<0.01	0.06
	1938	196 370	17 558	0.92	<0.01	0.09
Germany	1925	161 689	9 856	0.99	<0.01	0.01
	1929	199 107	12 698	0.98	<0.01	0.02
	1938	223 368	13 534	0.96	<0.01	0.03
France	1925	75 515	32 219	0.96	0.39	0.04
	1929	89 534	40 120	0.95	0.39	0.05
	1938	78 144	34 470	0.86	0.28	0.16
Japan	1925	30 483	2 750	0.92	0.06	0.03
	1929	38 181	6 805	0.87	0.09	0.08
	1938	62 425	13 813	0.84	0.11	0.11
Canada	1925	31 139	19 703	0.82	0.50	0.13
	1929	42 551	25 865	0.74	0.41	0.19
	1938	37 443	20 642	0.63	0.32	0.23
USSR	1925	25 320	790	0.65	0.03	<0.01
	1929	52 966	1 250	0.71	0.02	<0.01
	1938	176 349	1 493	0.73	<0.01	<0.01
India	1925	19 036	1 578	0.85	0.03	0.06
	1929	20 899	1 713	0.84	0.01	0.07
	1938	25 696	3 241	0.86	0.02	0.11
Brazil	1925	3 228	2 740	0.69	0.60	0.25
	1929	4 027	3 515	0.65	0.58	0.30
	1938	4 375	3 343	0.52	0.36	0.40

* Columns 3 and 4 are in thousand metric tons coal equivalent

Source: J. Darmstadter et al., *Energy in the World Economy: A Statistical Review of Trends in Output, Trade, and Consumption Since 1925*, Baltimore: The Johns Hopkins University Press for Resources for the Future (1971), Tables VI and XI.

capita energy consumption hardly changed during the interwar years. São Paulo experienced further industrialization. Steel works and small petrochemical plants appeared; Firestone and Goodyear, American tire companies, opened plants in the city. Hydroelectric generation contributed to the establishment of a well developed industrial complex before World War II. High rise housing rose in the central city and suburban developers hooked into the expanding electric and telephone networks. But, as in Cairo (undergoing little industrial development), new housing, the utilities, and other paraphernalia of industrialized societies remained the privilege of a relatively small middle and upper class. Even though most Paulistas were poor, ill-housed, and not in the market for many consumer goods, Brazil's cities were identified as good markets for American electrical appliances, unlike Alexandria or Cairo. While Americans were purchasing one million gas ranges annually during the 1930s and additional millions of electrical appliances, most Brazilians, and assuredly most Egyptians and Indians, had never seen these marvels.

As in São Paulo, so in Bogata and Caracas and urban centers in other non-industrial countries. Generating stations, pylons, street cars, and oil tank farms appeared, comprising the skeleton of a modern energy structure. But they were superimposed upon societies lacking the mass demand and mass purchasing power that sustained the energy industries in the USA, UK, and Germany.[3]

The energy transition in Japan achieved a stage midway between that of the highly industrialized western nations and the lesser developed states. Rapid industrial growth, initiated before World War I, centered on indigenous steel, heavy machinery, textile, and shipbuilding

Table 3.2 *Per capita* consumption of energy in selected countries*

	1913	1925	1929	1933	1938
World	0.7	0.8	0.9	0.7	0.8
USA	5.1	6.2	6.7	4.6	5.2
UK	4.2	4.0	4.1	3.5	4.1
Germany	2.7	2.6	3.1	2.1	3.2
Japan	0.4	0.5	0.6	0.6	0.9
USSR	0.3	0.2	0.3	0.6	0.9
Argentina	0.5	0.5	0.7	0.6	0.7
Brazil	0.1	0.1	0.1	0.1	0.1
Egypt	na	0.1	0.1	0.1	0.2
India	<0.1	0.1	0.1	0.1	0.2

* 1913 shows metric tons of coal consumption; all other data expressed in metric tons of coal equivalent

Sources: J. Darmstadter *et al.*, *Energy and the World Economy: A Statistical Review of Trends in Output, Trade, and Consumption Since 1925*, Baltimore: The Johns Hopkins Press for Resources for the Future (1971), pp. 652–91.

industries. Competition from foreign imports forced some retrenchment during the 1920s but the core remained intact even through the worst of the depression. Industrial production, valued at 5.1 billion yen in 1931 had doubled by 1937, transforming an adverse balance of trade into a favorable balance. Japan's industrial structure, in part called into being by the demands of a growing and aggressive military establishment, demanded ever larger imports of coal, oil, iron ore, and other minerals. By 1936, minerals accounted for 22 percent of the value of Japan's imports; petroleum and coal imports composed 7 percent of the total import bill.

Japan's evolving energy regimen resembled that of western European nations in certain respects and that of the USA in others. Coal as a contributor to total energy consumption declined more swiftly in Japan than in the UK or Germany, but less precipitously than in the USA. Concomitantly, Japanese industries turned more readily to fuel oil than did their counterparts in the UK or Germany. The electrification of urban Japan proceeded as quickly as in urban Britain and more quickly in industry and transport, partly because of Japan's superior hydro-power sites. During the interwar years,[4] Japan improved its electrical equipment manufacturing capabilities, but still purchased most large and custom-made equipment from the USA or Germany. In 1940, as war closed in on Japan and the USA, Japan awaited delivery of three hydroelectric generators from America for placement at gigantic dams in Manchukuo.

Though most Japanese households were connected to electric lines, domestic demand lagged far behind American. As in Germany, Sweden, Norway, and Italy, industry and transportation provided much the larger part of the electric load — above 70 percent compared with something over 50 percent in the USA. In all of these nations, electricity powered a rising share of industrial horsepower. These differences in energy use reflected the particular resource endowments of the indus-trialized countries, the size of their industrial sectors, and *per capita* income.[5]

During the 1920s, annual energy consumption in the USA exceeded the combined consumption of the UK, Germany, France, Japan, Canada, and the USSR (Table 3.1). The depression only marginally tempered this great disparity. Moreover, unlike each of the above states, excepting the Soviet Union, America was essentially energy self-sufficient. A mammoth industrial complex, rapid urbanization, a pro-ductive agricultural sector, and relatively high *per capita* income per-mitted Americans to consume energy profligately, seek and secure the control of overseas energy resources, and market energy and energy related goods and services around the globe.

Although the USA suffered a deeper and longer depression than did many industrialized nations, the energy use patterns of prior decades persisted and energy consumption remained at high levels. Coal production fell by 204 million metric tons between 1919 and 1932 and had not much improved by 1938 (Table 2.2). However, consumer expenditures in the USA for natural gas and oil declined between 1929 and 1932 by only 19 percent, compared with a fall of 70 percent in spending for food and beverages. Expenditures for oil and gas surpassed the 1929 total in 1936 and increased by another 35 percent by 1939, attesting to the strength of the retail gasoline market. The depression did not prevent a substantial rise in the number of residential electric hook-ups. Between 1929 and 1939, the percentage of all dwellings with electric service rose from 68 percent (35 percent in 1920) to 77 percent. *Per capita* annual consumption surged upward from 502 kwh in 1929 to 897 in 1939. But the pattern of growth during the depression differed from that of the 1920s. During the latter years, industrial electric use alone accounted for 53 percent of new consumption while residential took but 10 percent. During the depression decade, new residential use roughly equaled new industrial use, in part because of the linkage of several hundreds of thousands of rural residences to power lines under the Rural Electrification Administration program and in part because of an apparent steady decline in average real prices for residential users.[6] Still, the 60 percent of American families that earned under $2000 annually in 1929 were infrequent participants in the evolving consumer society. These folk, urban and rural, were not in the market for new homes complete with the latest energy intensive gadgets.

The advance of energy consumption in the modernized nations during the interwar years was impressive. The number of electric consumers in the UK climbed from 730,000 in 1920 to 8.9 million in 1938. During those years, some 4 million new dwellings were constructed, many under public housing programs, and all of which included electric service. *Per capita* kwh consumption in Germany advanced from 330 in 1925 to 807 in 1937. The number of registered motor vehicles in America soared from under 10 million in 1920 to 34 million in 1941 while the gasoline consumed per vehicle grew from 400 gallons to 648 gallons. In Cairo perhaps 14,000 autos sped along the streets in 1940.[7] As one contemplates the statistics, it is an inescapable conclusion that most people around the world had still to experience the modern age of energy.

Energy exports

As in earlier years, trade in energy furthered the energy transition but contributed unevenly to the economies of the nations so engaged.

Demand, dulled by low incomes in most countries, was further dead-
ened by depression. While the total value of international trade grew
less impressively after the war than before, the value of mineral fuel
exports rose from 4.8 percent of total world exports in 1913 to 6.3
percent in 1929 and 7.5 percent in 1937. An expanding proportion of
total energy production entered world trade and a larger proportion of
all energy consumed arrived as imports (Table 3.1). In the USA, energy
related exports formed an average of 17 percent of all exports during the
five years, 1926–30, only ranking below cotton.

Petroleum replaced coal as the most valuable mineral export. In
1913, coal and coke formed 71 percent of mineral fuel exports, a
percentage that fell to 43 in 1929 and 40 in 1937. Petroleum products
alone, with an export value of $1.1 billion in 1937, exceeded the export
value of wheat and flour, cotton, and all ores. One-third of all oil
consumed in 1925 arrived as an import; 45 percent in 1938.[8]

Two basic flows characterized world energy trade: the export of
crude oil from non-industrial societies to the refineries of the MNOCs;
the sale of refined products, coal, fossil fuel burning equipment, and
electrical goods by industrialized countries to industrialized countries.
Non-industrial producers such as Venezuela or Iraq reaped few benefits
from this exchange.

The spread of electric utilities throughout the world during the 1920s
owed little to the direct intervention of governments, except in the case
of mother country and colony. As in the past, most generating stations
were constructed, equipped, owned, and operated by Americans or
Europeans. In Latin America, USA, British, and German firms furnished
a large proportion of all the electrical equipment in operation and
owned the larger utilities and street railways. American and western
European electrical equipment manufacturers created investment holding companies which financed power companies at home and abroad.
The two largest German holding companies, Siemen & Halske and
Allgemeine Elektrizitats-Gesellschaft (AEG) owned operating companies throughout Europe, Latin America, and Japan. GE's subsidiary,
Electric Bond and Share Company, the largest utility firm in the USA,
owned dozens of utilities in Latin America and elsewhere while GE,
through its subsidiary, International General Electric Company, owned
electrical manufacturing plants in the UK and other nations.

By far the largest share of electrical goods traded passed between
the developed states with Europe and Canada importing over one-half
of the value in 1925 and the USA, UK, and Germany exporting above
80 percent of a total volume that increased threefold between 1913 and
1925. Britain, the leading exporter, was also the largest importer in
1925, host to the largest of GE's foreign subsidiaries. Britain, as well

as Venezuela, took notice of this foreign presence. But such was the financial power of GE and AEG that they could not be displaced. Of the non-western countries, Japan accommodated most skillfully to the power of the electric multinationals (and the MNOCs as well) and, after World War II, reborn zaibatsu closed the technology gap and overcame the foreign multinationals at home and abroad.[9]

Energy intensive technologies fostered higher living standards in 1938 compared with 1913, a sign of progress far less visible in Venezuela than in Europe. Widespread poverty, infrastructure inadequacies, unstable and elitist governments and colonialism in vast areas of Africa and Asia fastened millions around the world in a seemingly permanent state of economic marginality.

Coal — a troubled industry

The League of Nations in 1927 published the results of an inquiry into the world coal industry, replicating on a global scale earlier investigations of the domestic industry conducted in the USA and Britain. At the end of the interwar period, the International Labour Office released its study of world coal.[10]

All agreed that the leading coal producing nations carried a large and growing excess productive capacity, estimated for 1929 at 30 percent in the UK, USA, and Germany. This imbalance between capacity and demand derived from a number of interconnected pressures. Nations with coal reserves sought coal self-sufficiency by increasing production, protecting domestic markets from foreign penetration, and promoting coal sales abroad. Concurrently, the substitution of other fuels for coal and the improved efficiency of coal use attenuated markets. These conditions, somewhat tempered by modest economic growth in the West between 1924 and 1929, were greatly exacerbated when depression struck and led to cutthroat competition in national and international markets.

Compared with the prewar period, demand for coal and coal production after the war, allowing for short-term ups and downs, remained static over a twenty year period. Production in 1929 exceeded the 1913 output by some 218 million metric tons (mmt), fell below prewar levels during the depth of the depression, and only regained the 1929 level in 1937. In contrast, crude oil production tripled between 1913 and 1929, and rose again by just under twofold by 1939 (see Tables 2.2 and 2.7). As in the prewar years, the great bulk of production occurred in the USA and Europe, together accounting for 90 percent of output in both 1913 and 1937. Negative influences on coal demand, then, affected most seriously the USA and European producers.

Political events caused serious dislocation in the coal industries of the major producers, closing markets to some and opening markets to others. Strikes in the USA in 1919 and 1922 and in Britain in 1921 and 1926, in response to the lowering of wages by owners, disrupted coal production, permitting competitors to muscle their way into the traditional overseas markets for British and American coal (largely Canada). France emerged from the war with half of her productive capacity destroyed. The Treaty of Versailles awarded France large reparations from Germany, paid in part by Ruhr coal, and control of the Saar coal mines. Reparation coal from Germany reduced British markets on the Continent.

Coal's many afflictions, the consequence of labor-management strife, postwar recession and lackluster recovery, fuel substitution, and improved coal burning technologies failed to motivate serious reorganization of domestic industries. Many voices called for reform in both Britain and America. In the latter, nothing was done until 1933 while in the former the measures enacted dealt primarily with labor issues. Neither nation attempted to improve the competitive position of coal in world markets, in spite of recommendations from various coal commissions — the Sankey Commission (1919) and Samuel Commission (1925) in the UK and the US Coal Commission (1922) in the USA — to restructure the industry. These coal commissions advocated the abandonment of marginal mines and the amalgamation of efficient but small units into larger units as well as the organization of joint sales agencies to reduce the debilitating effects of slashed wages and destructive price competition.[11]

While both the British and American (bituminous) industries experienced some concentration after the war, they remained highly fragmented and contentious if compared with continental coal industries. Weaker collieries were eliminated in Britain, leaving 1,860 in 1938 compared with 2,549 in 1919 and some amalgamation occurred, a process encouraged by the Mining Industry Act of 1926 and made compulsory by the Coal Mines Act of 1930. In the USA, attrition weeded out some 2,000 marginal mines. The number of mines producing over 500,000 metric tons *per annum* also fell by several hundred. Some 6,000 mines remained in 1929, compared to 9,331 in 1923. The depression wiped out hundreds of others. In contrast, thirty-three firms in the Ruhr Valley, about one-half owned by integrated steel companies, produced the entire output and all of the Saar mines were owned by the state. Twenty-eight firms produced 90 percent of French output. The trend toward fewer and larger producing units also prevailed in Japan where eight large firms controlled 80 percent of production.[12]

The consolidation characteristic of continental European industries enabled Germany, Poland, the Netherlands, and others to strengthen their cartels as regulators of production and sales. The prewar Rhenish–Westphalian Coal Syndicate survived the war; new cartels arose elsewhere in Europe. These organizations, essentially arms of the state and benefiting from export subsidies, undersold British coal in many markets. Laggard and feeble British efforts to organize regional sales agencies posed no threat to her competitors.[13]

Coal marketers in Europe and the USA confronted slack markets during the postwar years. Productive capacity in metals and raw materials far exceeded demand in the industrial countries while no new and large markets materialized. Large stocks of primary goods accumulated, depressing prices and foreign trade. Petroleum, directly linked to high growth industries, sustained its upward momentum; coal did not. Lagging demand, competition from other fuels, and technological progress combined with the appearance of new producers and national efforts to achieve coal self-sufficiency, to reduce substantially the foreign coal trade.

Shifting patterns of coal consumption

The proportion of national coal consumption attributable to major categories of consumers (Table 2.4) underwent some change between the wars.[14] Industry remained the largest consumer, followed in most countries by residential–commercial. In general, the share of production burned by electric utilities rose, but this gain — in total tonnage as well as percentage — was partly offset in the UK and Germany by reduced coal use in manufactured gas works. Too, the tonnage and share of coal use by ships and railroads diminished in the USA, Germany, and Japan while remaining stable in Britain and France.

Two essential causes explain the shifts in coal consumption: fuel substitution and improved coal burning technologies. These trends were most advanced in the USA. All the major consumers replaced a portion of coal with fuel oil and electricity, and in some nations with natural or manufactured gas. Railroad use of coal in the USA declined by 50 million metric tons (mmt) during the period 1920–39, while diesel fuel use rose from about 8 mmt in 1920 to above 12 mmt in 1938. The improved efficiency of diesel engines and electrification speeded coal's decline and retarded diesel use, a trend descriptive of railroad coal use in Japan, Italy, and France where electrification proceeded quite rapidly. Coal bunkering also declined as merchant fleets converted to fuel oil. In 1914, 97 percent of all vessels over 100 metric tons burned coal. The tonnage of coal fired vessels declined from 48 mmt in 1914 to 38 mmt in 1932 while the tonnage of oil fired ships rose from 2 to 30 mmt. Britain's bunker trade, comprising a steady 25 percent of coal exports, was reduced from some 21 mmt in 1914 to an average of 11 mmt in 1938–39.

In 1900 few industries used electricity for any purposes; by the 1930s, however, electricity supplied almost 70 percent of factory motive power in the USA and Germany and above 40 percent in the UK and Belgium. Much of this substituted directly for coal. Industry in the USA burned 100 million fewer metric tons of coal in 1940 than in 1930. Coal use in iron and steel fell from 30 mmt in 1923 to 15 mmt in 1936, a reduction matched exactly by Britain's iron and steel industry. France, Europe's largest coal importer, consumed only slightly more coal in 1936 than in 1913, while fuel oil use increased tenfold. While thermal electric generating plants consumed a larger tonnage of coal the world over, the efficiency of those plants denied coal the full benefits of rising electric use. Whereas in 1922 2.75 pounds of coal were required to produce one kwh, in 1939 1.6 pounds served. Moreover, in the USA the use of natural gas and fuel oil in electric generating stations rose from 3 percent of total fuel use in 1922 to 13 percent in 1937 while in Japan, France, Italy, Sweden, and Norway, hydroelectric generation advanced swiftly.

Coal prices did not drive the railroads, shipping companies, or industries to an oil substitute. The generic advantages of oil or some other energy source prompted the switch. An equivalent amount of energy in fuel oil could be stored in a fraction of the space demanded by coal. Buried pipes moved oil from tanks, often buried also, to furnaces, whereas coal required an elaborate, space consuming system of automated shovels and belts, if not men with shovels, to fire the furnaces. These and other advantages of fuel oil also carried cost benefits but they were reflected in enhanced efficiency and convenience rather than in a cheaper initial price per energy equivalent unit of coal. Similar considerations motivated residential and commercial patrons to abandon coal for fuel oil or, in America, natural gas. Residential fuel oil consumption expanded more than sixfold between 1929 and 1941; millions of new residential oil furnaces were sold. In 1938, the International Labour Office estimated that one-half of normal coal demand was threatened by displacement by other fuels and water power and three-quarters of demand was materially affected by improved fuel economies.[15]

The international coal trade

Many factors impinged directly upon the volume of coal imports and exports. Prior to World War I, Britain outpaced rivals in an expanding market relatively unimpeded by political barriers. Chapter 2 specified the comparative advantages that sustained Britain's pre-eminence as a coal shipper. But World War I, the retributive quality of the peace, the softness of national economies during the 1920s, and the shocking slump and consequent emergence of warlike nations during the 1930s interposed political impediments in the path of the postwar trade.

The center of the foreign trade in coal remained in Europe. But the tonnage of coal exported tailed-off. The average annual volume of coal exported in 1909–13 amounted to 184 mmt; in 1925, 146 mmt were exported. Thereafter, exports ranged between a high of 179 mmt in 1929 to a low of 120 mmt in 1933. In 1909–13, 15 percent of all coal produced was exported; in 1938, 9 percent. While total world energy consumption climbed during the 1920s and did not decline during the depression, coal's share of total energy use slipped, as did the percentage of coal imports to total energy use (Table 3.1).

Prior to the war, Britain supplied about one-half of world coal exports, a share regained by 1925. Slippage occurred following the strike of 1926. By 1938, Britain's share had dropped to 35 percent. Germany and Poland were causes and beneficiaries of Britain's decline: Germany's share rose from 12 percent (1909–13) to 27 percent in 1937; Poland held 6 to 18 percent between 1929 and 1937. The above three nations accounted for 70 percent of total coal exports.

European nations after the war as before purchased the bulk of coal exports. The importing nations listed in Table 2.5 received 66 percent of total imports in 1936. Canada, still largely provisioned by the USA, accounted for 11 percent of coal imports. Of the ten leading importers, only Japan operated outside the European network.[16]

Britain's shrinking coal exports

Unremitting attrition ravaged Britain's foreign coal trade. At home, labor-management strife, lackadaisical mechanization, and continued fragmentation weakened the industry. Meanwhile, former markets expanded their domestic production. New and effective exporters invaded world coal markets. Fuel substitution and more efficient fuel use proceeded irreversibly. Hydroelectric power emerged as a significant energy source in several former British markets.

All of these changes damaged Britain's foreign coal trade. The changed postwar circumstances of Germany, a competitor and a market, of France, the largest market for British coal, and of Poland, an aggressive newcomer in the coal trade contributed directly to Britain's coal malaise.

The decline of Britain's coal industry stemmed from the loss of comparative advantages. Prior to the war, Buxton writes, superior output per manhour allowed British exporters to undersell competitors. After the war, rising wages and incomplete mine modernization forced production costs above those of competitors, particularly Germany and Poland. Buxton and Jones specify higher relative wage costs as erosive of Britain's competitive position in Europe. Lubin and Smart emphasize technical weaknesses, pointing to the more rapid mechanization of mines in Europe and the USA. Other weaknesses commonly noted include: fragmentation of the industry, costly excess capacity, deteriorating rail facilities, and neglect of the by-products industry.[17]

As coal trade analysts recognized, this itemization of domestic disabilities revealed some but not all of the causative factors that reduced exports. Jones, for one, asserts that the mine labor force declined rapidly after 1928, that mechanization proceeded quickly, and that productivity per man-shift improved. If Jones is correct, then British coal prices should have become more not less competitive. Perhaps they would have had not Britain returned to the gold standard in 1925. For the next several years, an overvalued pound negated the

Table 3.3   World markets for British coal, 1923, 1928, 1936

	1923	1928	1936
British exports			
(million metric tons)	103	67	47
% to France	17	14	14
% of above imports	62	48	29
% to Germany	14	8	7
% of above imports	52	50	51
% to Italy	8	10	<1*
% of above imports	90	51	<1
% to Sweden and Denmark	6	5	14
% of above imports	79	34	44
% to Belgium and Holland	13	7	3
% of above imports	94	27	11
% to all other Europe	8	12	17
% of above imports	65	51	48
% to South America	6	7	6
% of above imports	na	na	54
% to Brazil and Argentina	na	6	5
% for bunkers	17	25	24
% to all other markets	11	12	15

* Reflects Ethiopian war sanctions

Sources: See Table 2.6; International Labour Office, *The World Coal-Mining Industry. Studies and Reports. Series B. No. 31*, Geneva: ILO (1938), pp. 131–2; B.R. Mitchell, ed., *European Historical Statistics*, second revised edition, London: Macmillan (1981), pp. 433–5.

savings made through increased efficiency.[18] Nonetheless, coal exports plunged by 30 percent between 1928 and 1936 (see Table 3.3).

Stringent controls over coal exports to neutrals during World War I compelled many customers to seek other sources of fuel. The postwar depression reduced industrial demand for coal. Labor-management disputes (in the USA as well) periodically wrought havoc in the UK. Coal strikes in 1921 and 1926 cost Britain 68 mmt and 100 mmt, respectively (Table 2.2).[19] As British coal exports plunged to 29 mmt in 1926 (down from 73 mmt in 1925) the exports of key European nations rose by 15 mmt. More remarkably, US exports advanced from 23 mmt in 1925 to 39 mmt in 1926. US exports to Latin America, averaging 692,000 metric tons for 1922–5, reached 5 mmt in 1926. Shipments to Europe soared to 16 mmt, compared with 2 to 4 mmt during each of the four previous years. While the American invasion of new markets proved impermanent, the UK never recaptured fully its European markets.[20] Even more disconcerting to British coal interests, French fuel oil use, stable in 1924 and 1925, rose twofold by 1929 while western European fuel oil consumption increased by 73 percent.[21]

Competition for coal markets

The Treaty of Versailles created new and nationalistic states and stripped territory and resources from the vanquished. The rise of the Bolsheviks to permanent power in Russia struck fear into the hearts of the affluent around the world. But for Europe's coal industry, the birth of a new Poland that incorporated former German Upper Silesia, the retrocession of Alsace-Lorraine to France, French control of the Saar coal mines, and the coal component of Germany's reparations payments were of greater moment.

Territorial losses and reparations cost Germany one-quarter of coal reserves and some 50 mmt of coal production, or 18 percent of the output of 1913. Reparation coal from the Ruhr district amounted to 27 percent of annual output. Coal reparations, valued at 283 million gold marks, contributed between 25 and 30 percent of total reparation payments due under the Dawes Plan of 1924. Human and material losses during the war combined with territorial losses and reparations to cast Germany into a chaos of extraordinary unemployment and horrendous inflation. Germany's coal industry, however, exhibited remarkable recuperative powers.[22]

Between 1919 and 1924, the German coal industry reeled from the successive shocks of diminished productive capacity, reparations, and structural weaknesses. Germans in 1919–20 suffered from severe coal and food shortages, influenza — the more deadly because of chronic malnutrition and frigid homes, and joblessness. Anti-French and anti-reparation demonstrations in the Saar and the Ruhr in 1922, effectively stopping reparation coal deliveries, prompted the invasion of the Ruhr by French and Belgian troops in 1923. The acceptance of onerous terms by Germany, including annual coal reparations of 15 mmt, terminated the occupation. Thereafter, Germany's coal industry forged ahead, maintaining adequate production for home use and producing a surplus, above reparations, for export.[23] By the late 1920s, the German coal industry operated at a high level of productivity, much to the distress of British coal merchants.

The key to German success was the survival and regulatory effectiveness of the Rhenish–Westphalian Coal Syndicate (RWCS).[24] Reorganized between 1923 and 1925, RWCS produced and marketed the entire Ruhr output by 1929. Representing 40 coal firms, some the subsidiaries of the largest Ruhr steel companies, the size of the syndicate's members assured the capital necessary for mechanization and other internal improvements. Successive German governments encouraged modernization by authorizing domestic coal price increases and offering low interest development loans.

RWCS defended "contested" domestic markets against the competition of foreign coal. In the contested areas, the syndicate offered coal at prices competitive with imports and often below the cost of production; higher prices levied in non-competitive markets reimbursed cartel member losses. German imports fell from a prewar tonnage of 18 mmt annually to 9–10 mmt during the late 1920s and 6 mmt annually in 1934–6. German strategies cost the British dearly. Imports from the UK dwindled from an average of 9.5 mmt (1909–13) to about 3 mmt annually in 1934–6 (see also Table 3.3.). In 1925, Germany prohibited coal imports from Poland. Simultaneously, RWCS campaigned successfully for a larger share of foreign markets (Table 3.4). By 1929, German

Table 3.4 Destination of German coal exports, 1926–8, 1936

	1926–8 average (000 metric tons)	% of total imports	1936 (000 metric tons)	% of total imports
Netherlands	7840	86	4001	69
France	6352	37	8442	37
Belgium	5005	59	5185	70
Italy	4360	26	6030	71
Total Exports	29603			

Sources: H.M. Hoar, *The Coal Industry of the World*. U.S. Department of Commerce. Bureau of Foreign and Domestic Commerce. Trade Information Bulletin No. 105, Washington, D.C.: GPO (1930), p. 116; International Labour Office, *The World Coal-Mining Industry. Studies and Reports. Series B. No. 31*, Geneva: ILO (1938), pp. 131–2.

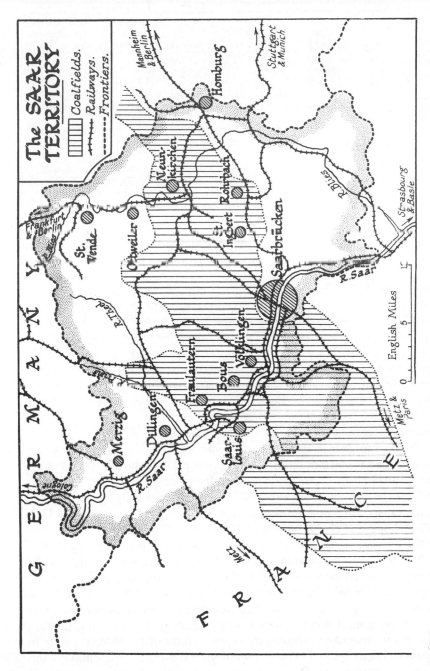

Map 3.1 Franco–German borderlands, 1920s. (*Source:* B.T. Reynolds, *The Saar and the Franco–German Problem,* London: Edward Arnold & Co. (1934), inside cover.)

Table 3.5 Energy supply in France, 1913–36 (thousand metric tons)

	Coal production	Saar production	Coal Imports	Refined oil imports	Hydroelectric production (million kwh)
1913	44 640	—	18 700		
1920	21 100	—	25 800		
1925	47 052	12 900	18 300	2 339*	4 000
1929	53 800	13 579	17 300	3 167	6 600
1934	47 600	11 318	20 700	5 778	7 195
1936	45 252	—	23 100	7 503	8 210†

* 1927
† 1935

Sources: J.H. Jones *et al.*, *The Coal Mining Industry: An International Study in Planning*, London: Sir Isaac Pitman & Sons (1939), pp. 28–9, 37, 82, 209, 213; B.R. Mitchell, ed., *European Historical Statistics*, second revised edition, London: Macmillan (1981), p. 439.

coal exports, not including reparations coal, had attained prewar levels and exceeded Britain's exports to Holland and Belgium.[25]

The consequences of Versailles and the emergence of new and aggressive coal marketers deprived Britain of markets in France and Italy. In 1913 and 1923, France received 60 percent of coal imports from the UK; in 1936, 29 percent (Tables 2.6, 3.3, 3.5). France restored rapidly its devastated mines to maximum output. Domestic coal supplied two thirds of its needs, compared with under one-half in 1920 while total demand in 1929 surpassed demand in 1913 by 21 mmt. French producers, organized into sales agencies by 1929, employed the same price cutting tactics against British coal that worked for RWCS. Taxes on imported coal favored domestic production. In eastern France consumers availed themselves of cheap Polish coal.

The coal market in Italy, a nation without coal or oil and dependent upon Britain for 90 percent of coal imports prior to the war (Table 2.6), was penetrated by German, Polish, Belgian, and Dutch coal. By 1935, one year before the trade sanctions imposed upon Italy by the League of Nations, Italy received 50 percent of coal imports from the UK. Reparations coal composed about 25 percent of total imports during the 1920s, other German coal, 13 percent, and Polish coal, 8 percent.[26]

Poland's rise to prominence in the European coal trade vividly demonstrated the power of non-market forces in restructuring the trade. The acquisition of Upper Silesian coal fields added 20 mmt to Polish production and, because of their location, created possibilities for exports to central and western Europe. Part of the Ruhr occupation settlement obligated Germany to import 6 mmt of Polish coal yearly in the three years, 1923–5. The termination of this trade compelled Poland to seek substitute markets, a search eased by the British coal strike of

1926. Coal exports to Scandinavia rose from 20,000 tons in 1924 to 4.3 mmt in 1926.

The Polish coal industry, accounting for 14 to 18 percent of the value of national exports and lacking strong internal demand, necessarily attracted government support. Public funds modernized the ports of Danzig and Gdynia, constructed new railroads to them, and subsidized the building of a fleet of colliers. Preferential rail freight rates to the sea and to the southern Polish frontier enabled Polish coal to enter markets in Scandinavia, France, Italy, and central Europe. Government authorized price cuts on coal exports assured Polish coal a price edge in distant markets such as Genoa.[27] Finally, the highly centralized Upper Silesian coal industry — three companies controlled three-quarters of production — organized a number of sales agencies endowed with the authority to set quotas and prices, allocate markets, and enforce the arrangements. These tactics lifted Polish exports from under 500,000 metric tons in both 1921 and 1922 to an average of 12.5 mmt annually during the period 1923–31, 23 percent above prewar levels.[28]

Britain and the USA did little to encourage exports. Other producing nations maximized domestic production and exports through preferential policies. Germany, France, Belgium, and Spain heightened tariff barriers against coal imports and, along with Holland and Poland, fostered central sales agencies that, favored by low rail freight rates, effectively reduced foreign imports. Concurrently, the sales agencies aggressively promoted their products in foreign markets once dominated by Britain, eroding Britain's position in Scandinavia and Italy. Far away, Chile and Argentina, formerly dependent upon British coal, raised duties on imported coal and switched to fuel oil, thereby virtually ending the coal trade. The quest for energy self-sufficiency, abetted by nationalistic trade policies, drastically attenuated Britain's coal trade. The depression completed this process.[29]

The shattering impact of collapsed industrial production, shrinking and unreplenished inventories, rising unemployment, and disappearing consumer demand cast the coal industry deeper into the economic abyss. Governments responded by intervening more forcefully in coal affairs, the net result of which further restricted international trade.

World energy use rose minutely between 1929 and 1938 while the share of coal shrunk (Table 3.1). *Per capita* energy consumption in major industrial states leveled off or declined (Table 3.2). Coal production in the UK, France, Germany, Poland, and the USA fell by 31 percent from 1929 to 1933, two-thirds of the loss attributable to the USA. Of the western coal producers, only a rearmed Germany had regained predepression production levels by 1938 (Table 2.3).

National coal policies in Europe generally involved some combination of production quotas, the allocation of market shares among producers, minimum prices for the home market, the licensing of importers, import quotas and/or high tariffs, and aggressive sales campaigns. To encourage exports, Germany, France, Belgium, and Poland offered export bonuses, permitted price shaving, further lowered coal freight rates, engaged in monetary manipulation, and negotiated bilateral preferential trade agreements. The consequences of these policies virtually eliminated coal imports in continental Europe.

Britain defended the foreign coal trade by negotiating bilateral agreements with several nations. Typically, those treaties assured the UK a stable percentage of total coal imports: in Denmark, 80 percent, in Sweden, 60 percent, in France, a fair share of allowable imports. The agreements improved Britain's position in Scandinavia, but overall her coal trade atrophied (Tables 2.2 and 3.3). Parliament also enacted several coal bills between 1926 and 1936 that addressed miner welfare and strengthened government authority to compel amalgamation, but nothing sufficed to restore health to the coal industry. In America, federal coal policies aimed to stabilize employment rather than to identify coal's role in the national energy mix. Ineffectual measures featuring incredibly complicated minimum price fixing and unenforceable prohibitions of unfair competition failed to revitalize the coal industry. Only the rise of German and Japanese militarism, compelling threatened nations to arm, temporarily injected new life into national coal industries. But, of course, war ended the coal trade.[30]

Coal, a summary

Depression and the anti-depression measures of industrialized states applied the *coup de grace* to a much diminished international coal trade. Even in 1929 prospects for the coal trade were poor and becoming poorer. Each year fuel substitution weaned consumers from coal while improved coal burning efficiency further dampened demand. The likelihood of the emergence of new industrial states, all clamoring for coal to feed dynamic and energy intensive industries, appeared dim. The nations with the most promising growth potential — Australia, Canada, the USSR, Argentina, Brazil — were well endowed with coal, petroleum, natural gas, or hydroelectric sites, the latter already of particular importance in Italy, Sweden, Norway, and Japan.[31]

While coal use did increase after World War II, the major consumers burned domestic coal. The coal trade narrowed to shipments of coke and other special purpose coals or to an exchange of coal and other goods within such political units as the Soviet bloc. Nuclear power generation posed an additional threat to coal, as did environmental protection laws.

The booming oil industry

The ubiquitous car symbolized, to Americans, a progressive age. Americans swiftly embraced the auto—one auto per fourteen people in 1919 and one auto per four people in 1938. This romance with the auto was far more intense in America than elsewhere; in the Europe of the 1930s, one car sufficed for every sixty-two people. So rapid did demand for oil accelerate after World War I that numerous American oil experts forecast a domestic oil shortage. However, enormous discoveries in California, Oklahoma, and Texas plus the onset of the depression turned the fear of shortage into the reality of an oil glut.

World demand for petroleum doubled between 1919 and 1926 and doubled again by 1940 (see Table 3.6 for trends). In the USA, gasoline composed 24 percent of total oil demand in 1919 and 46 percent in 1938. In the latter year, 522 million barrels of gasoline were burned, a figure equal to total oil consumption in 1918. Globally, gasoline consumption in 1938 accounted for 37 percent of total oil use. Americans used seven of every ten gallons of gasoline. To meet this exploding demand, for fuel oil as well, oil companies scoured the earth for new fields while exploiting older fields more intensively. Table 2.7 attests to their success.[32]

Such statistics are the bare bones. They cannot convey the extraordinary expansion of the oil corporations, the new technologies employed to develop new fields and concoct new products, the intense competitiveness for global resources and markets among the few but powerful international oil companies and their home countries, the

Table 3.6 Relationship to world petroleum demand of US demand and exports, 1913–39

	Total world demand (000 metric tons)	US demand (% of world)	US exports (% of non–US demand)
1913	54 298	55	30
1919	78 975	66	33
1924	141 236	68	36
1929	205 380	64	30
1932	195 308	59	18
1939	303 729	56	20

Source: L.M. Fanning, *American Oil Operations Abroad*, New York: McGraw-Hill (1947), pp. 225, 232.

reverberations of short-term economic cycles, or the angry nationalism evoked by oil company operations around the world.

Two powerful firms, Standard Oil (New Jersey) and Royal Dutch–Shell dominated the international oil industry. Pursuing expansionist policies that were frequently supported by their home governments, the oil giants forced responses from the producing countries in which they operated and from the non-producing countries in which they marketed. Necessarily, then, the following pages pay particular attention to the Anglo-American petroleum firms — the precipitators of action, the inducers of unanticipated and frequently negative reactions.

The oil producing regions

Schlumberger, Ltd, a leading purveyor of oil field services, introduced wireline logging in 1927 by passing a monitored electric current through the underground rock formations being drilled by an oil rig. The electrical signature provided an improved gauge of an oil well's prospects. Geologists regularly employed magnetometers, torsion balances and gravimeters, seismographs, and other instruments to locate potential oil bearing structures. The application of such devices, however, merely suggested places where oil might be present. Only the actual drilling of a well could prove out the pool. Geophysical and geochemical techniques raised the chances of success from one well in ten to two in ten. Modern technologies combined with an equal measure of intuitive experience and luck to open magnificent new fields during the interwar years. Development costs climbed as technologies improved.

Production in the USA rose steadily (Table 2.7), periodically leaping forward as prolific new fields were discovered in Oklahoma, Texas, and California. If brought in toward the end of the 1920s, as were the impressive Kern County, California pools (1928–32), the roaring Oklahoma City, Oklahoma, field (1929), and the even greater East Texas field (1930), the new finds not only added to reserves but contributed to troublesome oil surpluses. East Texas came in at an especially inauspicious moment and, in 1933, flowing uncontrollably, produced one-half of US demand.[33]

Table 2.7 pinpoints the ebb and flow of oil production in other nations. Of particular importance was the impact of war and revolution on Russian production, the erratic nature of Mexican output, the meteoric rise of Venezuela, the somewhat slower growth in the Netherlands East Indies (NEI) and Persia, and the appearance of Middle Eastern oil in world markets just before World War II. The US share of world production remained extremely high, but did drop from a peak of 72 percent in 1923 to 61 percent in 1939. Soviet oil production, under five percent of world production during the 1920s, accounted for over ten percent during the 1930s. Oil production in Latin America, notably Venezuela, Mexico, and Colombia, provided 16 percent of world oil in 1939. The Middle East accounted for some five percent during the 1930s.[34]

North and South America pumped 77 percent of all oil raised in 1938. The shallow waters of Venezuela's Maraicabo Bay and adjacent land near the mouth of the Orinoco River yielded a torrential flow. Huge investments by RDS subsidiaries over a decade culminated in the eruption of a 100,000 barrel a day gusher in 1922. Equally significant investments by SONJ failed to bring in a promising well until 1928 while Sun Oil Company invested above $750,000 in leases on two million acres, found nothing, and quit the search.

In the USA, the proximity of potential oil bearing terrain to settled areas and the private ownership of most of that land encouraged the proliferation of small scale wildcat firms or individuals. Relatively small firms also made their way in refining, wholesaling, and retailing. A peculiar brand of politics emerged from this mixture of the large and the small that was not replicated elsewhere. The larger firms established their dominance over all phases of the industry and were repeatedly attacked in state and federal political arenas by the small firms, so called independents, for monopolistic practices. In other nations, geographic isolation limited exploration to the well financed MNOCs. In Iraq, and later the Persian Gulf sheikdoms, political and geographic conditions demanded large scale operations, frequently in the form of consortia of MNOCs that received concessions directly from the government. Thorough exploration of Iraq's Mosul district was long postponed by Turkish claims to ownership. When that issue was resolved the production of oil, discovered in commercial quantities in 1927, awaited the construction of hundreds of miles of pipeline to the Mediterranean Sea. Geopolitical factors so intruded that even the giants could not be assured of gaining entry, let alone success.

Success graced the efforts of the MNOCs in the difficult Venezuelan and Middle Eastern environments. The real impact of discoveries in Iraq, Persia, Saudi Arabia, and Kuwait came during and after World War II and convinced oilmen of the wisdom of their investments in exploration and development. It was clear, by the mid-1930s, that the cost of retrieving a barrel of oil from the Middle East was far less than in the USA or even Venezuela. To phrase it somewhat differently, the total cost of adding a barrel to US reserves far exceeded the cost in the Middle East or Venezuela. The relative cheapness of Middle Eastern oil raised the possibility of exporting it to the USA to compete with more costly US oil. Imports of Mexican and Venezuelan oil had already aroused the hostility of producers of American oil. As a political issue foreign imports surfaced during the first years of the depression in the form of demands for high tariffs or oil import quotas. After World War II, a flood of Middle Eastern oil forced this issue, now linked to national security, to resurface.[35]

The behemoths of the oil trade

Multinational oil companies, predominantly American and British, consolidated their control over all phases of the industry and in all fields outside of Russia. SONJ outstripped all competitors in the size and scope of its operations. Its assets were twice as large as Standard Oil of New York (SONY), merged with Vacuum Oil Company in 1931 to form Socony–Vacuum, and as large as the combined assets of Gulf and Standard Oil of California (SOCAL). These firms competed internationally with Standard Oil of Indiana (SOIND), the Texas Company, RDS (treated as British) and the Anglo-Persian Oil Company (APOC).

During the interwar years, these and a few other Anglo-American firms owned a share of foreign oil production, a proportion shifting among them as old fields declined and new fields came in, that ranged between 65 and 80 percent. The foreign output of the British firms fell from 41 percent in 1929 to 35 percent in 1939 while the US share declined from 50 percent in 1921 to 25 percent in 1939. The shrinking Anglo-American portion attested to the success of the Soviet oil industry which contributed some 10 to 12 percent of total world production (Table 2.7) and almost 30 percent of non-US world production during the 1930s. Anglo-American oil interests also held equal parts of 80 percent of non-Russian foreign reserves.[36]

American and British enterprises extended their grasp over foreign deposits of minerals other than oil. British companies in 1929 produced one-third of the world's tin ore and one-fifth of the zinc. US transnationals owned 12 percent of zinc, 26 percent of copper, and 27 percent of bauxite. The US controlled an even larger share of ore refineries – 45 percent of zinc smelting capacity, 51 percent for aluminum, and 83 percent for copper. These patterns, laden with political implications, were even more pronounced in oil.[37]

American ownership of oil refineries on foreign soil expanded rapidly from 1920 to 1939. US firms may have controlled as much as 15 percent of foreign refining capacity during the early 1920s, a share rising to about 24 percent of a much larger throughput by the late 1930s. In 1939, American firms owned the entire refining capacity of Bolivia, Colombia, and Venezuela, five of seven refineries in Argentina, about 60 percent of Canadian refining capacity, above one-third in Germany, Hungary, and Yugoslavia, one-quarter in France and the NEI, and roughly 13 percent in the UK, Belgium, and Czechoslovakia. In addition, American refiners operated in the Dutch West Indies, Bahrain, and Saudi Arabia.

Data limitations preclude a calculation of the share of world oil production and refining capacity attributable to specific companies. Data for several firms suggestive of the actual figures are offered in Table 3.7. RDS and SONJ consistently pumped 18 to 23 percent of the world's oil from 1929 to 1935. In 1934, the nine firms listed accounted for at least 37 percent of the total. In the USA, too, concentration of production prevailed and intensified over time. By the late 1930s, the 20 largest US companies controlled 70 percent of proven reserves (94 percent in 1970) and 53 percent of production (74 percent in 1970), compared with 46 percent in 1926.

Concentration also occurred in refining. RDS owned 45 refineries in 15 countries and the Dutch colonies in 1937, but total barrel per day capacity (bpd) is unknown. In the USA, the Shell Oil Co. owned nine refineries by 1929 and produced six percent of all gasoline; only SONJ and SOIND were larger refiners. Both SONJ and RDS operated refineries in the NEI. RDS possessed a capacity of 104,500 bpd and SONJ, 45,500 bpd. APOCs large Abadan refinery (250,000 bpd) produced three million metric tons of products in 1932. APOC owned 32,500 bpd in England and other refineries in Australia, Burma, Iraq, and France. SONJ's wholly owned foreign refineries were capable of processing some 665,000 bpd in 1939. The Texas Co., SOCAL, Union, Socony–Vacuum, Sinclair, Gulf, and Pure owned a foreign capacity of 238,000 bpd. A small number of American firms controlled 70 percent of world refining capacity. The twenty largest US firms owned 53 percent of domestic capacity in 1933 (86 percent in 1970), up from 46 percent in 1926.[38]

Both Jersey Standard and RDS operated tanker fleets of some two million gross metric tons in 1937, or 35 percent of world tanker tonnage. Their subsidiaries managed thousands of miles of pipeline, a large proportion in the USA. This enormous complex of oil field equipment, refineries, tankers, pipelines, storage depots, and commercial outlets required huge investments. The USA ranked as the world's largest foreign investor as well as the largest exporter and importer (particularly of primary goods). Europe depended upon a buoyant and open American market for her goods in order to discharge a war debt estimated at $20 billion (90 percent owed by the UK, France and Italy). American capital kept Latin America afloat. The overwhelming American

Table 3.7 Crude oil production and percentage of world production for several oil companies, 1920, 1929–35 (thousand metric tons)

	SONJ	RDS	GULF	APOC	SOIND	SOCAL	UNION	IPC	TEXACO
1920	8 648	15 000	4 240	1 385	*				3 944
	0.09	0.16	0.05	0.01					0.04
1929	12 065	25 184	10 916	5 567					6 086
	0.06	0.13	0.05	0.03					0.03
1930	12 167	23 980	8 911	5 461	7 650				5 147
	0.06	0.13	0.05	0.03	0.04				0.03
1931	11 862	20 533	8 252	5 939	6 926				4 093
	0.06	0.11	0.04	0.03	0.04				0.02
1932	14 853	20 936	6 869	5 750	3 531[†]				3 952
	0.08	0.12	0.04	0.03	0.02				0.02
1933	19 024	21 957	7 051	6 450	1 559	5 005	1 555		4 308
	0.10	0.11	0.04	0.03	<0.01	0.03	<0.01		0.02
1934	23 117	24 078	6 886	7 087	1 973	5 264	2 073	1 031	4 341
	0.11	0.12	0.03	0.04	0.01	0.03	0.01	<0.01	0.02
1935	24 739	26 620	7 399	7 487	2 683		2 599	3 729	5 240
	0.11	0.12	0.03	0.03	0.01		0.01	0.02	0.02

* Data not available in empty spaces
† Sale of foreign producing properties to SONJ

Sources: *World Petroleum Directory, 1937*, New York: R. Palmer (1937), pp. 247, 269, 384; H. Larson et al., *History of Standard Oil Company (New Jersey). New Horizons 1927–50*, New York: Harper & Row (1971). p. 148; B. Shwadran, *The Middle East, Oil and the Great Powers*, New York: Praeger (1955), pp. 162, 252; R. McLean and R. Haigh, *The Growth of Integrated Oil Companies*, Boston: Graduate School of Business Administration, Harvard University (1954), pp. 96–8, 683.

presence contributed to numerous revolutions and the consolidation of oppressive regimes. Within this context, Table 3.8 suggests the magnitude of overseas oil investments by US firms.[39]

The structure of individual companies described in Chapter 2 provided the framework for further growth. Firms added subsidiaries, merging them into larger groups as necessary. The *World Petroleum Directory, 1937* listed over 100 subsidiaries of RDS while SONJ was credited with 113, many of which served as holding companies for still other units. Both firms reorganized during the 1920s with the parent organization becoming a holding rather than operating company, responsible for overall planning and supervision and performing banking functions for the group. Standard's annual investments, reaching $300 million in 1937, were financed largely through earnings rather than through new stock issues. RDS followed a similar course in launching its US and non-US subsidiaries. The subsidiaries of RDS, SONJ, Gulf, and other MNOCs frequently managed securities firms that traded in both oil and non-oil stocks and bonds and provided funds for particular capital expenditures.[40]

Seeking the improved market opportunities promised by enhanced self-sufficiency, the transnational firms further integrated their operations. APOC launched an ambitious program, expending £2.5 million in exploration from 1918 to 1928. The firm purchased existing transportation and marketing firms and created new marketing units, especially in Europe. APOC and RDS entered into joint marketing operations in the eastern Mediterranean and South Africa and, in 1931, in the UK. APOC gained new outlets for its oil and RDS won access to crude supplies. APOC also enlarged the capacity of the Abadan refinery and constructed refineries in the UK, France, and elsewhere.

In the USA, the MNOCs relied on domestic crude in competing vigorously for a larger share of the mammoth internal market while

Table 3.8 Direct investments of US abroad, 1919–40

	1919	1929	1936	1940
Total US investment abroad ($000 000)	3880	7527	6690	7000
Total US oil investment abroad ($000 000)	399	1116	1074	1277
% in oil in Western hemisphere	0.45	0.47	0.33	0.36
% in oil in Mexico		0.19	0.06	0.03
% in oil in Venezuela		0.20	0.16	0.20
% in oil in Colombia		0.05	0.06	0.06
% in oil in Europe	0.29	0.21	0.26	0.25

Source: L.M. Fanning, *American Oil Operations Abroad*, New York: McGraw Hill (1947), pp. 244–5.

seeking foreign crude and facilities to serve international markets. Standard, stripped of much of its productive capacity by the dissolution decree of 1912, integrated backward into production both at home and abroad.

During the period, 1912–17, SONJ purchased 87 percent of its crude requirements, in 1927, 62 percent, and in 1939, 39 percent. Meanwhile Jersey's crude needs had reached one million barrels daily, a sixfold increment since World War I. For the most part, Standard purchased companies with proven production records. In 1920, it bought the Colombian holdings of the Tropical Oil Company, transferring Tropical to its Canadian subsidiary, International Oil Ltd. Tropical's fields produced 2.8 mmt in each of 1928, 1929, and 1930, adding substantially to Standard's crude production (Table 3.7). An even larger acquisition in 1932 transferred to SONJ all the foreign properties of an SOIND subsidiary. Costing above $75 million—paid for in cash and stock— SONJ obtained four refineries, including the 115,000 bpd Aruba facility, 1,500,000 acres of Mexican leases, 3,100,000 acres in and around Lake Maracaibo, and other assets. Standard's Venezuelan production, under 1 mmt annually before 1932, soared to 4 mmt in 1932, and reached 14 mmt in 1939. Venezuelan output fully accounts for the rising production of SONJ presented in Table 3.7. By 1939, Venezuela provided 27 percent of SONJ's crude requirements, much of the crude transported to the great Aruba refinery, now enlarged to a capacity of 300,000 bpd. A portion of Aruba's refined output competed with domestic products in the large East Coast market of the USA.[41]

Concession holding subsidiaries of the MNOCs proliferated in South America, partly a consequence of host country laws which, as in Venezuela, limited the acreage awarded to any single firm. The Atlantic Refining Co. created three layers of holding companies to manage at least eight exploration firms in Venezuela; RDS employed four layers. SONJ's organization surpassed all others in complexity. It operated through three (or more) central holding companies, the largest a subsidiary of Imperial Oil. Each of the three holding companies controlled a score or more of producing and transportation firms. This confusing maze masked the connection between Standard, the bugbear of articulate nationalists the world over, and individual companies. Jersey Standard employed Imperial Oil of Canada for this purpose throughout South America.[42]

Sun Oil Company's unhappy exploration experience in Venezuela consumed money voraciously but yielded only dry holes. To spread the risks and costs, MNOCs increasingly resorted to joint ventures in developing promising oil fields in remote areas. Adhering to the wishes of the British government, Turkish Petroleum Company (Iraq

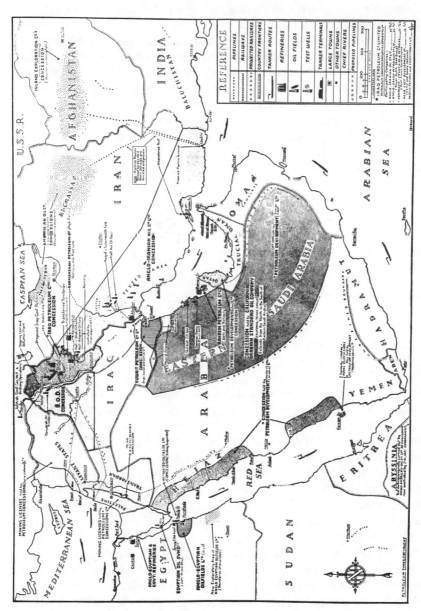

Map 3.2 Middle Eastern oil developments in 1937. (*Source: World Petroleum Directory, 1937*, New York: R. Palmer (1937).

Petroleum Co. in 1929), in 1926, enlarged the partnership to include several American firms. Similar, if smaller scale, arrangements occurred in Colombia and Venezuela during the 1920s, but the most significant joint ventures emerged during the 1930s.

SOCAL received oil concessions in Bahrain and Saudi Arabia in 1929 and 1932, respectively. Burdened by the initial high development costs, SOCAL sold one-half interest in each concession to The Texas Co. in 1935 and 1936. The Texas Co. added to its reserves while SOCAL benefited from widened market opportunities. By 1941, Bahrain oil moved to Asian markets through a network of Caltex terminals. Somewhat earlier, Kuwait awarded a concession to Gulf that aroused the ire of APOC (Anglo-Iranian Oil Co. in 1935). Gulf, in 1934, agreed to divide its interest with the British firm. These Persian Gulf ventures bore fruit during and after World War II. Lastly, SONJ and Socony–Vacuum formed in 1934 the Standard–Vacuum Company, with assets of $250 million, an agreement in which the two firms shared SONJ's production and refining capacity in the NEI and marketed through Socony–Vacuum's well situated Asian outlets.[43]

The expansion of the overseas refining capacity owned by US firms evolved logically from the decision to utilize foreign crude to supply foreign markets. Forwarding Venezuelan crude to refineries in the Dutch West Indies and then shipping finished products to Europe economized on transport and benefited from lower refining costs. Too, a number of countries, particularly during the depression, promoted greater domestic refining output. The effects of such decisions reduced the extent to which exports from the USA filled non-US demand (Table 3.6) and increased the volume and value of crude exports from the USA relative to refined exports. Between 1926 and 1934, the proportionate value of gasoline and kerosene exports declined from 63 percent to 32 percent. French and Italian crude imports, well under 1 million barrels annually during the 1920s, rose to 23 million barrels in 1938, reflecting an intense concern for national security as well as an accelerating demand for oil. The trend toward refined product self-sufficiency was pursued vigorously by European governments at the conclusion of World War I. Jersey Standard, RDS, and other MNOCs accommodated to this by reorganizing their foreign oil operations.[44]

The MNOCs pursued market oriented policies, expanding in response to steadily ascending demand during the 1920s. While practicing cautious and selective retrenchment during the worst years of the depression, they also grasped opportunities to augment their reserve position and improve their market share, often through joint venture agreements with other large firms. The oil policies of the USA and the UK affected their decisions, but did not determine the course chosen. The American multinationals would have arrived at about the same position in 1939 in all phases of operations had the USA government never uttered a word about oil. The encouragement and support offered the MNOCs by the US government provided but flimsy protection against the emergent nationalism of producing countries.

Oil nationalism

Undeveloped, quasi-independent producing countries such as Persia, underdeveloped but independent producers such as Mexico, backward non-producing nations such as Spain, and developed nations without oil and with weak domestic refining capabilities such as France, each manifesting a sharpened sense of nationalism, challenged the profit seeking and expansionist international oil companies. The leaders of the MNOCs and their apologists proclaimed the advantages of oil industry investments to national economies, praising company baseball teams, higher wages and worker housing, schools, and clinics. National leaders and governments, however, expected oil and other natural resource revenues to serve as a catalyst for economic growth. These expectations in the lesser developed countries whatever their justification, were dashed during the interwar years by the inherent weaknesses of their societies, by the deflation of natural resource prices in the 1920s and the depression of the 1930s, and by the expatriation of the greater share of natural resource revenues. The invading capitalists, in the eyes of the hosts, feasted upon and contributed to infrastructure inadequacies.

Among the developed and developing nations of Europe, France, Germany, Italy, Spain, and Romania devised policies designed to inhibit the further growth of foreign MNOCs and to strengthen domestic firms. The Soviet Union nationalized the entire industry. Spain declared a state monopoly over oil distribution and expropriated SONJ properties in 1927, a direct response to the purchase by Standard in 1922 of Spain's largest oil marketing firm. France, the third largest Standard market in Europe, launched a two-pronged campaign to resurrect national refining: tariffs on refined products were raised; two state controlled firms were established, one to oversee French oil interests overseas, especially France's share of Mesopotamian oil, the second to refine and market. France permitted American firms to operate domestically, but they faced stiff competition from a revitalized home industry and from RDS. Italy and Germany also sought enhanced refining self-sufficiency as part of their military buildup during the 1930s.[45]

Romania followed a distinctively independent course after World

War I, countering RDS and SONJ efforts to reassert their supremacy with a series of mining laws that strongly favored domestic over foreign firms. As in the past, Standard was singled out for particularly discriminatory treatment. Standard's fortunes deteriorated, but so did the Romanian oil industry. While production advanced during the 1920s (Table 2.7), exploration and new well drilling fell off as hostile legislation and the persistent threat of nationalization convinced foreign firms to refrain from new investments. Dependence upon oil revenues prevented the Romanian government from adopting production restrictions or other conservationist measures as prices plummeted during the early 1930s. Nationalism notwithstanding, Romanians failed to gain control over the larger and more modern refineries. Romanian producers sold most of their crude to the foreigners. Lastly, military weakness and vulnerability to German attack compelled accommodation to rising German demands for oil in 1937–39, even though the terms of this trade were less advantageous than terms proffered by the UK and France. Ultimately, Nazi troops occupied and operated Romania's oil fields. Romanian oil nationalism had poorly served the national interest.[46]

Bolshevik nationalization of the oil industry and the confiscation without compensation of all foreign properties scandalized the West which hated the new regime. European governments and the USA and such influential oilmen as Henri Deterding of RDS and Walter Teagle of SONJ, deluded by the conviction that the USSR was an aberration soon to be replaced by a responsible Russian government, labored to weaken the infant regime. Recognition was denied—by the USA until 1933. Ineffective military intervention on the side of anti-Soviet forces and spasmodic economic coercion retarded reconstruction but failed to destroy the Soviet Union.

Ideological myopia blinded westerners to the unswerving commitment of Soviet leaders to communism, to the fearsome dynamism of this new and authoritarian state, to the willingness of the regime to sacrifice short- for long-term goals, to the essential competence of Soviet managers and technicians, and to the improbability of maintaining anti-Soviet unity in the West. Rapid advances in Soviet oil production after 1921 (Table 2.7) attested to the illusory quality of western opinion.

The former Allied powers schemed and maneuvered against the USSR. Various combinations of western oil and financial interests pressured the USSR for compensation and to reopen the Baku fields to foreign exploitation. The Soviets skillfully played one set of interests against another, weathered oil boycotts, and rebuilt the petroleum industry. So foolish were the oilmen, that SONJ in 1920 purchased 50 percent of the Nobel holdings in the dead Russia Empire while the stocks of other seized properties were traded regularly. The RDS and SONJ officials adhered staunchly to the notion that denying the USSR technology, capital, and markets would block the development of the oil industry and bring the Bolsheviks, hat in hand, to the West. But the Soviet delegation to the Genoa and The Hague conferences in 1922 offered no compensation and insisted upon recognition of the USSR as a precondition to establishing new producing consortia under the control of the state owned oil trust. Even the latter offer was quickly withdrawn as progress in the oil fields, by 1925, convinced Soviet managers that foreign participation was unnecessary.

The competitiveness of the key MNOCs in the European market corroded anti-Soviet unity. Between 1925 and 1929, SONJ, RDS, Sinclair, and other firms negotiated oil purchases with the USSR and, then, supported its recognition. These contracts reflected decisions by the American firms to utilize foreign oil to supply Europe. An RDS- Soviet arrangement in 1929 enabled oil from the Baku field to enter the British market through a Soviet retail outlet. As a result, Soviet oil exports rose impressively after 1925, supplying Germany with one-fourth of oil imports, France with 10 percent, and Italy with 41 percent. Soviet oil expors virtually ceased in 1932, as all resources were re-directed toward the development of heavy industry, agriculture, and the armed forces.[47] Two decades later, the reappearance of Soviet oil in European markets evoked renewed consternation among leaders of the Western alliance.

Pitted against a strong, purposeful, and self-reliant state, MNOC power wilted. The USSR, unlike the lesser developed nations of the Middle East, Latin America, and Asia, dealt with the oil giants on its own terms. In other countries, the MNOCs set the initial terms. The adoption of confrontational policies by the host governments, if damaging to the companies, weakened as well the entire industry.

Considerable attention has been lavished on the discovery and exploitation of Middle Eastern oil with the focal point being the controversy between the UK and the USA over the latter's desire to participate in Iraq's Mosul fields and the resolution of that issue. Earlier commentators couched their treatments in terms of the confrontation, brought to a head by the Treaty of San Remo (1920) which ostensibly divided Middle Eastern oil between Britain and France, between British oil imperialism and American "Open Door" policies. The exclusionary schemes of Britain, according to this rendition, aroused opposition in the USA, at this time gravely concerned over the magnitude of its domestic reserves. Urged on by SONJ, the US government exerted sufficient pressure to compel the UK to admit American firms to partnership in Iraq.[48]

Recent investigators, blessed with hindsight, widened the context of the discussion, considering, for example, Turkish nationalism and western insistence on regional order as essential elements. General agreement has been reached on key points.[49] Britain opted for American participation in Iraq not because of official US pressure but in order to spread the risk of developing Mosul among a larger number of companies. The firms involved in the reorganized Turkish Petroleum Company (Iraq Petroleum Company in 1929) accepted in 1928 the Red Line Agreement in which, as Gibb and Knowlton describe it, the members "bound themselves not to operate, except through the company, within. . .virtually all of the old Turkish Empire." This agreement became a dead letter when American MNOCs sought, obtained, and started operating concessions in the Arab Persian Gulf states. The Achnacarry Agreement of 1928 in which SONJ, RDS, and APOC attempted to stabilize world market shares and avoid an oil war also fell victim to the self-interest of individual firms.[50]

To safeguard investments, the USA accepted British political control in Iraq and Persia. The USA proclaimed the principle of the Open Door as a means of gaining access to commercial opportunities without shouldering attendant responsibilities for maintaining order. Insofar as US power allowed, the Open Door was closed in areas where US interests predominated. The fear of oil shortage is discounted as a factor in the American thrust, instead, the expansionist ambitions of the American MNOCs provides the essential motivational explanation. The wedding of oil and imperial defense led Britain to foster a partnership with American firms in Iraq and to refrain from adopting an uncompromising opposition to later concessions awarded American firms in the Persian Gulf region.[51]

Dependency — British military installations and the manipulation of governments, the power of APOC and TPC, fiscal subordination, the perceived inequity of concessional agreements — stoked the fires of latent Persian (Iran in 1935) and Iraqi nationalism. A bitter relationship evolved as Iraqi and Persian governments vigorously contested the terms of concessions demanded by TPC and APOC (Anglo-Iranian Oil Company in 1935).

Iraq, even prior to the termination of the British mandate in 1932 unsuccessfully demanded participatory rights in TPC but gained a revision in the calculation of royalties so that as production increased so too did royalties. To strengthen its hand against TPC, Iraq invited American firms to bid for concessions. This tactic did win more favorable terms from TPC in 1927 when commercial quantities of oil were discovered. In Persia, an escalation of demands considered extortionate by APOC accompanied the establishment of the authoritarian and nationalistic Pahlavi regime in 1921. In 1928–9 and again in 1932, APOC–Persian disputes flared. Despite the presence of British naval forces in the Persian Gulf, Persia persevered, forcing a favorable revision of the method of calculating royalties. Through 1940, AIOC (ex-APOC) paid £140 million in royalties to the Iranian government and invested vast sums in facilities. Still, handsome profits accrued with dividends in 1937 and 1938 exceeding 20 percent *per annum*.[52]

Nasty disputes between the MNOCs, particularly SONJ, and the governments of several Latin American states punctuated the interwar years. Mexico, Venezuela, Colombia, Peru, Bolivia, and Argentina distrusted the MNOCs and the USA and the UK. Unburdened by the presence of foreign troops, in full control of internal affairs, and, therefore, possessed of much greater political flexibility than Iran or Iraq, Latin American producers determined to assert full sovereign control over their oil resources. The leading producers, Mexico, Venezuela, Colombia, and Peru sought returns from oil sufficient to catalyze industrial growth. Economic diversification, they believed, would reduce their reliance upon exports of cheap raw commodities and imports of costly manufactured goods, improve their exchange position, and add to the capital available for internal investments.

In this struggle against Anglo-American economic hegemony and the dominance of RDS and SONJ — together controlling 75 percent of Latin American oil production in 1937, the producing states were doomed to disappointment. Raw commodity exports in 1938 composed 83 percent of the value of Colombia's total exports and petroleum, 23 percent; for Peru, like Colombia an oil infant at this time, 71 percent and 30 percent; for Mexico, 76 percent and 9 percent (reflecting the collapse of oil after 1922); and for Venezuela (the world's third largest producer), 95 percent and 91 percent. Five decades later, Venezuelan exports of oil composed 82 percent of the value of all exports while manufactured imports equaled 82 percent of the value of all imports.[53]

Argentina's earlier move toward state control provided a precedent and model for nationalization in Bolivia in 1937, in Mexico in 1938, and in Brazil in 1940. The path to state ownership was most tortuous in Mexico. Civil wars, intense foreign pressure, oil field labor-management disputes, in short, unstable political conditions faced foreign oil operators in Mexico for the two decades following the declaration of state ownership over subsurface minerals in the Mexican Constitution of 1917. Discouraged by the political climate, SONJ essentially abandoned Mexico until the purchase of SOIND properties in 1932 brought to Standard a large producing acreage. RDS, on the other hand, remained active, accommodating to uncertainty and arousing less Mexican animosity than Standard. Finally, after twenty years of stagnant production, President Cárdenas in 1938 seized upon a labor dispute with SONJ to expropriate all foreign oil properties. In 1940, he established Pétroleous Mexicana (PEMEX) to manage the industry. The expropriated firms orchestrated a boycott of Mexican oil to force compensation and Britain severed its diplomatic relations, whereupon Mexico increased its exports to Germany and Japan. Compensatory issues were resolved with American firms in 1942 and with British firms in 1947.[54]

While Venezuela, Colombia, and Peru chose not to nationalize or to create state owned oil companies, relations with the foreign firms were tense. *SONJ* dominance remained intact in Venezuela because of the favorable policies of the dictator, Juan Vincente Gómez, toward foreign investments, and because of Peruvian and Colombian weakness and dependence upon oil revenues. Nonetheless, the possibility of nationalization drew frequent concessions from the oil companies and the US government. The USA ratified the Colombian–USA treaty of 1920, compensating the former for the loss of Panama, partly as a consequence of Colombian threats to apply its oil laws and to refuse a pipeline concession necessary to SONJ. Indeed, during the 1930s, the US government frequently urged upon the companies a more moderate and less narrowly legalistic attitude toward their presumed rights. In return, the MNOCs received new leases from Colombia and Venezuela. During the controversy with Mexico, as Europe prepared to self-destruct, US insistence upon company forbearance became especially forceful.[55]

The immediate consequences of oil nationalism upon the fortunes of the MNOCs were, it seemed at the time, undetectable. The companies continued to grow even during the depression. World markets swam in oil. Production in East Texas, Venezuela, and the Middle East negated the impact of Mexico's fall. Producer states chose an unpropitious moment to assert their sovereignty but, those states responded to an emotional imperative rather than to an objective analysis of market opportunity.

Tradition, corruption, and the absence of a modern economic infrastructure prevented the funneling of Middle Eastern royalties into modernization projects. Latin American states, independent and with superior natural endowments, still lagged behind in the quest for economic progress, lacking the ability to generate sufficient local capital for development. The MNOCs drained wealth from the producing states. To maintain their dominance, the companies assiduously protected their production and refining technologies from the locals, refusing to train nationals for technical or management jobs. When they could, MNOCs prevented host countries from creating a domestic or external marketing apparatus. Coercion was employed against nationalization in Mexico. MNOCs, then, must bear part of the onus for the persistent economic backwardness of the lesser developed producing countries. But, the governments and ruling classes of those nations also share the blame.

War, the cure for depression

Nations struggled desperately and in isolation to extricate themselves from the depression, relying upon unprecedented government economic intervention and pursuing, in Foreman-Peck's words, "beggar-thy-neighbor" trade policies. Recovery between 1933 and 1937, like a false spring buoyed up the spirits of many only to be dashed by the violence of new storms. In fact, recovery came most swiftly to Japan, already at war in China, and to Germany, consciously preparing for war. In the more pacific states of the West, the threat of aggression finally turned economies upward, but only the USA derived full benefit.[56]

The energy industries suffered as other industries contracted and purchasing power deteriorated. As noted above, national coal control schemes proliferated in western Europe, the USA, and Japan, but excepting for Germany and Japan, failed to achieve their goals. In the USA, despite oil policies designed to reduce production, oil production far exceeded demand during the 1930s. US energy policies failed to induce either stability or recovery; war in Europe achieved both goals. In Japan and Germany, coal production marched ahead during the late 1930s, keeping abreast of a general economic recovery stimulated by war or preparations for war.

The depression, smoldering hatred for the Versailles Treaty, French control in the Saar, and other frustrations and delusions permitted Adolf Hitler to come to power in Germany in 1933. Japan, in the meantime, had struck at China in 1931 and seized Manchuria, converting it into the puppet state of Manchukuo in 1932, and quit the League of Nations in 1933. Both nations rapidly armed and militarized. Both nations, complaining of assorted plots to deny them access to raw materials, stared covetously at the colonies of their perceived enemies. Japan presented convincing arguments demonstrating western European and American control over the world's principal minerals, a case undented by spurious western rejoinders pointing to the small proportion of strategic mineral production derived from colonies.

Germany and Japan initiated programs to moderate their energy deficiencies. Each, harnessing their coal resources, funded ambitious and moderately successful synthetic fuel industries, in which area Germany was the world's technological leader. The Japanese invested heavily in hydroelectric installations in Manchukuo and Korea, partly to provide power for coal liquefication plants. Both nations, dangerously dependent upon oil imports, shored up their domestic stockpiles through regulations controlling the oil trade, promoting domestic refining, and subjecting foreign refiners to mandatory stockpiling quotas.[57]

These measures, as Japan and Germany fully realized, would not fuel the wars that each contemplated. Plans evolved to conquer the oil producing territories of their enemies, particularly Romania, Soviet Caucasia, the Middle East, and the NEI. Myopically and soporifically, the USA, Britain, and France watched the aggressor states openly prepare to strike.

Notes

1. A quote taken from J.G. Clark, *Energy and the Federal Government: Fossil Fuel Policies, 1900–1948*, Urbana: University of Illinois Press (1986), p. 169.
2. League of Nations, Economic and Financial Section, *International Economic Conference, Geneva, May, 1927, Memorandum on Coal, Vol. I*, Geneva: League of Nations (1927), pp. 74–5; J. Darmstadter *et al.*, *Energy in the World Economy: A Statistical Review of Trends in Output, Trade, and Consumption Since 1925*, Baltimore: The Johns Hopkins Press for Resources for the Future (1971), pp. 652–91.
3. For the above two paragraphs: J. Abu-Lughod, *Cairo: 1001 Years of the City Victorious*, Princeton: Princeton University Press (1971), pp. 96, 158–74; W. Dean, *The Industrialization of São Paulo, 1880–1945*, Austin: University of Texas Press for the Institute of Latin American Studies (1969); pp. 110–17; P. Monbeig, *La Croissance de la Ville de São Paulo*, Grenoble: Institut et Revue de Géographie Alpine (1953), pp. 56–76; Electrical Equipment Division, *Electrical Development and Guide to Marketing Electrical Equipment in Brazil*, US Department of Commerce, Bureau of Foreign and Domestic Commerce. Trade Information Bulletin No. 496, Washington, DC: GPO (1927), pp. ii, 4–7.
4. Interwar does not precisely fit the Japanese experience. The Sino-Japanese conflict of 1931 — the Mukden incident — led to the occupation of Manchuria and the establishment of the puppet state of Manchukuo in 1932.
5. For the above two paragraphs: *The Japanese–Manchoukuo Year Book, 1938*, Tokyo: The Japan–Manchoukuo Year Book Co. (1938), pp. 386–7, 402; Mitsubishi Economic Research Bureau, *Japanese Trade and Industry Present and Future*, London: Macmillan (1936), pp. 135, 311–22; T. Yazaki, *Social Change and the City in Japan From the earliest times through the Industrial Revolution*, translated by D.L. Swain, San Francisco: Japan Publications, Inc. (1968), p. 384; E.B. Schumpeter, ed., *The Industrialization of Japan and Manchukuo, 1930–1940: Population, Raw Materials, and Industry*, New York: Macmillan (1940), pp. 415–17, 832; League of Nations, Economic and Financial Section, *International Economic Con-*

ference, Geneva, May 1927, Electric Industry, Geneva: League of Nations (1927), p. 40; World Power Conference, *Transactions of the World Power Conference. Vol. II. Electrical Energy. 1933*, Stockholm: Svenska Nationalkommittén For Vorldskraftkonferenser (1934), pp. 224, 584; US Bureau of the Census, *Historical Statistics of the United States, Colonial Time to 1970, Bicentennial Edition, Part II*, Washington, DC: GPO (1975), p. 828.

6. *Ibid.*, I, p. 319, II, p. 827–30.

7. P.M. Hohenberg and L.H. Lees, *The Making of Modern Europe 1000–1950*, Cambridge, Mass.: Harvard University Press (1985), pp. 313–4; R.A.S. Hennessey, *The Electric Revolution*, Newcastle-upon-Tyne: Oriel (1977), p. 177; *The Japanese–Manchoukuo Year Book, 1938*, p. 401; Darmstadter, *Energy in World Economy*, p. 655; World Power Conference, *Electrical Energy*, p. 39; H.F. Williamson *et al.*, *The American Petroleum Industry: Vol. II. The Age of Energy, 1899–1959*, Evanston, Ill.: Northwestern University Press (1963), pp. 446.

8. For the above two paragraphs: P L Yates, *Forty Years of Foreign Trade*, London: George Allen & Unwin (1959), p. 223; E.A. Tupper, *United States Trade with World, 1934*, US Department of Commerce Bureau of Foreign and Domestic Commerce. Trade Information Bulletin No. 822, Washington, DC: GPO (1935), p. 27.

9. Electrical Equipment Division, *Electrical Development in Brazil*, pp. 8–13; League of Nations, *Electrical Industry*, pp. 21, 69–70, 82; M. Wilkins, *The Maturing of Multinational Enterprise: American Business Abroad from 1914 to 1970*, Cambridge, Mass.: Harvard University Press (1974), pp. 16, 65–7.

10. League of Nations, *Memorandum on Coal*; International Labour Office, *The World Coal-Mining Industry. Studies and Reports. Series B. No. 31*, Geneva: ILO (1938). For the USA, see Clark, *Energy and the Federal Government*, Chapter 5 for citations to numerous executive and congressional studies of coal, the most important being, US Coal Commission, *Report of the United States Coal Commission in Five Parts*, Washington, DC: GPO (1925). For comments on various UK coal commissions see, M.W. Kirby, *The British Coalmining Industry 1870–1946: A Political and Economic History*, Hamden, Conn.: Archon Books (1977), pp. 36–8, 43–8, 75–81 and H. Townshend-Rose, *The British Coal Industry*, London: George Allen & Unwin (1951), pp. 15–16, 20–3.

11. See note 10 above. Also, see M.P. Jackson, *The Price of Coal*, London: Croom Helm (1974), pp. 13–21 and I. Lubin and H. Everett, *The British Coal Dilemma*, New York: Macmillan (1929), pp. 288–303.

12. Kirby, *British Coalmining*, pp. 67, 139, 153–68; J.H. Jones, *The Coal Mining Industry: An International Study in Planning*, London: Putnam & Sons (1939), p. 803; Clark, *Energy and the Federal Government*, pp. 172, 256; N.J.G. Pounds and W.N. Parker, *Coal and Steel in Western Europe: The Influence of Resources and Techniques on Production*, Bloomington: Indiana University Press (1957), pp. 342–4; ILO, *World Coal-Mining*, pp. 222–4; K. Wang, *Controlling Factors in the Future Development of the Chinese Coal Industry*, New York: King's Crown Press (1947), p. 104.

13. A number of sales agencies were launched and on the verge of organization in the USA by 1932. Viewed as a panacea by many operators, the sales agency approach was rejected by New Deal policy makers in favor of the universal recovery program of the National Industrial Recovery Act

of 1933 which encompassed the coal industry, Clark, *Energy and the Federal Government*, pp. 257–8.

14. A single composite account of shifting coal use is lacking, therefore I relied on numerous sources, including: ILO, *World Coal-Mining*, p. 48; M.M. Hoar, *The Coal Industry of the World*, US Department of Commerce. Bureau of Foreign and Domestic Commerce. Trade Information Bulletin No. 105, Washington, DC: GPO (1930), p. 92; S.H. Schurr and B.C. Netschert *et al.*, *Energy in the American Economy, 1850–1975, an economic study of its history and prospects*, Baltimore: The Johns Hopkins Press for Resources for the Future (1960), p. 737; Clark, *Energy and the Federal Government*, pp. 251–5, 285–8; National Industrial Conference Board, *Oil Conservation and Fuel Oil Supply*, New York: NICB (1930), p. 159 and *The Competitive Position of Coal in the United States*, New York: NICB (1931), p. 123; Schumpeter, ed., *Industrialization of Japan*, p. 425; R.W. Ferrier, *The History of the British Petroleum Company, Vol. I. The Developing Years, 1901–1932*, Cambridge: Cambridge University Press (1982), p. 674; Jones, *Coal Industry*, pp. 55, 213; Jackson, *Price of Coal*, p. 180; WPC, *Electrical Energy*, pp. 88, 285.

15. ILO, *World Coal-Mining*, pp. 92–101.

16. For the above four paragraphs: *ibid.*, pp. 114–15, 118–25, 131–2; Darmstadter, *Energy in World Economy*, pp. 303–4; League of Nations, *Memorandum on Coal*, I, pp. 25–7. See above Chapter 2, p. 17.

17. N.K. Buxton, *The Economic Development of the British Coal Industry From Industrial Revolution to the Present Day*, London: Batsford Academic (1978), pp. 97–8, 171–2; Jones, *Coal Industry*, pp. 60–2; Lubin, *British Coal Dilemma*, pp. 130–55, 273–88; R.C. Smart, *The Economics of the Coal Industry*, London: P.S. King & Son (1930), pp. 46–7, 151; ILO, *World Coal-Mining*, pp. 10–11, 101–10.

18. Jones, *Coal Industry*, pp. 85–7; Kirby, *British Coalmining*, pp. 69–70.

19. For the strike, see *ibid.*, pp. 51–64, Chapter 5.

20. These statistics were derived from many sources, all of which have been cited in prior notes.

21. Jones, *Coal Industry*, p. 213; NICB, *Oil Conservation*, p. 157.

22. K. Hardach, *The Political Economy of Germany in the Twentieth Century*, Berkeley: University of California Press (1976), pp. 17–18; A.H. Stockder, *Regulating an Industry: The Rhenish–Westphalian Coal Syndicate, 1893–1929*, New York: Columbia University Press (1932), pp. 26–7; B. Reynolds, *The Saar and the Franco-German Problem*, London: Edward Arnold & Co. (1934), p. 87; League of Nations, *Memorandum on Coal*, I, pp. 49–52.

23. The substitution of cheaper lignite (brown coal) for bituminous (stone coal) in domestic heating and the electric and gas utilities freed a large tonnage of stone coal for industrial purposes and for exports. Brown coal production, 31 percent of total production in 1913, equaled bituminous production by 1922 and occasionally surpassed it thereafter. Given the very high sulfur content of lignite, this shift boded ill for the environment.

24. See above, Chapter 2, pp. 19, 24.

25. For German developments, see Stockder, *RWCS*, pp. 25–6, 33–5, 52–5, *passim*; Jones, *Coal Industry*, pp. 256, 266–71, 299; Hoar, *Coal Industry of the World*, pp. 25, 116; Lubin, *British Coal Dilemma*, p. 235.

26. For France and Italy: Smart, *Economics of Coal*, pp. 166–8; Reynolds,

The Saar, pp. 229–31; League of Nations, *Memorandum on Coal*, pp. 38–41; Lubin, *British Coal Dilemma*, pp. 235–7; 241–4; Jones, *Coal Industry*, p. 188; Hoar, *Coal Industry of the World*, pp. 87–8, 193–6.

27. As in Germany, Polish consumers subsidized coal exports by paying higher domestic prices.

28. For Poland: Hoar, *Coal Industry of the World*, pp. 130–2; Jones, *Coal Industry*, pp. 238–9, 243, 256; Buxton, *British Coal Industry*, p. 169–70; Smart, *Economics of Coal*, pp. 170–3; League of Nations, *Memorandum on Coal*, I, pp. 32–3; ILO, *World Coal-Mining*, pp. 131–2, 160–3.

29. For the above two paragraphs: Buxton, *British Coal Industry*, p. 162; Jones, *Coal Industry*, pp. 62–3, 189–91; Hoar, *Coal Industry of the World*, pp. 55–62, 189, 265–75; Smart, *Economics of Coal*, pp. 170–1, 176.

30. For the above three paragraphs: R.L. Gordon, *The Evolution of Energy Policy in Western Europe: The Reluctant Retreat from Coal*, New York: Praeger (1970), p. 21; ILO, *World Coal-Mining*, pp. 180–91, 247; Clark, *Energy and the Federal Government*, Chapter 10, J.P. Dickie, *The Coal Problem, A Survey: 1910–1936*, London: Methuen (1936), pp. 146–60.

31. Smart, *Economics of Coal*, p. 177; Lubin, *British Coal Dilemma*, pp. 237–41; WPC, *Electrical Energy*, pp. 399, 488; *Japan–Manchoukuo Year Book 1938*, pp. 401–2.

32. American Petroleum Institute, *Petroleum Facts and Figures*, Baltimore: Lord Baltimore Press (1931), p. 144 and *Petroleum Facts and Figures*, 6th edn, Baltimore: Lord Baltimore Press (1939), pp. 10–11, 18–20; L.M. Fanning, *American Oil Operations Abroad*, New York: McGraw-Hill (1947), p. 232. Clark, *Energy and the Federal Government*, pp. 147–9. For a lively and erudite account of America's automotive love affair see, W.J. Belasco, *Americans on the Road: From Autocamp to Motel, 1910–1945*, Cambridge: MIT Press (1979).

33. F.W. Zimmermann, *Conservation in the Production of Petroleum: A Study of Industrial Control*, New Haven: Yale University Press (1957), pp. 284–5; API, *Petroleum Facts 1939*, pp. 53–9; Clark, *Energy and the Federal Government*, pp. 173, 210–11, 230.

34. In addition to Table 2.7, see B. Shwadran, *The Middle East, Oil and the Great Powers*, New York: Praeger (1955), pp. 436–7.

35. For the above three paragraphs: E.H. Davenport and S.R. Cooke, *The Oil Trusts and Anglo-American Relations*, New York: Macmillan (1924), 231–4; Fanning, *American Oil Abroad*, p. 79; G.S. Gibb and E.H. Knowlton, *History of Standard Oil Company (New Jersey). The Resurgent Years 1911–1927*, New York: Harper & Brothers (1956), pp. 384–91; A.W. Giebelhaus, *Business and Government in the Oil Industry: A Case Study of Sun Oil, 1876–1945*, Greenwich, Conn.: JAI Press (1980), p. 85; Shwadran, *Middle East Oil*, pp. 250–3; Clark, *Energy and the Federal Government*, pp. 197–8, 298.

36. Fanning, *American Oil Abroad*, pp. 64–7; Ferrier, *History of BP*, pp. 436, 543, 674.

37. W.P. Rawls, *The Nationality of Commercial Control of World Minerals*, New York: The American Institute of Mining and Metallurgical Engineers, Inc. (1933), pp. 27–9.

38. For the above three paragraphs: Clark, *Energy and the Federal Government*, pp. 14, 188, 324, 459; *World Petroleum Directory, 1937*, pp. 583–4, 607–8; K. Beaton, *Enterprise in Oil: A History of Shell in the United*

States, New York: Appleton-Century-Crofts (1957), pp. 348–52, 422; A.L. ter Braake, *Mining in the Netherlands East Indies*, Bulletin 4, The Netherlands and the Netherlands Indies Council of the Institute of Pacific Relations, New York: Institute of Pacific Relations (1944), p. 75; Fanning, *American Oil Abroad*, pp. 235–42.

39. For the above two paragraphs: *ibid.*, p. 234; *World Petroleum Directory, 1937*, pp. 248, 629; P. Fearon, *War, Prosperity & Depression: The U.S. Economy 1917–1945*, Lawrence, Ks.: University Press of Kansas (1987), pp. 80–1; K.Q. Hill, *Democracies in Crisis: Public Policy Responses to the Great Depression*, Boulder, Colo.: Westview Press (1988), p. 15; F.B. Tipton and R. Aldrich, *An Economic and Social History of Europe, 1890–1939*, Baltimore: The Johns Hopkins University Press (1987), p. 233.

40. H.M. Larson *et al.*, *History of Standard Oil Company (New Jersey). New Horizons, 1927–58*, New York: Harper & Row (1971), pp. 12–13, 38, 797–800; Beaton, *Shell in the US*, pp. 166–70, 357–60; *World Petroleum Directory, 1937*, pp. 244–50, 581–3.

41. *Ibid.*, pp. 200, 532–41; Ferrier, *History of BP*, pp. 238, 463–504, 549; Gibb, *Standard Oil, 1911–1927*, pp. 46–8; Larson, *Standard Oil, 1927–50*, pp. 115, 148, 720; J.F. Rippy, "The United States and Colombian Oil," *Foreign Policy Association Information Service*, V (1929–1930), p. 26.

42. *World Petroleum Directory, 1937*, pp. 106, 245, 532–6; A. Pinelo, *The Multinational Corporation as a Force in Latin American Politics: A Case Study of the International Petroleum Company in Peru*, New York: Praeger (1973), pp. 31–40; Giebelhaus, *Sun Oil*, pp. 85–6.

43. For the above two paragraphs: *ibid.*; E.W. Chester, *United States Oil Policy and Diplomacy: A Twentieth Century Overview*, Westport, Conn.: Greenwood Press (1983), pp. 232–3, 246–50; Shwadran, *Middle East Oil*, pp. 298–300, 385–90; *World Petroleum*, 12 (June 1941), p. 26; I.H. Anderson, *The Standard–Vacuum Oil Company and United States East Asian Policy, 1933–1941*, Princeton: Princeton University Press (1975), pp. 3–4, 202–16; Larson, *Standard Oil, 1927–50*, pp. 52–6.

44. Tupper, *US Trade with the World*, pp. 16–19, 27; Fanning, *American Oil Abroad*, pp. 226–31.

45. Wilkins, *Multinational Enterprise*, pp. 84–5, 235–6; Larson, *Standard Oil, 1927–50*, p. 335; Jean Rondot, *Compagnie Francaise des Pétroles du franc-or au pétrole-franc*, Paris: Plon (1962), pp. 11–12, 25–38, 59–65; Gibb, *Standard Oil, 1911–1927*, pp. 507–11.

46. M. Pearton, *Oil and the Romanian State*, Oxford: Clarendon Press (1971), pp. 99–133, 155–81, *passim*; N. Foster and D. Rostovsky, *The Roumanian Handbook*, London: Simpkin Marshall (1931), reprinted by Arno Press (1971), pp. 168, 171; J.H. Nelson, *Petroleum Refineries in Foreign Countries*, U.S. Department of Commerce. Bureau of Foreign and Domestic Commerce. Trade Information Bulletin No. 494, Washington, DC: GPO (1927), pp. 29–30; Chester, *US Oil Policy*, pp. 68–71.

47. For the above four paragraphs: A. Fursenko, "The Oil Question in Soviet–American Relations at the Genoa Conference of 1922," unpublished paper (1983); H. Hassmann, *Oil in the Soviet Union: History, Geography, Problems*, translated by A.M. Leiston, Princeton: Princeton University Press (1953), pp. 33–61; L. Fischer, *Oil Imperialism: The International Struggle for Petroleum*, New York: International Publishers

(1926), pp. 110–49; Chester, *US Oil Policy*, p. 79; L. Heyman, *The New Aspect of the Oil Problem*, London: Petroleum Times (1933), p. 61–2; Gibb, *Standard Oil, 1911–1927*, p. 357.

48. In American parlance, an "Open Door" policy meant free trade. It was originally employed as an argument against the exclusion of the USA from economic participation in China by nations claiming exclusive spheres of interest there. In China, and elsewhere, Americans demanded commercial equality. F. Delaisi, *Oil, Its Influence in Politics*, translated by C.L. Leise, London: The Labour Publishing Co. (1922); J. Lepoutre, "La Lutte pour la Suprématie du Pétrole," *Revue Economique Internationale* (May 1922), pp. 246–74; P. de la Tramerye, *The World Struggle for Oil*, London: Allen & Unwin (3rd edn, 1923); Davenport, *Oil Trusts*; Fischer, *Oil Imperialism*; A. Mohr, *The Oil War*, New York: Harcourt, Brace (1926).

49. See: Shwadran, *Middle East Oil*; P. Sluglett, *Britain in Iraq, 1914–1932*, London: Ithaca Press (1976); W. Stivers, *Supremacy and Oil: Iraq, Turkey, and the Anglo American World Order, 1918–1930*, Ithaca, N.Y.: Cornell University Press (1982); Ferrier, *History of BP*; Chester, *US Oil Policy*.

50. Gibb, *Standard Oil, 1911–1927*, p. 306; Chester, *US Oil Policy*, pp. 13–15; Stivers, *Supremacy and Oil*, pp. 128–31.

51. Somewhat greater influence is ascribed to the US government in J.A. De Novo, "The Movement for an Aggressive American Oil Policy Abroad, 1918–1920," *American Historical Review*, LXI (July 1955), pp. 854–76, and G.D. Nash, *United States Oil Policy, 1890–1964: Business and Government in Twentieth Century America*, Pittsburgh: University of Pittsburgh Press (1968). Clark, *Energy and the Federal Government*, assigns greater significance to the perceived fear of shrinking US oil reserves as a factor in US domestic and international oil policies.

52. Sluglett, *Britain in Iraq*, pp. 112–13, 162–5; Wilkins, *Multinational Enterprise*, pp. 219–20; Stivers, *Supremacy in Oil*, pp. 118–24; Ferrier, *History of BP*, pp. 100–31; Chester, *US Oil Policy*, 256–7; Shwadran, *Middle East Oil*, pp. 153–60.

53. H. Trueblood, "Raw Material Resources of Latin America," *Foreign Policy Reports*, XV (August 1939), pp. 114–25; Chester, *US Oil Policy*, pp. 169–73, 195–6; Larson, *Standard Oil, 1927–1950*, pp. 328–9; the World Bank, *World Tables 1988–89 Edition*, Baltimore: Johns Hopkins University Press (1989), p. 615.

54. Foreign Policy Association, "The Mexican Land and Oil Law Issue," *Foreign Policy Association Information Service*, II (August 1938), pp. 246–53; C.A. Thomson, "The Mexican Oil Dispute," *Foreign Policy Reports*, XIV (August 1938), pp. 122–32; A.J. Bermúdez, *The Mexican National Petroleum Industry: A Case Study in Nationalization*, Stanford: Institute of Hispanic American and Luso-Brazilian Studies (1963); L. Meyer, *Mexico and the United States in the Oil Controversy, 1917–1942*, translated by M. Vasconcellos, Austin: University of Texas Press (1972); Chester, *US Oil Policy*, pp. 118–33.

55. Pinelo, *International Petroleum Co. in Peru*; J. Salazar-Carrillo, *Oil in the Economic Development of Venezuela*, New York: Praeger (1976); J.V. Lombardi, *Venezuela: The Search for Order, The Dream of Progress*, New York: Oxford University Press (1982); S.J. Randall, "The International Corporation and American Foreign Policy: The United States and

Colombian Petroleum, 1920–1940," *Canadian Journal of History*, 9 (August 1974), pp. 179–96; Rippy, "US and Colombian Oil," pp. 19–35; Chester, *US Oil Policy*, pp. 144–7; Wilkins, *Multinational Enterprise*, pp. 255–72.
56. J. Foreman-Peck, *A History of the World Economy: Inernational Economic Relations since 1850*, Brighton: Wheatsheaf Books (1983), p. 213; for a concise analysis of the worst years of the depression, see P. Fearon, *The Origins and Nature of the Great Slump, 1929–1932*, Atlantic Highlands, N.J.: Humanities Press (1979).
57. For the above three paragraphs: S. Takahashi, *Japan and World Resources*, Tokyo: Kenkyusha Press (1937) and Royal Institute of International Affairs, Information Department, *Raw Materials and Colonies*, New York: Oxford University Press (1936) summarize the conflicting positions of the Axis powers and their antagonists. See also, Schumpeter, *Industrialization of Japan*, pp. 43–4, 373–5, *passim*; Takahashi, *Japan*, p. 29; C.C. Concannon *et al.*, *World Chemical Developments in 1935*. US Department of Commerce. Bureau of Foreign and Domestic Commerce. Trade Information Bulletin No. 832, Washington, DC: GPO (1936), pp. 19, 23, 29, 36; M. Erselcuk, "Japan's Oil Resources," *Economic Geography*, 22 (January 1946), p. 16; Anderson, *Standard–Vacuum*, pp. 80–7; Chester, *US Oil Policy*, pp. 297–301; *World Petroleum*, 13 (January 1942), pp. 23–7.

4

Energy flows in a politically polarized world

World War II strongly influenced the energy future of the world. To the victor come the spoils. Had the war commencing in 1939 been concluded on terms favorable to the Axis powers, one might imagine them in possession of the Soviet Union's Baku fields, much of the Middle East, and the Netherlands East Indies. What an impact such an outcome would have had on the Allied powers and on the giant firms that dominated the world oil industry. Far more was at risk than oil or other natural resources, but one can still conjecture that the economies and societies of Britain, the USA, and other nations would have evolved quite differently had the Axis dictated terms of access to Middle East oil.

Energy and World War II

Each of the major belligerents committed substantial resources to securing a fuel supply sufficient for the prosecution of a highly mobilized conflict fought on distant and shifting fronts. Germany and Japan, without domestic oil reserves and the latter without adequate coal, planned campaigns to conquer fuel-producing regions while investing heavily during the 1930s in the development of synthetic fuel technologies. In both nations the production of coal, the chief feed stock for synthetics, enjoyed high priority.

Neither Britain nor the United States made provisions before 1939 for an emergency fuel supply. The UK felt reasonably secure. British companies controlled the largest oil fields in the Middle East and operated successfully in safe regions in the western hemisphere. A more than adequate domestic coal supply was available. For its part, the USA

95

possessed large and accessible petroleum and coal reserves and dominated the oil industries of South America and Saudi Arabia, the latter's
potential still unrecognized. The USSR, with enormous productive
potential in all fuels, experienced the destruction or seizure of much of
its western based coal industry and its Baku oil fields. With great effort
and the provision of several lend lease refineries by the USA, the Soviet
Union produced and refined about 60 percent of its petroleum needs.[1]

The belligerents grossly miscalculated their energy requirements.
Germany and Japan possessed stocks and access to supplies sufficient
only for a relatively short war. Germany's conquests in Europe added
the sizable coal production of Poland and France, some part necessarily
devoted to sustaining the conquered populations, the oil fields of
Romania, and the Maikop fields of the northern Caucasus, the latter so
thoroughly destroyed by retreating Soviets that they added nothing to
the oil stock of the Third Reich. Neither did the other conquests yield
more than marginal increments to fuel supplies. By 1943, heavy and
sustained Allied air attacks pulverized Germany's fuel industry, particularly the synthetics complex, and its transportation links. Oil became
desperately short by 1944. Shortages of aviation gasoline severely
hampered the operation of the Luftwaffe during the last year of the
war. As labor productivity declined, partially due to malnutrition
among miners, coal production in occupied France and Belgium fell off
severely by 1943. Maintenance and transportation services also became
increasingly inadequate. Forced labor in German mines maintained the
labor force at adequate levels, but dreadful working conditions resulted
in low productivity. Falling supplies of coal in 1943 and 1944 hamstrung
the production of iron and steel and synthetic fuels.

Japan launched its war against the USA and other European states
with a natural resource base more limited than that of Germany. The
need for oil determined that Japan would strike south to seize the
Netherlands East Indies. Japan's hopes rested on the fatally optimistic
assumption that the USA would not persist in a long and costly struggle.
With a much less developed synthetic fuel industry than Germany,
Japan depended upon ocean transport for the bulk of its oil and some of
its coal. American control of the sea lanes by late 1944 placed virtually
each Japanese oil tanker at risk. By early 1945, Japan's oil stocks had
dwindled to under one million barrels. An almost total blockade of the
home islands by US naval and air forces denied Japan access to the oil of
Southeast Asia. Shortages of oil and coal severely constrained war
industries. Perhaps even more deadly in 1945 was the looming specter of
widespread starvation.[2]

British complacency in 1939 about fuel supplies gave way to despair
by 1940. As German planes pounded the UK, submarines sunk an

increasing tonnage of tankers. The intercession of the USA in 1940 through the exchange of American destroyers for bases in British possessions, the Lend Lease Act of March 1941, and the transfer of fifty oil tankers to Britain in May 1941 relieved the situation. Petroleum stocks climbed well above the danger zone. Although Nazi submarines destroyed an enormous tonnage of tankers after America's entry into the war, supplies from America were not jeopardized. The destruction of Axis armies in North Africa in 1942 eliminated the threat to the Suez and the Persian Gulf oil fields. Thereafter, American production supplemented by Venezuelan and Middle Eastern oil provided more than adequate fuel to Allied forces.

Military demands for fuel compelled the heavy intervention of the British and American governments in their energy industries. In the USA, a complex of federal agencies successfully maintained adequate production of fuels, particularly aviation gasoline and chemical feedstocks for synthetic rubber, distributed fuels to the Allies and to domestic wartime industries without totally denying supplies to non critical industries or the civilian sector, and moderated inflationary pressures. But these agencies and the policies they implemented were swiftly abandoned in 1945 and 1946. America preferred, as in 1918, to return to an essentially unregulated regimen for petroleum and coal.[3]

A prewar heritage in the UK of intermittent government intervention in the coal industry and in the energy utilities combined with severe wartime conditions to propel Britain toward national ownership. Beginning in 1939 all energy was strictly rationed, far more so than in the USA. By 1943, the Ministry of Fuel and Power controlled coal prices and miners' wages, an intervention necessitated by inflationary pressures, labor scarcity, and other operational problems. The government operated the mines while the mine owners retained financial responsibility. The Labour Party called for the immediate nationalization of coal. While the Conservative Party resisted this demand, it supported continuing state authority to compel industry rationalization. Labour's electoral victory after the war led immediately to the nationalization of coal and the electric and gas utilities.[4]

While petroleum remained in private hands in both Britain and the USA, the foreign policies of both nations presumed continued access to cheap oil, thus assuring a competitive/cooperative Anglo-American relationship concerning foreign fields. Britain's dependency upon foreign oil was total but the national energy mix during and immediately after the war still reflected the dominance of coal which, in 1950, provided 90 percent of total primary energy requirements.[5] America's consumption of oil was far greater, with all but a fraction supplied domestically. In both nations, knowledgeable government and oil industry officials foresaw a dramatic rise in domestic oil consumption. Americans worried that domestic oil demand might outstrip additions to reserves, thus reducing the margin of oil security. Both governments also evinced vague fears about Soviet intentions in the Middle East and about the nationalistic aspirations of both independent and colonial oil producing countries. The USA and the UK attempted individually and cooperatively, under the untrusting eyes of France and other nations, to guarantee Anglo-American domination of the key foreign oil fields, safeguard private investments abroad, and assure private investors further opportunities in secured areas. One need not assert that postwar Anglo-American policies marched to a tune orchestrated by the powerful oil companies to recognize that concern about oil supply and investments contributed to the shaping of policy.[6]

Two specific oil policy initiatives — the Petroleum Reserves Corporation and the Anglo-American oil treaty — make clear the evolving purposes of both governments and reflect, as well, the inability of the US government radically to alter its traditional oil policies. Both programs demonstrated American awareness of the great significance of Persian Gulf oil wealth, a gnawing doubt about the extent of domestic oil reserves, suspicions about the intentions of the MNOCs operating in that area, and skepticism about the willingness of Britain to allow US companies to participate in Iraqi and Iranian production.

The Petroleum Reserves Corporation (PRC) issue involved a contract between PRC and the Aramco partners in 1943 providing government financing of a refinery and a pipeline to the Mediterranean Sea in exchange for an exclusive federal oil reserve. Arousing intense opposition from independent oil companies and others hostile to federal intrusion in the oil industry, the idea was abandoned. But the larger objectives of national security and security for American oil interests survived in a new policy, that of hammering out an oil treaty with the UK that would preserve and enlarge American participation in the world oil industry.

Between 1944 and 1947, American and British negotiators concluded two agreements, both cf which suffered defeat in the American political arena at the hands of a coalition of domestic oil companies and opponents of American entanglement in such international arrangements. The agreements themselves suited the interests of both governments by establishing a mechanism to assure bilateral control over Middle Eastern fields by American and British firms.

Britain gained the implicit commitment of American power to defend the fields. Grave doubts about the devotion of the MNOCs to the national interest motivated American negotiators, particularly Harold L. Ickes, Secretary of Interior (1932–46). To Ickes, the political ramifications of Middle Eastern oil required an active federal presence to counterbalance the egocentric multinationals. For the American MNOCs, the proposals offered equal participatory opportunities in areas dominated by the Anglo–Iranian Oil Company (AIOC) and the Iraq Petroleum Company (IPC). For AIOC, the accord minimized the risk of dangerous price competition and political turmoil in the Middle East, a threat attributed to Soviet machinations. However, the US Senate rejected the treaty in 1947.[7] Agreements relative to Middle Eastern oil would depend in the short-term on inter-firm arrangements. Over the long-term, the resounding impact on the producing governments of nationalism, anti-Zionism, and calculations of national self-interest would radically alter the shape of the Middle Eastern oil industry.

Anticipating a Nazi drive toward Middle Eastern oil fields, in 1941 British troops seized the fields of Iraq and Iran, including the great Abadan refinery. Thereafter, Anglo-American forces assured the security of Persian Gulf production. By the end of the war, Iranian, Iraqi, and Saudi oil production reached 27 million metric tons (mmt), an 88 percent increase over 1941, and provided about 10 percent of Allied oil needs.[8] When the Axis collapsed in 1945, the fields of Iran and Saudi Arabia were poised to enter an era of explosive production. Allied victory solidified the position of the MNOCs in that region, permitted their return to areas occupied by the Axis, excepting eastern Europe, and appeared to strengthen their bargaining position in Latin America. For a time the MNOCs exercised an informal governance over overseas oil. But this restored hegemony engendered the intense antagonism of host governments toward the MNOCs and their home governments.

Trends in world and regional energy use to 1960

However measured, world energy consumption soared after World War II. Between 1945 and 1950 primary commercial energy use rose by 25 percent, comparable to the growth rate of the 1920s. From 1950 to 1960 energy use rose by 55 percent (Table 4.1). During the first fifteen postwar years, total primary energy requirements (TPER) advanced by 1,600 million metric tons oil equivalent. This enormous leap in energy use, accelerating through the 1960s, occurred within particular national contexts and was, therefore, constrained by unique circumstances.

Energy consumption stormed ahead in the most highly industrialized countries of western Europe, Japan, the United States, and the Soviet Union. The USA assumed the key role in the political and economic reconstruction of western Europe and Japan, motivated by

Table 4.1   World total primary commercial energy requirements,
1938–70 (million metric tons oil equivalent)

	Mmtoc TPER	Percent				
		Solid fuels	Oil	Natural gas	Hydro-electric	Nuclear
1938	1217	72	21	6	1	0
1945	1600	66	23	10	2	0
1950	2059	62	25	12	1	0
1961	3185	48	33	16	2	<1
1970	5170	33	45	20	2	<1

Sources: Constructed from J. Darmstadter *et al.*, *Energy in the World
Economy: A Statistical Review of Trends in Output, Trade, and Consumption
Since 1925*, Baltimore: The Johns Hopkins University Press for Resources for
the Future (1971), p. 652; Gilbert Jenkins, *Oil Economists' Handbook 1985*,
London: Elsevier Applied Science Publishers Ltd (1985), p. 76; *BP Statistical
Review of World Energy*, June 1986.

humanitarianism, fear (obsession in the view of some) of global communist expansion, and economic self-interest. Conversely, the less
developed nations, many gaining their independence after the war,
failed to achieve self-sustained growth. They remained mired in economic backwardness, characterized by high birth rates, declining death
rates, marginal and primitive agriculture, grossly inadequate employment opportunities, an elitist and exploitive political leadership, and
dependence upon the technological, managerial, and capital inputs of
wealthier countries, including the former colonial masters. Only a
minority of the world's population, then, enjoyed the fruits and encountered the frustrations of a more energy intensive round of life.

The more highly developed nations, without exception, if at differing
paces, adopted oil intensive patterns of energy use. This emerging
energy regime damaged coal industries in the West while stimulating the
expansion of the global oil industry, still dominated by a handful of
American, British, French, and Dutch multinationals. Within this context, the critical factor was the shift of the USA from a net oil exporter
to a net oil importer. This shift further consolidated the producing
power of the MNOCs operating in the Middle East even as it evoked
noisy political controversy in the USA. Middle Eastern governments
quickly challenged the MNOCs and forced a drastic revision of the
oil pricing system. Permeating all of this in the West were consumer
preferences and governmental efforts to define the national interest with
regard to a particular energy mix. An array of international and regional
military/political/economic organizations operated on the fringes of the
energy arena. The United Nations Organization, the Arab League, the
European Coal and Steel Community (the European Economic Community in 1957), and the Organization of Petroleum Exporting Coun-

tries (OPEC, established in 1960) sought with varying degrees of success to intervene in energy issues.

The extraordinary rise in world energy use occurred during years of unprecedented general economic growth, the one both cause and effect of the other. The total value of world exports more than doubled from 1945 to 1958, reaching $109 billion, and had doubled again by 1967 while energy's share of world trade advanced from under 9 percent during the early 1950s to almost 10 percent in 1965. At that time the value of exported mineral fuels exceeded $18 billion.[9]

To appreciate the transformation in the composition of energy entering world trade requires greater specificity. Table 4.2 traces the demise of coal as the leading energy export, accomplished prior to World War II, and the remarkable relative position achieved by oil by 1965. Table 4.2 establishes the largely domestic character of the world coal industry in contrast to the predominantly international reach of the oil industry. By 1965, only 7 percent of mined coal entered foreign trade compared with 60 percent of oil production, a volume covering 89 percent of all energy exports.

Soaring statistics characterize analyses of world trade in general and of energy traffic in particular. Aggregate energy figures and the conclusions they support obfuscate the limited scope of energy traffic. Relatively few nations measurably participated or profited from energy trade. The favored nations, all intensive users of commercial energy, owned large shares of world trade and manufacturing output. As late as 1970, non-commercial (organic) fuels composed at least 35 percent of TPER in Brazil, India, Indonesia, and South Korea.[10]

Measurements of global energy trade are of marginal value unless

Table 4.2 Energy and world trade, 1925–65 (percent)

	1925	1938	1950	1960	1965
Commercial energy exports as percentage of world energy production	14	16	18	23	28
Coal exports as percentage of world energy production	9	7	4	3	3
Crude/refined oil exports as percentage of world energy production	4	9	14	20	25
Exports as percentage of total energy exports for:					
Oil	32	56	76	87	89
Coal	68	43	24	13	10
Exports as percentage of total production for:					
Oil	30	40	46	53	60
Coal	11	10	7	7	7

Source: Constructed from Darmstadter, cited in Table 4.1, pp. 224, 423

Table 4.3   National–regional shares of world primary energy production, 1925–65 (percent)

	1925	1938	1950	1965
USA	49	39	44	31
Western Europe	34	32	19	10
USSR	2	9	11	18
Middle East	<1	1	5	11
Latin America	3	4	6	7
Eastern Europe	4	5	7	6
All others	7	10	8	17

Source: Same source as Table 4.2, pp. 224–62.

framed comparatively. Production of mineral fuels occurred within certain countries and specific fuels passed to individual markets. The number of national or institutional actors that influenced those trans-actions were few. A handful of nations consumed the bulk of the world's energy. In 1950 and 1970, the USA and Canada, OECD-Europe*, the USSR, and Japan accounted for 80 and 73 percent, respectively, of global TPER.[11] Similarly, the USA, USSR, and a few Middle Eastern states contributed 60 percent of the world increase in primary energy production from 1950 to 1965. As Table 4.3 suggests, the locus of world energy production shifted to those nations with substantial oil reserves.

Energy in western Europe after World War II

World War II left continental Europe in a shambles, with much of its industry and infrastructure destroyed, with the eastern regions about to be isolated from the western by force of Soviet arms, and with its potentially most powerful state utterly prostrate and soon to be divided into an eastern and a western Germany. By the mid 1950s, western Europe had risen from the ashes and was poised on the brink of re-markable economic growth. A transformed energy mix accompanied European recovery, one that further cracked the foundations of the coal industry, greatly expanded the market power of the oil industry, and intensified each nation's dependence upon energy imports.

Table 3.1 depicts the centrality of coal in Britain, Germany, and France in 1938. For the nations that formed the European Coal and Steel Community (ECSC) in 1952 — Germany, France, the Benelux

---

* Including Austria, Belgium, Denmark, Finland, West Germany, Greece, Iceland, Ireland, Italy, Luxembourg, Netherlands, Norway, Portugal, Spain, Sweden, Switzerland, Turkey, the United Kingdom. Unless otherwise specified, references to western Europe include the above nations.

nations and Italy — coal provided 87 percent of TPER in 1937, 81 percent in 1950, and 74 percent in 1955. In Britain, coal accounted for 85 percent of TPER in 1955. Crucial to European recovery, then, was reconstruction of the coal industry which had suffered severe damage toward the end of the war. An impressive effort through 1947 reconstructed and equipped the mines of Belgium, France, the Netherlands, and West Germany, but only in France did production equal prewar output. Shortages of coal caused widespread suffering during the winters of 1945–8 while seriously impeding the rebuilding of electric utilities and the iron and steel and other heavy industries.

The coal producing nations devised individual and collective strategies to overcome the bottlenecks and were joined in this campaign by the USA. Despite the frequent and debilitating strikes that wracked the American coal industry in 1946–8, the USA shipped a significant tonnage of coal to ECSC states during this emergency. In 1947, US coal provided 94 percent of ECSC coal imports. To coordinate these deliveries, the USA and the UK made use of the European Coal Organization (ECO), set up in 1945. ECO possessed full allocative powers, duties absorbed after 1948 by administrative units involved in the Marshall Plan. Britain and France nationalized their coal industries in 1946. British occupation forces terminated the prewar Ruhr coal cartel but ultimately failed to prevent the concentration of German coal output in the hands of a few large mining and steel companies.

These initiatives notwithstanding, European economic recovery required the massive input of the Marshall Plan. Marshall Plan funds permitted the large scale reconstruction of the coal industry and the achievement of coal sufficiency by the late 1950s. Thereafter, the national coal policies of Britain, France, and West Germany and the coal stabilization programs of ECSC proved incapable of resisting a slippage in coal demand that began during the late 1950s and early 1960s (Tables 2.2 and 4.4).

In the UK, inadequate capital investment in new mines and new equipment prevented the industry from meeting demand and kept coal prices relatively high, thus attracting imports from the USA. British coal exports withered away to insignificance (see Table 3.3). West Germany's increasingly efficient coal industry produced a surplus for export to its ECSC partners, particularly France. But Germany also imported a sizable tonnage; in 1960, for instance, imports equaled 38 percent of exports. As was the case before the war, French coal production fell short of domestic demand by 25 to 30 percent with the deficit supplied primarily by the USA and Germany. Overall, ECSC members required more coal than they produced.

American coal remained competitive in Europe during the 1950s

Table 4.4   Coal production in world and selected nations, 1945–73 (million metric tons)

	1945	1950	1955	1960	1965	1973
World[1]		1861	2191	2486	2861	3029
USA[2]	578	516	465	416	512	543
UK	186	220	225	197	191	130
West Germany[1]	70	188	223	240	239	222
France	35	53	57	58	54	36
USSR[1]	149	261	390	510	578	615
East Germany[3]	108[4]	137	201	225	251	246
Poland	49[4]	83	101	114	142	195

[1] All coals
[2] Bituminous only
[3] Brown coal or lignite equivalent
[4] 1946

Sources: Darmstadter, cited in Table 4.1, p. 191; U.S. Bureau of the Census, *Historical Statistics of the United States, Colonial Times to 1970. Bicentennial Edition. Part 1*, Washington, D.C.: USGPO (1975), p. 589; B.R. Mitchell, ed., *European Historical Statistics*, 2nd revised edition, London: Macmillan (1981), pp. 365–8, 386–8; A.R. Griffin, *The British Coal Mining Industry: Retrospect and Prospect*, Buxton, Derbys: Moorland (1977), p. 186.

despite the distance; from 1947 through 1958, the USA supplied from 44 to 65 percent of annual imports. After World War II, US aid packages fostered the use of American coal. As this political advantage waned, the rapid mechanization of American mines and the progress of strip mining raised productivity to levels far superior to even the most advanced German mines. While coal prices in the USA declined markedly from 1947 through 1960, domestic coal became more dear in western Europe. The higher fixed costs of European coal mines were partially attributable to ECSC and national efforts to protect the standard of living of miners by supporting prices. Western European nations did not consider reducing the number of miners by scaling down national coal industries. Coal was still viewed as essential to national security. Miners still possessed considerable political clout. Into the 1960s, then, the European coal industry could neither defend itself against foreign coal nor, and more threatening in the long run, counter the price and efficiency advantages of fuel oil.[12]

Between 1945 and 1953, even before the sudden reversal of coal industry fortunes in western Europe, oil consumption advanced sharply. OECD-Europe's coal use increased by some 100 mmt between 1948 and 1960, or by 24 percent, but coal's share of TPER fell from 83 percent in 1950 to 61 percent in 1960 (Table 4.5). Over the same period, oil's share moved from 14 to 30 percent and natural gas from less than 1 percent to almost 3 percent. In the Netherlands, oil use equaled coal use by 1960.[13]

Favorable oil prices relative to coal prices, the convenience of oil for residential and industrial purposes, and the flood of Marshall Plan dollars accelerated an energy use transition initiated prior to the war. Competitive oil prices generated positive responses among consumers. Several factors help explain the attractiveness of oil prices: the availability of Middle East oil (not so secure as Europeans learned during the 1950s), the abandonment of a price system designed to protect the overseas marketability of US oil, the construction of a European refining industry that quickly reduced the need to import more expensive refined products, and, as some insist, the effort of the US government to

Table 4.5 Total primary commercial energy requirements of selected countries, 1950–75 (percent)

	1950	1955	1960	1965	1973	1975
OECD–Europe						
Solid fuels	83	73	61	43	23	23
Liquid fuels	14	21	30	45	59	55
Natural gas	<1	<1	2	3	10	13
Hydroelectric	2	3	3	3	6	6
Nuclear	0	0	<1	<1	1	1
UK						
Solid fuels	92	85	74	62	37	38
Liquid fuels	8	14	25	35	48	44
Natural gas	0	0	0	<1	11	15
Nuclear	0	0	<1	2	3	3
West Germany						
Solid fuels	95	90	76	57	32	31
Liquid fuels	4	9	23	41	55	51
Natural gas	0	<1	<1	2	10	14
Nuclear	0	0	0	0	1	2
France						
Solid fuels	77	68	54	41	17	17
Liquid fuels	20	29	32	46	68	63
Natural gas	<1	<1	3	4	8	10
Hydroelectric	3	3	10	9	6	8
Nuclear	0	0	<1	<1	2	2
Italy						
Solid fuels	49	33	19	15	9	8
Liquid fuels	32	42	56	62	72	74
Natural gas	4	14	15	8	9	11
Hydroelectric	15	11	10	14	9	7
Nuclear	0	0	0	<1	<1	<1
USA						
Solid fuels	42	31	25	25	21	21
Liquid fuels	38	43	42	42	44	45
Natural gas	19	25	29	30	30	28
Hydroelectric	1	1	3	3	4	4
Nuclear	0	<1	<1	<1	1	2

Table 4.5 (cont.)

	1950	1955	1960	1965	1973	1975
USSR						
Solid fuels	77	76	52	44	36	34
Liquid fuels	20	20	30	35	37	39
Natural gas	3	3	8	19	23	24
Hydroelectric	<1	<1	1	1	4	3
Nuclear	0	0	0	<1	<1	<1
Japan[1]						
Solid fuels	70	68	53	34	17	18
Liquid fuels	21	22	31	53	75	71
Natural gas	<1	<1	<1	1	1	2
Hydroelectric	9	9	15	13	5	6
Nuclear	0	0	0	0	0	2

[1] TPER figures would be lower if firewood and charcoal use were included. In 1953, in Japan, wood and charcoal provided at least 8 percent of energy supply. In Russia, in 1955, wood provided at least 7 percent of energy supply.

Sources: Largely constructed from J. Darmstadter *et al.*, cited in Table 4.1, Table 11, and IEA, *Energy Balances of OECD Countries, 1970/1982*, Paris: OECD/IEA (1984), pp. 387–9, 404, with occasional reference to annual issues of *BP Statistical Review of World Energy*.

restrict oil imports, this shortly after the USA became a net importer of oil.

Oil formed the largest single commodity in the dollar budget of most Marshall Plan recipients.[14] Few dispute the necessity of such a massive infusion of money into Europe in 1947–8, both as a humanitarian act and as a program that served the political and economic interests of western Europe and the USA. Certainly it stabilized and then induced growth in the North Atlantic economies, an achievement closely associated with US-led efforts to remedy severe foreign exchange shortages and worrisome balance of payments deficits that developed during and after the war.

American firms, drawing oil from the Middle East, supplied at least 70 percent of funded oil to Europe, paid for in dollars. To ease the acute dollar shortage which plagued the UK and other European nations, the Economic Cooperation Administration (ECA) campaigned with some success to force American MNOCs to reduce prices on Marshall Plan crude delivered to Europe. The US Department of State, pursuing a somewhat contradictory purpose, spearheaded American efforts to pry open British dominated sterling markets for the sale of "dollar" oil. Britain, desperate to preserve dollars, wished to replace "dollar" oil with "sterling" oil. ECA did not wholly subscribe to the State Department position which better served the interests of American MNOCs than the objectives of the Marshall Plan. Related to the sterling drain and impinging upon US oil interests was the issue of European refinery construction. ECA argued that such a program would reduce the dollar drain by substituting cheap crude for expensive refined products. The resistance of US refinery interests successfully restricted the application of Marshall Plan funds to refinery construction. European refining expanded nonetheless. These developments further eroded the justification for the so-called Gulf oil price system and, by widening the access of Europe to Middle Eastern oil, vastly increased the value of the concessions of the MNOCs.[15]

Western Europe, by the 1950s, had recovered from the worst effects of depression and world war. Gross national products rose steadily, driven principally by a dynamic manufacturing sector. By 1960, primary energy consumption in OECD-Europe exceeded use in 1950 by 43 percent, compared with a US growth rate of 26 percent. While 1960 *per capita* energy use in the USA was at least double that of any Western European nation excepting Britain, such highly industrialized states as Belgium, France, and West Germany produced a larger volume of gross national product per energy input than did the USA, attesting to superior energy use efficiency in those states. Accompanying accelerated economic growth and energy use was a persistent shift from oil to coal and slight increases in total natural gas and hydroelectric use.

The energy mix of European and other industrialized nations is summarized on Table 4.5. Substantial differences are apparent; compare Italy to the norm for OECD-Europe. The dissimilar patterns stem from the varying natural resource endowments of each nation. Italy, with little coal, emphasized hydroelectric development (the largest component of the "other" category) and quickly shifted to oil. France nationalized coal and the electric and gas utilities, and focused on reducing coal imports by the expansion of domestic coal mining and hydroelectric capacity. Still, French coal production remained inadequate and costly while oil seemed cheap and plentiful. France, therefore, adopted a goal of energy independence during the 1960s, emphasizing control of foreign oil fields, continued expansion of refinery capacity, and, finally, nuclear power. Germany and Britain, without domestic oil or gas, both of which the USA and USSR had in abundance, continued to rely primarily upon coal until the late 1960s. Both shored up the coal industry through various subsidies and protection against oil competition. Nonetheless, as Table 4.4 shows, coal production in Britain fell off substantially after 1955–6 while it plateaued in West Germany. In both countries and in the USA as well, electric generation emerged as the largest single market for coal but it was never immune from the competition of natural gas and fuel oil. During the 1960s, Britain, Holland, and Norway launched ambitious exploration ventures in the North Sea.

Substantial oil and natural gas fields were discovered. Dutch gas became a factor in the European energy mix during the 1960s and British and Norwegian oil during the 1970s.

The Treaty of Rome, creating the European Economic Community in 1957, committed the Common Market to a common energy policy. Critical differences in national energy wealth, as between the coal producers and the non-coal producers, obstructed the formulation of a unified approach to energy. Members desired cheap and secure energy but could not discover an acceptable policy to attain that objective. The problem of coal overcapacity and shrinking markets remained unresolved through the 1960s. Members protected their key energy industries without regard to the collective good, none volunteering to dilute full sovereignty over those crucial sectors.[16]

The recognition of dissimilarities in national energy use should not obscure the relentless progression toward rough congruence depicted on Table 4.5. Energy users in western Europe had fewer options from which to choose — and Japan fewer yet — than consumers in the USA or Soviet planners. But the choices became ineluctably convergent by the mid-1960s. There are only so many ways to produce energy economically. Thus, the generation and use of electricity, whatever the primary energy employed, exploded in the industrial countries after World War II, a process replicated by the lesser developed countries as expeditiously as possible. Nation pursued nation along roughly parallel paths.

The energy mix of Japan

Japan possesses the poorest energy and non-fuel mineral resource base of the world's fully industrialized economies. Troublesome import dependency, a factor in Japan's decision in the 1930s to acquire an empire, intensified after World War II. If only commercial fuels and hydropower are considered, Japan in 1950 imported almost 30 percent of TPER, a proportion rising to 40 percent by 1960 and 86 percent in 1970. Policy choices of a radical nature emerged in Japan during the 1960s, resting on assessments of national economic performance during the late 1950s.[17]

American occupation of a devastated Japan democratized Japanese politics. American policy also consciously aimed at the further consolidation of the power of multinational corporations, proffering direct benefits on the oil companies. Under American supervision, the reconstruction of Japanese industry hastened the shift to fuel oil and away from coal. American firms supplied the fuel oil. However, and pregnant with meaning for the future, the USA failed to destroy the zaibatsu. Once Japan became master of its own house, the zaibatsu reasserted their dominion in all leading industrial sectors, including the petroleum, electrical equipment, and nuclear industries. Japanese managers speedily rebuilt iron and steel using only the newest technologies. Concurrently, intense efforts and channeled investments flowed into the shipbuilding, chemical, auto, and electrical equipment industries, all of which fell under the sway of reborn zaibatsu.

The consequences for energy use in Japan were momentous, fully apparent as the catalytic effects of the Korean War propelled the economy into a great boom, underwritten in large part by swelling export earnings. The Japanese coal industry responded feebly to rising demands from industry, especially for coking coal for steel, and coal shortages caused occasional crises in electric generation. By 1960, such conglomerates as Mitsubishi were fully committed to petroleum as the leading industrial fuel and were importing growing volumes through subsidiary trading firms. As a result of occupation policies American oil companies reaped substantial rewards from this surge in oil consumption.[18]

The US government prohibited the operation of Japanese refineries until 1949 and then pressured the Japanese to permit the MNOCs to participate in refining on a 50:50 basis, an exaction not imposed upon Germany. American capital flowed into Japan and the American MNOCs secured the right to supply the required crude oil. Only gradually during the 1960s did the powerful Ministry of International Trade and Industry (MITI) assert national control over the participation of foreign firms in the oil industry. By this time, Japan was securely bound to oil (Table 4.5).

The security implications of oil import dependence fostered Japanese initiatives during the late 1950s and early 1960s to modernize the electric power industry, limit the freedom of electric utilities to import foreign electrical equipment, encourage research and development in nuclear power, nurture energy conservation practices, and support Japanese-owned ventures in foreign oil exploration and discovery. Not all of these policies bore immediate fruit. The Japanese surrendered to the siren-song of cheap oil during the 1960s. Nonetheless, they reflected the aims of successive governments. When an energy crisis struck in 1973, the Japanese government, directly connected through MITI to the powerful zaibatsu, wielded sufficient power to buffer the economy from the worst of the oil price shock. Japan's OECD colleagues could not make such a claim.[19]

The energy mix of the Soviet bloc

With its armies in place, the Soviet Union quickly imposed its rule over eastern Europe. From the Baltic States to Poland and south to Bulgaria, Soviet power forced the integration of eastern European economies with its own. Resources and technology from the bloc nations flowed eastward, some simply expropriated as the reward of victory and some gained on terms imposed on the powerless, to contribute to the massive task of rebuilding the Soviet economy. Such was the devastation visited on the USSR by advancing and retreating Nazis, that the ill effects of the war lingered on for decades, with recurrent shortages of critical goods and glaring industrial and agricultural inefficiencies exacerbated by a rigid economic system.

For all the difficulties facing the nation after 1945, not the least being the bloody paranoia of Joseph Stalin and the gulf separating East and West, the Soviets reconstructed their economy and greatly expanded primary energy production. In the immediate postwar years planners concentrated on the coal industry but peat and wood remained important supplemental fuels. Transportation inadequacies, lack of modern equipment and spare parts, and, perhaps, the insecurities of Stalin's last years hampered the rehabilitation process. But sheer muscle power, some no doubt belonging to forced laborers, pushed production up-

Table 4.6 World crude oil production, 1945–70 (million metric tons)

	1945	1950	1955	1960	1965	1970
World	365	528	781	1066	1536	2322
USA	238	274	345	357	396	488
Venezuela	45	78	109	145	176	188
USSR	21	38	71	150	248	354
Iran	18	32	17	54	96	194
Mexico	6	10	12	14	16	25
Romania	6	4	11	12	13	14
Iraq	5	6	35	49	67	79
Saudi Arabia	3	26	49	63	103	180
Canada	1	4	18	26	41	64
Indonesia	<1	7	12	21	25	43
Algeria	<1	<1	<1	9	29	52
Kuwait	0	17	55	83	110	138
China			<1	3	7	20
Nigeria			0	<1	14	55
Libya				0	62	168
United Arab Emirates				0	14	39
Above percentage of world production	95	94	94	93	92	90

Source: DeGolyer and MacNaughton, *Twentieth Century Petroleum Statistics,* Dallas, Texas: DeGolyer and MacNaughton (1984), pp. 4–11.

ward. By the mid-1950s, the Soviets prepared to mineralize thoroughly their energy system, initiating a great campaign to exploit oil and natural gas resources. Coal production — Table 4.4 — rose by 242 percent between 1945 and 1965. Oil production, at 21 million metric tons in 1945, shot upwards, reaching 248 mmt in 1965 (Table 4.6). Natural gas production also surged ahead after 1955, climbing from about 9 billion cubic meters (bcm) to 45 bcm in 1960 and 128 bcm in 1965.[20]

The changing Soviet energy mix displayed in Table 4.5 mirrored these production gains. But unyielding bottlenecks somewhat constrained output. While enormous reserves of fossil fuels existed, their distance from centers of population and industry severely challenged the capabilities of the delivery system. Electric power generation lagged sadly behind demand because of coal shortages — a prompt for the development of nuclear power. Throughout the Soviet coal industry, mechanization, and, therefore, labor productivity, lagged behind western standards. The key oil fields of the Urals–Volga region produced low quality crude necessitating the opening of the far distant oil and gas fields of Siberia and the construction of thousands of miles of pipeline by a pipeline industry hampered by technological and materials shortcomings. Similarly backward technologically, the refining industry produced inferior products, particularly lubricants, compared with western or even Romanian refineries.[21]

Eastern Europe depended far more heavily upon coal than the USSR or western Europe. In 1965, solid fuels composed 82 percent of TPER, a substantially greater coal dependency than in western Europe (Table 4.5). Only Romania possessed significant oil reserves, but these were rapidly depleted by the Soviet Union which disposed of at least 60 percent of Romanian production, obtained at a fraction of the world price. Into the 1950s, eastern European resources, technologies, captive scientists and technicians, and manufactured goods streamed into Russia. This traffic was conducted under the terms of bilateral trade agreements, or Soviet reparations imposed upon such formerly hostile countries as Czechoslovakia, Hungary, and Romania. So great were internal Soviet needs, that bloc countries received relatively little in return, and that on unfavorable terms. Western European nations, economically more advanced than all but Czechoslovakia prior to the war, sped far ahead of eastern Europe, which lacked a generous Uncle Sam.

Persistent energy scarcity obstructed eastern European modernization. The use of bloc resources to strengthen the Soviet economy contributed to the backwardness of all bloc economic sectors as did the national totalitarian political regimes. The properties of foreign oil companies in Romania were nationalized in 1948 under the aegis of

Sovrompetrol, a joint Soviet–Romanian company fastened on Romania in 1945 for the purpose of funneling oil to the USSR. Denied foreign capital and technology, neither of which the Soviets could (would) furnish, crude production fell during the late 1940s, reaching prewar levels only in 1953. Existing fields were pumped vigorously, but new drilling equipment was unavailable, exploration languished, and reserves declined.[22]

The captive resources of eastern Europe contributed to the diversification of a Soviet energy mix that moved toward a three-fuel balance during the 1960s (Table 4.5). Soviet oil exports, initially to bloc and allied countries, but then to the general world market, rose dramatically from the late 1950s through the 1960s, precipitating an adverse reaction from the USA and her allies. Americans, in particular, accused the Soviets of dumping oil in order to disrupt western markets and otherwise sow confusion and discord in the West. All of this reflected the impressive performance of the Soviet energy sector, accomplished partly at the expense of bloc members.[23]

The Soviets did not escape certain final costs. Dissidence in the leading bloc states forced concessions to national economic aspirations. Resources, notably oil, began to flow in large volumes from Russia to its partners. In the 1970s, Soviet officials complained loudly about the oil drain and fretted about the intrusion of western capital and influence. Such was the outcry that one would think that the captives had captured the captor.

The US energy mix

America's seemingly insatiable energy appetite developed well before World War II. Somewhat dampened by the depression and the war, energy use gathered momentum after 1945. Tables 3.1 and 3.2 documented the gross prewar trends. Although the USA share of world TPER declined steadily from 47 percent in 1929 to 40 percent in 1950 and 30 percent in 1970 (Table 6.1), America's share of world oil consumption remained above 60 percent in 1950, but had declined to 38 percent by 1965. To maintain this reduced share of oil use in 1965, Americans required 236 mmt more than consumed in 1950. Western Europe's total annual consumption only equaled 236 mmt in 1962. US *per capita* consumption of primary energy exceeded global *per capita* use by 7.6 times in 1929 and was still 6.6 times greater in 1970 (Table 6.4). Domestic production of primary energy supplied all but a fraction of TPER: 95 percent in 1950 and 91 percent in 1970.[24]

From 1945 well into the 1960s, as the mantle of US economic and military power enveloped the so-called free world, US energy and economic policies emphasized the cheapness and abundance of energy supplies.[25] American foreign policies focused intensely on the containment of international communism, exemplified by the Truman Doctrine, the Marshall Plan, the creation of the North Atlantic Treaty Organization, and the commitment of US forces in Korea. These strategies affected oil, but they were hardly oil-driven. Energy formed only one of myriad considerations during the presidential administrations of Truman, Eisenhower, Kennedy, and Johnson.

To mold a reasonable generalization that integrates energy matters with foreign policy, one must emphasize an unflinching dedication to anti-communism, global free trade, and free enterprise. In the view of American policy makers, the achievement of those *overarching goals* would benefit all American industries at home and abroad. Thus, the Truman Doctrine in serving notice to the Soviets that communist con spiracies would be strenuously resisted also reassured American investors of the security of their Persian Gulf properties. Nothing in this implied federal subservience to the MNOCs.

During and after the war, the USA adopted a conciliatory attitude toward both the Mexican and Venezuelan governments, the former having nationalized oil before World War II and the latter, in 1948–49 and again after 1958, maneuvering to obtain a better deal from the MNOCs. In these and other Latin American states, the US government refrained from applying full leverage to protect American firms from the nationalism of host governments. The USA, particularly after the Cuban Revolution in 1959 and the rise of Fidel Castro to power, dedicated itself to arrest the spread of communism even if this mandated recognition and support of governments that threatened foreign investments or that trod upon civil liberties. In Latin American and elsewhere, the USA responded passively to the nationalization of American interests. The USA exerted little influence over its multinationals and often remained uninformed of multinational policies until after the fact, as was the case in the Middle Eastern price cuts of 1959–60.[26]

After the war, the US government assigned energy policy a low priority and eschewed the formulation of a coherent national energy policy. Instead, successive administrations tinkered with energy on a fuel-by-fuel basis, only rarely considering the effect of any one fuel policy on the other primary energy sources. Efforts to deregulate natural gas succumbed to Truman and Eisenhower vetoes. That the artificially low natural gas prices fixed by the Federal Power Commission and by dozens of state and municipal regulatory bodies robbed the coal industry of markets, encouraged wasteful use of a premium fuel, and acted as a disincentive to the development of new reserves seemed a matter of supreme indifference to everyone save the gas industry. Electricity remained highly regulated. Prices were kept low, partially by using cheap natural gas and fuel oil as boiler fuels. Electricity use shot upward; US *per capita* consumption rose from 1,136 kwh in 1937 to 5,947 kwh in 1965, 2.6 times greater than average EEC consumption.

Analysts of US energy policies have lavished especial attention on the emergence of the USA as a net oil importer after 1948 and on the imposition of voluntary oil import quotas in 1955 and mandatory quotas in 1959. Suffice it to remark here that quotas were adopted at the behest of the domestic oil industry and aimed at raising domestic production, stimulating exploration, and shoring up domestic prices, all of which, it was argued, were necessary to national security. A rare breed these quotas, perhaps the only fully implemented federal energy policy before the 1960s. This, rather than their intrinsic importance, may partly explain their magnet-like attraction for analysts.

Perhaps more important in the long run, defense considerations stymied research on the peaceful application of nuclear energy until President Eisenhower's Atoms for Peace address at the UN in 1953 partially raised the lid of secrecy. This new tack encouraged the private sector and the Atomic Energy Commission to cooperate in research and development. While private sector markets for nuclear reactors failed immediately to materialize in the USA or in Europe, the new policy did promote bilateral agreements and led to subsequent payouts. Prior to the speech, the tightly veiled nature of atomic research fostered the pursuit of dead ends and less efficient reactor technologies. By the mid-1950s, the USA, France, Britain, and the USSR were committed to their own schemes, as Canada and Sweden would be soon after. Once the USA adopted a policy of promoting nuclear power it pursued this goal without regard to its impact on coal, with inadequate attention to reactor safety and siting, and with callous indifference to the inevitable need to dispose of irradiated waste and obsolete equipment.

Great publicity and ballyhoo attended the "freeing" of nuclear energy for peaceful uses. The American public, however, received little information about costs, about federal subsidies, about the concentration of research funds and knowledge in very few firms, about who should own and pay for nuclear plants, or about safety and environmental impacts. Scientists and government officials in the USA and elsewhere apparently believed the general public incapable of understanding such complex technical issues.

The forces governing the energy mix of the USA were well recognized prior to the war. Coal's share declined after World War I as oil and natural gas use spread. This process was essentially complete by 1955 (Table 4.5). Overall, the US energy mix reflected the domestic availability of fossil fuels and consumer preferences for gas or oil rather than coal, choices abetted by gas prices that were fixed too low and by access to cheap oil. The absence of focused energy policies in the USA encouraged results similar to the more comprehensive policies of European nations, that is a growing dependence upon oil imported from potentially insecure countries and a coal industry in disarray.[27]

The energy mix of the lesser developed countries (LDCs)

Dozens of former colonial peoples trod the exhilarating but painful path to independence after World War II. Other peoples, possessed of sovereignty for generations, as in Latin America, labored under economic, social, and political disadvantages hardly less burdensome than those shouldered by the recently liberated. In some countries, Indonesia and Algeria for example, independence only came as a result of bloody revolutions. In few places did independence pour forth the sweet fruits of economic prosperity and political stability. Decades, if not centuries, of exploitative colonial rule had not prepared the newly free nations for the competitive conditions of the modern world. Internal divisions, based on class, race, and tribe, precluded the evolution of political stability and spawned recurring coups and counter-coups. Overwhelmingly rural and agricultural, engaged in primitive, subsistence farming, enmeshed in a colonial economy even after independence, with high fertility rates and declining death rates unaccompanied by the creation of sufficient employment, these peoples remained mired in abject poverty.

The energy mix of the LDCs reflected their economic backwardness. Indonesia, with significant oil reserves, depended in 1970 upon noncommercial (organic) energy sources for 75 percent of its total energy requirements, a proportion that remained over 50 percent in 1982. Brazil, energy dependent, consistently used non-commercial fuels for over 30 percent of TPER from 1970 through 1982, a share that exceeded 50 percent until the mid-1960s. In 1970, India relied on traditional organic fuels — wood, cow dung — for 90 percent of its energy and managed to reduce that figure to 70 percent by 1983.

Raising the *per capita* consumption of commercial energy necessitated the introduction of new technologies, both large and small. More easily accomplished in urban areas than rural, LDC governments naturally focused their efforts on the cities, foolishly permitting rural areas to stagnate. Nothing seemed to work. Shortages of funds, ignorance of technologies, autocratic governments, landed elites, a smothering illiteracy, and on and on, obstructed steady progress. Within each LDC a few benefited from modernization, but most did not. Rural villagers unable to make a living on their small plots fled to the permanent unemployment and cultural despair of life in Lagos, São Paulo, or Manila.[28]

The wealthy nations of the West provided insufficient development aid via bilateral arrangements or through such institutions as the International Bank for Reconstruction and Development (World Bank) and the International Monetary Fund. The World Bank preferred to support giant projects when less complex and smaller-scale technologies might have been more suitable. Into the 1970s, the World Bank refused to lend money to national oil companies, always advocating development through private enterprise. Neither India nor Brazil, seeking a modicum of oil independence through state ownership of production and refining, were able to secure financing from the West. Electrification efforts in the LDCs received support if the utility was privately owned, which usually meant that it was a subsidiary of a British or American holding company.

For the most part, the energy importing LDCs remained captive markets for the MNOCs. India, countries in West Africa, and other LDCs entered into importing and refining agreements with the MNOCs when weak and ignorant of the oil industry. Competition was eliminated and prices kept high. India's effort to break this stranglehold by building national refineries and importing Soviet oil at cheaper prices encountered stiff MNOC resistance. The question for India (and other LDCs), as Dasgupta suggests, was the binding nature of agreements concluded when India possessed neither knowledge nor leverage and which fastened disadvantageous terms on the nation.

During the 1950s, a mixed response to that question emanated from the LDCs. Iran answered with a resounding "no" and nationalized the oil industry in 1950. This step was not emulated by other Middle Eastern nations. Host government resentment smoldered for a time. Latin American states waffled, motivated on the one hand by nationalistic pressure for state control over resources and key economic sectors, and, on the other hand, by a persistent and increasing need for foreign capital. India forced the American & Foreign Power Company to relinquish control of its electric plants; confiscations occurred in Colombia and Argentina. By 1960, national oil companies in Latin America operated in Colombia, Peru, Uruguay, Venezuela, Argentina, Bolivia, Chile, and Mexico.[29] A stiff and ill-wind blew into the face of the international energy companies.

The post World War II oil boom

Into the 1960s American and British commentators on oil affairs wrote with exuberant optimism of the fantastic upsurge in oil consumption and of the performance of the oil companies in filling that demand. Observers were particularly attentive to the benefits bestowed by the MNOCs upon the producing nations in the form of wages and social and welfare services. This positive appraisal was dampened only by an amorphous fear of Russian aggression in the Middle East and distrust of producing government intentions regarding concessionary terms.[30] Non-westerners penned less charitable assessments of western and MNOC policies in the Middle East, questioning their motives and their performance and accusing them of ignorance of and indifference to the aspirations of producing states.[31] To such criticisms, the MNOCs responded by emphasizing the sanctity of contracts, the Russian menace, and the inability of host states to manage an industry as complicated as oil.

For a time after World War II, the industry's impressive growth deflected criticism. Global withdrawals more than doubled from 1945 to 1955 and almost doubled again by 1965 (Table 4.6). As Table 4.2 demonstrates, oil ruled global energy exchanges after the war. The 53 percent of total oil production exported in 1960 equaled 87 percent of total energy exports and was accompanied by a dramatic transformation in national roles.

Oil production in the USA declined from 52 percent of world output in 1950 to under 20 percent after 1970. In 1973, the USSR surpassed the USA as the largest producer. US liftings, although rising, were inadequate to domestic demand. Formerly the leading exporter, the USA became a net importer in 1948. By 1960, US exports and imports of oil formed 2 percent and 21 percent, respectively, of the world total. Simultaneously, America's production-reserve ratio fell off again after 1958, following a trend visible since World War I. Oil lifted from the well-worked American fields cost much more per barrel than oil taken from Venezuela or the flush fields of Saudi Arabia or Kuwait. From 1953 to 1962, a $42 billion investment in domestic fields added 4 billion metric tons to reserves; in the Middle East, an investment of $2 billion added over 19 bmt.[32]

While domestic American producers inveighed against New Deal production regulations, the rising costs of exploration and production, and the competition of cheaper foreign oil, the MNOCs focused their efforts overseas. The average daily output of a Middle Eastern well reached 3,860 barrels in 1958 compared with 250 in Venezuela and 12 in the USA. Middle Eastern fields produced 28 percent of world production in 1965, compared with 7 percent in 1938. Those fields contained 61 percent of world proven reserves. Kuwait, Saudi Arabia, Iran, and Iraq, each the preserve of a consortium of MNOCs, led the way (Table 4.6), exporting, in 1960, 233 mmt of oil, or just over one-half of all oil moving in international trade.[33]

Venezuela reigned as the premier oil producer in Latin America, with Mexico a distant second (Table 4.6). Venezuela produced 80 percent of Latin American oil in 1960 and accounted for over 90 percent of regional exports, a large portion in the form of crude transfers to refineries in Aruba and Curacao. Regional demand for oil was far greater in Latin America than in the Middle East; thus a rising proportion of oil remained in the region after World War II. The most marked trend, however, was the growing global marginality of Latin American oil. Between 1950 and 1960, the volume of Venezuelan oil entering the USA rose by over 8 mmt, but the share fell from 69 percent to 51 percent. The Middle Eastern contribution rose from 21 to 30 percent. The position of Venezuela in the US market suffered further attenuation in subsequent years. In Europe and Latin America, competition from cheaper Middle Eastern oil steadily eroded Venezuelan sales during the 1950s and thereafter. Within the region, oil producing but importing nations such as Argentina, Brazil, and Mexico strove to reduce oil imports by developing production capacity. Only marginally successful, they shifted from Venezuela to the Middle East for oil. Brazil, by 1960 the region's largest importer, trimmed its purchases from Venezuela by 25 percent during the 1960s while quadrupling its imports from the Middle East. The shift away from Venezuela intensified during the 1970s.[34]

Following World War I, an outraged western oil industry had watched helplessly as the Soviet Union nationalized its oil industry, refused to compensate former owners, and revitalized the industry in the face of invasion, civil war, and boycotts. Soviet oil production plummeted during World War II but recovered quickly, increasing by 3.4 times from 1945 to 1955 and more than doubling again by 1960 (Tables 2.7 and 4.6). New fields discovered in the Volga–Urals region and developed at great expense supplied 58 percent of total production in 1955 and 71 percent in 1965. Pushing further east into the incredibly difficult topography of the Siberian and Central Asian fields challenged the technological capabilities of the nation during the 1980s. Despite severe obstacles, Soviet exploratory drilling, accounting for some one-third of total oil industry investment, added substantially to Soviet reserves. By 1983, Russia held three times the reserves of the USA and 13 percent of world reserves.[35] The reappearance of Russian oil in western European markets in the 1950s, reflecting production successes and foreign exchange needs, caused consternation within some circles of NATO. What were Soviet intentions?

The multinational oil companies

In 1965, western Europe, the USA, and Japan purchased two-thirds of the $17.9 billion in mineral fuels entering world markets, receiving 598 mmt of oil compared with 191 mmt in 1955. OPEC members sold 51 percent of the value of fuel. Fully integrated MNOCs produced, refined, and marketed virtually all of the oil sold by OPEC states and others, excepting the USSR.[36]

The eight firms appearing in Table 4.7 lifted some 165 mmt in 1950, a volume constituting 85 percent of world producton, excluding the USA, Canada, the Soviet bloc, and China, and 100 percent of Middle Eastern, Indonesian, and Venezuelan production. Table 4.7 summarizes the non-US production and refining shares of the MNOCs. Although their portion gradually narrowed, the MNOCs retained a strong predominance. SONJ produced 74 mmt in 1950 (14 percent of world total) of which 50 mmt originated outside of the USA. SONJ's global share equaled 13 percent in 1965. SONJ, BP, and RDS produced 71 percent of non-US oil in 1950 and 56 percent in 1966 while the remaining five listed in Table 4.7 withdrew 23 percent in 1950 and 44 percent in 1966. As of the late 1950s, these MNOCs sat on 92 percent of proven reserves, owned 75 percent of world refining capacity, and marketed over 70 percent of oil products.

The MNOCs retained the organizational configuration described earlier, adding to it as units were created to reflect entry into new concessions or marketing areas.[37] The MNOCs listed on Table 4.7 wielded enormous financial strength, owning almost 40 percent of world fixed assets in petroleum of $97.2 billion in 1960, of which SONJ accounted for $10.6 billion. While SONJ's share of global fixed assets declined, the value of its holdings doubled from 1950 to 1960. To the assets of these giants could be added those of five additional firms, four of which were American—Standard Oil of Indiana, Phillips Petroleum, Continental Oil Co., and Marathon Oil Co.—and one, Petrofina, a Belgian firm. Together these five possessed assets worth $10.1 billion in 1966, $3 billion less than SONJ reported for that date.[38]

Investments in the petroleum industry soared after World War II (see Table 3.8 for US direct investments abroad). Annual total investments of $2.7 billion in 1946 reached $8.2 billion in 1955, for a ten-year total of $56.2 billion, of which the US oil industry received $38.1 billion. US direct investments abroad from 1946 to 1960 rose from $7.2 billion to

Table 4.7 MNOC shares of crude production and refinery throughput, 1950–66 (million metric tons)

	1950 Production	1950 Refining[2]	1957 Production	1957 Refining[2]	1960 Production	1960 Refining	1966 Production	1966 Refining
SONJ	50	38	79	67	96	88	158	150
BP	40	30	50	30	75	45	125	80
Shell	23	44	61	79	80	97	120	137
Gulf	20	3	51	8	59	15	89	29
Texaco	10	20	24	25	40	33	72	58
SOCAL	10	6	26	13[3]	28	16	74	26
Mobil	6	5	17	15	29	22	48	42
CFP	2	na	9	na	na	na	36	na
Above total[2]	165	146	317		407		722	
Percentage of production[1]	100		100					
Percentage of production[2]	85	72	81	68	72	53	76	61

[1] Including Iran, Iraq, Saudi Arabia, Kuwait, Qatar, Indonesia, and Venezuela
[2] Excluding USA, Canada, USSR, eastern Europe, and China except where otherwise noted
[3] Eastern hemisphere only

Sources: Constructed from data in E. Penrose, ed., *The Large International Firms in Developing Countries: The International Petroleum Industry*, London, Allen and Unwin (1968), pp. 78, 98, 107, 115–33, and M.G. Adelman, *The World Petroleum Market*, Baltimore: The Johns Hopkins University Press for Resources for the Future (1972), pp. 80–1.

$31.8 billion with petroleum's portion climbing from 15 to 34 percent and reaching $10.8 billion in 1960. Then, from 1955 to 1970, the industry invested some $215 billion in the search for and marketing of oil. The share devoted to production in the USA fell off sharply in response to more lucrative opportunities elsewhere.

The investments of individual MNOCs cannot be tabulated but reference to capital expenditures hints at their magnitude. From 1950 to 1966, SONJ's capital expenditures totaled $13.9 billion out of a net income of $21.8 billion. Standard's income–expenditure ratio averaged 0.63 over that period, reflecting its self-financing capability and its low long-term debt, a characteristic of other giant oil companies as well. In 1960, the firms listed in Table 4.7 provided 30 percent of a total global oil investment of $10.8 billion.[39]

Suffocation by numbers? Perhaps! But such figures, at the least, capture the essence of aggregate and individual Big Eight dominance. Few observers, excepting oil industry officials and inveterate advocates of giant enterprise, perceived such control of the industry as a natural consequence of economies of scale and as a boon to consumers.[40] Adelman, Al-Otaiba, Leeman, Luciani, Odell, Penrose, among others, each specified the political and institutional forces that permitted the evolution of such concentrations of power in the oil industry.[41]

Historically, the early concessions in Latin America and the Middle East resulted from the application of overwhelming US and European economic and political pressure on the weak governments in those areas. Ruling cliques in Turkey and Persia (and then Iraq and Iran), Saudi Arabia, Venezuela, and Mexico, entranced by visions of immense royalties and other payments, turned the national patrimony over to foreigners on terms wholly favorable to the MNOCs. Furthermore, western governments deliberately fostered the emergence of such giant firms as AIOC and RDS. In the USA, anti-trust legislation and occasional anti-trust indictments failed to retard industrial concentration at home or abroad. Rarely were American MNOCs inconvenienced by anti-trust proceedings. In an oblique way, then, the US government fostered the evolution of the highly concentrated structure of the post World War II oil industry.

Into the 1950s, Big Eight concessions in the Persian Gulf encompassed the entire producing area with the only significant deviation occurring in Iran as a result of the revolutionary turmoil of the early 1950s. The concessionary status in 1950 was as follows: Iran, AIOC with 100 percent; Iraq, IPC, a consortium of all the firms listed in Table 4.7 except Texaco, Gulf, and SOCAL with 100 percent; Kuwait, divided between Gulf and BP; Saudi Arabia, exploited by Aramco, a joint venture of SOCAL and Texaco (the original partners) and SONJ and

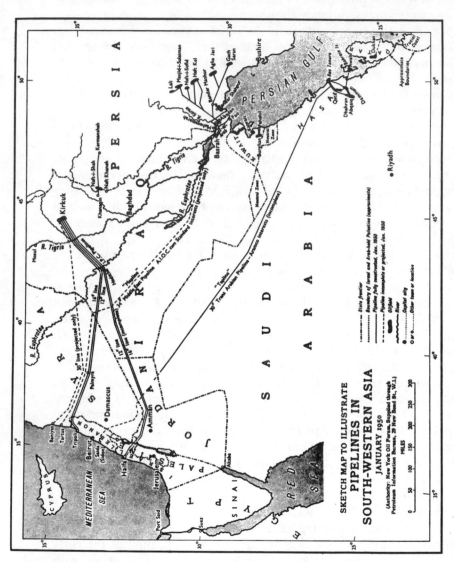

Map 4.1 Middle Eastern pipelines, 1950. (*Source:* Olaf Caroe, *Wells of Power: The Oilfields of South-Western Asia. A Regional and Global Study,* London: Macmillan (1951), facing p. 94. Reprinted with permission.)

Socony–Vacuum (soon Mobil); and Venezuela, where SONJ, RDS, and Gulf accounted for 78 percent of production.

The production and marketing capacity of each MNOC determined its attitude toward consortium participation. SOCAL and Texaco, awash with Saudi oil, gained stability and much needed capital by taking in SONJ and Socony–Vacuum. SONJ's agreement with AIOC to purchase a large volume of crude over twenty years defused AIOC's opposition to the expansion of Aramco. The Gulf–BP partnership in Kuwait protected each from the market competition of the other. In 1947, Gulf and RDS negotiated a contract in which the crude-long Gulf produced huge quantities for the crude-short RDS. The latter refined and marketed that crude and the two divided the profits evenly. As RDS and BP already marketed jointly, RDS functioned as a *de facto* partner in the Kuwait concession. No less than the Aramco relationship, the Kuwait arrangement and other market sharing agreements constrained competition in many parts of the world.[42]

The MNOCs also controlled the transportation of crude by tanker and pipeline with almost 90 percent of carrying capacity owned by the Big Eight. A spectacular expansion of total tanker tonnage and in the size of tankers occurred after World War II. By 1960, deadweight tonnage reached 64 million long tons and tankers of over 100,000 dead weight tons (dwt) were being launched. Pipelines such as Aramco's Tapline, connecting Saudi Arabia and the Mediterranean, were completed. Some 65 percent of Middle Eastern oil moved toward Europe via the Suez Canal and the Mediterranean pipelines, routes vulnerable to closure by the transit states. The remaining 35 percent was shipped via the Indian Ocean. Into the 1950s, the MNOCs successfully thwarted penetration of this near monopoly. A Saudi Arabian scheme to create a national tanker company fell afoul of Aramco opposition. The MNOCs successfully repelled producing state efforts to enter downstream operations until the 1970s.[43]

Consortia and contractual arrangements afforded each MNOC member intimate knowledge of the operations of its partners and greatly reduced the possibility of an intra-Big Eight oil war. The MNOCs, an oligopoly, globally, but exercising monopolistic power in the Persian Gulf fixed the revenues of producing states by controlling liftings and by defending a price structure that served their collective interests. The American multinationals justified their performance through recourse to free market arguments. Few, outside America, believed them.

The hegemony of the MNOCs did not go unchallenged during the 1950s and challenges intensified during the 1960s. Independent oil companies such as Continental and Phillips sought concessions in Libya and other newly discovered oil fields. Long on crude but short on markets, partly as a result of the US import quotas, the new producers competed with the MNOCs in Europe. State oil companies proliferated after World War II, following the precedent of Argentina, France, and Mexico. Some, such as Italy's Ente Nazionale Irdocarburi (ENI) sought concessions in the Middle East. With government encouragement and protection, Japan launched an exploration venture in Saudi Arabia that discovered a rich field in 1959. French state companies monopolized production in colonial Algeria. National and private sector firms slowly whittled away at MNOC control over production. But the most dire threat to MNOC monopoly originated in the key producing states. At first demanding a larger financial share from their oil wealth, they next asserted their right to equal participation in their oil industry, and eventually asserted full control over all phases of the industry.

The price of oil

In 1959 and 1960, the MNOCs unilaterally reduced the posted price of crude. This radical step followed several years of selling at concealed discounts from the posted price. The price cuts, inimical to the interests of Middle Eastern producers and to Venezuela whose revenues were linked to the price of oil, precipitated the formation of OPEC.

Free market theorists and MNOC officials offered a market-driven explanation for crude oil production and prices. They argued that supply (and the exploratory endeavors undergirding supply) and price, its minimum level determined by the cost of production, fluctuated in conjunction with the demand of the moment. Producers, attuned to market logic, would always produce the next barrel of oil that had a purchaser. Because substitutes for such products as motor fuels and lubricants were lacking, the price elasticity of oil was low. The purchaser would always be there. Refiners, for instance, ran at full capacity regardless of price. Consumers lacked the flexibility of energy substitution. Inherent to this interpretation was the operation of a free market in which competition moderated price. Producers, whether private sector or state, set prices rationally to reflect supply and demand factors rather than establishing prices that conformed to institutional, political, or ideological imperatives.

A free market in oil has never existed. Posted prices,* a convention invented by Rockefeller's Standard Oil Company, were only loosely related to actual costs of production which were only imperfectly

---

* Posted prices, set by the largest producers of crude, established the price buyers would pay for crude. The dominant buyers were also the largest producers.

known. The old Standard Trust utilized prices to drive competitors from business. The posted price system evolved into the Gulf-plus system whereby MNOCs fixed the price of internationally traded oil at the price of US Gulf Coast crude plus the cost of delivery from the Gulf. The landed cost of Persian Gulf oil to Japan equaled the price of more expensive Gulf Coast oil shipped over a much greater distance. The Gulf plus system, adopted at Achnaccary in 1928, prevailed during a time of weak and unorganized opposition to the MNOCs and when the US served as the world's leading exporter. However serviceable to the MNOCs, the Gulf system did not reflect market-driven pricing.

The Gulf system collapsed under the pressure of exploding Middle Eastern production and the transition of the USA from exporter to importer. The cost of Middle Eastern production rose less rapidly after World War II than production costs in the USA and then actually fell. The disassociation of Middle Eastern crude prices from Gulf prices quickly followed, matching the interests of the MNOCs who imported Middle Eastern oil into the USA and somewhat reducing import costs in Europe and Japan. But the abandonment of the obsolete Gulf system did not usher in an era of free market prices. It was simply replaced by a new system that conformed to MNOC interests.[44]

Price inelasticity favored the producers who were also the transporters, refiners, and marketers. The MNOCs, frequently partners in production and marketing, manipulated production within their concessions and avoided price competition in world markets. The price of Middle Eastern crude during the 1950s fluctuated in response to the institutional needs of the MNOCs, but always guaranteed the companies an immense profit per barrel as production costs declined and liftings rose. The cash dividends of SONJ rose by 145 percent from 1950 to 1956 and by another 66 percent over the next decade while RDS's cash dividends tripled between 1955 and 1966. After the war, posted crude prices peaked in 1947 at $2.20 per barrel and did not again reach that level until 1971. Between those anchor years, prices first fell through 1952, rose in response to the Iranian Crisis, the Korean War, and the Suez closure, fell in 1959–60 and then held firm at $1.80 per barrel from 1960 to 1970.[45] But posted prices from the mid-1950s through the 1960s inaccurately defined the price paid for oil.

The great bulk of Middle Eastern and Venezuelan crude passed to affiliates of the producing unit at a nominal, book-keeping, price that corresponded with the posted price of the moment. This price was not meaningful since the holding companies manipulated the book returns of downstream affiliates to meet corporate interests. Increasing quantities of oil were sold on long-term contracts to other MNOCs, an example being the Gulf–RDS contract noted above. Large discounts from posted prices characterized these sales. Spot market (open or arms length market) prices also diverged radically from posted prices, perhaps by as much as $0.35 to $0.50 per barrel. When independent oil companies became significant players in international markets, discounting became rampant, a practice further encouraged by the appearance of cheap Soviet oil and by the imposition of import quotas by the USA. Posted prices, then, were artificially high. They failed to reflect other price-shaving devices such as freight rate bargains that also lowered the terms of sale. Through the 1950s, the MNOCs jealously protected their power to manage prices.

Until the 1970s, most oil moved under contract. As ascending independent production sought buyers, spot markets for non-contract oil became more important. The largest spot market emerged at Rotterdam, the point of entry for crude purchased by an enormous number of giant refiners and other processors. With the breakdown of the old pricing system and the capture of the MNOCs by the producing countries — part of the drama of the post-1973 years — spot market prices became the key determinant of contract prices.

The subtle tactics employed by a handful of firms impinged hardly at all on the final price of oil products (minus such variables as import duties or excise taxes) relative to which there was little real competition. Shell and Esso (SONJ) regular gasoline cost the same within any given market area and were of equivalent quality. In uncontested markets, often uncontested because of an agreement among particular MNOCs, product prices were notably higher than in contested markets. Crude oil in Saudi Arabia and Kuwait could be produced at $0.10 per barrel compared with $1.51 in the USA, yet US crude prices in the 1950s were only $0.40 to $0.60 per barrel higher. Obviously, the MNOCs enjoyed great latitude in determining the posted price. The internal needs of the firms and agreements between firms provided criteria for establishing prices. An internal logic prizing stability and order prevailed over a market logic seeking enlarged market shares through price competition.

The MNOCs, as producers of the crude they bought, decided the timing and the dimension of price changes. From 1954 to 1960, world oil production jumped from 697 mmt to slightly over 1 bmt, an increase in volume almost two times larger than the increase from 1948 to 1954. As production surpassed demand, the US import quotas, said to restrict supply in that market, and Soviet exports exerted competitive pressure, especially in the European market. Companies new to international trade sought and gained concessions throughout the Middle East. The MNOCs reacted to the future threat of that production. Slack demand prompted the MNOCs to lower the posted price of Middle Eastern and Venezuelan oil in 1959 and 1960 without consulting the host governments, a grave error as it turned out. Outraged producing states quickly formed OPEC. Host governments, whose revenues were linked to posted prices, complained bitterly and concocted plans to restore revenues by gaining a larger share of oil wealth. This was the first step to wholly dispossessing the MNOCs.[46]

Trends in marketing to 1960

The oil markets of the USA, western Europe, and Japan absorbed two-thirds of world oil exports in 1955 and over three-quarters in 1965. The UK, France, West Germany, and Japan, lacking domestic production, contrived to reduce the cost of imports by developing a refining industry that met domestic needs. The USA engaged in a rancorous debate over the national security implications of foreign oil imports.

Demand for oil accelerated so sharply in the USA after World War II that imports exceeded exports in 1948. By 1959, net imports of 90 mmt equaled 18 percent of total demand. Refined products composed 44 percent of total imports, the larger part refined in the Caribbean refineries of MNOCs from Venezuelan crude. Venezuela crude accounted for 47 percent of crude imports and Middle Eastern for 30 percent. In 1950, virtually all of this oil was shipped by US MNOCs to their American affiliates for refining and marketing. SONJ and Gulf accounted for 41 percent of total imports in 1950. Eight other major firms shared 57 percent. By 1957, a number of new firms had entered the importing business, shaving the portion of the ten largest MNOCs to 64 percent.

In America, the high cost independent domestic producers and refiners without access to foreign oil bitterly opposed this invasion, charging the MNOCs with conspiracy to drive independents from the market. The coal industry jumped into the fray, blaming enormous dollar and tonnage losses on imported oil dumped at cutrate prices into coal's traditional markets. Skillfully appropriating the national security argument, the independents struck a sensitive nerve, as the Eisenhower administration was agonizing over the implications of the Iranian Revolution, the Suez closure, the Soviet threat in the Middle East, and Arab antagonism toward the US–Israel connection. These considerations, far more than independent rhetoric about MNOC conspiracy, convinced the Eisenhower administration that domestic production, the only truly secure source, demanded protection. Initially eschewing compulsion, the administration implemented voluntary import quotas which operated ineffectually from 1956 to 1959. A mandatory system went into effect in 1959.[47]

While the US market for imported oil increased by two times from 1955 to 1965, western European imports tripled and those of Japan multiplied by eight times. Within Europe, the UK, West Germany, France, Italy, and the Benelux states accounted for about 90 percent of imports. As noted earlier, western Europe developed a large refining complex during the 1950s so as to shift from costly refined imports to cheaper crude imports from the Middle East and thus realize significant savings in import bills. The USA possessed 55 percent of refinery capacity in 1952 and 39 percent in 1960; western Europe's share improved from 11 to 18 percent. By 1970, Europe's refining capacity accounted for 28 percent of world capacity, compared to 25 percent for the USA. In the non-Soviet bloc and non-US world, the MNOCs listed on Table 4.7 owned 67 percent of capacity. Into the late 1960s, those MNOCs handled an only slightly smaller percentage of total crude runs. European nations depended upon the MNOCs for initial refinery construction, employing a variety of tactics to induce MNOC cooperation.

West Germany did not intervene in the domestic oil market until the mid-1960s when it sought to mitigate the effects of oil use on its coal industry. France employed state power in all energy sectors. French regulations stipulating that foreign marketers obtain at least 90 percent of their product needs from local refineries compelled the foreign firms to build refineries in France. Import licenses and quotas protected CFP's share of the French market. France also attempted with minimum success to induce foreign refiners to increase crude oil purchases from the franc zone. Whether in response to these directives or not, French refining capacity expanded by 180 percent from 1955 to 1965. Britain permitted BP, RDS, and SONJ to expand refining at their own pace. UK refining capacity more than doubled between 1952 and 1960, doubling again by 1970. RDS, BP, and SONJ owned 98 percent of refinery capacity into the 1970s.

Britain's refiners developed substantial product markets in western Europe, particularly in West Germany, Sweden, and Italy, and in Japan. Three MNOCs divided Britain's market while many more sought German customers. In these markets, crude and products originated for the most part with MNOCs who engaged in product competition but evinced little interest in active price competition.[48]

Refining and marketing in postwar Japan evolved under the self-interested supervision of the USA. Policies were imposed that guaranteed US firms a substantial share of the product market and which endowed the US MNOCs with the right to supply the crude needs of the refineries jointly owned by the MNOCs and Japanese firms. As a result, about 80 percent of Japanese crude imports were supplied by US MNOCs. Ultimately, Japan reduced its foreign exchange drain by developing the refining sector. Remarkable growth occurred upon termination of the occupation. A capacity of 10 mmt in 1955, smaller than Iran's Abadan refinery, attained 88 mmt by 1965, inferior only to the USA and the USSR. By 1960, four of Japan's largest refineries were wholly owned by nationals. During the 1960s, the government intervened directly to bring all phases of the petroleum industry under comprehensive regulations and to develop Japanese-controlled foreign oil fields. Spectacular success eluded the latter strategy; only 10 percent of Japan's oil imports originated from its Saudi Arabian concession in 1974. Japan remained dependent upon Middle Eastern oil sold by MNOCs.[49]

Cold War jitters assured a paranoid reaction to the appearance of Soviet oil in western markets. Between 1951 and 1959, Italy, Sweden, Greece, Austria, India, and Japan received Russian oil, amounting to about one-half of Soviet exports. Altogether, Soviet exports to the West constituted about 5 percent of world imports, but in the eyes of the US government the implications loomed larger. Some foresaw dumping of cutrate Soviet oil to disrupt western firms and damage western economies. Others perceived Soviet oil as a weapon to divide NATO. As interpreted by H. Williamson, Soviet oil exports reflected the "everpresent possibility of a Russian attempt to undermine the free world petroleum industry."[50]

A simpler and less conspiratorial explanation for Soviet exports suffices. The Soviets produced a surplus and they needed foreign exchange in order to finance the purchase of machinery and technology. Western Europe required oil and responded favorably to offers from the Soviets. To the French or Italians, particularly after the Suez Crisis of 1956, the USSR appeared a more secure source of supply than the Middle East. Moreover, the importers wished to diminish their dependence upon the American MNOCs. Thus, the exchange offered benefits to both parties.

Soviet oil sales corresponded with a general improvement in western European trade with the Soviet bloc. However, the USA, during the John F. Kennedy presidency, succeeded in gaining the cooperation of its NATO allies in reducing the trade of strategic items to Soviet countries. Europeans lacked enthusiasm for this policy and frequently circumvented it. Soviet oil sales, at low but not giveaway prices, contributed to the pressures that prompted the MNOCs to reduce their posted price in 1959–60. That single act disrupted the oil industry in the Middle East more than anything done or contemplated by the USSR.[51]

The discontented producing LDCs

The MNOCs obtained the bulk of their oil after World War II from societies caught in a vortex of nationalistic fervor. The major producing states of Iran, Iraq, and Saudi Arabia, nominally independent but virtual dependencies of Britain before the war, cast off that inferior status and pursued their own national and regional goals. Elsewhere in that region, Kuwait and future producing states in north Africa would achieve independence by 1962. Algeria won its independence through armed struggle, as did Indonesia. Long established and fully independent states such as Venezuela and Mexico struggled to assert their national rights against the economic and political might of the USA.

Autocratic Middle Eastern regimes, frequently claiming an ancient heritage, sought to absorb the proto-nation into the regime or dynasty. Unlike the nations of Latin America, Middle Eastern states lacked strongly articulated demand for political democracy. Other imperatives moved those governments, none exciting fervor equal to anti-Zionism which must be considered an intrinsic component of their nationalism. Entrenched and apparently powerful regimes in the Middle East — Iran, Egypt, Iraq, Libya — disintegrated in a nationalist and anti-Zionist whirlwind, replaced by equally autocratic, if secular, strongmen. These regimes all escalated their demands against the oil companies. So, too, did the intermittent democratic governments of Venezuela. It was the totalitarian cliques in Venezuela that courted and feted the MNOCs.

Middle Easterners perceived the MNOCs from a different perspective than Latin Americans. In part, the distinction stemmed from cultural factors, in part from developmental potential and objectives. Most important, the MNOCs and the USA stood condemned in the Middle East as the allies of Zionism. In Latin America, democracy's advocates identified the oil oligopoly as hostile to free government and national goals. National self-interest, however defined by the contending political groups in Latin America, determined policies toward the multinational corporations. Transnational loyalties in the Middle East and inward-looking nationalism in Latin America, as well as economic markers, targeted the adversary.

The special requirements of economic modernization in Latin America and the Middle East clashed with political and ideological realities. Americans and Europeans lived in societies that recognized the primacy of private property, of contracts, and of individual rights. The peoples of Latin America and the Middle East exalted other values. Expropriation and nationalization strengthened the collectivity and asserted national sovereignty. However much those peoples were oppressed and exploited by their rulers, however meagerly

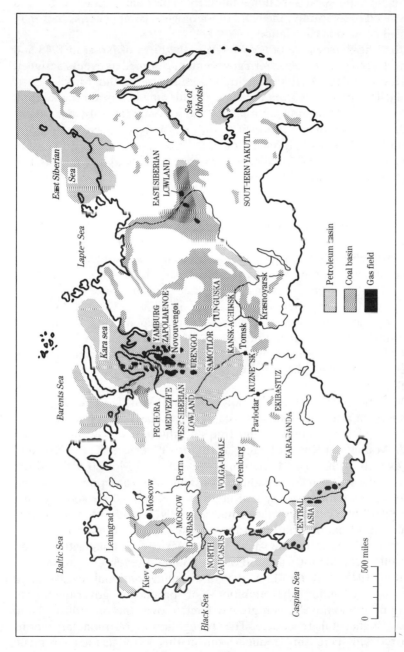

Map 4.2 Soviet energy fields. (*Source:* E.A. Hewitt, *Energy, Economics, and Foreign Policy in the Soviet Union*, Washington, D.C.: Brookings Institution (1984), p. 30. Reprinted with permission.)

nationalization advanced standards of living for the masses, the act was a legitimate expression of national integrity. This final solution might also be essayed prematurely, the child of ideological compulsion rather than rational economic calculation.

From the perspective of the MNOCs, the birth of Israel in 1948 and its quick recognition by western governments loomed as events designed to subvert their carefully nurtured dominance in the Middle East. Distancing themselves from Israel by abandoning her as a terminal for a Persian Gulf–Mediterranean pipeline and as a market or by not assigning Jews to jobs in the producing countries left unresolved the larger question.[52] Would Arab hatred of Israel and the equation of Zionism with imperialism drive Middle Eastern governments to acts that contradicted their economic interests?

The Arabian Peninsula producers evolved an agenda after 1948 that balanced precariously between demonstration of ardent anti-Zionism and the exigencies of national economic development. Whichever way policy tilted, furthering this agenda conflicted with the status quo. From 1948 through the Suez War of 1956, a tilt first in one direction and then in the other occurred, but for the most part the essence of Arab oil policy resembled the programs of Venezuela and Indonesia. Producers demanded as large a share of proceeds from oil as was politically realizable at a given moment, pressing forward step by step toward that day when full operational control could be established. At issue were rates of withdrawal, exploration, concessionary terms, including economic rents, pricing, the training of local personnel, and downstream development.

Oil nationalism emerged prior to World War I, achieving some successes during the interwar years, particularly in Argentina and Mexico, but serving in Iran and Iraq and the new producing states of Saudi Arabia and Kuwait largely as rhetorical devices. The AIOC and IPC as well as SONJ and RDS in Venezuela and Mexico asserted the sanctity of long-term concessionary contracts while accepting the necessity of renegotiating royalty and tax formulas and acknowledging host state ownership of sub-surface minerals. MNOCs admitted the theoretical right of nationalization at the conclusion of a concessionary contract but did not anticipate such results. Mexican nationalization failed to instill in the MNOCs a sense of foreboding or even of caution.

From 1945 into the late 1950s, a raging nationalism assaulted colonialism, feeding the ambitions of producing governments to function autonomously, win greater control over the oil industry, and realize higher oil revenues. The renegotiation of monetary terms occurred with increasing frequency during this period as the gains made by one state became the minimum demands of other states. Failed negotiations in Iran triggered a revolution, nationalization, and a counter-revolution. Egypt's daring nationalization and closure of the Suez Canal in 1956–7 satisfied both nationalistic and anti-Zionist injunctions, as well as inflating the domestic and Pan-Arab credibility of President Nasser. By 1959–60, widening fissures radiated throughout the structure of the international oil industry.

The Latin American experience is less susceptible to generalization. Oil alone drew multinational firms to the Middle East while agricultural and mineral products as well as such large urban markets as São Paulo and Rio de Janeiro, Caracas and Buenos Aires attracted a melange of international corporations to South America. Further along the tortuous path of economic development than all Middle Eastern states save Iran, states such as Argentina, Brazil, and Venezuela required the constant infusion of multinational capital, technology, and management expertise. Goodsell emphasizes the hardening stand of Latin America toward foreign companies, citing several examples of nationalization and of stringent controls imposed on multinational operations. But inconsistency appeared as well. Venezuela as the largest producer and Argentina and Brazil as the most developed states wavered in their posture toward the MNOCs, now hostile, now receptive. A short-lived, democratically oriented government in Venezuela forced a larger payoff from the oil companies. But this government fell in 1948 and was succeeded by a decade long dictatorship that treated MNOCs tenderly. The necessity of attracting private capital counseled moderation but pervasive nationalism demanded activism.[53]

In 1948, a democratic government in Venezuela imposed a tax system on the MNOCs which divided operating profits on a 50:50 basis. SONJ, RDS, and Gulf accepted this change without protest while fearful of greater exactions in the future. Venezuela's success in 1948 stimulated Middle Eastern governments to confront the MNOCs with similar demands. While the Venezuelan precedent buttressed the Arab case, the Arab producers prior to the Venezuelan contract had launched aggressive campaigns for a larger share of the take. Negotiations between Saudi Arabia and Aramco spanned the years 1946–9, with Saudi officials insisting that Aramco could afford to pay more. The Iraqi government criticized IPC for the slow development of the industry, demanding higher production and revenues. In 1950, Saudi Arabia and Aramco concluded a 50:50 arrangement which was replicated in Iraq and Kuwait and which replaced the fixed per ton royalty.

For the MNOCs, the 50:50 arrangement seemed the simplest solution for several reasons. The impact of the higher payments was softened for the American firms by the decision of the US government to grant a $1 credit on domestic income taxes for each $1 paid in taxes to a foreign government. Secondly, production was rising to meet the voracious demand of major consuming regions while costs declined. As SONJ's Middle Eastern liftings rose from 12 percent of total production in 1950 to 23 percent in 1960, its net income doubled. Finally, the MNOCs proclaimed the 50:50 agreement a principle, equitable to both parties and conducive to continued capital investment. But hardly had the new arrangements taken hold than host governments advanced additional claims against the companies and secured superior terms from the independents and state owned oil firms. Host governments denied the immutability of the 50:50 arrangement, none more so than Iran's.[54]

Longrigg considers Iranian nationalism misguided and irrational. Fesharaki portrays Muhammed Khan Mussadiq as a ruthless dictator. Shwadran views Mussadiq as an ambitious but patriotic politician. Mussadiq and nationalism coalesced in 1950, disrupting the oil industry until 1954. The crisis in Iran began when AIOC and Iran reached an impasse in renegotiating the terms of the AIOC concession. The national legislature, dominated by ardent nationalists, was determined to force terms on AIOC rather than negotiate. AIOC, amenable to a 50:50 division, refused to budge from the letter of past contracts. The uncompromising position of both parties precipitated the overthrow of the government, the ascension of Mussadiq to power, and the nationalization of AIOC.[55] Iran employed nationalization as a weapon against AIOC and Great Britain rather than as a strategy to achieve economic modernization. The Iranian example did not change the opinions of those who taught that market driven forces precluded actions that damaged economic self-interest.

Old regimes inevitably label as Jacobins dangerous challengers. In this unequal contest between a new, isolated, and naive Iranian regime and a coalition of MNOCs and the USA and British governments, Mussadiq's opponents deftly cast him as a Soviet tool, equating opposition to the West with support for the USSR. Levy, Hassmann, and Chester assumed that the Soviets pursued a policy in the Middle East designed to force Western abandonment of its regional interests. In fact, little evidence exists to support this contention. The first Iranian Revolution was home-grown. Communists in Iran supported but hardly controlled Mussadiq's government. Far more disruptive were the Arab–Israeli wars, the invasion of Suez by Britain, France, and Israel, the war in Algeria, the policies of the MNOCs, and the myopic and decidedly unsympathetic western response to LDC nationalism.[56]

In the short-term, the Iranian Revolution and nationalization severely damaged both the Iranian oil industry and the national economy. After the withdrawal of AIOC personnel in 1951, Iranian production fell from 38.1 mmt in 1950 to under 3 mmt in 1952, 1953, and 1954 and only surpassed the 1950 figure in 1957. The great Abadan refinery was virtually inoperative during the revolutionary ferment, depriving European and Asian markets of some 20 mmt annually for three years. Moreover, the MNOCs, with the blessing of the US government, imposed an effective boycott on Iranian oil. The shortfall was barely felt in oil markets. Production from Iraq and Kuwait climbed from a combined total of 24 mmt in 1950 to 80 mmt in 1954 while Saudi Arabian production increased by 20 mmt. This surge in withdrawals, in addition to advances elsewhere more than compensated for the absence of Iranian oil.

In 1953, Mussadiq fell to an army coup, contrived as some assert by America's CIA. Negotiations then recommenced between the Iranian government of the restored Shah and, at the insistence of the USA, a consortium of oil companies in which American firms were well represented. The USA exploited this opportunity to appropriate for Americans firms 40 percent of the old AIOC holdings. The Iranian Consortium consisted of BP with 40 percent, RDS, 14 percent, CFP, 6 percent, Gulf, Mobil, SOCAL, SONJ, and Texaco, each with 7 percent, and a group of eight American independents, organized as Iricon Agency Ltd, that held the remaining 5 percent.

The Consortium operated under a contract with the National Iranian Oil Company (NIOC) which owned all the oil in Iran. While the nation's oil moved through the Consortium, NIOC rapidly improved its skills. In 1957, a law endowed it with broad discretionary authority in planning for future oil development. Shortly thereafter, NIOC signed pioneering joint venture exploration and development contracts with Italy's ENI and Standard Indiana. During the 1960s, Saudi Arabia, Kuwait, and other states emulated these agreements. The Consortium appeared to exercise firm control over Iranian oil. Iran won nothing financially that had not been offered in 1949, that is a 50:50 split. But during the 1960s, NIOC expanded its purview, undertaking marketing, acquiring tankers, and concluding new joint venture contracts that mandated the sharing of technology and that improved Iran's take of oil. By the 1970s. NIOC possessed the necessary experience and skills to operate without the Consortium.[57]

Hardly had the Iranian Consortium restored normal operations than Egypt nationalized the Suez Canal in July 1956 and, in November, Britain, France, and Israel invaded with the intention of capturing the canal. President Nasser blocked the waterway through which passed nearly one-half of Middle Eastern oil. Simultaneously, the Syrian army blew up the IPC pipeline to the Mediterranean. Together, the two transportation systems carried some 85 percent of western Europe's oil supply. An acute, if temporary, oil shortage buffeted Europe, exacerbated in Britain and France by the imposition of an oil embargo by Saudi Arabia which Aramco could only obey. Prices rose. Only strenuous efforts by the MNOCs to marshal additional tankers for the long haul from the Persian Gulf, the renewal of European purchases in the western hemisphere, and transfers of American stocks to Europe prevented a scarcity of crisis proportions. Western Europe, with rationing imposed in several countries, made do with 80 to 85 percent of its normal oil supply.[58] In 1958, Suez traffic was resumed. The crisis ended, and memory of it soon faded.

Walter J. Levy perceived the Suez crisis as radically changing the context of the world oil trade.[59] But normal supplies for western Europe, by-passing the Suez, had been restored by 1957. The affected nations neither reformed their energy use practices nor moderated their oil dependency. In Britain, for example, shortages failed to stimulate interest in the coal industry. The USA and its European allies did not prepare plans for future contingencies. The Suez closure in 1956 was considered an aberration. But it was not; the past arrived again in 1967. The MNOCs and their governments ignored the lessons of the Iranian Revolution and the Suez closure. The MNOCs were powerful. However, during the late 1950s, host demands and the appearance of new oil firms in the Middle East demonstrated that the MNOCs no longer occupied unassailable heights.

NIOC denied new concessions to the Consortium, preferring to contract with newcomers so as to reduce the Consortium's hold on the industry. Iraq engaged the IPC in a vituperative controversy from 1958 to 1962 in which Iraq dictated terms and IPC slowed down production. In 1958, the government of Rómulo Betancourt replaced a dictatorial regime in Venezuela. Betancourt championed an oil policy that would diminish the autonomy of the foreign concessionaires and that envisaged the creation of an organization of oil exporting countries. Before its fall, the military junta raised the 50:50 division to 60:40, thus disabusing the oil firms of their faith in the immutability of the 50:50 arrangement. Betancourt urged Middle Eastern producers to adopt the new split.

Meanwhile, independent and state-owned or state-encouraged oil firms competed with the MNOCs for concessions. ENI in Iran, the Arabian Oil Company (Japanese) in off-shore Saudi Arabia and Kuwait, the Ohio Oil Company, Amerada Petroleum Company, and Continental Oil Company, partners in Libya, among others, won concessions by awarding superior financial and participatory terms to the hosts. RDS, in 1960, joined Kuwait in the first MNOC–host partnership to develop an off-shore concession.[60]

More exacting financial terms, joint ventures, the receptivity of host

governments to independent and state oil company offers, the intensi-
fication of nationalistic rhetoric, the Iranian and Egyptian examples, the
coalescence of LDCs into a loose anti-western bloc, thus formalizing
the so-called north–south dichotomy, the willingness of anti-communist
states to turn to the USSR for aid in an effort to apply leverage against
the US. . . . How many signs were necessary to force recognition among
the MNOCs that times had changed and to elicit a more balanced reply
to LDC grievances?

The MNOCs, model capitalistic organizations, lacked the intellectual
flexibility to evaluate external stimuli that controverted their simple-
minded economic faith. People or institutions or nations that refused to
maximize economic gain, that chose ideological goals over market
goals, thus imperiling the beneficial results of MNOC investments, were
incomprehensible to them. How else to explain their abrupt lowering of
the posted price of oil in 1959 without consultation with either their
home or host governments?

For the MNOCs, large surpluses of oil seeking market outlets required a price reduction. No matter that reduced posted prices lowered
the revenues of producing state governments. No matter that this
occurred just as the USA imposed mandatory import quotas. No matter
that the Arab League (1945), seeking to politicize oil, had created in
1951 an Arab Oil Exporting Committee to foster Arab control over oil
and the use of oil power against Israel. In 1959, the Arab League
sponsored the first Arab Petroleum Congress in Cairo, with Iran and
Venezuela in attendance. High on the agenda, and vigorously promoted
by Venezuela, was the creation of a permanent oil-coordinating body.
One year later, participants in a conference in Baghdad established
OPEC.[61]

Conclusion

The West and Japan careered down the road of energy import dependency. For OECD-Europe and Japan in 1960, the percentage of net
imports to TPER reached 35 and 40 percent, respectively, rising to 45
and 67 percent just five years later.[62] But the West, and particularly the
USA, mesmerized by the cheapness of oil, ignored the rumblings
of LDC producer states. Wilson poses a germane question: can oil
(energy) issues be dichotomized into categories of foreign policy problems and domestic problems?[63] The USA did this by opting for oil
import quotas. Europeans and Americans, MNOCs and governments,
discounted the menace of thwarted nationalism throughout the Third
World while neglecting to relate the anti-Zionist compulsion of Arab

states to the security of oil flow. Cold War warriors in the USA accused the Soviets of fomenting instability in LDC states, immediately labeling Mussadiq and Nasser as puppets of the USSR.

The price reductions of 1959 and 1960 reflected the great power of the MNOCs. But their ability to act unilaterally in production and price faced implacable challengers, both within the industry and without. Price reductions, notwithstanding, the MNOCs wielded less power in 1960 than in 1945. If the US government consciously depended upon American MNOCs to so manage affairs in producing areas that sources of supply remained secure, it was tied to an unreliable agent. A realignment of power had transpired, with OPEC a sign of the times. Some westerners sensed the drift and voiced warnings to a disinterested public. In Britain, an energy planning unit doubted the advisability of aggravating the nation's oil dependence upon producers that evidenced frightening instability. But this message emphasized new and reliable sources of oil rather then energy use diversification.[64] As a rule, only those with a particular stake in such forms of energy as coal or natural gas deplored the absence of diversification.[65]

Supply-siders ruled during the 1960s as they had in the past, exercising command from conference rooms in Washington, D.C., London, Amsterdam, and New York, and newly armed with the beguiling possibility of infinite energy through nuclear power. Oil in abundance existed. The optimism of supply-siders refused to accord any validity to either warnings of resource scarcity or of collective action by oil producers to withhold supplies.

Notes

1. For the above two paragraphs: A.S. Milward, *The German Economy at War*, London: Athlone Press (1965), pp. 3, 7, 12–15, 20, 119–20; C.C. Concannon *et al.*, *World Chemical Developments in 1935*. U.S. Department of Commerce. Bureau of Foreign and Domestic Commerce. Trade Information Bulletin No. 832, Washington, D.C.: GPO (1936), pp. 19, 23, 29; W. Levy, "Japanese Strategy Based on Inadequate Oil Supply," *World Petroleum*, 13 (January 1942), pp. 23–5; W.K. Hancock and M.W. Gowing, *British War Economy*, London: HMSO (1949), pp. 112, 118, 188–90, 257; I.H. Anderson, *Aramco, the United States and Saudi Arabia: A Study in the Dynamics of Foreign Oil Diplomacy, 1933–1950*, Princeton, N.J.: Princeton University Press (1981), pp. 33–4, 42; H. Hassman, *Oil in the Soviet Union. History, Geography, Problems*, translated by A.M. Leiston, Princeton, N.J.: Princeton University Press (1953), pp. v–vi, 59.
2. For the above two paragraphs: Milward, *German Economy*, pp. 49–52, 158–60, 168–89; S. Olsson, *German Coal and Swedish Fuel, 1939–1945*, Gothenburg: Institute of Economic History of Gothenburg University

(1975), pp. 100–28; Anderson, *Aramco*, pp. 194–5; J.B. Cohen, *Japan's Economy in War and Reconstruction*, Minneapolis: University of Minnesota Press (1949), pp. 131–47, 386; M. Erselcuk, "Japan's Oil Resources," *Economic Geography*, 22 (January 1946), p. 14.

3. J.G. Clark, *Energy and the Federal Government: Fossil Fuel Policies, 1900–1946*, Urbana: University of Illinois Press (1987), see Chapters 12–14.

4. M.W. Kirby, *The British Coalmining Industry, 1870–1946. A Political and Economic History*, Hamden, Conn.: Archon Books (1977), pp. 177–92; L. Hannah, *Electricity before Nationalisation: A Study of the Development of the Electricity Supply Industry in Britain to 1948*, Baltimore: The Johns Hopkins University Press (1979), pp. 301–6; Hancock, *British War Economy*, pp. 154–6, 175.

5. J. Darmstadter *et al.*, *Energy in the World Economy: A Statistical Review of Trends in Output, Trade, and Consumption Since 1925*, Baltimore: The Johns Hopkins University Press for Resources for the Future (1971), p. 107.

6 P.F. Cowhey, *The Problem of Plenty: Energy Policy and International Politics*, Berkeley: University of California Press (1985), pp. 96–100, portrays the US government as the initiator of the post World War II oil regime. M. Wilkins, *The Maturing of Multinational Enterprise: American Business Abroad from 1941 to 1970*, Cambridge: Harvard University Press (1974), pp. 286, and D.S. Painter, *Oil and the American Century, The Political Economy of U.S. Foreign Oil Policy, 1941–1954*, Baltimore: The Johns Hopkins University Press (1986), pp. 52, 95–6, 206, offer necessary qualifications to Cowhey's view.

7. For PRC and the treaty: Anderson, *Aramco*, pp. 68–71, 98–100, 125; B. Shwadran, *Middle East Oil and the Great Powers*, N.Y.: Praeger (1955), pp. 318–32; Clark, *Energy and the Federal Government*, pp. 346–7; 385–6; P. Odell, *Oil and World Power*, 8th edn, Harmondsworth, Middlesex: Penguin (1986), pp. 202–5; O. Caroe, *Wells of Power: The Oil-fields of Southwestern Asia, A Regional and Global Study*, London: Macmillan (1951), pp. 113–20, 222–7.

8. S.H. Longrigg, *Oil in the Middle East: Its Discovery and Development*, London: Oxford University Press (1961), pp. 119–27; De Golyer and MacNaughton, eds, *Twentieth Century Petroleum Statistics, 1984*, Dallas: De Golyer and MacNaughton (1984), pp. 4–5, 9.

9. Darmstadter, *Energy in the World Economy*, p. 126; United Nations, *1983 International Trade Statistics Yearbook. vol. 1, Trade by Country*, New York: UN (1985), pp. 1038–9, 1086.

10. International Energy Agency, *Energy Balances of Developing Countries 1971/82*, Paris: OECD/IEA (1984), pp. 14–25, 315, 318, *passim*.

11. *BP Statistical Review of World Energy, June 1986*, p. 31; IEA, *Energy Balances of OECD Countries, 1970/1982*, Paris: OECD/IEA (1984), pp. 387–9, 404.

12. For coal: L. Lister, *Europe's Coal and Steel Community*, N.Y.: Twentieth Century Fund (1960), pp. 27–8, 97–9, 258–70, *passim*; W.G. Jensen, *Energy in Europe, 1945–70*, London: G.T. Foulis (1967), pp. 2–10, 117; Clark, *Energy and the Federal Government*, pp. 374–8; G.L. Reid *et al.*, *The Nationalized Fuel Industries*, London: Heinemann Educational Books (1973), p. 16; M.P. Jackson, *The Price of Coal*, London: Croom Helm

(1974), p. 191; Statistical Office of the European Communities, *Energy Statistics Yearbook 1958–1968*, Luxembourg: Statistical Office (1969), pp. 92, 97; P. Gardent, *Le Charbon, Panorame Economique*, Paris: Denud (1961), pp. 130–3, 144–5; World Coal Study, *Future Coal Prospects: Country and Regional Assessments*, Cambridge: Ballinger (1980), pp. 461–2; W.F. Saalbach, *United States Bituminous Coal: Trends Since 1920 and Prospects to 1975*, Pittsburgh, Pa.: University of Pittsburgh Press (1960), pp. 33–4.

13.   Jensen, *Energy in Europe*, pp. 34, 117; M.T. Hatch, *Politics and Nuclear Power Energy Policy in Western Europe*, Lexington: University of Kentucky Press (1986), p. 25. Chapter 6 offers a more detailed account of internal energy systems in the developed states.

14.   In Europe, Marshall Plan participants were organized into the Organization for European Economic Cooperation. The US Economic Cooperation Administration implemented the Marshall Plan. In 1960, OEEC was replaced by the Organization for Economic Cooperation and Development (OECD) which included the USA, Canada, and Japan.

15.   For oil: D.S. Painter, "Oil and the Marshall Plan," *Business History Review*, 58 (Autumn 1984), pp. 359–83; M. Conant, ed., *Oil Strategy and Politics, 1941–1981*, Boulder, Colo.: Westview Press (1982), pp. 63–73, 91–3; E.W. Chester, *United States Oil Policy and Diplomacy: A Twentieth Century Overview*, Westport, Conn.: Greenwood Press (1983), pp. 95–7; W.A. Leeman, *The Price of Middle East Oil: An Essay in Political Economy*, Ithaca, N.Y., Cornell University Press (1962), pp. 116–17, 142–7; W.M. Scammell, *The International Economy Since 1945*, 2nd edn, London: Macmillan (1983), pp. 14, 22–32; C. Tugendhat and A. Hamilton, *Oil, the biggest business*, new and revised edn, London: Methuen (1975), pp. 124–5.

16.   For the above three paragraphs: J. Foreman-Peck, *A History of the World Economy: International Economic Relations since 1850*, Brighton, UK: Wheatsheaf Books (1983), pp. 293–4; A.J. Surrey and J.H. Cheshire, *World Market for Electric Power Equipment*, Brighton, UK: University of Sussex (1972), p. 5; Jensen, *Energy in Europe*, pp, 34, 117; Gardent, *Le Charbon*, pp. 155–6, 184–7; Lister, *Europe's Coal and Steel Community*, p. 45; Hatch, *Politics and Nuclear Power*, pp. 14–16; C. Robinson, *A Policy for Fuel?*, Occasional Paper 31, London: Institute of Economic Affairs (1969), pp. 16–17; L.E. Grayson, *National Oil Companies*, New York: Wiley (1981), pp. 228–9.

17.   Y-l. Wu, *Japan's Search for Oil: A Case Study on Economic Nationalism and International Security*, Stanford, Calif.: Hoover Institution Press (1977), p. 21; United Nations, *World Energy Supplies 1955–1958*, New York: UN (1960), p. 25; IEA, *Energy Balances 1970/1982*, pp. 387–9, 404.

18.   For the above two paragraphs: J. Hirschmeier and T. Yui, *The Development of Japanese Business, 1600–1980*, 2dn edn, London: Allen & Unwin (1981), pp. 266, 288–91, 300–3; Cohen, *Japan's Economy*, pp. 427–36; R.E.D. Driscoll and J.N. Behrman, eds, *National Industrial Policies*, Cambridge: Oelgeschlager, Gunn & Hain (1984), pp. 85–7; Y. Matsumura, *Japan's Economic Growth, 1945–1960*, Tokyo: Tokyo News Service (1961), pp. 44–57, 113–21, 134–6; L. Howell and M. Morrow, *Asia, Oil Politics and the Energy Crisis*, New York: IDOC/North America (1974), p. 57.

19. For the above two paragraphs: M.Y. Yoshino, *Japan's Multinational Enterprises*, Cambridge, Mass.: Harvard University Press (1976), pp. 36–7, 48; Matsumura, *Japan's Economic Growth*, pp. 35–7, 42–3; Odell, *Oil and World Power*, 7th edn, pp. 146–50; Hirschmeier, *Japanese Business*, p. 300; R. Dore, "Energy Conservation in Japanese Industry," in R. Belgrave, ed., *Energy – Two Decades of Crisis*, Aldershot: Gower (1983), p. 96.

20. De Golyer and MacNaughton, *1984*, p. 8; D. Park, *Oil & Gas in Comecon Countries*, London: Kegan Paul (1979), pp. 43, 50, 140, 171, 184.

21. Hassmann, *Oil in the Soviet Union*, pp. 33–5, 133; R.W. Campbell, *The Economics of Soviet Oil and Gas*, Baltimore: The Johns Hopkins University Press for Resources for the Future (1968), pp. 8–14, 23–38, 159–60, 168–9; E.A. Hewitt, *Energy, Economics, and Foreign Policy in the Soviet Union*, Washington, D.C.: Brookings Institution (1984), pp. 31–5; G. Modelski, *Atomic Energy in the Communist Bloc*, Carlton: Melbourne University Press (1959), pp. 100–1.

22. For the above two paragraphs: sources for Table 4.5; Jensen, *Energy in Europe*, pp. 63–4, Hassmann, *Oil in the Soviet Union*, p. 135; M. Dewar, *Soviet Trade with Eastern Europe, 1945–1949*, London: Royal Institute of International Affairs (1951), pp. 1–7, passim; G.W. Hoffman, *The European Energy Challenge: East and West*, Durham, N.C.: Duke University Press (1985), pp. 7–8; C.N. Jordan, *The Romanian Oil Industry*, New York: New York University Press (1955), pp. 1–29, 48; M. Pearton, *Oil and the Romanian State*, Oxford: Clarendon Press (1971), pp. 276–83, 287–384; De Golyer and MacNaughton, *1984*, p. 7.

23. M.I. Goldman, *The Enigma of Soviet Petroleum: Half-Full or Half-Empty?*, London: Allen & Unwin (1980), pp. 23, 50–1; Park, *Oil & Gas*, p. 48; Hassmann, *Oil in the Soviet Union*, p. ix.

24. Darmstadter, *Energy in the World Economy*, pp. 622–3, 652–3; IEA, *Energy Balances 1970/1982*, pp. 387–9, 404.

25. See J.F. O'Leary, "Price Reactive versus Price Active Energy Policy," in P. Tempest, ed., *International Energy Markets*, Cambridge: Oelgeschlager, Gunn & Hain (1983), pp. 169–70.

26. Wilkins, *Multinational Enterprise*, pp. 319–21; S.G. Rabe, *The Road to OPEC: United States Relations with Venezuela, 1919–1976*, Austin: University of Texas Press (1982), pp. 102–5; H.M. Larson *et al.*, *History of Standard Oil Company (New Jersey). New Horizons 1927–1950*, New York: Harper & Row (1971), pp. 426–9. For a full discussion of US foreign policy and oil, see Chester, *U.S. Oil Policy* and Painter, *Oil and the American Century*.

27. For the above three paragraphs: R.H.K. Vietor, *Energy Policy in America since 1946: A study of business–government relations*, Cambridge: Cambridge University Press (1984), pp. 80–9, 210–16; C.D. Goodwin, "Truman Administration Policies toward Particular Energy Sources," in C.D. Goodwin, ed., *Energy Policy in Perspective: Today's Problems, Yesterday's Solutions*, Washington, D.C.: The Brookings Institution (1981), pp. 132–8, 192–200; W.J. Barber, "The Eisenhower Energy Policy: Reluctant Intervention," in *ibid.*, pp. 264–5, 274–82; Darmstadter, *Energy in the World Economy*, pp. 653–4; J.M. Holl, "Eisenhower's Peaceful Atomic Diplomacy: Atoms for Peace in the Public Interest," draft mimeo paper, December 1977; B. Goldschmidt, *The*

Atomic Complex: A Worldwide History of Nuclear Energy, translated from French by B. Adkins, La Grange Park, Ill.: American Nuclear Society (1982), pp. 241–55; further material on nuclear energy appears in Chapter 6.

28. IEA, *Energy Balances of Developing Countries 1971/1982*, pp. 14–24, 114–26, 218–29, 315, 318; Darmstadter, *Energy in the World Economy*, Table XI.

29. For the above three paragraphs: Scammell, *The International Economy*, p. 14; Foreman-Peck, *History of World Economy*, pp. 267–8, 305; H. Cleveland, ed., *Energy Futures of Developing Countries: The Neglected Victims of the Energy Crisis*, New York: Praeger (1980), pp. 1–2, 26–31, 37; B. Dasgupta, *The Oil Industry in India, Some Economic Aspects*, London: Frank Cass (1971), pp. 11–32, 67–8, 142–3; G. Philip, *Oil and Politics in Latin America. Nationalist Movements and State Companies*, Cambridge: Cambridge University Press (1982), pp. 131–2; J.W. Mullen, *Energy in Latin America: The Historical Record*, Santiago de Chile: CEPAL (1978), pp. 63–5; H. Madelin, *Oil and Politics*, translated by M. Totman, Farnborough: Saxon House (1975), pp. 16–17.

30. L.M. Fanning, *American Oil Operations Abroad*, New York: McGraw-Hill (1947); Caroe, *Wells of Power*; K. Beaton, *Enterprise in Oil: A History of Shell in the United States*, New York: Appleton-Century-Crofts (1957); D.H. Finnie, *Desert Enterprise: The Middle East Oil Industry and Its Local Environment*, Cambridge: Harvard University Press (1958); Longrigg, *Oil in the Middle East*; H.F. Williamson *et al.*, *The American Petroleum Industry: Vol. II. The Age of Energy, 1899–1959*, Evanston, Ill.: Northwestern University Press (1963).

31. N. Fatemi, *Oil Diplomacy: Powderkeg in Iran*, New York: Whittier Books (1954); B. Shwadran, *Middle East Oil*.

32. G. Jenkins, *Oil Economists' Handbook 1984*, London: Applied Science Publishers Ltd (1984), p. 57 and for notes 33 and 34; De Golyer and MacNaughton, *1984*, pp. 18, 60–1; M.A. Adelman, *The World Petroleum Market*, Baltimore: The Johns Hopkins University Press for Resources for the Future (1972), pp. 31–3; J.E. Hartshorn, *Politics and World Oil Economics. An Account of the World Oil Industry and Its Political Environment*, New York: Praeger (1967), pp. 58–9; Chase Manhattan Bank, *Investment Patterns in the World Petroleum Industry*, New York: CMB (1956), p. 10.

33. De Golyer and MacNaughton, *1984*, pp. 58–9; Leeman, *Price of Middle East Oil*, pp. 67–79; Z. Mikdashi, *A Financial Analysis of Middle Eastern Oil Concessions, 1901–1965*, New York: Praeger (1966), pp. 321–2.

34. De Golyer and MacNaughton, *1984*, pp. 58–9; Mullen, *Energy in Latin America*, pp. 37–8, 42; Philip, *Oil and Politics*, pp. 87–8.

35. Park, *Oil & Gas*, pp. 35–7; Hewitt, *Energy in the Soviet Union*, p. 29; Campbell, *Soviet Oil and Gas*, pp. 66–7, 87–103, 122; Goldman, *Soviet Petroleum*, pp. 33–4; De Golyer and MacNaughton, *1984*, p. 1.

36. UN, *1983 Trade Statistics*, p. 1086–7.

37. See above Chapter 2, pp. 34–7 and Chapter 3, pp. 74–81.

38. For the above two paragraphs: N. Jacoby, *Multinational Oil: A Study in Industrial Dynamics*, New York: Macmillan (1974), p. 41; C. Issawi and M. Yaganeh, *The Economics of Middle East Oil*, New York: Praeger (1962), p. 211; E. Penrose, ed., *The Large International Firms in De-*

veloping Countries: The International Petroleum Industry, London: Allen & Unwin (1968), pp. 91, 98, 102, 110, 119, 123–4, 129, 137–41.

39. *Ibid.*; Chase Manhattan Bank, *Investment in World Petroleum*, pp. 17, 21, 35–40; Tugenhadt, *Oil*, pp. 300–2; Issawi, *Middle East Oil*, p. 41; N.A. White, *Financing the International Petroleum Industry*, London: Graham & Trotman (1978), pp. 48–9.

40. See for example, Beaton, *Shell in the United States*; Larson, *Standard Oil, 1927–1950*; Fanning, *American Oil Abroad*.

41. Adelman, *World Petroleum Market*; M.S. Al-Otaiba, *OPEC and the Petroleum Industry*, London: Croom Helm (1975); Leeman, *Price of Middle East Oil*; G. Luciani, *The Oil Companies and the Arab World*, London: Croom-Helm (1984); Odell, *Oil and World Power*; Penrose, ed., *The International Petroleum Industry*.

42. For the above two paragraphs: Adelman, *World Petroleum Market*, pp. 80–1; Shwadran, *Middle East Oil*, pp. 349–54; Anderson, *Aramco*, pp. 146–54; Leeman, *Price of Middle East Oil*, pp. 24–7, 30–5.

43. G. Lenczowski, *Oil and State in the Middle East*, Ithaca, N.Y.: Cornell University Press (1960), pp. 31–4; A. Ronaglia, *The International Oil Market: A Case of Trilateral Oligopoly*, edited by J.A. Kregel, Basingstoke: Macmillan (1985), pp. 15–17; Anderson *Aramco*, p. 21; Mikdashi, *Middle Eastern Oil Concessions*, pp. 189–90.

44. For the above two paragraphs: E.J. Wilson, "World politics and international energy markets," *International Organization*, 41 (Winter 1987), pp. 131–2; P.G. Groth, "Energy Development and Security and Supply-Side Ideology: Oligopoly, Monopoly, and Imperfect Competition Make Fossil Fuel Regulation a Necessity," *American Journal of Economics and Sociology*, 44 (April 1985), pp. 157–8; Tugenhadt, *Oil*, pp. 54, 124–5; H. Maull, *Europe and World Energy*, London: Buttersworth (1980), pp. 207–10; Leeman, *Price of Middle East Oil*, pp. 93–108.

45. Penrose, *International Petroleum Industry*, pp. 91, 102; Jenkins, *Oil Handbook 1984*, p. 10.

46. For the above three paragraphs: Leeman, *Price of Middle East Oil*, pp. 3–5; Tugenhadt, *Oil*, p. 157; R.M. Burrell and A.J. Cottrell, *Politics, Oil, and the Western Mediterranean*, Beverly Hills, Calif.: Sage (1973), p. 38; De Golyer and MacNaughton, *1984*, p. 4; Penrose, *International Petroleum Industry*, pp. 69, 187–90; Hartshorn, *Politics and World Oil*, p. 149.

47. For the above two paragraphs: Yoshino, *Japan's Multinational Enterprises*, pp. 38–40; De Golyer and MacNaughton, *1984*, pp. 58–62; Victor, *Energy Policy in America*, pp. 95, 100, 106–14; Barber, "Eisenhower Energy Policy," pp. 232–47.

48. For the above four paragraphs: P. Hepple, ed., *The Petroleum Industry in the United Kingdom*, London: The Institute of Petroleum (1966), pp. 28–30, 61–9; Jenkins, *Oil Handbook 1984*, pp. 106–7; Adelman, *World Petroleum Market*, pp. 95–6; Hatch, *Politics and Nuclear Power*, pp. 27–8; Grayson, *National Oil Companies*, pp. 28–30; N. Lucas, *Western European Energy Policies: A Comparative Study of the Influence of Institutional Structure on Technical Change*, Oxford: Clarendon Press (1985), pp. 7–13.

49. Howell and Morrow, *Asia and Energy*, pp. 48–50; Jenkins, *Oil Handbook 1984*, pp. 106–7; Matsumura, *Japan's Economic Growth*, p. 89; Yoshino,

144 *Energy in a politically polarized world*

Japan's Multinational Enterprises*, pp. 38–40.
50. Williamson, *Age of Energy*, p. 819.
51. Campbell, *Soviet Oil and Gas*, pp. 226–9; Park, *Oil & Gas*, pp. 43–8; Goldman, *Enigma of Soviet Petroleum*, pp. 67–8; B.W. Jentleson, *Pipeline Politics: The Complex Political Economy of East–West Energy Trade*, Ithaca, N.Y.: Cornell University Press (1986), pp. 76–85, *passim*.
52. Anderson, *Aramco*, pp. 71–8; Caroe, *Wells of Power*, p. 117.
53. C.T. Goodsell, *American Corporations and Peruvian Politics*, Cambridge: Harvard University Press (1974), pp. 8–9; Rabe, *Road to OPEC*, pp. 117–21, 127–38; Hartshorn, *Politics and World Oil*, pp. 251–2; C.E. Solberg, *Oil and Nationalism in Argentina: A History*, Stanford, Calif.: Stanford University Press (1979), pp. 163–8. Chapter 5 contains a discussion of host government oil revenues.
54. For the above two paragraphs: Tugendhat, *Oil*, pp. 126, 130–2; Rabe, *Road to OPEC*, pp. 102–4; Al-Otaiba, *OPEC*, pp. 31–2; Issawi, *Middle East Oil*, pp. 31, 35; Wilkins, *Multinational Enterprise*, pp. 321–3; Anderson, *Aramco*, pp. 187–97; Penrose, *International Petroleum Industry*, pp. 91, 98; Painter, *Oil and the American Century*, pp. 165–71; Mikdashi, *Middle Eastern Oil Concessions*, pp. 140–5.
55. Longrigg, *Oil in the Middle East*, pp. 170–3; F. Fesharaki, *Development of the Iranian Oil Industry: International and Domestic Aspects*, New York: Praeger (1976), pp. 43–4; Shwadran, *Middle East Oil*, pp. 117–27; Fatemi, *Oil Diplomacy*, pp. xv–xxvii, 366–73.
56. Walter J. Levy in Conant, ed., *Oil Strategy*, pp. 134–5; Hassmann, *Oil in the Soviet Union*, pp. 142–3; Chester, *U.S. Oil Policy*, pp. 94–5; Shwadran, *Middle East Oil*, pp. 68–79.
57. For the above three paragraphs: H. Lubell, *Middle East Oil Crises and Western Europe's Energy Supplies*, Santa Monica, Calif.: Rand Corp. (1963), pp. 13–15; Chester, *U.S. Oil Policy*, pp. 262–5; De Golyer and MacNaughton, *1984*, pp. 9–11; M. Tanzer and S. Zorn, *Energy Update: Oil in the Late Twentieth Century*, N.Y.: Monthly Review Press (1985), pp. 52–3; Issawi, *Middle East Oil*, pp. 28–9, 175–6; Fesharaki, *Iranian Oil Industry*, pp. 59–61, 66–8; I.M. Torrens, *Changing Structures in the World Oil Market*, Paris: The Atlantic Institute for International Affairs (1980), pp. 10–11; R. Johns and M. Field, "Oil in the Middle East and North Africa," in *The Middle East and North Africa 1987*, 33rd edn, London: Europa Publications Ltd (1987), pp. 100–2.
58. Lenczowski, *Oil in the Middle East*, pp. 319–28, 335–8; Finnie, *Desert Enterprise*, pp. 61, 81–2; Lubell, *Middle East Oil Crises*, pp. 16–18, 26–7.
59. Levy in Conant, *Oil Strategy*, pp. 113–14.
60. For the above two paragraphs: Mikdashi, *Middle Eastern Oil Concessions*, pp. 223; E. Lieuwen, "The Politics of Energy in Venezuela," in J.D. Worth, ed., *Latin American Oil Companies and the Politics of Energy*, Lincoln, Nebr.: University of Nebraska Press (1985), pp. 204–6; G. Coronel, *The Nationalization of the Venezuelan Oil Industry, from Technocratic Success to Political Failure*, Lexington, Mass.: Lexington Books (1983), p. 26; Longrigg, *Oil in the Middle East*, pp. 310–11; Painter, *Oil and the American Century*, p. 165; Tugendhat, *Oil*, pp. 154–5.
61. Al-Otaiba, *OPEC*, pp. 47–54; Mikdashi, *Middle Eastern Oil Concessions*, pp. 174–5; A. Al-Sowayegh, *Arab Petropolitics*, London: Croom Helm (1984), pp. 83–6; A. Maachou, *OAPEC, an international organization for*

economic cooperation and an instrument for regional integration, trans. A. Melville, Paris: Berger-Levrault (1982), pp. 34–7.

62. IEA, *Energy Balances 1970/1982*, pp. 387–9, 404.
63. Wilson, "World politics and international energy markets", pp. 139–40.
64. Political and Economic Planning, *A Fuel Policy for Britain*, London: PEP (1966), pp. 9–10, 110–13.
65. See for example, Derek Ezra, *Coal and Energy: The need to exploit the world's most abundant fossil fuel*, London: Ernest Benn (1978). p. 17.

5

The owners of the world's petroleum resources

The Anglo-American oil treaty (1944–7) has been described as an initiative to devise a liberal (Painter's word) system of international control over Middle Eastern oil that would avoid debilitating competition and bring stability to the region. Of the manifold constituents of a liberal system, which I interpret as meaning a fair and just order, the indispensable principle would be full control over this resource by its owners. A liberal international agreement, then, should recognize the rights of ownership. Instead, the treaty validated concessionary contracts and the equal opportunity to acquire exploration and development rights. Nor did the treaty promise full producer state control over the industry in the future. In a vague provision, the treaty assured the safeguarding of producer economic interests.[1]

As it stood when finally rejected in 1947, the treaty offered little more to the producing states than they already possessed. It was not in the perceived interest of the USA or the UK to become parents of a liberal oil order. Nor did developing producer states concern themselves with consumer equity, the less so as most consumers were citizens of states considered hostile to the national goals of producer states. In the absence of a liberal settlement, the adversarial relationship between consumer interests, the MNOCs, and the producers smoldered after the Iranian crisis, flared momentarily in 1959–60, and then flamed uncontrollably by the end of the 1960s.

Violent confrontations during the 1950s in Iran, Egypt, and Syria and radical producer demands combined with the appearance of aggressive new players on the international oil stage to exert intense pressure on the MNOCs. Without warning, the MNOCs unilaterally lowered posted prices in 1959–60. The uproar over that indiscreet act guaranteed escalated producer demands and further discord.

The forces emerging during the 1950s that, in combination, caused concern among the MNOCs gained momentum during the 1960s. What had been an irritation became a direct threat to MNOC concessionary authority. Extremely nationalistic and assertive new producers such as Libya and Algeria joined with older producers to challenge the concessionary status quo. Individual members of OPEC succeeded in wringing improved terms from the Big Eight firms (see Table 4.7), in part because of the willingness of numerous new international oil companies, such as the Oasis Group (Continental, Marathon, Amerada, and Shell) and Occidental, to offer terms to the host governments far superior to established concessionary agreements with the MNOCs. These and other newcomers sought markets just as the USA imposed import quotas and during a time of rising Soviet oil exports to the non-Communist world. Discounting and other price shaving tactics further alienated producer governments, particularly Venezuela.

The oil crisis of 1973 actually began in 1967 when yet another Arab–Israel war erupted. Between 1968 and 1972, producer demands, backed by potent oil power, emasculated MNOC control over oil. Buoyant western economies that gorged themselves on oil proved vulnerable to the application of producer state power. This chapter pivots on the intensifying confrontation between the MNOCs and members of OPEC; it reveals the evanescent quality of MNOC power.

Old and new sources of oil

During the 1960s, oil production was initiated in the United Arab Emirates (UAE, formed in 1971), Libya, and Nigeria while output from Algerian fields rose quickly (Table 4.6). Iran, Iraq, Saudi Arabia, and Kuwait achieved notable gains in production. By 1970, the above states contributed 39 percent of world oil production (47 percent of non-Communist production), compared with 24 percent in 1960. Simultaneously, Venezuela's global contribution declined by 6 percentage points, mirroring a decline in production growth rates first experienced during the 1950s. The US global share also fell, by 12 percentage points, even though total production rose by 37 percent. But US domestic output fell so far short of satisfying domestic demand that impressive production gains faded to insignificance compared with import requirements. US imports more than doubled from 1960 to 1972, rising from 91,000 metric tons (mt) daily to 237,000 mt daily. By 1970, US imports amounted to about one-half of domestic production. Furthermore, as

American oil demand rose, additions to reserves stagnated so that the reserve to production ratio fell from 12.8 in 1960 to 9.4 in 1969. Alaskan slope reserves reversed that decline only temporarily.[2]

International oil companies rushed into Libya, Algeria, the UAE states, and Nigeria while vast quantities of oil poured from the established fields of the older Persian Gulf producers. Each of the newer producers adopted different exploration and recovery policies. Libya consistently utilized the services of consortia. These consortia, some with a distinct Libyan interest, frequently joined independents with MNOCs. The only firms operating alone were Phillips, Amoco, and the largest single concessionaire, Continental. Libya denied the MNOCs the degree of control over oil production that they possessed in older producing states. In Algeria, independent in 1962, the national firm, Sontrach, replaced the state companies of France as the principal operator. Until 1971, France received a significant portion of domestic demand from Algeria, but on more and more onerous terms. By 1973, Libya and Algeria had essentially cast off dependency upon the larger western oil firms.

For the most part, the UAE and Nigeria relied upon the MNOCs for all phases of oil development. A subsidiary of Iraq Petroleum Company controlled Abu Dhabi's oil industry. Led by an RDS–BP joint venture, each of the Big Eight except SONJ launched exploratory efforts in Nigeria. The location of Nigeria and Libya and the low sulfur content of their oil gained them ready access to markets in Europe and the USA.[3]

Soviet oil production roared ahead during the 1960s as enormous volumes poured from the Volga–Urals fields (Table 4.6 and Map 4.2). The fields located between Kazan in the north and Orensburg in the south accounted for some 70 percent of annual output, drawn chiefly from the Tatar Republic. Beginning in the late 1960s, the Soviets launched an intensive oil and gas exploration program in western Siberia. Proven reserves in those giant but remote fields rose by over fifteen times between the mid-1960s and 1975 while production rose from 31 million metrc tons in 1970 to 148 mmt in 1975. By then, western Siberia contributed some 30 percent of total oil production and 81 percent of natural gas. Siberian oils yielded superior grades of gasoline, naphtha, and middle distillates.[4]

Vast natural gas reserves in western Siberia spurred the Soviets to search for markets in western Europe, an initiative arousing strong opposition from the Reagan administration in the early 1980s. The Soviets pressed forward with a massive pipeline construction program. While falling short of planned goals, the Soviets nonetheless built some 51,000 kilometers of oil and gas trunklines between the late 1960s and 1975. High on their list of priorities were lines from the giant gas fields of Urengoi to the borders of western Europe.[5]

Exploratory efforts in other parts of the world promised short-term benefits. Americans lavished attention on Alaskan fields, but as late as 1976 those distant pools yielded no more than 2 percent of US demand. Closer to the USA, investments in Canada by US firms escalated during the 1950s and garnered payoffs in the following decade, but profits there were by no means as lucrative as in Libya or the older producing states (Table 4.6). Exploration and discovery in Latin America fell afoul of the chameleon-like transformations of national policies toward MNOC investments. Peru's major firm, the International Petroleum Company (SONJ), harassed by the government, ceased drilling during the late 1950s. President Betancourt of Venezuela refused, in 1958, to grant new concessions which led directly to a sharp reduction in recoverable reserves and a level of production that actually fell during the 1970s. Notwithstanding Mexico's exploratory efforts during the 1950s and 1960s, the nation remained dependent upon foreign imports into the 1970s. Oil production in the western hemisphere, then, became ever more marginal to the international oil trade.[6]

In 1962, a number of oil companies initiated negotiations with the UK and Norway to obtain exploratory rights in the North Sea (Map 5.1). Between 1964 and 1972, Norway and Britain approved a number of contracts with various MNOCs, frequently operating in consortia, and reached agreement on partition of the North Sea with the Netherlands, Denmark and West Germany. Both Norway and Britain rejected traditional concessionary contracts, opting for terms that lodged control in the producing country. The licenses issued divided relatively small concessionary tracts among numerous MNOCs, the larger independents, and such state firms as France's Elf Acquitaine. Both states chose firms with successful exploratory records and financial resources capable of underwriting expensive operations.

Numerous oil and gas fields were discovered in the North Sea between 1965 and 1972. Among the joint venturers, Shell and Esso, Amoco and the UK Gas Council, Phillips and Petronord (Statoil, in 1972) led the way along with BP which operated independently. New discoveries by still other firms occurred after 1972. Natural gas production from the British sector commenced in 1967. Four years later, the Norwegian sector produced oil and gas. Oil from the British sector was first landed in 1975. The high risks assumed by these developers paid off in the mid-1970s as liftings rose just as prices ratcheted upward. Prior to the price revolution, Norway and Britain independently had decided to increase the participation of the state and/or national companies. In 1972, Norway created Statoil to manage its oil properties. Britain raised the participatory shares of British oil companies and, in 1976, created the British National Oil Corporation.

During these years, the early tentativeness evinced by the British and

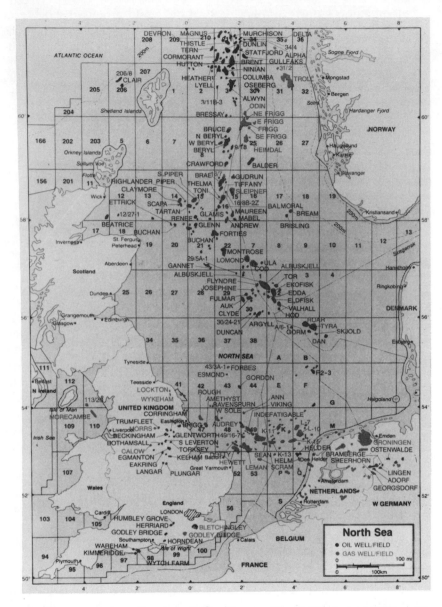

Map 5.1 North Sea oil and gas fields. (*Source: World Oil*, August 1987, p. 51. Reprinted with permission.)

Norwegian governments toward the experienced international oil companies disappeared, replaced by a confident stance that more precisely defined the national interest in North Sea oil and compelled obedience from the licensees, numbering almost 150 by 1972. As Kuczynski points out, by 1972, Norway "had significantly hardened its terms for exploration and discovery," establishing a contractual system that assured Norway fair remuneration from foreign lessees for its oil. Britain's terms were more lenient until 1973, but did have the advantage of quickening development and securing a large British stake in future production. Compared with Norway, Britain had more interests to serve, including British oil companies and American firms with the expertise to open difficult fields. Also, by the time oil flowed from the North Sea, the concessionary terms had been amended in favor of the British government.[7]

Noreng argues that the early and risky decisions and agreements struck between the governments and the firms reflected a dynamic assessment of future oil demand and prices.[8] For my part, I would suggest that the firms, endowed with no particular power of foresight, experienced incredibly good luck, plunging into a physically treacherous but politically secure area during the late 1960s when oil prices hovered around $2 per barrel and, then, reaping a bonanza when unpredictable political events forced oil prices to spectacular levels in 1973 and thereafter.

Splendid natural gas discoveries thrust first the Dutch and then the British into the natural gas business. The Netherland's Groningen field and then North Sea fields in the Dutch, Norwegian, and British sectors supplied northern Europe. The Dutch rapidly converted to natural gas use, a course followed by Britain during the late 1970s, and completed arrangements for export of gas to Germany and elsewhere. By 1970, natural gas provided 33 percent of Dutch TPER while for OECD-Europe that proportion rose from 2 to 10 percent from 1960 to 1970. As with oil exploration and development, the North Sea gas lessors awarded production contracts to MNOCs working in partnership with agents of the host governments; the government owners also participated in transport and sales.[9]

The MNOC hegemony

As in the past, the MNOCs lifted, transported, refined, and marketed most of the oil moving internationally. While their shares declined somewhat as both government-owned and independent firms entered the business, as of 1972 the Big Seven (Table 4.7 minus CFP) still produced 73 percent of non-Communist oil, refined 56 percent, and marketed 54 percent. State oil companies and independents enjoyed the largest share gains in refining and marketing but purchased a large portion of their crude from the MNOCs. American MNOCs controlled virtually all of Venezuela's oil. Aramco pumped, refined, and distributed just under 100 percent of Saudi oil. The Iranian Consortium shared the area with several NIOC–non-Consortium firms but the latter produced a mere trickle compared with the Consortium. Throughout the Persian Gulf and in Nigeria, the same results obtained. Only in Algeria, where an increasingly tenuous special relationship with France held, and in Libya, where first a traditional monarchy and then a radical revolutionary regime ruled, were the MNOCs denied concessionary hegemony.[10] The crude poor independents relied heavily on Libyan production to meet market requirements. In the mid-1960s, Libya shrewdly exploited this dependence.

World refinery capacity doubled between 1960 and 1970. Of a total increase in throughput of 1.3 bmt, the USSR and the USA added 18 and 13 percent respectively while western Europe added 39 percent and Japan 10 percent. The developed world, then, provided 80 percent of new refinery capacity during the decade. Although producing 39 percent of world oil, Middle Eastern capacity advanced by only 49 mmt. The Caribbean basin, including Venezuela, and South America added a capacity of 109 mmt, or 8 percent of the increase. By far the lion's share of Latin American and Middle Eastern capacity remained under MNOC control. The Iranian Consortium operated Abadan, Aramco owned Ras Tanura, and SONJ, RDS, SOCAL, and Texaco dominated the Latin American industry.

The ambitions of producing LDCs to raise their equity in downstream operations were frustrated. Into the late 1960s, the Big Eight controlled about 80 percent of Middle Eastern refining, a proportion technically reducible by the *de jure* ownership of Abadan by NIOC. In Latin America, new and old state companies carved out somewhat larger shares at the expense of the MNOCs. In Argentina, the Big Eight's share fell from 55 percent in 1955 to under 35 percent by 1970. In Venezuela, however, the share of SONJ and others remained above 95 percent until nationalization in 1975.[11]

A diminution of MNOC shares characterized production. From 1961 to 1971, the portion of state-owned and independent firms rose from 16 to 23 percent while the proven oil reserves of the MNOCs shrank from 92 percent to 67 percent of the total. Formerly, the MNOCs accounted for an overwhelming part of capital investment in foreign oil fields but that decreased from a 75 percent share in 1948 to 35 percent in 1970. Despite these share reductions, less than 20 percent of oil moving internationally during the late 1960s managed to bypass the MNOCs. However aggressively such independents as SOIND, Continental, Marathon, Occidental, or Getty battled for a niche in the industry, they were, more often than not, forced to seek either crude, refinery space and/or products, or transportation from the MNOCs.[12]

Developing pressures on world oil markets

Students of the world oil scene have chronicled during the 1950s and 1960s numerous shifts and turns that cumulatively eroded the dominance of the MNOCs. Maull observes an industry poised on the verge of restructuring by the late 1950s. He cites such catalysts as the intrusion of the independents in the Middle East, accelerated Soviet exports, the aggressive national policies of France, Italy, and Japan, the impact of US oil import quotas in stimulating competition in Europe, further discounting and rebating in the 1960s, and the formation of OPEC. Cowhey, Odell, and Mendershausen acknowledge such pressures while advancing their own priorities and dating significant restructuring to the late 1960s or early 1970s. Odell and Cowhey assign responsibility to the USA for this radical transformation and are of the opinion that the USA successfully defended its oil interests until the 1970s. Cowhey identifies the USA as the initiator and conservator of the postwar oil regime.[13]

These authorities weave masses of informative detail into their multifaceted tapestries. Painter's focus on US foreign oil policy complements the work of Cowhey and Odell but with an emphasis on the central role of the US oil industry in influencing that policy. Depicting an oil regime reflecting government–industry cooperation, Painter follows the older work by Nash. According to Painter, key areas of cooperation included control of Middle Eastern oil, containment of the Russians, and opposition to nationalization. Madelin, Tugenhadt and Hamilton, and Leeman note an earlier erosion of MNOC hegemony, essentially attributing this to the successful entry of state-owned and independent oil companies into Middle Eastern and other fields.[14] Invariably, these excellent studies highlight the same events and trends. Each provides a slightly different focus, no one of which offers a markedly different interpretation.

Competition for markets intensified during the 1960s, particularly in western Europe and Japan and in such developing countries as Argentina and Brazil. The immense American market for imported oil also beckoned to producers but access was somewhat limited by the oil import quotas of 1959. The West's unquenchable thirst for energy conjured up an image of market forces at work that reflected reality only partially. In 1987, an article by Ernest J. Wilson, III, offered perceptive criticisms of various models of world oil markets that purported to explain the recent and radical structural changes.[15]

One such model, termed "neoclassical economic," is faulted for its indifference to all but market forces. A second construct, the regime model, directs attention to the key institutional and political players that establish the essential rules under which all participants engage. Cowhey, for example, casts the USA as the guarantor of the system into the 1960s. The regime model allows for the introduction of new players and for shifts in power among the participants. According to Wilson, Mendershausen and Noreng[16] have contributed studies that strengthen the regime approach. Penrose's study of the internal institutional needs of the MNOCs exhibits an affinity for the interpretive intent of the regime model.[17] Wilson objects to this model as ignoring "the chaos of the market" and as attributing excessive rationality and purpose to firms and governments.[18] A third model, labeled "policy/political" and associated with such authors as Quandt and Yergin,[19] seems very similar to the regime model with, perhaps, a heightened attention to the role of policy-making elites. It is criticized on the same grounds as the regime model.

Wilson offers his own interpretive framework, the "petro-political cycle," which appears to be an amalgam of the three discarded models.[20] It accommodates the interacting influences of markets, political pressures, and industrial organization within the context of a particular (temporal) demand–supply situation. In a period of rising market expectations, sellers gain an advantage and the politics will differ from periods of falling markets and expanding purchaser power. Buyers and sellers exact maximum advantages when the market turns in their favor. The moment of opportunity for the producers occurred in 1970–71 when Libya and Algeria rode a rising market and changed the rules of the game.

Wilson may attribute excessive significance to that "moment" in 1970–1. The presumed advantages derived from a seller's market that producers had much to do with creating and from a series of past political decisions reaching back to Mexican nationalization in the face of American and British opposition. During the 1950s, producer states persistently upped the ante in the battle for control over oil even though competition was minimal and prices stable. In seeking the causes of structural change, Wilson, Cowhey, and others attribute an aggressive and formative role to the West while assigning a far too passive role to the major producer states. Apposite here are the Six Day War (1967), the second closure of Suez, another partial Arab embargo (including the turning off of Aramco's Tapline), Qadhafi's seizure of power and the subsequent radicalization of Libyan oil policies, the onset of Vietnam-induced inflation in the USA, and the supine response of western governments and MNOCs to the incremental demands of the oil producers, notably Libya.

The producers marched to their own drumbeat. Neither prices nor western policies deterred them. A reduction in price in 1959–60 led to the formation of OPEC as a counterforce to the western core. True the producing states were not prepared, yet, to act in concert; each was locked into financial and technological dependency upon the MNOCs. But their ultimate objective, complete control over their oil with a downstream capability, was not hidden from view. Nationalistic aspirations could be temporarily deflected but not defeated. Anti-Zionism could not be moderated.

Prices remained low during the 1960s; little spot market oil sold at posted prices. The competitiveness of the 1960s was not a manifestation of a suddenly liberated free market but rather a consequence of government policies. Consumer governments in the USA, Europe, Japan, India, and elsewhere fostered high energy use at the cheapest price. Europe and India welcomed cheap Soviet oil while the USA maintained natural gas and electricity prices at low levels. The consumer governments evidenced no intention to develop policies that moderated oil import dependence. The producing states, increasingly incensed at what they perceived as an unfair return on their oil, intensified their pressure on the MNOCs. Led by Iran, Middle Eastern governments invited newcomers to participate in oil development. Libya, then, exploited the absence of oil company unity by establishing new terms by fiat rather than through negotiations. The MNOCs, without support from their governments could only bow to producer demands or pull out.

The initiative, then, began to shift to the producing states well before the critical Tripoli and Teheran negotiations of 1970–1. The well-chronicled impact of the newcomers — consuming state-owned companies and independents — furthered the interests of the producer states but did not dramatically lessen the hold of the MNOCs on Middle Eastern oil. Indeed, only in Libya did the newcomers, mostly American firms, account for a significant portion of the withdrawals. Of the leading US independents only Continental, Marathon, and Occidental (Oxy) in 1973 drew over one-half of their oil from outside the USA, with Oxy, the largest single producer in Libya, obtaining 97 percent of its oil from overseas. Oxy's Libyan withdrawals accounted for 20 percent of Libyan production in 1970. Oxy was especially vulnerable to a Libyan action that threatened a reduction in production. As the largest Libyan producer, Oxy's exposed position may have weakened other producers.[21]

The importance of the state-owned companies has been somewhat inflated. Excepting the French firms in Algeria and CFP as a member of the Iranian Consortium, they produced miniscule amounts of oil compared even with the larger independents such as Continental. Only for a brief moment during the 1960s did French controlled Algerian oil satisfy a significant part of domestic demand. Italy's ENI obtained most of the its oil from the Libyan concessionaires and from the USSR. The Japanese met with continuous disappointment in pursuing a policy of disengagement from reliance on the MNOCs. By 1974, some 49 Japanese exploration and development companies were operating. From these efforts the Japanese received 13 percent of their total imports in 1965 and 8.5 percent in 1973.[22] The MNOCs ruled the roost. Only one adversary, the producing states, could tumble them from their perch.

Numerous studies have ascribed to the US oil import quotas an extraordinary influence on world oil markets in the 1960s. The following consequences are cited as typical:[23]

1. Quotas burdened US oil independents with surplus oil production from the Middle East (Leeman, Odell, Vietor).
2. This spurred intense competition for western European markets through price cutting and discounting (Longrigg, Odell, Tughenhadt and Hamilton).
3. The market shares of MNOCs were reduced while shares of independents expanded (Vietor).
4. These results antagonized Middle Eastern producers whose revenues were diminished due to price cutting (Al-Otaiba, Mikdashi, Odell, Vietor).
5. Quotas severely damaged Venezuela and precipitated retaliation (Barber, Coronel, Lieuwen, Odell, Rabe).
6. The above led directly to the formation of OPEC (Al-Otaiba).
7. Quotas conferred great price benefits upon western Europe and Japan (Blair, Hartshorn, Hoffman, Odell).
8. Conversely, quotas disadvantaged the USA in its economic competition with western Europe and Japan (Gisselquist, Blair).
9. The above prompted the USA to conspire with MNOCs and OPEC in the early 1970s to raise prices so as to disadvantage the industries of Japan and western Europe (Gisselquist, referred to in Park).
10. Quotas stimulated a Soviet export campaign in western Europe that triggered US anti-Soviet trade policies (Jentleson).

A book would be required to substantiate, qualify, or refute each point. My own view is that all of these assertions require at least modest qualification.

Competition for western European markets (points 1–3) by means of discounting, rebates, and other price shaving devices antedated the mandatory quotas. The unilateral cuts in posted prices of 1959–60 generated such consequences as modestly falling product prices before the quotas could have had an impact. By 1963 or so, the quotas might have reinforced these lower prices. Landed crude in the UK fell to the pre-Suez price in 1959. From 1959 to 1961, the price of crude imports to the UK declined by 10 percent. For the next four years, 1961–4, prices fell by 2 percent. Then, from 1964 to 1966, prices dropped by 12 percent, perhaps partly in response to an additional supply available as a result of the quotas. Landed crude prices to EEC countries displayed a similar pattern. But product prices in EEC nations from 1960 to 1967 did not manifest a pattern that suggests a strong quota influence.[24] Middle Eastern enmity toward the West evolved quite naturally well before the quotas (points 4–6). Neither OPEC, the organization spawned by the price cuts of 1959–60, nor producer disgruntlement over reduced revenues can be attributed to the quotas because posted prices were frozen during the 1960s. However, Venezuela did suffer a diminution of exports to the USA. The effects of the quotas on Venezuelan oil nationalism are unclear. Venezuela occupied an advanced position in the confrontation with the MNOCs (recall the 50:50 split and Betancourt's dedication to the founding of a producer's organization) before the US policy took effect. The quotas only added to the Venezuelan list of grievances against the MNOCs.

US imports from the Middle East continued to increase, as did on a far smaller scale imports of Canadian oil. Venezuela absorbed those losses. But Venezuelan oil cost much more than Middle Eastern oil. Moreover, Venezuela and the MNOCs were engaged in a vituperative controversy over the alleged neglect of the MNOCs to pay past taxes. That issue combined with a niggardly concessionary policy provoked the MNOCs to reduce exploratory efforts and hold production down. Between the two Suez crises, Venezuelan production rose by 21 percent compared with 164 percent in the Middle East.[25]

The quotas hardly staunched American imports. Crude and product import growth rates are shown on Table 5.1. The larger reductions in this chronology occurred in 1957–8 (the Suez Crisis), 1962–3, 1966–7 (Arab–Israel War and Nigerian Civil War), and 1969–70 (unilateral producer cutbacks in production, embargo by Middle Eastern producers, and continued impact of the Nigerian war). Imports

Table 5.1   Annual growth rates of US crude and product imports, 1955–70

	Crude imports annual growth rate %	5-year average %	Product import annual growth rate %	5-year average %
1955–6	20		8	
1956–7	9		10	
1957–8	−6	1.2	35	12.2
1958–9	1		9	
1959–60	6		−1	
1960–1	3		9	
1961–2	8		9	
1962–3	<1	3.8	5	9.6
1963–4	6		7	
1964–5	3		18	
1965–6	<1		10	
1966–7	−8		4	
1967–8	14	1.6	10	11.2
1968–9	9		13	
1969–70	−6		19	

Source: De Golyer and MacNaughton, *Twentieth Century Petroleum Statistics 1984*, Dallas, Texas: De Golyer and MacNaughton (1984), p. 51.

contributed to 18 percent of total US supply in 1959, 21 percent in 1965, and 26 percent in 1971, at which time domestic production peaked and went into decline. Between 1970 and 1976, US production dropped by 13 percent.[26]

As for the prices paid for oil by the USA and her economic competitors (points 7–8), it is not possible to detect any telling advantages for the latter. Crude and product prices declined after the Suez Crisis of 1957. The second Suez Crisis of 1967 jacked prices upward during the final two quarters of the year. In most European markets and in the USA, prices then fell moderately in 1968, thereafter holding steady until the first marked price increases in late 1970 and 1971. Those advances reflected the price agreements concluded at Tripoli and Teheran. Wholesale price indices for all goods closely paralleled those for oil. The landed price of crude oil in Europe exceeded that in Japan but neither price differed significantly from the wellhead price in the USA. During the years, 1962–6, the retail price per gallon of gasoline in Germany exceeded that in the USA by about two times while the French price was over three times higher. The wholesale price of heavy fuel oil in the USA averaged about $15 per barrel for the five years, 1962–6; in six major German cities, prices ranged from a low of $19 to a high of $31. Heavy government taxes in Europe accounted for a major part of these differentials. It may be true that high cost producers in the USA were buffered from the competition of low cost producers by the quota system as well as by market demand prorationing. These programs may have somewhat inflated oil prices in America. But energy inputs accounted for only a tiny fraction of the cost of manufactured products.[27] Whatever competitive superiority Germany and Japan achieved over the USA during those years did not derive from lower oil costs.

Americans managed to inflate the threat from Soviet oil exports out of all proportion, consistently attributing the most devious motives to their enemy. Competitively priced Soviet oil did win a place in the Italian, Greek, Austrian, and Swedish markets and penetrated Japan and other markets as well. But the Soviets did not leap wildly into the disturbed markets of 1967–8. Soviet exports, at 51 mmt in 1963, rose in the following increments: 1963–4, 5.3 mmt; 1964–5, 7.8 mmt; 1965–6, 9.2 mmt; 1966–7, 5.4 mmt; 1967–8, 7.2 mmt; 1968–9, 1.6 mmt; 1969–70, 5 mmt. These steady advances reflected a gradually widening circle of buyers. But in 1970 OECD-Europe received only 6 percent of total oil imports from Russia. As for dumping, Soviet prices were not always the lowest nor her discounts the highest. To impute to the Soviets an oil policy of purposeful disruptiveness, as Levy does, is untenable, blithely ignoring the benefits to all non-Soviet bloc trading partners and the foreign exchange requirements of the USSR. In any event, Soviet oil exports owed little to US oil import quotas (point 10).[28] The ninth item on this list, a typical example of unproven, if not unprovable, conspiracy, flies in the face of extant evidence and clothes the conspirators with a skill in covert manipulative diplomacy worthy of John le Carré.

India during the 1960s managed to reduce the costs of oil imports by applying pressure on the MNOCs. Soviet oil was imported despite MNOC claims that contracts prohibited such imports. The nationally owned Indian Oil Corporation (1959) launched a refinery construction program that prompted the MNOCs to lower prices modestly.[29] Even a weak nation, with a small market and just commencing the tough journey toward economic development, could extract concessions from the powerful MNOCs.

The grievances of the producing LDCs

The so-called rules of the game, imposed by the West–MNOC coalition, were challenged and fractured well before 1969–73. The oil regime as depicted by Cowhey, or by Roncaglia who packages the MNOCs, producer governments, and major consuming governments into a "trilateral oligopoly," is difficult to detect by the mid-1960s.[30] Encroachment on the domain of the rule-setters, manifest prior to World War II in Argentina, Bolivia, Mexico, and Spain, gained further ground after the war. The Venezuelan and Saudi Arabian profit sharing agreements represented notable infractions of the rules. So, too, did nationalization in Iran and the creation of NIOC, Brazil's establishment of Petrobras, and the formation of the Indian Oil Corporation, all achieved prior to the organization of OPEC. A well-conceived case against continued MNOC dominance braced these outbreaks of LDC nationalism.

Resource nationalism encompasses more than oil and reflects aspirations far transcending control over resources. The battle for control over oil, however, unleashed its most vigorous expressions. Lax, Maull, and Morse agree on the essential elements that comprise resource nationalism. They stress the enhanced risks to transnational firms and the danger to the national security of the industrial states explicit in the doctrine. For the LDCs, assertion of permanent sovereignty over resources accentuates three basic imperatives: to proclaim the integrity of the nation; to reverse the unfair terms of trade that the West defended, in other words to change the rules of the game; and to speed economic growth by employing the earnings gained by redistributing the take from resource exploitation. Lax views as unsavory the identification of foreign companies as agents of imperialism by the LDCs. He condemns the proclivity of LDC governments to use the firms as scapegoats to divert attention from domestic policy failures and/or political repression.[31] Deplorable though this may be in the abstract, it is a tactic with which developed democracies are familiar.

In drawing attention to Arab proclamations of full sovereignty over their oil wealth, Hurst clearly evokes Arab perceptions of the MNOCs as monopolistic agents of western imperialism. Latin Americans, according to Goodsell and Penrose, never doubted this claim and, as Fatemi demonstrates, the belief transfixed Iranians by 1950. These and other authors, particularly Mikdashi and Salazar-Corrillo, translate nationalist goals into more specific economic development objectives. As Mikdashi suggests relative to the Middle East, by 1960 the earlier demands of kings, shahs, or sheikhs for a larger cash income to distribute as they pleased had metamorphosed into a demand for income for development and to finance the eventual takeover of the oil industry. This requires some qualification: neither Cadillac sheikhs nor elites engorged with wealth disappeared; the military competed effectively for their share of oil revenues. Still, takeover or participatory arrangements that replaced the old concessions would endow the producing state with the authority to adjust production and price to the dictates of the market, a point cogently made by Alnasrawi, Hartshorn, and others. The massive outward flow of oil income to the MNOC-consuming states would be much reduced, with the producers retaining the bulk of the earnings.[32] How producing states employed this augmented income is a separate question from that of their right to that income.

Oil income and LDC economic growth

The leading non-industrial oil exporting countries were essentially single-crop economics, oil constituting by far the largest, if not the only, export. The economy of each nation rested firmly on the value of oil export earnings. As of 1970, for the nations included in Table 5.2, petroleum exports comprised in excess of 90 percent of the value of all exports, except in Nigeria where it accounted for 58 percent but would rise to 93 percent by 1974. Oil was virtually the only export of Saudi Arabia and Libya.

That portion of the export value retained by the producing states as economic rent consisted of payments from the MNOCs in the form of royalties, taxes, and profit sharing. At first royalties were calculated on the basis of a sum per barrel of production, then as a percentage of the value of gross sales, and, increasingly after 1960, as a percentage of the volume sold multiplied by the posted price. Tax rates rose steadily and a profit sharing breakthrough occurred when Venezuela gained a 50:50 split in 1948, a division that producing countries inexorably widened in their favor in subsequent years. This income formed an ever larger share of producer government revenue during the 1950s and 1960s (Table 5.2). For Venezuela, the share never dipped below 50 percent after 1956 and ranged between 65 and 70 percent during the 1960s. In Iran, the portion reached 87 percent in 1971, an advance from 30 percent in 1960. Kuwait's revenues from oil exceeded 95 percent of total revenues in 1954 while Saudi Arabia's oil revenues contributed 75 percent of total revenue in 1953 and over 85 percent by 1972.

Table 5.2 summarizes the substantial revenue gains attained by the leading OPEC states from 1956 to 1972 and the phenomenal addition after 1973. In each nation a greater share of the total value of exports remained at home. For the seven countries listed the proportion of revenues to total export value rose steeply: 33 percent in 1961; 49 percent in 1970; 60 percent in 1972; and 73 percent in 1974. The ability of the producing governments to recapture an ever greater share of the value of oil exports attests to the radical tilt of the balance of oil power in favor of the producers.[33]

Table 5.2 Producing country oil revenues and value of exports in parentheses, 1958–75 ($ million)

	1956	1961	1965	1970	1972	1975
Iran*	98	291 (900)	514	1 109 (2 600)	2 396	17 821 (21 600)
Iraq*	169	265 (500)	368	521 (800)	575	5 700 (5 600)
Kuwait*	194	461 (1 000)	598	820 (1 700)	1 403	6 542 (9 900)
Saudi Arabia*	362	378 (1 000)	664	1 214 (2 400)	2 745	22 575 (31 200)
Libya	<1	3 (na)	351	1 351 (2 800)	1 563	5 999 (7 100)
Venezuela*	na	843 (2 200)	1 097	1 378 (2 600)	1 902	9 270 (11 100)
Nigeria		19 (na)	36	247 (1 200)	1 117	6 654 (9 900)
Total above	843	2 439 (7 500)	3 906	7 526 (15 458)	13 673	87 197 (119 400)

* Founding members of OPEC in 1960

Sources: G. Lenczowski, *Oil and State in the Middle East*, Ithaca, N.Y.: Cornell University Press (1960), pp. 37–9; A. Al-Sowayegh, *Arab Petropolitics*, London: Croom Helm (1984), p. 47; J.W. Mullen, *Energy in Latin America: The Historical Record*. Santiago de Chile: CEPAL (1978). p. 40; A. Alnasrawi, *OPEC in a Changing World Economy*. Baltimore: Johns Hopkins University Press (1985). p. 108.

The producing governments, then, depended to an extraordinary degree on the revenues and foreign exchange earnings from oil sales. However, they were not alike in their revenue requirements. Saudi Arabia and Kuwait, with small populations and no resources other than oil, possessed much less capital absorptive capacity than Venezuela or Iran. The latter two, while quite different, ambitiously embarked upon costly modernization programs that required more capital than oil earnings provided. Iraq, Syria, and Libya, with considerably less economic potential than Iran or Algeria, espoused a radical brand of anti-Zionism. Iraq and Syria, as front line states, required huge sums for military purposes. Colonel Qadhafi of Libya also planned expensive adventures supported by a costly armaments program. Iran's hegemonic ambitions in the Persian Gulf and its role as a US surrogate against Soviet aggression encouraged the Shah to create a massive war machine while simultaneously launching a gigantic economic modernization effort. Both objectives were to be funded from oil revenues. In Iran, Iraq, Syria, and Libya, political goals based on military power increased the capacity to absorb capital far above the investment required for economic development.

The so-called low absorbers, too, sought to maximize income prior to the price and revenue explosion of 1973. The direct investments of MNOCs and other oil companies were but a fraction of the total foreign investments of the industrialized states. Earnings from oil investments as a share of all foreign investment earnings were substantially greater than oil investments as a proportion of total foreign investments. The direct investments of OECD members in the Middle East accounted for 9 to 10 percent of the OECD total in 1967 and in 1973. While the Middle East received between 10 and 15 percent of US investments in foreign oil, the region contributed one-third of all foreign investment earnings. US investments in Latin America dropped off sharply as a proportion of global investments. Venezuela, in particular, felt the pinch. MNOCs retaliated against Venezuelan tax and concessionary policies by reducing investments in exploration just as the initial impact of the US import quotas was being recorded.[34]

The West and the MNOCs were investing elsewhere, were disinterested in financing producer state projects, and were positively hostile toward the emergence of downstream capabilities among the producers. To raise oil income by revising concessionary agreements, increasing tax rates, tying royalties and profit sharing to posted prices, and opting for nationalization would resolve, producers argued, foreign exchange and indebtedness difficulties and would provide funding for defense and development. Many of the producer states, however, were sorely disappointed during the 1960s in their efforts to transform the oil industry into the leading sector of industrial growth.

The challenge was to stimulate growth in other economic sectors through the direct investment of oil incomes. Obviously, the circumstances of individual countries dramatically affected performance. Algeria, independent in 1962, determined to force oil revenues to serve national development. Through Sonatrach, Algeria controlled all oil operations. Algeria received substantial aid from the USA but the critical factor was the annual investment of a large part — over 30 percent — of oil earnings in natural gas pipelines and liquefication plants, petrochemicals, refining, light industry, and infrastructure. By the early 1970s, Algeria's import substitution tactics were progressing rapidly and would, or so planners believed, reduce dependence upon oil earnings and provide a firm economic base when the nation's relatively small oil reserves were depleted.

On a far larger scale, Iran moved along a parallel path, but one which tied her very closely to the strategic interests of the USA in the Middle East. Prior to 1973, inadequate revenues and a political structure that, in effect, rested on personal rule constrained both modernization and militarization. NIOC did improve forward and backward linkages to the national economy. Iran ranked as among the more assertive states in demanding a larger share of oil earnings, a posture exaggerated with the price ratcheting of 1973, and after, when Iran always supported prices that maximized oil revenues. Enormous revenues after 1973 fed the Shah's ambitions and the combined costs of economic modernization and militarization escalated wildly. The value of Iranian arms imports from the USA, under $500 million annually prior to 1973, climbed to $1 billion by 1975 and peaked at almost $4.5 billion in 1977. Iran's dependence upon oil earnings intensified. Unlike Algeria, Iran lacked the ability to employ import substitution to save foreign exchange. Virtually all oil industry and other equipment was imported, along with military hardware. These huge imports necessitated substantial borrowing with oil earnings serving as collateral, thus binding Iran ever more tightly to oil. Modernization's psychological shocks spawned increasing political dissent and threatening socioeconomic factionalism, neither of which the Shah accepted passively.[35]

Both Iran and Algeria owned and operated their oil and gas industries, and during the 1960s they implemented policies to improve their share of downstream activities, aiming at independent sales of both crude and products and, in Algeria's case, liquefied natural gas. Nigeria and Venezuela had not nationalized their oil industries. While they expanded oil revenues by imposing more exacting terms on the MNOCs, the linkages between oil and the economy remained more tenuous than in Algeria or Iran. Nigeria's colonial experience left behind a small commercial agricultural sector, a vast multitude of subsistence farmers, and very few trained and technologically sophisticated people. Tribalism and deep-rooted cultural differences between the north and the south led to the Biafran rebellion against the central government in 1967, a tragedy that took many lives and severely stunted economic and oil industry growth. Nigeria had no option but to turn over the oil industry to the MNOCs, albeit on terms more and more advantageous to the government.

Prior to the Biafran conflict, Nigerian authorities committed the nation to rapid economic growth financed by oil revenues. But no miracle occurred then, or after Biafra. *Per capita* GDP and *per capita* energy consumption in Nigeria remained very low (see Table 8.7, p. 300). As late as 1982, non-commercial fuels provided 71 percent of TPER. Connections failed to evolve between the economy and oil revenues that rose by thirteen times between 1961 and 1970 (Table 5.2). The absence of a large consumer market frustrated the implementation of import substitution policies. A developmental focus on large-scale industrial and urban projects obstructed the emergence of economic self-reliance. Lagos, Port Harcourt, and Bonny, for instance, benefited from investments in infrastructure and petrochemicals while the rural–agricultural sector suffered from egregious neglect. True, Nigeria had just gained its independence. Much more time was required. But time alone would not suffice. Balanced political and economic policies were required before oil wealth could be transformed into broadly shared national wealth.[36]

Venezuela, with a more advanced economy, a far less volatile society, and long experience with oil, worked no magic in turning oil income into balanced economic growth. An in-depth analysis of petroleum's contribution to Venezuelan economic development by Salazaar-Carrillo argues that from 1945 to 1973 revenue from oil exports spurred growth in other economic sectors through the creation of a modern infrastructure. Missing from this economic evaluation is attention to such critical political and social factors as the shifts between dictatorial and democratic governments that happened between 1947 and 1958, Venezuelan–MNOC relationships, economic nationalism, oil market weaknesses, and slackening oil exploration during the 1960s.

Rabe portrays Venezuela as a petroleum factory during the 1950s, controlled politically by the Jiminez dictatorship and economically by the MNOCs favored by Jiminez. Venezuela entered and emerged from the 1960s a very poor country. Betancourt's democratic government did confront the MNOCs over taxes and concessions but this resulted in diminished MNOC investments just as US import quotas and cheaper Middle Eastern oil undermined Venezuela's market position. Petroleum induced growth rained benefits upon economic sectors—steel and urban electric services—that meant little to the vast majority of the population. Agriculture received minimal notice from the developers. Rural migrants fled to the cities from stagnating rural areas. By the 1970s, with one-third of the population in Caracas, the nation was 75 percent urban. But wages remained very low and urban employment absorbed but a small portion of the new city dwellers. Urban elites emulated the lifestyles of the affluent in New York and Paris. To the extent that such populous LDC producers as Nigeria, Venezuela, and Indonesia neglected agricultural development and emphasized industrial development over the construction of a basic national infrastructure, to that extent oil wealth was misused. The mistaken belief that a solid industrial structure could be quickly developed produced an exacerbated maldistribution of income and created festering concentrations of urban poor and deepening rural poverty.[37]

For the producing nations, expansion into downstream operations promised a means of retaining a larger share of oil earnings while cashing in on the rising market of the 1960s. As noted earlier, however, the industrialized nations accounted for the greater part of new refining construction during the 1960s. In Latin America, for example, oil refining capacity more than doubled from 1954 to 1970, with Argentina and Venezuela responsible for most of the increase, but as a percentage of world capacity the region's share fell from 6 to 5 percent. Moreover, outside of Mexico and Argentina, MNOCs operated the refineries. In Iran, nationally owned refineries supplied only the domestic market. A Kuwait plan to foster downstream capabilities with the cooperation of the Kuwait Oil Co. (BP–Gulf) was rebuffed by the latter. Kuwait proceeded on its own; the Kuwait National Petroleum Co. (1960) opened its first refinery in 1968. During the 1960s, the MNOCs had every reason to discourage producer entry into downstream activities. MNOC power flowed from their command over necessary technologies. World Bank policies aided and abetted the MNOCs by refusing credits for oil and gas development and by denying funding to nationally owned ventures.[38]

More forceful producer government policies toward the MNOCs and more purposeful development strategies were imperative if producer economies were to improve. Nigeria advanced a step with the Petroleum Decrees of 1969 which mandated a great increase in the employment and training of Nigerians in managerial and technical jobs. But during the 1960s, a thin strand bound large oil sectors to national economies. Oil wealth was well-integrated in the economies of the industrialized states, but in the producer states that wealth generated little sound economic progress. In Indonesia, the successive dictatorships of Sukarno and Suharto turned Pertamina into a fief, unconnected with the economy. As in Nigeria and Venezuela, Indonesia's oil and other resources favored a few, widening already gross income disparities. The government ignored most farmers and encouraged the start-up of inefficient heavy industries. Clearly, the MNOCs were but one obstacle to LDC advancement. LDC political instability, corruption, and embedded structural inequity proved more intractable, seemingly impervious to remedy, than powerful foreign corporations.[39]

The transfer of oil power to host governments

The structure of the international oil industry underwent striking transformations during the 1960s. In the face of unrelenting pressure, the MNOCs, by 1972, were stripped of their hegemonic authority over production and price. Looman, in 1962, accurately predicted the steady movement toward nationalization by Arab producers.[40] Each host cleared its own path and not all chose immediate or total nationalization. Each state did compel the abandonment of the old concessionary system. The vaunted solidarity of the MNOCs, manifest in their stand against Iranian nationalization, crumbled like an empty wasp's nest.

Such was the success of the producers that Sheikh Yamani, Saudi Arabia's oil minister, observed in 1971 that "the role being played by the oil companies is now properly that of purchaser, refiner, and provider of technology."[41] Of the major producers, the states of the Arabian Peninsula viewed total nationalization as a step to be taken very cautiously. Saudi Arabia and Kuwait felt no immediate need to threaten their MNOC-operated consortia with expropriation. Venezuela eschewed nationalization until 1975 largely because of the lack of sufficient capital to undertake independent exploration and development. In impoverished and populous Nigeria, the government also approached nationalization warily until the second price shock of 1978–9 precipitated a flurry of expropriations. Algeria, Libya, Iraq, Peru, Bolivia, and Indonesia all nationalized, at least partly, prior to 1973.

Nationalization represented the final step in asserting full producer sovereignty over their valuable resource. But whether taken or not, the host states effectively diluted MNOC control by first winning a larger than 50:50 share of the profits from concessions and then by upgrading their role from lessor to that of full partner in the working of established concessions. Saudi Arabia achieved this in 1959 when it seated two nationals on Aramco's board of directors and participated, as did Kuwait, in the management of the Japanese-owned Arabian Oil Co. Iran's NIOC negotiated similar arrangements with ENI and SOIND. New concessions of the traditional type were offered less and less frequently.

Table 5.3 Producing government national companies

Argentina	Yacimentos Petroliferos Fiscales	1922
Peru	Empresa Petrolera Fiscal	1934
Bolivia	Yacimentos Petroliferos Fiscales Bolivianos	1936
Mexico	Petroleos Mexicanos	1938
Colombia	Empresa Colombiana de Petroleos	1951
Brazil	Petroleo Brasileiro	1953
Iran	National Iranian Oil Company	1954
Kuwait	Kuwait National Petroleum Company	1960
Venezuela	Corporación Venezolana del Petroleo	1960
Saudi Arabia	Petromin	1962
Algeria	Sonatrach	1963
Iraq	Iraq National Oil Company	1965
Indonesia	Pertimina	1965
Libya	Libyan National Oil Company	1969
Nigeria	Nigerian National Oil Company	1971

Sources: H. Madelin, *Oil and Politics*, translated by M. Totman, Farnborough: Saxon House (1975), pp. 16–17; A. Al-Sowayegh, *Arab Petropolitics*, London: Croom Helm (1984), p. 42.

The new contracts also designated a date for the relinquishment of concessions to the host government. Most dramatically, in 1961 Iraq wrested from IPC 99 percent of the concessionary area. Quietly, Qatar and Kuwait reclaimed one-third and one-half, respectively, of their concessionary areas in the same year. Libya's contracts with oil companies contained relinquishment provisions as did virtually all Middle Eastern contracts by 1973.[42]

In a striking departure from the norm, several host states replaced old style concessions with joint-venture contracts between the producer's national oil company (Table 5.3) and foreign firms in which the former shared fully in management and profits while the foreigners provided most of the capital and technology. In contracts of this type negotiated by the state companies of Algeria, Libya, and Nigeria, the foreign firms held equal rights of ownership. The terms of these cooperative enterprises were considerably less favorable to the oil companies than the joint-venture arrangements pioneered by Iran in 1957 and 1958. The new versions bound the producer governments for a shorter period of time, tied royalty payments and other bonuses to actual production, and linked all payments to posted prices. Contracts frequently bound the foreign partners to purchase at posted prices all of the host's share of production. Such buy-back provisions were necessary only until the producer governments developed their own marketing networks.[43]

Participation in the management of older concessions and joint-ventures in the development of new fields were not considered as permanent alternatives to nationalization. Such contracts normally vested the foreign firms with property rights in the oil fields. Second, even though the hosts shared in management decisions, the MNOCs retained control over the introduction and operation of technologies and, thus, over most production decisions. Also, the hosts as yet lacked refining, transportation, and marketing facilities and expertise. The oil had to be sold and only the MNOCs possessed worldwide distribution networks. Still, joint venture operations emerged as a favored form of participation. These arrangements promised full sharing of information between the expert — the firm — and the learner — the host government — minimizing the likelihood that the less competent partner would be exploited. Gradually, participation and the initiation of direct government-to-government sales diminished historical MNOC advantages.

Iran and Indonesia, among the major producers, and Brazil, Latin America's third largest producer and largest oil market, adopted policies that further attenuated the MNOC role. Brazil's Petrobras, formed in 1953, was a well-capitalized and financially independent firm that monopolized all phases of the oil industry. While Petrobras's production fell far short of meeting national demand, its record was impressive, advancing from a mere 127,000 metric tons in 1953 to 8.3 million metric tons in 1970. Refining profits financed exploration and paid for a large tanker fleet. The firm's refining capacity substantially reduced oil product imports. Unfortunately, production in Brazil leveled-off during the 1970s just as prices soared. Trade imbalances and debts plagued the nation into the 1980s. As of 1973, however, Brazil had successfully consolidated its control over the national oil industry.[44]

Total nationalization threatened negative consequences, among which were the flight of the larger firms and their expertise and technology. Reasonable contractual commitments led to retention of the MNOCs without vesting in them any property rights. Iran and Indonesia pioneered contractual arrangements that avoided the disadvantages of total nationalization without diminishing national authority.

Into the 1960s, Caltex (SOCAL and Texaco) and RDS controlled 90 percent of Indonesian oil production. In 1963, the MNOCs rejected Indonesian demands that the split in profits be raised to something above the 60:40 division agreeable to the companies. In 1965, the state seized British and American oil properties. RDS sold out to Indonesia which created Pertimina as an integrated state company. Caltex hung on, but no longer as an autonomous operator. Pertimina assumed full legal control over all operations. To retain Caltex and to attract other foreign firms, Pertimina then negotiated a series of contracts with Caltex, Japanese, French, and Italian firms, and with several American independents.

Caltex, the leading producer and responsible for at least one-half of production, functioned under a work (service) contract. The firm provided all the financing and technology for exploration and development and received about 60 percent of all production as reimbursement for expenses and as buy-back oil. Pertimina received title to all production equipment. Management was legally vested in Pertimina but, recognizing its lack of expertise, the firm rarely exercised that prerogative. The service contract framework persisted into the 1980s, although by then Pertimina's share had risen to 85 percent, a division still considered advantageous to the foreign firms.[45]

Iran and other producers utilized variations of the Indonesian model. Iran often required guaranteed loans to finance further exploration by NIOC. In a 1966 contract with ERAP, Iran received 90 percent of all profits. Gradually, joint-ventures with various foreign firms were transformed into service contracts. In Iran's case, the service contracts covered a much smaller proportion of national production than in Indonesia. Consortium wells yielded 93 percent of Iran's oil in 1973. Using the leverage of the work contracts, improved terms were pried from the Consortium. Venezuela, too, through its Corporacion Venezolana del Petroleo (CVP; Petroven since 1975) concluded long-term service contracts with foreign firms to work the national oil reserves. CVP, however, did not develop a strong national presence. Prior to 1975, the year in which Venezuela nationalized oil, the MNOCs dominated the industry.[46]

Work contracts endowed state firms with flexibility in managing their oil domain without relinquishing any rights. Complementary to nationalization, these arrangements turned the oil companies into hired hands. Joint-venture operations required mixed management. A service contract might stipulate foreign management but on terms that suited the employer. Service contract incentives could be frequently changed. They might even provide for sales that bypassed the MNOC networks, as was the case in a sales contract negotiated in 1965 between Pertimina and Japan's Far East Trading Company, endowed with the exclusive right to import Indonesian oil. By then, Japan was committed to a ten year investment program in North Sumatra from which Japan would receive 40 percent of withdrawals.[47] For the LDC producer, work contracts kept an avenue clear for foreign capital and expertise, regularized relationships with large oil companies or government agencies, commonly stipulated a training program for LDC personnel, and could embrace any or all phases of operations. Once the LDC firms developed marketing strengths, the old style arrangements with the MNOCs were doomed. Direct sales between Indonesia and Japan presaged the future.

Algeria, Iraq, Libya, and Peru nationalized their oil industries prior to 1973. In each case a successful revolution had replaced an old regime during the 1960s. The new governments quickly struck at the vulnerable concessionary companies. Algeria followed its own development rhythms in expropriating French and other firms between 1967 and 1971. Rapid improvement in Sonatrach's proficiency, Algeria's less intense dependence upon oil earnings, and a potentially valuable foreign trade in natural gas offered some economic justification for nationalization at that time.[48]

Iraq and Peru were veterans of oil wars against a single large concessionaire. When Iraq, in 1972, decided to nationalize a portion of IPC, consortium members imposed a boycott against Iraqi oil and drastically reduced production. This, in addition to antagonism toward US support of Israel in the Yom Kippur War of 1973, led to the expropriation of Exxon and Mobil, both partners in IPC, and the effective termination of the consortium.[49] Peruvian politics rather than economics explains the nationalization of SONJ's subsidiary in 1968-9. As part of a campaign to drive foreign businesses from the country, Peru, in a series of acts, struck at the USA and at multinational enterprise while simultaneously broadcasting its independence from foreign control. Pinelo claims that Peruvian self-assertiveness reflected political maturity and the ability to confront injustice, an astounding conclusion. He offers no evidence, nor does Goodsell, that the International Petroleum Company during the 1960s acted as an agent of imperialism or was other than a model employer. The company had long been the political football of the ruling elites that struggled for power in Peru. These wealthy factions had oppressed and exploited the Peruvian people. Nationalization represented nothing more than elite manipulation of anti-foreign sentiments for their own ends. With one of the lowest *per capita* incomes and one of the highest infant mortality rates in South America during the 1970s and 1980s, it appears that Peruvian nationalization spread few benefits among the impoverished population.[50]

In Libya, piecemeal nationalization between 1971 and 1973 garnered few economic benefits that had not already been won by forcing price increases and favorable joint-venture agreements. Nationalization, however, conformed to the dictates of Colonel Qadhafi's eccentric socialist ideas, served anti-Zionist purposes, and enhanced his Pan-Arab reputation. Of the above four nations, only Algeria developed persuasive arguments for nationalization. But, of course, nationalism, wherever expressed, derives little sustenance from logic.

The role of OPEC

Participation in the operation of older concessions and joint ventures and service contracts negotiated by national companies with foreign firms endowed the hosts with the power to influence the rate of production. While identifying nationalization as the ultimate means of controlling withdrawals, most approached that first step with caution. Libya, in 1971–2, erased the power of the oil companies to fix production rates, but the MNOCs remained entrenched in Iran, the Arabian Peninsula, and Venezuela where they lifted 90 percent of the oil in 1970.

Concurrently with the enhancement of their managerial role, the producers desired to establish the price they received for oil. By the mid-1960s, producer state demands reflected their belief that demand in the West warranted both augmented production and higher crude prices. In pressing relentlessly for both after 1965, the producers benefited from the activities of OPEC. As the most influential voice of producer opinion, OPEC's policy formulations, its consistency, and its organizational competence added substantially to its reputation during the 1960s.

OPEC,* however, did not set policy; individual states did. In its armory, OPEC stockpiled only the weapon of moral suasion. The action of separate states squeezed price hikes from the transnational firms. OPEC emerged as choreographer only in 1970–2. Representing a diverse constituency including non-Arab LDC producers, OPEC's survival required non-entanglement in the Arab–Israel vendetta. The establishment of the Organization of Arab Petroleum Exporting Countries in 1968 provided a vehicle to carry the war to Israel and its supporters. OPEC concentrated on price, production, and management.[51]

Although OPEC achieved an immediate victory in forestalling the further lowering of posted prices after 1960, the organization experienced but modest success until 1970–1. For example, it viewed overproduction as a threat to price stability, but proved unable to generate a consensus in favor of production quotas among members whose revenue needs and proven reserves varied widely. This issue was dropped — for a time. With regard to the price issue, while OPEC contributed strong advocacy, Libya and Algeria, the leading risk-takers after 1965, served as the shock troops. OPEC did intrude forcefully in the Libyan–oil company dispute of 1966 when its members agreed to deny new concessions to operators who refused to accept Libyan terms.

On a very practical level, OPEC developed acceptable positions on income tax rates and the use of posted prices for the payment of taxes,

---

* Saudi Arabia, Iran, Venezuela, Iraq, and Kuwait in 1960 and Qatar (1961), Libya (1962), Indonesia (1962), UAE (1967), Algeria (1969), Nigeria (1971), Ecuador (1973), Gabon (1975).

the expensing of royalties, and on revenue security in general. It agitated among its members for renegotiation of all revenue-related issues, particularly income tax rates, capitalizing upon the imposition of 60 percent tax rates by Venezuela and Indonesia during the 1960s. Similarly, in 1968, OPEC orchestrated demands for expanded producer participation, already achieved by Iran, Indonesia, and other members.

OPEC's "Declaratory Statement of Petroleum Policy" of 1968 codified its price policies, leaving no doubt as to its objectives. Pointedly, the declaration asserted the right of producer governments to determine the posted (tax reference) price. Reflecting a sensitivity to the erosive impact of inflation on government revenues, OPEC further demanded that the posted price be indexed against the value of imported goods and services. Indexing never became common. Rising spot market prices after 1973 and again after 1978 minimized the advantages of this technique, as did the moderate inflation experienced by the developed countries during the later 1980s. In addition, the statement called for the general extension of producer government control over petroleum policies, for relinquishment, and for expanded participation in established concessions.

The members of OPEC through collective and individual initiatives improved their revenue security after 1960. Demonstrating a sound understanding of political realities, OPEC abandoned discussions of prorationing while pressing ahead on issues conducive to consensus building. Members adopted OPEC's decisions voluntarily, applying them at the opportune moment. Lacking power over price and production, OPEC did not act as a cartel before 1973. The organization did establish itself firmly as the voice of the producers. Trailing in the wake of members during most of the 1960s, OPEC's pronouncement of 1968 strongly influenced the pivotal negotiations at Tripoli and Teheran in 1970–1. OPEC's strategy, fleshed out by Libya and Saudi Arabia, of turning the oil firms against one another and of separating price talks about North African oil from discussions of Persian Gulf prices suceeded spectacularly. In late 1973, the moment arrived to demonstrate producer power now lodged in OPEC.[52]

The producer drive toward full control

A series of strikes against the MNOCs beginning in 1966 undermined the foundations of MNOC power and subverted their will to resist producer demands. The host governments, especially in the Middle East, exploited these openings, playing one firm against another, threatening all with closure, escalating demands for larger shares of profits, stiffening the terms of service contracts, and colluding in OPEC. Were not the producers nearing a conjunction capable of propelling the incremental process of industry restructuring into a wholly new phase? Producer spokespersons and OPEC did not hide their objectives: total producer power.

A Libyan law of 1965 provided that the assessment of income taxes on oil profits be calculated on the basis of posted prices regardless of the actual price realized on the oil sold. At that time twenty-four companies worked Libyan concessions. SONJ, one of the largest producers, readily agreed to conform to the law but the Oasis group balked. Oasis and other independents lacked international marketing networks and were forced to sell their Libyan oil at discounted prices. Libya had absorbed the discounts as reduced income. To compel acquiescence, Libya's monarchy threatened to halt all exports; the firms gave in.

Hartshorn ascribes pivotal influence to this confrontation. For the first time since the Iranian Revolution, a producer broke a contract. By coercing some companies to accept terms agreed to by other companies, the custom of renegotiation of contracts was abandoned. Alterations in terms were now achievable by command. The fragility of the producing company position was apparent to all. Nor did the hard terms deter a continuing scramble for new concessions in Libya: thirty-seven concessionaires operated in 1968 with an output — 150 mmt — only slightly inferior to that of Iran and Saudi Arabia.[53]

Libya exerted pressure on the MNOCs just as an invigorated sellers market emerged and just prior to renewed warfare between Israel and the Arabs. By 1970, World TPER exceeded that of 1961 by 62 percent, reflecting an absolute increase equivalent to total TPER in 1950 (Table 4.1). While the demand for oil in the industrialized nations rose steadily during the years, 1960–5, demand increased even more sharply between 1965 and 1970. Refined product requirements in the USA, OECD-Europe, and Japan advanced by 300 mmt from 1960 to 1965 and by over 500 mmt from 1965 to 1970.[54] For the years, 1960–70, the West accounted for 68 percent of the global increase in demand for refined products.

Less dramatic but no less crucial than the Six-Day War of 1967 was the declining value of the US dollar, the currency used to fix oil prices and, therefore, to determine the value of producer government revenues. Into the late 1980s, the American dollar continued to weaken. The nation's falling dollar fostered the deterioration of its foreign trade account and stimulated the sale of American assets to foreign owners and the flight of American manufacturing capacity to lower cost industrializing nations such as Korea and Brazil. The "deindustrialization" of America attracted much attention but no policies to counter it. The cost of petroleum imports formed a major component of the burgeoning current accounts deficit from 1970 to 1990.

The falling dollar of the late 1960s reduced producer income. OPEC, articulating the opinion of its members in its "Declaratory Statement" of 1968, demanded the upward adjustment of oil prices as compensation for the dollar's weakness, a weakness made official by US devaluations between 1971 and 1973.[55] The Arab–Israel War of 1967 afforded the opportunity to force higher prices, and to achieve even more.

The Six-Day War of 1967 further radicalized Arab attitudes toward the USA and its western allies. As in 1956–7, Egypt closed the Suez Canal; it remained closed until 1974 at great cost to Egypt. Gradually, the route lost its primacy in oil traffic to supertankers traveling around the Cape of Good Hope. Oil flow through the IPC pipeline was disrupted. The diversion of western hemisphere and Indonesian oil to Europe averted a serious supply crisis. A poorly organized Arab embargo on oil exports to the USA, West Germany, and Britain proved costly and temporarily inconvenient to the latter. As in 1956, prices increased sharply but quickly fell again. Oil from Libya, Algeria, and Nigeria plus unused capacity in Venezuela substituted for embargoed supplies and, after the termination of the political crisis, provided crude that did not require Suez passage. At the peak of the crisis, Saudi Arabia, without enthusiasm, reduced production by 10 percent and threatened to shut down altogether if US aid to Israel persisted. The USA, as Chester observes, ignored this threat.[56]

Remedial steps minimized the war's dislocative effects on oil flow. But the conflict brought the cauldron of Arab nationalism and anti-Zionism to near boiling point and energized the confrontational attitude of the Arab producers. Much had changed since 1965. Greater changes followed at a dizzying pace.

The haphazard use of oil as a political weapon disturbed the conservative regimes of Saudi Arabia, Libya, and Kuwait. In 1968, they created the Organization of Arab Petroleum Exporting Countries (OAPEC) as an instrument to prevent the political use of oil. However, the overthrow in 1969 of the Libyan monarchy, neutral in the war of 1967, by Colonel Qadhafi and the admission of other Arab producers to memberships by 1972 subverted OAPEC's original purpose. Despite Saudi resistance, OAPEC in 1972 thoroughly subscribed to the political exploitation of oil power. It awaited only another war. By 1969, then, Arab and non-Arab producers were prepared to confront the MNOCs through OPEC while OAPEC marshaled its collective power for use against Israel's supporters.[57]

Western MNOCs and governments relinquished control over events in 1970 and after. Chester's study depicts frequent intervention by the US government in behalf of the American MNOCs.[58] But from 1965 forward, the MNOCs steadily retreated before the host government offensive. The US government, despite its presumed influence in Iran and Saudi Arabia, watched passively as producer states encroached upon the managerial rights of the oil companies. The USA responded hardly at all to OPEC or OAPEC. The Libyan Revolution of 1969 spawned a zealous antagonist in Colonel Qadhafi. As with Castro, US efforts to isolate and neutralize Qadhafi were futile. Without a voice in Libya, the USA offered little protection to American oil investments of over $1 billion. Producer state nationalization of American properties in Peru, Indonesia, and Libya generated no useful response. The USA at this time was preoccupied with Vietnam and inflation. In the Middle East, the USA maintained a presence in the Mediterranean and the Persian Gulf, built up the military power of Iran, guaranteed the security of Saudi Arabia, and honored its commitment to Israel. So imperfectly had the USA assimilated the meaning of past events in the Middle East that a House of Representatives report of 1972 concluded that the states of the Persian Gulf were more concerned with local problems than with the Arab–Israel conflict.[59]

American passivity, the bowing of France before Algerian demands, the non-influence of Britain, and the enormous oil dependence of Japan exposed the MNOCs to attack and defeat *en ensemble* and in detail. As Cowhey perceptively observes, the shared interests of the MNOCs and their hosts vanished after 1967. Algeria and Iran reduced their reliance upon the companies. Iraq, in 1968, disposed of them altogether. The hosts realized that new oil from the North Sea or Alaska would not be forthcoming in sufficient volume to dilute their collective strength.[60]

Qadhafi and the Algerian government first sensed these fissures in the MNOC battlements. French dependence upon Algerian oil, peaking at 35 percent of domestic demand in 1963 and still at 27 percent in 1970, and Algeria's ambitious schedule for economic development encouraged the latter's complete nationalization of oil between 1968 and 1971. Elf withdrew totally while CFP accepted the *fait accompli* and reached an agreement with Sonatrach. But the upward ratcheting of the per-barrel tax on Algerian oil greatly reduced the company's margin of profit and drove French receipts from Algeria down to 7 percent of total imports in 1971. The end of France's preferred position in Algeria forced France into greater oil dependency upon Libya and other Middle Eastern states. This, coupled with the events of 1970–3, greatly enhanced the attractiveness of nuclear power.[61]

Oil production advanced more rapidly in Libya during the 1960s than in other producing countries (Table 4.6). Western Europe looked to

Libya as a primary source of supply; in 1970, Italy received 35 percent of crude imports from Libya, Britain, 25 percent, France, 14 percent, and West Germany, 12 percent. The Libyan monarchy had wisely divided the earliest concessions among seven producing groups, of which the Oasis consortium, Oxy, and SONJ accounted for 66 percent of liftings in 1970. Qadhafi, flushed with the success of the 1969 *coup* and ardently anti-Zionist and anti-western, challenged the concession-aires in 1970 over the issue of price and production.

Qadhafi demanded an increase in posted prices. Oxy and others initially refused, whereupon Qadhafi ordered a stringent reduction in Oxy's production from 800,000 barrels daily to 400,000. Completely dependent upon Libyan production, Occidental sought to purchase its requirements from SONJ. According to Roncaglia, Jersey refused, thereby committing a serious blunder, the consequence of a myopic view of Oxy as a competitor rather than as a defender of operator in-terests. Wall, however, offers a different and better documented ac-count. Oxy sought oil at cost. Jersey demurred, but offered oil at the lowest contract price and, additionally, volunteered to help Oxy obtain similarly priced oil from RDS. Oxy snubbed this offer, later claiming that SONJ's refusal to sell forced the capitulation of all concessionaires to Qadhafi's terms. Jersey, however, insisted that even a sale at cost would not have deterred Qadhafi who was willing to assume great losses to achieve his goal. As he said, "we must show we are the masters here." Roncaglia, then, identifies MNOC disunity as the reason for Libya's success. Wall, adopting Jersey's view, discounts the utility of MNOC cooperation in this instance.[62]

Qadhafi's coercive tactics shattered the current price structure. The Persian Gulf states and Venezuela imposed similar terms. In one rapid assault, the MNOCs were denuded of authority over price and pro-duction. With the MNOCs reeling, OPEC seized the opportunity to demand direct producer government negotiations with all the com-panies. The MNOCs favored a single bargaining encounter but OPEC insisted on regional negotiations, one for North Africa at Tripoli and the other for Persian Gulf states in Teheran. OPEC shrewdly separated the negotiations involving the volatile Qadhafi and the radical Algerians from those of the more conservative Arabian Peninsular states and non-Arab Iran. The MNOCs would not be able to pit those two groups against one another. The companies deferred to OPEC's ultimatum.

The consequences of the Tripoli and Teheran agreements of 1971, soon overshadowed by the Yom Kippur War of 1973, the OAPEC embargo, and the price explosion forced by OPEC, were nonetheless momentous. The producers achieved the power to legislate price in-creases. Posted prices were jacked up in 1972 and 1973 by over $1 per barrel. Equally critical, tax rates moved to an average of at least 55 percent for all producers, with escalator clauses adopted to compensate for inflation. The improved bargaining position of the hosts encouraged them to demand larger equity rights in established concessions. When the companies balked at this, Saudi Arabia threatened to reduce Aramco's liftings. Aramco then agreed to sell a 20 percent interest to Saudi Arabia and to grant the latter the option of raising that equity to 51 percent by 1982. In 1973, similar terms were accorded to other Arabian Peninsula states. With the oil industry in Algeria, Iraq, and Iran already nationalized and Libya in process, the remaining producer states now embarked along that path. In Venezuela, new legislation in 1971 and 1972 assigned to the state penultimate control over the industry with the final transfer of ownership completed in 1975.

Finally, guided by Libya's imposition in 1971 of strict production controls, other states recognized oil as a non-replenishable resource. They discovered that income could be raised without increasing production. Libya permitted the withdrawal of 32 percent less crude in 1972 than in 1970 and reduced liftings again in 1973 and 1974. The Kuwait Oil Company's planned increases in production for 1971 were restricted by the government; production stabilized between 1970 and 1973 and actually fell in 1974 and 1975.[63]

Alnasrawi characterizes OPEC as a follower in all of this. However, it did accelerate action, exploiting Libya's successes by orchestrating the Tripoli and Teheran conferences. At the Caracas meeting of 1970, OPEC adopted a minimum 55 percent tax rate. One year later, OPEC urged members to demand greater equity shares. Perhaps, as Odell suggests, the MNOCs accepted the principle of collective bargaining through OPEC, believing that the agreements reached would more likely be honored by individual members. Indisputably, OPEC's status was markedly enhanced between 1960 and 1972.[64]

Conclusion

The producer states seized power from the MNOCs during the 1960s while western governments watched helplessly. A number of Arab producers, first united in the Arab League and then in OAPEC, challenged western support of Israel. The unilateral cut in posted prices in 1959–60 produced OPEC. These producer actions engendered a weak response in the West and no motion toward consumer government cooperation. By 1971, as Levy asserts, the MNOCs were required to act as if they were owned by the host states.

Producers generated the initiatives that shifted power in their favor.

Each MNOC protected its interests as best it could, viewing other firms as adversaries rather than as firms entangled in the same web. Acquiescence to each demand held out the hope that the final demand had been made. Western governments were, in Tugenhadt and Hamilton's view, unwilling to jeopardize supply by taking the side of the MNOCs. Consumer governments were incapable of substantially reducing demand for oil or of stockpiling oil against future contingencies.

Finding the causes of MNOC–western vulnerability in the entry of newcomers in the international oil business, mandatory US import quotas, or, as with Levy, in the machinations of the Soviet Union is less rewarding than charting the consequences of the swollen energy demands of the industrialized states, the subject of the next chapter. It is also essential to understand producer government objectives.[65] Nationalism and anti-Zionism combined with specific development objectives to motivate some producers to confront the MNOCs. Peru, Iran, and Indonesia were no less adversarial toward the domineering MNOCs than the Arab front line states. While often permitting expectations to overreach capabilities, the host nations correctly perceived increasing oil revenues as a prerequisite of autonomous economic growth. Individually and through OPEC, they won not only higher revenues but control over price and production — power.

Notes

1. D.S. Painter, *Oil and the American Century. The Political Economy of US Foreign Oil Policy, 1941–1954*, Baltimore: The Johns Hopkins University Press (1986), p. 52; for the text of the treaty, see O. Caroe, *Wells of Power: The Oilfields of South-Western Asia, A Regional and Global Study*, London: Macmillan (1951), pp. 222–7.
2. De Golyer and MacNaughton, *Twentieth Century Petroleum Statistics, 1986*, Dallas, Texas: De Golyer and MacNaughton (1986), pp. 6, 18, 60; Z. Mikdashi, *A Financial Analysis of Middle Eastern Oil Concessions, 1901–1965*, New York: Praeger (1966), pp. 321–2.
3. R.M. Burnell and A.J. Cottrell, *Politics, Oil, and the Western Mediterranean*, Beverly Hills, Calif.: Sage (1973), p. 72; M.S. Al-Otaiba, *OPEC and the Petroleum Industry*, London: Croom Helm (1975), pp. 97–9; H. Mendershausen, *Coping with the Oil Crisis*, Baltimore: The Johns Hopkins University Press for Resources for the Future (1976), pp. 28–9; F.A. Olaloku, *Structure of the Nigerian Economy*, London: Macmillan (1979), pp. 56–8; S.R. Pearson, *Petroleum and the Nigerian Economy*, Stanford, Calif.: Stanford University Press (1970), pp. 13–14.
4. Naphtha is the basic source for ethylene, butadiene, ammonia, and other chemical feedstocks; middle distillates include domestic and jet kerosene, gas oils, and diesel fuels.
5. M.I. Goldman, *The Enigma of Soviet Petroleum: Half-Full or Half-Empty*,

London: Allen & Unwin (1980), pp. 33–4, 44–8; D. Park, *Oil & Gas in Comecon Countries*, London: Kegan Paul (1979), pp. 40, 54–6, 61–4, 78–9; E.A. Hewitt, *Energy, Economics, and Foreign Policy in the Soviet Union*, Washington, DC: The Brookings Institution (1984), pp. 65–70. President Reagan's offensive against the Soviet–Western European gas deal is discussed in Chapter 9.

6. De Golyer and MacNaughton, *1986*, pp. 20, 26; A.J. Pinelo, *The Multinational Corporations as a Force in Latin American Politics: A Case Study of the International Petroleum Company in Peru*, New York: Praeger (1973), pp. 70–1; G. Coronel, *The Nationalization of the Venezuelan Oil Industry, from Technocratic Success to Political Failure*, Lexington, Mass.: Lexington Books (1983), p. 27; E. Lieuwen, "The Politics of Energy in Venezuela," in J.D. Wirth, ed., *Latin American Oil Companies and the Politics of Energy*, Lincoln, Nebr.: University of Nebraska Press (1985), pp. 206–11; J.W. Mullen, *Energy in Latin America: The Historical Record*, Santiago de Chile: CEPAL (1978), pp. 24–8; A.J. Bermúdez, *The Mexican National Petroleum Industry: A Case Study in Nationalization*, Stanford, Calif.: Institute of Hispanic American and Luso-Brazilian Studies (1963), p. 45; G. Philip, *Oil and Politics in Latin America. Nationalist Movements and State Companies*, Cambridge: Cambridge University Press (1982), pp. 87–8.

7. For this and the above two paragraphs: I. Kuczynski, *British Offshore Oil and Gas Policy*, New York: Garland Publishing (1982), pp. 2-26–27, 6-13–14, 7-20–23; O. Noreng, *The Oil Industry and Government Policy in the North Sea*, London: Croom Helm (1980), pp. 14–23, 39–42, 59, *passim*; J.C. Ausland, *Norway, Oil, and Foreign Policy*, Boulder, Colo.: Westview Press (1979), pp. 68–71; L.E. Grayson, *National Oil Companies*, New York: Wiley (1981), pp. 175–80.

8. Noreng, *Oil in the North Sea*, pp. 87–8.

9. M. Peebles, *Evolution of the Gas Industry*, London: Macmillan (1980), pp. 113, 138–42; J.D. Davis, *Blue Gold: The Political Economy of Natural Gas*, London: Allen & Unwin (1984), pp. 156–64; J. Russell, *Geopolitics of Natural Gas*, Cambridge, Mass.: Ballinger (1983), p. 66; IEA, *Energy Balances of OECD Countries, 1970/1982*, Paris: OECD/IEA (1984), pp. 387–9, 404.

10. R.A. Ajami, *Arab Response to the Multinationals*, New York: Praeger (1979), pp. 17–20; N.A. White, *Financing the International Petroleum Industry*, London: Graham & Trotman (1978), p. 18; G. Luciani, *The Oil Companies and the Arab World*, London: Croom Helm (1984), p. 11; Al-Otaiba, *OPEC*, pp. 97–9.

11. For the above two paragraphs: G. Jenkins, *Oil Economist's Handbook 1984*, London: Applied Science Publications Ltd (1984), pp. 106–7; Mullen, *Energy in Latin America*, pp. 45–6; B. Dasgupta, *The Oil Industry in India, Some Economic Aspects*, London: Frank Cass (1971), pp. 178–9; W.A. Leeman, *The Price of Middle East Oil: An Essay in Political Economy*, Ithaca, New York: Cornell University Press (1962), p. 42; M.A. Adelman, *The World Petroleum Market*, Baltimore: The Johns Hopkins University Press for Resources for the Future (1972), p. 96.

12. White, *Financing International Petroleum*, p. 18; Park, *Oil & Gas*, p. 20; Mendershausen, *The Oil Crisis*, p. 53.

13. H. Maull, *Europe and World Energy*, London: Butterworth (1980), pp.

212–13; P.F. Cowhey, *The Problem of Plenty: Energy Policy and International Politics*, Berkeley: University of California Press (1985), pp. 16–17, 96–100, 112; P. Odell, *Oil and World Power*, 7th edn, Harmondsworth, Middlesex: Penguin (1983), pp. 17–22, 27, 31–2, 37; Mendershausen, *The Oil Crisis*, pp. 4–6.

14. Painter, *Oil and the American Century*, p. 207; G.D. Nash, *United States Oil Policy, 1890–1964: Business and Government in Twentieth Century America*, Pittsburgh: University of Pittsburgh Press (1968); H. Madelin, *Oil and Politics*, translated by M. Totman, Farnborough: Saxon House (1975), p. 199; C. Tugendhat and A. Hamilton, *Oil, the biggest business*, London: Methuen (1975), pp. 147–9, 289–90: Leeman, *Price of Middle East Oil*, pp. 38–9.
15. "World Politics and International Energy Markets," *International Organization*, 41 (Winter 1987), pp. 125–49.
16. Mendershausen, *The Oil Crisis*; Noreng, *Oil Politics in the 1980s*, New York: McGraw-Hill (1978)
17. E. Penrose, ed., *The Large International Firms in Developing Countries: The International Petroleum Industry*, London: Allen & Unwin (1968).
18. Wilson, "World Politics," pp. 135–6.
19. W. Quandt, *Saudi Arabia in the 1980s*, Washington, DC: The Brookings Institution (1981); D. Yergin and M. Hillenbrand, eds, *Global Insecurity: Beyond Energy Future, A Strategy for Political and Economic Survival in the 1980s*, Harmondsworth, Middlesex: Penguin (1983).
20. Wilson, "World Politics," pp. 144–7.
21. Mendershausen, *The Oil Crisis*, pp. 53–4; Al-Otaiba, *OPEC*, pp. 97–9; Borrell and Cottrell, *Oil and the Mediterranean*, p. 72.
22. Mendershausen, *The Oil Crisis*, pp. 26–9; M. Tanzer and S.Z. Zorn, *Energy Update: Oil in the Late Twentieth Century*. New York: Monthly Review Press (1985), pp. 64–6; Grayson, *National Oil Companies*, pp. 24–8, 107–13; J.E. Hartshorn, *Politics and World Oil Economics. An Account of the International Oil Industry and Its Political Environment*, New York: Praeger (1967), pp. 278–81; Y-l. Wu, *Japan's Search for Oil: A Case Study on Economic Nationalism and International Security*, Stanford: Hoover Institution Press (1977), pp. 62–9; Luciani, *Oil Companies and the Arab World*, p. 137.
23. Only those authors not previously cited in this chapter are now cited: W.J. Barber, "The Eisenhower Energy Policy: Reluctant Intervention," in C.D. Goodwin, ed., *Energy Policy in Perspective: Today's Problems, Yesterday's Solutions*, Washington, DC: The Brookings Institution (1981), pp. 205–86; J.M. Blair, *The Control of Oil*, New York: Vintage Books (1978); D. Gisselquist, *Oil Prices and Trade Deficits: US Conflicts with Japan and West Germany*, New York: Praeger (1979); G.W. Hoffman, *The European Energy Challenge, East and West*, Durham, N.C.: Duke University Press (1985); B.W. Jentleson, *Pipeline Politics: The Complex Political Economy of East–West Energy Trade*, Ithaca, New York: Cornell University Press (1986); S.H. Longrigg, *Oil in the Middle East: Its Discovery and Development*, London: Oxford University Press (1961); S.G. Rabe, *The Road to OPEC: United States Relations with Venezuela, 1919–1976*, Austin: University of Texas Press (1982); R.H.K. Vietor, *Energy policy in America since 1945: A study of business–government relations*, Cambridge: Cambridge University Press (1984).

24. Jenkins, *Oil Handbook 1985*, pp. 21, 23, 35.
25. Rabe, *Road to OPEC*, 161–76; De Golyer and MacNaughton, *1986*, pp. 6, 9.
26. *Ibid.*, p. 51.
27. Jenkins, *Oil Handbook 1984*, pp. 20–1, 35, 37, 42; De Golyer and Mac-Naughton, *1984*, pp. 98–9; Maull, *Europe and World Energy*, p. 208. In the USA, market demand prorationing was initiated in 1935 with the organization of the Interstate Oil Compact. Actually, each state member of IOC determined its own quota. Moral suasion kept the states more or less in line.
28. W.J. Levy in M. Conant, ed., *Oil Strategy and Politics, 1941–1981*, Boulder, Colo.: Westview Press (1982), pp. 153–4; Park, *Oil & Gas*, p. 48; Hartshorn, *Politics and World Oil*, pp. 235–41; Goldman, *Enigma of Soviet Petroleum*, p. 23.
29. Dasgupta, *Oil Industry in India*, pp. 186, 192–3.
30. Cowhey, *The Problems of Plenty*, Chapters 2 and 10; A. Roncaglia, *The International Oil Market: A Case of Trilateral Oligopoly*, J.A. Kregel, ed., Basingstoke: Macmillan (1985), pp. 4–5.
31. H.L. Lax, *Political Risk in the International Oil and Gas Industry*, Boston: International Human Resources Development Corporation (1983), pp. 32–6; H. Maull, *Energy, Minerals, and Western Security*, Baltimore: The Johns Hopkins University Press (1984), pp. 8–18; E.L. Morse, "Introduction: The International Management of Resources," in R.W. Arad *et al.*, *Sharing Global Resources*, New York: McGraw-Hill (1979), pp. 6–16.
32. D. Hirst, *Oil and Public Opinion in the Middle East*, London: Faber and Faber (1966), pp. 18–26, 35–7; Penrose, ed., *International Petroleum Industry*, p. 275; C.T. Goodsell, *American Corporations and Peruvian Politics*, Cambridge: Harvard University Press (1974), pp. 8–9, 12–17; N.S. Fatemi, *Oil Diplomacy: Powderkeg in Iran*, New York: Whittier Books (1954), xxv–xxvi, *passim*; Mikdashi, *Middle Eastern Oil Concessions*, pp. 227–38; A. Alnasrawi, *OPEC in a Changing World Economy*, Baltimore: The Johns Hopkins University Press (1985), pp. 7–8, 27, *passim*; J. Salazar-Carrillo, *Oil in the Economic Development of Venezuela*, New York: Praeger (1976), pp. 72–7, *passim*; Hartshorn, *Politics and World Oil*, pp. 30, 158–64.
33. For the above three paragraphs: Alnasrawi, *OPEC*, p. 111; Maull, *Europe and World Energy*, p. 134; Salazar-Carrillo, *Oil in Venezuela*, pp. 77, 102, 135; D.H. Finnie, *Desert Enterprise: The Middle East Oil Industry and Its Local Environment*, Cambridge: Harvard University Press (1958), p. 153.
34. Goodsell, *American Corporations and Peruvian Politics*, pp. 7–9; Ajami, *Arab Response to Multinationals*, pp. 8–14; Burrell and Cottrell, *Oil and the Mediterranean*, p. 46; US Bureau of the Census, *Historical Statistics of the United States, Colonial Times to 1970, Bicentennial Edition, Part 1*, Washington, DC: USGPO (1975), p. 870; Rabe, *The Road to OPEC*, pp. 157–8, 195; Lieuwen, "Politics of Energy in Venezuela," pp. 209–16; Coronel, *Nationalization of Venezuelan Oil*, pp. 28–31.
35. For the above two paragraphs: Madelin, *Oil and Politics*, p. 161; Burrell and Cottrell, *Oil and the Mediterranean*, pp. 52–4; F. Fesharaki, *Development of the Iranian Oil Industry: International and Domestic Aspects*, New York: Praeger (1976), pp. 130–48, 211–14; W.W. Rostow, *The World Economy: History and Prospect*, Austin: University of Texas Press

(1978), pp. 500–4; P.L. Ferrari *et al.*, *US Arms Exports: Policies and Contractors*, Washington DC: Investor Responsibility Research Center (1987), pp. 101–2.

36. IEA, *Energy Balances of Developing Countries, 1971/1982*, Paris: OECD/IEA (1984), pp. 114–26; F.A. Olaloku, *Structure of the Nigerian Economy*, *passim*; Pearson, *Petroleum and Nigerian Economy*, *passim*; C. Wilcox *et al.*, *Economies of the World Today, Their Organization, Development, and Performance*, New York: Harcourt, Brace & World (1966), pp. 127–47; C.O. Ikporukpo, "Petroleum Exploration and the Socio-Economic Environment in Nigeria," *International Journal of Environmental Studies*, 21. no. 2 (1983), pp. 193–203.

37. Salazar-Carrillo, *Oil in Venezuela*, *passim*; Rabe, *Road to OPEC*, pp. 131–4, 166–7; Lieuwen, "Politics of Energy in Venezuela", pp. 209–16; John V. Lombardi, *Venezuela: The Search for Order, The Dream of Progress*, New York: Oxford University Press (1982), pp. 36–9.

38. Mullen, *Energy in Latin America*, pp. 29–35, Fesharaki, *Iranian Oil Industry*, pp. 211–14; Luciani, *Oil Companies and the Arab World*, p. 115; II. Collier, *Developing Electric Power: Thirty Years of World Bank Experience*, Baltimore: The Johns Hopkins University Press for the World Bank (1984), p. 172.

39. Pearson, *Petroleum and Nigerian Economy*, p. 164; L. Howell and M. Morrow, *Asia, Oil Politics, and the Energy Crisis: The Haves and the Have-Nots*, New York: IDOC/North America (1974), pp. 73–104; C.C. Stamos, Jr., "Energy and Development in Latin America," *Latin American Research Review*, XXI. no. 1 (1986), p. 198, Maull, *Europe and World Energy*, p. 116.

40. Leeman, *Price of Middle East Oil*, pp. 212–17.

41. Quoted in A. Al-Sowayegh, *Arab Petropolitics*, London: Croom Helm (1984), p. 13.

42. Leeman, *Price of Middle East Oil*, pp. 189–94; Al-Otaiba, *OPEC*, pp. 158–9.

43. Fesharaki, *Iranian Oil Industry*, pp. 73–8; Madelin, *Oil and Politics*, pp. 101–2; *Africa South of the Sahara 1987*, 16th edn, London: Europa Publications (1987), p. 777.

44. De Golyer and MacNaughton, *1986*, p. 6; Philip, *Oil and Politics*, pp. 371–82, 387–400, 481–3; J.D. Wirth, "Setting the Brazilian Agenda, 1936–1953," in J.D. Wirth, ed., *Latin American Oil Companies*, pp. 134–8.

45. E.W. Chester, *United States Oil Policy and Diplomacy: A Twentieth Century Overview*, Westport, Conn.: Greenwood Press (1983), pp. 303–5; M. Nishahara, *The Japanese and Sukarno's Indonesia: Tokyo–Jakarta Relations, 1951–1966*, Honolulu: University Press of Hawaii (1976), pp. 120–1; Howell and Morrow, *Asia and Energy*, pp. 76–7, 157; I.M. Torrens, *Changing Structures in the World Oil Market*, Paris: The Atlantic Institute for International Affairs (1980), pp. 11–12.

46. Fesharaki, *Iranian Oil Industry*, pp. 73–89; Al-Otaiba, *OPEC*, pp. 92–4; Lieuwen, "Politics of Energy in Venezuela," pp. 206–7; Coronel, *Nationalization of Venezuelan Oil*, p. 29; Philip, *Oil and Politics*, pp. 105–13.

47. Nishahara, *Japan and Indonesia*, pp. 118–21.

48. N. Lucas, *Western European Energy Policies: A Comparative Study of the Influence of Institutional Structure on Technical Change*, Oxford:

Clarendon Press (1985), pp. 26–7; Madelin, *Oil and Politics*, pp. 102–3, 109–11.

49. Z. Mikdashi, *The International Politics of Natural Resources*, Ithaca, New York: Cornell University Press (1976), p. 148; Odell, *Oil and World Power*, pp. 95–8.

50. Pinelo, *International Petroleum Company in Peru*, p. 145, *passim*; Goodsell, *American Corporations and Peruvian Politics*, pp. 52–4, 217–22.

51. A.L. Danielsen, *The Evolution of OPEC*, New York: Harcourt, Brace, Jovanovich (1982) is, in my view, the best study of OPEC.

52. For the above four paragraphs: *ibid.*, pp. 128, 247–8; Alnasrawi, *OPEC*, pp. 73–82; Hartshorn, *Politics and World Oil*, pp. 158–64, 336; Al-Otaiba, *OPEC*, pp. 112–17, 141–52, 161–5; Tugenhadt, *Oil*, pp. 199–202; *OPEC Oil Report, 1977*, London: Petroleum Economist (1978), pp. 9–10; Lax, *Risk in International Oil and Gas*, pp. 27–8; A.D. Johany, *The Myth of the OPEC Cartel: The Role of Saudi Arabia*, New York: Wiley (1980), pp. 27–8.

53. Hartshorn, *Politics and World Oil*, pp. 17–26; Al-Otaiba, *OPEC*, pp. 97–9; Chester, *US Oil Policy*, p. 272; De Golyer and MacNaughton, *1986*, pp. 9–10.

54. *Ibid.*, p. 16.

55. Al-Otaiba, *OPEC*, pp. 154–6; Alnasrawi, *OPEC*, p. 67; *OPEC Oil Report 1977*, p. 10.

56. Chester, *US Oil Policy*, pp. 100–1, 213, 246–8; Odell, *Oil and World Power*, pp. 198–200; Penrose, *International Petroleum Industry*, p. 85; Adelman, *World Petroleum Market*, p. 160.

57. Danielsen, *Evolution of OPEC*, pp. 153–4; Al-Sowayegh, *Arab Petropolitics*, pp. 89, 99–101; A. Machow, *OAPEC, an international organization for economic cooperation and an instrument for regional integration*, translated by A. Melville, Paris: Berger-Levrault (1982), pp. 43–7.

58. Chester, *US Oil Policy*, pp. 314–17.

59. United States House of Representatives. Committee on Foreign Affairs, Subcommittee on the Near East, *The United States and the Persian Gulf, September 29, 1972*, 92nd Congress, 2nd session, Washington, DC: USGPO (1972), pp. 7–9.

60. Cowhey, *The Problem of Plenty*, pp. 107–8.

61. Grayson, *National Oil Companies*, pp. 40, 52–4; Lucas, *European Energy Policies*, pp. 26–7; Madelin, *Oil and Politics*, pp. 102–3; Luciani, *Oil Companies and the Arab World*, pp. 51–4; Adelman, *World Petroleum Market*, p. 235.

62. Roncaglia, *International Oil Market*, p. 79; B.H. Wall, *Growth in a Changing Environment: A History of Standard Oil Company (New Jersey) Exxon Corporation, 1950–1975*, New York: McGraw-Hill (1988), pp. 705–7.

63. *BP statistical review of world energy 1971*; B.R. Mitchell, ed., European Historical Statistics, 2nd revised edn, London: Macmillan (1981), pp. 439, 441–3; Burrell and Cottrell, *Oil and the Mediterranean*, pp. 43–4, 57; Al-Otaiba, *OPEC*, pp. 97–9, 165–75; Tugenhadt, *Oil*, pp. 183–95; Coronel, *Nationalization of Venezuelan Oil*, pp. 35–8; *OPEC Oil Report 1977*, pp. 11–13; Chester, *US Oil Policy*, pp. 246–8; De Golyer and MacNaughton, *1986*, pp. 9–10.

64. Alnasrawi, *OPEC*, pp. 6–7; *OPEC Oil Report 1977*, pp. 12–13; Odell, *Oil and World Power*, p. 218.
65. For the final three paragraphs: Levy in Conant, ed., *Oil Strategy*, pp. 115–17; Tugenhadt, *Oil*, pp. 197–8; Adelman, *World Petroleum Market*, pp. 215–16.

6

Cheap energy, security, and the industrialized nations, 1960–73

With the industrialized states far in advance, the world economy experienced exponential growth rates between 1950 and 1970. Cheap food, raw materials, and energy nourished a boom in the advanced economies and spurred rapid industrial progress in such modernizing nations as South Korea, Brazil, and Argentina. World population growth, a mixed blessing, averaged 2 to 4 percent annually while economic output advanced at an annual rate of 4 to 5 percent. Sustained growth in the industrialized states seemed assured; green revolutions and expectations of steady economic growth promised unprecedented prosperity in the lesser developed countries. The failure of the LDCs to realize their hopes further embittered relations between the so-called North and South. In the West, where performance appeared to satisfy wants, a confident atmosphere prevailed.

However, the dominant position of the USA in the world economy, the product of its industrial and military might, sagged during the late 1960s. The cost of war in Vietnam and new social programs at home swelled budgetary deficits just as stiff competition in international markets and accelerating foreign penetration of domestic markets occasioned worrisome balance of payments deficits. A weakening US dollar triggered an import spree; wages and interest rates rose and labor productivity fell. The global consequences of American economic and political frailty were manifest during the 1970s and 1980s.[1]

Energy policy common denominators

The energy policies of the industrialized states reflected the conviction that rapid economic growth was the norm. Within those states, such high energy intensive industries as chemicals–plastics and light metals and the mass producers of consumer goods led the charge during this prosperous period. With fuel and other raw materials prices stable or declining, few devoted much attention to the question of finite resources. A surfeit of food and fuel seemed available. While the leading industrial and military nations necessarily factored resources into calculations of national security, national policies in the USA, western Europe, and Japan promoted consumption and the virtually uninhibited use of resources. Visions of long-term abundance made tolerable increasing energy import dependence and submerged warnings of future scarcity.

Energy deficient states, now including the USA, relied upon market mechanisms and the subtle touch of diplomacy and economic aid to maintain access to raw materials. Supremely confident in the power of technology, the major consumers of raw materials assumed that materials substitution (plastics for scarce metals) and efficiency improvements in the burning of fuels and in reducing ores to usable metals would dramatically extend the life of mineral resources. Few challenged the dogma that energy at the cheapest price was a positive good for national economics.

Cheap and abundant energy and raw materials over the long run formed the common denominators linking the economic policies and development goals of both advanced and industrializing states. The LDCs, too, imbibed this optimistic spirit. In general, voters in the stable democracies emphatically demanded and endorsed policies productive of higher wages, more jobs, improved economic security, and controlled inflation. The age of high mass consumption, anticipated by Rostow, enshrined by Galbraith, and eyed ruefully by Riesman and Bell precluded serious consideration of possible resource shortages.[2]

High living in the USA and its emulation in western Europe muzzled concern over inequities in the international distribution of wealth. Americans, having rediscovered poverty at home, focused on its amelioration. In Japan, less inclined than the West to induce high domestic consumption of consumer goods, workers and managers worked so efficiently that their high quality and low cost consumer goods flooded occidental markets. In the West, rising incomes for more people even nurtured, and especially in the USA, a politically potent environmental protection movement. Masses of people, now able to vacation at the seaside or lake, demanded clean water. During the 1960s and early 1970s, US administrations implemented a host of environmental protection policies mandated by a plethora of laws designed to protect the air, water, and land. These policies, and similar ones later adopted in western Europe, had proved inadequate by the 1980s. The crucial weakness with virtually all of the early environmental laws was that they did not yield an absolute decline in fossil fuel burning.

OECD-Europe, the USA, and Japan accounted for one-half of the global growth of total primary energy requirements (TPER) from 1950 to 1970. Table 6.1 displays the significant shares of TPER ascribable to the West and to the Soviet bloc and verifies the rapid switch from coal to oil as well as the greater employment of natural gas. A glance back to Table 4.5 suggests that the USA and the USSR accounted for the larger part of the natural gas increase shown in Table 6.1. The transition from coal to oil occurred swiftly within OECD (Tables 4.4 and 6.6) but much more slowly in Eastern Europe.[3]

The national energy policies of the leading OECD states during the 1950s and the 1960s reflected acceptance of common assumptions concerning present and future availability and costs of energy. Of course, each country shaped policies to conform to its individual resource endowment, energy requirements, and political customs. The fact that the governments of France, Great Britain, and Italy owned or

Table 6.1   Global and national total primary energy requirements, 1950–75

	1950	1960	1970	1973	1975
World TPER[1]	2059	3185	5170	5923	5957
Percentage of:					
Solid fuels	62	48	32	30	29
Oil	25	33	43	47	46
Natural gas	1	16	19	19	18
Nuclear	0	<1	2	2	6
Hydroelectric	<1	2	2	2	6
Percentage share of World TPER:					
USA	40	33	30	29	28
OECD-Europe	22	20	21	20	19
Japan	2	3	5	6	6
USSR	12	14	14	15	16
Eastern Europe	6	7	6[2]	6	7
All Others	18	23	24	24	24

[1] All TPER in million metric tons oil equivalent
[2] 1971

Sources: BP Statistical Review of World Energy, June 1986, pp. 31–3, passim; IEA, *Energy Balances of OECD Countries, 1970/1982,* Paris: OECD/IEA (1984), pp. 387–9, 404; D. Park, *Oil and Gas in Comecon Countries,* London: Kegan Paul (1979), p. 45; UN, *World Energy Supplies, 1955–58,* New York: UN (1963), p. 35; *ibid., 1960–1963* (1965), p. 33; *ibid., 1961–1970* (1972), pp. 55, 57; G. Jenkins, *Oil Economist's Handbook 1985,* London: Elsevier (1985), pp. 125–7; J. Darmstadter *et al., Energy in the World Economy. A Statistical Review of Trends in Output, Trade, and Consumption Since 1925,* Baltimore: The Johns Hopkins Press for Resources for the Future (1971), pp. 622–32.

Table 6.2 Net energy imports as percentage of TPER for OECD states, 1960–75

	1960	1965	1970	1973	1975
USA	6	8	9	17	17
Japan	40	67	86	93	91
OECD-Europe	35	50	63	65	59
West Germany	11	34	49	55	56
Britain	26	37	47	48	44
Netherlands	61	78	60	26	−6
Italy	65	83	85	87	83
France	44	56	72	81	75

Source: IEA, *Energy Balances for OECD Countries, 1970/1982,* Paris: OECD/IEA (1984), pp. 387–9, 404.

controlled most of their energy industries did not yield results markedly different from the less interventionist governments of West Germany and the USA. The search for secure and cheap energy supplies impelled each nation to react to Middle Eastern instability and producer government demands, the policies of MNOCs, the rundown of the coal industry, the uncertainties of nuclear energy, and to other energy matters impinging upon national security.

France, Italy, and Japan sponsored adventurous projects to provide oil produced by nationally controlled firms. The USA and West Germany relied wholly on the MNOCs for their oil imports. As Table 6.2 attests, these divergent policies produced strikingly similar results. Energy import dependence, mirroring enormous increases in petroleum imports (Table 6.3), escalated steeply in western Europe and Japan. America's enormous production of energy masked the impact on the dependency ratio of a doubling of oil imports during the 1960s. The sudden turnaround in Holland's situation and the initial reversal in Britain's position resulted from the development of North Sea gas and oil, a boon that would have occurred without direct government participation.

Indigenous political structures and practices influenced energy policy outcomes. In the coal producing states of western Europe sensitivity to the well-being of the coal industry, virtually the only source of domestic energy, and the political power of sizable miner unions somewhat retarded the displacement of coal by other fuels. But until the oil price hikes of 1973 and after, the lure of cheap oil, the increasing availability of natural gas, and the promises of nuclear energy were difficult to resist. In the USA, regulated and artificially low natural gas prices, relatively cheap domestic and imported oil, huge public subsidies for nuclear power, and consumer preferences critically affected the unprotected coal industry.

Each state recognized the relationship between energy costs and

Table 6.3 Net national crude oil and product imports, 1955−73 (million metric tons)

	1955	1960	1965	1970	1973
USA	45	85	116	160	305
Japan	12[1]	30	89	211	292
OECD-Europe	117	201	392	657	776
West Germany	7	26	68	118	139
Britain	31	50	76	106	117
Belgium and Netherlands	10	16	33	63	86
Italy	12	21	49	83	97
France	20	27	52	96	130
World	300	456	759	1263	1656[2]
Percentage rows 1−3 to World	58	69	79	81	83

[1] 1956
[2] 1974

Sources: DeGolyer and MacNaughton, *Twentieth Century Petroleum Statistics 1986*, Dallas, Tex.: DeGolyer and MacNaughton (1984), pp. 58−9; Y. Matsumura, *Japan's Economic Growth, 1945−1960*, Tokyo: Tokyo News Service Ltd (1961), p. 89; G. Jenkins, *Oil Economist's Handbook 1985*, London: Elsevier (1985), p. 57; B.R. Mitchell, ed., *European Historical Statistics, 1750−1975*, 2nd revised edn, London: Macmillan (1981), pp. 442−3.

industrial output. In iron and steel, chemicals and petrochemicals, in aluminum and other industries applying electrolytic processes or other process heat, the costs of energy to total input could reach 25 or 30 percent. In the transportation industries the costs of energy were still higher. The industrial nations, particularly those heavily reliant upon foreign trade such as West Germany and Japan, would not increase energy input costs by buffering domestic coal industries against oil or natural gas.[4]

In the following pages, I discuss the generally parallel evolution of national energy mixes in the leading economies and the tactics that led to similarity. The chapter will conclude with a discussion of the international trade in thermal electric equipment and the changing circumstances that first retarded and then stimulated the growth of nuclear power, a technology that promised cheap, safe, and reliable power.

The western European energy equation

European economic recovery from the destruction of World War II was in full swing by the late 1950s and the momentum was sustained during the 1960s. The economies of western Europe surged forward, although the UK experienced less dramatic and, to many Britons, inadequate progress. Cities were rebuilt, transportation networks re-established and modernized, and new industries emerged and older industries were revitalized. Crude steel output in West Germany almost tripled between 1950 and 1960 and did triple in Italy. In France, steel production rose twofold during that decade. Belgium and the Netherlands experienced similar rates of growth. Less spectacular but still impressive growth occurred from 1960 to 1970. Britain, however, recorded lower growth rates in steel and in other sectors of the economy.

Foreign trade increased markedly in Germany, France, Italy, the Low Countries, Denmark, and Norway. While serious balance of payments deficits retarded British domestic growth and were a recurrent problem in France and Italy, Germany's industrial prowess and foreign demand for her products fashioned a surplus in the external trade account. Throughout western Europe, gross national product ascended more rapidly than in the USA, as did *per capita* GNP. European standards of living approached the heights of American standards of living and far exceeded those of other nations and regions.[5]

The rebuilding of Continental Europe's economic and social infrastructure required massive inputs of energy. OECD-Europe's TPER expanded from 624 million metric tons oil equivalent (mtoe) in 1960 to slightly over 1.2 billion mtoe in 1973, an increase of 92 percent. In 1960, Germany consumed 114 percent more energy than in 1950 and consumption climbed an additional 82 percent by 1973. French energy use in 1960 exceeded use in 1950 by 64 percent; from 1960 to 1973, French TPER rose by 108 percent. Italy's TPER advanced fivefold between 1955 and 1973, with a tripling of consumption occurring between 1955 and 1965. In the Netherlands, energy use tripled from 1955 to 1973. In contrast, British growth in energy use lagged far behind, rising only 15 percent from 1950 to 1960 and 29 percent from 1960 to 1973, a record in keeping with lower economic growth rates. These countries accounted for 77 percent of OECD-Europe's TPER in 1960 and 72 percent in 1973; Germany, alone, used 23 percent of TPER in 1973.[6]

In Chapter 4, I noted that the energy mix of particular European nations varied noticeably during the 1950s, reflecting different national energy resource endowments. Table 4.5 depicts the heavy coal dependency of OECD-Europe during the 1950s, a reliance radically diminished during the next decade. Each western European nation, whether a major coal producer or not, moved from coal to other fuels. By 1973, solid fuels provided but one-quarter of OECD-Europe's TPER. Britain and Germany, with large coal reserves and a high fixed investment in the coal industry, relied upon coal for more than 30 percent of energy requirements. Coal use in the Netherlands declined from 69 percent of TPER in 1955 to 5 percent in 1973.[7]

In Germany, the UK, France, and Italy, among other nations, the process of oil substitution for coal was far advanced by 1973 while natural gas had become a key component of national energy mixes (Table 4.5). Cheap and accessible oil poured into European markets. Net oil imports for OECD-Europe reached 726 mmt in 1973, compared with 201 mmt in 1960 (Table 6.3) while coal production stagnated and fell (Table 4.4). By 1973, Dutch natural gas supplied 13 percent of TPER in OECD-Europe. Domestic natural gas significantly moderated Dutch reliance upon oil and permitted the termination of coal production in 1975.

These shifts in national energy mix were not entirely market driven. Comparative fuel costs shaped political decisions. Consumer preferences, prospective technological advances, and the imperatives of national security could speed up, slow down, or abort what might appear as a natural process. Hefty government subsidization was essential to the birth and growth of the nuclear power industry. European governments after 1945 directed the rehabilitation of coal industries and several Continental states banded together in the European Coal and Steel Community. Having invested substantial capital in this rebuilding program, the UK, Germany, and France were understandably reluctant to permit the uninhibited use of a competing and imported fuel to damage the major domestic fuel producing industry.

European governments, with the exception of Germany, owned and operated their coal and energy utility industries which, combined with the existence of partly or wholly owned state oil companies, afforded potential leverage over energy consumption, both in the aggregate and in specific end uses. West Germany intervened directly least of all, pursuing policies more similar to the USA than to Britain or France.

Innumerable factors contributed to the evolution of national energy policies, including: energy resource endowment; comparative fuel costs; the political influence of energy industries, whether or not nationalized; the mix of foreign and native in energy industry ownership; the condition of the economy and its various components, each with some political clout; assessments of foreign competitive pressures; assessments of the reliability of foreign energy suppliers; customary practices regarding government economic authority; and nationalistic sentiments. These can be subsumed within two objectives: national security and self-sustained economic growth.[8]

Table 6.4 indicates that *per capita* consumption of energy in OECD increased far more rapidly from 1950 to 1970 than world *per capita* consumption. *Per capita* consumption in the USSR and eastern Europe replicated only the gross pattern of OECD. Given the necessary dedication of western European governments to rapid and permanent econo-

Table 6.4 *Per capita* consumption of energy, 1950–83 (metric tons coal equivalent)

	1950	1960	1970	1975	1981	1983
World	1.0	1.4	1.9	1.5	1.5	2.1
USA	7.9	8.6	12.5	12.2	12.0	10.8
OECD-Europe		2.8	4.3	4.5	4.6	
Germany	2.5	3.7	6.0	5.8	6.2	5.9
UK	4.4	4.9	5.4	5.0	4.9	5.0
France	1.9	2.6	5.0	4.6	5.1	5.0
Italy	0.4	1.2	4.0	4.3	3.0	4.3
Japan	0.6	1.2	4.0	4.3	3.1	4.3
USSR	1.7	3.0	4.5		4.4	
Eastern Europe	1.8	3.0	4.3			
Argentina	0.9	1.2		2.5[1]		
India	0.1	0.1		0.4[1]		

[1] 1972

Sources: IEA, *Energy Balances of OECD Countries 1970/1982*, Paris: OECD/ IEA (1984), pp 387–9, 404; *ibid.*, *1983 1984* (1986), pp. 120 1, 135, IEA, *Energy Balances of Developing Countries 1971/1982*, Paris: OECD/IEA (1984), pp. 190–3; Statistical Office of the European Communities, *Energy Statistics Yearbook 1969–1973*, Luxembourg: SOEC (1974), p. 33; G. Jenkins, *Oil Economist's Handbook 1985*, London: Elsevier (1985), pp. 99, 117, 132, 135–6.

mic growth, high employment, and higher wages, each nation's voracious energy appetite demanded satisfaction. OECD-Europe did not have the option of choosing between high and low energy intensive paths. Opting for the latter would have necessitated a revolution in values and, perhaps, spawned revolution in the streets as well. The higher energy intensive course had already been set. One-half century of death, destruction, and economic crisis elevated the anticipation of western Europeans for the material benefits of a high energy intensive society. An energy intensive strategy promised prosperity and economic power, achievable, in a period of stable and low energy prices, at modest cost.

European governments could manipulate the energy mix, and that is what they attempted. As observed above, most states held common assumptions about energy, chief among them being its cheapness and abundance. During the first postwar decade, Britain, Germany, France, Belgium, and Holland, each with large coal industries, relied on a resurrected coal industry for the bulk of domestic energy needs. Through 1955 or so the diminution of coal's contribution to TPER was slight; thereafter, coal's share fell precipitously. This reversal in coal's fortunes, concurrent with the first Suez crisis, compelled the producing states to reassess the national stake in a vigorous coal industry.

The lesson of Suez might have suggested the wisdom of protecting coal's role through research that would enhance its value by improving its efficiency as a fuel and reducing its polluting effects, and through programs that improved rates of productivity and lowered the cost of coal. The Suez crisis did not inspire such a practical response. The policies that did emerge from western Europe's re-evaluation of the role of the coal industry necessarily encompassed more than coal's proper share in meeting national energy needs. The policies of each state differed in detail but, as Cowhey observed, the consequences were similar. Gordon criticized European governments for retarding the rundown in coal production, suggesting that the industry should have been consolidated and reduced to special purpose mining.[9]

Might not criticism of national coal companies for delaying the rundown of coal as reasonably be directed at government policies that permitted and encouraged the decline of the coal industry? Having assumed ownership of a valuable resource, the individual governments and ECSC neglected to improve its worth by increasing its utility. Dreams of nuclear power, hints of rising natural gas supplies, and the short-lived effects of the Suez closing precluded the application to coal of value-enhancement programs.

Gordon asserts that decades of reliance on coal, national ownership in the UK and France, significant state participation elsewhere in Europe, and mine employment numbering in the hundreds of thousands obstructed policies founded on a realistic projection of comparative price and demand. A rundown that permitted mass miner unemployment and that jeopardized the security attending domestic coal availability was politically unacceptable. The thorough-going reform of the industry was similarity unattractive.

Coal, however, cost more than oil per Btu produced. Suez notwithstanding, oil supplies seemed secure. Cheapness, accessibility, and obvious consumer preferences tilted the case in oil's favor, but politicians accepted the results slowly and reluctantly. ECSC, assuming the inevitability of coal contraction, provided financial assistance for scaling down the industry to Belgium, France, and the Netherlands, the first two deciding to reduce coal production drastically, and Holland opting to abandon it entirely.[10]

Dutch natural gas production permitted the termination of domestic coal production in 1975. Between 1965 and 1970, coal's share of Dutch TPER declined from 31 to 10 percent, oil's share dipped from 63 to 57 percent, and the share of natural gas rose from 4 to 31 percent. Neither France, Belgium, nor Germany possessed an alternative domestic energy source. The North Sea promised both gas and oil to the UK during the 1970s. Italy, with the poorest energy endowment of the European states, switched rapidly during the 1950s from imported coal to imported oil and gas while developing a substantial hydroelectric capacity.[11]

France fashioned the most highly defined energy policy in western

Europe; Germany, the least. In 1946, France nationalized the coal, electric, and gas industries. Initially, policy focused on rebuilding the coal industry (Table 4.4) and obtaining ECSC sanction for price controls for coal that protected it from oil competition. Concurrently, France reorganized the state owned oil companies, preparatory to launching a grand exploratory campaign throughout the French empire. While oil from French colonial territories and French companies participating in Middle Eastern consortia received preferential treatment in the domestic market, the primary concern into the late 1950s was with coal, and secondarily with expanding hydroelectric capacity. However, coal's defenses were inadequate against the advantages of oil. By 1960, penetration of the home market by oil products had damaged coal's marketability. Coal production, peaking in 1958, began to slide (Tables 4.4 and 4.5).

Bowing to the reality of oil competition, France revised its energy policies after 1960, vesting government agencies with augmented powers of implementation and administration. The emphasis shifted from protecting high cost coal to the importation of low cost oil, preferably produced in French possessions by state oil companies. During the 1960s, France favored coal with less protection against competition than Britain or Germany.

In opting for cheaper imported energy, France announced its intention to defend the international competitiveness of national industries and its confidence in the security of its overseas oil concessions. Hardly initiated, the Algerian revolution cast this policy into disarray. Nonetheless, the new policies encouraged vastly increased oil use. Table 6.3 shows that imports rose by 7 mmt from 1955 to 1960, 25 mmt from 1960 to 1965, and almost doubled from 1965 to 1970. French import quotas and other regulations guaranteed the domestic market share of French produced crude. Natural gas received no particular attention. Hydroelectric production grew more rapidly than total electric production from 1950 to 1960 but fell thereafter while a modest nuclear power complex emerged (Table 6.5).[12]

To strengthen the competitiveness of French industry, Lucas suggests, France designed its energy policy to obtain secure energy at the lowest possible price. Hatch interprets French intentions more narrowly. Although articulated in terms of independence and security of supply, French policy, Hatch believes, "had less to do with the total amount of domestic energy consumption that was supplied by imports than with control over the domestic oil market and assured 'French' crude oil production."[13] Import dependence (see Table 6.2) was an acceptable risk given French company control over a substantial portion of oil imports and the persistence of low oil prices.

The policies of Germany, Italy, and Britain while less dirigiste than

Table 6.5   Electricity production, 1950–84

	1950	1960	1970	1980	1984
OECD-Europe					
Total[1]	257	569	1146	1743	1925
% hydro	41	40	28	24	24
% nuclear	0	<1	4	17	26
Germany					
Total	47	119	243	369	395
% hydro	19	11	7	5	5
% nuclear	0	0	2	12	23
France					
Total	37	75	147	258	343
% hydro	47	55	39	27	21
% nuclear	0	0	4	24	59
UK					
Total	67	139	249	285	283
% hydro	2	2	2	2	2
% nuclear	0	2	10	13	19
Italy					
Total	25	38	83	186	183
% hydro	88	81	35	na	25
% nuclear	0	0	3	1	4
Japan					
Total	46	116	396	576	649
% hydro	82	51	23	16	12
% nuclear	0	0	1	14	21
USA					
Total	410	892	1740	2401	2563
% hydro	25	17	15	12	13
% nuclear	0	<1	1	11	14

[1] All totals in billion kwh

Source: IEA, *Energy Statistics 1983/1984*, Paris: OECD/IEA (1984), pp. 130–2.

the French were all characterized by state intervention. Until the late 1960s, Germany confined its activities to shoring up the coal industry. But various tax disincentives to fuel oil use, incentives to such coal users as power plants and steel, and concentration of the coal industry into larger and more efficient units were rather ineffectual. Stagnant coal demand during the late 1950s was followed by decline during the 1960s. Between 1957 and 1968, coal employment plunged from 604,000 to 272,000. By 1973, coal provided only one-third of German TPER while coal production descended to a tonnage below that of 1955 (Tables 4.4 and 4.5). Germany relied upon the MNOCs for oil. By 1969, foreign oil companies, led by Esso (SONJ), BP, and RDS, owned 75 percent of German refining capacity.

Policy directions altered markedly after 1968. Germany decided to establish a national oil company, Deminex, to explore and develop overseas oil concessions. Oil regulations were imposed that aimed to guarantee German-owned firms at least one-quarter of the domestic market. These innovations reflected German distrust of the supply performance of the MNOCs during the second Suez crisis. Policy makers in the Federal Republic decided to reduce supports for coal and invest large sums in the nuclear industry. Germany moved slowly in the French direction but without essential reliance upon national energy firms or agencies.

Italy's policies resembled those of France. ENI, the state owned oil company, dominated an energy market that confined coal use to electric generation. Italy sought natural gas suppliers more assiduously than either France or Germany. Italy's nuclear development program, however, yielded disappointing results.[14]

Britain's less dynamic economy relied more heavily on coal than her Continental neighbors (Table 4.5). *Per capita* consumption of energy in the UK recorded negligible growth from 1950 to 1970, compared with her European allies (Table 6.4). Britain did not become more energy efficient. Indeed, the reverse occurred. Government policies that improved welfare failed to stimulate managerial and technological initiatives necessary to confront an increasingly competitive global economy. TPER in Britain advanced 45 percent during those years while TPER in Germany, only 57 percent of Britain's in 1950, exceeded the latter's by 10 percent in 1970. The invasion of domestic coal markets by oil and by American coal met resistance in the form of imported oil and coal licensing requirements, high excise duties on fuel oil, and restraints on the use of fuel oil by power plants. But coal's disadvantages — pollution, ineffective marketing, poor reputation among consumers — were beyond the remedial powers of purely fiscal measures. Protecting the electric power market of coal while simultaneously promoting the rapid introduction of nuclear power (Table 6.5) made sense as an employment policy but not as an energy policy. In any event, oil was cheaper per Btu than coal. Left to its own devices, coal's rundown would have been even more rapid. As it was, coal production fell sharply after 1965 (Table 4.4).

By late 1960s, however, the energy outlook for the UK was superior to that of most other European countries. British oil companies commanded a sizable production in the Middle East and Venezuela and considered those to be secure sources. Native firms controlled one-half of the domestic oil market. About one-half of Britain's £700 million net oil import bill in 1970 was payable to British firms, notably BP and RDS. Moreover, the UK could anticipate a flow from the North Sea that promised oil independence. The British Gas Council in joint ventures with several American firms actively explored the North Sea for natural gas. By 1973, natural gas supplied 11 percent of TPER (Table

4.5) and a thorough-going conversion from manufactured to natural gas was in midcourse. The British government orchestrated and managed the exploitation of North Sea energy.[15]

Throughout western Europe the transition from coal to other fuels accelerated. The Netherlands moved expeditiously to complete this transition with the discovery of the Groningen gas field in 1951. This enormous field, with reserves equal to the Hugoton field in the USA but less than one-half the size of the three major Soviet fields, provided sufficient gas for Dutch use and a large surplus for export to western Europe. The Dutch immediately incorporated Gasunie, a state owned company, which, in association with RDS and Esso, organized the market in Europe. Exports of 5 million cubic meters in 1963 climbed above 11 billion cubic meters (bcm) in 1970 and reached 31 bcm by 1973. From 1963 through 1973, German distribution firms purchased about 35 percent of Dutch exports with the remainder piped to France, Belgium, Switzerland, and Italy.[16]

The quantity of Dutch gas sold abroad in 1973 equaled in caloric value about 47 mmt of coal, much directly substitutable for coal, and oil as well, in homes, commercial buildings, factories, and power stations. In Europe, the price of gas, pegged to fuel oil, was cheaper than coal.[17] Tables 6.6 and 6.7 summarize the consequences for coal of conversion to natural gas and oil.

Demand for coal by the electric power industry ceased expanding in the mid-1960s as gas became available (Table 6.6). The marginal growth of coal use in Germany occurred only because of various taxes on oil use and laws passed in 1964, 1965, and 1973 that subsidized coal burning in power plants.[18] In 1969, natural gas produced 4 percent of thermally generated electricity; in 1973, 12 percent (Table 6.7). Holland, understandably, turned to natural gas. France and Italy converted rapidly to fuel oil and Belgium to oil and natural gas. Britain slowed the replacement of coal by oil by limiting oil burning in power plants and selling coal to electric authorities at the lowest possible prices. The policies of Tory and Labour governments did not prevent the capture by fuel oil of 29 percent of the thermal power plant market in 1973 (Table 6.7). Without this protection, the power market for coal probably would have slipped badly, perhaps justifying lower electricity rates and stimulating the more thorough electrification of the realm (Table 6.5).[19]

Steady decline characterized coal use in industrial, residential, and commercial sectors (Table 6.6). The steel industry was the second largest consumer of coal. The unimpressive pace of steel industry growth in France and the UK combined with new technologies, adopted rapidly in Germany, that lowered coke inputs per ton of pig iron output to reduce overall coke consumption.[20] For the nations detailed in Table

Table 6.6 Coal use in western Europe, 1960–73 (million metric tons)

	1960	1964	1968	1973
West Germany				
Consumption	227	262	223	217
Converted to:				
Electricity	61	92	102	113
Manufactured gas	7	7	3	2
Coke	60	58	48	44
Briquettes, etc.	43	44	28	7
Final Deliveries to:				
Steel industries	24	28	21	21
Other industries	14	11	6	6
Domestic–commercial	12	11	10	10
France				
Consumption	61	61	50	36
Converted to:				
Electricity	8	13	14	9
Manufactured gas	1	<1	0	0
Coke	18	18	16	15
Briquettes, etc.	<1	<1	<1	<1
Final deliveries to:				
Steel industries	15	16	14	9
Other industries	14	15	9	4
Domestic–commercial	11	12	9	6
UK				
Consumption	197	187	143[1]	116
Converted to:				
Electricity	51	67	65	62
Manufactured gas	22	20	5	<1
Coke	29	26	20	24
Briquettes, etc.	1	1	1	1
Final deliveries to:				
Steel industries	3[3]	3[3]	11	9
Other industries	3[3]	3[3]	19	11
Domestic–commercial	30[2]	20[2]	34	21

[1] 1969
[2] House coal only
[3] Jackson's categories do not correspond with EC categories

Sources: Statistical Office of the European Communities, *Energy Statistics Yearbook, 1958–68*, Luxembourg; SOEC (1969), pp. 26–8; *ibid.*, *1969–1973* (1974), pp. 34–8.

6.6, coke making demanded 24 mmt tons less coal in 1973 than in 1960. Adding to coal's woes by 1970, as Tables 4.5 and 6.5 suggest, nuclear power made its presence felt and expanded swiftly in succeeding years. In Germany and in Britain, public moneys devoted to nuclear power development diluted the protective effects of subsidization of the coal industry.

Table 6.7 Western European thermal electric production, by source of fuel, 1960−73

	1960	1969	1973
Germany			
Total thermal production[1]	106	192	254
% all coal	92	70	59
% oil	2	13	14
% manufactured gas	5	3	4
% natural gas	<1	4	12
France			
Total thermal production	34	74	113
% all coal	67	61	24
% oil	8	24	61
% manufactured gas	13	6	6
% natural gas	12	8	9
Italy			
Total thermal production	8	60	95
% all coal	20	10	3
% oil	47	77	89
% manufactured gas	6	3	3
% natural gas	27	9	4
Netherlands			
Total thermal production	17	35	49
% all coal	76	28	3
% oil	20	39	13
% manufactured gas	3	4	3
% natural gas	1	28	81
Belgium			
Total thermal production	15	27	38
% all coal	76	39	13
% oil	12	46	53
% manufactured gas	12	10	10
% natural gas	<1	5	24
UK			
Total thermal production	139	192	234
% all coal	99	82	69
% oil	<1	17	29
% manufactured gas	<1	<1	1
% natural gas	0	<1	1

[1] All totals in billion kwh

Sources: Statistical Office of the European Communities, *Energy Statistics Yearbook 1958−1969*, Luxembourg: SOEC (1969), pp. 289−93; *ibid.*, *1969−1973*, pp. 226−7; G.L. Reid *et al.*, *The Nationalized Fuel Industries*, London: Heinemann Educational Books (1973), pp. 186−7.

Table 6.8 Sources of OECD-Europe oil, 1961–75 (percent)

	1961	1966	1970	1971	1973	1975
Middle East	64	51	48	57	68	70
North Africa	8	25	34	24	16	12
West Africa	2	5	7	8	7	7
USSR	9	8	6	6	6	7
Latin America	16	9	4	4	2	3
All other	1	3	1	1	1	1

Source: G. Jenkins, *Oil Economist's Handbook 1985*, London: Elsevier (1985), pp. 59–64.

The price, performance, and convenience advantages of competing fuels caused the stagnation or decline, and even abandonment, of western European coal industries. Britain and Germany retarded the decline while the Netherlands, France, and Belgium hurried it along. The cost of this policy in heightened dependence upon imported oil and natural gas resonated into the 1970s and the 1980s. By 1973, each of the European nations detailed in Table 6.2, except Holland and Britain, relied upon imports for over one-half of TPER, a dependence chained to imported oil.[21]

The strategies employed by western European governments to develop secure oil sources and to lessen the burden of oil imports yielded meager results. The consistent intervention of France and the less comprehensive policies of Germany led to a similar vulnerability by 1973. Oil imports by OECD-Europe rose from 117 mmt in 1955 to 776 mmt in 1973 (Table 6.3). The UK, France, the Low Countries, and Germany, the recipients of almost 90 percent of western Europe's imports in 1959, still received over 80 percent in 1973. As Table 6.8 specifies, the Middle East provided two-thirds of this oil except during the latter half of the 1960s when North African oil poured into Europe. Libya, alone, supplied 21 percent of western Europe's oil in 1971. From 1960 to 1970, France received some 30 percent of its oil and Italy and Germany, together, some 10 percent from Algeria. But, during the early 1970s, Algeria and Libya reduced their output compelling their customers to turn again to the Persian Gulf.

Representative of the Continental European position were the drastic shifts in the sources of French oil that occurred between 1970 and 1974. During the 1950s, France derived over 80 percent of its oil from the Persian Gulf. As Algerian and then Libyan oil came in, France substituted Algerian oil and as much Libyan oil as possible for the more costly Persian Gulf crude. The Persian Gulf share of the French market slipped to 44 percent in 1970 while Algeria and Libya, combined, provided 45 percent. One year later, the Persian Gulf portion rebounded to 61 percent, reaching 77 percent by 1974. At that time, Algeria's share rested at 7 percent and Libya's at 3 percent. Algeria's nationalization of all French companies 1970–1 and the virtual withdrawal of those firms from the country in addition to Libya's decision to severely limit output produced this change. It signified the defeat of French oil policy.

These events affected Britain, ensconced in Kuwait, Iraq, and Iran, less dramatically than France, although Britain had turned to Libya and also to Nigeria and Venezuela in an effort to diversify her sources of oil. Germany, importing twice as much from Libya as the UK, was constrained to turn to Algeria and the Persian Gulf to replace the lost Libyan tonnage. Reliance upon Libya for 43 percent of German requirements in 1968 diminished to 24 percent in 1973; the Persian Gulf percentage, at 68 in 1961, fell to 38 in 1968, and then climbed above 50 percent in 1973. Italy was forced to make similar adjustments in oil purchases.[22]

Western European energy policies fell far short of success if avoiding, or at least moderating, energy import dependence was the central objective. Only the Dutch, and only because of Groningen, actually reduced net energy imports as a proportion of TPER (Table 6.2). French efforts to develop secure sources of oil seemed fulfilled in 1961 as Algerian production rose, but the French position eroded as Algeria won independence in 1963, raised prices in 1969, and nationalized in 1970–1, thus terminating whatever special relationship France had enjoyed. Germany, relying on the MNOCs, exercised little control over its crude oil supply and permitted foreign firms to dominate the domestic market. Europe did not alleviate its dependence upon a few volatile nations in an unstable region. The exposed position of Europe encouraged Middle Eastern producers to raise prices in 1970–1 and again in 1973.

Achieving energy security through the diversification of oil supplies was not feasible for western Europe. Only Middle Eastern producers could satisfy swollen European demand. The USSR, Venezuela, and Nigeria, regarded as more reliable, filled only a marginal part of demand. Unfortunately, the European draw upon those states actually declined during the 1960s (Table 6.8). Diversifying the domestic energy mix offered a method of dampening oil demand. Holland, alone, enjoyed the developed resource flexibility required for that approach. Although North Sea gas deliveries to Britain mounted after 1967, flexibility lay in the future. Even at the higher prices of 1970–2, oil and natural gas were cheaper than coal. Coal's environmental impacts counseled against more coal burning with available technologies. Moreover, to raise coal production in 1970, reversing a decade of neglect, would require substantial capital investment. Given the price of oil and gas, and in Britain the promise of North Sea gas and oil, the diversion of funding and other resources to coal was adjudged uneconomical.

To reduce the risks of interruption in oil supply, already experienced on two occasions, and enhance the security of domestic supply, Europeans could have: offered attractive political and economic concessions to the Arab producers; pursued Soviet supplies more assiduously; cultivated Latin American production, even at higher prices; reduced the share of oil in national energy mixes through substitution and conservation; stockpiled oil; cooperated through the European Community to eliminate contradictory energy policies and the duplication of energy research. These real options were not discussed because of the cheapness of oil in the summer of 1973. Cooperation through the Community produced rhetoric but no common policies. Non-coal producers opposed the subsidization of coal. The Community played no role in North Sea development. Despite Euratom, Community members competed in the nuclear field instead of cooperating to reduce US technological and marketing supremacy. European nationalisms precluded the exploration of the above possibilities. In fall 1973, each European state found itself in a similar predicament.[23]

Japan's oil dependency

The Japanese economy expanded at a prodigious rate during the 1960s, attaining an average annual growth rate in real output of over 10 percent from 1963 to 1973; few other industrial countries reached 5 percent. Exports pulled Japanese growth along. The rapid absorption and creation of new production technologies and innovative and high quality products enhanced the price advantages and marketability of Japanese wares. Unencumbered by enormous military expenditures, in contrast to the USA, Britain or France, and the Soviet Union, the reinvestment of earnings in industry yielded new earnings, high savings, and a consistently high rate of investment in research and development. As remarked in Chapter 4, a coalition between government and business generated carefully wrought industrial policies that included the coordination of all mineral imports and the refusal to protect domestic energy industries against foreign competition, the latter necessitating the gradual rundown of the domestic coal industry.

Japan's energy import dependence comprised only part of its general resource import dependence. By 1973, Japan imported more than 90 percent of its energy (Table 6.2), aluminum, copper, nickel, iron ore, and manganese. Most of these strategic materials were imported, processed, and fabricated into products by giant zaibatsu. These conglomerates, Mitsubishi and Mitsui being the largest, controlled the general trading companies that essentially monopolized external trade. The Ministry of International Trade and Industry (MITI) possessed the authority to subsidize or invest directly in mining ventures, support new technologies, and in general nudge the zaibatsu into conformity with national policies, a power almost unheard of in the USA and even in Europe. In this era of low natural resource prices, Japan's purposeful economic policies produced a bonanza. From 1958 to 1968, Japanese gross domestic product rose from $32 billion to $142 billion. Japanese GNP equaled 20 percent of the GNP of the original six European Community members in 1958 and 37 percent in 1968. In 1966, Japan matched and then exceeded British GNP. Japan's external trade advanced from $10 billion in 1961 to $26 billion in 1968. But, one cost of high economic growth rates was almost total energy import dependence.[24]

This striking economic growth increased Japan's share of global TPER, in contrast to a falling share for the USA and western Europe (Table 6.1). Japan, strongly influenced by US policies during the occupation, swiftly turned from coal to oil, and by 1973 was more dependent upon oil than its OECD partners (Table 4.5). TPER in Japan tripled between 1950 and 1965 and more than doubled again by 1973. Japanese energy consumption in 1960 equaled 9 percent of American use, 64 percent of German, and 53 percent of British. By 1973, that comparison read: 20 percent, 125 percent, and 147 percent, respectively.[25] In 1960, Japan ranked third as an oil importer, behind the USA and UK; in 1965, Japanese imports surpassed Britain's and Japan ranked first in 1970 (Table 6.3). By 1973, three-quarters of TPER derived from oil.

The costs of oil imports were monumental, in current dollars rising from $673 million in 1960 to $2.8 billion in 1970, $6.5 billion in 1973, and over $15 billion in 1975. These sums represented an ever larger portion of the total imports bill: 9 percent in 1960, 16 percent in 1973, and following the OPEC price shock, almost 35 percent in 1975.[26] Until 1973 these costs seemed bearable because energy prices remained relatively low and because Japan utilized its energy with an efficiency superior to the USA and equal to OECD-Europe. In 1973, Japan produced $2,391 of gross domestic product per input of one metric ton of TPER oil equivalent, compared with $1,226 for the USA and $2,552 for OECD-Europe.[27] Japan enjoyed little maneuverability in energy decision making. Other than oil, no feasible fuel options existed. To moderate oil dependence, Japan could reduce internal consumption and pursue nuclear and liquefied natural gas (LNG) opportunities. To better secure its oil supply, Japan could explore for oil independently, own its own tankers, and spread its purchases among numerous suppliers.

The domestic energy mix of Japan mirrored its intense oil dependency. During the 1960s, oil was cheaper by one-third than coal as a boiler fuel for industry and thermal electric generation. Hydroelectric production stagnated after 1965 (Table 6.5) while oil burning power plants, producing 17 percent of electricity in 1960, generated well over one-half in 1973. *Per capita* consumption of energy in Japan advanced at a faster pace from 1950 to 1970 than in the USA or most of OECD-Europe (Table 6.4). But the distribution of internal energy consumption differed from American and European patterns.

In Japan, direct personal consumption of energy in the home and in private transportation accounted for a much smaller proportion of total end use than in the USA or Europe. In America, transportation, alone, consumed 29 percent of primary energy in 1970 and residential–commercial burned another 25 percent. Together, those uses composed only 25 percent of Japanese TPER. A wide variance in the proportion of total oil consumption claimed by gasoline distinguished the USA from both Japan and western Europe: 39 percent, 15 percent, and 16 percent, respectively. This reflected, in part, the superior public transit systems of the latter two and the importance of commercial trucking in the USA distribution system. Japanese industry ran on fuel oil, consuming 56 percent of all oil compared with 16 percent for European industry and 38 percent for American. American industry burned large volumes of natural gas, unavailable in Japan, and much more coal than Japanese counterparts.

Electricity consumption replicated oil use patterns. The bulk of power was fed to Japanese industry. In America, residential–commercial use was larger by a small margin than industrial use, reflecting increasing numbers of families lodged in single-family housing packed with electric appliances. In western Europe, industrial uses of power exceeded domestic commercial use more narrowly than in Japan.[28]

It is worth noting here that the concentration of energy use in Nipponese industry offered a highly defined target for conservation during the decade following 1973. The Japanese could achieve significant savings through more efficient industrial energy use. In the USA, the personal character of energy use presented a diffused target for government commands and/or moral suasion and yielded disappointing results.

Resource scarcity in the home islands elicited vigorous government responses beginning in the 1930s. The pre-World War II solution, conquest, led to disaster. Following the war, and once American occupation terminated, Japanese resource policies concentrated on the cultivation of diverse sources of supply and on winning some control over supply through direct investments or long-term contracts. To secure raw materials, Japanese capital and management and technical expertise spread throughout the world. By 1970, Mitsui was engaged in dozens of overseas mining operations to extract iron ore, copper, tin, salt, and petroleum at an investment cost of $25 billion. Mitsubishi possessed three energy companies, one involved in natural gas development in Indonesia, and the others exploring for oil around the world.

Recognizing its limited energy options, the Japanese government induced and supported nationally owned oil discovery ventures but did not create a state owned oil company. The first and most successful firm was the Arabian Oil Company, operating concessions jointly with Saudi Arabia and Kuwait in 1957. Interest then slackened until 1967 when MITI created the Japanese Petroleum Development Corporation (JPDC) to assist private investors with guaranteed loans and technological aid. JPDC spurred dozens of firms to initiate overseas exploration. The four largest conglomerates and the five largest electric utilities were involved in 26 of the 49 joint ventures active in 1974. The utilities were particularly interested in gas development, viewing LNG, expensive though it was, as preferable to coal or oil. Both Mitsubishi and Mitsui formed oil development subsidiaries to consolidate their exploration endeavors. In turn, these development companies negotiated joint venture agreements with the large MNOCs. In Abu Dhabi, Mitsubishi owned the Middle East Oil Company and JPDC bought out the BP interest in the Abu Dhabi Marine Areas Ltd.[29]

JPDC's goal of importing 35 percent of oil requirements from national producing firms seemed far from realization in 1973. Japan remained dependent upon a few producers and on foreign oil companies. American firms and BP and RDS delivered almost 75 percent of the oil while Japanese firms brought in 10 percent. In 1973, the Persian Gulf states, including Iran, supplied 78 percent of imports and Indonesia provided another 18 percent. The Indonesian relationship had developed after 1965 when Sukharno seized British and American oil properties and established a special oil relationship with Japan. An oil deal concluded in 1972 committed Japan to a $234 million oil development loan to Indonesia in return for a guaranteed ten-year supply of 51 mmt annually, or about 17 percent of oil imports. Japan also drew on Indonesia for bauxite, nickel, lumber, foodstuffs, and, commencing in 1972, LNG.[30]

In Wu's opinion, Japan's efforts to diversify its sources of oil were disappointing. In 1973, investments of 131 billion yen in foreign oil field operations yielded 8.5 percent of oil imports. Indonesian oil deliveries rose but reliance upon the Persian Gulf remained fixed. In 1961, 1973, and 1978, the latter region provided 74, 78, and 77 percent, respectively, of oil imports. To some extent, Japanese firms and government to government contracts lessened the role of the foreign MNOCs as deliverers and as refiners.[31] Into the 1970s, Japan doggedly held to these policies, turning to Latin America, the USSR, West Africa, Australia, and other places for energy. But the quantities available were a trickle, and higher priced than the volumes received from the Middle East. The great price shock of 1978–9 catalyzed Japanese conservation efforts and in the 1980s receipts from the Middle East dropped to about two-thirds of a reduced internal demand. LNG imports also rose, filling some 10 percent of TPER by 1985 while nuclear filled 9 percent. But for all of this, an interruption of Persian Gulf supplies remained a clear and present danger to Japan.

Energy in the Soviet bloc

Energy production and consumption accelerated smartly in the Soviet Union during the 1950s and 1960s, propelled by annual GNP growth rates that excelled those in both the USA and the European Community. In the eastern European satellites, however, economic and energy growth rates use trailed behind those of the dominant partner. The bloc states continued to rely heavily on coal which, as late as 1965, still accounted for 82 percent of TPER. Soviet bloc coal production soared between 1950 and 1965. Total output reached 760 mmt. The bloc contributed 53 percent of the increase in world coal production of which the Soviets accounted for one-third (Table 4.4). Thereafter, the role of coal declined more quickly, falling to 66 percent of TPER in 1973 while oil and natural gas climbed to 21 and 12 percent, respectively. Meanwhile, the USSR brought to maturity a three-fuel energy system that superficially resembled the primary energy mix of the USA (Table 4.5).

The Soviet decision of the late 1950s to shift resources from coal to petroleum and natural gas production, while by no means reducing coal production, resulted in marked increases in oil (Table 4.6) and natural gas supply. Gas production, at 128 billion cubic meters in 1965, reached 289 bcm in 1975. Production advances of such magnitude necessitated enormous annual investments in exploration, pipeline construction, and the expansion of refining capacity along with a progressive improvement in Soviet technologies or access to western technologies. Modernization of the railroad net, particularly between eastern sources of oil and western points of consumption, further taxed available Soviet capital. Hewitt suggests that as the costs of energy development increased, additional capital was withheld from other economic sectors. Oil pipeline mileage tripled between 1950 and 1961 and doubled again by 1970 while the tonnage of oil hauled by rail also grew rapidly. Refining capacity expanded at an equal rate: a capacity of 89 mmt in 1957 reached 189 mmt by 1965. Spurring both oil and gas production, in addition to general economic growth, was Soviet recognition of market possibilities in western Europe, the greater efficiency of those fuels in industrial processes, and eastern European demands for energy that required satisfaction to some degree.[32]

Costs rose and technological demands intensified as older coal and oil reserves were depleted, as exploration and development moved ever eastward after 1960, and as the Soviets concentrated on exploiting their enormous natural gas fields in western Siberia. As noted earlier, the need to import foreign equipment, particularly large diameter pipe and turbines for pipeline compressor stations, persuaded the Soviets to seek markets in western Europe for their surplus oil and gas. Simultaneously, the real politick of hegemonic power required increasing energy exports to their bloc partners. The fuel surplus was not a true one, available as it was only at the expense of domestic consumption.

The domestic energy mix of the USSR resembled America's in that coal remained a significant fuel, natural gas use increased, and a relatively low degree of oil dependence obtained — all of those fuels drawn from domestic fields (Table 4.5). But the similarities cease at that point. The Soviet bureaucracy planned and directed each aspect of energy production, distribution, and end use. Little or no central planning intruded into the American system. The ability of Americans to substitute one fuel for another, as in the residential shift from coal to oil, natural gas, and electricity, could not be replicated in the USSR, nor was it considered desirable. Ideology and the exigencies of Soviet economic growth demanded the programmed distribution of energy among users. Given the high priority of industrial development and defense, the Soviet domestic sector was the loser in energy allocation. In the USA, hospitals, homes, and schools were favored over industry during periods of tight natural gas or electricity supply.

In the Soviet system, price was of no importance to most domestic consumers. Agencies of the state, for example, supplied coal or fuel oil to other state agencies for distribution to public housing authorities. Virtually everyone lived in public housing whether a high-rise in the city or in a collective in the countryside. Gasoline or diesel fuel powered trucks, tanks, buses, and a handful of autos driven by or for officials. Soviet apartments were not furnished with the latest kitchen appliances as was French working class and middle class housing beginning in the 1960s. In the Soviet Union, energy was moved around according to centrally determined priorities. The producers and distributors of energy felt no particular urgency to move energy expeditiously to end use points. Bottlenecks proliferated in cities and industrial regions.

The Soviet industrial sector claimed in excess of one-half of energy use in 1970, compared with one-third in America. The industrial fuel mix also differed. By 1970, natural gas accounted for one-half of the fuel burn in American factories while the Soviets relied essentially on coal and oil. Private transport was not a factor in the USSR. All transportation in America consumed about 30 percent of TPER compared with 11 percent in the Soviet Union. The residential–commercial sectors of both nations required similar proportions of TPER. But the quality of American residential fuel was far superior. Until the late 1970s, little natural gas entered Soviet residences while it was the leading American residential fuel. In Russia, chemical and industrial uses of natural gas predominated. By the late 1970s, however, Soviet plans included the reduction of domestic oil use and the increase of natural gas, not in response to consumer demand but in order to free more oil for export. At the end of the 1970s, the domestic market for natural gas remained largely untapped. *Per capita* electric consumption in Russia reached 3,074 kwh in 1970. In Germany, that figure stood at 3,984, in the UK, 4,259, and in the USA, 8,487. Non-industrial electric use in the USSR lagged even further behind America and western Europe.

Soviet energy use conformed to a self-imposed preoccupation with the build-up of heavy industry and the industrial-transportation infrastructure. If GNP per unit of TPER did not vary substantially from the US—$1,380 to $1,231 (US), it should have. A vast amount of US energy flowed toward such non-productive uses as private transportation and residential heating, cooling, cooking, and lighting. In western Europe and Japan, less locked into private consumption patterns than Americans, GNP per unit of TPER far surpassed that of Russia. Moreover, so inflexible were Soviet energy use habits that, during the 1970s, while the USA significantly improved the efficiency of energy use, the Soviet Union hardly improved at all.

The Soviets were more concerned with gross industrial output and less concerned with maximizing GNP/TPER than Japan or western Europe because fuel was so plentiful for industrial purposes and because industrial output neither entered non-bloc foreign trade nor catered to consumer needs. Fuel use efficiency in the steel industry, for example, was of little significance compared with total production of steel ingots. GNP per unit of TPER in American industry attained a figure more comparable with that of Japan and western Europe than of Russia because US manufacturers operated under constraints similar to those affecting their OECD competitors.[33]

Net Soviet energy exports as a percentage of total energy production rose from 7 percent in 1960 to 12 percent in 1970: oil accounted for 85 percent and coal for all but a fraction of the remainder.[34] Tables 6.9 and

Table 6.9   Soviet crude oil and product exports, 1955–75 (thousand metric tons)

	1955	1960	1965	1971	1975
Total	8006	32318	64419	105200	130448
Eastern Europe	2201	9200	22397	44760	63280
Other bloc	1997	6000	6529	7520	9920
Western Europe	2364	14395	23833	33100[1]	34250[1]
West Germany	0[2]	1240		6090	7630
Italy	290[2]	4703	7345	9000	6880
Finland				8570	8770

[1] Includes only EC-9 plus Austria, Sweden, and Yugoslavia
[2] 1956

Sources: R.W. Campbell, *The Economics of Soviet Oil and Gas*, Baltimore: The Johns Hopkins University Press for Resources for the Future (1968), p. 238; D. Park, *Oil and Gas in Comecon Countries*, London: Kegan Paul (1979), pp. 168–9; B.W. Jentleson, *Pipeline Politics: The Complex Political Economy of East-West Energy Trade*, Ithaca: Cornell University Press (1986), pp. 91–113.

Table 6.10   Soviet oil exports as a factor in world oil trade, 1955–75

As percentage of:	1955	1960	1965	1971	1975
World exports	3.0	7.2	8.4	7.7	8.8
Soviet production	11.0	22.0	26.0	27.0	26.0
OECD-Europe net imports	2.0	7.2	6.0	6.8	7.6
West German net imports	0	4.7		4.9	6.5
Italian net imports	2.0	21.9	14.5	10.2	7.8

Sources: G. Jenkins, *Oil Economist's Handbook 1985*, London: Elsevier (1985), pp. 57–64; B.R. Mitchell, ed., *European Historical Statistics 1750–1975*, 2nd revised edn, London: Macmillan (1981), p. 442; sources for Table 6.9.

6.10 summarize global Soviet oil exports which expanded more rapidly than the world total until 1965 or so and again after the embargo of 1973. Accelerated oil deliveries to eastern Europe pushed the volume of exports upward while their world share leveled off. The bloc states received 46 percent of Soviet oil exports in 1960, 50 percent in 1971, and 56 percent in 1975. Deliveries were far more crucial to bloc states than were western European imports of Soviet oil. OECD-Europe receipts from the USSR in 1971 composed 7 percent of all imports; for Germany, 5 percent. Westerners paid in hard currency or in essential manufactured items, particularly producer durables, and that provided the compelling reason to develop the energy trade with the West.

Until 1973, Soviet exports of machinery and equipment ranked first in value earned while ores and concentrate metals equaled fuels in value earned. But, whereas the value of fuel exports accounted for 18 percent of the ruble value of all exports, compared with 22 percent for machinery, fuel brought in 27 percent of hard currency, with oil, alone accounting for 22 percent. A large proportion of exported machinery, ores, and fuels flowed to bloc nations in return for other products, particularly foodstuffs. With the price shock of 1973 and the emergence of a large trade in natural gas with western Europe after 1974, the ruble value of fuel exports climbed substantially above other export product groups: fuels accounted for 50 percent of hard currency earnings in 1976 and 80 percent in 1982. Oil and gas were among the very few Soviet products of any value to western Europe.[35]

Italy, Germany, and Austria during the 1960s and France and other OECD states during the 1970s benefited from the availability of Soviet oil. Hewitt concludes that after 1971 Soviet prices adhered closely to world spot market prices. During the 1960s, however, Moscow offered prices competitive with the discounted prices quoted by the MNOCs. To Italy's ENI, mindful of the Suez crisis of 1956–7, the USSR proffered secure contracts for large volumes at prices below discounted Middle Eastern oil. ENI's receptivity was the greater because the deal diminished dependence on the MNOCs. While substantial Italian reliance on Soviet oil tapered off during the 1960s (Tables 6.9 and 6.10), in part due to US pressure, the Russian reputation for reliability persisted into the 1970s, prompting western nations to continue Soviet oil imports and to commence natural gas purchases. This exchange suited both parties, however it may have angered US strategists who viewed the trade as a plot to fracture NATO.[36]

The USSR possesses some 40 percent of known natural gas reserves, including the biggest field, Urengoi, and four of the six largest, all discovered in the 1960s and all far to the east of consuming territories. During the 1960s, Soviet policy makers decided to utilize this gas to replace oil used internally and to export the freed oil to western Europe and the bloc states. Such were the volumes of gas available that exports were also feasible. Pipeline construction, despite difficulties, accelerated. By the mid-1960s, 50,000 kilometers of trunk line existed and another 12,000 were being laid. Production soared. Concurrently, gas use in Europe quickened because of the availability of Dutch gas. In the European Community of Nine, gas consumption climbed from 10 billion cubic meters in 1964 to 74 bcm in 1970 and 140 bcm in 1973. The Netherlands accounted for one-half of total consumption, so some 70 bcm (minus fractional non-Dutch production) represented the size of the import market. Dutch gas filled that demand until the early 1970s. The Soviets planned to share that large market.

An erratic American opposition, especially during the administration of John F. Kennedy, confronted Soviet oil and gas export plans. US leverage in NATO succeeded in temporarily blunting the Soviet oil export campaign and in limiting western European exports of vital energy equipment to Russia. Such barriers, serving only ill-defined American purposes, quickly toppled. Presidents Johnson, Nixon and Ford liberalized trade restrictions with the Soviets, permitting American firms to negotiate lucrative energy equipment sales with their erstwhile enemies. Moreover, the Soviets proved adept at either producing their own equipment or circumventing American restrictions. Americans, unwilling to allow this and other business to escape by default to Europe and Japan, could not sustain an embargo.[37]

The Soviet–western Europe gas trade commenced in 1968, with shipments to Austria exchanged for steel products. These exports remained fairly insignificant until 1974. Since then, and following a decade of careful planning, impressive growth has characterized the volume and value of Soviet gas exports. As an example, in 1970 energy officials arranged to import Iranian gas for use in the southern regions, thus freeing Siberian gas for sale to western Europe.[38] The flowering of the gas trade during the 1980s and US efforts to impede it will be returned to in subsequent chapters.

Eastern European economies lagged far behind the leading OECD-European states through the 1980s. Continued Soviet political control, exercised through minions of Moscow and propped up by the might of the Red Army (manifest in Hungary in 1956 and during the Prague Summer of 1968) was deemed essential to the security of the USSR. This political reality determined the pace and character of economic growth in the European bloc states. Beginning in the late 1950s, the Soviets orchestrated a force-fed campaign of Soviet-style industrialization which, as at home, immediately felt the retarding influence of backward agriculture. To modernize and hopefully to allay the deep-rooted disaffection of national populations toward their heavy-handed regimes required the transfer of energy and other resources from the USSR to its subject states.

An imperative of modernization was the rapid substitution of oil and natural gas for coal in both industrial and domestic sectors. Poland, East Germany (GDR), and Czechoslovakia contained sufficient coal, but aside from Romania's diminishing oil reserves, the region overlay little oil or gas. Although sizable oil imports from Russia commenced during the 1960s (Table 6.9), followed by gas imports during the 1970s, coal remained the leading regional fuel, composing 66 percent of TPER in 1973 and still at 60 percent in 1985. In the coal states mentioned above over 70 percent of TPER derived from coal in 1975. As oil and gas use rose, eastern Europe became more dependent upon the USSR. Energy import dependence, low relative to OECD-Europe or Japan (Table 6.2), increased from less than 10 percent in 1960 to 16 percent in 1970 and continued upward during the 1970s. Poland, GDR, and Czecho-slovakia, in 1970, imported from Russia 85, 87, and 70 percent, respec-tively, of total energy imports.

Energy supplies from the Soviet Union during the 1960s carried a stiff price, literally. According to Hewitt, until 1974 eastern Europe paid substantially more for Soviet oil than western Europe and more than world spot prices. In 1971, GDR, Poland, and Czechoslovakia each received between 9 and 10 mmt from the Soviet Union, or 97 percent of all oil receipts. Oil, cheaper by 50 to 60 cents per barrel, was available but the Soviets prohibited purchases from the Middle East. Beginning in the late 1960s, the Soviets also compelled their partners to help finance energy development projects. Czechoslovakia, as an example, invested 500 million rubles in Russian oil exploration in exchange for guaranteed deliveries of costly oil. Bloc states also diverted funds from weak domes-tic sectors to the construction of Soviet nuclear power plants. Into the 1970s, eastern Europe contributed an estimated $5 billion to assure the continued flow of Soviet oil and gas.[39]

Left to their own devices, eastern Europe would have embarked upon a program of industrialization that attracted western capital and technology. North African and Persian Gulf oil was readily available and little Russian oil would have been imported. Deals would have been struck for Soviet gas. The financing of electric generation and trans-mission facilities, too, would have drawn in western financial and tech-nological aid. Some of the advantages of a free relationship with Russia might have dissipated between 1973 and 1979 when Soviet oil prices to eastern Europe were held below world spot prices. As for the Soviets, it is difficult to ascertain the economic advantages of the energy traffic with the bloc states. Each barrel of oil shipped to eastern Europe had a more productive use at home. In the Soviet view, such valuable commodities as fuels constituted goods to exploit politically. Oil and gas earned western currencies and technology. Oil could also be used as a weapon. The Soviets curtailed oil deliveries to Czechoslovakia in 1968, and to Cuba which opposed the invasion of Czechoslovakia. In later years, Moscow employed an oil embargo to force the Polish government to crush internal dissidence.

Energy policy confusion in the United States

Compared with its OECD partners, the USA luxuriated in energy and mineral wealth. As in western Europe and Japan, the supply of energy and minerals was firmly linked to the goals of national security and sustained economic growth. The USA assumed that its worldwide market power, managed by giant oil and mineral multinationals and protected by a global military presence, would assure the continued inward flow of necessary natural resources at low prices. Since abundant domestic reserves of fossil fuels and other minerals existed, a comprehensive national resource policy failed to emerge for lack of compelling reasons.

By the 1960s, however, US dependence on imports of critical metals and oil reached unprecedented levels. Prices, however, remained low; supply remained adequate. Assertions of producer sovereignty in Mexico and Iran were treated as isolated incidents. The USA, then, was unprepared for the disintegration of US–MNOC hegemony in Middle Eastern oil fields during the 1960s. As producer governments acted in concert to control production and price, the USA did nothing to protect its vested interests, sanguinely believing that producers always sold their wares at market determined prices.

The belief that energy supply was basically secure precluded serious consideration of resource policies that would extend the life of reserves or moderate demand through conservation, resource substitution, processing or refining improvements, and recycling.[40] Whatever was essayed in the energy policy arena was inspired by internal energy politics rather than by a realistic appraisal of global energy politics. Despite prior warnings, American officials rejected the possibility that Saudi Arabia would turn its oil power against the USA.

The energy transition in America, initiated during the 1920s, manifested persistent fluctuations in the shares of TPER distributed among primary energy sources into the 1980s (Tables 4.5 and 7.1). The energy crises of the 1970s encouraged a modest revival of coal use that seems to have settled at a stable level since 1980, as it has in OECD-Europe and Japan. Sporadic shortages in gas supply, declining reserves, and higher prices caused a reduction in both the share of gas in TPER and in the amount consumed. The fall in gas use was compensated by rising coal and nuclear contributions to supply. In Japan and OECD-Europe, as in the USA, the troublesome factor lay in the inability substantially to reduce the proportion of net energy imports to TPER, specifically petroleum imports (Table 6.3). US oil imports doubled from 1960 to 1970, despite the oil import quotas. For the four years, 1970–3, oil imports rose by 91 percent, carrying import dependence to 17 percent in 1973 (Table 6.2). Oil import dependence moved from 36 percent in 1970 to 40 percent in 1973, and 51 percent by 1975.[41]

America recorded an average energy use growth rate of about 5 percent annually during the 1960s, compared with 6 to 7 percent in the USSR, West Germany, and OECD-Europe, and certainly unremarkable compared with Japan's 21 percent.[42] The USA, notwithstanding its plentiful oil and gas reserves, a superabundance of coal, and strong nuclear technology, found itself with less energy than it required. It joined a lengthening list of oil importing industrialized and industrializing nations. The magnitude of the American demand did not mark it off from all other markets. Japan's oil imports often equaled and even surpassed America's while the cumulative imports of OECD-Europe greatly exceeded America's (Table 6.3).

America's prodigious consumption of energy, documented in Tables 6.1 and 6.3–6.5, must be placed within the context of the nation's global economic position. Trade deficits accumulated during the late 1960s as the competitive strength of American industry weakened both at home and abroad. For the five years prior to the OPEC price hike, 1968–72, the value (1980 dollars) of American imports surpassed exports by an annual average of $68 billion, small potatoes compared with the 1987 deficit of $211 billion.[43] The escalation of the war in Vietnam and a moderately expensive campaign to create a poverty and pollution free Great Society yielded budgetary deficits. After 1968, an inflationary surge ripped into the purchasing power of many Americans whose real incomes declined. The Vietnam conflict fractured domestic political unity and, combined with such issues as inflation and social reform, left energy issues smoldering in a forgotten corner of the backyard. The ramifications of OPEC's victories at Teheran and Tripoli induced little discussion and no action.

R.H.K. Vietor and C.D. Goodwin offer insights into and details of domestic energy politics since World War II that cannot be duplicated here.[44] The American government, after World War II as before, perceived energy resources simply as commodities. Concern about competitiveness within each industry, deviations from the mandates of antitrust legislation and, in the case of coal, anxiety over the volatility of labor–management relations, defined the paramount issues. Energy, as a thing in itself, as the bedrock upon which the economy rested, hovered indistinctly at some far edge of American political consciousness.

The American coal industry offers a convenient point of entry since US policies toward other fuels keenly affected its fortunes.[45] Table 6.11 shows the decline of coal and its partial recovery from 1965 to 1973. The rundown was most pronounced between 1947 and 1961, years in which intense competition from fuel oil and natural gas eroded coal's markets. As the railroads dieselized and electrified, coal disappeared as a railroad fuel. Between 1947 and 1965, residential and commercial demand plunged by over 80 million metric tons as former users happily replaced dirty and inconvenient coal furnaces with fuel oil or natural gas apparatus. Total industrial consumption fell off by a significant margin: demand in 1947 for 251 mmt dropped to 172 mmt by 1973. These losses were not recovered through exports.

Only power plant demand rose, and quite rapidly at that. In this

Table 6.11 Consumers of US coal, 1947–73 (million short tons)

	1947	1955	1961	1965	1970	1973
Production	631	465	403	512	603	543
Electric utilities	86	141	180	243	320	387
Railroads	109	15	0	0	0	0
Coke plants	105	107	74	95	96	94
Cement and steel	22	16	15	16	13	6[1]
All other manufacturing	124	90	77	86	75	72[2]
Residential– commercial	97	53	28	19	12	11
Exports	69	51	35	50	71	50

[1] Steel only
[2] Includes cement

Sources: U.S. Bureau of the Census, *Historical Statistics of the United States, Colonial Times to 1970. Bicentennial Edition. Parts 1 and 2*, Washington, D.C.: USGPO (1975), pp. 589–91; R.H.K. Vietor, *Environmental Politics and the Coal Coalition*, College Station, Tex.: Texas A & M University Press (1980), p. 129; Ching-yuan Lin, "Global Pattern of Energy Consumption before and after the 1974 Oil Crisis," *Economic Development and Cultural Change*, 32 (July 1984), pp. 781–802.

market, too, stiff competition was encountered, but coal successfully increased the tonnage sold to buyers that consumed 71 percent of production in 1973, a far higher proportion of total production than the norm in western Europe (Table 6.6). But thermal plants burned a rising volume of natural gas and fuel oil as boiler fuels, reducing the market share of coal from 69 percent in 1955 to 56 percent in 1973. In that year, an amount of oil and natural gas equivalent to 300 mmt of coal produced 655 billion kwh, a severe deprivation from the perspective of the coal industry.[46]

Excluding coal demand in the utilities and overseas markets, coal consumption fell from 457 mmt in 1947 to 183 in 1973 (Table 6.11), compelling a shrinkage in the labor force from 416,000 in 1950 to 140,000 in 1970. This occurred despite coal prices that declined from an average of about $15 per ton, f.o.b. mines, in 1947 to under $8 in 1969, the result of increasing mechanization and reduced labor costs. Improving productivity per man hour did not, however, lower coal prices by a margin sufficient to compete with fuel oil or natural gas.

Coal operated in a market in which regulated natural gas and electricity prices were fixed, according to critics of regulation, at levels below the intrinsic value of those energy forms. Lin's calculations indicate that the price of oil relative to coal declined by more than 40 percent between 1955 and 1973. In power plants, the technology of coal burning raised the kwh output per unit of coal. The coal industry remained labor intensive and the bargaining power of its dominant union precluded the wage slashing that characterized the industry during the 1920s and early 1930s. Coal's disabilities included very high freight rates compared to the pipeline rates prevailing for oil and natural gas.[47]

Coal, an unregulated industry, felt the heavy hand of government. Legislative efforts to deregulate natural gas failed during the Truman and Eisenhower administrations. Gas remained tightly regulated until the Carter and Reagan presidencies. Artificially low prices encouraged the inefficient use of natural gas as a boiler fuel and discouraged the search for supplemental reserves. Withdrawals consistently exceeded new discoveries after World War II with rapid depletion occurring after 1969. Some sections of the country suffered gas delivery curtailments in 1970 and from the interdiction of new service hookups. The coal industry vigorously supported gas deregulation and emergency curtailments, hoping that uncertainty of gas supply would attract new orders for coal. Demand for coal did rebound during the 1960s (Table 6.11) as some older thermal power plants switched from gas to coal and as wartime demand reinvigorated a hitherto slumping steel production.

The National Coal Association mobilized industry opposition to both public hydroelectric projects and to subsidization of nuclear power. Pursuing, as it had during the 1920s and 1930s, an inveterately self-interested course, its self-serving position elicited little sympathy from government circles. Federal promises to support research in coal synthetics and to promote overseas markets came to nothing.[48]

In 1963, the Clean Air Act presented a new danger to coal. Although not immediately threatening to coal interests, this law, as Vietor explains it, engendered further efforts to put teeth in it, resulting in the Clean Air Act of 1970. Mounting concern over the deleterious effects of coal burning on air quality formed but a part of a more comprehensive crusade to protect natural ecosystems. In addition to the air quality acts, Congress responded to public demands for environmental protection by enacting laws regulating the disposal of solid wastes and controlling water pollution. In 1969, the National Environmental Policy Act won passage and, in the following year, the Environmental Protection Agency was established. This flurry of legislation, much of it amended during the 1970s to improve its effectiveness, promised to add substantially to the cost of coal burning. Air quality standards affected coal burning power plants, water quality controls impinged upon mines that contaminated surface water and groundwater supplies, and health and safety regulations required investments in and around the mines to bring units into compliance. Other laws provided compensation to many thousands of miners (or their survivors) who suffered from black lung disease. The cost of compliance to these regulations, though still fairly

light in 1973, became progressively steeper thereafter, perhaps dampening a resurgence in coal production stimulated by the sharp increase
in oil prices in 1973.[49]

Coal's dilemma, traceable to the ubiquitous use of oil and natural gas
and exacerbated by environmental protection legislation, seemed irreversible during the 1960s. The earlier failure of gas deregulation did
not prompt renewed efforts during the 1960s. Both the Kennedy and
Johnson administrations emphasized natural gas rate reductions, despite industry-wide concern over reserves and general agreement that
only higher wellhead prices would induce exploratory drilling. Gas
curtailments to industrial consumers, beginning in 1970, became more
serious in subsequent years. Although beneficial to the coal industry,
curtailments raised fuel prices, adding to the burden of the OPEC price
increases after 1973, forced plant closings and worker layoffs, and
jeopardized municipal service. But these untoward consequences struck
most sharply after 1973.[50]

Back in the 1920s and again in the 1930s, the independent oil firms,
enthusiastically supported by the coal industry, demanded federal
action to reduce or prohibit the import of cheap foreign oil. The Suez
closure of 1956 and augmented sensitivity to the connection between
national security and America's domestic oil industry led to the adoption of voluntary import quotas in 1957 and mandatory quotas in 1959.
By limiting oil imports to growth rates matching internal consumption,
prices would be raised sufficiently, or so it was averred, to stimulate
domestic exploration and, secondarily, to improve the competitive
situation of coal. The reinvigoration of domestic energy industries
would reduce dependence on foreign oil and fasten national energy
security to a firm domestic foundation.[51]

The international ramifications of the quota system were discussed in
Chapter 5. Domestic impacts are no easier to isolate. Crude oil production rose by 34 percent during the ten years, 1961–70 and then
began to fall; during the previous ten-year period, production had risen
by only 14 percent. However, the number of producing wells drilled
declined from 30,641 in 1956 to 12,398 in 1970 while the number of
exploratory wells dropped from 16,173 to 7,693. The quotas failed to
induce domestic exploration. Crude oil reserves in 1970 were even lower
than in 1959 while the reserve–production ratio, holding at 12 from 1958
to 1963, fell off to under 10 in 1969 and 1970. Old fields and old wells
provided the new production.[52]

Eisenhower's successors tinkered with the import quotas. The
northeastern seaboard, the nation's largest fuel oil market, was permitted to import more fuel oil than the quotas allowed, a trend reflected
in the growth rates of product imports provided by Table 5.1. Refined

product imports more than doubled from 1961 to 1969 and rose by an additional 71 percent from 1969 to 1973. Fuel oil shortages in 1969–70, a result of the lingering effects of the second Suez closure, production cutbacks in Libya, and aggravated by natural gas scarcity in 1970, convinced Nixon to open the dike even wider. By this time, significant pressure was exerted from within the Nixon administration to abandon the quotas. Nixon finally terminated the program in April 1972.[53]

American energy import dependence intensified between 1970 and 1973 (Table 6.2) even as the share of domestic oil demand filled by imports reached 40 percent in 1973. Natural gas and fuel oil shortages occurred after 1969. The coal industry was besieged by competitive and environmental forces. The caustic touch of Vietnam eroded national unity. Inflation sapped the strength of the domestic economy, compelling President Nixon to impose a nationwide wage and price freeze in 1971 and successive price controls thereafter. Holding oil prices down from 1971 through the embargo of 1973 (oil controls remained in effect until 1981), just as world prices rose, further discouraged domestic oil exploration and development and stimulated even greater volumes of imports, thus worsening dependence upon a few producing countries.

Many policies impinged upon America's energy supply from 1960 to 1973, but an energy policy did not surface. The regulatory practices affecting natural gas conformed to consumer demand for low rates. Pressure from within the domestic oil industry and a poorly conceived notion of national security produced oil import quotas which achieved nothing positive. The federal government hardly responded to the transfer of production and price power to the oil producing states. The short-term implications of soaring energy use appeared on few agendas in Washington, D.C. From 1971 to 1973, the Nixon anti-inflation program treated oil as just another commodity. On the bright side, a surge of new orders for nuclear power plants occasioned some optimism regarding future energy supply. But in 1973, America's glaring energy vulnerability, replicated in western Europe and Japan, invited radical Arab action following the Arab attack on Israel during the Yom Kippur holy days.

International traffic in electrical equipment and plant

Burgeoning electricity production in the OECD states and in various industrializing countries characterized the 1950s and 1960s. Thermal plants and hydroelectric facilities generated the great bulk of new production, the share for each type dependent upon the water power resources of particular countries. Argentina, Brazil, Colombia, Mexico, and Venezuela generated four-fifths of a Latin American output that in 1975 was eight times larger than in 1950. In 1975, thermal plants in Argentina produced 82 percent of the total while in Brazil hydropower generated 92 percent. Impressive advances were achieved in Turkey, India, and other LDCs. Expansion required huge investments in plant and equipment and, for the LDCs, necessitated the importation of technology and technicians and large amounts of capital from the developed states.[54]

Fewer than a dozen firms located in the USA, UK, West Germany, Switzerland, Italy, and Japan dominated the electrical equipment industry, with the USA clearly the leader in nuclear into the 1970s and West Germany replacing the USA as the leading exporter of thermal plant equipment by 1969. For such large firms as General Electric, the world's largest electrical equipment manufacturer, and the merged Siemens-AEG of Germany, the world market was divided into several parts.

Western European and US firms dominated their national markets. So powerful and capable were GE and Westinghouse that the USA, which installed over one-half of global generating capacity between 1955 and 1969, composed but a small fraction of the international market for such large items as steam turbine generators. Conversely, only a small part of US turbine production left the country. Western European manufacturers exported one-half of electrical equipment output to other European countries. Firms such as Switzerland's Brown Boveri relied almost wholly upon exports while German and Japanese firms such as Siemens-AEG and Hitachi defended market shares at home and successfully cultivated sales around the world, including sales in the USA. In the US market, sophisticated buyers selected the best technology available. Siemens-AEG and Brown Boveri discovered a thriving US market for high voltage transmission equipment when US manufacturers carelessly failed to meet delivery schedules. Japanese firms won contracts in the USA for hydroelectric equipment. These incursions cost American firms a share of the home market that could have been retained by better management.[55]

In addition to the markets of western Europe and the USA, demand in Latin America, South Korea, South Africa, and elsewhere afforded opportunities for the sale of entire plants as well as for specific equipment. Electrification, considered essential to economic modernization, provided a standard by which to measure progress. Brazil nationalized the assets of the American and Foreign Power Company in 1963 and 1964, assumed responsibility for all investments in new facilities, and launched a massive electrification program. From 1967 through 1973, Brazilian investments in power rose from $474 million to $1.4 billion, and totaled $5.7 billion. Electricity production reached 80 billion kwh, up 3.5 times since 1960. Other Latin American governments also bought out American and Foreign Power and promoted electrification, although on a scale more modest than Brazil.

The World Bank loaned significant sums to the LDCs for power planning. Bowing to the trend toward government ownership of power systems, the Bank encouraged the development of autonomous government power agencies, the construction of nationwide grids, and the employment of rate structures designed to attract private investment. US, European, and Japanese firms competed vigorously for consulting and construction contracts in the LDCs. Hitachi and Mitsubishi vied for Brazil's hydroelectric contracts, employing a low price strategy backed by decades of experience in hydroelectric operations. World Bank regulations required open bidding and Bank approval of the victors, requirements that caused serious decline in the Commonwealth business of British electrical firms. European and Japanese firms penetrated such former British markets as Hong Kong, Australia, and South Africa.[56]

Until the mid-1960s, LDC projects consisted largely of thermal and hydroelectric construction. At that time, the cost of nuclear generation appeared to have fallen to a level competitive with a thermal plant of equivalent capacity. Based entirely on the reduction in the price of a complete plant per unit of generating capacity, these cost estimates neglected a host of pertinent factors. Nonetheless, such cost analyses presented a new power option to the LDCs and, during the 1960s, India, Pakistan, Argentina, Brazil, Egypt, South Korea, and Taiwan decided to pursue the nuclear alternative. India pushed ahead rapidly, its Canadian contractors bringing a plant on line in 1969.[57]

Nuclear power contributed a negligible portion of global and national TPER in 1973 (Table 4.5). Only in Britain did nuclear stations produce as much as 10 percent of electricity (Table 6.5). During the 1950s and 1960s, the American attempt to monopolize the technology collapsed in the face of nuclear development in Britain and the USSR. Abandoning a monopolistic stance, President Eisenhower's "Atoms for Peace" speech to the UN in 1953 announced America's willingness to share nuclear technology for peaceful purposes with non-hostile nations, both developed and undeveloped. Reactor technology and research capabilities were transferred to civilian firms. The USA obviously anticipated that GE and Westinghouse would dominate the global market for nuclear plants and that the US monopoly of enriched uranium would provide the leverage to prevent the spread of nuclear weapons.

Initially, the USA employed bilateral agreements, as with India and Pakistan, to regulate the transfer and use of nuclear technology and fissionable materials. Then, in 1957, more than 100 nations founded the

International Atomic Energy Agency (IAEA), each signatory pledging to abide by IAEA's non-proliferation safeguards. The explosion in 1964 of a nuclear device by China, a non-IAEA member, galvanized a joint US–USSR campaign to obtain worldwide ratification of a Non-Proliferation Treaty in 1968, an achievement marred by the failure to gain the adherence of China and France, each the possessor of nuclear weapons, and Argentina, Brazil, India, Pakistan, South Africa, and Israel, each with the potential for nuclear weaponry. The American interest in international safeguards stemmed from a somewhat egocentric desire to prevent the spread of such destructive weaponry to states considered unstable and aggressive and to strengthen the competitiveness of its nuclear industry in world markets. India's triggering of a bomb in 1974 and subsequent weapons development in Israel, Pakistan, and perhaps elsewhere accentuated the shortcomings of the Non-Proliferation Treaty and IAEA's safeguard procedures.

A large market for reactors in western Europe and the USA did not immediately materialize following the implementation of the Atoms for Peace program, despite an agreement between the USA and Euratom that favored American equipment and promised large US subsidies. From 1957 to 1961, GE and Westinghouse exported only seven plants, all under bilateral agreements, to Japan and western Europe. Neither did a domestic market emerge in the USA, which possessed only three operational plants in 1963. Britain's nuclear industry exported plants to Japan and Italy, but its prospects dimmed when further orders did not arrive. Although the sales atmosphere seemed poor, Canada, France, and West Germany supported an active nuclear research and development program. Nationally owned agencies in Canada and France and Kraftwerk Union, one of Germany's three largest electrical equipment firms, achieved the capability of producing an entire plant. From 1951 to 1960, those nations received seven orders for plants, Britain, twenty (all but one domestic), and the US firms, ten. During the 1960s, Sweden and Japan joined the club of nuclear plant exporters.

Increasing confidence in the safety and cost effectiveness of nuclear power produced a market breakthrough in the mid-1960s, accompanied by a rush of orders through 1974 which revitalized the American and European nuclear industries. By far the larger share of orders originated from the highly industrialized nations. The USA logged 186 new orders from 1966 through 1974, western Europe, 84, and Japan, 14. By 1974, 53 plants were operational in the USA, and 44 in OECD-Europe (with an additional 30 under construction). Many of the non-US plants were constructed during the 1960s under licensing agreements with GE or Westinghouse. But American supremacy waned thereafter. Siemens-AEG abrogated its licensing arrangement with Westinghouse in 1970 while Japanese firms quickly developed their own competence and became independent of their American mentors. France, Canada, Britain, and Sweden vigorously searched for orders. Competition intensified just as inflation and the rise of organized opposition to the safety and environmental hazards of nuclear power brought to a sudden halt this avalanche of orders for new plants. New orders in the USA fell from 109 (1971–5) to 12 (1976–80). Equally sharp declines were experienced in Germany and Japan. Hard times plagued the nuclear industry into the late 1980s; only France and the Soviet Union sustained a relatively high level of new construction.[58]

The advocates of nuclear power claimed that it would be too cheap to meter. Costs, however, spiraled to unimaginable heights during the 1970s. Nuclear electricity was no cheaper than hydro or thermal. Moreover, as opponents emphasized during the 1970s, the hidden costs attending plant safety, nuclear waste disposal, plant decommissioning, and public subsidization pushed the real price of nuclear electricity well above thermal generation. Even more damaging than cost inflation, there arose a ubiquitous public disenchantment with the assurances of nuclear adherents concerning the safety of the technology. But Three-Mile Island and Chernobyl were in the future. As of 1973, organized opposition was only emerging in the USA and almost unheard of in Europe or Japan. To many, nuclear power looked good.[59]

Conclusion

The industrialized states of the West experienced impressive economic growth after the Korean War. Economic policies promoted high employment and rising wages while dampening inflationary pressures. Constant economic growth was predicated on cheap, abundant, and uninterrupted energy and mineral supplies. The western nations, and others, recognized the close relationship between energy supply and national security. But none of the OECD states were self-sufficient in energy resources. Rapid economic growth, sought by all, fostered energy consumption which intensified energy import dependence. Rising levels of energy imports during the 1960s weakened national security, but policies promoting domestic consumption overrode equally weighty objectives of national security. Abundance and cheapness made energy import dependence acceptable.

Energy policies in the capitalist West served domestic political demands. In the Soviet Union, energy policies had to take cognizance of basic needs in the satellite states, but not to the detriment of Soviet industrial and defense goals. Each nation pursued narrow and short-term goals, thus precluding the possibility of formulating even inter-mediate-term plans. Thus, in western Europe and in the USA, the coal industry was allowed to deteriorate even though it was the largest and most valuable internal source of energy. In the USA, artificially low natural gas prices harmed the coal industry while speeding the depletion of gas reserves and discouraging exploration.

Interventionist and non-interventionist nations had all tumbled into the same empty barrel by 1973 when oil import dependence reached high levels. Western countries neglected to formulate policies protective of domestic energy resources or to foster the development of renewable energy. Aside from very controversial and costly nuclear technology, no substitute energy forms appeared on the horizon. New oil and gas finds in the North Sea and Alaska promised a few nations temporary ameli-oration of energy import dependence. As the oil producing states of OPEC gained control of production and prices in 1970–1, western consuming nations observed, lethargically. Professional politicians, whatever their personal beliefs, were quick to spot a non-issue.

Notes

1. For the above see: W.W. Rostow, *The World Economy: History and Prospect*, Austin: University of Texas Press (1978); P.F. Chapman and F. Roberts, *Metal Resources and Energy*, London: Butterworths (1983); W.M. Scammell, *The International Economy Since 1945*, 2nd edn, London: Macmillan (1983).
2. W.W. Rostow, *The Stages of Economic Growth: A Non-Communist Manifesto*, 2nd edn, Cambridge: Cambridge University Press (1971); J.K. Galbraith, *The Affluent Society*, Cambridge, Mass.: The Riverside Press (1958); D. Riesman, *Abundance for What? And Other Essays*, New York: Anchor Books (1965); D. Bell, *The Cultural Contradictions of Capitalism*, New York: Basic Books (1976).
3. OECD-Europe included: Austria, Belgium, Denmark, *Finland*, France, West Germany, Greece, Iceland, Ireland, Italy, Luxembourg, The Netherlands, Norway, Portugal, *Spain*, Sweden, Switzerland, Turkey, and Britain. Other members include: *Australia*, Canada, *Japan*, *New Zealand*, and the United States. *Yugoslavia* is an associate member. In 1960, OECD superseded the Organization for European Economic Cooperation which was established in 1948. The original members of OEEC included all of the above excepting those in italics.
4. The points alluded to in the above four paragraphs are treated in greater detail in subsequent sections. A few of the studies dealing with these matters are: P.F. Cowhey, *The Problems of Plenty: Energy Policy and International Politics*, Berkeley: University of California Press (1985); R.L. Gordon, *The Evolution of Energy Policy in Western Europe: The Reluctant Retreat from Coal*, New York: Praeger (1970); L.E. Grayson, *National Oil Companies*, New York: Wiley (1981); M.T. Hatch, *Politics*

and Nuclear Power: Energy Policy in Western Europe, Lexington: The University Press of Kentucky (1986); G.W. Hoffman, *The European Energy Challenge: East and West*, Durham, N.C.: Duke University Press (1985); W.G. Jensen, *Energy in Europe, 1945–1980*, London: G.T. Foulis (1967); H. Maull, *Europe and World Energy*, London: Butterworths (1980).

5. B.R. Mitchell, ed., *European Historical Statistics, 1950–1975*, 2nd revised edn, London: Macmillan (1981), pp. 423, 518–19.
6. IEA, *Energy Balances of OECD Countries, 1970/1982*, Paris: OECD/IEA (1984), pp. 387–9, 404; *BP Statistical Review of World Energy, June 1986*, pp. 31–3; J. Darmstadter *et al.*, *Energy in the World Economy: A Statistical Review of Trends in Output, Trade, and Consumption Since 1925*, Baltimore: The Johns Hopkins University Press for Resources for the Future (1971), pp. 624–7.
7. IEA, *Energy Balances, 1970/1982*, pp. 387–9, 404.
8   Cowhey, *Problems of Plenty*, pp. 134–44, Gordon, *Energy Policy in Western Europe*, pp. 63–94; N. Lucas, *Western European Energy Policies: A Comparative Study of the Influence of Institutional Structures on Technical Change*, Oxford: Clarendon Press (1985), pp. 9–17; H. Mendershausen, *Coping with the Oil Crisis*, Baltimore: Johns Hopkins University Press for Resources for the Future (1976), pp. 22–35; P.R. Odell, "The Energy Economy of Western Europe: a return to the use of indigenous resources," *Geography. Journal of the Geographical Association*, 66 (January 1981), pp. 1–14.
9. Cowhey, *Problems of Plenty*, pp. 134–5; Gordon, *Energy Policy in Western Europe*, pp. 52–8.
10. The High Authority of the European Coal and Steel Community *et al.*, *Memorandum on Energy Policy (June 25, 1962)*, np (August 1962), pp. 17–21; Gordon, *Energy Policy in Western Europe*, pp. 67–71, 244; L. Lister, *Europe's Coal and Steel Community*, New York: Twentieth Century Fund (1960), pp. 50–1, 280, 336; Hoffman, *European Energy Challenge*, pp. 2–4.
11 IEA, *Energy Balances, 1970/1982*, pp. 387–9, 404.
12. For the above three paragraphs: Lucas, *European Energy Policies*, pp. 9–11, 16–17; Gordon, *Energy Policy in Western Europe*, p. 62; Grayson, *National Oil Companies*, pp. 26–8, 34–6; Hatch, *Politics and Nuclear Power*, pp. 16–19.
13. *Ibid.*, p. 19; Lucas, *European Energy Policies*, pp. 14–15.
14. For the above two paragraphs: Hatch, *Politics and Nuclear Power*, pp. 12–14, 27–30; Mendershausen, *The Oil Crisis*, p. 26; Grayson, *National Oil Companies*, pp. 115–24; C. Tugenhadt and A. Hamilton, *Oil, the biggest business*, revised edn, London: Eyre Methuen (1975), p. 317.
15. For the above two paragraphs: IEA, *Energy Balances, 1970/1982*, pp. 387–9, 404; Political and Economic Planning, *A Fuel Policy for Britain*, London: PEP (1966), pp. 29–31, 97–101, 203; M.P. Jackson, *The Price of Coal*, London: Croom Helm (1974), p. 127; G.L. Reed *et al.*, *The Nationalized Fuel Industries*, London: Heinemann Educational Books (1973), pp. 18–19, 23; P. Hepple, ed., *The Petroleum Industry in the United Kingdom*, London: The Institute of Petroleum (1966), pp. 42–3; M. Peebles, *Evolution of the Gas Industry*, London: Macmillan (1980), 33–41.
16. Jensen, *Energy in Europe*, pp. 108–9, 112–14; J.D. Davis, *Blue Gold: The*

Political Economy of Natural Gas, London: Allen & Unwin (1984), pp. 14, 183–5; Peebles, *Gas Industry*, pp. 139–40.

17. O. Noreng, *The Oil Industry and Government Policy in the North Sea*, London: Croom Helm (1980), pp. 95–6.
18. Mendershausen, *The Oil Crisis*, p. 24.
19. Lucas, *European Energy Policies*, pp. 17–18; PEP, *Fuel Policy for Britain*, pp. 62–3.
20. G. Manners, *Coal in Britain*, London: Allen & Unwin (1981), p. 69.
21. R.M. Burrell and A.J. Cottrell, *Politics, Oil, and the Western Mediterranean*, Beverly Hills, Calif.: Sage (1973), p. 47; E.S. Simpson, *Coal and the Power Industries in Postwar Britain*, London: Longmans (1966), pp. 98–100.
22. For the above three paragraphs: Burrell, *Oil and the Mediterranean*, pp. 45–9; Grayson, *National Oil Companies*, p. 40; Mendershausen, *The Oil Crisis*, pp. 21, 26–7, 30; H. Madelin, *Oil and Politics*, translated by M. Totman, Farnborough: Saxon House (1975), p. 182; Hepple, *Petroleum Industry in UK*, p. 34; PEP, *Fuel Policy for Britain*, p. 227; Tugenhadt, *Oil*, p. 251; F.A. Olaloku, *Structure of the Nigerian Economy*, London: Macmillan (1979), p. 58.
23. For the above two paragraphs: Mendershausen, *The Oil Crisis*, pp. 19–21; Hatch, *Politics and Nuclear Power*, pp. 30–1; Grayson, *National Oil Companies*, p. 166; E.A. Hewitt, *Energy, Economics, and Foreign Policy in the Soviet Union*, Washington, DC: Brookings Institution (1984), p. 153; I. Kuczynski, *British Offshore Oil and Gas Policy*, New York: Garland Publishing (1982), p. 6–12; ECSC, *Memorandum on Energy*, pp. 14–16; Tugenhadt, *Oil*, pp. 251–7.
24. For the above two paragraphs: Ching-yuan Lin, "Global Pattern of Energy Consumption before and after the 1974 Oil Crisis," *Economic Development and Cultural Change*, 32 (July 1984), p. 792; Rostow, *World Economy*, p. 273; J. Foreman-Peck, *A History of the World Economy: International Relations since 1850*, Brighton: Wheatsheaf Books (1983), p. 297; J. Hirschmeier and T. Yui, *The Development of Japanese Business, 1600–1980*, 2nd edn London: Allen & Unwin (1981), pp. 292–5, 322–3; J.A. Wolfe, *Mineral Resources: A World Review*, New York: Chapman and Hall (1984), pp. 16–17; Chapman, *Metal Resources and Energy*, p. 163; Z. Mikdashi, *The International Politics of Natural Resources*, Ithaca, New York: Cornell University Press (1976), pp. 27–30; H. Shibata, "The Energy Crises and Japanese Response," *Resources and Energy*, 5 (June 1983), pp. 130–4; Statistical Office of the European Communities, *Basic Statistics of the Community...1968–1969*, 9th edn, Luxembourg: Statistical Office (1970), pp. 23, 73–5.
25. IEA, *Energy Balances 1970/1982*, pp. 387–9, 404; Darmstadter, *Energy and the World Economy*, pp. 623–4, 627, 642.
26. Y-l. Wu, *Japan's Search for Oil: A Case Study in Economic Nationalism and International Security*, Stanford, Calif.: Hoover Institution Press (1977), p. 27; United Nations, *1983 International Trade Statistics Yearbook, vol. 1. Trade by Country*, New York: UN (1985), p. 1087.
27. IEA, *Energy Balances 1983/1984*.
28. For the above three paragraphs: A.J. Surrey and J.H. Chesshire, *World Markets for Electric Power Equipment*, Brighton: University of Sussex (1972), p. 92; Wu, *Japan's Search for Oil*, p. 24; J.L. Cochran and G.L.

Griepentrog, "U.S. Energy: A Quantitative Review of the Past Three Decades," in C.D. Goodwin, ed., *Energy Policy in Perspective: Today's Problems, Yesterday's Solutions*, Washington, DC: The Brookings Institution (1981), pp. 686–7; G. Jenkins, *Oil Economists' Handbook 1985*, London: Applied Science Publishers (1985), p. 99; Statistical Office of the European Communities, *Energy Statistics Yearbook 1969–1973*, Luxembourg: SOEC (1974), p. 216.

29. For the above two paragraphs: Hirschmeier, *Japanese Business*, p. 343; L. Howell and M. Morrow, *Asia, Oil Politics and the Energy Crisis: The Haves and the Have-Nots*, New York: IDOC/North America (1974), p. 57; J. Russell, *Geopolitics of Natural Gas*, Cambridge, Mass.: Ballinger (1983), pp. 42–3; G. Luciani, *The Oil Companies and the Arab World*, London: Croom Helm (1984), p. 133; M.Y. Yoshino, *Japan's Multinational Enterprises*, Cambridge: Harvard University Press (1976), pp. 40–53; M.S. Al-Otaiba, *OPEC and the Petroleum Industry*, London: Croom Helm (1975), pp. 84–7

30. Howell, *Asia and Energy*, pp. 47, 52–3, 62–3, 73; Burrell, *Oil and the Mediterranean*, p. 55; Wu, *Japan's Search for Oil*, pp. 23–6; M. Nishahara, *The Japanese and Sukarno's Indonesia: Tokyo–Jakarta Relations, 1951–1966*, Honolulu: University Press of Hawaii (1976), pp. 118–21.

31. Wu, *Japan's Search for Oil*, pp. 72–4, 137; Cowhey, *The Problem of Plenty*, pp. 139–40.

32. For the above two paragraphs: Hewitt, *Energy in the Soviet Union*, pp. 15, 36, 38; UN, *World Energy Supplies, 1955–1958*, New York: UN (1963), p. 35 and *1961–1970* (1972), pp. 55, 57; Park, *Oil and Gas*, pp. 44, 50, 79, 84, 140, *passim*; R.W. Campbell, *The Economics of Soviet Oil and Gas*, Baltimore: The Johns Hopkins University Press for Resources for the Future (1968), pp. 141–54, 159–60, 168–9.

33. For the above two paragraphs: Hewitt, *Energy in the Soviet Union*, pp. 105–7; Cochrane, "US Energy," in Goodwin, ed., *Energy Policy*, pp. 686–7; Davis, *Blue Gold*, pp. 128–30, 178; Campbell, *Soviet Oil and Gas*, pp. 208–16; Peebles, *Gas Industry*, pp. 160–6; IEA, *Energy Balances 1983–1984*, *passim*; Lin, "Global Pattern of Energy Consumption," pp. 786, 792–6.

34. Hewitt, *Energy in the Soviet Union*, pp. 150–2.

35. Park, *Oil and Gas*, p. 165; J.P. Stern, *International Gas Trade in Europe: The Policies of Exporting and Importing Countries*, London: Heinemann (1984), p. 65.

36. Hewitt, *Energy in the Soviet Union*, p. 156; B.W. Jentleson, *Pipeline Politics: The Complex Political Economy of East–West Energy Trade*, Ithaca, New York: Cornell University Press (1986), pp. 92–3; M.I. Goldman, *The Enigma of Soviet Petroleum: Half-Full or Half-Empty?*, London: Allen & Unwin (1980), pp. 68–72; J.E. Hartshorn, *Politics and World Oil Economics: An Account of the International Oil Industry and Its Political Environment*, New York: Praeger (1967), p. 236.

37. For the above two paragraphs: Davis, *Blue Gold*, pp. 14, 17, 120; Jensen, *Energy in Europe*, pp. 115–16; Park, *Oil and Gas*, pp. 17–18, 48–9; SOEC, *Energy Statistics Yearbook 1969–1973*, p. 186.

38. Jentleson, *Pipeline Politics*, Chapters 4–5; Stern, *International Gas Trade*, pp. 46–7; Peebles, *Gas Industry*, pp. 167–9.

39. For the above three paragraphs: Hoffman, *European Energy Challenge*,

pp. 7–8; Rostow, *World Economy*, p. 281; J.P. Stern, "East European Energy and East–West Trade in Energy," in R. Belgrave, ed., *Energy– Two Decades of Crisis*, Aldershot: Gower (1983), pp. 23, 32–4; Park, *Oil and Gas*, pp. 98, 114–15, 121, 168–9; Hewitt, *Energy in the Soviet Union*, p. 163; Goldman, *Enigma of Soviet Petroleum*, pp. 60–7; G. Modelski, *Atomic Energy in the Communist Bloc*, Carlton: Melbourne University Press (1959), p. 215.

40. Chapman, *Metal Resources and Energy*, p. 163; Mikdashi, *International Politics of Natural Resources*, pp. 24–6.

41. De Golyer and MacNaughton, *Twentieth Century Petroleum Statistics 1986*, Dallas, Tex.: De Golyer and MacNaughton (1986), p. 64.

42. IEA, *Energy Balances 1970/1982*, pp. 387–9, 404.

43. World Bank, *World Tables 1988–89 Edition from the Data File of the World Bank*, Baltimore: Published for the World Bank by the Johns Hopkins University Press (1989), pp. 600–3.

44. R.H.K. Vietor, *Environmental Politics and the Coal Coalition*, College Station, Tex.: Texas A & M University Press (1980) and *Energy policy in America since 1945: A study of business–government relations*, Cambridge: Cambridge University Press (1984); Goodwin, ed., *Energy Policy in Perspective*.

45. Only bituminous is considered here; by 1970, anthracite accounted for 1 percent of total coal production.

46. US Bureau of the Census, *Historical Statistics of the United States, Colonial Times to 1970. Bicentennial Edition. Parts 1 and 2*, Washington, DC: USGPO (1975), Part 1, pp. 589–92; Lin, "Global Pattern of Energy Consumption," p. 787; W.F. Saalbach, *United States Bituminous Coal: Trends Since 1920 and Prospects to 1975*, Pittsburgh: University of Pittsburgh Press (1960), pp. 11–13.

47. For the above two paragraphs: Bureau of the Census, *Historical Statistics Part 1*, pp. 590–1; World Coal Study, *Future Coal Prospects: Country and Regional Assessments*, Cambridge, Mass.: Ballinger (1980), pp. 460–2; Saalbach, *Bituminous Coal*, p. 21; Gordon, *Energy Policy in Western Europe*, p. 157; Vietor, *Energy policy in America*, pp. 272–7; W.J. Barber, "Studied Inaction in the Kennedy Years," in Goodwin, ed., *Energy Policy in Perspective*, pp. 320–4; Lin, "Global Pattern of Energy Consumption," p. 783; J.G. Clark, *Energy Policy and the Federal Government: Fossil Fuel Policies, 1900–1948*, Urbana: University of Illinois Press (1986), pp. 178–80.

48. For the above two paragraphs: C.D. Goodwin, "Truman Administration Policies toward Particular Energy Sources," pp. 132–8, 182–92, and Barber, "Kennedy," pp. 316–20 in Goodwin, ed., *Energy Policy in Perspective*; Vietor, *Energy policy in America*, pp. 80–9, 167–78, 273–4; De Golyer and MacNaughton, *Petroleum Statistics 1986*, p. 75; Bureau of the Census, *Historical Statistics. Part 2*, p. 820; B. Goldschmidt, *The Atomic Complex: A Worldwide Political History of Nuclear Energy*, La Grange Park, Ill.: American Nuclear Society (1982), p. 328.

49. Vietor, *Coal Coalition*, pp. 137–60; D.M. Gates, *Energy and Ecology*, Sunderland, Mass.: Sinauer Associates (1985), pp. 126–32, 251–3; R. Mills and A.N. Toke, *Energy, Economics, and the Environment*, Englewood Cliffs, N.J.: Prentice Hall (1985), pp. 330–5, 352.

50. Vietor, *Energy policy in America*, pp. 274–7; Barber, "Kennedy," in Goodwin, ed., *Energy Policy in Perspective*, pp. 320–4.

51. Clark, *Energy and the Federal Government*, pp. 197–201, 298; P. Odell, *Oil and World Power*, 7th edn, Harmondsworth, Middlesex: Penguin (1983), pp. 39–43; W.J. Barber, "The Eisenhower Energy Policy: Reluctant Intervention," in Goodwin, ed., *Energy Policy in Perspective*, pp. 252–9.
52. De Golyer and MacNaughton, *Petroleum Statistics 1986*, pp. 18, 20, 27–8.
53. *Ibid.*, p. 60; Barber, "Kennedy," p. 312 and J.L. Cochrane, "Energy Policy in the Johnson Administration: Logical Order versus Economic Pluralism," pp. 391–2 and N. de Marchi, "Energy Policy under Nixon: Mainly Putting Out Fires," pp. 404–6, in Goodwin, ed., *Energy Policy in Perspective*; Vietor, *Energy policy in America*, pp. 142–3; E.W. Chester, *United States Oil Policy and Diplomacy: A Twentieth Century Overview*, Westport, Conn.: Greenwood Press (1983), pp. 46–7.
54. J.W. Mullen, *Energy in Latin America: The Historical Record*, Santiago de Chile: CEPAL (1978), p. 54; H. Collier, *Developing Electric Power: Thirty Years of World Bank Experience*, Baltimore: The Johns Hopkins University Press for the World Bank (1983), pp. 168–9.
55. For the above two paragraphs: Surrey, *Electric Power Equipment*, pp. 5, 40–5, 56–8, 93–7, 106–19, *passim*.
56. For the above two paragraphs: Collier, *Electric Power*, pp. 30–8, 69–72, 83–4, 168–9, *passim*; Wilkins, *Multinational Enterprise*, pp. 361–2; Mullen, *Energy in Latin America*, p. 54; C. Flavin, *Electricity's Future: The Shift to Efficiency and Small-Scale Power*, Worldwatch Paper 61, November 1984, Washington, DC: Worldwatch Institute (1984), p. 13; Surrey, *Electric Power Equipment*, pp. 42, 93–103.
57. The LDC experience with nuclear power is discussed in Chapter 9. L.C. Nehrt, *International Marketing of Nuclear Power Plants*, Bloomington, Ind.: Indiana University Press (1966), pp. 342–4; J.E. Katz and O.S. Marwah, *Nuclear Power in Developing Countries: An Analysis of Decision Making*, Lexington, Mass.: Lexington Books (1982), pp. 12–17; M.A. Khan, "Nuclear Energy and International Cooperation: A Third World Perception of the Erosion of Confidence," in I. Smart, ed., *World Nuclear Energy: Toward a Bargain of Confidence*, Baltimore: The Johns Hopkins University Press (1982), pp. 51–3.
58. For the above two paragraphs: F. Fesharaki *et al.*, *Critical Energy Issues in Asia and the Pacific: The Next Twenty Years*, Boulder, Colo.: Westview Press (1982), pp. 126, 140–6; Goldschmidt, *Atomic Complex*, pp. 244–6, 251–5, 267, 306–9, *passim*; Barber, "Eisenhower," pp. 216–17 and Cochrane and Griepentrog, "US Energy," p. 702, in Goodwin, ed., *Energy Policy in Perspective*; L.S. Spector, *The New Nuclear Nations*, N.Y.: Vintage Books (1985), pp. 6–7; Khan, "Nuclear Energy," pp. 50–5 and M. Lonnroth and W. Walker, "The Viability of the Civil Nuclear Industry," p. 206, in Smart, ed., *World Nuclear Energy*; Jensen, *Energy in Europe*, pp. 94–6; Nehrt, *Marketing Nuclear Power*, pp. 128–9, 192–3, 350; SOEC, *Energy Statistics Yearbook 1969–1973*, pp. 266–7.
59. C. Flavin, "Reassessing the Economics of Nuclear Power," in L.R. Brown, director, *State of the World 1984: A Worldwatch Institute Report on Progress Toward a Sustainable Society*, New York: W.W. Norton (1984), p. 119; W. Shawcross, "Nuclear Power: The Fifth Horseman," *The Spectator*, October 25, 1986, p. 10.

7

The West and the energy crisis of 1973–8

Simultaneous Egyptian and Syrian attacks on advanced Israeli positions on October 6, 1973 coincided with a scheduled OPEC meeting in Vienna on October 8. The Arab assault, launched as Jews celebrated the high holy day, Yom Kippur, precipitated a protracted energy crisis, the causes of which are still debated and the consequences of which are still being sorted out. This chapter describes the varied responses of OECD-Europe, the USA, and Japan to a sudden and steep rise in the price of oil, a temporary embargo and resultant oil scarcity, and gnawing uncertainty about the security of oil supplies. The chapter concludes as Moslem fundamentalists in Iran overthrew the Shah's government, sending the Shah into exile in July, 1979, and thereby precipitating an astounding jump in oil prices. The following chapter employs the same time frame to investigate the impact of these events on the Soviet bloc and on the producing and non-producing LDCs.

The OPEC price hikes and the OAPEC embargo

OPEC officials wending their way to Vienna in early October were firmly resolved to set prices above those established at the Tripoli and Teheran meetings by producer fiat. The Yom Kippur War presented a propitious moment for OPEC to jack prices up without negotiation or consultation with the MNOCs or their governments. The energy supply and demand predicament of the industrialized states assured the success of OPEC's price decisions and encouraged the Organization of Arab Petroleum Exporting Countries (OAPEC) to impose an oil embargo on October 17, 1973.

As energy use in the West became ever more intensive and ever more oil based, reliance upon energy imports intensified. Net energy imports as a percentage of total primary energy requirements (TPER) for the USA, Japan, and OECD-Europe stood at 17, 93, and 65, respectively (Table 6.2). Oil composed the bulk of those imports. Together, those three markets received 1,373 million metric tons of oil in 1973, or 83 percent of world imports (Table 6.3). As Table 7.1 indicates for 1973, oil provided well over half of TPER in OECD-Europe and Japan and 44 percent in the USA.

Had this oil been obtained from many sources, each supplying but a small proportion of overall demand, the West would have been less vulnerable to OPEC and OAPEC pressure. Table 7.2 identifies the key regions from which the West obtained its oil. It appears that the USA drew from more diverse and less insecure producers than its OECD associates. But, as it happened, that offered little protection. In the USA, the world's largest energy and oil producer (in 1973), output from aging domestic fields declined between 1970 and 1973 while TPER and oil's share of TPER rose (Table 7.1). American crude oil imports soared from 67 mmt in 1970 to 164 mmt in 1973. Members of OPEC supplied 74 percent of the latter tonnage. OPEC sellers dominated western European and Japanese markets even more completely. Europe drew 89 percent of its crude and Japan 80 percent from OPEC which provided 64 percent of world supply.

Surging western demand for oil, particularly in the USA where both oil and natural gas production exceeded discoveries, created the moment for OPEC price action. Supplies were tight and transportation fully employed in 1973. The West evinced no capacity for united resistance to an OPEC price increase. The producing states were convinced that the MNOCs would not object to higher prices and would follow orders. The Yom Kippur War, then, did not cause a price increase but did, in association with the OAPEC embargo, cause a higher price to be selected. The West had no choice but to acquiesce to the OPEC price. Readily available alternatives to petroleum did not exist.[1]

The political might of oil was used by OAPEC to punish the friends of Israel. On October 17, OAPEC announced a production cutback of 5 percent each month until Israel both withdrew from the territories seized in 1967 and agreed to recognize Palestinian rights. The next day, Saudi Arabia, the erstwhile friend of the USA, reduced oil production by 10 percent and imposed a total embargo on the USA which, by then, had undertaken the resupply of Israel's armed forces. Libya followed suit. Saudi Arabia then reduced production by 25 percent. By October 22, OAPEC's members had joined Saudi Arabia in the embargo and

Table 7.1   TPER and fuel mix of industrialized states, 1970–87

	TPER*	% Solid fuels	% Oil	% Natural gas	% Hydro	% Nuclear	% Net imports to TPER
USA							
1970	1563	21	42	33	4	<1	9
1973	1742	21	44	30	4	1	17
1979	1916	25	45	25	3	3	21
1985	1792	24[1]	40	25	5	6	12
1987	1840	24	43	23	4	6	16
Japan							
1970	282	23	69	1	7	<1	86
1973	340	17	75	1	5	<1	93
1979	377	15	70	5	6	5	90
1985	372	20	55	10	6	9	84
1986[4]	380	18	56	10	5	11	86
OECD-Europe							
1970	1044	30	57	6	7	1	63
1973	1197	23	59	10	6	1	65
1979	1286	22	54	14	7	3	54
1985	1236	20	46	16	8	10	40
1986[4]	1277	20	44	15	7	11	40
USSR[3]							
1970	789	38	35	22	4	<1	
1973	874	36	37	23	4	na	
1979	1134	30	38	27	4[2]	1[2]	
1985	1376	26	33	35	4	3	

* Million metric tons oil equivalent

[1] 28 percent in 1984
[2] 1980
[3] The Soviets were net exporters
[4] Estimates

Sources: IEA, *Energy Balances Of OECD Countries, 1970/1982,* Paris OECD/IEA (1984), pp. 387–9, 404; *ibid., 1983/1984,* pp. 16–17, 76–7, 120–1, 135; *BP Statistical Review of World Energy, 1981, 1982, 1984, 1986, passim;* IEA, *Coal Information 1987,* Paris: OECD/IEA (1987), *passim.*

production slashes. Also subject to the embargo were the Netherlands, Portugal, Canada, Rhodesia, and South Africa.

The aggressive Saudi response should not have taken the USA by surprise. In April, 1973, the Saudi government had warned the Nixon administration that oil would be used politically against the USA if it persisted in favoring Israel over the Arabs. The Aramco partners, trying to distance themselves from America's commitment to Israel, publicly criticized Israel's Arab policies. But the Nixon administration, preoccupied with the Watergate scandal, dismissed the Saudi warning as a bluff. American foreign policy in the Persian Gulf rested on the assumption that the Soviet menace tied Saudi Arabia and Iran so firmly to the USA that neither could afford to weaken their protector. American policy makers shared the belief that Saudi self-interest and, by extension, Arab Persian Gulf self-interest, precluded radical action on behalf of anti-Zionism. The USA was wrong. As Al Sowayegh asserts, the Arab world was less concerned with the Soviets than with Israel and the Palestinians.[2]

Oil withdrawals by the OAPEC states declined from 19.8 million barrels daily* in September 1973 to 15.5 mbd in December. After subtracting from this loss the increased production of the non-Arab producers, the net loss approximated 3.5 mbd. The non-embargoed industrialized nations suffered supply deficiencies along with the embargo's targets. The 5-month embargo denied the USA about 25 mmt, or 8 percent of 1973 crude imports while domestic production fell from 480 mmt in 1972 to 444 mmt in 1974. This loss sufficed to cause real oil shortages in America.

Diminished production, distribution inefficiencies, and MNOC decisions combined to deny normal supplies of oil to most western European nations and to Japan. While France was not included in the embargo, minimally reduced shipments were experienced as the MNOCs diverted some oil intended for France to embargoed markets. France complained mightily of discrimination and blamed oil difficulties on the machinations of foreign oil companies. Oil scarcity was more onerous in Germany than in France or the UK. MNOCs and the independents delivered 12 mmt less to Germany in 1974 than in 1973, a reduction of 8 percent. Japan, reliant upon a few producing countries and a few Anglo-American oil firms for most of her oil, was in a precarious position. Japan's largest producing firm, the Arabian Oil Company, like Aramco, was forced by Saudi Arabia to reduce production. The MNOCs, too, notified Japanese refineries of a diminution in crude

---

* Multiply by 50 to obtain the metric ton equivalent for twelve months.

Table 7.2   Sources of oil for industrialized states, 1973–85 (percent)

	1973	1979	1982	1985
USA				
Net imports (mmt)	305	420	249	248
Middle East	13	25	15	8
North Africa	6	15	5	4
Latin America	43	30	41	41
Canada	21	5	9	15
All others	17	25	30	32
OECD-Europe				
Net imports (mmt)	776	647	466	412
Middle East	68	66	49	35
North Africa	16	14	16	20
West Africa	7	8	7	12
Soviet Bloc	6	9	16	20
All others	3	3	12	13
Japan				
Net imports (mmt)	292	276	206	202
Middle East*	76	74	66	64
Southeast Asia	19	21	21	19
Western hemisphere and China	3	4	11	13
All others	2	1	2	4

* Includes North Africa

Source: BP Statistical Review of World Oil Industry, 1970–86.

deliveries. The foreign MNOCs delivered a larger proportion of available crude to their Japanese affiliates than to Japanese owned firms.[3]

Arab oil politics elicited immediate diplomatic responses from the beleaguered OECD states. To curry favor with the Arabs, both the European Community and Japan hurriedly assured the world of their sympathy for Palestinian rights. An EC meeting in November, 1973 called upon Israel to withdraw her troops from Egyptian lands seized in late October and early November, a demand seconded by Japan in December. Both EC and Japan, in keeping with a 1967 United Nations' resolution, stated that Israel should withdraw from the lands conquered in 1967. The EC also undertook joint meetings with the Arabs, culminating in a 1974 gathering with the Arab League and the Palestinian Liberation Organization (PLO). In return, OAPEC exempted Japan and EC members from the production cutbacks of November and December. Neither was the USA wholly immobile. Despite its scream of blackmail, the USA pressed Israel to reach an immediate accord with Egypt, permitting the Sadat government to retire from the field with some honor. As a result of this subtle American shift, the OAPEC states, excepting Libya and Syria, ended the embargo in March 1974.[4]

The pro-Arab maneuvering of EC and Japan secured fewer benefits than the initiation of direct bargaining for oil supplies with the governments of the producing states.

As intended, the production cuts and an effective embargo shocked the industrialized states. Panicky buyers, unassured by their governments or the oil companies, imagined the disappearance of oil from local markets. But the psychological consequences of the embargo had evaporated by 1974 or 1975. The impact of the price weapon lasted longer and had greater effect. National economies had hardly accommodated to the first round of price increases when the Iranian Revolution precipitated an even more extreme ratcheting upwards of oil prices in 1979–80. The price increases of 1973 and following years were programmed by OPEC; western panic rather than OPEC design precipitated the price explosion of 1979–80.

Opinions regarding OPEC's prices from 1973 through 1978 range from the wildly accusative which cast OPEC in the role of an arrogant price gouging cartel blamable for all the ills — inflation, in particular of the 1970s to those essentially absolving OPEC of all responsibility for the economic maladjustments of that decade.[5] Most analysts avoid the polar positions, recognizing western and OPEC responsibility for unstable and, in many LDCs, damaged national economies. But even on the middle ground, disagreements abound regarding the motivation of OPEC. Some emphasize profit maximization objectives and others focus on political goals. Still others have concluded that OPEC, the USA, and the MNOCs conspired to raise prices to serve the profit maximization objectives of OPEC and the MNOCs and to weaken the competitive position of western Europe and Japan *vis-à-vis* the USA.[6] These interpretations will be explored in Chapter 8. To provide context for the ensuing discussion of the energy crisis in the OECD states, I merely mention at this point a set of goals to which OPEC's members seemed to adhere.[7]

OPEC and OAPEC cannot be considered truly distinct bodies. The key members of OAPEC were equally important to OPEC. The pursuit of higher oil incomes for development purposes and anti-Zionist political goals were not mutually exclusive. OAPEC wielded its oil weapon while driving prices up through OPEC. Prices soared without linkage to either proven reserves or costs of production. These price hikes reflected:

1. A producer assessment of the true value of crude to users.
2. Producer insistence that oil prices move with the inflated costs of imports from the industrial nations.
3. Producer intention to gain compensation for earlier losses resulting

from MNOC price and production authority and the relatively weak bargaining power of the producers.
4. A compromise between producers such as Iran, desirous of the highest possible price, and Saudi Arabia which sought to avoid price increases that severely damaged the West or that stimulated active conservation and/or the search for alternative fuels.
5. Internal political rather than market forces.

Prior to the oil price revolution of late 1973, a gnawing inflationary pressure troubled the economies of the industrialized states. In western Europe, annual rates of inflation during the 1960s had been held, for the most part, under 5 and even 4 percent. By 1972, however, the rate exceeded 5 percent and surpassed 6 in France and 7 in Britain. In the USA, the wage and price controls of the Nixon administration temporarily checked inflation. Wage increases and a buoyant consumer demand in Europe coupled with a contracting surplus of raw materials and a 70 percent increase in crude oil prices between 1970 and the summer of 1973 thrust general prices upward. These trends were exacerbated in the USA by large annual domestic budgetary deficits, rising interest rates, and, spurred by an increase in the exchange value of the dollar, a swelling balance of trade deficits. Inflation rates in both Germany and Japan reached higher levels than in the USA. Unlike America, however, industrial expansion continued in the former Axis partners and unemployment rates advanced less severely. Higher wages in Germany and Japan were justified by improved productivity and the successful marketing of technologically advanced goods and services in international markets. In the USA, and in the UK, France, and Italy as well, soaring wages accompanied industrial stagnation or decline and the loss of foreign markets. Both Germany and Japan demonstrated greater capability in redirecting industrial emphases and thus proved more resilient when confronted by the OPEC price hikes than the American, British, French, or Italian economies. None of the latter could so easily counter the blow of rising import bills by throwing their export sectors into higher gear.[8]

Table 7.3 encapsulates the course and volatility of oil price changes during the years since 1973. Posted prices (OPEC's official prices) quadrupled from August 1973 to 1975. A second price revolution followed between 1978 and 1981. A third period of instability commenced in 1986 with prices plunging as low as $9 and then gradually rising to a somewhat stable level during 1989.

The striking oil price bargains enjoyed by the West during the 1960s ended in 1973. Until then the net cost of oil imports comprised a small, if unavoidable, part of the total import bill. In Germany which, alone

Table 7.3 Oil prices, 1973–88

Date	Posted crude price ($ bbl)	Annual average regular gasoline prices		
		UK (Pence per UK gallon)	USA (Cents per US gallon)	Germany (Cents per US gallon)
August 1, 1973	3.07	36	40	150
October 16, 1973	5.12			
1974*	11.25	52	53	
1975	12.38	72	57	
1978	12.70	75	63	195
1979	24.00	116	86	209
1980	32.00	128	119	253
1981	34.00	145	131	
1983	29.00	180	116	
1985	28.00		11?	
1986	14.00		86	
1986 low	9.00			
1987†	18.00		90	
1988	18.00			

* Year end prices
† Saudia Arabian light

Sources: G. Jenkins, *Oil Economists' Handbook 1985*, London: Applied Science Publishers Ltd (1985), p. 20; De Golyer and MacNaughton, *Twentieth Century Petroleum Statistics 1986*, Dallas, Tex.: De Golyer and MacNaughton (1986), pp. 13, 41; Energy Information Administration, *Monthly Energy Review November 1987*, Washington, D.C.: USDOE (1988), p. 96; Congressional Quarterly, *Energy Policy*, 2nd edn, Washington, D.C.: CQ (1981), p. 43; L.R. Brown *et al.*, *State of the World 1988*, Washington, D.C.: W.W. Norton (1988), p. 26; *Lawrence Journal World*, March 10, 1988.

of the major OECD-European states, maintained a positive current accounts balance, the oil bill was hardly noticed. The staggering oil price advances of 1973–1975 worsened the trade deficits of the UK, France, Italy, and the USA while transforming a favorable balance in Japan to a negative balance.

Imported oil as a percentage of the value of all imports climbed swiftly between 1972 and 1975. In 1972, that percentage rested under 9 in Germany, France, and Britain and at 12 percent in energy poor Italy. By 1975, oil's share had reached 22 percent in Italy, 18 percent in France, 15 in Britain, and 14 in Germany. In Japan, in 1974, imported oil accounted for 32 percent of the import bill. Translated into dollars this meant that the Japanese oil import bill rose from $4.4 billion in 1972 to $24 billion in 1975. The US oil import tab leaped from $3.3 billion in 1970 to $27 billion in 1975. By 1978, the annual import bill of over $35 billion represented 20 percent of the cost of American imports that had more than doubled in value since 1973.[9]

The economic consequences of the oil price explosion while varying in detail and duration within OECD were most severe from 1973 through 1975. Current accounts deficits fostered deflationary policies designed to reduce the currency drain. The ensuing economic slowdown, especially in such energy intensive industries as chemicals and steel, pushed unemployment within OECD from 11 million in 1973 to above 18 million in 1976. The contraction of the US economy was attested to by negative growth in 1974 and 1975, declining growth in productivity rates between 1973 and 1978, and unemployment rates that rose from 5 percent in 1973 to over 8 percent in 1975. Rising oil prices in the industrialized states further exaggerated existing cost-push inflationary pressures by impelling consumer prices upward to levels far exceeding actual new costs of production and distribution. Consumer prices in Japan rose by as much as 30–35 percent in both 1974 and 1975. Italy's 6 percent rate of inflation in 1972 jumped to an average of 18 percent for 1974 and 1975. The British faced 24 percent inflation in 1974, three times higher than in 1972. France, also, experienced double-digit inflation in 1974 and 1975. Since wage increases rarely matched the rate of inflation, the real wages of workers stagnated or declined, resisting improvement until the mid-1980s.

Excepting Germany, which contained inflation and sustained a favorable balance of trade, economic malaise, characterized by recession and inflation, belabored the industrial world in 1974 and 1975. Many billions of dollars were drained from the oil importing countries by the oil exporting countries. The global value of OPEC's oil exports in 1978 reached the stupendous sum of $136 billion, compared with $15 billion in 1970. The European Community contributed 30 percent of this increase, the USA, 22 percent, and Japan, 17 percent. The three, together, paid out $83 billion more for oil in 1978 than in 1970. Japan's fuel imports consumed 5 percent of gross domestic product in 1975. OPEC received 4 percent of Japan's GDP, OPEC captured 3 percent of the GDP of the EC-9 and 1 percent of US GDP. Money shifted in extraordinary amounts to states with limited spending ability, at least in the short-term. Chapter 8 will discuss the employment of those petrodollars, a portion of which the oil producing countries returned to the industrialized importing nations in the form of investments.

The siphoning from the industrialized states of tens of billions of dollars, most of which languished in savings in 1973 and 1974, contributed to a severe contraction of spending, causing reduced inventories, investment, and production, and spawning high unemployment. These developments, instead of forcing prices down were accompanied by galloping energy and other costs that propelled prices skyward. The term "stagflation" was coined to describe this strange amalgam of industrial recession and inflation.[10]

The inflationary pressures directly attributable to huge increases in oil prices terminated in 1975, with stable oil prices holding into 1978. The levels attained by 1975, justifiable in the opinion of OPEC, had intensified inflation and had retarded economic growth. However, as Alnasrawi convincingly argues, OPEC alone cannot be blamed for stagflation. Western economic difficulties, particularly American and British, and widespread import dependence were entirely self-inflicted, exposing the unshielded West and the even more vulnerable oil import-ing LDCs to the full force of OPEC's prices. The stability of pre-1970 prices ended. The MNOCs, formerly the price managers, were replaced by a cohort of oil producers with widely divergent interests but joined in OPEC. While not the only cause of stagflation, OPEC was the prime mover in 1973–5.[11]

The embargo and price revolution signaled the final transfer to the leading oil producers of control over their oil industries. The power-ful MNOCs, and the larger independents as well, were casualties of a forced structural transformation of the international oil industry. Chapter 8 offers a more elaborate discussion of the transformed func-tions of the MNOCs. Here several questions are posed that relate to the effects of the energy crisis on the industrialized states and their MNOCs.

Under the regime of the MNOCs, the oil supply of the West seemed assured. After 1973, however, the national companies of producing states encroached upon or assumed the functions of the MNOCs as principal lifters. What role would the MNOCs play in exploration and development? How would their enormous investment potential and technological expertise be utilized? Would they respond to the political risks of Middle Eastern oil operations by withdrawing to more stable, if more costly, oil fields? Producer governments harbored downstream ambitions. How successfully would the producing states penetrate re-fining and marketing sectors? The MNOCs confronted not only the producing state oil firms but new or revitalized consumer state com-panies. Importing states exhibited distrustful or skeptical attitudes to-ward the policies of the MNOCs and demanded that they serve national interests. Did the MNOCs possess sufficient acumen to serve their own interests as well as those of producer and consumer governments?

The crisis of 1973 encouraged government intervention in energy that went beyond the formation of state energy companies. Rising oil prices enhanced the value of other forms of energy. Was it possible for consumer states to loosen the OPEC stranglehold through the substi-tution of coal, natural gas, nuclear power, or other forms of energy? Did effective fuel substitution require state intervention? Were supply side solutions adequate or was it imperative that the consuming states shave total energy use by practicing conservation? Were western nations politically capable of responding forcefully and purposefully to the energy challenge, including the possibility of irreversible environmental damage posed by their own voracious appetite for energy?

The coordination of western energy policies

Scarcity of oil in the ground formed no part of the crisis of 1973–5. The producing states contained sufficient reserves to supply global demand into the twenty-first century. The OAPEC embargo caused temporary inconvenience and demonstrated the ability of united producing states to disrupt oil flows. The OPEC price increases were enduring and costly. Cast into oblivion were western assumptions about the security and cost of oil. While the response of the West to the two-pronged assault of the producers varied from state to state, they continued, for the most part, to embrace similar energy objectives.

Critical to each nation was strengthening security of energy supplies. This encompassed relations with traditional suppliers, the foremost of which were the source of current problems, active efforts to exploit domestic energy sources, and the development of new and more secure sources of overseas oil. Dependence upon unstable and/or hostile suppliers could be reduced; the volume of oil imports could be cut. This required either replacement by some other fuel or a diminution of TPER or some combination of both. Diversification of the internal energy mix, earlier recognized in the abstract as desirable, emerged after 1973 as a "new" policy objective. The crisis also thrust into prominence an appreciation, long taken for granted because of plentiful and cheap energy, that the energy sector was vital to national economic stability and growth. Higher costs of energy affected the competitiveness of industries in world markets.[12]

Within OECD this congruence in broad energy policy goals was filtered through and supported or constrained by the political configuration, resource endowment, and current economic strength of each nation. Unique national situations also seriously impaired western co-operative endeavors through such existing institutions as the European Community, expanded to nine states in 1973, OECD, and NATO. National attitudes, egocentrism and jealousies, leaders reflecting the collective limitations of their constituents, all obstructed the formulation of collective responses to protect the developed consumer states from new disruptions of supply or to dull the price power of the producers. The International Energy Agency (IEA) did emerge in 1974 as an autonomous organization housed within OECD, but its usefulness has still to be tested.

The producer campaign gave birth to two cooperative approaches to the western energy dilemma. An aggressive anti-OPEC strategy, reflecting the US proclivity to label OPEC as the author of its economic woes, underlay a US proposal to create an international energy organization among the industrialized importers that would confront producer power with consumer power. Europe and Japan drew back, however, from the adversarial nature of the US initiative. The European states, and France in particular, preferred a conciliatory approach to OPEC and the Arab states. EC envisioned the development of a special relationship with Arab producers, one that would buffer them from the taint of America's pro-Israel policies and, perhaps, undermine the dominant position of the USA in Iran and Saudi Arabia.[13]

A conference attended by the USA, Canada, Norway, Japan, and the EC states in February 1974 revealed profound disagreements over suitable policies. The USA advocated the application of collective pressure against OPEC and opposed individual national arrangements with the producers that would further weaken the MNOCs. The EC bloc regarded this position as self-serving. France, intensely nationalistic and a welcome host for the virus of anti-Americanism, refused to sign an initial communique and ultimately eschewed membership in IEA. While this diluted the collective influence of EC in IEA, French objections forced the USA to moderate its demands and mute its public expressions of hostility of OPEC. The USA won the adoption of a plan to share oil among IEA members during an oil supply emergency. France seized upon this scheme to justify its refusal to join. In truth, France, jealously guarding a narrow conception of national sovereignty, rarely accepted the lead of any other state. Norway, about to become an oil producer, displayed no enthusiasm for oil sharing and choose a partial rather than full membership in IEA. With an EC–Arab dialogue already in progress, the USA agreed to a non-confrontational approach to OPEC by the new organization. In November 1974, IEA was constituted as a part of OECD. In 1975, IEA met with OPEC and accomplished nothing; thereafter, OPEC ignored IEA.

IEA has played no discernible role in international energy affairs. The oil crisis management system has not been applied. For the most part, IEA functions as an information dispenser and as a voice of persuasion, preaching oil import reduction and advocating realistic domestic energy prices, conservation, fuel switching, nuclear development, and vigorous energy R&D. IEA's members pledged in 1975, and frequently thereafter, to pursue those goals. They were only honor bound to do so. During the 1980s, the utter indifference of successive American administrations towards IEA's objectives further obscured its relevance.

EC courted the Arab states but gained little thereby. Neither did the evolution of the European−Arab discussions into conferences between the EC and the lesser developed nations − the so-called North−South dialogue − produce more than mutual recrimination. The oil producing countries, led by the OPEC states, presumed to speak for the LDCs and defined the agenda to include all natural resources, LDC indebtedness, and economic development. The South's demands, in European eyes, were unreasonable. So acrimonious did the talks become that OPEC, in 1975, threatened to raise prices unless Europe adopted the Arab position, the gist of which would guarantee the commodity prices of exporters, and thus their incomes, and liberalize the extension of credit to LDCs while easing up on debt collection. Meetings continued under UN auspices but the developed and underdeveloped states were unable to reach a consensus. An international treaty was signed in 1982 to regulate the uses of the deep seabed but American, German, and Japanese refusal to sign thwarted implementation.[14]

The European Community has been unsuccessful, in the opinions of El-Agraa and Kohl, in fashioning a significant role in international energy decision making. A common energy policy failed to emerge after 1973. Norway, a key North Sea producer, rejected membership in 1973. Britain, the major North Sea oil and gas producer and achieving energy self-sufficiency in 1981, uncovered few reasons to shape its energy policies in conformity with Community wishes. The energy policies of members with significant energy resources and technological strength fostered national rather than collective goals. Members competed rather than cooperated in developing nuclear energy, despite Euratom. Britain and the Netherlands adopted oil and gas production and price policies that aroused the resentment of their Community partners. The oil crisis of 1979 generated mere reiterations of previously announced objectives. Grayson, writing in 1981, doubted that future EC energy initiatives would amount to much.[15] National interests subdued collective energy interests.

Alone among the multi-state energy organizations, OPEC possessed the power to influence events. Of the western energy organizations, the International Atomic Energy Agency (IAEA) appeared to be the most active because of its responsibility to verify the peaceful uses of nuclear materials moving across national boundaries. But the IAEA does not formulate broad energy policies. Policies after 1973, as before, originated with the separate states. Although the developed states shared energy policy objectives, the detailed agenda of any one nation frequently clashed with that of other nations. American price controls on domestic oil encouraged consumption and rising levels of oil imports after 1973, thereby supporting OPEC's high prices. In the view of other OECD members, US price controls damaged their interests.

National responses to the energy crisis

The OECD nations were acutely vulnerable to an oil action by the Persian Gulf and North African producers, the suppliers of 80 percent of OECD-Europe's oil imports, 74 percent of Japan's, and 40 percent of America's (Table 7.2). Prior to 1973, the industrialized states had recognized the implicit danger of heavy oil import dependence (Tables 6.2 and 6.3), but low prices and plentiful oil dissipated any sense of urgency to moderate that dependence. More compelling was the commitment to sustained economic growth. The embargo and price increases shattered assumptions about security and constant economic growth. Continued reliance upon the MNOCs now seemed foolhardy to Europeans and Japanese. The risks attending production ventures in the Middle East and other LDCs became glaringly apparent. Among political goals, the containment of inflation assumed paramountcy. The beguiling lure of nuclear energy, the renewed attractiveness of coal, the production of North Sea oil and gas became critical agenda items in various OECD states. Conservation and renewable energy, even in the short-term more promising sources of energy than the fossil fuels, struggled, mostly unsuccessfully, for a prominent place on the agenda.

In one sphere, that of American foreign policy, American objectives remained constant. America's OECD partners, many also members of NATO or otherwise linked to the USA in military pacts, evidenced a willingness to alter attitudes and policies toward the Soviet bloc and the Arab states. The USA held staunchly to its own truths. From the Nixon Doctrine to the Carter Doctrine, America clung tenaciously to the conviction that the Soviet Union threatened the stability of the Middle East. Nixon's reliance on surrogate powers to stave off the Soviets disintegrated in 1979 when the Shah's power crumbled, while Carter's promise to intervene unilaterally to protect the Persian Gulf was meaningless.[16] American military power and diplomacy proved impotent against implacable Arab hatred of Israel, strident nationalism, and such manifestations of violence and chaos as the Lebanese imbroglio, the Iran–Iraq War, and the West Bank Palestinian rebellion of early 1988. Western oil ventures faced multiple risks in the Middle Eastern tinderbox. It behooved the importing states and their oil companies to reassess the costs of maintaining production in the region.

According to Luciani's calculations, the 10 largest MNOCs (the Seven Sisters plus Amoco, CFP, and Elf) controlled 73 percent of Middle Eastern/North African production in 1972. By 1980, they had direct access to but 47 percent, the bulk of which they received under contract from producing state oil companies. Concomitantly, MNOC ownership of non-Communist world production fell from almost 70 percent in 1973 to under 50 percent by 1980. National firms handled a rising share of production, processing, and marketing. Given the risks inherent in Middle Eastern operations, BP, Gulf, and Elf virtually abandoned the region while RDS cut back sharply the scale of its operations (Table 8.6). The Aramco partners, all US firms, continued to invest in Saudi Arabia, believing it relatively secure and unlikely to proceed arbitrarily against them.[17]

The advanced importing states, after 1973, extended their authority over the domestic oil industry. Italy's ENI and France's CFP antedated the energy crisis. In addition, France, in 1976, formed Elf-Acquitaine through an amalgamation of firms. New state companies, Norway's Statoil (1973) and the British National Oil Company (1976) were created to protect national security and assure the state a fair share of the proceeds from North Sea oil production. Both firms were endowed with offshore oil properties, engaged in joint ventures with private firms, and refined and marketed oil. Germany, too, experimented in 1974 with an amorphous sort of national oil company but when it failed to advance German interests it was terminated in 1979. Britain also turned away from state control when the government of Prime Minister Thatcher succeeded in privatizing both BNOC and the British Gas Corporation.[18]

To assess the performance of the state owned firms requires identification of their official objectives. Three goals seem paramount: to strengthen the security of oil supply, to gain preferential treatment from producing states, and to reduce substantially MNOC shares of domestic markets. ENI dominated the Italian market only because RDS, BP, and Exxon withdrew. ENI consistently operated at a loss and was dependent upon the MNOCs and the USSR for a large portion of its crude. ENI did not win particular favor from the producing states. French oil companies lost direct access to Middle Eastern oil during the 1970s while dependence upon that region for oil continued unabated. After 1978, revolution and war virtually dried up the flow of oil from Iran and Iraq, forcing French companies to search for supplies in less chaotic areas. The goal of a 50 percent share of the domestic market for state firms was abandoned in 1978. Statoil and BNOC owned safe oil. By most accounts they performed satisfactorily. But did they better serve the national interest than the private firms would have, functioning under a regulatory agency with no hands-on role? Labour created BNOC; Socialists, Statoil. Evaluations of both depend upon the ideological eye of the beholder.[19] French, Italian, and German vulnerability to sudden supply disruptions in the late 1980s remained acute. Britain and Norway enjoy energy self-sufficiency for some finite period of time only because of the North Sea.

For a steady flow of crude, America relied upon its special relationship with Iran and Saudi Arabia and the private firms operating there and in such other producing areas as Latin America, Canada, and Nigeria. European efforts to improve oil security by initiating government to government contacts with Saudi Arabia and Iran yielded little oil above that covered by existing contracts with the Iranian National Oil Company and Saudi Arabia's Petromin. While Aramco in Saudi Arabia, the Iranian Consortium, and the BP–Gulf partnership in Kuwait experienced severe contraction in controlled liftings, these firms continued to receive most of the oil that the Gulf states did not process or market themselves.[20]

Changes in the location of world energy reserves and centers of world production into the 1980s were insufficiently remarkable to augur a more secure energy future for the industrialized states. The TPER of the USA, Japan, and OECD-Europe declined by 5 percent between 1979 and 1985; global TPER climbed 7 percent. Oil as a proportion of global TPER fell from 46 percent in 1975 to 38 percent in 1985, a reduction reflected in the energy use patterns of the industrialized states (Table 7.1). A commensurate increase in the use of coal, natural gas, nuclear, and hydropower accompanied oil's decline. But this modest alteration hardly justified complacency regarding future fuel supplies in the economically advanced states.

Oil remained the premier fuel. Production in 1985 matched that of 1973. Virtually the same countries in 1985 produced a portion of world oil similar to that of 1973 and earlier (Tables 7.4 and 4.4). New producing areas in the North Sea and Alaska offered but temporary relief. North Sea reserves of 3 billion metric tons (bmt) were a mere seven times greater than annual oil consumption in OECD-Europe. Alaska added 1.4 bmt to US reserves, the equivalent of two years of domestic consumption. Moreover, the declining volume of Middle Eastern and North African production after 1979 reflected conscious policy rather than depleted reserves. OPEC's members sat on more than 60 percent of world reserves in the late 1980s. Middle Eastern states controlled over 50 percent of reserves. This oil is far cheaper to produce than offshore oil or oil from other fields in the western hemisphere.[21]

The oil price advances of 1973–4 and 1979–80 induced a flurry of oil exploration and development ventures in areas other than the Middle East. New oil from the North Sea or Alaska cost anywhere from 15 to 30 times more to produce than Middle Eastern oil, but with prices 60 to 80 times greater than the cost of production, the new oil reaped large profits. Global reserves, however, remained quite stable, rising but 2 or 3 percent from 1973 to 1979 and not at all during the 1980s.

Substantial oil discoveries in Latin America after 1975 added over 7 bmt to regional reserves by 1985. Mexico owned 6 bmt of this increase and Venezuela, 1 bmt. Mexico elected to accelerate production, lifting 47 mmt more in 1979 than in 1973; Venezuela's production fell by 52 mmt (Table 7.4). Latin American output rose by only 11 mmt over those years and its share of world oil exports remained at about 10 percent.

The most significant long-term trend in world oil production occurred after 1979. Middle Eastern producers substantially reduced output while Britain, Norway, and Mexico raised the volume of their liftings (Table 7.4). OPEC producers husbanded their reserves. Saudi Arabia, with 24 percent of global reserves in 1986, contained 141 years of production at 1986 levels; Britain's North Sea fields, contributing less than 1 percent to world reserves, would last for less than a decade at current withdrawal rates, as would US reserves.[22]

Regions considered secure by OECD states yielded only marginal additions to natural gas reserves. US gas reserves continued to fall while no large finds augmented western Europe's reserves. During the 1970s, the USSR and Iran discovered new fields which gave the Soviets some

Table 7.4 World crude oil production, 1973–87 (million metric tons)

	1973	1978	1979	1980	1985	1987
World	2829	3078	3156	3049	2828	2767
USSR	430	568	593	612	607	590
USA	467	441	433	436	455	415
Saudi Arabia*	372	409	488	490	165	231
UK and Norway	2	73	97	108	165	123[1]
Mexico	27	62	74	98	137	127
China	51	102	108	107	127	134
Iran*	297	264	154	84	114	122
Brunei[†]	15	21	27	25	93	
Venezuela*	171	110	119	110	86	86
Canada	90	67	76	72	79	75
Nigeria*	104	97	117	105	75	64
Iraq*	102	127	176	84	73	102
Indonesia*	68	83	82	80	67	66
United Arab Emirates*	77	93	77	87	59	75
Libya*	110	100	105	93	53	49
Algeria*	56	56	61	58	50	32
Kuwait*	140	96	112	71	48	61
Egypt	8	23	27	30	45	
Above % of World production	91	91	93	90	88	83

* OPEC states
[†] Includes Malaysia
[1] UK only

Sources: De Golyer and MacNaughton, *Twentieth Century Petroleum Statistics 1986*, Dallas, Tex.: De Golyer and MacNaughton (1986), pp. 4–11; Energy Information Administration, *Monthly Energy Review November 1987*, Washington, D.C.: USDOE (1988), pp. 112–13.

35 to 40 percent of global reserves and Iran 20 to 25 percent. Iran contains more natural gas than all of North America, as do the Arab Persian Gulf states. But Middle Eastern gas is of little use to Europe or the USA. Indeed, flaring wastes over 60 percent of the gas produced. Earlier expectations of a large liquefied natural gas trade did not materialize, except to Japan where LNG imports substituted for oil in electric generation. Soviet gas exports to western Europe filled a rising demand.[23]

The security of OECD's future supply of oil and natural gas remains problematic, in spite of the reduced rate of energy use achieved since 1979. Since the mid-1970s, OECD states have rapidly depleted their safest sources of oil. Adequate reserves of natural gas exist, particularly in western Europe, but that fuel cannot substitute for oil in road transportation. Coal use has not contributed to a diminution in gas or oil use while nuclear, even under the most favorable conditions imaginable, will not displace fossil fuels in the production of electricity. This suggests that the West did not use to advantage the time gained by its temporary access to secure oil and gas by reducing its reliance on those potentially scarce fuels. As the 1980s ended, the West's energy position remained fragile.

During the 1960s, the dominant position of western MNOCs in the oil fields of the non-Communist world assured, or so the West believed, an uninterruptible supply of energy to the cheapest price. But even while the oil spigot ran freely, not every nation hewed undeviatingly to the cheapness standard. France opened its doors to cheap oil, at the expense of the coal industry, but neither Britain nor Germany could afford simply to abandon coal, their sole domestic source of energy. Various forms of subsidization buffered those large coal industries against the full effects of oil and gas competition, a protection persisting in Britain even as North Sea oil and gas penetrated the domestic market. Simultaneously, the West committed substantial funds to develop nuclear power, despite the absence of accurate cost data and reliable safety procedures. The incongruities characteristic of pre-embargo fuel policies extended into the post-embargo years.

The supply side reaction of the West

Western European nations and the USA (Japan will be treated separately) responded to the price and supply shock of 1973 with policies that I would label as minimally incremental. Each state operated within parameters set by a particular energy endowment and a unique political structure and style. Each aimed to diversify its internal energy mix by reducing oil imports through the substitution of indigenous forms of energy and/or fuels obtained from producers more reliable than the Arab states. Simultaneously, several European states launched diplomatic initiatives to placate Arab producers and, hopefully, to foster with them a special state-to-state relationship through the medium of national oil companies. The USA relied upon its Persian Gulf security role to maintain the flow of oil from Iran and Saudi Arabia. Soaring oil prices aggravated inflation and worsened trade imbalances. The pricing of energy products posed a complex dilemma: allowing an uninhibited market driven rise in domestic prices risked a political backlash; artificially restricting prices might obstruct energy exploration while encouraging habitual use.

Supply considerations dominated the energy strategies of the USA and western Europe, and Japan as well, from 1973 through 1979. In addition, the governments of the USA, Britain, Italy, and France employed price controls to moderate inflation while Germany permitted oil prices to rise to market levels, necessitating concomitant increases in regulated electricity and natural gas prices. US price regulations prevented product prices from increasing as sharply as they did in western Europe. Most commentators agree that controlled prices in the USA retarded the discovery of new oil and gas, stimulated energy consumption, thereby serving the purposes of OPEC, and excited the hostility of America's OECD partners.[24]

Of the major OECD members, France acted most directly to curb oil imports. Impelled by security considerations as well as by a high current accounts deficit in 1974, which could not be alleviated by larger exports, France imposed, in 1975, a ceiling on the value of allowable oil imports. Germany, on the other hand, while offering some incentives to improve the efficiency of energy use, essentially allowed home demand to determine the level of oil imports. In contrast to France, Britain, Italy, and the USA, Germany's comprehensive industrial policies encouraged a rapid acceleration of exports, the earnings of which paid the higher cost of oil imports. In Germany, as Ikenberry explains it, energy policy formed an integral part of industrial policy. In America, the crisis produced, in November 1973, the misleading rhetoric of President Nixon's "Project Independence," an impossible scheme to "meet America's energy needs from America's own energy resources" by 1980.[25] Thereafter, a hotchpotch of energy legislation achieved little. Most significantly, Presidents Nixon and Ford failed to win legislation to decontrol oil and gas prices and to tax imported oil.[26]

The volume of oil imports after 1973, displayed in Table 7.5, attests to the success or failure of each nation's effort to reduce oil imports. Note, however, that a reduction of oil imports was not synonymous

Table 7.5 Net national crude oil and product imports, 1973–85 (million metric tons)

	1973	1977	1978	1979	1980	1984	1985
USA	305	432	409	420	337		248
Japan	292	279	270	284	253	217	
OECD-Europe	776	657	648	647	589		413
West Germany*	151	143	144	151	138		95
Britain	117	53	42	26	7	−37	
Italy	131	115	118	123	109	92	
France	130	117	116	126	109	68	

* Gross imports

Sources: De Golyer and MacNaughton, *Twentieth Century Petroleum Statistics, 1986,* Dallas, Tex.: De Golyer and MacNaughton (1986), pp. 60–1; *BP Statistical review of the world oil industry,* issues, 1970–85, *passim*; IEA, *Energy Statistics, 1971–1981,* Paris: OECD/IEA (1983), pp. 311–31, 343–53, 626–38, *1983–1984* (1984), pp. 51–3, IEA, *Energy Balances of OECD Countries, 1970/1982,* Paris: OECD/IEA (1984), pp. 387–9, 404.

with resolution of the energy crisis. Over the period, 1973–7, net American oil imports rose by 38 percent, French imports declined by 13 percent, and German imports fell by 5 percent. Britain's import dependence was dramatically reduced after 1975 when North Sea oil arrived. By 1978, domestic oil filled in excess of one-half of British demand while oil consumption had dropped by 11 percent. Britain achieved self-sufficiency in 1981. TPER dropped more rapidly than in other industrialized nations, not as a consequence of a programmed effort but due rather to a stagnant economy. Both TPER and net import dependence in the USA steadily advanced from 1973 to 1979 (Table 7.1). In Germany, net import dependence remained unchanged through the 1970s while TPER rose modestly, both trends reflecting Germany's willingness to pay for more expensive energy. French TPER also grew, but at a much slower rate than during the 1960s. Import dependence was essentially unchanged because of rising coal and natural gas imports.[27] In short, TPER trends reveal no purposeful campaign among the above states to reduce energy use; instead they sought to substitute other fuels for oil. Conservation, from 1973 to 1978, was not identified as an essential new source of energy.

The supply side policies implemented by the industrial states aimed at increasing the use of coal and/or natural gas and expanding nuclear power, objectives not easily accomplished. Resource constraints, institutional structures, environmental concerns, interest group politics, and domestic energy use habits frustrated the fulfillment of energy supply goals, particularly in nations that lacked access to new and plentiful sources of energy.

The role of coal

The large coal industries of Britain and Germany suffered severely from oil competition during the 1960s (Table 6.6). Production in America reached its nadir during the early 1960s and then rebounded. But, the industry was burdened by large overcapacity and, by the early 1970s, was constrained by stiff environmental laws (Table 6.11).

Theoretically, high oil prices enhanced the value of coal as an available and lower cost substitute for oil, and of gas in America, as a boiler fuel in power plants and industry. In the coal producing nations, post-embargo energy plans were partly predicated upon a resurgent coal industry. Projections of electricity consumption through the 1970s optimistically employed as their guide the 6 to 8 percent annual growth rates of the 1960s which, if accurate, would create a demand requiring additional coal and nuclear generation.

In America, the Nixon and Ford administrations counted on vastly increased coal production to reduce oil imports swiftly. Ford called for 250 new coal mines that would add 125 mmt to US coal production which equaled 655 mmt in 1975, already 55 mmt higher than output in 1973. President Carter, in 1977, established the goal of 1 bmt by the 1980s. Not to be outdone, the Economic Commission for Europe, in 1978, anticipated a doubling of US coal production to 1.2 bmt by 1985. Even more incredibly, the World Coal Study (1980) predicted 2 billion short tons by the year 2000.

Somewhat less wild projections for production in Germany and the UK assumed a production in 1980 at least equal to 1973. However, in both countries and in EC as a whole, coal production declined through 1978, rose from 1979 to 1981, and commenced to slip again. Of the numerous factors that precluded achievement of coal production objectives, environmental opposition, infrastructure deterioration of the coal industry, a rash of nuclear plant openings, and falling rates of growth in electricity consumption were telling.[28]

In Europe and the USA during the 1970s, a body of environmental protection and health and safety laws added substantially to the costs of coal mining and coal use. Federal legislation in Germany regulated coal-burning emissions and water quality. German environmental groups concentrated on nuclear power rather than on coal mining and burning. In contrast, bitter political fights ensued in the USA over legislation designed to prevent and correct abuses of land and water by underground and surface mining. Proposals to regulate strip mining precipitated a battle royal. When finally passed in 1977, despite two previous presidential vetoes, the Surface Mining Control and Reclamation Act increased the cost of producing the low sulfur coals of America's western mines. Similar struggles erupted over efforts to reduce the emission of various solid and gaseous pollutants during coal combustion. Emission control laws doubled the time consumed in siting and constructing a coal-fired power plant. Other laws mandated the application of state-of-the-art anti-pollution equipment. This legislation added to the cost of construction. Environmental objections, including heightened concern over acid rain, clashed with the equally compelling need to prohibit or strictly limit the production of electricity by natural gas and oil.

Necessary environmental laws were constantly subjected to the oblique assault of governments committed to increased energy production as the solution to the energy crisis. The German government and the Nixon and Ford administrations in America resisted the imposition of stricter environmental standards and sought to dilute existing rules. President Reagan undermined environmental defenses, virtually nullifying, for instance, the effectiveness of the strip mining law. The Reagan, Thatcher, and Kohl governments denied responsibility for the export of and damage caused by acid rain. Also, those leaders ardently supported nuclear power.[29]

The coal industry of Great Britain declined precipitously after 1955

Table 7.6 Coal production in world and selected nations, 1973–86 (million metric tons)

	1973	1977	1980	1982	1984	1985	1986
World	3029		3733	3903	4113	4359	4399
USA	599	697	753	838	896	886	807
UK	130	106	130	125	51	105	104
West Germany	222	215	225	224	212	210	201
USSR	615	665[1]	653	647	642	647	670
East Germany*	246		258	276	296	312	315
Poland	195	234	230	210	243	250	255
China[†]	398	550	620	641	789	845	873
Australia	88		105	128	138	156	169
India	81		114	136	153	158	168
South Africa	62		116	144	163	174	181

* Brown coal only
[†] Hard coal only
[1] 1978

Sources: W.A. Rosenbaum, *Energy, Politics, and Public Policy*, 2nd edn, Washington, D.C.: CQ Press (1987), pp. 166–7; *BP Statistical Review of World Energy*, issues, 1970–86; IEA, *Energy Statistics, 1971–1981*, Paris: OECD/IEA (1983), pp. 332–52, 643–8, *1983–1984* (1984), pp. 54–6; IEA, *Coal Information 1985*, Paris: OECD/IEA (1985), pp. 48, 432–3 and *1987* (1987), pp. 53–4.

(Tables 4.4 and 7.6). In Germany, a steeper fall was prevented by increased coal use in electric generation. Rising electric generation in America fostered a revival of the coal industry. The coal industries of Britain and Germany, however, were plagued by great overcapacity and only maintained by government subventions.

Electric power plants in Europe consumed about two-thirds of total coal production, and in the USA above 80 percent. Coal industries had received niggardly capital inputs during the 1960s. Archaic plant, hostile miner unions, deteriorating transport and, in the USA, outdated deep sea coal ports obstructed coal industry exploitation of the tantalizing market opportunities created by the energy crisis. Britain, in 1974, announced a £600 million investment plan for coal, but by 1982, coal output fell short of the 1973 figure and slid again in 1985. In Britain especially, but in Germany and France as well, the coal industry suffered from decisions made in the 1960s to shift from coal to oil and gas as power plant boiler fuels and to nuclear plants. Apparently shut off from power markets, coal companies and coal governing boards laid no plans to expand or modernize during the 1970s. Reversing this proved impossible. German coal production exceeded 210 mmt only because electric rate payers helped pay for utility coal use and because the utilities earned subsidies when they agreed to burn a stipulated tonnage over a number of years. Increased imports, not greater local production, satisfied expanded coal demand in Europe.[30]

The great coal bonanza anticipated in 1973 never materialized in Europe and appeared to have run its course in America by 1984. Sharply falling oil prices after 1985 and heightened concern about the environmental impact of coal burning dimmed the economic luster of coal. Rising production in the USA was solely the consequence of the electric industry shift from oil and gas to coal, a process beginning during the 1950s and accelerating after 1973 — by 1985, electric plants consumed 85 percent of US coal output. The inability of Europe's coal industries to fill demand encouraged a modestly expanded international coal trade after 1973. But World Coal Study projections for substantial increases in the coal trade during the 1980s were very inaccurate. America hardly needed a 2 bmt output to fill foreign orders that peaked in 1981 at over 100 mmt and dropped to 80 mmt by 1986. Total world coal exports accounted for but 9 percent of world production. Ten nations, led by the USA, Australia, Poland, Russia, and South Africa provided more than 95 percent of all exports. Japan purchased the largest share of imported coal. Coal imports of EC countries amounted to over 70 mmt annually during the early 1980s, a small volume but reflecting the failure of European coal industries to satisfy demand. American and South African coal undersold British coal in Europe, and in Britain as well.[31]

Turning toward natural gas

Natural gas offered OECD-Europe an efficient replacement for coal and oil in such uses as space heating and cooking and industrial heat processes. From 1970 through 1985, natural gas provided a rising proportion of TPER (Table 7.1). Growth in France, Germany, and Italy matched that of OECD-Europe. For the Netherlands, with its domestic gas fields, the share of gas in TPER fluctuated around 50 percent from 1975 into the mid-1980s. North Sea gas permitted the UK to expand gas use from 5 percent of TPER in 1970 to 24 percent in 1985. While gas use rose in Europe, it declined in the USA (Table 7.1). Natural gas reserves depleted during the late 1970s were not restored thereafter. Supply problems intensified after 1969, reaching crisis proportions in some areas by 1979 and necessitating the curtailment of gas supply to some users and the prohibition of new gas hookups.

Natural gas exports from Holland's Groningen field commenced during the 1960s. With the discovery of North Sea gas, new supplies became available to Europeans. Such was the rise in gas consumption in western Europe — 74 billion cubic meters (bcm) in 1970 and 230 bcm* in 1985 — that imports from the USSR and Algeria grew in importance after the mid-1970s. The international gas trade centered in western Europe which received 52 percent of world imports. Japan and the USA, each receiving a comparable volume, accounted for another 30 percent. The USSR, Netherlands, and Norway shared 68 percent of world exports.[32]

During the 1970s and early 1980s, natural gas prices lagged behind oil prices so that gas competed favorably against a range of energy alternatives. Because of price controls, this held true in the USA as well, but scarcity ruled out an augmented role for natural gas. Each western European nation sought to increase the share of natural gas in its energy mix. Ideological preferences determined the structures that evolved to produce, transmit, and distribute the fuel. The North Sea producers delegated authority to administer gas production and transmission to national firms which operated through contracts with MNOCs. Phillips Petroleum operated oil and gas terminals for Statoil while a joint venture between RDS, Esso, and the Dutch government performed those functions. Gaz de France and Italy's ENI controlled their domestic markets. MNOCs dominated the German gas industry. RDS and Esso owned large shares in Ruhrgas, the giant gas utility which distributed 67 percent of domestic gas requirements. Ruhrgas, Thysingas, and other German utilities negotiated directly with Gasunie of

---

* Roughly 200 million metric tons oil equivalent.

Holland and Statoil regarding volume, prices, and duration of contract.

In the early 1970s, the British decision to prohibit exports of natural gas and the Dutch decision to conserve its gas fields and not to renew old contracts or let new ones diminished potential supply. Importers such as Germany, France, and Italy seeking gas as a substitute for oil, increasingly turned to the USSR and to North Africa. Only in 1981, in response to falling government revenues, did the Dutch reverse their export policy and initiate a search for new North Sea gas. By 1981, Soviet and North African gas provided about 30 percent of French imports. Soviet natural gas composed 30 percent of German natural gas imports and, by 1990, might exceed 50 percent. Russian gas provided one-third of total Italian gas consumption and may rise to 40 percent by 1990. By the mid-1980s, Soviet gas was a better bargain than Dutch or Norwegian gas.[33]

Soviet gas rode a rising tide and North African an ebb tide in western Europe.[34] Europeans considered the Soviets a reliable supplier of reasonably priced gas. Algeria's persistent efforts to reopen negotiations on the price of committed gas and even to unilaterally abrogate contracts earned for it a reputation of unreliability. With Soviet gas available and Holland once again an active gas merchant, Europeans turned away from LNG, a very expensive fuel and dangerous to transport and handle.[35]

US natural gas production and reserves each declined by about 25 percent from 1972 to 1985. Vietor and the contributors to the Goodwin volume identify federal and state price controls as the culprit. But fears of monopolistic pricing by gas producers, often subsidiaries of the major oil companies, and the large pipeline companies thwarted full federal deregulation until the 1980s. Obtaining gas from Canada, Mexico, and Algeria proved difficult. Each producer demanded the most lucrative deal. Negotiations with Algeria were abrogated between 1979 and 1981 because of Algeria's price demands. Similarly, in 1978 and 1979, disagreements over price prompted the USA to break off talks with Mexico. Under the best of circumstances, those sources could fill but an infinitesimal portion of domestic gas demand. Adjustments in gas use, however, did augment the gas available to residential and commercial users and to certain industries. Federal laws promoted nuclear power and conversion of electric plants from oil and gas to coal while prohibiting, in 1978, the use of gas as a boiler fuel in industry. As a result, power plant consumption of natural gas remained stable at 17 percent of gas production after 1973. In contrast, electric power in Japan took 57 percent of supply in 1985. American industries reduced their gas use, consuming 43 percent in 1985, compared with one-half in 1973, amounting to a 4 billion cubic feet cutback.[36]

From 1973 through 1979, US gas use declined by 8 percent; from 1979 through 1985, as deregulation took effect and prices rose, gas use declined by 6 percent. This diminution seemed more the consequence of economic slowdown, doubts regarding adequate supplies, and, after 1985, cheaper oil than a product of federal policies. Since 1979, savings have been no more substantial than before 1979. Estimated reserves continued to decline despite higher prices.

Significant relief from reliance upon foreign oil, the centerpiece of post-embargo energy policy, required: the discovery of large domestic oil and/or gas reserves; a vast expansion of coal use; significant additions of nuclear power; the commercial development of renewable forms of energy; conservation. Domestically owned oil and gas carried Britain to energy self-sufficiency by 1975. Substituting gas for oil reduced Holland's net energy imports from 78 percent of TPER in 1968 to under 10 after 1975.[37] Germany, France, Italy, and the USA lacked the domestic fossil fuels necessary for massive fuel substitution. In Germany and the USA, strong environmental interest groups slowed the rush to coal. Among available domestic resources, nuclear power beckoned in 1973 as the fastest way to reduce fossil fuel use in the power industry.

Nuclear power, a Faustian bargain?

The ebullient mood of nuclear power adherents turned sour during the 1970s while the role projected for the technology in 1973 fell far short of expectations. In 1973, OECD predicted an installed nuclear capacity for all members of 500 GW* by 1985 and 1,000 GW by 1990. In 1983, the capacity of operating plants within OECD equaled 142 GW with 169 GW ordered or under construction. Although well below OECD projections, a total capacity of 311 GW, if those in process came on line, represented a significant productive capacity (see Table 6.5). However, only part of the 169 GW in process materialized.

In the USA, the utilities canceled 116 nuclear plants with a capacity of 130 GW between 1970 and 1984 while no new orders were announced after 1979. Between 1975 and 1987, Germany ordered only two nuclear plants and suspended construction on eight others. From 1967 to 1978, Britain ordered no new reactors but then ordered five in 1980. Between 1978 and 1987, Austria, Sweden, Denmark, Italy, and Holland abandoned the nuclear alternative. In 1970, Italy laid plans for 100 plants; in 1988, two of the three plants built were shut down. Switzerland, in

---

*GW = Gigawatt = 10,000,000,000 watts.

1988, elected to phase out the technology. Of the industrialized powers, only France and the Soviet Union (even after the Chernobyl disaster of April 26, 1986) evinced an unswerving dedication to nuclear energy.

As of 1986, nuclear power provided some 11 percent of TPER in OECD and generated 28 percent of electricity. In the USA, those figures were, respectively, 6 and 16 percent. France, by 1988, derived over 70 percent of electricity from some fifty nuclear power plants, and Belgium over 60 percent. Switzerland and Germany depended upon nuclear for about one-third of electric output, the UK about one-fifth. With the exception of France, these 1986 figures reflect very slow growth since the late 1970s.[38]

Within a decade, then, nuclear power ceased to be a viable option in America and much of western Europe. The extravagant promises of the nuclear industry and its powerful government supporters were buried under the realities of cost inflation and justifiable uncertainty regarding the safety of the technology.

"Two, four, six, eight, we don't want to radiate," chanted the anti-nuclear throng gathered on the Mall in Washington, DC, in 1978. One hundred thousand demonstrators crowded into Bonn in 1980 to protest against nuclear technology. Much had gone awry for the nuclear industry. Prior to the embargo, the cost of nuclear plants escalated to mind-boggling heights. Electric utilities, especially in the USA, risked their financial health by encumbering themselves with such capital obligations. In the USA, as Table 7.7 indicates, final costs greatly exceeded initial cost estimates. Plants finished during the late 1980s will be burdened by cost overruns of 500 to 1,000 percent. If these plants generate, ratepayers will shoulder the final costs.

A recent mass mailing by the US Council for Energy Awareness, a nuclear advocacy organization, alleged that "... *right now, extremists are working in over a dozen states and in Congress to shut down all the nuclear power plants in America.*" The nuclear industry in America blames cost overruns on the regulatory stranglehold of the federal government and on uninformed and ideologically driven radicals who dominate the environmental movement and command a broad constituency within a general public ignorant of the true facts. This self-justifying stance contains a mite of truth. In the USA, Germany, and elsewhere some of the more vociferous opponents of nuclear energy are simply anti-technology and/or dedicated to restructuring thoroughly the social order. But, it seems fair to say, most Americans and western Europeans are comfortable with and receptive to advanced technologies. Nuclear technology, however, makes their gorge rise. While experts endlessly debate the cost competitiveness of nuclear versus coal generated electricity and arrive at diametrically opposed conclusions,

Table 7.7 Nuclear plant cost inflation in USA ($ million)

	Projected cost	Actual cost
Diablo Canyon, Calif.	450	4400
Shoreham, N.Y.*	241	4000
Marble Hill, Ind.*	1400	7000
Midland, Mich.	267	4400
Seabrook, N.H.	973	5800
Trojan, Ore.	235	4600
Grand Gulf, Miss.	300	2800

* Abandoned or non-operative

Source: Time, February 13, 1984, pp. 34–42.

a large segment of the general public deems the technology too risky and associates it with the proliferation of nuclear weapons.[39]

That such negative attitudes, as measured in numerous public opinion polls, attained their current political effectiveness can be partially attributed to the disingenuousness of industry and government spokespersons since the birth of the industry. Despite a history of frequent plant accidents and shutdowns, including the near reactor meltdown at Three Mile Island in America in March 1979 and the fearsome reactor explosion at Chernobyl in the Soviet Ukraine in April 1986, reactor manufacturers and governments deny the dangers implicit in this technology. The US Council for Energy Awareness, in 1988, insisted that "nuclear energy is a safe, clean way to generate electricity." The Council assured Americans that nuclear plants "have a whole series of multiple backup safety systems to prevent accidents." Yet studies in America, Sweden, and Germany in 1987 estimated at 70 percent the probability of an accident such as Chernobyl occurring within the next five or six years.[40]

Equally erosive of the nuclear cause are the unresolved problems of nuclear waste disposal and the decommissioning of aged plants. The cost of burying an abandoned plant could equal the original cost. What will be done with irradiated material that remains lethal for thousands of years? The states of the federal republics of Germany and the USA have forcefully resisted the deposit of nuclear wastes within their territories. States, communities, and private groups have rendered ineffective national laws designed to locate waste disposal sites. "Put it somewhere else, not in my backyard" expressed the attitude of those dwelling in proximity to possible nuclear waste dumps. Faced with cost escalation, public fears of nuclear accidents, irresolution regarding waste disposal, and lower than predicted rates of growth in electricity demand, it is not surprising that nations in Europe and the utilities in America withdrew from the market for nuclear plants. A General

Electric official conceded in 1988 "that the domestic nuclear market for new plants has disappeared, with no hope of return in the foreseeable future."[41]

France persists as a world leader in nuclear technology, particularly the fast breeder reactor. Anti-nuclear opposition in France is ineffectual due to a highly centralized governmental structure comfortably insulated from such dissent. The Conservative Party in Britain and the Christian Democratic Union in Germany, victorious in elections in 1987, reaffirmed their commitment to nuclear power. In both nations, the opposition advocated the abandonment of the technology. Prime Minister Thatcher's government announced a twenty-five-year program of nuclear and coal-fired power plant construction estimated to cost £70 to £100 billion. Thatcher and Chancellor Kohl regard nuclear as indispensable to future economic growth, and both hope to capitalize on this revival through overseas sales of reactors.[42]

Central to the success of these programs are the development of reliable waste disposal methods and the safety of a new generation of reactors. Britain, Germany, and France are gambling on a future technological quick-fix.

In spring 1987, British newspapers reported a much higher incidence of leukemia among children living near nuclear reactors than among children living at a distance. If the causal nexus is corroborated, does the need for power outweigh such a clear and present danger? Some argue that achieving the greater good of the many justifies the occasional suffering of the few. They embrace the "Faustian bargain." Many people had, by 1988, rejected a Faustian bargain with the technology. Chernobyl warned that a nuclear mishap spread suffering among more than a few and among people far removed from the site.[43]

Nuclear power has not emerged as the dominant source of energy in the western world. Those nations now retreating from the technology cannot be applauded for a wise choice. While rejecting nuclear for the moment, few nations have made provisions for alternatives to fossil fuels.

Conservation, a low priority

The leading industrial states have cavalierly ignored the most obvious new source of non-polluting, reliable, and safe energy, that derived from using less — conservation. A second source, equally untapped, is renewable energy: solar, water, biomass, the wind. Writing of West Germany, Lucas opines that "to say that support for renewable energy . . . is lukewarm would be something of an exaggeration."[44] Considered exotic, few nations supported the research and development necessary to derive even marginal value from conservation or renewables.[45]

Between 1973 and 1979, western Europe and the USA focused attention on increasing the supply of energy and on substituting other fuels for oil. TPER in the USA rose uninhibitedly. Americans used an additional 174 million metric tons oil equivalent (mmtoe) during those years, or just under half of total Japanese TPER in 1979 (Table 7.1). Equally damaging, the USA became even more dependent upon foreign oil. OECD-Europe compiled an only slightly better record. Europeans used more energy in 1979 than in 1973, but did reduce net oil imports by 16 percent (Table 7.5). More effective conservation occurred after the second price shock in 1979. Thereafter, prices, aided by policies, worked to reduce energy use and improve efficiency of use, at least until 1984 when tumbling oil prices sparked a renewed upward march of energy consumption. In 1985, US and OECD Europe TPER surpassed that of 1973.

Shifting to indigenous energy reserves reduced western European net energy import dependence after 1973 and, in America, after 1979 (Table 7.1). In Europe, natural gas and nuclear power, and in America, coal and nuclear power, substituted for oil. Europe's conversion to natural gas entailed risks even if local resources were well husbanded. Switching from oil to gas, both purchased from foreign suppliers, at best temporarily alleviated the supply problem.[46]

Laws in the USA mandating slower driving speeds (changed to a higher speed in 1987) and improved gas mileage for automobiles (made less effective by President Reagan) provide some evidence for those who claim success for energy conservation. Proof abounds that industry adopted energy saving techniques. In the USA — and in western Europe and Japan — one unit of GDP required less energy to produce in 1980 than in 1973 (Table 7.8). The improved gasoline efficiency of new cars after 1973 moderated American oil consumption into the 1980s. But, in both Europe and America, bigger and more powerful cars reappeared after 1986. Automobile advertisements no longer emphasized better gas mileage.[47]

Economic stagnation reduced energy use in Britain. Investment in conservation fell far short of investment in the North Sea, nuclear power, and coal mines. Investment in R&D for conservation and renewables totaled £9 million in 1980–1 compared with at least £346 million in all other energy industries. The German Ministry of Economics proposed a conservation program in 1974 but it was rejected as detrimental to economic growth. Rising prices served as the sole conservationist weapon. The federal and state governments offered limited financial incentives to improve the energy efficiency of buildings, but

Table 7.8 US dollars of GDP produced per energy input, 1970–86*

	1970	1973	1980	1984	1985	1986[1]
USA	1227	1266	1418	1602	1693	1747
Japan	2386	2391	2902	3272	3440	3455
Germany	2618	2610	2980	3196	3243	3285
UK	2136	2261	2653	2924	2905	2922
France	3038	2998	3378	3582	3572	3499
Italy	2528	2472	2805	2960	2937	3010
OECD-Europe	2581	2552	2849	3038	3059	3088

* GDP divided by TPER (mtoe)
[1] Estimated

Sources: IEA, *Energy Balances of OECD Countries, 1983–84*, Paris: OECD/ IEA, *passim*; IEA, *Coal Information 1987*, Paris: OECD/IEA (1987), *passim*.

reducing speed limits and increasing the fuel performance of autos were unachievable due to opposition from drivers and auto manufacturers. Increased supplies remained the central objective of the government. In 1980–1, the German coal industry received DM15 billion in federal subsidies; conservation schemes received about DM1 billion in each year, 1978–82. In 1977 and 1978, the French government rejected a series of broad conservation proposals, but the Iranian Revolution compelled some rethinking and the acceptance of some measures. Still, French subsidies to an uneconomic coal industry exceeded investments in conservation by four times. In the absence of broad and effective conservation measures, it is no wonder that energy use in western Europe climbed as energy prices fell after 1984.[48]

Price regulation in the USA held energy prices below world market levels, thus encouraging energy use and partly negating the effects of conservation measures applied to private transportation. Rising prices in Europe inhibited increased energy use but were unaccompanied by government incentives to save energy. Consumers in America and Europe adjusted rapidly to the higher prices and failed to discard old energy use habits. Energy intensive industries responded more permanently to higher prices, learning to produce more without added energy inputs. Industry led the way as the price crunch of 1979 catalyzed a more dynamic conservationist thrust. But, prior to that watershed event, neither Americans nor Europeans imbibed a conservationist élan.

Japan and the first energy shock

Japan, with the poorest energy endowment and the highest import dependence of the industrialized states, responded quickly and pointedly

Table 7.9 Total energy import bill, 1970–87 ($ billion)

	USA	Japan	EEC
1970	3	3	10
1973	8		
1975	27	24	56
1976	33	29	67
1977	44	29	71
1978	44	41	112
1979	65	64	162
1980	87	65	153
1985	56	43	124
1986	40	37	94
1987	44		

Sources: UN, *1983 International Trade Statistics Yearbook, vol. 1. Trade by Country*, New York: UN (1985), pp. 1086–7; OECD, *Foreign Trade by Commodities. Imports. vol. 2. 1985* and *1986*, Paris: OECD (1986), p. 146; Energy Information Administration, *Monthly Energy Review November 1987*, Washington, D.C.: USDOE (1988), p. 13.

to the price increases and supply disruptions of 1973–4. Even before that crisis, the Japanese government devised strategies to improve energy security. Mentioned earlier were efforts to bring more oil and other natural resources under Japanese control, reduce dependence upon MNOCs, and diversify the sources of oil imports by investing in non-Middle Eastern oil fields. Tables 6.2, 6.3, and 7.2 suggest only limited success in achieving those goals both before and after 1973.

The oil price increases terminated more than a decade of export-led economic growth and exacerbated prior inflationary trends. To pay for energy imports, Japan gave up some 6 percent of GDP during both the first and second energy crises, compared with about 2 percent for the USA and 3 percent for West Germany. Table 7.9 presents the cost of energy imports in current dollars. As a proportion of the entire import bill, energy imports in Japan reached 46 percent in 1980 and 34 percent in the USA. For the latter, an energy import bill of $87 billion produced a trade deficit of $24 billion; for Japan, energy imports caused a deficit of $11 billion.[49]

To combat this debilitating trend, the USA did little until 1979. Japan acted first to contain inflation and, then, to address the energy dilemma by improving energy use efficiency, de-emphasizing energy intensive industries, diversifying the sources of oil, and reducing the role of oil in the energy mix. While unmitigated success escaped them, the Japanese had something to show for their efforts by 1979.[50]

Inflation, already approaching 15 percent before the oil crisis, jumped to about 30 percent in 1974 and 1975. Targeting inflation as the most pressing threat, the government curtailed monetary growth, reduced spending, imposed lower wage settlements on labor, and inveighed against high interest rates. Inflation fell to under 10 percent by 1977 at the cost of slower rates of economic growth. Industrial policies paralleled fiscal policies. Like Germany, Japanese economic growth was export-led. The energy crisis weakened such heavy industries as iron and steel and petrochemicals, currently facing stiff competition from such places as South Korea. Rather swiftly, Japan shifted its industrial focus from high energy intensive industries to less resource intensive and higher technology intensive industries. Along with Germany, Japan re-energized its quest for international markets, counting on larger earnings from exports of electrical equipment and lightweight, fuel efficient cars, as examples, to pay the added cost of imported fuels. Favored industries benefited from government research support; the nuclear industry was most favored.[51]

Japan's energy-specific policies employed conservation, particularly after 1979, and technological change to reduce overall energy consumption and lower oil imports. The substitution of nuclear power and liquefied natural gas (LNG) for oil received high priority. As in the USA and Germany, Japan prohibited new orders for oil-fired electric plants. Fiscal incentives were employed to encourage industry to conserve energy. But, as with Germany, the Japanese government manifest reluctance to deal rigorously with consumption in the private transportation and residential–commercial sectors. As auto use increased, so, too, did gasoline consumption. Residential–commercial energy use marched ahead until 1980. Between 1973 and 1980, Japanese electricity production advanced by 23 percent while consumption in the residential–commercial sector rose by 50 percent, spurred on by the sale of air conditioners and domestic appliances. Shibata considers Japanese energy policies cautious and unimaginative.[52]

Greater attention was directed toward assuring supply than at conserving energy. Efforts to achieve greater control over oil through the medium of Japanese oil companies were no more rewarding than in earlier years. Table 7.2 indicates a somewhat diminished reliance upon Middle Eastern oil, but 64 percent from that region — 40 percent from the Arab producers — confirms persisting vulnerability. Imports of Japanese developed crude never exceeded 10 percent from 1970 to 1985. Indeed, Japan's oil supply became less secure. In 1972, eight major oil companies delivered 75 percent of total imports. During the next decade, the MNOCs were replaced as the dominant suppliers, but by producing governments rather than by Japanese firms. By 1982, producing governments provided 47 percent of imports compared with 41 percent for the MNOCs.

A trade agreement with China in 1978 in which Japanese technology was exchanged for oil and coal provided little of either and resulted in the cancellation of contracts in 1981. In 1985, China provided about 7 percent of Japanese oil imports. Investments there, however, and in Malaysia as well, may bear fruit in the future, as does participation in Indonesian energy development.[53]

Greater quantitative success has been achieved in replacing coal- and oil-fired power plants with nuclear and LNG. Despite LNG's very high cost, Japan imports a large volume because it is environmentally acceptable. While the number of gas customers has expanded rapidly, power plants consume some 75 percent of LNG. Coal is environmentally unacceptable; oil can no longer be burned in power plants. Japan contains very little natural gas. Thus, Tokyo Electric Power has entered long-term contracts for LNG from Alaska, Brunei and Indonesia, Abu Dhabi, and Malaysia. LNG provided 5 percent of TPER in 1979 and 10 percent in 1985 (Table 7.1). It provides over 20 percent of electric power. Nuclear provides 21 percent (Table 6.5; see Table 7.1).

Indifference to conservation meant that only LNG and nuclear power were available to meet the demand for household energy and for electric power. As an earlier section emphasized, the costs of and risks attending nuclear power were substantial. Despite awareness of such disadvantages, Japan developed a fully self-sufficient nuclear complex, complete with the domestic manufacture of all components, fuel reprocessing, and a breeder reactor. Whereas ninety-seven contracts in the USA were canceled after 1975, thirty new Japanese reactors were planned or under construction at the end of 1986, with a total capacity larger than that on-line in 1986. By 1984, nuclear generation produced 63 percent more electricity than in 1980, meeting some five-sevenths of the increased electric demand over that period.

The industry and its government sponsors confront, however, ardent political opposition from both socialists and environmental groups, linked in a configuration similar to the anti-nuclear movement in Germany. Operating reactors, numbering thirty-four in 1986, concentrated in such densely populated areas as Tokyo–Yokohama and Osaka–Kyoto. Few Japanese were far removed from a reactor; few reactors were far removed from an earthquake fault. Stringent construction and safety regulations have prevented a Three Mile Island-type accident. Frequent shutdowns, however, plagued the industry. As in America and Europe, no long-term plans have been formulated for the secure storage of nuclear wastes. Information emanating from nuclear officialdom glibly overlooked the waste problem.[54]

Energy consumption in Japan rose from 1973 through 1979, fell from 1979 to 1982, and renewed its upward movement thereafter. However, oil consumption and oil imports fell (Table 7.5). Energy use efficiency in Japanese industry registered impressive advances. In 1980, the petrochemical industry consumed 84 percent of the energy burned per unit of output in 1973; steel consumed 43 percent. Other industries ranged between those two marks.[55] The data in Table 7.8 attests to the superior performance of Japan.

Despite the progressive record, Japan remains highly dependent upon Middle Eastern oil. Diversifying the fuel mix by substituting LNG required the acceptance of high costs and acknowledged dangers in transporting and processing the volatile fuel. Nuclear plants produce electricity at lower costs than LNG and other fuels. But the long-term viability of nuclear power remains clouded. From the embargo through 1979, *per capita* consumption of energy in Japan rose slightly while TPER registered an 11 percent gain. The Iranian price shock induced a modest reduction of 9 percent through 1982. By 1985, TPER was again 10 percent above that of 1973 (Table 7.1).

Constraints on energy policy formulation

The energy crisis of 1973–4 only temporarily disrupted the flow of oil to the industrialized democracies. World crude output dipped by 5 percent from 1974 to 1975 and then rose by 11 percent between 1975 and 1980. Although OPEC's production stabilized after 1975, output from Saudi Arabia and the North Sea added 131 mmt to available supply between 1973 and 1980. Oil was available (Table 7.4).

Immediate and lasting consequences attended the oil price increases (Table 7.3). Throughout OECD, annual rates of economic growth slowed and even became negative in 1974 and 1975, the annual rate of inflation climbed, along with unemployment, and, with the exception of West Germany, balance of payments deficits accumulated. By 1978, none of the OECD states had recaptured the growth position of 1972–3. The Iranian price shock occasioned renewed disarray, but markedly less so in Japan and Germany than in the USA, Britain, Italy, or France.[56]

Not surprisingly, political constraints and ideological predilections shaped the policy responses of the industrialized democracies to the supply and price squeeze. Each of the governments, its leadership vulnerable to the ebb and flow of electoral results, marched to the tune of influential constituencies peculiar to each country.

Motorists and household consumers of electricity and gas cast many votes. The USA, Germany, Italy, France, Britain, and Japan cushioned those interests against the full force of surging oil prices. The posted price of crude advanced by 680 percent from 1973 to 1979; retail gasoline prices in Germany rose by 32 percent; in USA, by 115 percent; in

France, by 138 percent; and in the UK, by 226 percent (Table 7.3). The tax portion of retail prices in the USA changed scarcely at all. French, British, and Italian gasoline taxes were raised but at a rate much below the rise in posted prices.[57] Treating drivers and householders tenderly undoubtedly salvaged votes but such expediential politics also dampened the conservationist effects of rising prices.

Political fragmentation in Italy and America precluded the formulation of a workable energy policy. Italy scrapped its ill-conceived nuclear program without devising a viable alternative. In Britain, Labour governments relied on state companies to manage North Sea energy development, but dealt irresolutely with nuclear power. Prime Minister Thatcher's regime privatized the state oil and gas companies and, while planning to sell the assets of the Central Electricity Generating Board by 1991 and British Coal by 1993, firmly committed Britain to a nuclear future. The ideological incantations of left, center, and right in France were suffused by nationalistic emotions. The abandonment of NATO, the articulation of a pro-Arab-anti-Zionist position, dialogues with the Arabs, the rejection of IEA membership, refusal to accept nuclear non-proliferation accords reflected a pervasive nationalism, personified in the memory of Charles de Gaulle. France's nuclear complex and her *force de frappe* of nuclear weapons are displayed as triumphs of autonomy. Thus, the Socialist government of 1981, owing some part of its electoral success to its anti-nuclear promises, adopted the essence of its opponent's nuclear program. The rhetoric of German center-right governments expressed an unabashed devotion to free enterprise and market driven solutions to the energy crisis. In fact, Germany relied heavily on the policies and cooperation of powerful cartel-like utility combines and the central commercial banks. Federal and state governments, in America as well, regulated, subsidized, and otherwise intruded in energy affairs. Lucas perceives the "great firms as the initiators of policy" in Germany.[58] Understandably, they focused on nuclear development and other supply side solutions.[59]

The USA lacks a center of power and never was this more true than during the 1970s. Powerful and diverse constituencies competed for political preference and economic gain. People and organizations blended into myriad interest groups. Their common refrain demanded government intervention on their behalf while opposing, in the name of free enterprise, government favoritism toward other groups. Presidents Nixon, Ford, and Carter, successively, occupied the White House between 1973 and 1980. None succeeded in wringing approval for their comprehensive energy plans from the thoroughly Balkanized Congress.

Prior to the Iranian crisis, the USA may well deserve the lowest

grade for its energy policy response, but the marks of its OECD partners were not much better. The USA proved unwilling to plug the dike
against oil imports which, in 1979, were 100 mmt greater than in 1973.
The non-producing OECD states maintained their imports at a stable
level after 1973 (Table 7.5). Just as elements within the US government
blamed OPEC, Germany, and Japan for American balance of payments difficulties, so did the larger OECD states attribute economic
instability and high oil prices to American oil imports. The Iranian crisis
impelled the USA to cooperate with Japan and the EC nations in jointly
reducing oil imports. A scheme to that effect was announced at the
Bonn and Tokyo summit meetings of 1978 and 1979 and reconfirmed
at the Venice meeting in 1980. Even before those meetings, President
Carter labored to win congressional approval for the deregulation of
oil and natural gas prices.[60]

Assigning the scapegoat role to the USA was as unjustifiable as it
was for the USA to reproach Germany and Japan for America's industrial weakness. Each industrial state applied supply side solutions
to the crisis. Indeed, the USA adopted more diverse and stringent conservation measures than its critics. To be sure, other measures, particularly price controls, canceled out the full effects of the conservation
laws. Guilty of indifference to conservation and the use of renewable
energy, the USA and its allies pushed full steam ahead to discover new
sources of oil and to expand nuclear power. But, America's pluralistic
politics and the federal system permitted a robust anti-nuclear coalition
to block expansion even as consumer interests obstructed the abandonment of controlled oil prices and defeated efforts to raise taxes on imported oil. Political fragmentation and executive weakness stifled efforts
by Carter to pull together a broadly based constituency favoring conservation. The governments of western Europe fared no better.

European governments and IEA correctly chided the USA for ir-
responsibly neglecting to stem the flow of oil imports. America's critics
were no less supply driven. The IEA, in the mid-1970s, displayed an-
noyance at Norway's decision to maintain moderate North Sea oil production and not produce immediately from new fields. The frustrated
importers contended that this forced them to pay more for oil.[61] At that
time, those importers had no conservation policies in place.

One half of the reduction in oil imports accomplished in OECD-
Europe from 1973 to 1977 were attributable to Great Britain and her
North Sea oil (Table 7.5). The remainder occurred because of stagnant
economies. Thereafter, increased natural gas use and nuclear power
made possible a diminution of oil imports. Conservation, arousing no
enthusiasm, contributed but marginally to the slackening of European
energy use. Politically influential utilities, whether private of state

owned, sought greater not lesser sales, more not fewer appliances in households. Convincing people to burn less energy yielded no political gain to politicians accustomed to promising the best of all possible worlds at half price. As Rosenbaum wisely observes, "President Carter's advocacy of energy conservation as duty, sacrifice, and discipline added the stigma of moral obligation to conservation's other unfortunate implications. Conservation should not seem to require for its success a nation of Calvinists."[62]

So, the leaders of market driven democracies acted predictably, scurrying after new, expensive, and, frequently, dangerous sources of energy and loath to confess the shortcomings of their policies. Diversifying the domestic energy mix resolved few problems. Each of the fuels substituted for oil harbored serious drawbacks. In 1979, Carter, embarrassed by the negative reception of fellow citizens to his call for energy conservation, quickly turned to an $88 billion scheme to produce synthetic fuel. Big money and giant technology legitimated such programs.[63]

Notes

1. For the above two paragraphs: H. Maull, *Energy, Minerals, and Western Security*, Baltimore: The Johns Hopkins University Press (1984), p. 108; De Golyer and MacNaughton, *Twentieth Century Petroleum Statistics 1986*, Dallas: De Golyer and MacNaughton (1986), p. 60; International Energy Agency, *Energy Policies and Programmes of the IEA Countries, 1985 Review*, Paris: OECD/IEA (1986), p. 38; P. Odell, *Oil and World Power*, 7th edn, Harmondsworth, Middlesex: Penguin (1983), pp. 112–13; C. Tugendhat and A. Hamilton, *Oil, the biggest business*, London: Methuen (1975).

2. For the above two paragraphs: Congressional Quarterly, Inc., *Energy Policy*, Washington, DC: Congressional Quarterly, Inc. (1981), p. 15; C.P. Bradley, *Recent United States Policy in the Persian Gulf: (1971–1982)*, Grantham, N.H.: Tompson & Rutter (1982), pp. 47–51; E.W. Chester, *United States Oil Policy and Diplomacy: A Twentieth Century Overview*, Westport, Conn.: Greenwood Press (1983), pp. 246–8; USHR Committee on Foreign Affairs, Subcommittee on the Near East, *The United States and the Persian Gulf, September 29, 1972*, 92nd Congress, 2nd session, Washington, DC: USGPO (1972), pp. 7–9; A. Al-Sowayegh, *Arab Petropolitics*, London: Croom Helm (1984), pp. 71–80, 123–9.

3. For the above two paragraphs: A.D. Johany, *The Myth of the OPEC Cartel: The Role of Saudi Arabia*, New York: Wiley (1980), p. 48; De Golyer and MacNaughton, *1986*, p. 5; M.T. Hatch, *Politics and Nuclear Power: Energy Policy in Western Europe*, Lexington, Ky.: The University Press of Kentucky (1986), pp. 40–1; H. Mendershausen, *Coping with the Oil Crisis: French and German Experiences*, Baltimore: The Johns Hopkins University Press for Resources for the Future (1976), pp. 71,

85–6; B.R. Mitchell, ed., *European Historical Statistics 1750–1975*, 2nd revised edn, London: Macmillan (1981), pp. 442–3; Y-li. Wu, *Japan's Search for Oil: A Case Study of Economic Nationalism and Economic Security*, Stanford: Hoover Institution Press (1977), pp. 2–3, 26.

4. Al-Sowayegh, *Arab Petropolitics*, pp. 140–1; Wu, *Japan's Search for Oil*, pp. 1–2; W.L. Kohl, *International Institutions for Energy Management*, Aldershot, Hampshire: Gower (1983), pp. 44–8; Congressional Quarterly, *Energy Policy*, pp. 20–1.

5. J.A. Wolfe, *Mineral Resources: a World Review*, New York: Chapman and Hall (1984), pp. 17–18, reflects the accusatory extreme; F. Fesharaki, *Development of the Iranian Oil Industry: International and Domestic Aspects*, New York: Praeger (1976), pp. 155–70 and A. Alnasrawi, *OPEC in a Changing World Economy*, Baltimore: The Johns Hopkins University Press (1985), pp. 93–7, approach the other extreme.

6. See D. Gisselquist, *Oil Prices and Trade Deficits: US Conflicts with Japan and West Germany*, New York: Praeger (1979), pp. 62–3 and, with some qualifications, Odell, *Oil and World Power*, pp. 224–9.

7. For a general discussion of producer goals, see E.J. Wilson, III, "World politics and international energy markets," *International Organization*, 41 (Winter 1987), pp. 125–49.

8. Hatch, *Politics and Nuclear Power*, p. 197; A.M. El-Agraa, ed., *The Economics of the European Community*, 2nd edn, Diddington, Oxford: Phillip Allan (1985), p. 55; W.W. Rostow, *The World Economy: History and Prospect*, Austin: University of Texas Press (1978), pp. 286, 290, 294–5; G. Jenkins, *Oil Economists' Handbook 1985*, London: Applied Science Publishers Ltd (1985), p. 20; Mendershausen, *The Oil Crisis*, pp. 91–3.

9. For the above two paragraphs: see sources for Table 7.3; Mitchell, ed., *European Historical Statistics*, pp. 518–20; Wu, *Japan's Search for Oil*, p. 27; UN, *1983 International Trade Statistics Yearbook. vol. 1. Trade by Country*, New York: UN (1985), pp. 1086–7; J.L. Cochrane, "Carter Energy Policy and the Ninety-Fifth Congress," in C.D. Goodwin, ed., *Energy Policy in Perspective: Today's Problems, Yesterday's Solutions*, Washington, DC: The Brookings Institution (1981), p. 587.

10. For the above three paragraphs: Hatch, *Politics and Nuclear Power*, p. 197; P. Tempest, "The International Energy Investment Dilemma," *The Energy Journal*, 4 (July 1983), pp. 3–4; N. Choucri, *International Politics of Energy Interdependence*, Lexington, Mass.: Lexington Books (1976), p. 56; IEA, *World Energy Outlook*, Paris: OECD/IEA (1982), p. 63; H. Shibata, "The Energy Crisis and Japanese Response," *Resources and Energy*, 5 (June 1983), pp. 136–8; J. Foreman-Peck, *A History of the World Economy: International Economic Relations since 1850*, Brighton: Wheatsheaf Books (1983), p. 350; UN, *1983 Trade Statistics*, pp. 1086–7.

11. Alnasrawi, *OPEC*, pp. 93–7; H. Askari and J.T. Cummings, *Oil, OECD, and the Third World: A Vicious Triangle*, Austin: University of Texas Press (1978), p. 2; A.E. Safer, "World Oil Markets and the Business Cycle," *Energy Communications*, 5. no. 5 (1979), pp. 334–7.

12. For thoughtful discussions of energy policy objectives see: P.F. Cowhey, *The Problems of Plenty: Energy Policy and International Politics*, Berkeley: The University of California Press (1985), pp. 37–8; Wilson, "World politics," p. 129.

13. G.J. Ikenberry, *Reasons of State: Oil Politics and the Capacities of Ameri-*

can Government, Ithaca, New York: Cornell University Press (1988), pp. 80–103, suggests that the US launched its collective initiative because it could not respond to the energy crisis with forceful domestic policies.

14. For the above four paragraphs: IEA, *World Energy Outlook*, Paris: OECD/IEA (1977); N.J.D. Lucas, *Energy and the European Communities*, London: Europa (1977), pp. 60–5, 71–3; L. Turner, "UK Interests and the International Energy Agency," in R. Belgrave, ed., *Energy-Two Decades of Crisis*, Aldershot: Gower (1983), pp. 157–8, 161–3; Mendershausen, *The Oil Crisis*, pp. 60–1; Kohl, *International Energy Management*, pp. 10, 17–18, 23–5; R.C. McWilliams, "Deep Seabed Minerals: The Common Heritage of Mankind," unpublished seminar paper, Lawrence, Kan., April 25, 1985, pp. 8, 18.

15. El-Agraa, ed., *European Community*, pp. 254–9; Kohl, *International Energy Management*, pp. 34–6; D. Ezra, *Coal and Energy: The need to exploit the world's most abundant fossil fuel*, London: Ernest Benn (1978), p. 169; Lucas, "Energy, the UK and the European Community," in Belgrave, ed., *Energy*, p. 269; Turner, "UK Interests," in *ibid.*, pp. 200–3; L.E. Grayson, *National Oil Companies*, pp. 229–32.

16. For a more detailed account of US foreign policies in the Gulf, see Bradley, *US Policy in the Gulf*. See also, W.I. Levy, "Oil and the Decline of the West," *Foreign Affairs*, 58 (Summer 1980), pp. 999–1015.

17. For the above two paragraphs: G. Luciani, *The Oil Companies and the Arab World*, London: Croom Helm (1984), pp. 11, 36–58; I.M. Torrens, *Changing Structures in the World Oil Market*, Paris: The Atlantic Institute for International Affairs (1980), pp. 15–19; Mendershausen, *The Oil Crisis*, p. 46; R.A. Ajami, *Arab Response to the Multinationals*, New York: Praeger (1979), pp. 17–20.

18. Lucas, *Western European Energy Policies: A Comparative Study of the Influence of Institutional Structure on Technical Change*, Oxford: Clarendon Press (1985), p. 38; Grayson, *National Oil Companies*, pp. 75, 146–60; 210; O. Noreng, *The Oil Industry and Government Policy in the North Sea*, London: Croom Helm (1980), pp. 147–50; D. Goodermote and R. Mancke, "Nationalizing Oil in the 1970s," *The Energy Journal*, 4 (October 1983), pp. 69–71.

19. H. Madelin, *Oil and Politics*, translated by M. Totman, Farnborough: Saxon House (1975), p. 103; Lucas, *European Energy Policies*, pp. 39–40; Grayson, *National Oil Companies*, pp. 41, 66, 114; Luciani, *Oil Companies and the Arab World*, pp. 126–30; M.G. Visher and S. Remoe, "A Case Study of a Cuckoo Nestling: The Role of the State in the Norwegian Oil Sector," *Politics and Society*, 13. no. 3 (1984), pp. 335–6.

20. N. Grimaud, "L'OPEP: De L'Exercise Difficile du Monopole," *Afrique et L'Asie Moderne*, 32 (Summer 1984), pp. 14–16; S. Hunter, *OPEC and the Third World: The Politics of Aid*, London: Croom Helm (1984), pp. 122–8; Bradley, *US Policy in the Gulf*, pp. 26–9, 33–40.

21. *BP Statistical Review of World Energy, June 1986, passim*: J.F. O'Leary, "Price Reactive versus Price Active Energy Policy," in P. Tempest, ed., *International Energy Markets*, Cambridge, Mass.: Oelgeschlager, Gunn & Hain (1983), p. 165; M. Tanzer and S. Zorn, *Energy Update: Oil in the Late Twentieth Century*, New York: Monthly Review Press (1985), p. 144; De Golyer, *1986*, pp. 4–11, 18, 62.

22. J.W. Mullen, *Energy in Latin America: The Historical Record*, Santiago

de Chile: CEPAL (1978), p. 13; The Economist Intelligence Unit, *1986/ 1987 Yearbook. Energy in Latin America and the Caribbean*, London: Economist Publications Ltd (1987), p. 2; *BP Review 1986*, p. 18; Mendershausen, *The Oil Crisis*, pp. 42–8, E.L. Morse, "An Overview: Gain, Costs, Dilemmas," in J. Pearce, ed., *The Third Oil Shock: The Effects of Lower Prices*, London: Routledge & Kegan Paul (1983), p. 4; Ezra, *Coal and Energy*, pp. 29–33; De Golyer, *1986*, p. 1.

23. For the above three paragraphs: EIU, *1986/1987 Yearbook*, p. 3; De Golyer, *1986*, p. 14; J. Birks, "Oil and Gas," in T.L. Shaw *et al.*, eds, *Policy and Development of Energy Resources*, Chichester: Wiley (1984), 143–5; B. Mosaavar-Rahmani, *Energy Policy in Iran: Domestic Choices and International Implications*, New York: Pergamon Press (1981), pp. 15– 16; J. Russell, *Geopolitics of Natural Gas*, Cambridge, Mass.: Ballinger (1983), pp. 42–3; J.P. Stern, *International Gas Trade in Europe: The Policies of Exporting and Importing Countries*, London: Heinemann Educational Books Ltd (1984), pp. 157–8.

24. For the above three paragraphs: G.W. Hoffman, *The European Energy Challenge: East and West*, Durham, N.C.: Duke University Press (1985), pp. 44–6, 62–3, 108–9; Grayson, *National Oil Companies*, pp. 19, 25–6; Lucas, *European Energy Policies*, p. 40; R.H.K. Vietor, *Energy policy in America since 1945: A study of business–government relations*, Cambridge: Cambridge University Press (1984), pp. 270–1, 292–303; *The Economist*, January 3, 1987, p. 73.

25. Nixon's 1973 energy speech in Congressional Quarterly, *Energy Policy*, p. 241.

26. Mendershausen, *The Oil Crisis*, pp. 91–3; G.J. Ikenberry, "The irony of state strength: Comparative responses to the oil shocks of the 1970s," *International Organization*, 40 (Winter 1986), pp. 111–15, 125; N. de Marchi, "Energy Policy under Nixon: Mainly Putting Out Fires," and "The Ford Administration: Energy as a Political Good," in Goodwin, ed., *Energy Policy in Perspective*.

27. See sources for Table 7.5.

28. For the above three paragraphs: P. James, *The Future of Coal*, 2nd edn, London: Macmillan (1984), pp. 179, 189; Hoffman, *European Energy Challenge*, p. 6; H.T. Franssen, "OECD Coal Demand in the 1980s," in D. Hawdon, ed., *The Energy Crisis: Ten Years After*, London: Croom Helm (1984), pp. 109–10; Congressional Quarterly, *Energy Policy*, pp. 249, 254; United Nations Economic Commission for Europe, *Coal: 1985 and Beyond*, Oxford: Pergamon Press (1978), pp. 23, 41, 43; World Coal Study, *Coal–Bridge to the Future*, Cambridge, Mass.: Ballinger (1980), p. 432.

29. World Coal Study, *Future Coal Prospects: Country and Regional Assessments*, Cambridge, Mass.: Ballinger (1980), pp. 166, 489; James, *The Future of Coal*, pp. 64–97, 187–8, 196; Ezra, *Coal and Energy*, pp. 148– 53, 157–8; Congressional Quarterly, *Energy Policy*, pp. 108–9; de Marchi, "Ford," *passim*; W.A. Rosenbaum, *Energy, Politics, and Public Policy*, 2nd edn, Washington DC: CQ Press (1987), pp. 109–10, 127–8.

30. James, *The Future of Coal*, pp. 54–7, 192; World Coal Study, *Coal Prospects*, p. 398; M. Sill, "Coal in Western Europe: 1970–1981," *Geography. Journal of the Geographical Association*, 69 (January 1984), p. 69; Hatch, *Politics of Nuclear Power*, p. 43; G. Manners, *Coal in Britain*, London:

Allen & Unwin (1981), pp. 54–7; Lucas, *European Energy Policies*, pp. 213–4.

31. C-yuan Lin, "Global Pattern of Energy Consumption before and after the 1974 Oil Crisis," *Economic Development and Cultural Change*, 32 (July 1984), p. 787; Rosenbaum, *Energy and Public Policy*, p. 165; World Coal Study, *Coal Prospects*, p. 432; IEA, *Energy Statistics, 1971–1981*, Paris: OECD/IEA (1983), pp. 134–55, *1983–4* (1984), pp. 118–20; *World Coal*, 9. no. 4 (August 1983), p. 20; F.R. Anton, *The Canadian Coal Industry: Challenge in the Years Ahead*, Calgary: Detselig (1981), pp. 136–7; Hoffman, *European Energy Challenge*, p. 57; Manners, *Coal*, pp. 80–2.

32. For the above two paragraphs: Vietor, *Energy policy in America*, pp. 275–7; Hoffman, *European Energy Challenge*, pp. 6–7; E.A. Hewitt, *Energy, Economics, and Foreign Policy in the Soviet Union*, Washington, DC: The Brookings Institution (1984), p. 218; B.I. Greer and J.L. Russell, "European Reliance on Soviet Gas Exports: The Yamburg–Urengoi Natural Gas Project," *The Energy Journal*, 3 (July 1982), pp. 24–5.

33. For the above two paragraphs: J.P. Stern, *International Gas Trade*, pp. 153–4, 158–9; J.D. Davis, *Blue Gold: The Political Economy of Natural Gas*, London: Allen & Unwin (1984), pp. 167–8, 199–202; J.C. Ausland, *Norway, Oil, and Foreign Policy*, Boulder, Colo.: Westview Press (1979), pp. 75–8; Lucas, *European Energy Policies*, pp. 195–7; Russell, *Geopolitics of Natural Gas*, pp. 66–9; P. Odell, "Natural Gas in Western Europe: Major Expansion in Prospect," in W.F. Thompson and D.J. De Angelo, eds, *World Energy Markets: Stability or Cyclical Change*, Boulder, Colo.: Westview Press (1985), pp. 286–8.

34. These trades will be returned to in Chapters 8 and 9.

35. Stern, *International Gas Trade*, pp. 79–88; Russell, *Geopolitics of Natural Gas*, pp. 93–5; C. Cragg, "Natural Gas in the Middle East and North Africa," in *The Middle East and North Africa 1987*, 33rd edn, London: Europa Publications Ltd (1987), p. 136.

36. De Golyer, *1986*, pp. 75–6; Vietor, *Energy policy in America*, pp. 292–303; Goodwin, ed., *Energy Policy in Perspective, passim*; R. Gutierrez, "Mexican Economic and Oil Policies of the 1970s and Strategies for the 1980s," in M. Wionczek and R. El-Mallakh, eds, *Mexico's Energy Resources: Toward a Policy of Diversification*, Boulder, Colo.: Westview Press (1985), p. 30; Congressional Quarterly, *Energy Policy*, pp. 68–9; Maull, *Energy and Western Security*, pp. 82–3.

37. IEA, *Energy Balances of OECD Countries 1970/1982*, Paris: OECD/IEA (1984), pp. 387–9, 414, *1983–1984*, pp. 84–5, 135; *BP Statistical Review 1986*, pp. 31, 33.

38. For the above three paragraphs: IEA, *World Energy Outlook (1982)*, pp. 332–3; C. Flavin, *Nuclear Power: The Market Test. Worldwatch Paper 57*, Washington, DC: Worldwatch Institute (1983), pp. 8, 43, and "Reforming the Electric Power Industry," in L.R. Brown *et al.*, *State of the World 1986*, New York: W.W. Norton (1986), p. 100; World Resources Institute, *World Resources 1988–1989*, New York: Basic Books (1988), p. 305; *New York Times*, April 1, 1984; *World Watch*, 1 (January–February 1988), p. 7; *Time*, January 2, 1989, p. 39; W. Shawcross, "Nuclear Power: The Fifth Horseman," *The Spectator*, October 25, 1986, pp. 9–12.

39. USCEA letter (January 1989). The complexity of the cost issue is exemplified in L.J. Perl, "The Current Economics of Coal and Nuclear

Power in the United States," in Thompson, ed., *World Energy Markets*, which suggests that as of 1983 "nuclear plants are less economic than coal in the US....," p. 508. The advertisements of the USCEA provide pro-nuclear arguments. See Flavin, *Nuclear Power: The Market Test* for the counter-argument.

40.   For the above four paragraphs: Rosenbaum, *Energy and Public Policy*, p. 139; Hatch, *Politics and Nuclear Power*, pp. 102–9; *The Guardian*, September 4, 1986; A. Marsh, "Environmental Issues in Contemporary European Politics," in G.T. Goodman *et al.*, eds, *The European Transition from Oil: Societal Impacts and Constraints on Energy Policy*, London: Academic Press (1981), pp. 141–5; US Council for Energy Awareness advertisements in *Time*, Spring issues, 1988; Flavin, "How Many Chernobyls?" *World Watch*, 1 (January–February 1988), p. 14–15.

41.   Quoted in *EPRI Journal*, 13 (December 1988), p. 13.

42.   Rosenbaum, *Energy and Public Policy*, pp. 148, 154–5; Lucas, *European Energy Policies*, p. 202; Hatch, *Politics and Nuclear Power*, pp. 141–8; M. Lonnroth and W. Walker, "The Viability of the Civil Nuclear Industry," in I. Smart, ed., *World Nuclear Energy: Toward a Bargain of Confidence*, Baltimore: Johns Hopkins University Press (1982), p. 205; Ikenberry, "Responses to the oil shocks of the 1970s," pp. 125–6; *The Guardian*, September 2, 1986, October 6, 1986. February 1, 1987.

43.   A.M. Weinberg, "Social Institutions and Nuclear Energy,", *Science*, 177 (July 1972), pp. 27–34.

44.   Lucas, *European Energy Policies*, p. 233.

45.   D. Hays, *Energy: The Case for Conservation. Worldwatch Paper 4*, Washington, DC: Worldwatch Institute (1976), p. 7, *passim*; C.P. Shea, *Renewable Energy: Today's Contribution, Tomorrow's Promise. Worldwatch Paper 81*, Washington, DC: Worldwatch Institute (1988).

46.   Stern, *International Gas Trade*, pp. 65–7; Russell, *Geopolitics of Natural Gas*, pp. 78–80.

47.   S.H. Schurr, "Energy Efficiency and Production Efficiency: Some Thoughts Based on American Experience," in Tempest, ed., *International Energy Markets*, pp. 56–7.

48.   M. Carpenter, "The Response of the European Community," in Tempest, *International Energy Markets*, pp. 118–19; E.A. Hewitt, *Energy in the Soviet Union*, p. 218; A.F. Pexton, "A fuels policy into the 21st century," in Shaw *et al.*, eds, *Energy Resources*, p. 15; Lucas, *European Energy Policies*, pp. 56–8, 155, 231–3, 256; H.W. Maull, "Time Wasted: The Politics of European Energy Transition," in Goodman *et al.*, eds, *European Transition from Oil*, pp. 286, 292–5; D.J. Spooner, "Energy: 1973–1983 the diversification decade," *Geography. Journal of the Geographical Association*, 69 (August 1984), p. 156.

49.   *The Far East and Australasia 1987*, 18th edn, London: Europa Publications Ltd (1987), p. 488; Wu, *Japan's Search for Oil*, p. 27; US Department of Energy, *Monthly Energy Review, July 1981*, Washington, DC: USGPO (1981), p. 10.

50.   H. Shibata, "The Energy Crises and Japanese Response," p. 129, advances the thesis that general industrial and anti-inflationary policies produced greater results than energy-specific policies; *Lloyds Bank Group Economic Report 1983, Japan*, London: Lloyds Bank Group (1983), pp. 3–6.

51. *Ibid.*, pp. 6, 10–12; Shibata, "The Energy Crisis and Japanese Response," pp. 138–9, 148–52; J. Hirschmeier and T. Yui, *The Development of Japanese Business, 1600–1980*, 2nd edn, London: Allen & Unwin (1981), p. 298; *Far East and Australasia 1987*, pp. 487, 498; Wu, *Japan's Search for Oil*, pp. xiii–xiv; R.E. Driscoll and J.N. Behrman, eds, *National Industrial Policies*, Cambridge, Mass.: Oelgeschlager, Gunn & Hain (1984), pp. 85–7.

52. Wu, *Japan's Search for Oil*, pp. 5–8, 12; R. Dore, "Energy Conservation in Japanese Industry," in Belgrave, ed., *Energy*, pp. 91–6; J. Watanuki, "Japanese Society and the Limits of Growth," in D. Yergin and M. Hillenbrand, eds, *Global Insecurity: A Strategy for Political and Economic Survival in the 1980s*, Hammondsworth: Penguin Books (1983), pp. 179–80; Jenkins, *Oil Handbook 1985*, p. 96; Shibata, "The Energy Crisis and Japanese Response," pp. 140–3.

53. For the above two paragraphs: Luciani, *Oil Companies and the Arab World*, p. 137; H. Ishihara, "Energy demand and supply conditions in Japan," *OPEC Review*, VIII (Autumn 1984), pp. 283–4, 294; Odell, *Oil and World Power*, pp. 153–7; R. Kokubun, "The Policy of Economic Policy Making in China: The Case of Plant Cancellations with Japan," *The China Quarterly*, 105 (March 1986), pp. 21, 31.

54. For the above three paragraphs: Stern, *International Gas Trade*, p. 149; M. Peebles, *Evolution of the Gas Industry*, London: Macmillan (1980), pp. 100–10; Maull, *Energy and Western Security*, p. 8; H. Takahashi, "Rush of Big Projects Promises Glut in LNG," *The Oriental Economist*, May 1985, pp. 14–17; N.W. Davis, "Nuclear Power Generation in Japan," *ibid.*, October 1983, pp. 30–5; IEA, *Energy Statistics 1983/1984*, pp. 180–2; Flavin, *Nuclear Power*, p. 51; World Resources Institute, *World Resources 1988–89*, p. 311.

55. Dore, "Energy Conservation," p. 120.

56. DeGolyer, *1986*, p. 4; *BP Statistical Review 1980*, p. 18; Hatch, *Politics and Nuclear Power*, p. 197; Rostow, *World Economy*, pp. 602–3.

57. Congressional Quarterly, *Energy Policy*, p. 43.

58. Lucas, *European Energy Policies*, p. 259.

59. *Ibid.*, pp. 53–6, 160, 252–6.

60. *The Washington Star*, June 26, 1979; *The New York Times*, June 29, 1980; Kohl, *International Energy Management*, pp. 19, 28–9.

61. Ausland, *Norway*, pp. 42–7; Maull, *Europe and World Energy*, London: Butterworths (1980), pp. 77–8.

62. Rosenbaum, *Energy and Public Policy*, p. 206.

63. Congressional Quarterly, *Energy Policy*, pp. 210–11, 223; see Ikenberry, *Reasons of State*, Chapter 6 for an exposition of the view that the US government turned to high tech energy R&D because of its inability to "alter prevailing government roles in the energy arena . . . .," p. 139.

8

The lesser developed countries and the oil boom of the 1970s

The industrialized societies possessed a variety of economic, technological, and managerial defenses against oil shortages and price increases which, if utilized, would have lessened the impact of the oil producers' actions in 1973 and largely avoided the repercussions of plummeting Iranian production after 1978 (Table 7.4). Political considerations within the western states precluded the application of effective counter measures during the 1970s.

Other nations lacked the capacity to respond flexibly to the price shock. In Tanzania, Bangladesh, Taiwan, the Philippines, or Brazil, each an energy importer, and in Saudi Arabia, Venezuela, and Mexico each with a sizable energy surplus, the quest for rapid industrial development established the parameters for policy responses to soaring prices.

Russian *per capita* GNP is similar to that of Italy, Singapore, and Hong Kong. During the mid-1970s, income in eastern Europe compared favorably to incomes in Ireland, Spain, Greece, and South Korea. East Germany's income may have exceeded Britain's. While the Soviet bloc states created welfare, industrial, and agricultural sectors more modern than most of the oil importing LDCs, they were much less profitably linked to western economies than such nations as South Korea or Taiwan.

Some characteristics of underdevelopment

Within the large array of LDCs, states manifest a wide variety of economic, social, and political conditions. Political scientists, sociologists, and economists might organize a discussion of underdevelopment around categories that differentiate nations according to types of state structures and degrees of state power. The range among LDCs includes: the authoritarian and command economies of eastern Europe, in which states control the entire economy but operate within parameters defined by the USSR;* the strong state economies of South Korea, Brazil, or Saudi Arabia, in which the state established overall policies within which public and private enterprise operated; the weak state structures in Tanzania, Nigeria, or Bangladesh, in which governments, whether tending toward authoritarianism or democracy, have failed to impose control or exert firm leadership over their economies.

The LDCs are largely planned economies, but not necessarily socialist. Their development strategies reflected the distribution of internal wealth and power, assessments of resource strengths and weaknesses, industrial potential, levels of urbanization, nationalistic desires, and other elements. Thus, South Korea and Taiwan, recipients of munificent US aid, developed export led economies based upon specialized manufactured goods, much like Japan. Brazil and Argentina, less energy dependent than South Korea or Taiwan, but with much larger domestic economies coupled import substitution with raw materials exports. Mexico, energy self-sufficient, vacillated between import substitution and export led programs. The export led policies of Saudi Arabia contrasted sharply in size and composition with the commodity export dependence of Tanzania and much of Central America.

This chapter employs energy import dependence as the organizational device. Two groups of energy import dependent states are featured: the eastern European satellites of the USSR; and other oil importing LDCs. The oil exporting states comprise a third group. Within and between the import dependent groups great diversity reigns. East Germany (GDR), Argentina, Brazil, and South Korea generate incomes and health and welfare indicators far superior to Bangladesh and the Philippines (Table 8.1). Variable opportunities characterized the abilities of these states to fulfill economic development objectives and to respond successfully to the energy price escalation of the period, 1973–82. The least advanced states, forming the bottom group of Table 8.1, enjoyed the fewest policy options in confronting the energy crisis.

All LDCs were variously afflicted by world inflationary trends which

---

* By early 1990, the Soviet bloc had collapsed. The reunification of Germany seemed imminent. Elsewhere in eastern Europe dictators had been chased from office and even executed. The shape that political and economic institutions might assume remained unclear. Democratization seemed a popular and achievable demand. Much depended, however, upon the resilience of domestic economies and the willingness of the West to provide a financial safety-net while new institutions were created.

Table 8.1   Indicators of development for selected states

Country	1982 Per capita TPER (mtoe)	Country	1986 Per capita kwh	Country	1986 Infant mortality rate*	Country	1976 Per capita GNP ($)
World	1.5	World	1875	World	6		
USA	7.5	USA	10258	Japan	6	USA	7890
East Germany	5.0	East Germany	6253	USA	8	West Germany	7380
West Germany	4.7	West Germany	6173	West Germany	9	Japan	4810
USSR	4.4	USSR	5332	East Germany	10	East Germany	4220
Czechozlovakia	3.2	Japan	5306	Czechoslovakia	16	Poland	2860
Japan	3.1	Bulgaria	4955	Bulgaria	17	Czechoslovakia	2841
Bulgaria	3.0	Czechoslovakia	4899	Poland	19	USSR	2760
Poland	3.0	Poland	3547	Hungary	20	Bulgaria	2360
Romania	2.5	Romania	3153	Romania	24	Hungary	2280
Hungary	2.4	Hungary	2390	South Korea	31	Romania	na
Argentina	1.6	Argentina	1448	USSR	31	Argentina	1550
South Korea	1.5	South Korea	1352	Argentina	35	Brazil	1140
Brazil	1.0	Brazil	1228	China	50	South Korea	640
China	0.6	Egypt	448	Philippines	51	Ecuador	640
Egypt	0.5	Ecuador	440	Ecuador	70	China	410
Nigeria	0.4	China	377	Brazil	71	Philippines	410
Ecuador	0.4	Philippines	359	India	110	Nigeria	380
India	0.2	Pakistan	214	Egypt	111	Egypt	280
Philippines	0.2	India	211	Pakistan	120	Pakistan	170
Pakistan	0.1	Nigeria	84	Nigeria	127	India	150
Bangladesh	0.04	Bangladesh	41	Bangladesh	128	Bangladesh	110

* Infant deaths per 1000 live births, 1986

Sources: 1986 World Population Data Sheet, Washington, D.C.: Population Reference Bureau (1986); World Resources Institute, *World Resources 1987*, New York: Basic Books (1987), pp. 303–13; Sources for Table 7.1; V. Smil and W.E. Knowland, eds, *Energy in the developing world. The real energy crisis*, Oxford: Oxford University Press (1980), pp. 372–85.

rising energy prices exacerbated. Among the poorest LDCs, invariably those utilizing significant quantities of non-commercial fuels, the economies were so weak that energy prices alone cannot be said to have radically derailed development programs. Tanzania and most of Central America, in the absence of radical energy price increases, would have arrived at a level of development by 1983 similar to that actually achieved. The Brazilian economy, however, evidenced sufficient sophistication by 1973 to suffer seriously from inflated prices for energy and other imports. Energy in Brazil was more crucial to development schemes than in Tanzania or Central America (Table 8.2).

Brazil's development constraints differed from those of poorer states in degree rather than in kind. Brazil might represent that level of development to which the least developed societies can most reasonably aspire in the near future. For that reason, economic and social trends in Brazil might be considered somewhat characteristic of lesser developed societies.

Intense urbanization stands out as a most striking feature of contemporary Brazilian society. Brazil contains the third — São Paulo — and tenth — Rio de Janeiro — largest cities in the world. Already 36 percent urban in 1950, that proportion reached 73 percent in 1985 (Table 8.2). Declining (but still very high relative to the West) death rates, including infant mortality, and high birth rates generated redundant rural populations. The stream of jobless rural folk into the cities of India, Egypt, Nigeria, and many other countries precipitated urban growth rates that exceeded rural rates by two times. At 1985 rates of growth, the population of Brazil, Egypt, Nigeria, India, and Bangladesh will double within 26 to 31 years. Given the distribution of resources and current conditions in the urban areas, services will deteriorate. In Brazil, 8 of 10 urbanites have access to safe water (1 of 2 in rural areas) and 1 of 3 city dwellers are hooked into sanitation systems. The availability of such services lags far behind in the less advanced countries. Unhealthy conditions and nutritional deficiencies inevitably yield very high infant mortality rates (Table 8.1). Enormous numbers of poor, many squatting on unused land, exist in Brazil's teeming and polluted cities. In Cairo and Alexandria, Karachi and Lahore, Lagos, and Dhaka essential urban services reach but a fraction of residents while unemployment can exceed 50 percent, this despite the claim of urban areas to a lion's share of development money.

Early on, Brazil and other LDCs patterned development plans on models provided by the advanced western states. This choice locked the LDCs into techniques and industries available only from the West, often purchased with loans obtained from such western dominated insitutions as the World Bank, and all of which necessitated the adoption of western

Table 8.2 Energy mix of selected LDCs

	% rural[3]	% net energy imports to TPER average 1973–8	% non-commercial fuels to TPER average 1973–8	% oil to TPER 1973	% oil to TPER 1978
Argentina	15	15	9	68	67
Brazil	27	38	33	43	42
South Korea	35	40	43	34	41
Egypt	53	0	8	68	67
Central America[1]	53	47	37	40	na
India	75	11	43	19	18
Nigeria	77	0	80	11	17
Tanzania[2]	85	100	92	7	na

[1] 1975 only
[2] 1980 only
[3] 1985

Sources: IEA, *Energy Balances of Developing Countries 1971/1982.* Paris: OECD/IEA (1984), *passim*; J.W. Mullen, *Energy in Latin America: The Historical Record,* Santiago de Chile: CEPAL (1978), p. 20; G. Schramm, "Managing Urban/Industrial Wood Fuel Supply and Demand in Africa," *The Annals of Regional Science,* XXI (November 1987). pp. 61, 66; World Resources Institute, *World Resources 1987,* New York: Basic Books (1987), pp. 260–1.

energy use practices. As an example, Brazil, around 1980, contained 13 million motor vehicles, mostly operated in the cities which housed almost 110 million, or 1 vehicle per 8 urban residents and 1 per 12 Brazilians (the US ratio was 1:2). A fractional portion of Brazilians, then, owned a car. Yet funds poured into highway construction in the southern fifth of the country where the urban population concentrated. Brazil's enormously costly "energy from alcohol" program removed land from food production in a country where 40 million peasants are landless and focused entirely on a mode of transportation affordable to a small minority. The market imperatives of food supply and the social–political dangers of landlessness assure that the Amazon's rain forests will continue to lose ground to pasture, cropland, and infrastructure development that does not generate permanent employment.[1]

The process of industrialization in Latin America, Szekely asserts, aggravated an already severe maldistribution of income. By 1975, one-half of the population received only 8 percent of the income compared with 13 percent in 1960. Industrialization made the wealthy wealthier and more powerful, but, in Brazil for instance, it also conferred some benefits upon a rapidly growing middle class. Few benefits trickled down to the rural populace, many of whom were forced from the land into urban unemployment.[2] By the mid-1980s, improvements in key welfare sectors should be noted among even the poorest LDCs. Infant and child mortality rates declined in many LDCs, but were still five to ten times greater than in western Europe. Concurrently, life expectancy rose. *Per capita* GNP rose by 58 percent in Brazil between 1976 and 1986, triggering a relative gain in household income for each of the lowest four quintiles. However, in Central America and Brazil, inflation severely eroded purchasing power. Remaining unresolved were the questions of how to provide jobs for swelling populations and how to reduce population growth.[3]

Some few LDCs experienced striking economic gains during and after the 1960s. Singapore, South Korea, and Taiwan, authoritarian and single party states into the 1980s, evolved impressive industrial sectors that competed fiercely with the USA, Japan, and western Europe for market shares in manufactured goods. From 1966 through 1981, the growth rate of South Korea's GNP hit double digits six times and never fell below 7 percent. In Taiwan and South Korea, industrial growth rested upon wage rates below those in Japan and on acquiescent labor. South Korea's *per capita* GNP rose from $676 in 1976 to $2,010 in 1983, but few gains spread among the 40 percent living in the countryside or among urban factory workers. Stark income maldistribution persisted despite rapidly growing economies. Still, a successful international trade permitted these nations to respond more effectively to high energy prices than Brazil, despite its domestic oil production, and other poor countries.[4]

The price shock of 1973 and the energy importing LDCs

Several score of states with *per capita* annual incomes ranging from under $100 to about $600, a few of which are included in Table 8.1, compared with incomes exceeding $7,500 in the USA, West Germany, and Canada, possessed neither the resources, technologies, nor management skills to cope successfully with the energy crisis. There is little doubt that China and those nations ranked below it in the *per capita* TPER column of Table 8.1, of which Nigeria alone was a significant energy seller, can be categorized as undeveloped. Argentina, Brazil, and South Korea belong in a category of developing LDCs with lower middle incomes. The Soviet bloc states are lodged in a cohort of almost developed middle income states. Japan and East Germany represent developed nations with upper middle incomes while the USA and West Germany, along with other European Community of six countries, are highly developed upper income nations.

In terms of quality of life, the true meaning of these incomes is debatable. Most westerners would assign a superior quality of life ranking to Japan and West Germany than to Russia and East Germany. The nuances and cultural differences that complicate such comparisons at the upper end of the ranking in Table 8.1 are absent at the lower end. Whatever the measurement used, Bangladesh is recognizable as a land mired in poverty and lacking the means for broad and rapid improvement. India, with a self-sufficient nuclear program and other accouterments of modernity, displays a stronger affinity with Egypt, Pakistan, and Nigeria than with South Korea, Argentina, or Brazil.

In the developed states of the West, the energy problems of the 1970s can be considered discrete, resolvable with available political and economic tools. In 1974, the USA could have effectively stemmed the inflow of foreign oil by imposing oil import fees, deregulating oil and gas prices, and fostering conservation. The appropriateness of such remedies varied widely among the oil importing LDCs. Tanzania, Bangladesh, and several Central American states used tiny quantities of commercial fuel compared with non-commercial fuel. Such states enjoyed little room to maneuver. India and Brazil, however, had developed economic sectors requiring large volumes of commercial fuel even while other sectors used virtually none (Tables 8.1 and 8.2). Brazil's options were greater than India's because it possessed substantial oil reserves and hydroelectric potential. But, for both, any marked reduction of commercial energy use would retard the development of vital economic sectors. Their options were much narrower than those available to the West.

Traditional and modern energy sectors

Bifurcated societies characterized the oil importing LDCs. A relatively small number of affluent people, mostly urban, supported military or civilian governments that kept down the urban and rural poor. Economic policies redounded to the benefit of the few. Two energy regimes coexisted: an urban based system resting on the fossil fuels, overwhelmingly oil, hydroelectric power where feasible, and the availability, after 1970, of the first nuclear reactors; and a rural energy system using non-commercial organic fuels but into which commercial fuels gradually penetrated.

As a general rule, Latin America and sub-Saharan Africa relied primarily upon oil while in Asia coal provided a substantial share, a leading share in India, of total commercial energy consumption. Table 8.2 offers a distilled view of the LDC energy mix. It includes two oil exporting countries, Nigeria and Egypt, and several in which the exploitation of biomass fuels provided over one-third of TPER — 80 percent in Nigeria and 92 percent in Tanzania. The size of the industrial sector determined the relative magnitude of commercial energy use. *Per capita* TPER in Argentina and South Korea far outstripped that of the bottom eight nations listed in Table 8.1. The high use of non-commercial fuel in South Korea, an economically advanced state compared with the Central American republics, vividly reflects a division between an urban centered industrial sector and a traditional agriculture more comparable to Brazil than to Argentina.

Brazil ranked as the second largest oil producer in South America (Argentina ranked third). Its output exceeded 30 mmt by 1986, three times the production of 1980. This impressive volume notwithstanding, one-third of Brazilian TPER derived from non-commercial fuels and the country was quite energy import dependent. Such states as Pakistan, Bangladesh, and the Philippines were even more import dependent than Central America. The former group relied heavily on traditional fuels and were among the lowest *per capita* users of energy. Tanzania represents a very low income country — $180 *per capita* GNP in 1976 and $240 in 1983 — into which commercial fuels have barely penetrated.[5]

The rapid increase in oil prices after 1973 had multiple effects of varying severity on the different layers of LDC societies. In Tanzania, the Philippines, and Central America, without energy resources, in oil rich Nigeria, and in poorly endowed India, the vast majority of people relied for their energy upon firewood or other biomass. Enormous numbers of Brazilians also depended upon non-commercial fuels. The price crunch of the 1970s exacerbated a fuel wood crisis in those countries. Rising prices of kerosene and LPG forced villagers who used those fuels for domestic purposes or in cottage industries to revert to wood, thus increasing demand for a resource not only relatively scarce but essential to the preservation of ecosystems. Deforestation intensified, especially in Africa, Indonesia, and Brazil, those areas of the world with the most magnificent rain forests. Lumbering and clearing land for tillage also contributed to a pace of deforestation that destroyed 0.06 of the forests each year in the above areas. Ten trees were felled for each one planted. The destruction of groundcover by country people struggling to survive hastened desertification in the northern reaches of sub-Saharan Africa.[6]

No immediate resolution of this energy crisis is in sight. Too many people and very slow economic growth prevent the integration of most Tanzanians into commercial fuel regimes and guarantee a rising demand for firewood. In some parts of Africa, the nearest fuel wood is over a day's walk from the village. Small things like efficient cook stoves would help, but most of the affected countries are unable, alone, to manage such programs. Besides, as Brazil's record in the Amazonian forests suggests, governments exploit resources to satisfy short-term objectives.[7]

The poor rural inhabitants of the LDCs, weakened as they were by decades of economic neglect, political manipulation, and cultural invasion, were made only marginally poorer by the energy crisis. Where possible the agrarians moved to cities, to São Paulo, Mexico City, Bombay. There, the sharp rise in energy costs further dampened whatever hopes these urban villagers entertained of improving their lot.

The modern energy sector concentrated in the cities but did not thoroughly integrate all city dwellers even though a greater use of commercial fuels necessarily accompanied urban growth. In most LDC cities, the majority of residents were poor, used a minimum of heating of cooking oil, scrounged for burnable refuse, and did without. The urban poor frequently lived in shanty towns, unlinked to water, gas, or electric service. Economic development during the 1960s favored the more affluent. Great office buildings, high-rise apartment houses, refineries, and hydroelectric projects generated insufficient work to absorb available labor.

Even in the absence of an energy price revolution, most LDCs lacked the resources to improve significantly the living standards of the majority of their citizens. Tanzania and other sub-Saharan states, virtually all of Central America, much of South America, India, and most of the

Indochinese Peninsula practiced traditional agriculture, often within a semi-feudal structure, depended upon low price commodity exports to earn foreign exchange, and were ruled by governments that, for whatever reasons, paid little attention to modernizing the agricultural sector. Import substitution and the development of a dynamic export sector based upon specialized manufactured goods, so successful in South Korea, was beyond the realm of possibility for Tanzania and, probably, for India.[8]

The LDCs and energy costs

Western governments and financial institutions closely monitored the impact of rising energy prices in the LDCs, but concern focused primarily on the swelling external debt and current accounts deficits rather than upon deteriorating welfare. As the brief consideration below of Brazil, Argentina, South Korea, Tanzania, and India demonstrates, LDC governments differed in their ability to respond flexibly to ascending oil prices, rising global inflation, and slower growth in the industrial states (see Tables 8.1 and 8.2). Such states, however, faced a similar conundrum: how to reduce energy import bills so as to moderate the debt burden without retarding development or damaging already low standards of living.

Most dismaying to the raw commodity exporting LDCs, the value of their exports rose more slowly than the cost of their imports; reduced economic activity in the West further deflated the value of their goods. Table 8.3 depicts the degree to which energy imports among a group of LDCs consumed a higher value of exports. From 1972 through 1980, the cost of energy imports as a percent of export earnings reflected staggering increases in energy import bills and a much more rapid growth in cost than in volume. India paid $976 million more for oil in 1974 than in 1972, a rise of 516 percent, but imported only 14 percent more in volume. For most LDCs, the second price shock added hugely to the economic costs already incurred.[9]

Brazil's experience exemplified this unfortunate concatenation of events. Beginning in the 1950s, Brazil endeavored to build an industrial sector by protecting domestic manufacturers against foreign competition. For two decades, import substitution was consistently applied, often in conjunction with an emphasis on the export of coffee and other raw materials. These policies yielded impressive gains: gross domestic product advanced at an annual rate of 11 percent from 1968 to 1974. However, non-plantation agriculture and the plight of the landless poor suffered from this intense concentration upon the urban–industrial

Table 8.3 Value of oil imports as a percent of all exports for oil importing LDCs, 1972–81

	1972	1975	1976	1978	1980	1981
Tanzania	10	21	20	29	57	26
Kenya	11	36	38	23	54	59
India[1]	8	27	19	30	73	na
Pakistan	5	24	23	28	34	39
South Korea	13	25	21	17	33	30
Philippines	13	31	32	27	32	37
Taiwan	6	12	13	13	na	na
Costa Rica	4	5	4	5	20	18
Honduras	7	19	11	8	21	21
Brazil	14	39	40	36	51	50
Argentina[1]	2	8	7	6	7	4

[1] Crude oil only

Sources: IMF, *International Financial Statistics. October 1979*, Washington, D.C.: IMF (1979) and *November 1983* (1983).

Table 8.4 Brazilian energy imports, 1970–80

	1970	1975	1980
($ million) Value of:			
All imports	2 845	13 578	24 922
All exports	2 739	8 669	20 132
Energy imports	351	3 551	10 749
Energy imports as % of exports	13	41	53
Oil imports (mmt)	16	35	50

Sources: Statistical Bulletin of the OAS, 9 January–June (1987), pp. 53–5, 64; J.D. Wirth, ed., *Latin American Oil Companies and the Politics of Energy*, Lincoln, Neb.: University of Nebraska Press (1983), p. 272.

sector. As a large urban middle class emerged, the distribution of wealth became more inequitable.

Brazil's energy import bill suddenly shot upward in 1973 (Table 8.4), sharply raising the costs of creating high energy intensive industries. To sustain industrial momentum, Brazil cut back in welfare, shaved investments in rural development, and borrowed heavily to pay for capital equipment unavailable domestically. By the early 1980s, Brazil sacrificed three-quarters of export earnings to external debt service. Debt restructuring, moratoria on interest payments, and further debt followed. In 1988, only the USA owed more money than Brazil. In the case of Brazil, then, the energy price shocks of 1973 and 1979 derailed development programs that, while undervaluing rural reform, might have created a stronger economy in the urban south and provided a firm base from which to distribute benefits more evenly throughout the country.[10]

In contrast with Brazil, Argentina, possessed an energy regime only marginally dependent upon imported fuels. Domestic oil production provided 86 percent of requirements in 1973 and over 100 percent by 1982. Hydroelectric and nuclear facilities contributed 13 percent of TPER in 1980, up from 2 percent in 1973. Between 1975 and 1979 and again after 1981, its agricultural exports and a maturing manufacturing sector earned foreign trade surpluses. Notwithstanding these accomplishments, Argentina's economy succumbed to a rate of inflation surpassing 100 percent in 1974, reaching 600 percent in 1976, and soaring to a horrendous 1,100 percent by 1985. Chaos in government prevailed, but this did not deter lenders and cash-short Argentine governments from doubling the external debt between 1980 and 1983, when it reached $45 billion. One authoritarian regime succeeded another, with the last of the military juntas leading the nation to its costly Falklands defeat in 1982.[11] In Argentina, the energy crisis aroused little concern.

In sharp contrast with Brazil and Argentina, South Korea shaped a dynamic industrial sector and a strong export program despite its overwhelming reliance upon energy imports, the cost of which climbed to burdensome levels by 1981. Consumption of coal and oil, expressed in coal equivalence, rose by nine times from 1961 to 1975 and, as prices roared upward, increased by another three times from 1975 and 1981. By 1981, imports met 71 percent of commercial fuel requirements. Industrialization proceeded even as the countryside remained locked in a traditional agriculture dependent upon non-commercial energy. In 1982, one-third of Korean TPER consisted of wood and other organic materials.

Korean exports, a mix shifting among several heavy industries, textiles, electronics, engineering services, and foreign investments and borrowing sustained the economy. Korean goods competed successfully in American and European markets and found new outlets among the Middle Eastern oil exporting states. Dependent during the 1960s upon the MNOCs for its refined products, Korea first induced the MNOCs to refine jointly with Korean companies and, then, nationalized the industry. During the 1980s, Korea refined 100 percent of its oil demand while purchasing, transporting, and distributing the whole of its crude imports.[12]

The US connection, strong government planning, the protection of domestic markets against foreign imports, artificially low export prices, and the work habits of its industrial labor force contributed to Korea's remarkable economic performance. Its repressive, single-party government, very low wages, and poor working conditions were, as Harris comments, "all additional constituents of the Korean miracle."[13] Those weaknesses and the sensitive issue of Korean unification threatened the old regime during the late 1980s.

Tanzania, India, and other poor nations possessed neither the resources of Argentina nor the industrial base of South Korea. While Argentina's difficulties may be attributable to the ineptitude of authoritarian regimes, such was not the case in Tanzania or India.

India consumed over 200 times more commercial energy than Tanzania in 1986, reflecting an increase in Indian energy use of almost 200 percent since 1970. Tanzanian energy use rose only 18 percent over the same period. The sheer size of India's population and economy dwarfed Tanzania's. But, even though *per capita* energy consumption in India exceeded Tanzanian by eight times, this meant that while the average Tanzanian used 5 gallons of kerosene annually, the average Indian used 40 gallons. Conservation in Tanzania had little relevance while India could not afford the technological retooling necessary to improve the efficiency of its commercial energy sector.

Energy demand in such states was relatively inelastic. As the crude import bill claimed an increasing proportion of export earnings (Table 8.3), India complained loudly about MNOC and OPEC price gouging. Efforts to increase domestic oil production yielded some results by 1985 when withdrawals surpassed those in 1975 by about four times. Domestic production replaced some imports, but more, not less, oil was required if India's development projects were to advance. The severe price shock of 1979–81 compelled cutbacks in imports that, in turn, retarded development projects.

In the meantime, India's population, and Tanzania's as well, spun out of control. Stimulated by improvements in health care, India's population rose from 635 million in 1976 to 785 million in 1985, an addition of more people than lived in the six original countries of the EC plus Czechoslovakia and East Germany in 1986. Tanzania's average natural population increase was among the world's highest. Since the 1960s, Tanzania has suffered from declining agricultural production *per capita* and recurrent food supply crises.

Population explosion constitutes a most dire threat to state and social viability in Brazil, Central America, India, sub-Saharan Africa, and elsewhere. These places are energy poor. They rely heavily upon noncommercial fuels. Mounting population, unmatched by proportionately greater commercial energy use or by the dedication of funds to agricultural improvement, leave masses of people on lands of declining fertility or, where new lands are available, drives vast numbers to clear everything in sight in order to cultivate and to cook.

As Gerner points out, numerous other concerns impinge on development that may be as relevant as population. The rational peasant argument alerts us to some of the reasons for large families and the difficulties involved in controlling population without instituting other changes in the socio-economic structure of society. Population, resources, opportunities all enter the calculus. An adverse person–resource ratio is at once the cause and effect of virtually all other problems.[14]

Development and emergency aid for the LDCs

Considerable scholarly attention has been directed at the flow of aid and investment capital to the oil importing LDCs. Corporate investors shied away from unstable countries, spending only nominal sums for energy development in such places as Bangladesh, Sri Lanka, or Tanzania. The investment strategies of the MNOCs favored the more stable historic producers and such new areas as the North Sea and Alaska. Aid dispensing institutions proliferated during the 1970s, supplementing such existing agencies as the World Bank, the International Monetary Fund, and the Inter-American Development Bank. Kuwait established its Fund for Arab Economic Development while Venezuela's Puerto Ordaz Agreement (1974) provided credits to help Caribbean and Central American importers pay their energy bills. Regional organizations included the Arab Fund for Economic and Social Development and, in Latin America, the San José Pact (1980) between Mexico and Venezuela which guaranteed adequate oil supplies and provided preferential credits to specific Central American and Caribbean nations. OPEC's Special Fund for International Development operated globally.[15]

Disagreement is rife regarding the effectiveness of aid funds distributed during the 1970s and 1980s. Alnasrawi and Shihata point out that OPEC's Arab producers provided in official development assistance a much higher percentage of their GNP (in 1981, 4.4 percent) than OECD (0.35 percent). Kuwait, Qatar, Saudi Arabia, and UAE led all donors. Kuwait, in 1977, donated 10 percent of GNP to aid, compared with Holland's 1 percent, the high among western states. Hunter and Al Sowayegh join the above authors in proclaiming the significance and generosity of Arab aid to the LDCs. Pachauri demurs, concluding that OPEC or Arab aid was not significant to most Third World nations. More critically still, Foreman-Peck depicts the OPEC relationship with the LDCs as more exploitive than the MNOC–LDC connection. The disputants present compelling evidence that Arab-OPEC aid was highly politicized, lavished upon a few LDCs, and of marginal productive value to most recipients.[16]

Shihata, a former director-general of OPEC's Special Fund, in supporting his case for adequacy, effectiveness, and distributive evenness, glosses over key facts and issues. In justifying the spread of Arab-OPEC aid, his discussion ignores the Arab–Israel conflict. In excess of one-half of all OPEC bilateral aid went to the front line states of Egypt, Syria, and Jordan. Much of the aid money reaching Egypt, amounting to 31.5 percent of the total, financed the purchase of Soviet arms during and immediately after the disastrous 1973 War. Thereafter, Arab aid and credits to Egypt that may have reached $17 billion through 1978 financed a wide variety of development projects and the external debt. This aid came to an abrupt halt when Egypt signed a peace treaty with Israel in 1979. Shihata also neglects the clear geographical–religious dimensions of Arab aid. Arab countries received 73 percent of all OPEC aid while 20 percent flowed to Muslim countries in Africa and Asia, leaving virtually nothing for non-Arab and non-Muslim states.

OPEC's total disbursements were substantial if compared with the aid dispensed by individual western states. In 1977, OPEC aid amounted to $6 billion exceeding US aid by 30 percent and West German aid by 167 percent. The oil price hikes engineered by OPEC greatly increased LDC balance of payments deficits with OPEC. OPEC aid equaled about 28 percent of that deficit from 1974 through 1977. This was sticking plaster treatment for hemorrhage. Aid to India averaged $269 million annually from 1974 to 1977 while the higher oil prices transferred, on the average, an extra $711 million annually from India to OPEC. The UN and IMF also initiated aid programs to ease balance of payment difficulties, but neither accumulated enough funds to offer much relief.[17]

OPEC swam in money during these years. Its members returned a pittance to states that failed to meet political or religious criteria. OPEC's most promising aid institution, the Special Fund, directed its attention exclusively toward the least developed states, but it disbursed only 6 percent of total OPEC aid from 1976 through 1982, frequently in cooperation with the World Bank. After 1977, the Special Fund did spread its funds to such previously ignored states as Tanzania. But in selecting projects, the Fund followed the lead of the World Bank which, I believe, established priorities that were the reverse of need. Energy development received some 40 percent of the funds (energy projects were also the largest single category of Inter-American Development Bank loans), followed by transportation, and, finally, by agriculture which received but 10 percent of the aid. Lenders and borrowers preferred drilling for oil or building highways to redistributing land or encouraging family planning. The World Bank financed projects that entailed minimum political risk. Applicants for loans tailored their projects to fit lender preferences.[18]

Aid from the West also increased after 1973, but especially after 1978. So, too, did loans from private western banks, particularly to Argentina, Brazil, and Mexico. Some portion of those loans represented recycled Arab petrodollars invested in western financial houses, thus linking the Arab producers to Latin American states which received no official OPEC aid. However, the sum total of OPEC–OECD development moneys in 1977, estimated at $22 billion, only equaled the trade deficit of the LDCs with OPEC. In that year the total trade deficit of the LDCs approached $77 billion. The amount of development money made available was negligible relative to need. Much aid was wasted or stolen, as the fall of the Marcos regime in the Philippines revealed. Saudi Arabian, Libyan, and OPEC Special Fund aid to Uganda during the genocidal regime of Amin could not have been productive. Tanzania spent $500 million to topple Amin, far in excess of its energy import bill.[19]

Western lending institutions were hardly exemplary models. World Bank funds flowed to energy intensive, high-tech projects, thus compounding the economic problems of the borrowers. The IMF, then, disbursed large sums to help countries defray energy import costs in part fostered by the World Bank.

OPEC's success in driving up oil prices may have offered some moral satisfaction to other LDCs, as would any humbling of the West. But the economic viability of many LDCs deteriorated. Higher oil and manufactured goods prices and relatively low commodity prices eroded their purchasing power and reduced their ability to pursue necessary development objectives. The second price shock dried up the credit of many LDCs, forcing them to reduce imports of necessities.[20] Uncontrolled population growth and a stagnant, antiquated agriculture cast a pall over their future. Famine and near famine endangered all or parts of many countries, particularly in sub-Saharan Africa. The disappearance of forests and groundcover and unrelieved drought promised slow death to millions. The West, the Soviet bloc, and OPEC shared some responsibility for this as did the leaders of the imperiled societies.

The producing state bonanza

OPEC's new price regime shifted tens of billions of dollars from oil importers to oil exporters. In 1970, global oil exports were valued at about $16 billion; in 1974, an increase of 31 percent in the volume traded generated a 738 percent increase in current value to $134 billion.

Table 8.5   Value of international oil trade and revenues of exporters, 1970–81 ($ billion)

	1970	1974	1981
Global value	16.0	134.0	349.0
Oil revenues:			
OPEC	7.5	112.0	287.9
Arab Persian Gulf,	4.8	51.4	159.4
of which:			
Saudi Arabia (percentage)	48	61	71
Iran	1.1	17.8	11.6
Venezuela	1.4	10.0	14.2
Indonesia	0.3	1.4	10.5

Sources: See Table 7.3; R.K. Pachauri, *The Political Economy of Global Energy*, Baltimore: The Johns Hopkins University Press (1985), p. 77; D. Gerner, "Petrodollar Recycling: Imports, Arms, Investment, and Aid," *Arab Studies Quarterly*, 7 (Winter 1985), p. 3.

The price effect of the Iranian Revolution climaxed in 1981, by which time the volume of oil traded equaled but 85 percent of the volume of 1974 while the cost had escalated to $349 billion (Table 8.5). For the nations receiving this extraordinary transfer of wealth, identified in Table 8.5, and for Mexico as well, oil exports provided from 60 to 100 percent of export earnings and the bulk of government revenues. Ayubi and Pachauri accept the sum of $250 billion as the surplus revenue disposed of by OPEC during the years, 1974–80.[21]

Responses to this unprecedented transfer of money were predictable. The USA, most vociferously anti-OPEC of the OECD group, led an abortive campaign against OPEC. To most Americans, the Arab producers were thieves and all ills traceable to OPEC. Western experts anticipated that the petrodollars amassed by the exporters would, because of their withdrawal from productive investment, derange the world economy, the assumption being that the industrial states were more capable of channeling investments into productive ventures than the exporting states. The Arabs perceived themselves as Ali Babas, unlocking the treasure of the 40 thieves, here a dozen or so MNOCs. Before 1971, the producers were powerless to prevent the siphoning of their wealth to the West. As producers explained it, they merely reclaimed the full value of their oil, virtually their only marketable asset.[22]

To what ends were the oil revenues directed? Were the petrodollars invested in assets that added to productive capacity or that enhanced welfare? Conventionally, the leading exporting states are divided into two groups: the low absorbers and the high absorbers. Normally in-

cluded in the former are the Arabian Peninsula producers* and Libya
(Table 8.7, see page 300). The high absorbers, or states with sizable
populations and/or development potential encompassed Iran, Algeria,
Egypt, Nigeria, Indonesia, Mexico, and Venezuela. That the low
absorbers earned the preponderant share of oil income is apparent from
Table 8.5. Saudi Arabia, in 1981, accumulated one-third of global
revenues from traded oil and 40 percent of OPEC's oil revenues. The
Arab Gulf states, unable to utilize their entire earnings domestically,
possessed vast sums to dispose of.

Within OPEC, the high absorbers contained 91 percent of OPEC's
population and earned 26 percent of OPEC's oil revenues in 1980. The
governments of these states and Mexico were highly dependent for
revenues upon the earning power of oil. By 1980, oil exports equaled 75
percent of Mexico's total export earnings. Despite their large revenues,
each of these states spent more than they earned, thus assuming large
external debts.

While the oil export cultures differed widely from one another in
their social and political arrangements, they all experienced a sudden
and fortuitous influx of great wealth and they all suffered from economic
underdevelopment. Each quickly devised plans to dedicate oil earnings
to modernization and to reduce their economic dependence upon oil or
other energy and raw material exports. As a group they differed from
the oil importing LDCs only by virtue of the oil windfall. Most analysts
express disappointment in the development purchased with oil wealth,
particularly if, as Howell and Morrow and Brogan do, inquiry is focused
upon the domestic distribution of oil bonanza benefits.[23]

Development and the employment of oil money

Mexico, Iran, and Nigeria will be used to adduce the array of difficulties
confronting the oil exporters as they attempted to convert their oil
profits into an engine of economic growth. Mexico, with a larger
domestic economy and a more stable polity than most LDC exporters,
purposefully exploited ascending oil prices and the discovery, at a most
propitious moment, of new oil fields to join the ranks of the exporters.
By 1980, Mexico exported almost one-half of its oil (Table 7.4). Under
the Shah, Iran launched perhaps the most ambitious modernization
campaign of all the LDCs while simultaneously creating a large military
machine. In Nigeria, still recovering from a bloody civil war, modernization had hardly begun. Lacking all but the most rudimentary

---

* Saudi Arabia, Kuwait, UAE, Bahrain, Qatar.

infrastructure, Nigeria's birth and infant mortality rates were among the world's highest.[24]

Each of the above nations relied primarily upon the government to manage the oil sector and income investments. National oil companies acted as development leaders. In 1978, President Lopez Portillo of Mexico stated, "This opportunity will come only once in history. We have to transform a non-renewable resource into a permanent source of wealth."[25]

During the 1960s and 1970s, Mexico applied import substitution policies. Coincidentally, an abundance of low wage labor attracted an increasing number of American manufacturing firms to sites along the US border. This specialized foreign trade sector did not require Mexican capital. Nor was the employment and income generated sufficient substantially to improve welfare or to finance necessary infrastructure additions. Still largely dependent upon raw material exports, Mexico resorted to heavier foreign borrowing just as its new oil fields proved out.

The enticing potential of oil prompted Portillo virtually to abandon import substitution in favor of oil export earnings as the means of forcing domestic growth. Portillo orchestrated an ambitious program of public sector spending in health, education, agriculture, and other areas. Internal demands, however, were so great that swollen oil earnings failed to suffice. Confident that oil prices would remain high, Mexico resorted to new borrowing just as severe inflation swept through an overheated economy. Burgeoning oil production and exports contributed to an inflation that made Mexican manufactured exports more costly and imports and borrowing less dear. By 1982, oil furnished over 60 percent of export earnings. Additionally, investments in agriculture favored a tiny minority of large commercial farmers and ignored the vast majority of small farmers. Agricultural growth ceased by the late 1970s and the food import bill mounted.

Mexican GDP grew at a real rate of 8 percent annually from 1977 through 1981, but was accompanied by annual inflation rates of 30 percent. Although *per capita* GNP rose, the real incomes of the working class and many middle income earners did not rise. The bottom 20 percent of society earned 5 percent of total income in 1978 and 3 percent in 1980. Mexico's current accounts deficit rose dangerously as imports surged forward, stimulated by inflation. By 1982, before the fall in oil prices, Mexico's debt approached $80 billion; inflation now attained 100 percent. The oil bonanza had reaped confusion and stagnation.

Modernization had not taken firm root. Linkages between the oil and gas industries and the economy were thin. Agriculture did not improve. Rural people swarmed into Mexican cities and the USA, joining the ranks of job seekers. Urban Mexico grew at an incredible pace, adding 50 million between 1960 and 1989, or more people by 17 million than lived in Mexico in 1960. The population of Mexico City climbed toward 16 million while Mexico became a food importer. The drastic fall in oil prices during the 1980s further battered Mexico's oil reliant economy. New loans were required to service oil ones. Retrenchment replaced growth and reform as the objectives of national policy.[26]

Oil sustained the modernizing segment of Iran's economy and the power of the Pahlavi dynasty since the pre-World War II years. During the oil boom of the 1960s, Iran's revenues from oil rose from $291 million to $1.1 billion and more than tripled by 1973. OPEC prices brought in between $17 and $22 billion in each year from 1974 through 1979, exceeding the returns of every OPEC state save Saudi Arabia. During the 1960s, the Shah committed a rising share of oil revenues, amounting to 95 percent of export earnings, to industrialization and increased that commitment after 1973. Consumer goods output rose as did industrial employment, but the lack of most raw materials and the inability to design and fabricate machinery necessitated a high level of imports. Parallel to this thrust, the Shah assumed the role of US military surrogate in the Persian Gulf. Tolerating no opposition, the regime spawned an insidious internal security apparatus which, leagued with the armed forces, absorbed vast, if unspecified, sums of money. Iran became the largest importer of arms in the Middle East.

The Shah's government devoted negligible sums to agricultural reform while alienating the dominant rural and small town population by its disdain for traditional religion and its oppressive character. The National Iranian Oil Company evolved into a modern and fully integrated organization, even investing in foreign energy and non-energy firms, but its linkages with the economy were weak, as were those of the chemical, steel, and electric generation industries. Such sectors offered some employment, but they did not rest upon a firm supporting industrial substructure. Technology, maintenance and parts, and even the technical staff came from abroad. The industrial and military sectors siphoned resources from agriculture which became, according to Looney and Jazayeri, increasingly marginal and detached from the economy. Food imports rose from the mid-1970s to the mid-1980s with the volume of cereal imports doubling and meat imports tripling. Reliant upon oil earnings for the bulk of government revenue, Iran, in OPEC, normally pressed for high prices.

Iran's GNP increased almost fivefold between 1972 and 1978, yet income differentials widened, engendering social discontent that repression could not fully squash. The Shah's regime and the entire energy sector, well integrated into the political economy of the West, were viewed by the religiously and politically disaffected as alien bodies existing parasitically within the body politic. The Shah's regime was judged inimical to the futures envisaged by the Iranian people.[27]

The oil bonanza of 1973–81 rewarded Nigeria with enormous revenues from oil exports, perhaps totaling in excess of $40 billion for the five years 1974–8 and as much as $35 billion total for 1979 and 1980. In 1975, an ambitious development plan projected investments of $50 billion over a five-year period, 11 times greater than the prior plan. Included in this development war chest were anticipated oil and gas investments by the major oil companies that operated under contract and in participatory agreements with the Nigerian National Petroleum Company. A huge steel industry entirely dependent upon foreign technology and management, two hydroelectric units, two new refineries, port facilities at Port Harcourt, and billions expended in making Lagos a gleaming capital city consumed most of the development funds but produced a paltry number of permanent jobs. The new industries required massive imports of technology and support services. Oil income enriched the few with access to unstable Nigerian governments,[28] and stimulated the urban middle class minority to spend lavishly for imported goods. Inappropriate development choices and government mismanagement, as in Iran, turned bounty into waste.

By 1980, Nigeria, formerly a food exporter, devoted 12 percent of its import bill to food. In the southeastern region, long a source of national food supply, population pressure forced the further shrinkage of farms. Erosion reduced arable lands to dust; yields per acre declined. In the Niger Delta, oil and gas exploration pushed farmers from the land while oil pollution severely damaged the fishing industry. Overexploitation of its hardwood forests reduced hardwood exports in 1980 to a mere 8 percent of the 1960 value. Meanwhile, fuel wood provided some 80 percent of TPER (Table 8.2). Nigeria's standard of living in the early 1980s remained frozen, in real terms, at the low level of 1970. Periodic food shortages occasionally threatened famine, compelling costly emergency imports to avoid disaster.

Public sector wage increases and rising urban welfare expenditures, an ill-conceived campaign to industrialize, and rising food imports pushed inflation to crisis levels. With expenditures exceeding revenues (virtually all from oil), Nigeria resorted to foreign loans, convinced, like Mexico, in the permanence of rising oil prices. The small farmers and urban workers, perhaps the beneficiaries of improved health care and access to elementary education for their children, won few other economic gains from the oil boom. The chosen projects were urban, capital intensive, and, often, cosmetic. They meant nothing to the Niger Delta fisherman whose world, like his fish, turned belly-up when the oil rigs arrived. Far from lessening Nigerian dependence upon the West, the oil boom tightened it.[29]

Mexico, Iran, and Nigeria differed markedly in individual circumstances. Yet each chose a somewhat similar path, one that attempted to force modernization upon a society of limited absorptive capacity. "Petromania," as Amuzegar dubs it,[30] stimulated overambitious development plans and, in Iran, the creation of a costly military machine. Inefficient and/or corrupt bureaucracies demonstrated a proclivity for large and highly visible projects only tenuously linked to the larger economy. Agriculture and rural areas suffered from inopportune neglect. Food production, particularly cereals, failed to keep up with population growth, necessitating ever larger imports. Mexico and Nigeria evaded, except rhetorically, facing up to the population crisis.

These nations spent what they earned and then some, but their systems could not ingest the input beneficially, that is to improve the income security and social welfare of the impoverished 40 to 50 percent of the people and to absorb them into the national polity. Tanzer and Zorn charge ruling elites and those with access to power with turning state capital—oil revenues—into private wealth.[31] A small group of nationals replaced the MNOCs as plunderers of the national patrimony.

Internal economic development in Saudi Arabia and other desert oil producers with relatively small and homogeneous populations hewed closely to the patterns already described. The desert states are, and will continue to be, totally reliant upon oil for revenues. For that reason, the larger share of internal investments flowed into the energy industries, and especially into downstream ventures. Saudi Arabia's efforts to diversify and move away from oil, symbolized by large industrial complexes at Jubayl and Yanba, are disparagingly called "Saudi pyramids."[32] Welfare and irrigation projects were also funded. But there remained an enormous sum of disposable income.

According to Fesharaki, westerners much exaggerated the petrodollar problem of the 1970s. The producing states proved more absorbent than anticipated. Capital markets in Europe and the USA handled the petrodollars efficiently. Pachauri estimates that OPEC's investible surplus for the three years, 1975-77, averaged $35 billion annually. On the average, bank deposits took $12 billion while a category called "other capital flows" amounted to $12 billion. Gerner surmises that much of this surplus was invested in western capital markets, particularly in the USA where the giant surplus holder, Saudi Arabia, enjoyed intimate connections. Funds entering the USA purchased short-term instruments, including government securities, but funds were also invested in various US and European companies. This accounts for about $26 billion of the surplus. An additional $8 billion was invested in the IMF, World Bank, and developing countries.

The oil exporters also increased their imports from the West. While the value of oil exports far exceeded the value of those imports, the latter rose in importance. For the nine countries of the EC, the value of exports to the seven largest oil suppliers equaled 3 percent of total exports in 1973 and over 6 percent in 1976. The value of West German exports to OPEC states doubled between 1978 and 1981. Arms sales composed part of these exports, particularly from the USA and to Saudi Arabia and Iran.

The total amounts recycled, according to Pachauri's calculations, equaled less than 5 percent of the GDP of the OECD countries, and considerably less for the USA, West Germany, and Japan. Western bankers employed a portion of their share of petrodollars to lend, by 1980, over $170 billion to Mexico, Brazil, Argentina, and Venezuela, one-third from US banks. The total foreign debt of these countries approached $250 billion and had reached crisis proportions in Mexico. This and other strains on Western economies were self-generated.

No doubt the West would have been better off had this enormous income transfer not occurred. From 1974 through 1980, OPEC's oil revenues totaled $981 billion, roughly 75 percent derived from the West. This unabated payout can be attributed in part to western energy decisions, or non-decisions. The oil import bill of America, however, cannot carry full blame for the economic woes that harried the USA during the 1970s and 1980s. Federal budgetary deficits, wages chasing prices, weakened competitiveness in domestic and foreign markets, the transfer of manufacturing abroad, all attacked the American system. Gerner and Pachauri argue that recycling was of much greater significance to the surplus holders than to the West. Only the West could absorb such surpluses. Only the West could provide the goods and services desired. Only western oil demand kept the exporters' economies afloat.[33]

The oil exporters and the MNOCs

Following the precedents of the 1960s, the oil exporters further consolidated their control over domestic oil industries and the foreign operating firms. Ecuador (1972), Iraq (1972–5), Nigeria (1974–84), Kuwait (1974–6), Venezuela (1975), Saudi Arabia (1976–83), and Qatar (1976–7) assumed full control over all phases of their industries. The revolution in Iran terminated the Iranian Consortium.

Producing governments lavished attention on national oil companies, where feasible expanding their functions to include a monopoly over domestic sales, the operation of new downstream facilities, and overseas joint ventures with foreign companies. Oil exports wholly owned by the producing states composed a rising share of the volume exported. None of these changes could be resisted by the MNOCs or by their home governments. Events had shifted the balance of power to producers.

With the exception of Saudi Arabia, the OPEC states during the 1970s radically diminished the equity shares owned by the MNOCs. Saudi Arabia assumed full ownership of Aramco's assets in 1983. Iraq, Iran, Kuwait, and Venezuela, among OPEC members, and Mexico, prohibited direct foreign participation in oil. In Kuwait, the former owners of Kuwait Oil Company, BP and Gulf, retained access to oil through contracts under which the MNOCs performed a service and earned a fee paid in oil. In the states permitting equity ownership, such as Libya, Algeria, Nigeria, Ecuador, and Indonesia, the oil companies owned minority shares.[34]

Between 1971 and 1980, MNOC control over foreign production fields declined precipitously in the Middle East and North Africa. The eighteen largest oil companies lost ownership over 19 mbd during those years. For the "Seven Sisters," ownership of production fell from 82 percent in 1963 to 22 percent in 1981. By then, the producing countries owned 60 percent of output. Other MNOCs owned the remainder. These losses affected the MNOCs in various ways. Table 8.6 summarizes the supply (production, buy-back, or contract payments) situation of the Seven Sisters plus Elf, CFP, and Amoco. The regional take for BP and Gulf fell by 3.1 mbd and 1.2 mbd respectively, leaving them only the oil earned through service to Kuwait. The marked decline after 1979, particularly for Exxon, Texaco, and Chevron, reflected termination of supply from Iran. The Aramco partners remained in Saudi Arabia, basically working for the state. As their total world supply declined, their dependence upon Saudi Arabia mounted.

Of the Seven Sisters, RDS responded most successfully to the oil exporter's offensive. RDS quickened the pace of exploration and production in the North Sea, Canada and Alaska, on- and off-shore America, Venezuela, Nigeria, and Indonesia. RDS gained American production in 1984 when it absorbed Shell USA. By 1986, the firm controlled 85 percent of the volume owned in 1974, compared with 32 percent for Exxon, and was far less dependent upon Arab producers than the Aramco partners.

The Middle Eastern and North African oil supply of the six non-Aramco partners fell more swiftly than did their total world supply. BP, through its purchase of Standard of Ohio, obtained Alaskan oil, but the

Table 8.6   Worldwide crude supply of ten MNOCs and percentage from Middle East and North Africa, 1974–86

	1974	1975	1976	1977	1978	1979	1980	1985	1986
*Exxon**									
000 bd	5320	4957	5325	5091	4723	4479	4008	1720	1796
% supply from ME/NA	51	46	50	53	52	52	55		
*Texaco**									
000 bd	4507	3770	4015	3923	3552	3626	3316	1328	1146
% supply from ME/NA	61	59	64	64	64	64	64		
*Chevron**									
000 bd	3814	3025	3542	3403	3289	3198	3009	1543	1610
% supply from ME/NA	70	66	73	72	72	71	81		
*Mobil**									
000 bd	2462	2240	2156	2370	2117	2180	1991	1295	1306
% supply from ME/NA	60	63	65	69	63	62	59		
Gulf									
000 bd	2585	2185	1992	2147	2015	1988	1224		
% supply from ME/NA	52	45	42	35	36	33	16		
BP									
000 bd	4440	3440	3540	3390	3720	3260	2590	2748	2733
% supply from ME/NA	82	79	71	61	46	35	18		
RDS									
000 bd	5917	4786	4732	4847	4714	4555	3735	4427	5049
% supply from ME/NA	42	40	43	42	38	33	25		
Amoco									
000 bd	874	945	921	1004	1032	849	836	847	810
% supply from ME/NA	5	16	19	24	27	15	17		
CFP									
000 bd	1741	1454	1510	1430	1437	1422	1273		
% supply from ME/NA	81	92	84	81	78	75	65		
Elf									
000 bd	415	452	366	370	372	378	364		
% supply from ME/NA	29	32	12	9	8	9	8		
Total above	33 122	26 856	28 099	27 985	26 971	25 935	22 146		
% ME/NA	69				52		47		

Sources: G. Luciani, *The Oil Companies and the Arab World*, London: Croom Helm (1984), pp. 36–58; G. Jenkins, *Oil Economists' Handbook* 1985. London: Applied Science Publishers Ltd (1985), p. 74; *Petroleum Economist*, LIV (June 1987), 214.

* Aramco partners

firm focused on its North Sea shares. The Aramco firms also sped up Alaskan and North Sea activity. RDS, Gulf, and Mobil, in partnership with the Nigerian National Petroleum Company, accelerated drilling and production. Fifteen firms concluded agreements with Indonesia. China negotiated seventeen contracts for off-shore exploration with various firms or consortia between 1980 and 1983. In the early 1980s, several Latin American producers were seeking increased MNOC participation in oil development.[35]

Each of the producing states wished to enlarge their take from crude by refining a larger share of production and by engaging in direct selling. Globally, refining remained concentrated in the USA, western Europe, and the USSR. America and Europe, together, possessed the same share of refining capacity in 1983 as in 1973, that is 33 percent. Saudi Arabia, Kuwait, Algeria, and Venezuela strove to maximize their advantages by expanding petro-chemical output. Soaring prices in 1979–81 stiffened their resolve and investment in refining rose. The threat of cheaper refined products alarmed western refiners. By the mid-1980s, several had reduced or terminated their refining operations in Europe. The share of refining held by the ten firms in Table 8.6 did drop from over 50 percent to less than 40 percent in 1980 as independents, now purchasing directly from the LDCs, entered the business in Europe and America.

The market share of the producing states increased dramatically from 1970, when it was about zero, to 1980, when the state companies of OPEC's members exported one-half of total shipments. The competition of state companies, including European, and independents shaved the non-Communist world marketing share of Aramco from 35 percent in 1970 to 29 percent in 1979 and the share of the Seven Sisters from 60 to 50 percent while the share of state enterprises rose from 6 to 18 percent. Saudi Arabia's Petromin increased its direct sales from under 200,000 bd in 1973 to 2.2 million bd in 1981, 23 percent of production. The gains of these new sellers in a world in which consumption in 1979 was merely 7 percent higher than in 1973 explains the 28 percent drop in world crude supply of the firms listed in Table 8.6.[36]

Augmented producer state power was not a harbinger of imminent MNOC disappearance. Aramco remained the most efficient channel to major markets for the Saudis. Other LDCs, Venezuela for one, found it necessary to negotiate technological support contracts with the MNOCs. Few could dispense with them, and only at considerable cost. While Kuwait, in the mid-1980s, purchased marketing facilities in western Europe, Saudi Arabia chose not to replicate the wellhead to gas pump network of the Aramco partners. However, Aramco receives a quantity of oil determined by Saudi Arabia. The partners feared a production cutback in 1981 that would leave them virtually no oil and, in fact, their entitlements were reduced in 1981 and 1982.[37]

OPEC's price decisions

Something of OPEC's diversity is captured in Table 8.7. The Arab Gulf states, led by Saudi Arabia, produced 621 mmt in 1976, 47 percent of OPEC's total, and held 60 percent of OPEC's proven reserves. The Arab Gulf states are extraordinarily wealthy, with *per capita* incomes far above those of OECD nations (Table 8.1), but the high incomes mask gross maldistribution. If, as Quandt reveals, one of the Saud clan's 5,000 princes can receive $100 million in a single oil transaction, how many billions of Saudi income were sucked up by the royal family?[38] UAE and Qatar and Saudi Arabia and Libya permitted infant mortality rates comparable to those in Nigeria and Indonesia.[39]

OPEC's members carried their cultural baggage to each meeting. Each member responded to its own economic imperatives. Each fashioned international political goals. Iran viewed itself as the Persian Gulf power. Saudi Arabia reluctantly displayed its anti-Zionist credentials while carefully protecting its ties with the USA. As the San José Pact

Table 8.7   Characteristics of the OPEC states

	1986 Population (millions)	1983 *Per capita* GNP ($)	1986 Infant mortality rate	Crude production* (mmt)	1981 Proved reserves (mb)
Indonesia	168.4	560	84	69	9 800
Nigeria	105.4	770	127	101	16 500
Iran	46.6	1 930	115	288	57 000
Algeria	22.8	2 320	88	48	8 080
Venezuela	17.8	3 830	39	136	20 300
Iraq	16.0	1 390	77	115	29 700
Saudi Arabia	11.5	12 230	100	393	164 600
Ecuador	9.6	1 420	70	9	850
Libya	3.9	8 460	97	79	22 600
Kuwait	1.8	16 200	23	103[1]	64 480
UAE	1.4	23 700	45	71	30 600
Gabon	1.2	3 430	112	11	480
Qatar	0.3	21 160	38	23	3 400

* Average 1974–6
[1] 1976

Sources: 1986 Population Data Sheet; BP statistical review of world oil industry 1980, London: BP (1980), p. 18; V. Smil and W.E. Knowland, eds, *Energy in the developing world. The real energy crisis,* Oxford: Oxford University Press (1980), p. 398; M.E. Ahrari, *OPEC, The Falling Giant,* Lexington, Ky.: The University Press of Kentucky (1986), p. 202.

proved, Venezuela acted responsibly within its region. OPEC's decisions, then, were a compound of political, economic, and social elements and necessarily arrived at only through debate and compromise. OPEC could not possibly became a monolithic group even though the adhesive that bound it together was a single resource.

OPEC set world oil prices unilaterally until the panicked western response to diminishing Iranian oil 1979–80 caught it unawares. The price increases of 1974–5 and 1978 were reached after intense internal debate and associated with the imposition of higher royalty rates and income taxes on the MNOCs which permitted the producing states to lever revenues upward without raising prices. To none of this did the companies object since the extra cost could be passed through to consumers or to everyone if governments elected to protect consumers from the full effects of rising prices.[40]

Profits accruing to the companies as a result of OPEC decisions have been unnaturally mixed together with the alleged advantages that higher energy prices offered to the USA to fashion, à la Gisselquist and Odell, a conspiracy thesis. The USA, the MNOCs, and OPEC colluded, we are told, to force prices up. Presumably, higher prices would improve the trade position of America by weakening the productive competitiveness of Germany and Japan, both of which would face higher energy prices than the fossil fuel rich USA.[41] But, neither the USA nor the MNOCs could offer anything that OPEC did not already possess. OPEC did not need to conspire with anyone.

Did OPEC's official prices reflect compromises between two groups of states with divergent interests? Conventionally, Libya, Algeria, Iraq, Iran, Nigeria, and, periodically, Venezuela and Indonesia are labeled price hawks. They sought the highest price in order to maximize government revenues urgently needed for economic development, welfare improvements, arms, and international purposes. Deemed price doves, Saudi Arabia and the Arab Gulf states, resisted price levels that seriously threatened the economic stability of western economies or that, by inducing conservation, lessened the future value of their enormous reserves.[42]

Saudi Arabia possesses the ability substantially to raise or lower OPEC production, and thus affect world prices. Within OPEC, the Saudis exerted an influence that was at one time, dovish, at another time, hawkish. Saudi Arabia put teeth in the embargo of 1973–4 by reducing its production, thereby assuring a radical increase in price, but in 1977 resisted more than a moderate 5 percent hike. Saudi Arabia reduced production by 2 mbd in early 1980 and cut again in the spring. Prices spiraled upward. Perhaps they had succumbed to pressure from the hawks. More likely, they were responding hostilely to the Camp

David Accords. The Saudis repeatedly warned the USA that only a Middle Eastern settlement favorable to the Palestinians, including Israeli departure from East Jerusalem, would guarantee future oil supplies. Gottheil identified the Saudis as leading the price surge of late 1979. Iran, on the other hand, agreed to a price freeze for all 1978 after the Shah had concluded a favorable military supply agreement with the USA. Nigeria, Venezuela, and Indonesia inclined toward profit maximization, but also favored producing at capacity even as those choices lost their complimentarity just prior to the Iranian Revolution.[43]

Prices stabilized between 1973–4 and the second shock of 1979, rising less rapidly than the rate of western inflation (Table 7.3). With the end of the embargo, OPEC production increased through 1977, but then sagged in 1978 as a surplus developed. As Iranian, and then Iraqi, production fell in 1979–81 to only 25 percent of their norms, such OPEC states as Nigeria, Venezuela, and Kuwait raised production so as to benefit from the higher prices. But the Saudi reduction, directly affecting US and Japanese supplies, was the key action.

The history of prices before the turmoil in Iran reflected a fair balance of power within OPEC. Certainly, the price hawks failed to impose their demands on the group. OPEC, however, could agree about little more than official selling prices, and it could not enforce them. The organization lacked the mechanisms to respond effectively to the soft market developing in 1978 as a consequence of slumping western economies and to new supplies of oil. Saudi Arabia, with a withdrawal capacity of approximately 11 million bd and claiming that 6 or 7 mbd satisfied revenue requirements, enjoyed more flexibility than other OPEC states. But Saudi Arabia could not coerce OPEC, nor did it want to. Instead, the Saudis preferred that OPEC adopt enforceable production quotas as a defense against an oil glut and soft prices. Although powerful, Saudi Arabia failed to win this objective until prices started to slump in 1981. The failure speaks to the essential nature of OPEC, a loose confederation of producers of varying productive capacity and with divergent interests. Members refused to yield their newly gained sovereignty over production.[44]

OPEC slid unsuspectingly into the second oil bonanza. Each member demanded the highest possible price. By 1980–1, recession swept over the West and energy demand contracted. OPEC, however, appeared incapable of acting in concert. In the mid-1980s, Ghamen, prematurely, wrote of fading OPEC importance. To Ahari, OPEC seemed to drift, after 1981, "with the ebb and flow of events, waiting for another political crisis to tighten the market for them." More perceptively than many, Pachauri believed OPEC sufficiently robust to remain a "force . . . in the world's energy future." Pachauri's opinion was justified by the

Table 8.8 CMEA–6 energy import reliance, 1960–82 (percent, in million tons oil equivalent)

	1960	1974	1978	1980	1982
Primary energy	2.1	16.5	22.3	26.4	23.7
Gaseous fuels	1.9	14.8	26.5	32.4	32.9
Liquid fuels	12.9	76.7	84.3	na	83.9

Source: G.W. Hoffman, *The European Energy Challenge: East and West,* Durham, N.C.: Duke Press Policy Studies (1985), pp. 164–76.

improved stability and market control exercised by OPEC as 1989 ended.[45]

The Soviet bloc and the energy opportunities of the 1970s

Estimates of CMEA–6* average annual real GNP and national income growth rates during the 1970s indicate performance superior to the USA or European Community. Other measurements place CMEA–6 states, excepting East Germany, well below the West in 1976 (Table 8.1) and in 1986 and more comparable to Argentina and South Korea. Recent revelations of Soviet economic frailty, its increasing dependence upon western currency, technology, and food, and similar, even exaggerated, characteristics manifest among the bloc states, tied to the USSR by force, have prompted me to include the Soviet bloc within this discussion of LDCs. With regard to energy, the Soviets are exporters while a comparison of Tables 7.1 and 8.8 indicates that the oil import dependence of CMEA–6 matched Japan's.[46]

Only the USA consumed more energy than the Soviet Union, and the gap substantially narrowed since 1973. Russia's TPER, 50 percent of America's in 1973, equaled 77 percent by 1985 and had surpassed that of OECD-Europe (Tables 7.1 and 8.1). The USSR produced enormous quantities of oil, coal, and natural gas, ranking first, second, and third, respectively (Tables 7.4 and 7.6). Although eastern Europe contributed a large tonnage of coal, the region depended upon the USSR for some 40 percent of its primary energy supply.[47] Rising energy prices during the 1970s presented the USSR with lucrative opportunities to sell oil and gas to the West; the dependency of the satellite states became a burden to Russia.

---

* The Council for Mutual Economic Assistance, founded in 1949, now includes: Russia, Cuba, Mongolia, Vietnam, and the CMEA–6 — Bulgaria, Czechoslovakia, East Germany, Hungary, Poland, and Romania, the subjects of this discussion.

Soviet oil production shot forward after World War II, increasing sevenfold by 1960 and then doubling by 1970. With production shifting deep into Western Siberia by the mid-1970s, production climbed 73 percent by 1980 (Tables 4.6 and 7.4). Then, Soviet production tapered off, plateauing during the early 1980s and even declining in 1984 and 1985, reflecting the gradual loss in productive capacity of older fields and the absence of significant discoveries. However, production recovered in 1986 as new fields proved out in Western Siberia and the Northern Caspian Basin, thus confounding a CIA study of 1977 which predicted that the Soviets would be net importers by the mid-1980s.[48]

As Soviet oil production peaked, the exploitation of giant natural gas reserves gained momentum. The 198 billion cubic meters (bcm) produced in 1970 rose to 435 bcm by 1980. Almost the entire increase in global natural gas production between 1973 and 1983 occurred in Western Siberia. This outpouring of gas partly compensated for disappointing oil, coal, and nuclear electric output.

Natural gas served as the swing fuel in Russia's domestic energy mix and in the critical energy export sector. It became the primary fuel used in Russia by 1985 (Table 7.1), substituting for coal and oil in the industrial and residential sectors and holding a steady share as a boiler fuel in electric generation. The great volume of natural gas production released oil for export and supported a marked rise in the volume of gas exports. The emergence of a dynamic natural gas industry occurred at a most propitious moment. With western Europe scurrying about in search of reliable supplies of oil and for oil substitutes, the Soviets reaped the benefits of OPEC price increases in the oil and gas contracts negotiated with eastern and western Europe.[49]

OPEC and OAPEC significantly improved Russia's ability to obtain hard currency and necessary technology from the West and facilitated the improvement and/or initiation of relations with Middle Eastern states, even those so vigorously anti-Communist as Saudi Arabia, Kuwait, and Iran. The NATO states knew that major Russian industries, oil and gas transmission in particular, obtained their reliable technologies from the West. However pointedly the USA might inveigh against the transfer of advanced technology to the Russians, western Europe stood to gain from a technology/cash–oil/gas exchange with the "enemy." Thus, the USSR and Austria initiated the gas trade by bartering gas for pipe. Other western European countries quickly signed agreements with the Soviets. The USSR demonstrated flexibility in gas export arrangements and was considered a reliable energy supplier. In one deal, Soviet gas sales to France were diverted to Italy while Dutch sales to Italy were piped to France. During the 1970s, the Soviet Union burned Iranian gas in its southern republics, thus freeing Soviet gas for export to Europe. The USSR proved amenable to any reasonable proposition, if it returned either hard cash or technology.

At this critical juncture, Russian oil and gas served as an equilibrating force. Economic exigencies in the West forced the abandonment of ideological and strategic objections to the purchase of Soviet fuels. Western demand strengthened the Soviet energy sector which, already providing 27 percent of Russia's hard currency earnings in 1971, contributed 80 percent in both 1981 and 1982. In the latter year, oil earned $11.2 billion and gas, $4.5 billion.

Soviet oil exports to western Europe supplied the latter with some 16 to 20 percent of total imports in each year from 1982 to 1985, an improvement in market share since the years, 1971–5 (see Tables 6.9 and 6.10). Russian oil, priced very closely to spot market prices for Middle Eastern oil but cheaper to transport, permitted some diminution of Middle Eastern imports. This "benefit" should not be exaggerated. OECD-Europe's reduced purchases from the Middle East (Table 7.2) resulted mainly from the availability of North Sea oil, the oil self-sufficiency of Britain and Norway, and virtually no growth in TPER from 1973 through 1985 (Table 7.1). European buyers realized that Russia approached the upper limits of oil export capacity during the early 1980s. The Soviets were all too aware of this and resented the oil committed to the bloc states.

Natural gas earnings of $4.5 billion in 1982 yielded 19 percent (3 percent in 1975) of total earnings from exports to the West. Gas transmitted to western Europe, conceived in oil equivalence, earned no more than 70 percent and as little as 40 or 50 percent of the spot market price of a barrel of oil. The superior profitability of oil exports over gas exports explains the Soviet design to substitute gas and nuclear electricity for oil. This required a vast transmission and distribution system. Each of the gas delivery contracts signed with western European importers at favorable prices included partial payment for the gas with gas transmission equipment. In this way, the larger European importers paid for part of the construction of Russia's far flung transmission system. The largest deal of all between Russia and Europe, the Yamburg–Urengoi natural gas pipeline project, was announced in 1980. It precipitated President Reagan's efforts to stymie the project by prohibiting the delivery of critical equipment to the Soviet Union, a dispute investigated in the following chapter.

In 1980, West Germany received 42 percent of total Soviet gas exports and Italy and France, together, 44 percent. Soviet gas in 1980 provided 14 to 19 percent of gas consumption in those three states, a figure that may rise to 30 or 35 percent if the 1990 terms are met. But western European oil and gas imports from Russia did not, as of 1980, add up to a dangerous reliance upon NATO's only enemy. Expressed in oil equivalence, Soviet oil and gas provided roughly 15 mmt of TPER, or 5 percent.[50]

Western Europe perceived Russia as an energy supplier of marginal overall importance, but preferred because of price and reliability. Western Europe served a larger purpose in the Soviet scheme of things, but by no means did Soviet leaders believe that the western alliance could be subverted by the sale of a little oil and gas. Russia pursued this trade to achieve balanced internal economic growth, a goal that seemed as distant in 1980 as in 1970.

The enormous revenues accumulated by the Arab producers after 1973 and recurrent violence in the Middle East assured profitable markets for arms traders. As the leading purveyors of armaments, the USSR and the USA shared, during the 1970s and early 1980s, 65 to 70 percent of the business, with the remainder divided among their European allies. Menon calculates that arms sales provided from 15 to 27 percent of Soviet hard currency earnings, second only to energy earnings, between 1971 and 1981, and some 55 percent of the value of exports to the LDCs.[51] In the Middle East, the Soviets garnered 31 percent of arms purchases, with Syria, Iraq, Libya, and Algeria taking 40 percent of the total between 1975 and 1982. Saudi Arabia and Iran (to 1979) were America's best customers. In 1977 and 1978, the USA delivered almost $20 billion worth of arms to the region; Iran received $4.4 billion and Saudi Arabia, $4 billion. The Saudis spent, in 1980–1, some $21 billion on defense, or 18 percent of GNP. Saudi arms purchases rose to even higher levels during the worst of the Iran–Iraq War.[52]

The Soviets shrewdly coupled the arms and oil trades, especially after the outbreak of the Iran–Iraq conflict. Munificent grants from the Arabian Peninsula states funded Syrian arms purchases from Russia, amounting to over $8 billion from 1978 through 1982. More fascinating was the tacit cooperation extended by Saudi Arabia to Iraq which permitted the landing of Soviet arms in Saudi Arabia for final delivery to Iraq. Gawad maintains that the Saudis transferred oil to the Soviet account in partial payment for Iraqi-bound arms. The staunch anti-Communism of the Saud family gave way before the common Saudi and Soviet interest in preventing Iran from defeating Iraq. Not surprisingly, the Soviets also slipped arms into Iran in exchange for oil. Exhibiting a similar morality, the USA sold arms to Iran notwithstanding its publicly expressed antagonism to the Khomeini regime. France, West Germany, and Italy, ostensibly supporting the existence of Israel, jumped at the opportunity to sell arms to such implacable foes of Israel as Libya and Syria.[53]

Soviet energy policies in western Europe and the Middle East earned currency, technology, food, good will, and occasional international political advantage. Linking these policies with global schemes of disruption and conquest is a fruitless exercise. The superpowers wished to maximize their opportunities in the Middle East. Their maneuvers contributed little to the welfare of the region's societies. The regimes that rule throughout the region, however, have repeatedly sacrificed welfare objectives for the sake of self-perpetuation and in the name of anti-Zionism. Neither the USSR nor the USA should be condemned in isolation.[54]

Eastern European energy dependence

Soviet modernization has been both aided and retarded by the subordination of the bloc states. The official Soviet line emphasizes mutuality of purpose, coordination of effort, and a deeply rooted cooperative relationship between CMEA–6 and the Soviet Union.[55] The power of the Red Army, the use of force on several occasions, and the induced economic and political dependence of the CMEA–6 on the Soviet Union more credibly explains the bond than voluntarism.

Chapter 6 described the intensifying eastern European energy dependence upon Russia. CMEA–6 reliance upon energy imports, overwhelmingly from the USSR, is summarized in Table 8.8. Demand for Russian oil and gas was only mitigated by the use of regional coal. While diminishing gradually during the 1970s, coal still claimed a 60 percent share of regional TPER in 1985. Prior to 1974, Russia charged its partners higher prices for oil than western European importers paid. Superficially, this followed the normal Soviet (or MNOC) practice of charging those customers without alternative suppliers more than customers who also purchased elsewhere. Thus, Russia exacted premium prices from Finland and Austria. However, unlike the latter states, the CMEA–6 were prohibited from drawing upon other markets. The CMEA–6 was a classical captive market, much more so than India was captive to the MNOCs.

The paucity of energy resources in CMEA–6 has, overall, retarded industrialization. The German Democratic Republic, Poland, and Czechoslovakia, each with valuable coal reserves, contain almost no oil or gas. Moreover, both Czechoslovakia and GDR were deficient in hard coal and reliant upon Russia for necessary supplies. Poland, the largest hard coal producer in eastern Europe, exported coal to its bloc neighbors, and to the West as well (Table 7.6). But, Poland's need for hard currency during the 1970s prompted it to reduce internal consumption of coal in order to increase exports to the West, a decision that damaged heavy industry. Coal exports did not rise sufficiently to pay for imports. By 1980, the government's policy of increasing energy and consumer goods prices while freezing wages merged with other grievances to generate considerable social unrest. Just as the Iranian price shock occurred, Polish coal production faltered. The Soviet decision to freeze oil exports to eastern Europe at 1978 levels and falling coal production precipitated severe energy shortages during the 1980s. Poland's foreign debt rose as the modernization process ground to a halt.[56]

Romania, an important source of oil for western Europe prior to World War II, became, like Poland, a net importer of energy during the 1970s. Romanian oil production slipped in 1976 just as domestic demand and world prices ascended. Production declined by 33 percent between 1976 and 1985 as a result of decisions of the state oil industry, essentially under Soviet control since World War II, that emphasized maximum production while neglecting exploration and the adoption of secondary and tertiary production techniques. Still a net exporter in 1974, Romania imported 31 percent of its oil use in 1978 and turned to imported low grade coals to diminish more expensive oil imports. Although other CMEA members received preferentially priced oil from Russia, Romania did not. Moreover, allotments of oil to Romania were slashed by almost 30 percent in 1981 and frozen at that level. Thus, the Soviets punished the Ceauscecu regime for foreign policy independence. Russia employed the stick more frequently than the carrot when dealing with its eastern European allies.[57]

During the 1960s, indigenous coal reserves in GDR, Poland, and Czechoslovakia supported rapid industrialization. But, by the 1970s, industrial growth could no longer depend entirely upon coal which, in many industrial processes, was less efficient and more costly than natural gas or oil. These states received, however, only as much oil as Russia wished to ship. As a result, the low efficiency of such high energy intensive industries as glass, paper, chemicals (and fertilizers) diminished the ability of CMEA–6 to offer high quality–low cost goods to non-Communist buyers. In 1975, coal provided the above states 70 percent of TPER. Persistent high use of coal caused environmental damage, the severity of which only became widely known a decade later.[58]

The oil price increases of the post–1973 decade confronted the USSR with a true dilemma. Suddenly, Moscow stood to gain fat profits by selling oil (and then gas) to western Europe. But more than 50 percent of oil that could be spared was committed to eastern Europe. Permitting the cost of CMEA–6 imports to rise along with world spot prices would severely damage their struggling economies while stirring up smoldering antagonisms to Soviet domination. To avert confrontation with its partners, the Kremlin sold oil to CMEA–6 (except Romania) at prices below world levels and purchased CMEA–6 goods at prices above world levels.[59]

As Goldman wryly describes them, Soviet leaders wrung their hands in self-pity, complaining about being exploited by eastern Europe. Look how much more we could have earned, they intoned, had we been less generous and charged our Socialist neighbors higher prices. Although Soviet oil prices to CMEA–6 fell below those charged to the West between 1973 and 1975, prices to the bloc still doubled. By 1978, the price gap had all but disappeared. A price break was never offered for natural gas; indeed, eastern Europe paid more than double the price charged Italy. The second price shock of 1979–80 presented the Soviets with the same dilemma.

In response to this new opportunity, the Soviet offered a price to eastern Europe lower by half than world spot prices but froze the volume delivered at roughly the level of 1979. This forced CMEA–6 into world markets to obtain the oil necessary to modernization. The bloc states paid $10 billion to Russia in 1981 at prices 50 percent lower than spot market prices. Middle Eastern imports cost $2 billion. In 1982, imports of non-Soviet oil cost $3 billion while receipts from the USSR declined in value by about $1.7 billion. By 1987, the "price bargain" had ended; eastern Europe paid Russia $25 per barrel, compared with $18 on the spot market. The USSR also entered into gas export deals with CMEA 6 that provided more Btus per ruble than oil, but at rates higher than charged to western Europe. In addition, CMEA recipients were obligated to contribute labor, technology, and equipment to the construction of pipelines.[60] The Soviets gave little away.

While not entirely unresponsive to eastern European energy needs, the Soviets much preferred to reduce exports within the bloc. But neither an abrupt cut off nor sharp price increases could be essayed without considerable political risk. Moscow verbally encouraged the bloc states to develop nuclear energy, but could extend only modest aid and that at a stiff price. The Soviets dragooned Poland, Hungary, and Czechoslovakia into nuclear reactor joint ventures with construction on Soviet sites. The minor partners paid a substantial share of the cost and, together, would receive one-half of the electricity generated. Given the existence of greatly underused reactor manufacturing capacity in the West, there is little doubt that eastern Europe could have purchased plants from the West, with liberal credits, providing cheaper electricity than Soviet plants.

The Soviet nuclear industry languished compared with western Europe, Japan, or the USA. As of 1980, nuclear output contributed less to national energy supply than the nuclear component of the West (Table 7.1). Russia assigned high priority to nuclear energy but lacked the capacity to manufacture the necessary equipment quickly. In 1980, twenty-six reactors operated in the USSR, compared with thirty-two in the UK, twenty-three in Japan, seventeen in France, and ten in West Germany.

As of 1984, nuclear energy accounted for 10 percent of Soviet electric production, considerably less than the percentage generated by East German, Czech, or Hungarian nuclear plants. A crash program was initiated to push the nuclear portion of electric production to 25 percent by 1990. Western observers warned that the Soviets pursued those goals at the expense of reactor safety. Even before the Chernobyl accident in 1986, the program was far behind schedule. The accident cast the program into disarray and threatened the progress of the industry in the bloc states.[61]

Just prior to the Iranian Revolution and the invasion of Afghanistan, the Soviet energy balance induced much speculation in the West. As it turned out, the famous CIA report of 1977, predicting that the Soviets would become net importers by 1985, was not entirely accurate. While Soviet oil production ceased to advance and a tightness of energy supply developed, oil and gas continued to be exported to Europe, at high prices, through 1982. Since 1983, falling oil prices and slack foreign demand for natural gas forced adjustments in economic development goals, perhaps contributing to General Secretary Mikhail Gorbachev's program for economic revival (*perestroika*) and political liberalization (*glasnost*).

The energy and general economic difficulties experienced in eastern Europe during the 1970s seemed less the consequence of intrinsic resource or technological deficiencies than of the consequences of political and economic decisions imposed upon them by the Soviet Union. Japan and South Korea each fashioned dynamic economies from resource bases inferior to those possessed by the bloc states.

Conclusion

Escalating energy prices severely exacerbated pre-existing inflationary pressures during the years, 1973–81, weakening the economies of many nations while offering unbelievable development opportunities to a fortunate few.

For the energy deficient states, Tanzania and Brazil among many others, oil price increases far outstripped the prices received for commodity exports. Huge trade deficits accumulated, requiring extensive borrowing from foreign sources and depriving crucial development projects of funds. Within eastern Europe, poorly endowed with fuels other than coal, but possessed of excellent industrial potential, dependence upon the Soviet Union for oil and gas intensified. The Soviets benefited from the OPEC windfall but shared little of this manna with its satellites. GDR, Czechoslovakia, Hungary, and Poland were trapped like mammoths in a tar pit, their agricultural and industrial sectors suffocated by institutional rigidity and by decades of Communist mismanagement.

Brazil and India were caught in an economic–demographic snare that appeared inescapable. Soaring energy costs battered their fragile economies. But far more deadly was the population explosion. Energy at the cheapest price could bring little succor to societies containing so many millions of impoverished and landless people. Aid from the West and OPEC funded projects that offered few tangible benefits to the many. For Tanzanians and most sub-Saharan Africans, the price of commercial energy was irrelevant. Eroded land, encroaching desert, deforestation, and malnutrition were the pertinent facts of life. Africa, self-sufficient in food in 1960, imported just under one-half its needs in 1980.

The unprecedented revenues of the oil exporting LDCs did not magically transform their economies. Nigeria and Indonesia remained encumbered with layers of intractable difficulties. Self-sustained economic growth proved difficult to induce in Mexico, however much money was available. Mexico in 1980 was in worse condition than in 1970. A few producers, mostly Arab Gulf states, appeared to register solid economic improvement. But, Saudi Arabia and Kuwait remained tightly bound to oil and to western markets; their high average standard of living masked severe internal inequities and tensions.

Development could not be bought, simply, like a refinery, steel mill, or hydroelectric dam. It required a balanced approach, one that emphasized agriculture and rural employment as well as large scale industry and urban growth. A reformed energy mix and more appropriate energy technologies could contribute strongly. This might mean, at least in the short-term, greater but more efficient use of wood fuel in tandem with the application of such small energy devices as well-engineered coal stoves and water purification equipment rather than giant technologies. But, most of all, population must be brought into balance with available resources.

Notes

1. For the above two paragraphs: World Resources Institute, *World Resources 1987*, New York: Basic Books (1987), pp. 260–1; J. Goldemberg,

"Brazil: energy options and current outlook," in V. Smil and W.E. Knowland, eds, *Energy in the developing world: The real energy crisis*, Oxford: Oxford University Press (1980), pp. 227–8, 233–4; *1986 World Population Data Sheet*, Washington, D.C.: Population Reference Bureau, Inc. (1986); J. Sathaye *et al.*, "Energy Demand in Developing Countries: A Sectoral Analysis of Recent Trends," *Annual Review of Energy*, 12 (1987), p. 268; *New York Times*, July 3, 1985; S.E. Stamos, Jr, "Energy and Development in Latin America," *Latin American Research Review*, XXI, no. 1 (1986), pp. 194–5.

2. F. Szekely, ed., *Energy Alternatives in Latin America*, Dublin: Tycooly (1983), pp. 8–14.

3. See Table 8.1 and WRI, *World Resources 1988–89*, pp. 236–7, 242–3, 250–1; A.M. Strout, "Energy and Economic Growth in Central America," in Smil and Knowland, *Energy*, pp. 354–5.

4. South Korean *per capita* GNP in 1983 fell just under Argentina's and above Brazil's, *1986 World Population Data Sheet*; J.E. Katz and O.S. Marwah, *Nuclear Power in Developing Countries, an Analysis of Decision Making*, Lexington, Mass.: Lexington Books (1982), p. 233; P. Hallwood and S. Sinclair, *Oil, Debt, and Development: OPEC in the Third World*, London: Allen & Unwin (1981), pp. 21–3.

5. IEA, *Energy Balances of Developing Countries 1971/1982*, Paris: OECD/ IEA (1984), pp. 206–17, 266–77, 315–18; De Golyer and MacNaughton, *Twentieth Century Petroleum Statistics 1986*, Dallas, Tex.: De Golyer and MacNaughton (1986), p. 6; Smil and Knowland, eds, *Energy*, p. 372; G. Schramm, "Managing Urban/Industrial Wood Fuel Supply and Demand in Africa," *The Annals of Regional Science*, XXI (November 1987), p. 61.

6. J.R. McNeil, "Agriculture, Forests, and Ecological History: Brazil 1500–1984," *Environmental Review*, 10 (Summer 1986), p. 40. Deforestation in Brazil consumed 30,000 square miles in 1982. President Sarney, in 1988, declared a temporary freeze on government subsidization of the cattle, mining, and lumber interests which caused most of the damage, N. Lenssen, "Reprieve for the Rain Forest," *World.Watch*, 2 (January–February 1989), p. 35. For a description of the Brazilian subsidies, see WRI, *World Resources 1988–89*, pp. 211–12.

7. For the above two paragraphs: See Lester Brown, *State of the World 1988*, New York: W.W. Norton (1988) and other Worldwatch Institute publications on deforestation, soil erosion, and so forth; *New York Times*, April 26, 1987; G. Foley, "Outside the oil economy — rural energy in developing countries," in T.L. Shaw *et al.*, eds, *Policy and Development of Energy Resources*, Chichester: Wiley (1984), pp. 31–54; K. Openshaw, "Wood-fuel — a time for reassessment," in Smil and Knowland, eds, *Energy*, pp. 72–86; Goldemberg, "Brazil," in *ibid.*, pp. 227–44.

8. For the above two paragraphs: Sathaye *et al.*, "Energy in Developing Countries," pp. 268–72; H. Cleveland, ed., *Energy Futures of Developing Countries: The Neglected Victims of the Energy Crisis*, New York: Praeger (1980), pp. 21–5; J. Foreman-Peck, *A History of the World Economy: International Economic Relations Since 1850*, Brighton, Sussex: Wheatsheaf Books (1983), pp. 302–9; R.E. Driscoll and J.N. Behrman, eds, *National Industrial Policies*, Cambridge, Mass.: Oelgeschlager, Gunn & Haine (1984), pp. 33–6.

9. Hallwood and Sinclair, *OPEC in the Third World*, pp. 62–5; *Statistical Bulletin of the OAS*, 9 (January–June 1987), pp. 48, 50, 52, 58, 60, 64, 70.
10. Sources for Table 8.4; D. Dowd, *The Waste of Nations: Dysfunction in the World Economy*, Boulder, Colo.: Westview Press (1989), p. 99; N. Harris, *The End of the Third World: Newly Industrializing Countries and the Decline of an Ideology*, London: Penguin Books (1987), pp. 70–5.
11. *Statistical Bulletin of the OAS*, 9 (January–June 1987), pp. 50–1; The Economist Intelligence Unit, *1986/87 Yearbook. Energy in Latin America and the Caribbean*, London: The Economist Publications Ltd (1987), p. 13; C.E. Solberg, *Oil and Nationalism in Argentina: A History*, Stanford, Calif.: Stanford University Press (1979), pp. 172–6.
12. For the above two paragraphs: Katz and Marwah, *Nuclear Power*, pp. 233–4; IEA, *Energy Balances of Developing Countries*, pp. 266–77, 315–18; Hallwood and Sinclair, *OPEC in the Third World*, p. 53; Driscoll and Behrman, *National Industrial Policies*, pp. 137–46; C. Harvey, "The Impact of World Recession and World Prices on a Sample of Developing Countries," *IDS Bulletin*, 16 (January 1985), pp. 25–6; Harris, *End of Third World*, pp. 34–8; R. Mardon, "The Bureaucratic Authoritarian Industrializing Regime and the Control of Foreign Capital Inflows: The Case of the Republic of Korea," for delivery at the 1987 Annual Meeting of the American Political Science Association, September 3–6, 1987. Copyright by the American Political Science Association, pp. 23–5.
13. Harris, *End of Third World*, p. 37.
14. For the above four paragraphs: *1986 World Population Data Sheet*; WRI, *World Resources 1988–89*, pp. 53, 272, 306–7; De Golyer, *1986*, p. 11; M.B.K. Darkoh, "Combatting desertification in the arid and semi-arid lands of Tanzania," *Journal of Arid Environments*, 12 (March 1987), pp. 87–99; H. Madelin, *Oil and Politics*, translated by M. Totman, Farnborough: Saxon House (1975), pp. 213–15; L. Howell and M. Morrow, *Asia, Oil Politics, and the Energy Crisis*, New York: IDOC/ North America (1974), pp. 63–70; Smil and Knowland, eds, *Energy*, pp. 372–3; *New York Times*, November 8, 1981, February 14, 1982; D. Gerner to author, June 14, 1989.
15. Howell and Morrow, *Asia and the Energy Crisis*, pp. 63–70; Z. Mikdashi, *The International Politics of Natural Resources*, Ithaca, N.Y.: Cornell University Press (1976), pp. 139–40; N. Choucri, *International Politics of Energy Interdependence*, Lexington, Mass.: Lexington Books (1976), pp. 140–2; G.W. Grayson, "Venezuela and the Puerto Ordaz Agreement," *Inter-American Economic Affairs*, 38 (Winter 1984), pp. 56–63; V. Sordo-Arrioja, "The Mexican–Venezuelan Oil Agreement of San Jose: A Step Toward Latin American Cooperation," in M.S. Wionezek and R. El Mallakh, eds, *Mexico's Energy Resources: Toward a Policy of Diversification*, Boulder, Colo.: Westview Press (1985), pp. 109–10; S. Hunter, *OPEC and the Third World: The Politics of Aid*, London: Croom Helm (1984), pp. 46, 219–20.
16. A. Alnasrawi, *OPEC in a Changing World Economy*, Baltimore: The Johns Hopkins University Press (1985), pp. 128–32; I.F.I. Shihata, *The Other Face of OPEC: Financial Assistance to the Third World*, New York: Longman (1982), pp. 258–9; Hunter, *OPEC*, xv; A. Al-Sowayegh, *Arab Petropolitics*, London: Croom Helm (1984), pp. 23–6; R.K. Pachauri, *The Political Economy of Global Energy*, Baltimore: The Johns Hopkins

University Press (1985), p. 145; Foreman-Peck, *History of World Economy*, p. 306.

17. For the above two paragraphs: Shihata, *OPEC Financial Assistance*, pp. 9–11, 258–60 and Shihata *et al.*, *The OPEC Fund for International Development: the formative years*, London: Croom Helm (1983), pp. 4, 98; R. Menon, *Soviet Power and the Third World*, New Haven: Yale University Press (1986), p. 195; *The Middle East and North Africa 1987*, 33rd edn, London: Europa Publications Ltd. (1987), p. 361; N.N.M. Ayubi, "OPEC Surplus Funds and Third World Development: The Egyptian Case," *Journal of South Asian and Middle Eastern Studies*, V (Summer 1982), pp. 39–56; Hallwood and Sinclair, *OPEC in the Third World*, pp. 98–101, 108, 114; Pachauri, *Global Energy*, p. 145; Hunter, *OPEC*, pp. 192–209.

18. Shihata, *OPEC Fund*, pp. 50, 99–102, 205–6; Hallwood and Sinclair, *OPEC in the Third World*, p. 99.

19. Pachauri, *Global Energy*, p. 112; Alnasrawi, *OPEC*, pp. 128–32; Hallwood and Sinclair, *OPEC in the Third World*, p. 60; Cleveland, ed., *Energy Futures*, p. 64; Inter-American Development Bank, *Annual Report 1983*, Washington, DC: IADB (1983), p. 18.

20. IMF, *World Economic Outlook April 1985*, Washington, DC: IMF (1985), pp. 51–2.

21. Ayubi, "OPEC Surplus Funds,", p. 39; Pachauri, *Global Energy*, pp. 77, 100.

22. For the above two paragraphs: A.E. Safer, "World Oil Markets and the Business Cycle," *Energy Communications*, 5. no. 5 (1979), pp. 334–6; Hallwood and Sinclair, *OPEC in the Third World*, pp. 31–2; F. Fesharaki, *Development of the Iranian Oil Industry: International and Domestic Aspects*, New York: Praeger (1976), pp. 156–70; Alnasrawi, *OPEC*, pp. 7–8, 111; *OPEC Oil Report, December 1977*, London: Petroleum Economist (1978), pp. 4–14.

23. J. Amuzegar, "Oil Wealth: A Very Mixed Blessing," *Foreign Affairs*, 60 (Spring 1982), pp. 816–17; M. Tanzer and S. Zorn, *Energy Update: Oil in the Late Twentieth Century*, New York: Monthly Review Press (1985), pp. 83–6; A. Gelb, "From Boom to Bust—Oil Exporting Countries over the Cycle 1970–84," *IDS Bulletin*, 17 (October 1986), pp. 22–4; Howell and Morrow, *Asia and Energy*, pp. 73–95; C. Brogan, *The Retreat from Oil Nationalism in Ecuador, 1976–1983*, London: University of London Institute of Latin American Studies (1984), p. 19.

24. P. Odell, *Oil and World Power*, 7th edn, Harmondsworth, Middlesex: Penguin (1983), pp. 101–2; The Economist Intelligence Unit, *1986/1987 Yearbook*, p. 97; Amuzegar, "Oil Wealth," pp. 820–1; F.A. Olaloku, *Structure of the Nigerian Economy*, London: Macmillan (1979), pp. 248–52.

25. Quoted in W. Tuttle, III, "The Mexican Oil Industry, 1970–1984", History 696 Research Paper. University of Kansas. Spring 1985, p. 13.

26. For the above three paragraphs: *ibid.*, pp. 7–16, *passim*; Harris, *End of Third World*, pp. 74–83; 87; E. Duran, "Pemex: The Trajectory of a National Oil Policy," in J.D. Wirth, ed., *Latin American Oil Companies and the Politics of Energy*, Lincoln, Nebr.: University of Nebraska Press (1985), pp. 147–51; R. Gutierrez, "Mexican Economic and Oil Policies of the 1970s and Strategies for the 1980s," in Wionezek and El Mallakh, eds,

Mexico's Energy Resources, pp. 7–14; *Lloyds Bank Group Economic Report, Mexico*, London: Lloyds Bank Group (1983), pp. 10–11, 16, 39; EIU, *1986/1987 Yearbook*, pp. 98–9; Smil and Knowland, eds, *Energy*, p. 378; A. Bressand *et al.*, "Oil Exporting Countries," in J. Pearce, ed., *The Third Oil Shock: The Effects of Lower Prices*, London: Routledge & Kegan Paul (1983), pp. 33–6; F. Szekely, "Recent Findings and Research Suggestions in Oil and Mexico's Development Process," *Latin America Research Review*, XX. no. 3 (1985), pp. 236–42; WRI, *World Resources 1988–89*, pp. 246, 266.

27. For the above three paragraphs: Al-Sowayegh, *Arab Petropolitics*, p. 47; Pachauri, *Global Energy*, pp. 80–1; S.M. Ghanem, *OPEC: The Rise and Fall of an Exclusive Club*, London: KPI (1986), p. 46–8; Menon, *Soviet Power*, p. 188; Fesharaki, *Iranian Oil Industry*, pp. 182–93; R.E. Looney, "Origins of Pre-Revolutionary Iran's Development Strategy," *Middle Eastern Studies*, 22 (January 1986), pp. 104–13; A. Jazayeri, "Prices and Output in Two Oil-Based Economies: The Dutch Disease in Iran and Nigeria," *IDS Bulletin*, 17 (October 1986), pp. 16–18; Alnasrawi, *OPEC*, p 118; WRI, *World Resources 1988–89*, p 279

28. Military rule (1966–79) was replaced by an elected civilian government in 1979. The military ousted that government in 1983.

29. For the above three paragraphs: Ghanem, *OPEC, an Exclusive Club*, p. 63; F.C. Okafor, "Population pressure and land resource depletion in southeastern Nigeria," *Applied Geography*, 7 (July 1987), pp. 243–56; C.O. Ikporukpo, "Petroleum Exploitation and the Socio-Economic Environment in Nigeria," *International Journal of Environmental Studies*, 21. no. 2 (1983), pp. 195–8, 200–3; S. Postel and L. Heise, *Reforesting the Earth*, Worldwatch Paper 83, April 1988, Washington, DC: Worldwatch Institute (1988), p. 25; Olaloku, *Nigerian Economy*, pp. 140–1; Al-Sowayegh, *Arab Petropolitics*, p. 47; Jazayeri, "Oil-Based Economies," pp. 18–19; *Lloyds Bank Group Economic Report 1982, Nigeria*, London: Lloyds Bank Group (1982), pp. 2–9, 17–18.

30. Amuzegar, "Oil Wealth," p. 832.

31. Tanzer and Zorn, *Energy Update*, pp. 88–92.

32. E. Kanovsky, "The Diminishing Importance of Middle East Oil: A Harbinger of the Future?" *Middle East Contemporary Survey*, 5 (1980–81), pp. 382–90; Pachauri, *Global Energy*, pp. 85–6.

33. For the above four paragraphs: Fesharaki, *Iranian Oil Industry*, pp. 156–70; Alnasrawi, *OPEC*, pp. 85–6, 99–105; Pachauri, *Global Energy*, pp. 98–102; D. Gerner, "Petrodollar Recycling: Imports, Arms, Investment, and Aid," *Arab Studies Quarterly*, 7 (Winter 1985), pp. 1–2, 6; H. Maull, *Europe and World Energy*, London: Buttersworth (1980), pp. 104–6; *Lloyds Bank Group Economic Report, West Germany*, London: Lloyds Bank Group (1982), pp. 25–7; Editorial Research Reports, *World Economy, Changes and Challenges*, Washington, DC: Congressional Quarterly, Inc. (1983), pp. 4–8; Al-Sowayegh, *Arab Petropolitics*, p. 47.

34. For the above two paragraphs: J.R. Presley, *A Guide to the Saudi Arabian Economy*, New York: St. Martins (1984), p. 38; *The Middle East and North Africa 1987*, pp. 104–5; H.L. Lax, *Political Risk in the International Oil and Gas Industry*, Boston: International Human Resources Development Corporation (1983), p. 58; I.M. Torrens, *Changing Structure in the*

World Oil Market, Paris: The Atlantic Institute for International Affairs (1980), pp. 14–15; M. Quinlan, "Nigeria's oil industry," in Smil and Knowland, eds, *Energy*, pp. 272–4; Ghanem, *OPEC, an Exclusive Club*, pp. 49–50, 63.

35. For the above three paragraphs: G. Luciani, *The Oil Companies and the Arab World*, London: Croom Helm (1984), pp. 14–16; R.A. Ajami, *Arab Response to the Multinationals*, New York: Praeger (1979), pp. 17–20; Tanzer and Zorn, *Energy Update*, pp. 130, 148; Odell, *Oil*, pp. 16, 26; *New York Times*, November 11, 1981; G. Jenkins, *Oil Economists' Handbook 1985*, London: Elsevier Applied Science Publications Ltd (1985), pp. 235–6; G. Philip, *Oil and Politics in Latin America. Nationalist Movements and State Companies*, Cambridge: Cambridge University Press (1982), pp. 481–3; Brogan, *Oil in Ecuador*, p. 12.

36. For the above two paragraphs: Jenkins, *Oil Handbook 1985*, pp. 74, 162; Luciani, *Oil Companies and the Arab World*, pp. 11, 36–58; Lax, *Risk in International Oil and Gas*, p. 52; Tanzer and Zorn, *Energy Update*, p. 140; *The Middle East and North Africa 1987*, pp. 104–5; Ajami, *Arab Response to the Multinationals*, pp. 131–4; EIU, *1986/87 Yearbook*, pp. 151–2; *The Wall Street Journal*, May 1, 1981.

37. *The Middle East and North Africa 1987*, pp. 104–5.

38. W.B. Quandt, *Saudi Arabia in the 1980s: Foreign Policy, Security, and Oil*, Washington DC: The Brookings Institution (1981), p. 91. *The Wall Street Journal*, May 1, 1981 featured an article that corroborated the charge that Saudi princes exacted secret payments from the oil companies.

39. In fairness to UAE and Qatar, an impressive reduction in infant mortality occurred between 1976 and 1986, Qatar's falling to 38 and UAE's to 45. IMR rested at 100 in Saudi Arabia and 97 in Libya, attesting to niggardly attention to basic health care. Improvement in Indonesia excelled that for Saudi Arabia. *1986 World Population Data Sheet 1986.*

40. Ghanem, *OPEC, an Exclusive Club*, pp. 156–7; M.E. Ahrari, *OPEC, the Failing Giant*, Lexington, Ky.: University Press of Kentucky (1986), pp. 136–43.

41. D. Gisselquist, *Oil Prices and Trade Deficits: US Conflicts with Japan and West Germany*, New York: Praeger (1979), pp. 1–2, 10–13, 57–63; Odell, *Oil*, pp. 224–9.

42. Pachauri, *Global Energy*, pp. 72–3; Choucri, *Energy Interdependence*, pp. 167–73; Mikdashi, *International Politics of Natural Resources*, p. 75; Alnasrawi, *OPEC*, p. 67; Maull, *Europe and World Energy*, pp. 218–19.

43. Pachauri, *Global Energy*, pp. 63–4; C.P. Bradley, *Recent United States Policy in the Persian Gulf (1971–82)*, Grantham, N.H.: Tompson & Rutter (1982), pp. 47–9; Quandt, *Saudi Arabia*, pp. 128–31; F.M. Gottheil, "Oil and the Middle East: The Impact of Ideology on Performance and Policy," *Middle East Review*, 16 (Summer 1984), pp. 43–4; *Washington Post*, January 24, 1978.

44. *BP statistical review of world energy, 1980*, p. 18, *1986*, p. 4; A.D. Johany, *The Myth of the OPEC Cartel: The Role of Saudi Arabia*, New York: Wiley (1980), p. 21; Ahrari, *OPEC*, pp. 143–4; Alnasrawi, *OPEC*, pp. 3, 32–9; Hallwood and Sinclair, *OPEC in the Third World*, pp. 48–50.

45. Ahrari, *OPEC*, p. 4; Ghanem, *OPEC, an Exclusive Club*, p. 190; Pachauri, *Global Energy*, p. 69.

46. E.A. Hewitt, *Energy, Economics, and Foreign Policy in the Soviet Union*,

Washington, DC: The Brookings Institution (1984), pp. 15, 209; WRI, *World Resources 1988–89*, pp. 236–7; G.W. Hoffman with Leslie Dienes, *The European Energy Challenge: East and West*, Durham, N.C.: Duke University Press (1985), p. 176; IEA, *Energy Balance of Developing Countries*, pp. 387–9, 404. World Bank and OECD/IEA publications of economic indicators refer to Soviet bloc GNP as unavailable.

47. Hoffman, *European Energy Challenge*, pp. 157–60.
48. Hewitt, *Energy in Soviet Union*, p. 50; IMF, *World Economic Outlook 1985*, p. 147; M.I. Goldman, *The Enigma of Soviet Petroleum: Half-Full or Half-Empty*, London: Allen & Unwin (1980), pp. 5, 112–15; *World Oil*, August 1987, pp. 62–3.
49. For the above two paragraphs: D. Park, *Oil & Gas in Comecon Countries*, London: Kegan Paul (1979), pp. 44, 50; J.P. Stern, *International Gas Trade in Europe: The Policies of Exporting and Importing Countries*, London: Heinemann Educational Books Ltd, (1984), p. 65; Hewitt, *Energy in Soviet Union*, pp. 83–5; J.D. Davis, *Blue Gold: The Political Economy of Natural Gas*, London: Allen & Unwin (1984); E.L. Morse, "An Overview: Gains, Costs, Dilemmas," in Pearce, ed., *Third Oil Shock*, p. 26.
50. For the above six paragraphs: M. Peebles, *Evolution of the Gas Industry*, London: Macmillan (1980), p. 172; Davis, *Blue Gold*, pp. 143–4, Stern, *International Gas Trade*, pp. 46–7, 62, 65; *BP statistical review of world energy, 1981–85*, Park, *Oil & Gas*, p. 175; Hewitt, *Energy in the Soviet Union*, pp. 60, 119–20, 155, 157; B.I. Greer and J.L. Russell, "European Reliance on Soviet Gas Exports: The Yamburg–Urengoi Natural Gas Project," *The Energy Journal*, 3 (July 1982), pp. 24–5.
51. Menon, *Soviet Power*, pp. 183, 186–7, 206–12.
52. P.L. Ferrari *et al.*, *U.S. Arms Exports: Policies and Contractors*, Washington, DC: Investor Responsibility Research Center (1987), pp. 97–103; E.A. Kolodziej, *Making and Marketing Arms: The French Experience and Its Implications for the International System*, Princeton: Princeton University Press (1987), Appendix C.
53. A.A. Gawad, "Moscow's Arms-For-Oil Diplomacy," *Foreign Policy*, 63 (Summer 1986), pp. 154–8; Quandt, *Saudi Arabia*, p. 163; M.N. Katz, *Russia and Arabia: Soviet Foreign Policy toward the Arabian Peninsula*, Baltimore: The Johns Hopkins University Press (1986), pp. 147–51.
54. For a Soviet interpretation of US oil policy in the Middle East, see S. Losev and Y. Tyssovsky, *The Middle East: Oil Policy*, translated by D. Sventsitsky, Moscow: Progress Publishers (1984).
55. I. Kozlov, *Socialism and Energy Resources*, translated by G.A. Kozlov, Moscow: Progress Publishers (1981).
56. P. James, *The Future of Coal*, 2nd edn, London: Macmillan (1984), p. 138; K. Poznanski, "Economic adjustment and political forces: Poland since 1970," *International Organization*, 40 (Spring 1986), pp. 455–88; R. Belgrave, ed., *Energy—Two Decades of Crisis*, Aldershot: Gower (1983), p. 11.
57. De Golyer, *1986*, p. 7; Kozlov, *Socialism and Energy*, p. 29; Belgrave, ed., *Energy*, p. 8; Hoffman, *European Energy Challenge*, pp. 31–3, 175; R.H. Linden, "Socialist patrimonialism and the global economy: the case of Romania," *International Organization*, 40 (Spring 1986), pp. 347–80; M. Marrese, "CMEA: effective but cumbersome political economy," *ibid.*, pp. 288–327.

58. H.F. French, "Industrial Wasteland," *World.Watch*, 1 (November–December 1988), pp. 21–30.
59. For the above two paragraphs: A. Scanlan, "Communist Bloc Energy Supply and Demand," in P. Tempest, ed., *International Energy Markets*, Cambridge, Mass.: Oelgeschlager, Gunn & Haine (1983), pp. 18–19; Hoffman, *European Energy Challenge*, pp. 9–12; Park, *Oil & Gas*, pp. 114–15, 121; Marrese, "CMEA", pp. 303–6.
60. For the above two paragraphs: Goldman, *Enigma of Soviet Petroleum*, pp. 60–1; Kozlov, *Socialism and Energy*, pp. 32–5; Park, *Oil & Gas*, pp. 168–9, 171–2, 180–7; Hewitt, *Energy in the Soviet Union*, pp. 157–65; J. Stern, "East European Energy and East–West Trade in Energy," in Belgrave, ed., *Energy*, pp. 48–50; Hoffman, *European Energy Challenge*, p. 10.
61. For the above two paragraphs: Hewitt, *Energy in the Soviet Union*, pp. 96–7; *New York Times*, January 16, 1983, April 11, 1984; Goldman, *Enigma of Soviet Petroleum*, pp. 66–7, 107–8; WRI, *World Resources 1988–90*, pp. 119–20, 311; Hoffman, *European Energy Challenge*, pp. 14–15.

9

A second energy crisis: the Iranian Revolution and its aftermath

A year or two of relative energy price and supply stability ended in 1978 and 1979 with the outbreak of the Iranian Revolution. A decade of wild fluctuation in price and supply followed, punctuated by political crises of varying intensity and longevity, mostly centered around the volatile Persian Gulf. Buyer's panic first forced prices upward to $40 per barrel, weakening the economies of energy importing states sufficiently to induce a significant reduction in the demand for oil and a concomitant increase in the employment of substitutes for oil. Despite Iraq's attack on Iran in 1980, an oil surplus had accumulated by 1981. The availability of non-OPEC oil and reduced oil and energy consumption in the leading oil importing nations added to the surplus and depressed oil prices in 1982–83. Thereafter, powerful deflationary pressures dominated. Oil prices plunged as low as $8–$9 in mid-1986, rose to the $20 range in 1987, but slipped below $14 in fall 1988. By late 1989 OPEC had fashioned a new production agreement that stabilized prices just under $20.

Sudden, sharp price gyrations created new groupings of winners and losers and forced new quandaries to the fore. OPEC grappled with the thorny problem of production quotas. Price deflation blunted the incentive to explore and develop high cost oil or to hurry along the commercialization of synthetic fuels. Oil at $20 and abundant supply deadened the impulse to conserve. The remarkable revenue windfalls enjoyed by the exporting states from 1973 through 1981 afforded no final cure for underdevelopment and little protection against subsequently shrinking revenues. Neither did greatly reduced energy import bills smooth the path to development for the importing LDCs. Lower energy costs after 1982 permitted renewed economic growth within OECD but did not much affect the balance of power among the highly developed countries.

Reinvigorated economies in the West and elsewhere, but particularly in southeast Asia, in the absence of conservation and environmental policies quickly spawned interrelated ecological crises. Fossil fuel consumption was ever more positively linked with acid rain, ozone depletion, and global warming. The nuclear power industry buckled under the reaction to Chernobyl, but it could not be counted out in the future. The heavy oil importers, as of 1989, appeared no better prepared than in 1978 to withstand another energy supply crunch. Worse still, in ignoring environmental stresses during the 1970s and 1980s, they had squandered two whole decades. This happened because of their myopic focus on short-term economic growth.

The Iranian Revolution and panic in the West

Protests and violent acts against the Shah's government erupted in Iran in 1978. Striking oil workers, virtually shutting down Consortium production in late 1978, hurried along the demise of the Pahlavi dynasty. The Shah was deposed in 1979 and the victors, adhering to Shiite teachings, proclaimed the establishment of a Muslim republic, as pure a fundamentalist theocracy as the world had witnessed since John Calvin's Geneva. Panic spread throughout the West as Iranian exports dried up. Spot prices of $15 per barrel in December 1978 surged upward to a peak of $42 by May 1979 and remained at about $40 throughout 1980.

The Iranian shortfall, amounting to some 2 million barrels a day, or 100 million metric tons annually, reduced world production by only 3 percent, but precipitated a tripling in price. It is difficult to understand why such a modest shortfall engendered such distorted behavior. True, Iranian exports were heavily concentrated in the USA, western Europe, and Japan. Iranian exports to the USA were halved from 1978 to 1979 and then virtually ended. Japan lost some 25 mmt and Europe some 50 mmt. Panicked purchasers, particularly European and Japanese, searched frantically for oil in the spot market. Other producers rushed into the spot market to fill the void, only too happy to receive the extreme bids of nervous buyers. Bidders outbid one another, propelling prices upward in spite of the overall adequacy of oil supplies.[1]

The West in 1979 was as unprepared to act in concert to minimize the impact of the Iranian shortfall as it had been in 1973 to counter the embargo. The International Energy Agency's emergency oil allocation program was not invoked. Little had been essayed to moderate dependence upon oil from the Middle East (Table 7.2). Total energy use had not diminished (Table 7.1). Most of the West had recovered from the dog days of 1974 and 1975, enjoying renewed economic growth in 1977 and 1978. The West easily absorbed the modest price increase imposed by OPEC in 1978. The new equilibrium seemed durable.

Sharply declining Iranian production (Table 7.4) resurrected the fear of oil shortage in Japan, Germany, France, and Italy. Dependent on the MNOCs for a large portion of their supply, they searched elsewhere for oil. Since much oil was under contract, the Japanese entered the spot market. Suppliers, particularly OPEC members, reneged on their contracts with the MNOCs to secure spot prices that shot ahead of official OPEC prices. The MNOCs also entered spot markets and upward bidding for oil gained an irrespressible momentum.

OPEC's price setting authority disappeared. Each producing state exploited the panic to maximize its income. Saudi Arabia, the most powerful OPEC state, preferred price and production stability as a general rule. But the Saudis only half-heartedly resisted the price explosion. Saudi irritation over the Israeli–Egyptian Peace Treaty of 1979 numbed their motivation to hew faithfully to a moderate course. Indeed, the Saudis lowered their output in April and May 1979, thereby quickening the price escalation.[2]

OPEC's official prices moved upward in response to spot prices with the Saudis lobbying for unified prices. Even more threatening to the West, OPEC reopened discussions about production quotas. At the Caracas meeting of OPEC in December 1979, members agreed to maintain demand and supply in balance to protect current high prices. Should demand continue to rise at pre-1978 rates, OPEC would wield enormous power. The frightening possibility loomed of the Arabs again employing an embargo to support the Palestinians. In 1980, few in the West foresaw an absolute decline in oil-energy consumption. A covey of prognosticators predicted many years of $40 oil (or worse) and persistent oil scarcity. A Venezuelan official in mid-1980 advised the USA and the West to "get ready for awesome oil problems during the '80s. The worst is still to come—in price and supply."[3] Much appeared to depend upon Saudi policy. If the Saudis won OPEC to a policy that maintained production at the level of demand, prices would remain stable, albeit in the $40 range. If OPEC repulsed the Saudi strategy, as western analysts gloomily warned, Arab producers could keep the West on tenterhooks and the oil market in chaos by merely threatening another embargo.[4] In retrospect, this fear appears exaggerated. The Arabs were already exploiting an apparent oil scarcity and raking in profits.

Fortunately, the astounding price ratcheting of 1979–80 had ended by 1981. The effects of $40 oil proved severe but not irremediable, catalyzing, as they did, natural defense systems that had only imperfectly responded in 1973–4.

The total energy import bill of the largest OECD countries more than doubled from 1977 through 1980 (Table 7.9), forcing, except in Germany and Japan, annual inflation to levels comparable with those of 1974 and 1975. With the exception of the latter states, unemployment rates surged upward, equaling or surpassing rates in 1974. GDP declined in several states and grew at slower rates in others.[5] Retarded economic growth combined with explicit conservation measures to reduce overall energy use. TPER in OECD-Europe fell by 8 percent from 1979 to 1982 and by 9 percent in both Japan and the USA (see Table 7.1). Oil imports plummeted more radically than TPER, invigorating the natural gas and primary electricity industries and, in some countries, the coal industry. New sources of oil, foreign and domestic, emerged. By 1982, the Middle Eastern and North African share of the western oil market had declined from 71 percent in 1979 to 53 percent while total imports contracted by 31 percent (Table 7.2).

In the West, recovery was well along by 1984. The great bonanza had ended for the oil exporters, few of whom had used their great wealth with sufficient skill to guard against the day of declining oil revenues. Falling prices offered some relief to the oil importing LDCs, but so endemic were their problems that the future of many remained uncertain.

Persian Gulf instability took a turn for the worse when Iraq attacked Iran in 1980. While this war did not unleash another round of price hikes and supply shortfalls, oil importers anticipated the worst. Iraq struck at Iranian oil installations and Iran launched attacks on Gulf shipping, a tactic that prompted US naval intervention in the Gulf in 1987.

Shock and uncertainty about energy and natural resources, the LDCs and their accumulated debts, and about the global environment characterized the ten years, 1978–88. But, in 1988, most westerners viewed the future complacently. As America ran up to a November 1988 presidential election, the two candidates, Michael Dukakis and George Bush, the winner, articulated no new, or even old, thoughts about energy or the environment. For almost all Americans, energy was not an issue.

The Iranian crisis and western energy security

Western responses to the price and supply challenge of 1979–80 consisted of involuntary knee jerk reactions as economic growth slowed or ceased and a varied set of energy programs that amounted to more than a mere elaboration of policies stimulated by the price and supply crunch of 1973. Exorbitant oil prices speedily reduced demand for oil. But the key national policies of OECD members almost without exception emphasized security of energy supply, a goal sought but not attained since 1973.

To the conventional supply side approach were appended measures that promoted fuel substitution, including use of renewables, energy use efficiency, and explicit conservation incentives. Conservationist measures, however, were vulnerable to short-term changes in supply and price as well as to the hostility of supply side ideologues. Environmental considerations also retreated before the superior political strength of supply siders and business interests. The electoral victories of Margaret Thatcher in 1979, Ronald Reagan in 1980, and Helmut Kohl in 1982, and their subsequent reelections, attested, at least in part, to the appeal of supply siders who remonstrated against intrusive government.

The continuing quest for security of oil supply

Discovering new sources of domestic oil and/or exploration for oil outside the endemically chaotic Middle East afforded the most direct route to oil security. Projections of energy requirements from 1979 to 2000, which assumed an increase ranging from 25 to 50 percent within OECD, made new oil discoveries imperative.[6] With prices so elevated, national oil companies and private firms pushed ahead in the North Sea and Alaska, searched for new reserves in Venezuela and Mexico, initiated costly exploratory ventures in the South China Sea and other promising Asian sites, and even explored the forbidding waters of the Barents Sea.

Success attended some of these endeavors, but none were so remarkable as to alter radically world reserves. Many exploratory sites were abandoned as prices softened after 1982. With some ballyhoo, China awarded exploratory contracts to western firms in the South China Sea and in Quandong Province but little oil was found. Penzoil closed down its mainland China rigs while BP, RDS, Exxon, and Japanese interests demanded better terms for continued operations. A similar lack of success discouraged exploration off Taiwan, South Korea, and the Philippines. Japanese ventures in the above areas as well as in Malaysia and Australia only marginally improved the security of oil supply.[7]

Global reserves in 1986 reached 100 billion metric tons (bmt), greater by 2 bmt than reserves in 1981. The Middle East contained some 55 percent of the total in 1986 as in 1973. US reserves suffered steady depletion through 1979 and grew slightly between 1979 and 1981, but in 1986 were only 70 percent of the peak reserve estimate in 1970 of 5.4 bmt. North Sea reserves of 2.7 bmt in 1986 were lower by one-third than the 1978 peak, and had declined by 5 percent from 1985 to 1986. Venezuelan finds, especially in 1985 and 1986, raised proven reserves to 7.7 bmt, compared with 1.8 bmt in 1973. Mexican reserves shot upward between 1977 and 1981 and then held steady at about 7.5 bmt through the 1980s. Soviet reserves declined by 23 percent from 1976 to 1986. Middle Eastern reserves, on the other hand, grew by 5 bmt between 1979 and 1986.

World reserves in late 1989 were about the same as in 1986. But global consumption had advanced steadily. In 1987, world consumption was in its third consecutive annual decline (see Table 7.4, p. 246). Consumption then began its current ascension. Whereas in 1988 world production equaled 86 percent of estimated world productive capacity, estimates for 1990 suggested that production would exceed 90 percent of capacity. Early in 1990, many oil industry analysts predicted sharp oil price increases by 1995 as growing demand outpaced additions to reserves and caught up with pumping capacity.

Declining North Sea and US reserves accompanied steadily falling production. Britain's North Sea production peaked in 1986 while oil withdrawals from Alaska's Prudhoe Bay and other American fields fell off in 1987–8. High prices had sustained development in those difficult fields; lower prices in 1981 and thereafter, especially 1985–6, discouraged exploration. As well, the policies of both the Thatcher and Reagan governments precluded any interference with the production decisions of the private firms operating in those fields. Falling production resulted from physical depletion in the fields, not from decisions of the MNOCs to seek price stabilization through conservation. In these very high cost fields, with the equipment in place, maximum production at almost any price is preferred to reduced production.

Total western oil imports declined after 1979, as did the share of oil in domestic fuel mixes. North Sea oil bestowed energy self-sufficiency upon Britain and Norway. Through 1987, France, Germany, and Italy reduced the share of TPER derived from energy imports. Japan's energy imports, however, claimed a higher share of TPER in 1985 and 1986 than in prior years (Table 7.1). Reliance upon oil, while narrowing after 1979, remains above 40 percent in western Europe and 55 percent in Japan. US energy import dependence jumped sharply in 1987 to 16 percent, reversing a downward trend initiated in 1978. Table 7.1 suggests no marked improvement in lowering oil's share of American TPER. In 1990, oil imports again exceeded domestic production. Mobil Corporation, an Aramco partner, viewed this as unexceptional. The advocates of nuclear power depicted America as the pathetic hostage of foreign oil producers. Few, save environmental groups, called for policies that would reduce oil (and other fossil fuel) consumption through substitution and efficiency improvements.[8]

Table 9.1 indicates that the leading importers, by 1986, drew from a few suppliers not used in 1973. The western market share of OPEC and the Arab OPEC states contracted, but remained above 50 percent. Western diversification efforts produced no striking changes. Not including the North Sea, French diversification policies added one new supplier, Mexico. Germany, too, drew heavily upon the North Sea and sought oil from Venezuela, its sole new supplier. Italy received 72 percent of its imports from OPEC in 1986, of which 38 percent came from Saudi Arabia and Libya. Japan acted most vigorously to diversify its sources of oil, turning to China, Mexico, and Malaysia. But Japan still purchased 72 percent of its oil from Arab OPEC states. None of the "secure" sources of supply, including the Soviet Union, were capable of significant production on short notice. Moreover, most experts agreed that North Sea and Alaskan fields had already achieved their peak output. Potential new fields in the Gulf of Mexico contained about the volume remaining in the North Sea.[9]

By decade's end, the West fell far short of attaining oil security. Oil remains the leading source of energy. The Middle East contains over one-half of the world's oil, and the cheapest oil at that. Far from advancing its energy security, the West narrowly escaped disaster. At any moment before the truce of 1988, the Iraqi–Iranian war could have engulfed neighboring oil producers. This war demonstrated that regional instability was to be anticipated, that any one nation in the area in a moment of frenzy could swiftly reduce the 7.5 million barrels per day passing through the Persian Gulf to a trickle. One-half of that oil is destined for western Europe and Japan. The West turned an almost absolute dependence upon Arab-OPEC oil in 1973 to acute and dangerous dependence in 1988.

In obtaining oil, consuming nations could not anticipate favorable treatment from the MNOCs, the latter increasingly reduced to serving as oil cans for the producers. By 1986, producing state oil companies sold Japan more than one-half of its supply while the share of the major oil companies—75 percent in 1972—fell to under 40 percent. Japan further limited the power of foreign firms by consolidating a dozen or so firms into seven groups, the better to manage imports, refining capacity, and emergency stockpiling. In the USA, the major oil importing firms were suspected of withholding oil from the domestic market in order to realize higher prices. The swollen profits of the MNOCs convinced many of their culpability in contriving the oil shortages of 1979–80. Opponents of the giant firms demanded anti-trust indictments and

Table 9.1   Sources of crude oil for developed states, 1973 and 1986 (percent)

	1973					1986				
	France	Germany	Italy	Japan	USA	France	Germany	Italy	Japan	USA²
UK and Norway	0	0	0	0	0	25	35	2	0	8
USSR	2	3	5	0	0	8	6	12	0	0
Mexico	0	0	0	0	0	4	0	<1	6	14
Venezuela*	1	2	<1	0	11	0	9	1	0	11
Indonesia*	0	0	0	18	6	0	0	0	12	6
Malaysia*	0	0	0	0	0	0	0	0	4	0
China	0	0	0	0	0	0	0	0	7	2
Canada	0	0	0	0	30	0	0	0	0	14
All OPEC of which:	92	95	89	95	63	59	56	72¹	72	50
Saudi Arabia	22	23	27	19	14	21	11	21	13	13
Iran	8	13	13	33	7	4	3	9	7	2
Iraq	14	2	14	0	0	7	1	6	5	2
Libya	4	24	20	0	4	3	11	17	0	0
UAE	10	5	2	9	2	3	0	2	22	1
Kuwait	11	4	9	8	1	0	0	5	3	1
Algeria	8	13	3	0	4	4	8	4	0	2
Neutral Zone	0	3	0	6	0	0	0	0	6	0
Nigeria	10	9	0	0	14	8	15	6	0	8
Total crude imports (mmt)	135	110	128	245	161	71	66	82	166	249

* OPEC members
¹ Qatar, 5%
² Trinidad, 2%

Sources: OECD, *1973 Oil and Gas Statistics. Supply and Disposal*, Paris: OECD (1973) and *1979* and *1987*. Now entitled *Quarterly Oil and Gas Statistics*.

unsuccessfully sponsored legislation to compel the firms to divest themselves of all but one phase of oil operations and to give up their holdings in other energy resources.[10]

The MNOCS lost further ground in their relationship with the producing states. The trends of the 1970s intensified as the national oil companies of the LDC producers sold a greater share of production directly to clients in crude or refined form. Most dramatically, Iran's convulsions terminated the Iranian Consortium, a heavy blow to BP which lost its 40 percent interest (see Table 8.6). Consumers neither mourned the Consortium's demise nor joined the USA in boycotting Iranian oil in response to the year-long captivity of American hostages in Teheran. Instead, customers flocked to the National Iranian Oil Company, paid the premiums demanded, and with the restoration of production following a temporary halt as war erupted with Iraq, competed heatedly for a share of Iran's much reduced production.[11]

Producing countries in the Middle East and North Africa owned 60 percent of the 1981 output. Mexico and Venezuela owned and marketed 100 percent of their production. The British National Oil Company and Norway's Statoil owned above 50 percent of North Sea production. A thorough update of Table 8.6 was not possible, but the new data available suggests the appreciation of control exercised by the producing countries, despite the privatization of BNOC in 1987. BP and RDS owned a volume of crude production at least equal to product sales. The four Aramco partners—the first four firms listed in Table 8.6—owned only one-half of the crude necessary for their markets, in the 1970s, they had enjoyed rough self-sufficiency. Direct Saudi ownership of crude during the 1980s contributed a large percentage of the crude production lost to Aramco.

As the direct sales of Saudi Arabia's Petromin reached and exceeded 1 billion barrels (some 140 mmt) during the 1980s and as Saudi output declined from 490 mmt in 1980 to about 250 mmt in 1986, the share of the Aramco partners shrank. Aramco drew from the oil remaining after Petromin's take—called residual oil—but was not guaranteed all of that. A portion of the residual crude defined as incentive oil, amounting to as much as 25 mmt, was allocated among the partners in proportion to their direct investments in Saudi refining and industrial projects. Non-Aramco firms could receive incentive oil as well as oil purchased from Petromin. Mobile and Exxon, Aramco partners, RDS, a non-partner, and Celanese, a chemical company, each ventured 50:50 with Petromin to modernize or construct refineries. The Saudis employed incentive oil to force Aramco investment in development projects. By 1987, Aramco could no longer be considered the backbone of Saudi Arabia.[12]

The producing LDCs maintained a high level of investment in refinery and petrochemical operations even as reduced consumption caused refinery overcapacity. Several major oil companies closed their European refineries or sold them to Arab oil firms. The Kuwait Petroleum Corporation marketed refined products in western Europe and Britain. To the consternation of the British, Kuwait became the largest shareholder of BP, owning 22 percent by late 1988. Allowing an OPEC member such a strong voice in BP could not be countenanced. Britain ordered Kuwait to reduce its holdings by more than half. KPC also acquired a large American exploration business and invested in Conoco, Phillips, Schlumberger, and other oil and oil service firms.

In Britain, the Tory government successfully privatized the national oil and gas industries, scheduled the sale of the electric industry in 1990, and planned for the sale of British Coal in 1992. Similar instincts prevailed in the USA and Germany and even captured the Socialist government in France. Conservatism held sway, at least for the moment. Liberal welfare governments, whether actually socialist or not, failed during the 1970s to deal effectively with energy crises, stagflation, and unemployment. Backlash thrust into power such free marketeers as Thatcher and Reagan. What had happened, Prime Minister Thatcher asked, to the billions of pounds of government oil and gas revenues? Had the opportunity been taken to moderate current accounts deficits? Neither Labour nor Tory governments seemed capable of dedicating those windfall revenues to special and productive purposes. Both Thatcher and Reagan made certain that any special costs of denationalization or deregulation would be born by all taxpayers rather than by the industries benefited. Among their other accomplishments were continued national environmental degradation, rising exports of pollutants overseas, and policies that distributed income to the wealthy.

Elsewhere, however, governments and national companies grasped more authority during the early 1980s. The China Petroleum Corporation fed refined oil to Japan where the Japan National Petroleum Corporation closely monitored refined and crude imports. Japan preferred to produce its own gasoline rather than to import cheaper foreign gasoline. Governments the world over whittled away at the discretionary authority of the MNOCs. No longer could the latter claim a monopoly of expertise. Petroleum engineers and geologists from Petroven and Petrobras and oil platform engineers from China and Pemex were in the field hustling business for their countries. The Saudi oil industry gradually became "Saudi-ized" at all levels. Petromin called on South Korea, Japan, and Italy for expertise. Each nation evaluated the role of the MNOCs from the context of its immediate energy, income, psychological, and ideological objectives. Most usurped MNOC functions, often at some cost. Americans preferred to leave them alone, but that was not proof of essentiality.[13]

The diversification of internal energy use

Energy policies and practices in the developed states that emphasized fuel substitution, energy use efficiency, and conservation earned larger energy security dividends than did the search for new oil and gas. Transforming internal energy mixes, however, touched off contentious political debates as numerous interest groups promoted their own versions of appropriate goals and policies. Policy responses to the 1973 crisis assigned the highest priority to energy supply. The crisis of 1978–80 compelled the further elaboration of that principal objective but also stimulated public and private action to reduce TPER and, especially, to lower oil consumption by fuel substitution and conservation. Protecting the environment imposed a new constraint upon and rested in tense juxtaposition to the supply side and substitution elements of energy policies.

Overall results for the western nations can be derived from Table 7.1. TPER declined after 1979. Energy import dependence was somewhat moderated through 1985. The proportion of oil to TPER fell. In Japan and western Europe, natural gas use rose. Nuclear plants generated a higher share of electricity (Table 9.2). Coal's position remained ambiguous, as attested to by Japan's augmented coal use after 1979 and the inability of Britain and Germany to define the role of coal. In its annual report of 1986, the IEA expressed confidence that the energy policies of its members were "well designed" to achieve "lower energy and oil prices, while realizing continued development of indigenous energy resources and improvements in the efficiency of energy use." IEA counseled its members to resist backsliding as oil prices softened.[14]

The domestic energy mix of the industrialized states in 1986 and 1987, while altered in detail since 1973, reflected missed opportunities, minimalist politics, and the power of vested interests. Natural gas and nuclear power were thrust to the fore. In western Europe, the two combined to provide 26 percent of TPER in 1986, compared with 11 percent in 1973; in Japan, the advance was from 2 to 21 percent. Extraordinary controversy enveloped nuclear power, leaving it with a dubious future. Current supplies of natural gas preclude much greater consumption. Since the industrialized countries devoted little attention to renewables, they are left with petroleum and coal. Together, in 1986–7, those fuels provided over 65 percent of TPER in the West (Table 7.1), a diminution since 1973 of insufficient dimensions to take comfort in.[15]

Table 9.2 Aspects of the fuel mix of industrialized states, 1973–87

	USA	Japan	Germany	UK	France	Italy
TPER*						
1973	1742	340	270	231	181	132
1985	1792	372	267	202	194	141
Coal as % TPER						
1973	21	23	32	37	17	8
1985	24	20	32	31	13	12
Industrial fuel use*						
1973	514	158	85	71	61	50
1985	436	128	72	45	49	41
Coal use as % of industrial energy use						
1973	15	23	21	22	20	8
1985	13	28	26	18	19	15
Electric utility fuel use*						
1973	467	103	75	72	42	32
1985	609	149	96	69	77	41
Coal use as % of electric utility TPER						
1973	46	12	67	63	25	5
1985	58	14	57	61	14	6
Nuclear as % of electric generation						
1973	5	2	4	10	8	2
1985	16	24	31	20	65	5
1987	17	26	31	20	70	0

* Million tons oil equivalent

Sources: IEA, *Coal Information 1987*, Paris: OECD/IEA (1987), *passim*; IEA, *Energy Policies and Programmes of IEA Countries. 1987 Review*, Paris: OECD/IEA (1987), *passim*.

Not surprisingly, the IEA, EC, and America's Carter administration called for the doubling of coal use by 1990. World coal production advanced more rapidly between 1973 and 1980 than in subsequent years (Table 7.6). The USA and China mined one-half of the new tonnage. South Africa, India, and Australia also recorded impressive production gains.

Earlier projections of coal consumption for the leading OECD states during the 1980s did not materialize. Neither did the international coal trade expand as rapidly as anticipated. Coal exports from the USA, the leading shipper, rose from 49 mmt in 1977 to 100 mmt in 1981 and then fell to under 80 mmt in 1986. OECD-Europe and Japan provided the largest global markets, taking 136 mmt of the 195 mmt traded in 1975 and 215 mmt of 236 mmt in 1986. Poland shipped coal to western Europe and, with the USSR, met eastern Europe's needs. New markets in Hong Kong, Singapore, South Korea, and Taiwan drew from the USA,

Canada, South Africa, and Australia. The share of steam coal to total coal exports rose from 80 to 85 percent between 1973 and 1986, reflecting a stagnant world steel industry, improved efficiency in coke burning, increased coal use by electric utilities, and the slowdown in nuclear plant additions.

In the industrialized states featured in Table 9.2, the role of coal diminished after 1973 in Japan, Britain, and France, rose in Italy and the USA, and remained unchanged in Germany. French policies discouraged coal use in all but a few basic industries while rapidly substituting nuclear for fossil fuel fired plants. In Britain, Germany, and the USA ambivalence reigned. Each acknowledged the dangerous polluting effects of coal burning, yet each contained a large domestic coal industry, considered a hostile political force by Britain's Conservative government. Each manifest doubts about the wisdom of pursuing the nuclear alternative.

Germany persisted in subsidizing the use of domestic coal, more expensive than imported coal, in the iron and steel and electricity industries. From 1985 through 1987, subsidies protected one-third of production. Britain, like Germany, engaged in the process of phasing out uneconomic collieries, protected its coal industry through coal conversion incentives and long-term contracts between the national coal and electric authorities. Those policies discouraged coal imports. In Germany and Britain, unlike the USA, the governments offered some support to miners affected by mine closures. In addition, Britain's Tory government tentatively scheduled the sale of British Coal in 1992 or 1993. Just how this will be done and its impact on coal costs, of great moment to the soon-to-be privatized electric industry, remains unclear. At the least, one can surmise that privatization will be managed so as to dilute the power of the national miner's union. The latter has received more government attention than the polluting effects of continued large-scale coal burning.[16]

US coal policies under President Carter focused upon converting industries and utilities to coal, raising coal production, launching a monumental program to develop a synthetic fuels industry, and promoting coal exports. President Reagan abandoned the legislative foundations of these initiatives which had yielded meager results. Exports and utility use accounted for 60 to 70 percent of the gain in US production from 1973 to the peak year, 1984. The federal government offered only passive support to exports. Power plants consumed more coal, amounting to about 75 percent of coal production during the years, 1984–6, for reasons that had little to do with federal coal policies. Demand for electricity rose and coal prices per Btu were lower than oil or gas prices. Utility company disenchantment with nuclear power forced them back to the fossil fuels. The objectives of federal coal policies were glaringly at odds with the central goals of environmental legislation.[17]

Recent revelations that irrefutably link fossil fuel burning to fearsome environmental degradation have not retarded fossil fuel use which still provides about 80 percent of the world's energy. Britain has been labeled the "world's worst air polluter" by Friends of the Earth and stands accused by Germany and the Scandinavian states of exporting acid rain to those and other countries. Canada has similarly cited the USA as the source of acid deposition that, as in western Europe, destroys lakes and forests. American and British governments claimed the evidence linking pollution and climate change to be inconclusive. Each refused to formulate programs to reduce emissions of sulfur and nitrogen dioxides from coal fired power plants, ore smelters, and automobiles. However, the Thatcher government in 1987–8 laid the groundwork for a great expansion of nuclear generating capacity. The government justified this expensive program as a sure way to reduce acid rain and the greenhouse effect. Along the way, lowering coal use, however achieved, would also weaken the political power of the militant miners union.[18]

Under the auspices of the United Nations, fifteen European countries, Canada, and the USSR agreed in 1985 to reduce their sulfur dioxide emissions by 30 percent by 1995. Britain, Poland, and the USA declined to sign this treaty. Now, Norway and Sweden aver that a 60 or even 80 percent reduction is imperative to protect their environments. Germany, in 1984 and 1986, mandated stringent controls that promise to diminish the sulfur dioxide emissions of 1982 by two-thirds. However, Germany continues to subsidize coal burning in power plants.[19]

After four years of negotiations with Canada, the Reagan administration refused to engage in more than a dilatory research program. In 1986, a US Department of Energy spokesperson insisted that the USA pursued "reasonable measures for dealing with acid rain at this time."[20] Only in 1987 did Reagan agree to freeze nitrogen dioxide emissions at current levels. In Congress, efforts to control acid rain were stonewalled by members from polluting and coal mining states. Reagan's insensitivity to environmental degradation was reflected in his indifference to the warning voices of scientists about the warming of the atmosphere, the so-called greenhouse effect, expressed most forcefully by Dr James Hansen in June 1988. Hansen told a US Senate committee that greenhouse warming was not a threat but a reality. The US Department of the Interior acceded to energy industry demands by greatly increasing oil and gas leasing in fragile or hitherto protected areas. In

1987 and 1988, oil interests and the Reagan administration staunchly opposed a bill that would prevent drilling in the Arctic National Wildlife Reserve, on the Beaufort Sea in northeastern Alaska.[21]

The advent of the Bush administration has not produced a marked change in government policy. Attitudes, though, have been slightly modified. While the administration admits the need for an international agreement to resist global warming, it refuses to implement domestically the reduction of CO_2 emissions agreed to internationally. Presidential calls for clean air and water are hollow, unsupported by federal action to reduce fossil fuel use or to improve its efficiency. Prime Minister Thatcher seems more aware of the urgency of the matter than President Bush. In an impressive display of knowledge and analytic ability, Prime Minister Thatcher, in summer 1989, led a seminar on the relationship between energy policy and global warming. Perhaps, in 1990, the OECD states will unite on an enforceable policy to protect the ozone layer, reduce the emission of noxious chemicals, and deal with deforestation. In all of this, it is unfortunate that two of the largest polluters, the USA and the UK, must be dragged along reluctantly by other nations.

What action most be taken to reduce significantly the accumulation of pollutants on the land, in the sea, and in the air? Voluntarism is only marginally effective. On occasion, grass-roots organizations can stop pollution. Opposing coercive measures on the grounds of laissez-faire or individual freedom is the defense of the worst polluters, individuals, in their cars and in their creation of other wastes, ranking high among them. Doing next to nothing, apparently the preferred position of most nations, is life-threatening. The cost of reducing environmental pollution to levels that the earth can absorb will be enormous. But the annual costs of pollution are already horrendous and rising. Forest damage from acid rain in western Europe was reckoned at 22 percent of the total forest area as of 1986. Germany estimates pollution costs of $51 billion yearly, or 8.3 percent of GNP. The annual bill for soil erosion and water pollution in the USA is calculated at $26 billion.

Nations will not, generally, act alone to battle environmental threats that are transnational in cause and effect. They correctly point to the ineffectiveness of unilateral action. Any increment to production costs, they argue, would weaken their competitiveness. That leaves cooperative action with the costs prorated according to the quantity of pollution exported. Unless the industrialized states assume the burden of financing a global assault on pollution — the USA, Europe, and the Soviet bloc are responsible for two-thirds of global emissions from fossil fuels — the quality of the environment will continue to deteriorate.

334 The Iranian Revolution and its aftermath

Egocentric nationalism in the USA, Britain, the Soviet bloc, China, Japan, and Brazil, and a regiment of other states stands as the great deterrent to a cleaner world.[22]

The many disadvantages attending augmented consumption of coal, nuclear power, and imported oil prompted western Europe to utilize an expanding volume of North Sea, Dutch, and Soviet natural gas after 1973 (see Chapter 7). The share of TPER filled by natural gas grew rapidly in OECD-Europe and, in the form of LNG, in Japan. In the USA, where natural gas was in widespread use before 1973, gas price deregulation by Presidents Carter and Reagan did not reverse the decline in proven reserves. Since 1985, nothing has occurred to improve the limited capacity of natural gas to further reduce coal and oil use. In 1988, analysts of the US gas industry predicted a bright future for the fuel, pointing to accelerated residential use and, stimulated by the repeal in 1987 of the Fuel Use Act of 1978, the shift to gas by such industries as glass and chemicals. Besides ignoring the low quality use of a high quality fuel, these analyses focused on the next year or two and neglected to account for the steady shrinkage of US reserves, in 1987 down 7 percent from 1982 (Table 7.1). With gas consumption outrunning additions to reserves, a run of severe winters could raise demand above the delivery capacity of the pipeline companies. The industry, of course, would not utter a word of caution.

In Germany, France, and Italy, large importers of natural gas, the volume of gas burned and its share of TPER have plateaued since 1985. Those governments have sought contracts with their suppliers, the Netherlands, Norway, and Russia for Germany and France, and Algeria, Holland, and Russia for Italy, that sustain current levels of consumption. Japanese imports of LNG leveled off after 1985. Japan plans to increase LNG use. To further reduce dependence upon imported oil which is cheaper than LNG, the Japanese are investing heavily in the development of gas production and liquefaction facilities in Australia. Indonesia, and Malaysia.[23]

Coal and gas proffer but limited possibilities for dampening reliance upon imported oil. Gas, clean and efficient, exists in insufficient volume to broaden its use in western Europe or the USA. At this moment, the polluting qualities of coal negate the advantages of abundance. However, an energy crisis or a steady, guided series of oil price increases and OPEC-induced tightness of supply, predicted by some authorities for the 1990s, could trigger a coal binge.[24] A similar scenario could resurrect a presently debilitated nuclear power industry despite its costliness, inefficiencies, and clear dangers.

The energy crisis of 1979 did not revive the moribund nuclear industry in the USA. In western Europe, the intense opposition of organized environmentalists and others, a decline in the growth of electricity consumption, and the ever increasing costs of nuclear construction obstructed the addition of planned installations. France, with the most ambitious nuclear program in the world, forged ahead, bringing four new stations on line in 1987. But, the 1986 accident at Chernobyl convinced several European countries to cease new construction, close plants, and, effectively, to reject the nuclear option. The fearsome uncertainties unveiled at Chernobyl also constrained nuclear growth in the Soviet Union and in such densely populated and industrializing LDCs as South Korea and Taiwan.

Japan intends to double current nuclear capacity by 1995.[25] Britain and Germany plan fewer facilities than originally projected. For most of the OECD states, however, the contribution of nuclear power to electric production (see Table 9.2) has about peaked. Italy, in 1986, drew 5 percent of its power from three nuclear plants; in 1987, all three plants were closed. Austria abandoned its only plant. Nuclear generation will also recede in Belgium, Finland, Scandinavia, Switzerland, and the USA as older plants are retired and fewer new plants, or none at all, come on line. Britain plans to construct at least four nuclear plants, but this assumes the continued electoral success of the Conservatives. Current public opposition to new construction runs at over 50 percent in France and over 60 percent in several other OECD states.[26]

The nuclear moratorium in the USA severely damaged the technological competitiveness of American nuclear suppliers. General Electric, for example, confines its nuclear activities to servicing existing plants and is not a leader in developing advanced reactors. Indeed, America's electrical equipment manufacturers are also losing out to foreign suppliers. Foreign firms are buying American firms. Domestic power plants increasingly import heavy equipment. In 1988, no American companies produced extra-high voltage circuit breakers. Both GE and Westinghouse market Japanese breakers. A similar erosion of American technological leadership is apparent in other industries, as well.

While President Bush asserted the need for nuclear power, his constituents, in a Fall 1989 poll rejected new construction. Even more telling, voters in Sacramento, California, decided to close an operating nuclear plant because of its excessive cost and inefficiency. Construction and operating costs make nuclear power twice as costly as conventional coal plants. But more than costs are involved. Public opinion, in America or Italy, will only support the technology if industry and government can unequivocally demonstrate their ability to guarantee plant safety and to dispose of nuclear wastes safely. Public relations campaigns orchestrated by nuclear advocates blamed Chernobyl on human error rather than flawed technology, touted nuclear power as the only immediately viable substitute for imported energy, and heralded it as the answer to acid rain and global warming. Even if hopes materialize for a new generation of less dangerous reactors, a highly improbable accomplishment for the US industry, there remains the ever-present difficulty of waste disposal. Thus far, these appeals and promises have not altered the minds of those who distrust and fear the technology.[27]

When Italy shut down its nuclear plants in 1987, the government revealed plans to increase natural gas imports from the Soviets and North Africa. Coal imports were ascending prior to Chernobyl. Ominously absent from Italy's response was a renewed commitment to the conservation provisions of the 1981 National Energy Plan and the conservation law adopted in 1982. Indeed, softening energy prices in 1985–6 so obscured any recognition of conservation's benefits that a revision of the plan in 1986 assigned much lower priority to the development of renewable energy.[28]

Remissness in exploiting the potential energy savings of conservation characterized the energy policies of the industrialized states following the crisis of 1973–4. Falling Iranian exports and the ratcheting of prices in 1979–80 forced attention, for a time, to conservation. Some progress followed. Table 7.1 documents the decline in TPER between 1979 and 1985 while Table 7.8 demonstrates improved energy use efficiency. These coordinate trends, however, were as much the consequence of world recession and slower economic growth as of specific conservation measures.[29] Moreover, actual energy savings as of 1985, measured against consumption in 1973, were not evenly distributed among all domestic uses.

Table 9.3 denotes industry as the source for virtually all of the energy savings in each country. The table depicts a chronological pattern: the most pronounced savings occurred between 1979 and 1984 after which TPER (Table 7.1) again rose and energy use in industry ceased its downward slide. The transportation sector proved most resistant to conservation.

OECD economies stagnated from 1979 into 1983. The price of crude oil in 1981 exceeded that of 1973 by ten times and the annual growth of OECD GDP fell from 3.9 percent in 1978 to 0.3 percent in 1982. Slumping sales of metals and fabricated goods, an enormous rise in the energy costs of heavy industry, and intense competition for markets induced industries to pare energy costs. Closing obsolete plants and introducing newer production technologies, as in the US aluminum, copper, steel, and chemical industries, improved productivity and energy efficiency. Soaring electricity costs stimulated the aluminum industry to introduce energy saving procedures that improved energy efficiency by over 20 percent between 1975 and 1985, with three-

Table 9.3 Total final energy consumption of developed states, by economic sector, 1973–85 (million tons oil equivalent)*

	Industry	Transport	Other
UK			
1973	71	31	51
1979	61	34	58
1984	44	36	54
1985	45	37	58
Germany			
1973	85	34	79
1979	85	41	87
1984	73	43	77
1985	72	43	81
France			
1973	87	na	77[1]
1979	81	na	77
1984	69	na	69
1985	70	na	72
Italy			
1973	50	20	32
1979	49	26	35
1984	42	27	36
1985	41	28	36
Japan			
1973	158	41	52
1979	146	54	61
1984	129	57	66
1985	128	58	65
USA			
1973	514	411	497
1979	523	447	418
1984	448	442	402
1985	436	445	400

* Total final consumption = TPER − net losses in production and use
[1] All other

Sources: IEA, *Energy Policies and Programmes of IEA Countries. 1986 Review*, Paris: OECD/IEA (1987), *passim*, and *Coal Information 1987* (1987), p. 350.

quarters of the gain occurring after 1979. With a fuel bill of $475 million in 1979, Du Pont introduced an energy savings regimen consisting of conservation, often requiring new equipment, and fuel substitution, including cogeneration. German and Japanese industries responded to similar imperatives and won similar results. Germany and Japan applied a set of conservation rules and inducements to industry, including grants and loans for improvements in energy efficiency. American industries received few direct financial incentives to conserve. Indeed, just as energy prices began to slide, signals from the Reagan administration suggested the unimportance of conservation.

Between 1975 and 1980, the USA enacted a number of conservation laws, subsequently ignored or repealed by President Reagan, the most important being the Energy Policy and Conservation Act of 1975. In addition to setting energy efficiency standards for new buildings, this law imposed gasoline mileage standards for new autos. By 1985, fuel efficiency had improved from 13 miles per gallon (mpg) in 1973 to 25 mpg, lower by 2 mpg than the goal stipulated in the legislation, and far below western European or Japanese achievements. The Reagan administration, however, eased the standards for the car makers so that no improvement in the USA above the 1985 figure is likely during the 1990s. Unfortunately, cheaper oil since 1983 has drawn consumers away from fuel efficient cars, an inclination fostered by the world's auto-makers. Reagan's refusal (unreversed by his successor) to sanction higher, and readily achievable gasoline mileage standards coincided in time with the rise in the share of American petroleum consumption attributable to transportation to almost two-thirds between 1979 and 1987. In 1987, the USA contributed 22 percent of the world's carbon emissions from fossil fuels, an increase of 55 percent since 1960. Private autos alone are thought to contribute something over 30 percent of US carbon emissions.[30]

In the western industrialized countries, industrial conservation, re-cording savings of 10 to 20 percent between 1973 and 1980 and equi-valent savings from 1979 through 1984, far exceeded savings in other use sectors. Industrial savings were permanent gains and complimented by the somewhat improved energy efficiency of household appliances and new residential and commercial buildings. But transportation as a whole did not improve (Table 9.3). Governments preferred not to challenge the myopic preference of consumers for larger and less ef-ficient vehicles. To an extent, the force of Japan's energy savings were dissipated by inefficiency in transportation and agriculture. Japan re-mained heavily dependent upon imported oil, costing above $35 billion annually and exceeded only by the $46 billion US bill (1988). Two-thirds of Japan's oil originated in the Persian Gulf and met over one-half of TPER (Table 7.1). Energy security remained an elusive goal for Japan.[31]

The illusion of security

Softening oil prices between 1983 and 1985 and the sudden plunge of prices in 1986 blunted the conservationist trend in the industrialized states as well as the incentive to search for new energy supplies. Opti-mists gleaned comfort from the fall in TPER after 1979, the marked reduction in oil import bills (Table 7.9), the diversification of internal energy mixes, and the improvement in energy use efficiency. These positive signs, coupled with global oil reserves sufficient for 30 years and the mid-1988 truce between Iran and Iraq, dissipated fears of a third oil shock. Pessimists, however, considered this security illusory. Was the Middle East more stable in 1990 than earlier? Had the West won the battle to contain oil imports? Were the largest consumers significantly less dependent upon fossil fuels in 1990 than in 1973?[32]

Sufficient fossil fuel reserves exist to meet demand into the twenty-first century. But can the global environment survive the burning of coal and oil at current, and probably rising, rates for such a prolonged period? Western governments directed woefully inadequate attention to this most critical issue. While recognizing the savings possible by conservation, they clung to the primary goal of securing supply against a future disruption. To prepare for such an eventuality is imperative. The surest method of diminishing the likelihood or the impact of a new price-supply squeeze is not to stockpile some months supply of crude or to cast covetous eyes on the Arctic Circle, but to consume significantly less oil without turning to coal or nuclear power. Conservation, including the development of renewables, promises to contain the use of fossil fuels within safe limits without damaging economic efficiency. Britain's government proclaimed that the nation's annual energy bill of $38 billion could be reduced 25 percent through greater end use efficiency.[33] However, an expansive view of conservation, encompassing its geo-political, economic, and environmental impacts, appealed less to governments than adding to the supply of fossil fuels and, somehow, breathing new life into nuclear power.

Energy in the Soviet bloc during the 1980s

Within the Soviet bloc during the 1980s, overall energy supply and demand experienced no marked change from the trends sketched in Chapter 8. A decline in Soviet oil production after 1980 was apparently reversed by late 1986 while serious difficulties impeded the substantial increase of coal output (Table 7.6). The tragic Chernobyl reactor explosion of April 26, 1986 tarnished Russia's reputation in the West, nurtured anti-nuclear attitudes around the world, and defeated Soviet plans to supply at least 20 percent of Russian and bloc electric needs with nuclear power by 1990. Natural gas provided the bright spot in energy development: planned output for 1985 sought 630 billion cubic meters (bcm), actual production reached 643 bcm and, in 1986, 686 bcm.

Russia exacted immediate economic benefits from the price hikes and supply fears accompanying revolution in Iran. Although the volume of Soviet oil exports to the West exceeded exports in 1978 by only 5 percent, hard currency earnings rose by 2.5 times, reaching $14 billion. Natural gas earnings more than tripled to $3.7 billion, carrying the contribution of energy exports to total hard currency earnings in 1982 to 80 percent, compared with 54 percent in 1978. Arms sales boomed and the cost of Russia's largest import, grain, fell sharply. Believing, as did most western governments, that high oil prices and tight supplies would persist, Russia invested heavily in oil exploration in an effort to lift production to levels permitting greater exports to western Europe. Concurrently, the Soviets initiated an enormous natural gas pipeline program that would sharply accelerate production and shipments to the West. Ambitious economic modernization plans rested on the rapid advance of nuclear power and on augmented receipts of western money and technology.

Concomitantly, the Soviet Union, desirous of freeing oil for sale to the West and providing a market for Soviet nuclear technology, exerted pressure on CMEA–6 states to develop an energy regimen based on gas and nuclear power. To secure gas and oil imports required bloc commitments to Russia of foodstuffs and of capital, equipment, and labor to joint venture nuclear construction. Eastern European energy requirements, however, prohibited the achievement of phased cutbacks in Russian oil exports. Even before Chernobyl, nuclear expansion proceeded at a snail's pace, a victim of high costs and manufacturing deficiencies.[34]

Faced in 1981 with mounting oil import bills as Soviet prices rose by 10 times over 1976 prices, the German Democratic Republic exploited its large lignite reserves to raise coal production (Table 7.6). Thus, GDR avoided the intense energy dependence upon Russia that plagued other, less well endowed bloc states. In 1986, GDR relied on coal for 72 percent of TPER and suffered from intolerably high levels of pollution.[35] West German and UN sources estimate that nearly 30 percent of East Germany's forests have been destroyed by acid rain, a proportion similar to Poland's. Poland's internal instability obstructed gains in coal output while western European imports diminished. French imports of Polish steam coal declined from 3.5 mmt in 1979 to 280,000 mt in 1980 — a consequence of Solidarity action — rose to 1.9 mmt in 1983 and plunged again in 1985 to 883,000 mt. In 1986, Polish coal exports to the West equaled 57 percent of 1984 shipments.

Poland's foreign indebtedness and current accounts deficits, inflation of 60 percent, deep-seated labor unrest, smoldering consumer and political discontent, and the tantalizing vision of *glasnost* and *peristroika* gradually eroded the credibility of a regime that had demonstrated singular ineptness in managing the economy. In Fall 1989, the ruling

Communist government was repudiated in an exciting general election. An ex-Solidarity leader became Polish premier. Poland's economy, however, requires immediate treatment. The USA and its western allies must be generous with grants and credits that avoid fostering further environmental damage.

Soviet intentions to reduce oil exports to its allies proved impossible to accomplish. To avoid the further deterioration of weak CMEA–6 economies required Russia to sustain its annual exports at about 80 mmt from 1981 through 1986. That volume composed some 90 percent of CMEA–6 imports and 75 percent of total oil demand. Gas imports, all from Russia, rose from 29 bcm in 1981 to 38 bcm in 1986. None of this energy was obtained at bargain prices.

A dependent–subordinate linkage — apparently as intense in 1988 as in 1973 — defined the relationship between CMEA–6 and Russia. Soviet greed and Romanian irrationality combined to deny the latter the fruits of its oil, coal, and gas resources. Each winter, Bucharest and other areas suffer prolonged electricity and gas shortages. The West, too, shares culpability. Western creditors provided the late Ceausescu's regime a $10 billion loan which was used most foolishly. Canada sold nuclear plants to Romania on extended credits despite the gross inefficiency of the electric distribution system. To repay these debts, Ceausescu ordered the export of everything not bolted down. Romanians faced a regressing standard of living: food remains in very short supply and malnutrition is widespread. Heavy dependence upon coal constrains East German industrial efficiency and pollutes at home and abroad. Imports, largely from Russia, satisfy one-half of domestic energy consumption in Hungary which, along with Czechoslovakia, is concerned that nuclear power will not meet incremental electric demand during the 1990s. Unless accompanied by sweeping modifications, economic improvement resting on a more diversified internal energy mix will not be easily achieved in eastern Europe.[36]

Russia reaped a bountiful harvest in oil and gas sales between 1980 and 1982 but now confronts depleted hard currency earnings. Sales realizations from those fuels dropped from $16 billion in 1982 to under $7 billion in 1986, reflecting not only lower prices but also reduced western European oil imports (Table 7.5). Oil production fell while internal energy use advanced (Table 7.1). Should the decline in hard currency earnings persist over a prolonged period, economic modernization will be retarded, the more so unless substantial gains in cereal production are achieved. To speed up new oil discoveries through the application of state-of-the-art technologies, the Soviets are now contemplating joint ventures with foreign partners, a prospect that has attracted the interest of several large western firms.[37]

Great success rewarded the USSR's campaign to increase gas exports from its supergiant Yamburg–Urengoi field, located north of the Arctic Circle, via a 3,500 mile pipeline through the heart of European Russia to Prague and connections with western Europe. Initially conceived in 1978, the scheme quickly won the approbation of western European banking and industrial interests and their governments. The new line would carry an additional 40 bcm to Germany, Italy, France, and four other European countries by the late 1980s, compared with annual receipts of 25 to 27 bcm between 1978 and 1981. Russian gas, by 1990, would furnish some 20 to 25 percent of western Europe's gas requirements, thus lessening reliance upon Middle Eastern oil.

The proposal appealed to Europeans for several reasons. The Soviets offered gas at prices below North Sea and Dutch gas. Bankers in Britain, the Netherlands, France, Germany, Italy, and Japan extended loans covering virtually the whole cost of construction. In return, Russia purchased necessary equipment and pipeline valued above $15 billion from the creditor countries. Sales of turbines, computerized measuring equipment, heavy construction vehicles, and large diameter pipeline guaranteed thousands of jobs at Germany's A.E.F.-Telefunken, Britain's John Brown Engineering, France's Creusot-Loire, and Japan's Komatsu.

The Carter administration evinced no enthusiasm for the Soviet–European gas deal. In the name of human rights, Carter backed away from the less restrictive trade policies of his predecessors even before Russia's invasion of Afghanistan impelled him to suspend trade with the USSR. Unable to compete for Soviet orders, Caterpillar Tractor, GE, and other American firms lost millions of dollars in sales.

As presidential candidate, Ronald Reagan explicitly condemned the pipeline contracts. In July 1981, President Reagan embargoed the shipment of pipeline to Russia and extended the sanctions to the foreign subsidiaries and licensees of American firms in July 1982. Reagan's pipeline politics derived from unswerving hostility toward the USSR and from ill-founded assumptions that posited a direct link between the gas contracts and Soviet geopolitics. America's ideological response momentarily fractured the western alliance. Europe rebelled against the presumptuous American campaign to compel adherence to ideologically rooted policies and America's refusal to recognize Europe's economic and energy interests. France and other western European states prepared to ignore the sanctions and to retaliate if Reagan persisted along this course. He did not; in November 1982, the sanctions were abrogated.[38]

Scores of Japanese earth movers prepared the Siberian turf for the laying of German pipe while the USA pursued its futile policy. As it transpired, softening oil prices after 1983 and a stabilized rate of gas consumption led customers to lower their take from Russia. Moreover, the Netherlands and Norway, in 1985–6, offered gas at competitive rates which Germany and Austria accepted, thus reducing requirements from the USSR.[39]

The Soviets in 1987 and 1988 apparently reversed the downward slide in oil production. They cannot, however, anticipate augmented hard currency earnings from energy exports. Modernization, if it survives in the Soviet political arena, must proceed through the wise utilization of internal resources. Energy supplies should not pose severe problems. Indeed, energy pales to insignificance when compared with the unknowns faced by the Soviet Union as long suffering populations in eastern Europe abandon communism and initiate the task of shaping new political and economic structures.

Revelations in Moscow, in 1989 and early 1990, admitted to the feeble condition of the economy. The radically changed and changing relationships between the USSR and eastern Europe will undoubtedly compel the Soviets and eastern Europe to renegotiate their economic relationship. CMEA may not survive. In the USSR, plans for energy modernization will be affected by the particular decisions of former satellites. It seems unlikely that Moscow will subsidize oil shipments to CMEA–6. Eastern Europeans are unlikely to continue money or labor investments in giant Soviet nuclear and pipeline projects. In the near future, East Germany will merge with West Germany. While nervous Poles may likely continue for a time as members of the Warsaw Pact, their country, alone with Hungary and Czechoslovakia, will look to the West for aid. Western expertise and funds might be productively engaged in restoring Romania's oil industry. Poland desires to revitalize its coal industry. While eastern European peoples look forward to a time of greater material satisfaction, their economics are already among the world's greatest polluters. Like other advanced LDCs, demands for a higher standard of living will confront ecological imperatives.

The energy importing LDCs after the Iranian Revolution

Tanzania's external debt soared after 1973 and again after 1979, reaching $2.6 billion in 1984, three times the level of 1975 and equaling 68 percent of GNP. Simultaneously, high birth rates and declining death rates yielded an average annual population increase of 3.6 percent while food output *per capita* fell. Brazil's economic woes were of a different order of magnitude: a foreign debt of $69 billion in 1984, almost five times greater than in 1975; energy imports worth more than one-half of all exports (Table 8.4); population growth and rural poverty that generated a tidal wave of migration to unprepared cities (Tables 8.1 and 8.2); and a regressive agricultural sector.[40] The immediate future promised but slight amelioration of the dire poverty in which most Tanzanians and Brazilians lived.

The Iranian price hikes exacerbated the economic woes of many oil importing LDCs. Dozens of poor countries relied upon imported oil as their primary, or only, commercial fuel. Modernization demanded oil, but the exorbitant prices of 1978–81 compelled the slashing of imports. In Jamaica, Costa Rica, Sri Lanka, and the Philippines, the added burden forced postponement of road and other infrastructure construction, triggered rising unemployment, and encouraged efforts to increase food and raw materials exports. But the export value of raw commodities remained far below the cost of imported oil. In 1980, seven bushels of wheat purchased a barrel of oil that in 1973 cost less than a bushel.

The slackening of oil prices after 1983 afforded only temporary respite for such LDCs as Tanzania, Brazil, and India. Oil import bills declined, but the earning power of those nations improved only marginally. The total debt of Latin America, not including Venezuela and Mexico, reached $218 billion in 1985, 63 percent held by western banks. Schemes to avoid debt repudiation offered by western governments, the World Bank, and IMF uniformly called for fewer but more precisely dedicated loans, longer payment periods, lower interest rates, and a primary reliance upon internal capital formation. All of this sounded reasonable to a western ear. But who in Tanzania has such savings to be mobilized? Will the incredibly rich few in Brazil or Mexico voluntarily unlock their wealth for public purposes? In return for international aid, the debtor countries would introduce austerity programs, cut budget deficits, reduce inflation, and increase the role of the private sector at the expense of state owned companies. Inherent in these nostrums were political dangers for shaky LDC governments. The burden of service cuts and new unemployment caused by austerity and anti-inflationary recipes always falls most harshly on the underemployed and working poor and on the lower middle class. Those calling for retrenchment almost never feel any of its effects.

Few miracles occurred during the 1970s and 1980s to relieve the chronic poverty of the poor oil importing LDCs. A handful of LDCs — Taiwan, South Korea, Singapore, the colony of Hong Kong, each heavily dependent upon energy imports, fought their way out of the permanent poverty that afflicted all too many LDCs. Led by the manufacturing sector and exports, both protected by government policies, those Southeast Asian societies achieved impressive economic growth. Most other LDCs suffered from firmly embedded disabilities. Demand for their goods — Kenyan coffee, Sri Lankan rubber — shrank as did the prices received. Development faltered as the costs of imported modernization exceeded the ability of commodity exports to meet the bills.

The poor LDCs lacked the flexibility to respond to economic fluctuation. Although dozens of states, from the Congo to the Philippines, hired foreign developers to hunt for oil, few were so fortunate as Malaysia. Most, like Thailand, contained marginal reserves of limited attractiveness during a time of surplus.[41]

Several LDCs sought World Bank and other loans during the 1970s to initiate vast electrification programs, intending to create a strong nuclear component. The productive capacity of the nuclear industry in America and western Europe far surpassed demand. Whole markets disappeared under the fallout from Chernobyl. Framatome, Westinghouse, Kraftwerk Union, and a few other firms scoured the globe in search of business. The LDCs seemed to present sales possibilities but these proved mostly chimerical.

For most LDCs, nuclear power is not an option. A plant costing from $2 to $5 billion, requiring highly trained personnel and an efficient distribution system, is beyond their reach. In Africa, a nuclear plant costing $3 billion equaled at least one-half of the 1985 GNP of 39 of 45 countries. In Central and South America, the GNP of 16 of 24 states fell under $10 billion. Asian countries such as Pakistan and the Philippines, with GNPs above $30 billion, are mired in poverty. Potential purchasers were few. Eastern Europe, with seventeen plants and forty-seven in process in 1985, was the world's largest regional market. With the emergence of independent eastern European states, the market for nuclear plants might open up to western firms and nations willing to offer substantial credits.

Several of the LDCs decided that nuclear power made little sense. The increasing availability of gas and the cheapness of coal prompted Mexico to construct one rather than two plants and to plan no others. Venezuela never seriously considered a nuclear program. Iran, in 1980, abandoned the whole of the Shah's ambitious nuclear policy. Brazil, encumbered with a gigantic debt, reduced its nuclear program from eight reactors to two, and then suspended work on both. The primary contractor, Kraftwerk Union, lost billions of dollars in sales. Brazil's decision rested on several salient considerations: the high cost of borrowing money, unanswered questions concerning safety and waste disposal, reasonable doubts about the economic benefits of nuclear power and domestic hydroelectric potential.[42]

A primitive infrastructure and poverty precluded the emergence of a large nuclear component in such states as Pakistan and the Philippines. The paucity of energy resources, and in Pakistan's case, the desire to develop nuclear weapons, pushed them initially to embrace that option. Even India and China, both owning nuclear weapons, can marshal but limited funds to develop nuclear energy. Within India, an articulate opposition to nuclear power questioned its relevance to the enormous mass of poor rural people. The fall of the oppressive Marcos regime in the Philippines and revelations of corruption in the awarding of nuclear contracts to US firms caused the termination of work on the reactor under construction. Moreover, Filipinos voiced cogent objections to the intensified dependency upon the USA that would accompany nuclear power. China, after exciting western hopes of a vast nuclear market, turned instead to coal and hydroelectric. In the Chinese view, smaller scale hydro and coal units better fit the needs of its farming masses than giant facilities.

China well reflects the dilemma facing many LDCs. Rejecting nuclear power made sense; turning to coal, while the only substitute available, will severely retard global efforts to slow the warming of the atmosphere. In 1987, China ranked third in carbon emissions, fixing a greater tonnage in the atmosphere than West Germany, Britain, and Italy combined. These emissions will sharply increase as new coal fired electric plants are constructed. Meanwhile, already a food poor nation, air pollutants destroy a rising tonnage of grain.

Successful nuclear programs emerged in South Korea and Taiwan, both highly dependent on energy imports, which benefited US firms. However, they are small nations. South Korea's intention to derive 65 percent of its electricity from nuclear by 2000 — the nuclear contribution in 1984 reached 20 percent — will almost be achieved with the commissioning of seven reactors currently under construction.[43]

India, Pakistan, and Argentina, non-signatories to the 1968 Treaty on the Non-Proliferation of Nuclear Weapons (NPT), pursued the nuclear option most aggressively. India's explosion of a nuclear device in 1974 highlighted the essential weaknesses of the treaty. The USA, in 1978, responded forcefully, if not successfully, by adopting strict non-proliferation legislation that denied American nuclear fuel and technologies to non-signers of NPT. The USA also objected strenuously to the involvement of western European firms, especially German, in the nuclear projects of Brazil, a non-signer, and Argentina. President Carter's aims were easily circumvented. With the help of Canada, Germany, and Switzerland, Argentina mastered the entire nuclear fuel cycle by 1980.

President Reagan abandoned most controls over the export of nuclear fuel and plants. By the early 1980s, America's monopoly of re-processed fuel had been breached and its technology surpassed by France and Japan. America acted inconsistently, aiding Pakistan, a NPT non-signer, while convincing Belgium in 1984 to forgo a nuclear contract with Libya, America's *bête noire* but a NPT signatory. The NPT and American policies hardly affected the spread of nuclear technologies. Mandated inspections by the International Atomic Energy Agency cover but a portion of the nuclear plants within NPT nations, rarely monitoring facilities in the USA, UK, France, Russia, or China. India and China possess weapons capabilities; South Africa, Israel, Pakistan, Brazil, and Argentina may also. Whatever the weapons potential of these NPT non-signers, their decisions to proceed more slowly, if at all, with nuclear energy derived from the evaluation of more germane, non-military factors.[11]

The market potential of the LDCs for nuclear plants fades away under analysis. Most of those states cast aside their nuclear fantasies. Fossil fuels will meet the inevitable expansion of their energy needs. Some — Argentina, China, Malaysia — possess sufficient reserves to fill domestic requirements and even sell oil abroad. Others must rely upon imports. A variety of energy use initiatives such as small scale and locally managed hydro facilities, demonstration projects involving renewable energy, and a less obsessive desire for automobiles promise future benefits.

Criticism of Brazil's giant hydroelectric projects from both internal and external sources have caused a reassessment of power needs. Plans for dozens of new dams in the Amazon basin which would destroy a vast area of rain forest within which indigenous tribes live have been obstructed by the refusal of the World Bank to approve necessary start up loans. Instead, the Brazilian government and Brazilian utilities, with Bank aid, will dedicate $8 billion to transmission and end use efficiency improvements which should eliminate the need for much new generating capacity while saving 1,200 square miles from flooding. Brazil faces pressure from many quarters to adopt strong environmental policies. Developed states have a stake in Brazil's responses. This stake should translate into financial and technological aid to Brazil. Concurrently, Brazil needs to reciprocate by directing, as an example, investments away from the hydro–mining–ranching ventures that benefit the few while doing unalterable damage.[45]

A more realistic assessment by LDCs of domestic finances and energy requirements erects a natural defense against the promotion of large scale technologies by western vendors. However, the Brazilian and similar hopeful initiatives will wither unless population growth subsides.

Price fluctuations and the oil exporters during the 1980s

The average price of crude shot upward from about $17.50 per barrel in January 1979 to a peak of $42 in the last half of 1980, provoking a contraction in the global volume of oil traded of 3.4 million barrels per day, or 10 percent, from 1979 to 1980. The enormity of the price increase generated equally enormous earnings for the exporters (Table 8.5). A moderate, but steady, diminution of prices to the $32–$34 range occurred during 1982–3 as recession and conservation abated demand in the USA, western Europe, and Japan (Tables 7.2 and 7.5). In 1983, global oil shipments of 24.3 mbd fell short of the 1980 volume by 7.5 mbd.

Reasonably stable prices prevailed between 1983 and mid-1985. Although the rate of decline of western oil imports moderated, oil from non-Middle Eastern sources filled a rising proportion of western oil requirements. Then, in mid-1985, oil prices slipped more precipitously than they had risen in 1979–80, plunging to about $10 in early 1986. The development plans of the LDC exporters, already shaken by the earlier slackness in price and demand, were deranged by plummeting oil revenues. The damage sustained by the exporters, unrepaired by a price recovery to the $18–$20 range in 1987, were further aggravated by prices sliding toward $13 in September 1988. By early 1989, OPEC had adopted a viable quota system; prices rose again to $20.[46]

Estimates of the oil revenues of the LDC exporters differ from source to source. Pachauri's calculation of $288 billion for OPEC in 1981 exceeds the IMF figure by $48 billion.[47] This abbreviated discussion of OPEC revenues employs estimates derived from the latter. OPEC's revenues of $176 billion in 1979 rose to $250 billion in 1980. With the exception of Iran, each member gained income, but Saudi Arabia's increment of $42 billion equaled 57 percent of the total revenue increase. Only Saudi Arabia, and perhaps Kuwait, accumulated significant cash reserves. Total revenues slid in 1981 to $240 billion, a decline of only 4 percent. The gain by Saudi Arabia of $12 billion and of Indonesia of $6 billion masked larger percentage losses for wartime Iraq (−60 percent), Kuwait (−20 percent), Libya (−27 percent), Nigeria (−19 percent), and Venezuela (−18 percent). Substantial revenue slippage occurred in 1982 and 1983 among all OPEC states except Iran which steadily improved its sales despite the war. By 1983, OPEC's earnings had fallen to some $156 billion, still larger than 1978 but well below the bonanza years of 1979–82. Among the leading non-OPEC exporters, the oil revenues of Mexico, Norway, Britain, and Russia reached flood tide during the latter years.[48]

The elixir of windfall revenues aroused a renewed commitment to development among exporting LDCs, intoxicated by high prices that seemed durable. But the morning after the great binge arrived in 1983. Nine of OPEC's members, including Iran, Iraq, Libya, Nigeria, Saudi Arabia, Kuwait, and Venezuela, derived over 90 percent of export earnings from oil; Indonesia's dependency was 60 percent and non-OPEC Mexico's, 75 percent.[49] Diminished revenues presented a clear hazard to such populous and poor states as Nigeria, Indonesia, and Mexico whose development projects depended upon high oil earnings and the foreign loans secured by those earnings. For a number of LDC exporters, the boom of 1979–83 had become a bust by 1986. An oil glut, plunging prices, and overreaching development ambitions fueled the collapse. OPEC attempted to achieve consensus on workable production controls and an orchestrated market share campaign.

Oil moneys poured into the exporting countries between 1979 and 1982. The surprisingly high capacity of Saudi Arabia and Kuwait to absorb income had about reached its upper limit. Both accumulated adequate revenues to complete the massive non-oil and oil sector developments initiated after 1973. Of these two savers, Kuwait's employment of oil revenues reflected better balance. Kuwait invested more diligently than her neighbor, acting as a strong buyer in the financial markets of Europe and America and purchasing interests in a variety of foreign oil and non-oil companies. Less inclined to invest at home in monumental, non-oil related projects, Kuwait centered its efforts on refining and marketing its own oil. Kuwait, more than Saudi Arabia or any other LDC exporter, improved its natural strengths and, consequently, created a more balanced economy than other OPEC countries. Nonetheless, Kuwait remained an insecure country, dependent upon US naval forces in 1987 and 1988 to protect its oil exports from overt Iranian aggression. Neither did Kuwait's economic policies purchase immunity from the effects of falling oil prices.

The domestic use of Saudi Arabia's swollen oil revenues yielded only a marginal advance toward the goal of a diversified economy and the integration of its vast isolated parts. Its objectives differed conspicuously from Kuwait's, especially in the realm of foreign affairs and in OPEC's internal politics where the Saudis coveted the leading role. Ample expenditures — $19 billion spent in the USA and UK from 1980 to 1985 — bolstered its armed forces against the danger of an expanded Gulf war as well as for internal security purposes.[50] While Saudi Arabia's policies may have reasonably served its interests, as Quandt suggests, those policies manifested an external rather than internal orientation. In Pachauri's opinion, those policies left the nation with an economy that was generally weak and still wholly dependent upon oil earnings.

Kuwait and Saudi Arabia proved vulnerable to weakening oil prices, both experiencing current accounts deficits after 1982. For a year or so, the magnitude of their reserve funds allowed the continuation of internal development, but in 1985, both states reduced domestic spending and purchases of goods from abroad. Cuts in welfare expenditures, the firing of civil servants, the repatriation of foreign workers, and the cessation of work on infrastructure and non-oil industrial projects followed.[51]

The autocratic ruling houses of Kuwait and Saudi Arabia feared the democratic and liberalizing influence of the West as acutely as the fundamentalist Muslimism of Iran or the Marxism of the USSR. High oil incomes offered only material goods to their people, serving as an imperfect barrier against internal political and social changes that might flow from demands for expanded participatory rights. High oil incomes protected the family regimes. Lower oil earnings harmed the interests and imperiled the future expectations of the general public, of workers, of students, of lower and middle rank bureaucrats, of small entrepreneurs. Dissatisfaction could nurture disaffection.

Development projects funded by the windfall profits of 1979–82 carried the more populous LDC exporters only fractionally closer to their goals than had the programs initiated after 1973. The prerequisites for balanced growth in a diversified economy could not be purchased in a decade. Growth programs ignored the prevailing maldistribution of wealth and welfare. Maladroit use of new revenues contributed to the great debt burden pressing on several exporters even before the price collapse of 1982.

Nigeria, for instance, won a Pyrrhic victory in forcing the price of oil sky-high in 1979–80 and in threatening its largest buyer, the USA, with reduced supply unless it adopted correct policies toward southern Africa. The USA turned toward Mexico and Alaska and western Europe to the North Sea and the USSR, thus depriving Nigeria of markets just as prices and demand diminished. To protect its market share, Nigeria, in 1981 and after, undercut OPEC's official prices and ignored its quotas.

By 1983, Nigeria's oil based economy sagged badly, fomenting a military coup which accelerated economic decline. Nigeria's *per capita* gross domestic product slumped by 50 percent between 1980 and 1984 while the foreign debt jumped from about $7 billion in 1980 to above $20 billion in 1984. Debt service absorbed one-half of all export earnings. Development stopped. Construction of the new capital, Abuja, ceased. No highways entered that city and cattle grazed on abandoned building sites. Some one million workers lost their jobs. In 1986–7, the military government announced a severe austerity program. More workers, particularly white collar, were released. Food scarcity threatened many locales. Foreign creditors demanded greater retrenchment and less government activity in business as the price for restructuring the debt package. Predictably, those least able to earn an adequate income shouldered the greater burden.[52]

Nigeria's plight typified the pitfalls of sudden, great wealth that waylaid other LDC producers. Mexico and Indonesia counted on high oil earnings to fund growth and to attract foreign capital investment and loans. Indonesia, with a more diversified export base than Nigeria or Venezuela, reeled from the shock of tumbling oil earnings in 1984 and after. Oil revenues fell from $18 billion in 1981 to $9 billion in 1986 while exports of rubber, tea, tin, and other commodities remained at low levels. Sinking revenues forced postponement of work on large LNG facilities and other industrial projects. Unemployment rose as jobs failed to materialize for the two million people entering the work force each year. In all probability, the average annual income of Indonesians, the lowest in OPEC, declined.[53]

Mexico fell captive to the belief that oil earnings, spiced with large foreign credits, could carry the burden of economic growth. The nation's internal needs, however, far outstripped the earning ability of oil exports. The notion of oil as panacea for internal economic problems had been discredited by 1982. A foreign debt of under $30 billion in 1979 reached $108 billion in 1987, with American banks holding one-quarter of the total. Oil revenues declined after 1982, but most severely from 1986 to 1988, forcing intensified austerity and threatening Mexico's ability to service its debt. Retrenchment compelled a drastic cutback in subsidies that held food prices low. Rising food and other prices and a debt service burden exceeding 8 percent of GNP pushed inflation to 159 percent in 1987 and thoroughly eroded the incomes of workers and white collar groups.

Only the extension of new credits, organized by the USA, prevented Mexican bankruptcy. The creditors demanded, as they had in Nigeria, the opening of Mexico to private capital. Staggering from the price collapse and the devastation of the Mexico City earthquake, the government submitted. Japanese and American investments in oil and gas, hitherto the province of Pemex, rose. State owned industries were put up for sale. Mexico prepared to enter the General Agreement on Tariffs and Trade, requiring liberalization of restrictive import policies. Perhaps the most salient consequence of the economic crisis was the emergence of an apparently viable two-, or multi-, party system in 1988. In the short-term, the spread of internal opposition to government policies may exacerbate economic malaise. Resolution of vexing social and economic difficulties is unlikely, however, if the interests of the majority are ignored.[54]

OPEC loses control, 1979–88

The readiness of OPEC members to profit from western panic over supply drove oil prices to their upper limits in 1979 and 1980. The decision of Saudi Arabia, the so-called price dove, to reduce production in spring 1979, contributed to the price crunch. During the next two years, recession in the West and more efficient energy use reduced demand (Tables 7.2 and 7.5) while dearness of oil stimulated non-OPEC production and lessened western imports of OPEC oil. Something of an oil glut emerged in 1981, apparently induced by Saudi Arabia's efforts to maintain its global market share by shaving prices below those of OPEC colleagues. In demonstrating its power to dramatically raise output, Saudi Arabia pursued a broader purpose, that is to force upon OPEC a lower, uniform oil price and production quotas. Algeria, Libya, Iran, and Iraq, each seeking maximum revenues, resisted the Saudi campaign to determine OPEC policies.

The adverse consequences of diminished western oil consumption quickly spread among the producing LDCs as export earnings dropped and balance of payments deficits mounted. In 1982, and following a reunified price decision in 1981, OPEC tentatively agreed to reduce production by 10 percent, thus paving the way for the adoption of production quotas in 1983 (Table 9.4). Price stability and production quotas would, OPEC anticipated, moderate the pernicious effects of intra-

Table 9.4 OPEC's quotas and actual production, 1982–9 (million barrels per day)

	Quota	Production
March 1982 to	17.5	18.0 July 1982
November 1982		19.0 November 1982
December 1982	18.5	20.0 January 1983
March 1983	17.5	20.0 1983
1984	16.0	17.5 1984
1985	16.0	16.2 First quarter
		17.0 Third quarter
		15.5 Last quarter
First quarter 1986	15.0	20.0 August 1986
November 1986	15.8	21.0 November 1986
Last quarter 1987	17.5	18.5 Last quarter
April 1988	17.5	
April proposal 1988	16.6	18.0 April 1988
August 1988	15.0	20.0 August 1988
November 1988	18.5	
September 1989	19.5	22.5 September 1989

Sources: The Middle East and North Africa 1987, 33rd edn, London: Europa Publication Limited (1987), pp. 115–22; *New York Times*, October 4, 1985, April 29, 1988, September 24, 1989; *The Guardian*, October 23, 1986; *Time*, September 19, 1988, p. 45 and January 30, 1989, p. 53.

OPEC competition for markets into which poured Alaskan, North Sea, Mexican, and Russian oil. In reaching this accord, OPEC evinced far greater resilience than many in the West anticipated, or wished. But, OPEC, a voluntary confederation of states, could not impose policies that seriously disadvantaged any of its members.[55]

Recognizing that the production and price policies of non-OPEC oil exporters impinged sharply on the effectiveness of its decisions, OPEC sought the cooperation of Mexico, Britain, Norway, and the Soviets. In 1983, Mexico acceded to OPEC's request, at the sacrifice of some revenue. Britain, Norway, and the USSR, however, led the price break in 1983 with reductions of as much as 10 percent, taking oil down to $29–$30 per barrel. Saudi Arabia undermined OPEC's approach to those exporters by producing 25 percent more than its quota. OPEC and non-OPEC producers moved quickly to defend their market shares.

A modicum of price stability obtained in 1983 and 1984, but OPEC states, including the Saudis, constantly cheated, ignoring quotas (Table 9.4), shaving prices, and, as the Saudis preferred, bartering oil produced above the quotas for goods. The large foreign exchange reserves of the Saudis and their ability to raise and lower production at will enabled them to adapt to falling revenues, a flexibility absent in Nigeria, Indonesia, or Venezuela. In 1983 and 1984, the latter nations cut prices and produced above their allowable in a desperate attempt to stem revenue attenuation and maintain social and economic programs. Venezuela and Nigeria, for instance, both faced intense competition in the USA and European markets from non-OPEC oil. British and Norwegian price cuts in 1983 precipitated Nigeria's break with OPEC's posted price. The desertion of Nigeria sabotaged OPEC's strategy. In 1985, virtually all OPEC states, and especially Saudi Arabia, ignored the quotas. The Saudis had decided to maintain their 25 percent portion of OPEC production and protect their market share regardless of the effect on price. By default, this became OPEC's policy in 1985 and 1986.[56]

By 1985, OECD-Europe and the USA received a much diminished portion of lower total imports from the major OPEC exporters. OPEC's share of world oil production dropped from about one-half in 1979 to 30 percent in 1985 while its share of a shrinking global trade in oil — excluding the USSR and bloc states — declined from 88 percent in 1979 to 55 percent in 1982, but then improved to 64 percent in 1985. The Saudi decision to exceed its quota, thereby repudiating its role as swing producer, threw an additional 75 million metric tons of oil on the market in 1986, almost the whole of the OPEC increase from 840 mmt in 1985 to 925 mmt in 1986. OPEC's quota system self-destructed (Table 9.4).

As Saudi production forced prices toward $10 in spring 1986, the Saudi regime believed that it now commanded the leverage to win adoption of viable quotas that would push prices upward. Once again, OPEC approached non-OPEC producers. Informal talks between OPEC and Norway, Britain, and the USSR met with resistance in Britain and tacit commitments to cooperate in limiting production by Norway and Russia. But OPEC could not induce internal cooperation. In April 1988, OPEC met with a group of seven LDC exporters, including Mexico and Malaysia, proposing that an OPEC production cut of 5 percent be matched by non-OPEC states. Mexico, for one, agreed but OPEC failed to fulfill its end of the bargain. The great gap between quotas and production reversed the trend toward firmer prices commencing in 1987; prices dipped to around $14 in September and October 1988.[57]

Saudi Arabia acted as the leaven of change in the events just described. What purposes were served by Saudi machinations? Most agree that the Saudis sought to consolidate its dominance in OPEC by means of its productive power.[58] Prior to 1979–80, westerners viewed the Saudis as price moderates, seeking stability rather than profit maximization. However, Saudi Arabia did not perfectly fit that model before 1979 and certainly not after. By 1985–6, it sought revenue maximization through reduced prices and increased production. But, having brought about the great glut and price slide of 1986–7, Saudi power waned and the economy slipped into recession. Unable to herd other producers toward price stability, if that was their true objective, the Saudis defended their market share by producing above their ostensible quota.

The current era of relatively low oil prices directly benefited US, European, and Japanese oil companies. Aramco's take expanded as the Saudis defended their markets. Other LDC producers offered liberalized oil exploration and recovery contracts to foreign firms. Producers in 1988 were less concerned with ideological purity than with shoring up revenues and augmenting reserves. Of course, with prices at $10 in 1987 and at $14 in late 1988, the oil firms demanded stronger inducements to explore. Argentina, in 1985, sought foreign off shore exploration, signing risk contracts favorable to an Exxon-led group, Occidental, and others. Faced with a reduction of oil company drilling in 1987, Indonesia permitted foreign exploration in areas previously the preserves of Pertamina. Sinking oil revenues persuaded Egypt to improve production sharing terms for Texaco, Conoco, and other firms. Algeria, in 1987, offered the USA reasonable prices for delivery of LNG.[59]

OPEC lost control over prices after 1979 and was unsuccessful in preventing an erratic fluctuation between $10 and $20 per barrel until

November 1988, prior to which OPEC quotas and official prices were irrelevant. Economic decline and budget deficits among the rich Arabian Peninsula producers thwarted the expectations of their citizens (or wards) as less welfare trickled down from the top. In Saudi Arabia, the encroaching Gulf war stimulated large military expenditures and reduced service, welfare, and food subsidy spending. Economy remained, however, an alien term to many conspicuous consumers in the Saud family. With the possible exceptions of Algeria and Libya, the non-Peninsular members of OPEC suffered grievously from the price slump. But a remedy eluded OPEC. In Fall 1988, an accord to limit production seemed improbable. But OPEC confounded the experts. In November 1988, a new quota was adopted to which members adhered closely in January 1989.

At the end of 1989, as Table 9.4 indicates, a large deviation occurred between the OPEC quota and actual production. At that time, excess production in Kuwait, UAE, Nigeria, and Saudi Arabia accounted for the difference. Yet prices have remained reasonably stable which suggests that consumption is up and/or that other sources of oil are in decline or incapable of increase. Both seem to be the case. US oil consumption has risen while domestic production has declined. Simultaneously, western Europe's demand has increased while North Sea production has plateaued. Consumption in both South Korea and Japan rises steadily and can only be satisfied with Middle Eastern oil. As the final decade of this century of adversity commenced, OPEC producers alone possessed the productive ability to meet rising demand in the West and in East Asia. Within OPEC, the Arab producers along the Persian Gulf controlled vast reserves. It is not unreasonable to expect that new demand and Arab producer power will propel oil prices upward again, toward $30 per barrel or more over the next few years. Are the economics of western nations sufficiently stable to avoid the inflation, recession, and stagnation that accompanied the price hikes of 1979–80?[60]

Conclusion

The likelihood of a severe energy crunch seemed remote to consumers everywhere as 1989 ended. In the West, governments and energy experts acted as though open market forces could be relied upon to provide sufficient energy into some distant future. Advances in energy use efficiency were highly touted. Each new auto, building, or factory consumed less energy per unit of output than in 1973. Electricity captured a larger share of energy use. Despite Chernobyl, a new dawn for nuclear energy lit the horizon. Western economies roared ahead. In 1988, oil slid under $15 and those economies showed no ill effects even when prices rose to $20 at year's end. Analysts noted recent increases in western TPER but considered this trend of little consequence. They also pointed to the relative inefficiency of US energy use *vis-à-vis* other industrial states but neglected to link that to growing absolute demand for energy in the USA. They assumed that technology had created "an entirely new environment for energy users."[61]

As recently as 1988, many viewed OPEC as a mere shadow of its former self, wracked by internal divisions, members undercutting each other, and incapable of fashioning viable production quotas. OPEC's fall was attributed to greed. Squeezing the industrial states in 1973 and 1979 compelled them to seek new and efficient energy technologies, to conserve, and to draw oil from secure sources. The revenues of OPEC's members sank rapidly, lessening the international influence of such states as Saudi Arabia. Severe price wars wrecked OPEC's unity. OPEC appeared incapable of harming the West. Lulled into somnolence by energy supply forecasts, most western governments ignored their persistent oil import dependence.

The possibility of an even more formidable energy threat slowly penetrated the consciousness of governments and citizens during the 1980s. The accumulated impact of decades of uninhibited energy use and uncontrolled disposal of wastes seemed to achieve critical mass in the 1980s. Mounting evidence instructed global societies that rising fossil fuel use damaged, perhaps irreversibly, the environment. Individual states might devise some protection for their own space, but the potentially catastrophic effects of global warming and depletion of the ozone layer demanded immediate international action. This was the exact message of an ignored publication by the US Environmental Protection Agency in 1983, *Can We Delay A Greenhouse Warming?* — not "Is There a Greenhouse Warming?" Acknowledging the polarization of opinions, the authors argued the high risks of a wait-and-see attitude. Uncertainty regarding the precise character of the greenhouse phenomenon ought not to prevent an "expeditious response" to global warming that "is neither trivial nor just a long-term problem."[62] President Reagan, however, essentially rejected these findings while President Bush addresses these issues with the speed of a glacier.

Signs that nations recognized the danger gradually surfaced. Thirty-seven countries signed a treaty in 1987 to protect the ozone layer. In November 1988, the USA joined other industrial nations in Geneva to negotiate a treaty reducing carbon emissions. The UN and other groups have sponsored conferences on the climate. The popular magazine, *Time*, dedicated an issue in January 1989 to the "Endangered Earth."

US Senator Albert Gore, Jr, introduced a comprehensive, globally oriented environmental protection program at the opening of the 101st Congress.

Great obstacles, political and economic, faced even those wealthy nations disposed toward a cleaner world. Even more severe constraints impeded the poorer nations. Using less fossil fuel would retard the development of many LDCs while the more advanced countries worried that it would slow economic growth. The rape of the great rain forests evoked universal concern. But poor people demanded land to clear for farms and, unable to afford commercial fuels, chopped down more trees for firewood. While *Time* featured the essential biological role of tropical forests, it fell short of advocating that the wealthy nations assume most of the costs of forest preservation. Others were not so timid. Massive reforestation, exchanging part of the LDC debt for conservation programs, permitting continued LDC fossil fuel use while reducing it dramatically in the industrial countries were among the adventurous proposals of the *World Watch* staff.[63]

Nuclear energy's adherents offered that technology as a partial solution to environmental pollution while discounting the fear of future Chernobyls as the nightmare of the uninformed. At present, referendums in several industrialized states indicate that public opinion opposes new nuclear plants. Governments had abided by that opinion by canceling further construction. But nuclear proponents argue that it is the only alternative to thermal plants. That is not so. Conservation reduces noxious emissions. Solar electricity is not far from widespread commercial practicality. The technology exists to double the efficiency of automobile engines in the USA. But these concrete options to nuclear and thermal electricity and augmented fossil fuel use have no assured place on national agendas. Britain's recent commitment to the construction of numerous new coal burning and nuclear plants well-reflected the view of most western governments that high-tech solutions to future energy needs are more politically expedient than conservation. Conservation has yet to develop a constituency that matches evenly with electrical equipment manufacturers, electric utilities, miner unions, investors, or financial interests.

A respected voice assured his audience that while "future generations won't have the rich inheritance of natural resources that we have known...we can leave them rich technological capabilities to offset that loss."[64] A different, equally respected voice warned that "Unless we can quickly reduce our dependence on fossil fuels, cut back the loss of topsoil, reverse the deforestation of the earth, and check population growth a broad-based decline in the human condition may be inevitable."[65]

Notes

1. I.M. Torrens, *Changing Structures in the World Oil Market*, Paris: The Atlantic Institute for International Affairs (1980), pp. 20–5; E. Kanovsky, "The Diminishing Importance of Middle East Oil: A Harbinger of the Future," *Middle East Contemporary Survey*, 5 (1980–1), pp. 375–7; J.F. O'Leary, "Price Reactive versus Price Active Energy Policy," in P. Tempest, ed., *International Energy Markets*, Cambridge, Mass.: Oelgeschlager, Gunn & Hain (1983), pp. 171–3.
2. For the above two paragraphs: Torrens, *World Oil Markets*, pp. 20–5; E.J. Wilson, "World politics and international energy markets," *International Organization*, 41 (Winter 1987), p. 144; F. Fesharaki *et al.*, *Critical Energy Issues in Asia and the Pacific: The Next Twenty Years*, Boulder, Colo.: Westview Press (1982), p. 41; H. Maull, *Europe and World Energy*, London: Butterworths (1980), pp. 236–7; W.B. Quandt, *Saudi Arabia in the 1980s: Foreign Policy, Security, and Oil*, Washington, DC: The Brookings Institution (1981), pp. 114–17; A.L. Danielsen, *The Evolution of OPEC*. New York: Harcourt Brace Jovanovich (1982), pp. 194–6; *Washington Post*, April 10, 1979.
3. Quoted in the *Denver Post*, May 18, 1980.
4. *New York Times*, December 16, 1979, January 6, 1980; *Washington Post*, April 4, 1979, November 26, 1979, December 18, 1979.
5. IEA, *Energy Policies and Programmes of IEA Countries, 1983 Review*, Paris: OECD/IEA (1983), pp. 11–15 and *Energy Policies, 1985* (1986), p. 15; *Lloyds Bank Group Economic Report 1982, West Germany*, London: Lloyds Bank Group (1982), pp. 7–8; *New York Times*, September 28, 1983; P. Odell, *Oil and World Power*, 7th edn, Harmondsworth: Penguin (1983), pp. 230–5; A.M. El-Agraa, ed., *The Economics of the European Community*, 2nd edn, Deddington, Oxford: Phillip Allan (1985), pp. 52–4.
6. IEA, *World Energy Outlook*, Paris: OECD/IEA (1982), pp. 108–9.
7. *Beijing Review*, December 23, 1986, p. 2; A. Hammer, "On a Vast China Market," *Journal of International Affairs*, 39 (Winter 1986), pp. 19–21; J. Boatman, "China: Powering the People's Republic," *Multinational Monitor*, March 10, 1987, pp. 12–13; D.I. Hertzmark, "Energy in Southeast Asia: Responses to Energy Shocks, 1973–85," *Annual Review of Energy*, 12 (1987), pp. 27–8.
8. For the above three paragraphs: IEA, *Energy Policies 1982*, pp. 264–5 and *Energy Balances of OECD Countries, 1970/1980*, Paris: OECD/IEA (1984), pp. 387–9, 404; *World Oil*, August, 1987, p. 25; De Golyer and MacNaughton, *Twentieth Century Petroleum Statistics 1986*, Dallas, Texas: De Golyer and MacNaughton (1986), p. 18; Energy Information Administration, *Monthly Energy Review. April 1988*, Washington, DC: USDOE (1988), pp. 3–7; *BP statistical review of world energy. 1986*; *New York Times*, August 23, 1981, January 23, 1986, February 3, 1986, September 24, 1989; *The Guardian*, September 22 and December 31, 1986.
9. N. Lucas, *Western European Energy Policies. A Comparative Study of the Influence of Institutional Structure on Technical Change*, Oxford: Clarendon Press (1985), p. 39. N.W. Davis, "Consolidation in Japan's Petroleum Industry?", *The Oriental Economist*, February, 1984, p. 24;

The Economist, January 24, 1987, p. 62; *The Far East and Australasia 1987*, 18th edn, London: Europa Publications Ltd (1987), pp. 624, 632; H. Ishihara, "Energy demand and supply conditions in Japan," *OPEC Review*, VIII (Autumn 1984), p. 294; IEA, *Energy Policies 1986*, p. 198.

10. Ishihara, "Energy demand and supply in Japan," p. 294; N. de Marchi, "The Ford Administration: Energy as a Political Good," p. 506, and J.A. Yager, "The Energy Battles of 1979,", pp. 616–18, in C.D. Goodwin, ed., *Energy Policy in Perspective: Today's Problems, Yesterday's Solutions*, Washington, DC: The Brookings Institution (1981); R.H.K. Vietor, *Energy policies in America since 1945: A study of business-government relations*, Cambridge: Cambridge University Press (1984), pp. 210–16, 219–24; Congressional Quarterly, *Energy Policy*, 2nd edn, Washington, DC: Congressional Quarterly (1981), pp. 175–6; *Washington Post*, March 2, 1979; *New York Times*, October 3, 1987.

11. *The Middle East and North Africa 1987*, 33rd edn, London: Europa Publications Ltd (1987), pp. 106 7; B. Mossavar Rahami, *Energy Policy in Iran: Domestic Choices and International Implications*, New York: Pergamon Books (1981), pp. 56–9.

12. De Golyer and MacNaughton, *1986*, p. 9; *World Oil*, August, 1987, p. 82; *The Middle East and North Africa 1987*, pp. 104–5, 132–4; *Lloyds Bank Group Economic Report 1983, Saudi Arabia*, London: Lloyds Bank Group (1983), pp. 12–14; *New York Times*, February 5, 1985.

13. For the above two paragraphs: *ibid.*, May 1, 1984, January 21, 1985; *Time*, March 28, 1988, p. 51 and, relative to Kuwait–BP, October 17, 1988, p. 54; *The Economist*, November 12, 1988, p. 63 and December 10, 1988, p. 64; G. Luciani, *The Oil Companies and the Arab World*, London: Croom Helm (1984), p. 117; *Beijing Review*, September 29, 1986; *World Oil*, August, 1987, p. 82.

14. IEA, *Energy Policies 1986*, pp. 47–8.

15. For more positive evaluations of the energy mix transformation, see C-y. Lin, "Global Pattern of Energy Consumption before and after the 1974 Oil Crisis," *Economic Development and Cultural Change*, 32 (July 1984), pp. 781–802; J.W. Aitchison and D.W. Heal, "World patterns of fuel consumption: towards diversity and a low-cost energy future?", *Geography*, 72 (June 1987), pp. 235–9; International Monetary Fund, *World Economic Outlook 1986*, Washington, DC: IMF (1986), p. 154.

16. For the above four paragraphs: Lord Ezra, "Coal Supplies," in T.L. Shaw *et al.*, eds, *Policy and Development of Energy Resources*, Chichester: Wiley (1984), pp. 109–10, 114–16; CQ, *Energy Policy*, p. 253; IEA, *Coal Information 1987*, Paris: OECD/IEA (1987), pp. 41, 281 and *Energy Policies 1986*, pp. 191–3, 427–9; C. Simeons, *Coal: Its Role in Tomorrow's Technology*, New York: Pergamon Press (1978), pp. 18–19; *World Coal*, 8 (November–December 1982), p. 62; Bureau of Mines, *Minerals and Materials: A Bimonthly Survey, December 1987–January 1988*, Washington, DC: USGPO (1988), p. 31; *The Economist*, November 12, 1988.

17. J.L. Cochrane, "Carter Energy Policy and the Ninety-fifth Congress," in Goodwin, ed., *Energy Policy in Perspective*, pp. 573–6, 584–5; *New York Times*, October 13, 1980, February 8, 1981, May 16, 1982, May 23, 1983; EIA, *Monthly Energy Review, November 1987*, pp. 72, 78.

18. *The Economist*, December 10, 1988, p. 64.

19. Environmental Resources Limited, *Acid Rain: A Review of The Phenom-*

enon in the ECC and Europe, London: Graham and Trotman (1983), *passim*; P.L. Owen and S. Owen, "Resource Management," *Progress in Human Geography*, 10 (December 1986), pp. 575–6; A.S. Earl, "Lessons from Germany in Controlling Acid Rain," *Renewable Resources Journal*, 3 (Summer 1985), pp. 3, 32–3; *The [London] Sunday Times*, September 14, 1986; *The [Manchester] Guardian*, September 4, 12, 1986, November 24, 1986, January 17, 1987; *International Herald Tribune*, December 19, 1986.

20. *DOE This Month*, July 1986, p. 2.
21. *The Kansas City Times*, October 17, 1984; *New York Times*, August 7, 1984, March 16, 1985, January 9, 1986; *Christian Science Monitor*, March 21, 1986; EIA, *Annual Energy Review 1987*, Washington, DC: USGPO (1988), p. 129; *Climate Alert*, 1. no. 3 (Fall 1988), p. 1; *World Oil*, March, 1987, p. 17.
22. For the above three paragraphs: *Climate Alert*, Summer 1989, p. 5; C. Flavin, *Slowing Global Warming: A Worldwide Strategy. Worldwatch Paper 91*, October 1989, Washington, DC: Worldwatch Institute (1989), p. 64; *The Amicus Journal*, 12 (Winter 1990), pp. 2–3, 17–21; *The Guardian*, February 27, 1987; L.R. Brown and C. Flavin, "The Earth's Vital Signs," in L.R. Brown *et al.*, *State of the World 1988*, New York: W.W. Norton (1984), p. 14; *Time*, January 2, 1989, pp. 26–73.
23. For the above two paragraphs: *New York Times*, May 8, 1988; *Petroleum Economist*, August, 1987, pp. 295–6; IEA, *Coal Information 1987, passim* and *Energy Policies 1985*, p. 30 and *1986*, pp. 208, 247, 266; *The Wall Street Journal*, April 5, 1989.
24. *World Oil*, April, 1988, pp. 75–82; D. Yergin, "Crisis and Adjustment: An Overview," pp. 1–28 and R. Stobaugh, "World Energy in the Year 2000," pp. 29–57 in D. Yergin and M. Hillenbrand, eds, *Global Insecurity. Beyond Energy Future, A Strategy for Political and Economic Survival in the 1980s*, New York: Penguin (1983).
25. *Petroleum Economist*, February, 1987, p. 56.
26. *The Economist*, December 10, 1988, p. 64; C. Flavin, "The Case Against Reviving Nuclear Power," *World.Watch*, 1 (July-August 1988), p. 29.
27. For the above three paragraphs: *New York Times*, September 15, 1984, January 1, 1985; *Time*, February 13, 1984, pp. 34–42, June 19, 1989; *Lawrence Daily Journal World*, March 19, 1989; *Petroleum Economist*, August, 1987, p. 315; *EPRI Journal*, 13 (December 1988), pp. 7–13; EIA, *Monthly Review April 1988*, pp.118–19; Flavin, "Case Against Reviving Nuclear Power," pp. 27–35.
28. In 1986, Italy ranked first among OECD states in spending on energy R&D as a proportion of GNP. Nuclear energy claimed 86 percent of R&D spending. Italy ranked among the lowest in OECD in spending on renewables, only Britain being significantly lower. *Petroleum Economist*, August, 1987, p. 315; IEA, *Energy Policies 1986*, pp. 242–6; Flavin, "Creating a Sustainable Energy Future, pp. 36–7 and C.P. Shea, "Shifting to Renewable Energy," p. 81 in Brown, *State of the World 1988*.
29. G.W. Hoffman, *The European Energy Challenge. East and West*, Durham, N.C.: Duke University Press (1985), pp. 13–14; G. Manners, *Coal in Britain*, London: Allen & Unwin (1981), pp. 25–6; E.L. Moore, "An Overview: Gains, Costs, Dilemmas," in J. Pearce, ed., *The Third Oil Shock: The Effects of Lower Prices*, London: Routledge & Kegan Paul (1983), p. 6.

30. For the above two paragraphs: IEA, *World Energy Outlook* (1982), pp. 63, 65 and *Energy Policies 1986*, pp. 194–5, 244–5; Bureau of Mines, *Minerals and Materials, December 1987–January 1988*, pp. 12–15; *Du Pont Context*, 8. no. 2 (1979), pp. 21–2; CQ, *Energy Policy*, pp. 56–60; *Lawrence Journal World*, August 27, 1988, C. Flavin and A.B. Durning, *Building on Success: The Age of Efficiency*. Worldwatch Paper 82, March, 1988, Washington, DC: Worldwatch Institute (1988), pp. 24–5; L.R. Brown *et al.*, *State of the World 1990*, New York: W.W. Norton (1990), p. 19.

31. R. Dore, "Energy Conservation in Japanese Industry," in R. Belgrave, ed., *Energy—Two Decades of Crisis*, Aldershot: Gower (1983), pp. 102–7, 120; *The Economist*, February 7, 1987, p. 69; *The Far East and Australasia 1987*, p. 488; *Petroleum Economist*, February, 1987, p. 57.

32. *The Economist*, January 29, 1983, p. 59, November 22, 1986, p. 68, January 24, 1987, p. 65; IMF, *World Economic Outlook April 1985* (1985), p. 152; *New York Times*, February 13, 1986; *Washington Post National Weekly Edition*, August 24, 1987; O'Leary, "Price Reactive versus Price Active Energy Policies," pp. 166–7, J. Watanuki, "Japanese Society and the Limits of Growth," in Yergin and Hillenbrand, eds, *Global Insecurity*, p. 198; P.R. Odell and K.E. Rosing, "The Future of Oil: A Re-evaluation," *OPEC Review*, VIII (Summer 1984), pp. 203–28.

33. *The Economist*, December 10, 1988.

34. E.A. Hewitt, *Energy, Economics, and Foreign Policy in the Soviet Union*, Washington, DC: The Brookings Institution (1984), pp. 69, 155; *World Oil*, August, 1987, p. 62; World Resources Institute, *World Resources 1987*, New York: Basic Books (1987), pp. 100, 102–3; J.P. Stern, *International Gas Trade in Europe: The Policies of Exporting and Importing Countries*, London: Heinemann Educational Books Ltd (1984), p. 65; *The Christian Science Monitor*, February 5, 1986; *New York Times*, March 10, 1986; M. Marrese, "CMEA: effective but cumbersome political economy," *International Organization*, 40 (Spring 1986), pp. 307–9.

35. H.F. French, "Industrial Wasteland," *World.Watch*, 1 (November–December 1988), p. 22–5. In discussing the economies of eastern Europe, one needs to guard against analyses that present the worst case possible in order to condemn the Soviet system. Bloc experts are discommoded by serious lacunae in the data. Having taken this precaution, it seems that the weight of available evidence corroborates a reality resembling the worst case.

36. For the above two paragraphs: *New York Times*, April 1 and September 17, 1984; *Petroleum Economist*, May 19, 1987, pp. 174, 191–2; IEA, *Coal Information 1987*, pp. 48, 282, 344; *The Guardian*, September 16 and December 8, 1986; *Time*, September 5, 1988.

37. *BP statistical review of world energy 1986*, *passim*; *The Guardian*, August 14, 1986; *Christian Science Monitor*, March 22, 1986; *World Oil*, August, 1987, p. 62.

38. For the above four paragraphs: *New York Times*, August 16, 1981, February 14 and May 30, 1982; Stern, *International Gas Trade*, pp. 177–9; F.E. Banks, "Why Europe Needs Siberian Gas, " in Tempest, ed., *International Energy Markets*, p. 191; B.I. Greer and J.L. Russell, "European Reliance on Soviet Gas Exports: The Yamburg–Urengoi Natural Gas Project," *The Energy Journal*, 3 (July 1982), pp. 16, 18–20, 34–5; B.W. Jentleson, *Pipeline Politics: The Complex Political Economy of*

East–West Energy Trade, Ithaca: Cornell University Press (1986), pp. 138–45, 153–9; *Washington Post*, March 12, 1981; *The Chapel Hill Newspaper*, June 24, 1982; *Kansas City Times*, August 23, 1982; *Kansas City Star*, November 14, 1982.

39. For the most recent account of this affair see, A.J. Blinken, *Ally vs. Ally: America, Europe, and the Siberian Pipeline Crisis*, New York: Praeger (1987). B. Bergmann, "Natural Gas in Western Europe—perspectives of an attractive energy," *OPEC Review*, VIII (Spring 1984), pp. 63–8; Stern, *International Gas Trade*, pp. 52–60; IEA, *Energy Policies 1986*, pp. 132, 200.

40. WRI, *World Resources 1987*, pp. 242, 276.

41. For the above three paragraphs: Aitchison and Heal, "World patterns of fuel consumption," p. 238; J. Sathaye *et al.*, "Energy Demand in Developing Countries: A Sectoral Analysis of Recent Trends," *Annual Review of Energy*, 12 (1987), pp. 261–3; IEA, *World Energy Outlook* (1982), pp. 154–5; *Washington Post*, September 2, 1980; *New York Times*, February 14 and April 22, 1985, February 2, 1986; Hertzmark, "Energy in Southeast Asia," pp. 39–43; *World Oil*, August, 1987, p. 96.

42. For the above three paragraphs: WRI, *World Resources 1987*; Flavin, "Case Against Reviving Nuclear Power," pp. 28–31; J. Goldenberg, "Brazil: energy options and current outlook," in V. Smil and W.E. Knowland, eds, *Energy in the developing world. The real energy crisis*, Oxford: Oxford University Press (1980), pp. 236–7; J.E. Katz and O.S. Marwah, *Nuclear Power in Developing Countries. An Analysis of Decision Making*, Lexington, Mass.: Lexington Books (1982), pp. 10–17, 107–10; 210–17; The Economist Intelligence Unit, *1986/87 Yearbook. Energy in Latin America and the Caribbean*, London: The Economist Publications Ltd (1987), pp. 51, 105; Mossavar-Rahmani, *Energy Policy in Iran*, pp. 105–18.

43. For the above two paragraphs: Katz and Marwah, *Nuclear Power in Developing Countries*, pp. 235–6, 257, 273–91; Fesharaki, *Energy Issues in Asia*, pp. 138–9; *The Guardian*, September 24, 1986; Boatman, "China," pp. 11–13; *Beijing Review*, November 14, 1986, pp. 28–9 and December 29, 1986, p. 20; Brown, *State of the World 1990*, pp. 19, 62. WRI, *World Resources 1987*, pp. 302, 306.

44. For the above two paragraphs: L.S. Spector, *The New Nuclear Nations*, New York: Basic Books, (1985), *passim*; B. Goldschmidt, *The Atomic Complex: A Worldwide Political History of Nuclear Energy*, translated by B. Adkins, La Grange Park, Ill.: American Nuclear Society (1982), pp. 416–24; M.T. Hatch, *Politics and Nuclear Power: Energy Policy in Western Europe*, Lexington, Ky.: The University Press of Kentucky (1986), pp. 125–7, 130–4; S.C. Stamos, Jr, "Energy and Development in Latin America," *Latin American Research Review*, XXI. no. 1 (1986), p. 192; W.L. Kohl, *International Institutions for Energy Management*, Aldershot, Hampshire: Gower (1983), p. 125; *New York Times*, November 21, 1984; *The Guardian*, November 7, 1986; *World.Watch*, 2 (January–February 1989), pp. 10–16.

45. Flavin, *Electricity for a Developing World: New Directions*. Worldwatch Paper 70. June 1986, Washington, DC: Worldwatch Institute (1986), pp. 33–43; M.D. Lowe, "Bicycling into the Future," *World.Watch*, 1 (July–August 1988), pp. 10–16; N. Lenssen, "Brazil Sees the Light," *World.Watch*, 2 (May–June 1989), pp. 7–8.

46. For the above two paragraphs: G. Jenkins, *Oil Economists' Handbook 1985*, London: Applied Science Publishers Ltd (1985), pp. 19, 65–7; *BP statistical review of world energy, 1981 to 1986*; IEA, *Energy Policies 1986*, p. 13; *New York Times*, May 4, 1988; *Time*, October 24, 1988, p. 69 and January 30, 1989, p. 53.

47. R.K. Pachauri, *The Political Economy of Global Energy*, Baltimore: The Johns Hopkins University Press (1985), p. 77; IMF as reported in *New York Times*, October 29, 1985.

48. *Ibid.*, and August 23, 1981; Morse, "An Overview," p. 15; Hoffman, *European Energy Challenge*, p. 42.

49. *New York Times*, October 29, 1984.

50. P.L. Ferrai *et al.*, *US Arms Exports: Policies and Contractors*, Washington, DC: Investor Responsibility Research Center (1987), pp. 10–11, 106.

51. For the above three paragraphs: Quandt, *Saudi Arabia*, pp. 62–4, 127–8; Pachauri, *Global Energy*, pp. 82–6; H. Beblawi, *The Arab Gulf Economy in a Turbulent Age*, London: Croom Helm (1984), pp. 8–13; *The Washington Post National Weekly Edition*, August 24, 1987; *Kansas City Star*, September 18, 1983; P. Savigear, "Political Change in the Gulf: A Dilemma for Britain," *Contemporary Review*, 250 (January 1987), pp. 13–14.

52. For the above two paragraphs: *Washington Post*, March 16 and June 1, 1979; *New York Times*, October 20 and December 23, 1984, August 28, 1985; T.M. Shaw, "The State of Nigeria: Oil Crises, Power Bases and Foreign Policy," *Canadian Journal of African Studies*, 18. no. 2 (1984), pp. 398–400; N. Van Hear, "Nigeria. Price Drop Puts Babangida on the Spot," *Multinational Monitor*, April 30, 1986, pp. 13–14.

53. *The Far East and Australasia 1987*, p. 448; *New York Times*, October 29 and December 17, 1984.

54. For the above two paragraphs: WRI, *World Resources 1988–89*, p. 238; *Washington Post*, February 11, 1979; *New York Times*, February 2, 1982, February 11, 1985, January 23 and February 1, 10, 16, 1986; World Bank, *World Development Report 1989*, New York: published for the World Bank by Oxford University Press (1989), pp. 63, 205; EIU, *1986/87 Yearbook*, pp. 98–9; *World Oil*, August, 1987, p. 36.

55. For the above two paragraphs: IMF, *World Economic Outlook 1986*, pp. 149–50; *Washington Post*, March 11 and April 20, 1981; *New York Times*, June 14, 1981; *Middle East and North Africa 1987*, pp. 115–17; A. Alnasrawi, *OPEC in a Changing World Economy*, Baltimore: The Johns Hopkins University Press (1985), pp. 83–5.

56. For the above two paragraphs: *The Economist*, January 29, 1983, p. 60; L. Turner, "OPEC," in Pearce, ed., *Third Oil Shock*, pp. 86–8; *South China Morning Post*, May 29, 1983; *Lloyds Bank Group Economic Report 1982, Venezuela*, London: Lloyds Bank Group (1982), pp. 5–6, 21; *Kansas City Star*, February 20, 1983; *Time*, August 13, 1984, p. 74; *New York Times*, November 8, 1984; *Middle East and North Africa 1987*, pp. 96–8.

57. For the above two paragraphs: IMF, *World Economic Outlook 1986*, pp. 157–8; *BP statistical review of world energy. June 1986*, p. 4; *Christian Science Monitor*, April 14, 1986: *New York Times*, April 29, 1988; *Time*, May 9, 1988, p. 67, September 17, 1988, p. 45, and October 24, 1988, p. 69; *The Economist*, January 10, 1987, p. 26; *The Guardian*, January 23, 1987; *OPEC bulletin*, XIX (May 1988), pp. 23–7.

58. Pachauri, *Global Energy*, p. 86; A. Roncaglia, *The International Oil Market: A Case of Trilateral Oligopoly*, ed. by J.A. Kregel, Basingstoke:

Macmillan (1985), p. 123; E. Penrose, "OPEC and the World Oil Market of the 1980s," in D. Hawdon, ed., *The Energy Crisis: Ten Years After*, London: Croom Helm (1984), p. 41.

59. *World Oil*, August, 1987, p. 9.
60. *The Guardian*, December 31, 1986; *New York Times*, September 24, 1989; *The Wall Street Journal*, April 5, 1989.
61. *New York Times*, October 2, 1988.
62. US Environmental Protection Agency, *Can We Delay A Greenhouse Warming?*, Washington, DC: USGPO (November 1983), pp. i, 7–17.
63. *Time*, January 2, 1989; L. Brown *et al.*, "No Time To Waste: A Global Environmental Agenda for the Bush Administration," *World.Watch*, 2 (January–February 1989), pp. 10–19.
64. From an interview with John Gibbon, head of the US Congress Office of Technology Assessment, in *EPRI Journal*, 13 (December 1988), p. 27.
65. L.R. Brown, editorial, *World.Watch*, 2 (January–February 1989), p. 2.

10

Powering energy transitions and transactions: a summary and conclusions

How to package the transmutations in the political economy of global energy over the past century into a tidy model has eluded me. To cover events, often tumultuous, and key trends and to keep visible necessary chronological road signs has been difficult enough. The world's nations and peoples experienced diverse and complex energy transitions. The locus of national and world power constantly shifted. Power blocs rose and decayed. The material wealth of some societies underwent mind boggling growth while other peoples seemed frozen in want and despair. Technologies advanced beyond the ability of intelligent people to comprehend their workings or to predict their consequences. Most recently, people in many lands have become unhappily aware of the harsh, wounding impact on fragile environments of unrestrained, and fossil fuel propelled, economic growth. The many imponderables associated with these transformations assumed a magnitude too great for me to fold within a generalization or two or three.

Since the mid-nineteenth century, the compulsion and ability to augment material abundance stands out as the dominant characteristic of the advanced, as well as lesser developed, economies. The rise or fall of standards of living were charted by exclusively economic criteria. Into the post World War II years, quality of life considerations, less susceptible of quantification, were generally ignored. Even now, the quality of air or water, the distribution of educational opportunities, the adequacy of housing, and other socio-cultural variables rarely intruded into calculations of living standards. The environmental costs required to reach a certain level of income ought to give societies pause. Are the gratifications purchased by the generous incomes of many more valuable than the resources consumed to generate those incomes? Can,

365

will societies of abundance change their ways sufficiently to protect what is irreplaceable and to share their largess with poorer societies?

The industrialized states of the West, beginning with Great Britain in the mid-nineteenth century, achieved economic eminence through the melding of energy intensive processes with mass production. Energy resources were considered commodities to be traded as any other good. Water and air were considered free goods and, like energy, in infinite supply. Concomitantly, and with varied motives, the great powers of western Europe, joined by the emerging powers of the USA and Japan, won control over the energy resources — largely petroleum — of weaker states and societies. Internal resources, particularly rich in America but also substantial in Europe, and the unrestricted flow of resources from foreign lands, guaranteed the fossil fuels, food, and ores necessary to grand economic growth. The injustices of this system also assured the hostility of exploited societies, nurturing within them vigorous, unvanquishable strains of nationalism. The future consequences of a world economy divided between societies of great abundance and societies of scarcity rarely found a spot on political agendas. After World War II, the question of aid to the LDCs immediately became hostage to Cold War tensions.

From the years prior to World War I until the mid-1960s, the industrialized states and their multinational energy companies firmly controlled national and international energy regimes. Only rarely did the advanced states suffer from energy scarcity. Wars and depressions notwithstanding, the nations of western Europe, Japan, and the USA created mega-economies during the twentieth century. The global power of the West, the efficiency and capital might of the MNOCs, and the weakness and dependency of the oil producing LDCs in which the MNOCs operated guaranteed accessibility to oil. The advent of the Soviet regime which denied its oil to the West for a time caused minor inconvenience, however, how much it stirred up ideological animosities. High rates of production in the USA and elsewhere more than compensated for the loss.

Freely flowing and cheap oil, abundant coal, and new natural gas finds precluded serious concern about efficient end use or environmental degradation. The jet of cheap energy thrust energy transitions forward in Europe and America and, after World War II, in Japan, Canada, and a few other nations. Only occasionally were questions raised about the wisdom of unrestrained, energy intensive economic growth. More electricity, more gasoline, more cars, more refrigerators, more of everything was demanded. While other industrialized states lagged behind Americans in energy use *per capita*, by the late 1960s, they were as fully caught up as Americans in creating societies of abundance based on high energy use. With some variance in policies, governments complied with public demands for relatively cheap energy and hurried along the transition from coal to oil, natural gas, and, finally, nuclear power.

Was this conscious policy to keep energy costs fairly low the best path to follow? Prior to the 1970s, it may have been the only possible political course. Moreover, given economic rates of growth after World War II and the impressive reconstruction of western Europe and Japan, it seemed to be working. Even in nations which established public ownership, or some version thereof, of electric, coal, gas, and oil industries, competitive conditions prevailed. In Britain, France, and Italy, each with a national oil firm, foreign refiners and marketers operated without undue restriction.

Producers withdrew fuel resources from fields spread around the world. New technologies permitted utilization of a greater portion of a field's wealth while also allowing exploration and development in the most difficult topography. Concern about depletion, particularly of oil, and more particularly in the USA, surfaced from time to time, but new discoveries, somewhere, always dispelled such apprehension. Transporters and refiners, often subsidiaries of the major oil companies, met market demand with cheaply priced and high quality products. Intervention by government to promote fuel conservation seemed unnecessary since producers withdrew at the so-called maximum efficient rate of production while discovering as much or more than they withdrew. Until the 1970s, governments of the advanced states confined themselves primarily to protecting and expanding supply. After World War I, the USA supported efforts of its major firms to loosen Britain's oil monopoly in the Middle East.

From the narrow perspective of the West, market forces functioned under competitive conditions to assure socially optimal resource use.[1] But, even if each country used only its own resources and even if those resources were replaced at rates equal to depletion, socially optimal results would not necessarily obtain. Production cannot be separated from use if the standard employed is social optimization. Assurances are required that the resource produced is used in ways that maximize social welfare.

Since the early twentieth century, societies have known that coal mining destroyed landscapes and ruined groundwater. Cheap coal prices yielded low miner incomes which, in turn, produced ill-educated and sickly miner children. Non-interventionist governments permitted these consequences. In no way can one say that coal mining maximized social welfare. Since 1973, market forces have stimulated augmented coal mining, but now society is cognizant of the social and economic damage attending coal use. American taxpayers subsidize the compensation awarded to victims of black-lung disease while in Germany and Britain the various costs of eliminating unproductive mines are also socialized. The public is now paying for the harm done by coal mining. This bill rises steadily and now includes paying for the impacts of exported pollutants. Similarly, market forces may justify the revival of nuclear power, but since its employment damages local and global environments, no claims can be advanced for its welfare maximizing effects. Chernobyl spewed radiation into northern Italy and other areas, contaminating milk, vegetables, and other foods for scores of weeks. Compensation was not offered by the Soviet Union.

Cheap energy has attracted a stronger political constituency than has social welfare. Opponents of natural gas deregulation in the USA prevailed until the late 1970s. In Germany, subsidization assured competitive coal prices. By the early 1970s, the advanced economies drew a significant portion of their fuels from overseas sources at cheap prices. But, in the West, a conveniently narrow definition of the free market obscured recognition of the impact of oligopolistic MNOCs (and other resource multinationals) on the LDCs. Oligopolist or monopolist power inhibited the maximization of social welfare in the producing LDCs by undervaluing their goods and thus generating savings for the western users. Those savings, in effect, fired up demand for more energy in the West and discounted the potential benefits of efficient end use and conservation. The system did not work in the best interest of the LDC producers. The relevant fact is the undervalued resource, undervalued because of the disparity in power between the MNOCs/western governments and the LDC producers. This reduced LDC incomes. Whether they would have used additional revenues "efficiently" is unrelated to the fact of undervaluation.

A case can be made to the effect that the MNOC owners of Persian or Mexican oil before World War I or the owners of oil in Saudi Arabia or Kuwait after World War II should have treated the producers more fairly. Indeed, the native rulers so argued. At the time, however, this hardly seemed possible. To the disparity in power must be added the disdainful attitude of the West toward non-western races and cultures and their potential for advancement in the western image.

Would fairer treatment of the LDC exporters — higher prices or royalties, earlier joint venture arrangements, more liberal sharing of technologies and management skills — have moderated oil nationalism? Who knows! Among the Arab states, Pan-Arabism and anti-Zionism exercised a transcendent influence. Today, one may speculate that higher prices during the 1960s might have somewhat lessened the dependence of the West on imported oil and might have lessened the likelihood of a coalescence of producers into a power bloc. Western governments and MNOCs believed they followed reasonable policies toward the LDCs, despite constant and vigorous LDC denials. The benefits of cheap and abundant energy appeared incontestable because economies grew rapidly.

Oil dominated international energy commerce prior to World War II. Oil prices fixed the upper range of other fuel prices. Oil was a bargain and without competition for vehicular use. In local markets in America, the oil companies engaged in both price and product competition. In Europe, with fewer marketers and little local production, product competition prevailed. In the larger world of oil, in the connection between the Anglo–Iranian Oil Company and Iran or Jersey's International Oil Company and Venezuela, the price paid by the MNOCs depended more upon the power relationship between the two parties than upon competition for concessions or upon the costs of production. All of the advantages—capital, technology, management, market networks—concentrated on one side and when that side was also backed by the USA or UK, then the other side must concede or withdraw its resources and lose the income. So, the weaker party took what it could at the moment, perhaps fearing retaliation if it did otherwise. This was the system which the failed Anglo-American oil treaty intended to formalize after World War II.

Evidence accumulated during the 1950s and 1960s—earlier if Mexican nationalization is recalled—that the oil states, now mostly free from colonial bonds, would no longer accept untrammeled foreign ownership of their oil wealth. Freedom generated a sense of national integrity not easily cowed by western threats that no longer implied the use of military force. The MNOCs, sustained by the influence of America and Britain, made their final successful stand against resurgent nationalism in Iran, but could not undo the nationalization of Iranian oil. Algerian independence led immediately to the take over of French and other oil interests. The nature and locus of power were in transition.

The disparity in power between the MNOCs and the producing governments contracted even as the destructive capabilities of the superpowers achieved awesome levels. In terms of useable power, the negotiating parties approached equilibrium. After 1959–60, the MNOCs no longer dared to set prices unilaterally. While the western nations engaged more vigorously in the formulation of national energy policy and in the direct management of energy resources, endeavoring to maximize security of energy supplies and sustain economic growth, the dominance of the MNOCs in the LDC producing states deteriorated. As energy import dependence rose within OECD (Table 6.2), revealing a propensity for inelasticities of demand that had for a potential counter only the checkered future of nuclear power, the MNOCs suffered one setback after another.

OPEC was founded in 1960, the year Kuwait and Venezuela established national oil companies. Iraq, in 1961, repossessed 99 percent of its concessions and, in 1964, formed a national oil company. Algeria won its independence in 1962 and seized the properties of several oil companies in 1967, the year of the Third Arab–Israel War. Further nationalizations followed—in Peru, Indonesia, Bolivia, and Algeria, again, in 1971. Libya, in forcing concessionaires to accept higher prices, established the precedent that led to the capitulation of the MNOCs at Tripoli and Teheran in 1970–1. In the wake of the Yom Kippur War of 1973, producer states solidified their power over price and production.

Competition may have been an element in the prices American motorists paid at the gasoline pump, different by a few cents from station to station. In many markets the progeny of the old Standard Oil Trust served as price leaders. In Europe and elsewhere, the competitive element is difficult to discern. M.A. Adelman attributed oil prices before 1973 to the competitive structure of the oil industry. Challenging neo-classical orthodoxy, P.A. Frankel detected oligopolistic control of the industry by the MNOCs that thwarted competition through control of international production and oil technologies, especially refining.[2]

Adelman's theory presumed bargaining between equals that never prevailed in international oil markets. He ignored the political process, failing, as an example, to account for the role of consumer governments which pursued their own objectives relative to security and price, or of national oil companies which sought to enhance their autonomy from political control, as did Italy's ENI and Mexico's Pemex. The MNOCs, after World War I, abandoned the effort to undercut one another in seeking concessions and in expanding market shares. Frequently, they negotiated market sharing or dividing arrangements. Competition did occur between fuels in domestic markets. In America, coal faced severe oil and natural gas competition, the former pegged cheaply because of low production costs, and the latter kept at a low price by regulatory agencies. By the early 1970s, natural gas had penetrated coal markets in Europe while coal also suffered from the incursion of nuclear power, heavily subsidized by national governments.

The notion of oligopolist company power operating within a political framework has explanatory value. Even as Frankel wrote, however, that power had been eroding for a decade or more as national producers (including the USSR), national companies, and independent oil companies entered oil markets. These newcomers succeeded not because of competitive superiority but because the producing states sought to diminish the role of the MNOCs. Still, the essence of oligopolistic control may have been transferred to a new center of power—OPEC. Penrose, among others, recognized this shift while simultaneously debunking characterizations of OPEC as a cartel. These analyses emphasized power relationships rather than market forces as the moving force in world oil.[3]

Between 1973 and 1982, the dominant LDC producing states, all save Mexico members of OPEC, determined price and production. This power derived less from the measurable strengthening of the producers economies and polities than from weakness in the West. The OPEC states happened to sit on two-thirds of global oil reserves. The West, collectively, proved incapable of fashioning a defense against the embargo or price hikes and, individually, failed to alter internal energy mixes sufficiently to loosen OPEC's stranglehold.

The oil price offensive launched by OPEC and OAPEC's embargo, aimed at the supporters of Israel, did not provoke effective countermeasures in the West. Germany and Japan, more than their OECD partners, allowed the new, high prices to filter through their economies. Other states—lesser developed, too—adopted policies that protected consumers against the full impact of high prices. The USA maintained oil and other energy prices well below prevailing world prices, thus encouraging even greater energy consumption and its corollary, higher energy import dependence. In general, the OECD countries adhered to traditional objectives, seeking new oil/energy sources with some success in the North Sea and Alaska, focusing on security of supply, and emphasizing nuclear power as the only available substitute. Missing, and not a real option given artificially low prices, was a serious commitment to improved energy use efficiency or conservation.

In the West, a multiplicity of energy interests—coal miners, process heat manufacturers, automobile owners and makers, governmental bodies at various levels, to mention but few—promoted policies that served their particular needs. Shaping a national consensus proved an elusive goal for the politicians. How much more elusive was the effort within OECD or EC to mold an organizational view? OPEC, too, confronted difficulties but as it rode a high price tide, serious internal divisions could be by-passed.

Prior to the OPEC revolution, the oligopolist model, if employed flexibly enough to account for the diminution of MNOC power and the emergence of competing nodes of power, seemed effectively to capture reality. During these halcyon times of American-led western domination and satisfactory rates of economic growth, it was even possible to consider the western governments as an oligopolistic center in international energy transactions. While engaged competitively in global markets, less and less to the advantage of the USA, these states still subscribed to somewhat similar objectives and were capable of cooperation. From this was imputed an international "oil regime" model that presumed a common set of rules guaranteed by the most powerful states, the USA and its western allies. Roncaglia attempted to preserve the regime model by suggesting that a trilateral oligopoly, consisting of the USA and the West as consumer states, the MNOCs, and OPEC, secured the post-1973 order.[4]

No such regime is visible during the years after 1973. The ancien regime broke apart. The western nations, instead of solidifying extant partnerships, devolved into quarreling states. The USA demanded unity against the Soviets and the Arabs. Western Europe preferred non-confrontation. Neither the International Energy Agency nor the European Community assumed leading roles in developing energy policies. The MNOCs became adjuncts of the LDC producing states, following the orders of their masters. Only OPEC manifest the potential for wearing the oligopolist mantle and, perhaps, did so to a degree between 1973 and 1979. OPEC, however, could not emulate the standard of non-competitive cooperation achieved by British Petroleum, Royal Dutch Shell, or the Aramco partners during the period, 1920–60. During that time, MNOCS cooperated in production, refining, and marketing and priced their goods at remarkably similar levels in the same markets. OPEC found it difficult to agree on price and impossible to impose production quotas.

The Iranian Revolution collapsed OPEC's flimsy controls over international oil. More importantly, during the two years of "galloping, mad dog prices," as a Hong Kong landlord graphically expressed it, the industrialized states engaged seriously in conservation by developing new technologies to reduce fuel use. In some places and some economic sectors, import substitution proved feasible. North Sea and Soviet natural gas replaced some petroleum and coal in western Europe. Unfortunately, coal use also rose, an example of substitution that carried with it substantial environmental cost. Ironically, the nuclear solution fizzled, except in France, just when most needed, the victim of the duplicity of its proponents and managerial–political shortcomings as well as of technological failures. Remedying technological deficiencies, waste disposal in particular, and convincing evidence of its cost advantages, may still be insufficient to disarm its critics. The public has become inured to the egregious claims of nuclear's advocates.

Nonetheless, once the West shook itself free from the self-imposed panic of 1979–81, significant improvements in energy use efficiency and conservation yielded a decline in TPER and in net energy imports as a percentage of TPER. However, these positive developments proved transient. The sharp price decline of 1985–7 stimulated energy consumption and rising oil import dependence (Tables 7.1 and 7.3). In America, oil imports accounted for 42 percent of oil use in 1988 and right at 50 percent in 1989, compared with 31 percent in 1984. This confirmed an Amoco official's prediction of 50 percent imports by 1990, the same dependency rate obtaining in 1978.[5]

Permanent gains in energy use efficiency were achieved in several industries. The savings gained, however, were insufficient to maintain consumption at or below the levels of 1980–4. Since recovering from the recession of 1980–1, the advanced nations have promoted economic growth but have ignored conservation and have only hesitantly addressed the deleterious consequences on the environment of rising fossil fuel use.

While the industrialized democracies grappled with an energy problem resolvable with the tools available, many energy importing LDCs sank deeper into poverty. Such nations were not major factors in energy markets. But, as became clear during the 1970s and 1980s, insofar as the paucity of commercial energy use in those nations drove their steadily increasing populations to denude the landscape, to that degree those desperate people jeopardized their, and the world's, future. By 1989, desertification and deforestation had transformed vast areas in sub-Saharan Africa, Nepal and Bangladesh, and Brazil into wasteland.

Heightened sensitivity to the relationship between the environment and the economy of the poorer LDCs provided no catalyst for action. Indeed, the linkage has thrown into disrepute older theories of modernization that prescribed western-style economic development. Now these nations are between a rock and a hard place. Rapid and high energy intensive industrialization in the absence of agricultural reforms and population stabilization will further overload local environments and hasten global warming. The Soviet economic model is no longer an option. The LDCs are all too aware of the congenital weakness and environmental rot that characterizes ex-Soviet bloc economies.

Translating the *per capita* energy consumption of Honduras and the USA, expressed in oil equivalent, to Btu's *per capita* yields an astounding differential: Americans consumed 50,000 times more Btu's *per capita* than Hondurans in 1986. Multiplying that differential by 6 or 7 might express the differential between Americans and Tanzanians.[6] Yet each contributes to global decay. Americans, Europeans, Japanese, and other industrial nations pollute the atmosphere and their own and other's terrains as they fire up their economies; Hondurans, Brazilians, and Tanzanians and other poor peoples strip bare their lands in an effort to survive or to move out of poverty. How can these drives be so reconciled as to prevent further environmental destruction?

That question now engages the attention of innumerable groups and organizations, public and private, around the world.[7] One can offer a wild arithmetic to stabilize the environment, that is the reduction of one unit of energy consumption *per capita* in the industrialized states for each unit increase in the LDCs. Of course, western governments and their societies would reject such a sacrifice. But would it entail sacrifice? Methods abound to achieve substantial conservation and to employ renewable resources at reasonable cost and with measurable future profits.[8] The fuel use efficiency of automobiles is susceptible of substantial improvement, especially in the USA. Significant savings are realizable in the heating and cooling of buildings. These are appropriate areas for further and consistent government action.

Debate persists about the long-term sufficiency of world energy and natural resources and the probability of irreversible environmental damage. The case is made for increasing abundance through technological advances answering market demand. Julian L. Simons, a prominent neo-classical economist, offers an optimistic assessment. He assures us that:

> If present trends continue, the world in 2000 will be *less* crowded (though more populated), *less* polluted, *more* stable ecologically, and *less* vulnerable to resource supply disruption than the world we now live in.[9]

He finds little worrisome in current conditions: forests are safe; food supply is improving; water is plentiful; mineral resources are becoming less scarce; nuclear power is cheaper than coal or oil and as safe; threats of air and water pollution have been vastly overblown. Private initiative guarantees the future. The real threat to abundance and well-being lies in "constraints imposed upon material progress by political and institutional forces." Unrealistic reports that things are getting worse spur governments to counterproductive and potentially disastrous acts.[10]

Sustained by *laissez-faire* ideology, Simons and others dismiss as improbable, exaggerated, erroneous, willful, ideological the findings accumulated since 1960 by scientists from around the world. Simon's sanguinity about the future of the environment, others insist, have been shorn of its empirical foundations. His prescriptions for unfettered resource use as the means to abundance will lead to catastrophe. Interests, large and small, supported by governments, are savaging the world's rain forests and extinguishing countless species. In February and April 1989, oilspills in Antarctica and Alaska, respectively, killed thousands of creatures. The *Exxon Valdez* spill revealed unimagined incompetence and irresponsibility by Exxon, Alaska, and the USA. Americans are polluting Canada; Mexicans and Americans exchange pollutants; the UK exports pollution to Scandinavia. The road not to take is that of uncontrolled possessive nationalism.[11]

If the normative judgments are stripped from Simon's argument, a description of what is likely to happen remains, but the consequences will diverge radically from those he foresees. Despite his railing against government intervention, individuals, corporations, and governments mostly use resources as they will and in the name of economic progress. At present, no globally binding agreements safeguard the use of the oceans, the atmosphere, or space. The oil tanker befouling Antarctica was there not because she sailed a necessary route but because she carried tourists and thereby earned a bit more for the voyage. Western democracies recognize no obligation to promote and partly finance environmentally sustaining economic growth in the LDCs. The LDCs are torn by distributive inequities. Two percent of the population own one-half of El Salvador's farmlands. Capital shortages and entrenched elites foster the development and destruction of marginal agricultural lands.[12]

Simons may be correct in denying future resource scarcity. But at what cost will these resources be extracted? Large tracts of land in the western USA are being stripped and left unreclaimed and poisoned by modern gold hunters who can extract gold by chemical means. H. Maull and others argue that the West is extremely vulnerable to the disruption of strategic mineral supplies from South Africa.[13] Simons discounts the danger of future energy shortages. Nations, particularly in the West, act as though he is correct. He may even be right in downplaying the likelihood of future oil supply disruptions. That he will be wrong is just as likely. *World Oil* anticipates an oil crisis in the 1990s as non-OPEC sources run down and price power returns to OPEC.[14] Does that assessment reflect only the self interest of oilmen who wish to reverse a decline in exploration and production from on-shore and off-shore US fields and who lobby for the liberalization of concessional terms in the North Sea and elsewhere? A prominent oil economist, interviewed by Exxon's company magazine, *The Lamp*, considers future drilling in the Arctic National Wildlife Refuge as a necessary contribution to national security. Conservation was deemed of limited value. The oilmen and Simons preach a similar message — if it's there, produce it.[15]

The energy crisis has not been overcome. The consumer states evidence a hazardous reliance upon Arab oil. Arab–Israel hostility festers, flares, and periodically erupts. Tensions and instability perpetually threaten Persian Gulf supplies. The development of clean energy alternatives to fossil fuels lags. Current trends suggest augmented fossil fuel use during the 1990s, possibly mitigated by the resurrection of the nuclear industry.

Even if one accepts the probability of an adequate supply of fuel in the future, there is little reason to celebrate. The energy crisis has metamorphosed into a crisis of overconsumption which, over an uncertain time span, imperils the globe. Adhering to Simon's prescriptions will assure that the worst occurs sooner rather than later. While everyone wishes to prevent the worst from happening, just how will we protect ourselves? At the least, global cooperation is demanded, and not of the sort that may, in 1990, lead to the ratification of a treaty by some thirty nations permitting the exploration and development of Antarctica's mineral resources. Leadership must emanate from those nations with the greatest financial and technological wealth. People in the modern, affluent democracies must demonstrate awareness that their standards of living, or those of their children, are directly threatened by what happens to the tropical forests, the ozone layer, Lake Como and the Finger Lakes, and the birds of Antarctica. They must acknowledge that what happens is irrevocably linked to their energy consumption habits. If resolutions of this global dilemma are not blowing on the wind, more than metaphorically, the tragic consequences of irresolution are.

Notes

1. A theory to this effect was proposed by H. Hotelling, "The Economics of Exhaustible Resources," *Journal of Political Economy*, 39, no. 2 (1931), pp. 137–75. His ideas stirred up great controversy among resource conservationists, demanding public intervention, and neo-classical economists, some of whom accept occasional public regulation and do not advocate uninhibited private action.
2. Adelman, *The World Petroleum Market*, Baltimore: The Johns Hopkins University Press for Resources for the Future (1972); Frankel, *Essentials of Petroleum: A Key to Oil Economics*, 2nd edn, New York: A.M. Kelley (1969).
3. E. Penrose, ed., *The Large International Firms in Developing Countries: The International Petroleum Industry*, London: Allen & Unwin (1968) and "OPEC and the World Oil Market of the 1980s," in D. Hawdon, ed., *The Energy Crisis: Ten Years After*, London: Croom Helm (1984); H. Maull, *Europe and World Energy*, London: Butterworths (1980), pp. 200–7.
4. E.J. Wilson, III, "World politics and international energy markets," *International Organization*, 41 (Winter 1987), pp. 125–49; P.F. Cowhey, *The Problem of Plenty: Energy Policy and International Politics*, Berkeley: University of California Press (1985); A. Roncaglia, *The International Oil Market: A Case of Trilateral Oligopoly*, edited by J.A. Kregel, Basingstoke: Macmillan (1985).
5. *New York Times*, February 2, 1989. See also the gloomy assumptions of *World Oil*, December 1987, p. 9 and April 1988, pp. 75–82.
6. World Resources Institute, *World Resources 1988–9*, New York: Basic Books (1988), p. 306.

7. For an account of grassroots initiatives, numbering in the tens of thousands, see A.B. Durning, *Action at the Grassroots. Fighting Poverty and Environmental Decline*. Worldwatch Paper 88. January 1989, Washington, DC: Worldwatch Institute (1989).

8. See, for examples, R. Mills and A.N. Toké, *Energy, Economics, and the Environment*, Englewood Cliffs, N.J.: Prentice Hall (1985), pp. 400–32 and D.M. Gates, *Energy and Ecology*, Sunderland, Mass.: Sinauer Associates Inc. (1985), Chapter 14.

9. J.L. Simon, in C.H. Southwick, ed., *Global Ecology*, Sunderland, Mass.: Sinauer Associates Inc. (1985), p. 63.

10. *Ibid.*, p. 65.

11. Simon and H. Kahn, eds, *The Resourceful Earth: A Response to Global 2000*, New York: B. Blackwell (1984) set out to refute *The Global 2000 Report* (1982), a report commissioned by President Carter in 1977 and prepared by the Council on Environmental Quality and the Department of State. Virtually every publication of Worldwatch Institute, the United Nations Environment Programme, and World Resources Institute contradicts Simon.

12. P.H. Raven, in Southwick, ed., *Global Ecology*, pp. 309–10.

13. H. Maull, *Raw Materials, Energy, and Western Security*, London: Macmillan (1984) and "South Africa's minerals: the Achilles heel of Western economic security," *International Affairs*, 62 (Autumn 1986), pp. 620–6. See, O. Ogunbodejo, *The International Politics of Africa's Strategic Minerals*, London: Pinter (1985).

14. *World Oil*, April 1988, pp. 75–82.

15. Interview with J.H. Lichtblau, *The Lamp*, 71 (Fall 1989), pp. 4–7.

Index